CAREER OPPORTUNITIES IN THEATER AND THE PERFORMING ARTS

Third Edition

CAREER OPPORTUNITIES IN THEATER AND THE PERFORMING ARTS

Third Edition

Shelly Field

Checkmark Books®
An imprint of Infobase Publishing

Career Opportunities in Theater and the Performing Arts, Third Edition

Checkmark Books
An imprint of Infobase Publishing
132 West 31st Street
New York NY 10001

Library of Congress Cataloging-in-Publication data
Field, Shelly.
    Career opportunities in theater and performing arts / Shelly Field.— 3rd ed.
        p. cm.
    Includes bibliographical references and index.
    ISBN 0-8160-6288-9 (hc : alk. paper)—ISBN 0-8160-6289-7 (pb : alk. paper)
    1. Performing arts—Vocational guidance. I. Title.
    PN1580.F5 2006
    791'.023—dc22

Checkmark Books are available at special discounts when purchased in bulk quantities for businesses, associations, institutions, or sales promotions. Please call our Special Sales Department in New York at (212) 967-8800 or (800) 322-8755.

You can find Facts On File on the World Wide Web at http://www.factsonfile.com

Cover design by Nora Wertz

Printed in the United States of America

VB Hermitage 10 9 8 7 6 5 4 3 2 1

This book is printed on acid-free paper.

*This book is dedicated to the loving memory
of my grandparents Pauline and Samuel Kreisberg &
Frances and Richard Field.*

CONTENTS

HOW TO USE THIS BOOK

Purpose

Years ago, the reality of working in theater or the other performing arts was a pipe dream to many. Opportunities were not plentiful and those that could be located were often difficult to obtain.

Since 1992, when this book was originally published, the theater and performing arts industries have expanded, exploding into a multitude of career opportunities in a variety of areas. There are thousands of people working in various facets of the industry. There are many more who want to get in.

Before the first edition of this book was published there was no single reliable source describing the major career opportunities in theater and the performing arts. Three editions later, this book still serves as a guide for all those seeking a career in the field. This new edition of *Career Opportunities in Theater and the Performing Arts* includes all the updated information you need to prepare for and find an exciting and rewarding career in these fields.

Career Opportunities in Theater and the Performing Arts was written for every individual who aspires to work in the industry. The book will give you ideas of what the career opportunities are, where to locate them, and what training is required to be successful in your quest. The 72 careers discussed in this book encompass careers, not only for performing talent, but also for those in the business end of the industry and behind-the-scenes workers.

The performing arts industry requires a wide array of people with many different talents. It needs actors, writers, singers, dancers, costume designers, secretaries, receptionists, publicists, managers, teachers, production personnel, designers, electricians, critics, and more. The trick in locating a job in the industry is to develop your skills and use them to get your foot in the door. Once in, it's up to you to work hard, learn as much as you can, and climb the career ladder to other positions.

Read through the book to explore careers which interest you. See what the qualifications are and how you can obtain training in your chosen field. You can then start on your journey toward an exciting, financially rewarding career in theater and the performing arts.

Sources of Information

Information for this book was obtained through interviews, questionnaires, and a wide variety of additional sources. Some information came from personal experience working in the field. Other data were obtained from business associates and colleagues in various positions in the theater and performing arts industries.

Men and women in all aspects of the performing arts contributed their expertise. These people included individuals who work in the business and administration end of the industry; theaters; operas; ballets and orchestra companies; arenas, halls, and other venues; organizations; production companies; public relations and publicity firms; newspapers; magazines; radio and television stations; placement companies; arts councils; and more. Also interviewed were agents, managers, publicists, theater owners and employees, music therapists, dance therapists, educators, amateur and professional actors, actresses, dancers, singers, and administrators. Information was also obtained from schools, colleges, universities, personnel offices, unions, and trade associations.

Organization of Material

Career Opportunities in Theater and the Performing Arts is divided into 11 general employment sections. These include: Performing Artists; Writing and Composing for the Performing Arts; Production, Directing, and Design; Theatrical Administration and Business; Orchestra, Opera, and Ballet Company Administration; Behind the Scenes; Support Services for Performing Artists; Halls, Arenas, and Other Venues; Performing Arts Education; Performing Arts Journalism; and Miscellaneous Careers in Theater and the Performing Arts. Within each of these sections are descriptions of individual careers.

There are two parts to each job classification. The first part offers job information in a chart form. The second part presents information in narrative text. In addition to the basic career description, there is information on unions and associations as well as tips for entry.

Sixteen appendixes are offered to help locate information you might want or need to get started in looking for a job in the field. E-mail addresses and Web sites are included when available for universities, colleges, associations, and companies listed in the appendixes. This should make it even easier to obtain additional information.

These appendixes include practical, general information about college and university degree and nondegree programs in drama and theater arts, theater arts management and administration, dance, music therapy, and dance therapy; workshops, seminars, and symposiums; internships; trade associations, and unions; Broadway theaters; Off-Broadway theaters; Off-Off-Broadway theaters; dinner theaters; resident theaters; stock theaters; U.S. and Canadian orchestras; ballet companies; U.S. and Canadian opera companies; and arts councils and agencies. A bibliography of theater- and performing arts–related books and periodicals and a glossary are also included.

Whether you choose to be an actor, musician, dancer, composer, playwright, singer, arts council director, costume designer, wardrobe dresser, teacher, critic, coach, or usher, your job can be both exciting and fulfilling.

This book will help you prepare for a great career you will truly love. It will give you the edge over others. The job that you have been dreaming about is out there waiting for you. You just have to go after it.

It's interesting to note that the person who doesn't make it, is usually the one who just gave up a day too early. Don't let this person be you.

Persevere! You will make it.

Shelly Field
www.shellyfield.com

ACKNOWLEDGMENTS

I thank every individual, theater, opera company, orchestra, ballet company, agency, association, and union who provided information, assistance, and encouragement for this book and its previous editions.

I acknowledge with appreciation my editor, James Chambers, for his help and encouragement. I also must thank Neal Mailet, who as my initial editor, provided the original impetus for this book. I could not have successfully completed this project without the continuing assistance of Ed Field. Others whose help was invaluable include Actors' Equity Association; Alliance of Resident Theaters of New York; American Association for Music Therapy; American Dance Therapy Association; American Federation of Musicians; American Guild of Musical Artists; American Guild of Variety Artists; American Society of Composers and Publishers; American Society of Music Copyists; American Symphony Orchestra League; Barbara Ashworth, Beauty School of Middletown; Association of Theatrical Press Agents and Managers; John Balme; Dan Barrett; Ryan Barrett; Lloyd Barriger, Barriger and Barriger; Alan Barrish; Jan Behr; Eugene Blabey, WVOS Radio; Fredda Briant; Broadcast Music, Inc.; Broadway Unit of Makeup Artists and Hairstylists; Katrina Bull; Theresa Bull; Earl "Speedo" Carroll; Eileen Casey; Anthony Cellini, supervisor, town of Thompson; Lily an Chauvin; Sandra Clark; Karen Cobham; Dr. Jessica L. Cohen; Lorraine Cohen; Norman Cohen; Kathleen Conry, director/actress; Jan Cornelius; Crawford Memorial Library Staff; Meike Cryan; Daniel Dayton; W. Lynne Dayton; Charlie Devine; Mark DiRaffaele, Best Buy; Joseph Doucette, general sales manager, Middletown Honda; The Dramatists Guild; Dress Barn; Alex Dube, American Guild of Musical Artists; Britany Duffy, American Symphony Orchestra League; American Guild of Musical Artists; Michelle Edwards; Scott Edwards; Louis Ephan; Lisa Estrada, coordinator/director, Los Angeles Laker Girls; Ernest Evans; Pat Farell, Argosy Gaming; Field Associates, Ltd.; Deborah K. Field, Esq.; Lillian (Cookie) Field; Robert Field; Selma Field; Finkelstein Memorial Library staff; Forestburg Playhouse; Louise Fousy; John Gabarron; David Garthe; John Gatto; Sheila Gatto; Gina Giambattista; Sally Gifft; Sam Goldych; Pat Heavey; Hermann Memorial Library staff; Paul Holmes, stage manager; Joan Howard; International Alliance of Theatrical Stage Employees; International Association of Auditorium Managers; International Brotherhood of Electrical Workers; Tom Jamerson; Melik Jayawardena; Jimmy "Handyman" Jones; Dr. John C. Koch; Bruce Kohl; Lake George Opera Festival; Karen Leever; League of Resident Theaters; Ann J. Ledley; Local 162 IATSE; Bob Leone; Los Angeles Laker Girls; Ginger Maher; Phillip Mestman; Rima Mestman; Metropolitan Opera; Beverly Michaels, Esq.; Martin Michaels, Esq.; Jason Milligan; Monticello Central High School Guidance Department; Monticello Central School District High School Library staff; Monticello Central School District Middle School Library staff; Werner Mendel, New Age Health Spa; Sharon Morris; Music Business Institute; Music Educators National Conference; Florence Naistadt; National Association for Music Therapy; National Association of Broadcast Employees and Technicians; National Association of Broadcasters; National Association of Schools of Dance; National Association of Schools of Music; National Association of Schools of Theatre; National Dance Association; Chris Nelson; Earl Nesmith; New Dramatists; Jim Newton; New York State Employment Service; Nikkodo, U.S.A., Inc.; Organization of Professional Acting Coaches and Teachers; Don Paget; Barbara Pezzella; Karen Pizzuto; Ray Polgar; Anita Portas; Public Relations Society of America; Doug Puppel; Harvey Rachlin; Ramapo Catskill Library System; Doug Richards; Jim Ryan; Tito Sanchez, Association of Theatrical Press Agents and Managers; Craig Sandquist, producer; Richard Schaefer, lighting designer; Nelson Sheeley, freelance director; Beverly Sloan, Equity; Raun Smith, Casino Career Center; Society of Stage Directors and Choreographers; Laura Solomon; The Songwriters Guild; Matthew E. Strong; Sullivan County Performing Arts Council; Theatrical Wardrobe Union; Thrall Library staff; Marie Tremper; United Scenic Artists; University Resident Theatre Association, Inc.; Brian Vargas; Kaytee Warren; Tonaya Watts; Lisa Weiss, dancer; Carol Williams; John Williams; Dr. Diana Worby; and Rachael Worby. My thanks also to the many people, associations, companies, and organizations who provided material for this book and wish to remain anonymous.

INTRODUCTION

The song "There's No Business Like Show Business" says it all. Most people who work in theater and the performing arts are in the industry because they love it. Thousands of people work in this exciting industry. One of them can be you.

Almost any talent you have can be parlayed into obtaining a job in this multibillion-dollar business. The performing arts industry offers an array of career options; all you have to do is follow your dream.

Whether that dream is to be an actor, actress, singer, dancer, director, producer, or choreographer, your dream can come true. If being on the stage is not your dream, perhaps you would be more interested in a career backstage. You might want to be a stage manager, lighting designer, sound designer, makeup artist, hairdresser, wardrobe dresser, or costume designer.

You may dream of being the general manager of a theater, a conductor, an arranger, composer, or librettist. Or of working as a secretary, receptionist, fund-raiser, personnel manager, teacher, or coach within the industry.

The industry also needs critics, journalists, press agents, booking agents, managers, attorneys, accountants, and more. There is literally no skill that can't be incorporated into a career in the performing arts industry. Sometimes you might need to be a little creative to find a way in, but you usually can do it.

As you read the various sections in this book, searching to find the job you have always dreamed about, keep in mind that there are many ways to get your foot in the door of the performing arts industry. This book provides you with the guidelines. The next step is yours.

Within each section of this book you will find all the information necessary to acquaint you with the important jobs in both industries. A key to the organization of each entry follows:

Career Profile

At a glance, the career profile offers a brief description in chart form of job responsibilities and duties, salary range, alternate job titles, employment and advancement prospects, best geographic location, and any prerequisites necessary for the job.

Career Ladder

The career ladder illustrates a normal job progression. Remember that in the performing arts there are no hard-and-fast rules. Job progression may occur in almost any manner.

Position Description

Every effort has been made to give well-rounded job descriptions. Keep in mind that no two jobs in this industry are structured in exactly the same way. Job descriptions, areas of responsibilities, and job hierarchies vary from one organization to the next.

Salaries

Salary ranges for the 72 job titles in the book are as accurate as possible. Factors affecting salaries in the performing arts are based on many variables. These include the specific job, as well as the level of experience and degree of responsibility of the individual.

Earnings are also dependent on the type of theater an individual may be working in and its size, location, prestige, and geographic location. Compensation for those in the talent area is often dependent on the popularity of the individual.

Employment Prospects

If you choose a job that has an EXCELLENT, GOOD, or FAIR rating, you are lucky. You will have an easier time finding a job. If, however, you would like to work at a job that has a POOR rating, don't despair. The rating only means that it is difficult to obtain a job—but not totally impossible.

Advancement Prospects

Try to be as cooperative and helpful as possible in the workplace. Don't try to see how little work you can do. Be enthusiastic, energetic, and outgoing. Do that little extra that no one asked you to. Learn as much as you can. When a job advancement possibility opens up, make sure that you're prepared for it.

Education and Training

Although the book only gives the *minimum* training and educational requirements, this does not mean that it is all you should have. Try to get the best training and education possible. A college degree does not guarantee a job in any aspect of theater or the performing arts, but it does help prepare you for life in the workplace. Education and training also encompass theater-related courses, seminars, apprenticeships, programs, on-the-job training, and internships.

Experience, Skills, and Personality Traits

Experience, skills, and personality traits required will differ from job to job. You will need a tremendous amount of perseverance and energy for any job in the theater—it's hard work. You will also have to be articulate and pleasantly aggressive. Being outgoing also helps. Contacts are important facets of the business. Make as many as you can. Good contacts will help advance your career and expand your opportunities. Don't burn any bridges. The theater and performing arts world is small. You will encounter the same people over and over again throughout your career. Stay on good terms with everyone if possible.

Best Geographic Location

New York City is the theatrical capital of the country. This does not mean it is the only place to look for employment. Jobs in theater and the performing arts may be found throughout the country. Culturally active cities with theaters, orchestras, opera or ballet companies, halls, arenas, and other venues also offer good opportunities. Smaller or less prestigious theaters or companies can be excellent places to begin a career.

Unions and Associations

Unions and trade associations offer valuable help in getting access to many jobs in theater and the performing arts, as well as making contacts. They may also offer scholarships, fellowships, seminars, and other beneficial programs.

Tips For Entry

Use this section for ideas on how to get a job and gain entry into the areas in which you are interested. When applying for any job always be as professional as possible. Dress neatly and conservatively for interviews. Don't wear sneakers. Don't chew gum. Don't smoke in the reception area before an interview or during an interview. Don't wear heavy perfume or cologne. Always have a few copies of your résumé with you. These should look neat and professional. Have résumés typed and well presented. Make sure you check and recheck for errors in grammar, spelling, and content. Don't just rely on a spell and grammar checker.

If you are applying for a job as an actor, singer, or dancer, dress properly for auditions. Bring your résumé and professional photographs. Be thoroughly prepared for your audition.

Use every contact you have. Don't get hung up on the idea that you want to get a job without help. If you are lucky enough to know someone who can help you obtain the job you want, accept their generosity. You alone will have to prove yourself at the interview or audition and then later on the job. Nobody can do that for you.

Use the Internet as a resource. Research companies, look for jobs, get ideas, and keep up with trends. If you don't have Internet access at home, most schools, colleges, and libraries generally offer free on-site access.

Never be late. Be on time for everything. This includes job interviews, auditions, phone calls, work, meetings, sending letters, answering e-mails, etc. People will remember when you're habitually late, and it will work against you in advancing your career.

Learn something positive from every experience. Don't talk badly about prior bosses, clients, jobs, or colleagues.

The last piece of advice in this section is to do your best at all times. A good professional reputation will follow you throughout your career.

Have fun reading this book. Use it. It will help you find a career you will truly love. The world of theater and the performing arts can be both glamorous and exciting.

Don't get discouraged, and don't give up. Dealing well with rejection is part of the business. Not everyone gets the first job he or she applies for. Few become stars overnight. You may have to knock on a lot of doors, send out a lot of résumés, apply for a lot of positions, and attend a great many auditions before you get the job of your dreams.

Have faith and confidence in yourself. You *will* make it in the performing arts if you persevere. When you do get the job you have been dreaming about, share your knowledge and help others fulfill their dreams too! There really is no business like show business.

Success stories are great. If this book helped you in your quest for a job and you would like to share your story, go to www.shellyfield.com. Good luck!

PERFORMING ARTISTS

ACTOR/ACTRESS—THEATRICAL

CAREER PROFILE

Duties: Performing in theatrical productions; learning lines; attending rehearsals

Alternate Title(s): None

Salary Range: Impossible to determine earnings due to nature of business

Employment Prospects: Fair

Advancement Prospects: Difficult to determine

Best Geographical Location(s): Culturally active cities offer more opportunities.

Prerequisites:

Education or Training—No formal educational requirement; courses or workshops in acting and theater arts may be useful.

Experience—Experience acting in community and school productions is helpful.

Special Skills and Personality Traits—Excellent acting skills; ability to deal with rejection; good memory; articulateness; poise; good stage presence; dependability

CAREER LADDER

```
┌─────────────────────────────────────┐
│  Successful Actor/Actress Starring in │
│         Broadway Production            │
└─────────────────────────────────────┘

┌─────────────────────────────────────┐
│            Actor/Actress              │
└─────────────────────────────────────┘

┌─────────────────────────────────────┐
│   Aspiring Amateur Actor/Actress      │
└─────────────────────────────────────┘
```

Position Description

Actors or Actresses working in theater are the people who interpret dramatic roles in plays and other theatrical productions. Individuals may perform in acting roles only, or may also sing and/or dance.

Actors and Actresses working in theater usually start out working in community and/or school productions. Some, who have decided that this is the vocation they want to pursue, attend either a college with a theater arts major or dramatic schools, classes, and workshops.

Individuals then try to obtain experience in stock productions, touring or repertory companies, and dinner theater productions. The dream of most Actors and Actresses working in theater is to land a starring role in a Broadway play.

Actors and Actresses must audition for parts in plays. Individuals find out about auditions in a number of ways. They may have agents who set up auditions, or they may hear of open auditions through contacts or by reading the "trades." The trades are magazines and newspapers that report events in the entertainment industry.

Individuals may audition for many parts before they land a role. At an audition, the Actor or Actress may be asked to read a part of a script so that the director and producers can see if they are "right" for the role. Individuals may also be asked to leave a résumé of acting experience and an 8 × 10 glossy photograph of themselves.

In some situations, the Actor or Actress may be called back to read a part a second or even third time. Sometimes they get the part, often they don't. Individuals must be thick-skinned and have the ability to deal with rejection in this profession.

If they do get a part, the Actor or Actress will be required to learn their lines and attend rehearsals. In some situations, the individual will be hired as an understudy. An understudy must learn all his or her lines and movements just as the Actor or Actress who will be playing the part does. In the event that the Actor or Actress playing the part gets sick or is not able to play the role, the understudy will go on stage in his or her place.

While being an Actor or Actress in the theater is hard work, most individuals live for the day that they can see their name on the marquee of a Broadway theater.

Salaries

It is impossible to determine the salaries for Actors and Actresses who work in the theater. Earnings vary greatly depending on a number of factors, including the type of production that the individual is working in, his or her talent, experience, prestige, and drawing power. Earnings will also depend on the amount of work the individual has done. There are some actors who never get a paying job. Others may have annual earnings of $1 million plus, but this is rare.

In May 2005, Actors and Actresses working in a Broadway production earned a minimum of $1,381 per week, according to Actors' Equity Association. Those working in national tours or bus and truck tours earn a per diem.

Minimum weekly salaries for individuals working in off Broadway productions are set according to the seating capacity. For example, according to Equity, in May 2005 the minimum weekly salary of an Actor or Actress in an off Broadway production in a theater seating 100 to 199 people was $493; in a theater holding 200 to 250 seats the minimum weekly salary was $574; theaters seating 251 to 299 paid Actors and Actresses a minimum of $665 weekly; theaters seating 300 to 350 people paid a weekly minimum of $765; and theaters holding 351 to 499 seats had a weekly minimum salary of $857.

In order to be financially solvent, a great many Actors and Actresses are forced to work other jobs such as waiting on tables, teaching, or doing freelance assignments.

Employment Prospects

Employment prospects are determined by a number of factors including the talent of the individual as well as connections, luck, and being in the right place at the right time. Actors and Actresses who are talented may locate positions in summer stock, touring companies, and Off-Broadway and Off-Off-Broadway productions, etc.

Those aspiring to work in Broadway productions have very limited prospects. That is not to say that individuals cannot get a job on Broadway, but it is extremely difficult. There are only a limited number of Broadway plays and competition for the positions is fierce.

Advancement Prospects

Advancement prospects for Actors and Actresses are dependent on the same types of factors that help the individuals get jobs in the first place. These factors include talent, luck, being in the right place at the right time, and good contacts and connections.

The next rung up the career ladder might be obtaining a role in a more prestigious play, a larger role, or different type of theater. An Actor or Actress working in a touring company may advance his or her career by signing a contract for a Broadway production.

For some individuals, advancement might be landing a role in a major movie; for others it would be a starring role in a television series. There is no one career path to success as an Actor or Actress. A number of individuals start in the theater and move on to television or the movies and others go from TV or motion pictures to the theater to attain superstardom.

Education and Training

There is no formal educational requirement to become a theatrical Actor or Actress. Many individuals however, do have a college degree in theater arts or attend dramatic arts schools. Others take private acting lessons, participate in workshops, or attend seminars. Many Actors and Actresses continue taking lessons and workshops throughout their careers.

Experience, Skills, and Personality Traits

Most successful Actors and Actresses starring in Broadway productions have paid their dues by performing in a variety of situations including local, community, and school productions; summer stock; touring companies; etc. Others have worked in television, motion pictures, or other fields in the entertainment industry.

Actors and Actresses working in the theater should be articulate with clear, pleasant speaking voices. They should be poised and have the ability to perform in front of groups of people.

While the physical "look" of Actors and Actresses is important, there is no one appearance that can guarantee success. There are many good-looking men and beautiful women who do not make it as Actors and Actresses. What is important however, is that individuals are talented in their craft and have the creative ability to portray different parts effectively.

It is worth repeating that individuals working in any field of entertainment need a thick skin. They should be able to deal with rejection that all Actors and Actresses run in to at one time or another in their career.

It is helpful in building a successful career for the individual to be personable and easy to get along with. He or she should also be dependable and on time for appointments, rehearsals, and all performances.

Unions and Associations

The major union for theatrical Actors and Actresses is the Actors' Equity Association (AEA) also known as Equity. This organization sets minimum salaries and work conditions for its members. It also offers professional guidance and support. Individuals who work in unionized theaters must be members of this union.

Actors and Actresses who work in other fields may belong to other unions including Screen Actors Guild (SAG), the American Federation of Television and Radio Artists (AFTRA), or the American Federation of Musicians (AFM).

Tips for Entry

1. Get as much acting experience as possible. Perform in your school productions, community theater, summer stock, etc. The more you hone your skills, the better you will be.
2. Look for acting workshops, courses, and seminars. These, too, will help you improve your craft, give you valuable advice and experience, and offer you the opportunity to make important contacts.
3. Learn as much as you can about the entertainment industry. Take courses and seminars on business, law, management, etc. These courses will help prepare you for future success.
4. Prepare a professional résumé listing your acting experience. A résumé is often requested at casting calls and auditions. You may also be asked to leave an 8×10 glossy photograph of yourself. Many people have two different poses prepared, a head shot and a full body shot.

BALLET DANCER

CAREER PROFILE

CAREER PROFILE

Duties: Performing in ballets and recitals; attending rehearsals

Alternate Title(s): Dancer; Prima Ballerina

Salary Range: Minimum weekly earnings in unionized situation: $700

Employment Prospects: Poor

Advancement Prospects: Poor

Best Geographical Location(s): Culturally active cities hosting a number of ballet companies will offer more opportunities.

Prerequisites:

Education or Training—Extensive training and lessons through ballet company training programs and ballet schools

Experience—Experience in ballet is necessary

Special Skills and Personality Traits—Dedication; creativity; gracefulness; determination; physical fitness

CAREER LADDER

> **Principal Dancer in More Prestigious Production or Company**

> **Ballet Dancer, Member of the Corps**

> **Dance Student**

Position Description

Ballets are theatrical productions centered around dance. The story of a ballet is told through dance movement and music. Those who perform in ballets are called dancers, or principals, and are very highly trained.

Ballets, like most other theatrical productions, are elaborate, using scenery and lighting to help create the mood of the story. Dancers wear specially designed costumes which allow them freedom of movement when performing. They may wear regular ballet slippers or toe shoes depending on the type of dancing required.

The music in a ballet may be performed by a live orchestra or may be recorded. To a great extent, the music used determines the type of steps the dancers will perform. The dancers use combinations of basic movements to interpret the story. These combinations are developed and put together by the choreographer.

Individuals go through many years of training to become Ballet Dancers. Many go through apprenticeship and other training programs with regional or national ballet companies.

Ballet companies usually hold auditions for new dancers. Individuals may find out about these in a number of ways. Some Ballet Dancers have agents or managers who obtain auditions for them. Others find out about openings through word of mouth or reading about them in the trade papers such as *Backstage, Variety,* or in local entertainment publications. Many individuals contact various ballet companies on their own to determine when auditions will be held.

A dancer's training does not stop when he or she becomes part of a company or production. The Ballet Dancer continues taking classes through his or her career.

The dancer must attend all rehearsals set by the company. At the beginning of a production, the dancer will find out what his or her part will be and learn the combinations and movements involved in that part. After the individual dancers have learned their parts, they will practice putting them together with the other dancers in the company.

At some time during the rehearsal period, the dancers will be fitted for costumes. Ballet Dancers do not speak or sing during the performance. Costuming, therefore, is important to the story of the ballet. The costumes of the dancers help the audience relate to what is happening on stage. Special hair styling and makeup are also used to create the aura.

The lifestyle of a Ballet Dancer takes a great deal of self-discipline. Individuals must keep themselves physically fit and in good health at all times. They must also take extra precautions to avoid injuries. A sprained ankle before a performance could jeopardize an entire production. Ballet Dancers must eat well, choosing their foods wisely. They cannot afford to gain any extra weight.

Ballet Dancers are required to perform their parts at each production. Work hours may vary depending on the schedule of performances. Individuals may work in the afternoon, evening, and/or on weekends.

Salaries

Earnings vary greatly for Ballet Dancers. Individuals may be paid by the performance or on a weekly basis. Factors affecting earnings include the type of setting the individual is working in, the geographic location, and level, size, and budget of the ballet company. Other factors include the reputation and experience of the dancer and the type of part he or she is performing.

Ballet Dancers working in unionized halls have their minimum salaries set by the American Guild of Musical Artists (AGMA). Minimum weekly salaries for the 2004–05 season for individuals working in ballet companies range from approximately $700 to approximately $1,200. They are based on the specific ballet company, its size, budget, and location, as well as if the dancer is a principal, soloist, or in the corps de ballet. Dancers who travel with a company receive a per diem for room and board.

It should be noted that these figures are minimums. Dancers who are in demand can command much higher earnings.

Ballet Dancers working in nonunionized situations may earn between $350 and $1,000 or more per week.

Employment Prospects

While employment prospects are poor for Ballet Dancers, talented individuals who have a great deal of determination and drive will usually find jobs. While one can aspire to dance with a troupe that performs in New York or London, dancers may find opportunities with regional ballet companies throughout the country and the world. Culturally active cities hosting a number of ballet companies offer more opportunities for jobs.

Advancement Prospects

Advancement prospects are poor for Ballet Dancers. There are a number of paths a Ballet Dancer may take to climb the career ladder. The most common path for career advance-

ment is by auditioning for a position in a more prestigious ballet company. Another method of career advancement is to become a lead or principal dancer in a ballet.

Education and Training

Training is very important for Ballet Dancers. Individuals usually begin their training early in life. Many Ballet Dancers start taking lessons before they are six years old. By the time Ballet Dancers reach their late teens, they have already had extensive training and lessons in the art of ballet. Ballet Dancers obtain training through intensive lessons, workshops, and programs with ballet companies and ballet schools. As mentioned previously, lessons and other training continue throughout the dancer's career.

Experience, Skills, and Personality Traits

Most professional Ballet Dancers have had experience performing in front of audiences when they were amateur Ballet Dancers and students. By the time most of these individuals locate a paying job, they have danced hundreds of times in rehearsals and recitals.

Ballet Dancers must be extremely talented in the art of ballet. Successful dancers are very dedicated to their profession. Individuals must be willing to practice, train, and rehearse on a continuing basis. Ballet Dancers must be physically, mentally, and emotionally prepared to dance. They must be graceful in their movement. Creativity in expressing these movements is also helpful. Agility is necessary. Ballet Dancers must have a feeling for the music to which they dance.

Becoming a Ballet Dancer is not easy. Drive, determination, and perseverance are necessary for success.

Unions and Associations

Ballet Dancers working in unionized halls must be members of the American Guild of Musical Artists (AGMA). This union negotiates minimum earnings for its members as well as minimum working conditions and standards.

Tips for Entry

1. Look for intern, apprentice, and training programs. These can often be found in various ballet companies. The programs are a good way to get your foot in the door and help you obtain necessary experience.
2. Many ballet companies also offer summer workshops and programs. These offer opportunities to get additional training and experience.
3. Training is essential to this type of career. Get the best possible training. You may have to give up a lot of your free time taking classes but it will pay off.
4. Perform whenever you can. Experience in front of audiences is helpful.

CHOREOGRAPHER

CAREER PROFILE

Duties: Developing dances, movements, and routines for a theatrical production; assisting in casting of dancers; teaching dancers routines and movements; attending rehearsals

Alternate Title(s): None

Salary Range: Impossible to determine due to nature of the job

Employment Prospects: Fair

Advancement Prospects: Difficult to determine

Best Geographical Location(s): Culturally active cities offer more opportunities.

Prerequisites:

Education or Training—Training in dance required
Experience—Experience in theater and dance necessary
Special Skills and Personality Traits—Ability to teach; technical dance expertise; good communication skills; creativity; ability to conceptualize; assertiveness

CAREER LADDER

```
┌─────────────────────────────────┐
│  Choreographer for Larger, More │
│     Prestigious Production       │
└─────────────────────────────────┘

┌─────────────────────────────────┐
│         Choreographer            │
└─────────────────────────────────┘

┌─────────────────────────────────┐
│       Dancer or Student          │
└─────────────────────────────────┘
```

Position Description

The Choreographer of a theatrical production is responsible for staging the movements of the dancers. The individual may have varied responsibilities depending on the specific production.

Choreographers compose dances designed to suggest a story, interpret emotion, and enliven a production. The individual may choreograph a variety of different types of shows including ballet, musicals, and reviews. The job of the Choreographer begins when a producer or director contacts the individual and sends him or her a script. While the Choreographer is hired and paid by the producer of the show, he or she may be recommended by the director.

After reading the script and discussing specific responsibilities, the Choreographer and the producer negotiate a fee. If they can come to terms, the Choreographer gets the job. In most instances, the individual will sit in on the casting to determine which dancers should be hired for a production.

The Choreographer might meet with the director, musical director, stage manager, lighting, and set and costume design-ers to discuss each individual's concepts. He or she will also study the script and music. The individual will then develop routines and dance movements for the dancers and block them out on stage. A great deal of the Choreographer's job in planning dances is done on paper or in the mind of the individual. This preliminary work uses the Choreographer's most creative powers.

The Choreographer may work with assistants and dancers trying out the routines to make sure that they look good and fit into the time frame of the music.

The Choreographer may spend many hours teaching the dancers the steps and routines that have been developed and created. He or she will be responsible for rehearsing with the dancers until the routines are perfect. The Choreographer will usually begin rehearsing with the dancers separately and then run through the production and include the dancers with the rest of the cast. At this point, the choreography is adapted to changes in lines, entrances, exits, and movements by actors and actresses that inevitably occur in rehearsal. The Choreographer meets and discusses changes with the director throughout the rehearsal period. Choreographic changes are made in response to lighting, stage sets, and costuming changes.

The individual's job concludes on opening night. At that time, the Choreographer moves on to locate another production requiring the services of a Choreographer.

Salaries

Salaries for Choreographers vary. Factors affecting salaries include the type of production, amount of work the individual does annually, responsibilities, expertise, and experience. As of this writing the Society for Stage Directors and Choreographers sets a minimum fee of $52,925 to be paid to choreographer directors during the rehearsal period for Broadway musicals and $45,565 for Broadway dramas or plays. Choreographers at the top of their profession can earn hundreds of thousands of dollars annually.

Individuals working for theaters that are not unionized, community theaters, experimental theaters, etc. may work for nothing to obtain experience.

Employment Prospects

As with any creative endeavor, employment prospects for Choreographers are fair. Individuals must be willing to work in smaller regional theaters. Prospects become more difficult as individuals aspire to work on major productions such as Broadway shows or for well-known ballet companies.

Individuals may choreograph ballets, musicals, dramas, thrillers, mysteries, etc. They may specialize in ballet, modern, folk, ethnic, jazz, in different dance categories.

Choreographers get jobs in a variety of ways. They may send out their résumés to producers and directors of shows. Others get referrals from producers and directors they have worked with in the past or from organizations such as the Society for Stage Directors and Choreographers (SSDC).

It is important to note that as a rule, Choreographers working in theater work from job to job. Once a production is choreographed and opens, the individual must find another show to work with.

Advancement Prospects

Advancement prospects for Choreographers are difficult to determine. Factors affecting advancement include the individual's drive, determination, and experience, as well as contacts and being in the right place at the right time. Luck plays an important role too.

Advancement for a Choreographer can take a number of paths. The individual may climb the career ladder by getting the opportunity to choreograph a larger number of more prestigious productions. Choreographing a Broadway show or major ballet for a prestigious company is a great accomplishment in this profession.

Some individuals advance their career by choreographing television shows or movies. Others find career advance-

ment by moving into directing or producing theatrical performances.

Education and Training

There are no formal educational requirements for Choreographers. Most individuals begin their training as dancers. The best training is a combination of study with dance teachers and professional dancers. Workshops and classes with a number of different teachers give the individual the opportunity to learn a variety of different techniques.

Aspiring Choreographers might also get a college degree in theater or dance.

Experience, Skills, and Personality Traits

Most Choreographers have had previous experience in the theater and dancing. While individuals should know a great deal about dance, they do not have to be great dancers to be Choreographers. They should, however, be great communicators with the ability to teach. They must be able to get concepts across to dancers. Technical expertise in dance is imperative, as is a basic knowledge of music and music theory.

The Choreographer should be a team player, for he or she works with a wide variety of people—the producer, director, dancers, set designers, lighting designers, costume designers, etc. He or she should be easy to get along with yet assertive.

The individual should be creative and have the ability to conceptualize ideas. In this way, he or she will develop movements and combinations of movements for the dancers.

Unions and Associations

Choreographers working in unionized theaters must belong to the Society of Stage Directors and Choreographers (SSDC). This group sets minimum fees and working conditions for their members as well as offers professional guidance and support.

If the Choreographer was or is an actor or actress, he or she may also be a member of the actors' union, Actors' Equity.

Tips for Entry

1. Take as many dance and theater classes and workshops as possible with a great variety of teachers. The more classes you take the more you will learn.
2. A great deal of choreography is picked up watching others. Go see different types of plays, musicals, and other theatrical productions.
3. Go to the library and find books on choreography. Study the work of others.
4. Volunteer to choreograph your local community theater production. It is great experience.
5. Look for internships in choreography with theater groups, schools, and other organizations.

DANCER

CAREER PROFILE

Duties: Using body movements to express ideas, tell stories, and entertain

Alternate Title(s): None

Salary Range: Impossible to determine earnings due to nature of the job

Employment Prospects: Poor

Advancement Prospects: Poor

Best Geographical Location(s): Culturally active cities will offer more opportunities.

Prerequisites:

Education or Training—Extensive training through schools, private lessons, etc.

Experience—Experience in dance necessary

Special Skills and Personality Traits—Dedication; creativity; gracefulness; ability to deal with rejection

CAREER LADDER

```
┌─────────────────────────────────────┐
│  Dancer in More Prestigious Production │
│        or Dance Company              │
└─────────────────────────────────────┘

┌─────────────────────────────────────┐
│              Dancer                  │
└─────────────────────────────────────┘

┌─────────────────────────────────────┐
│   Dance Student or Amateur Dancer    │
└─────────────────────────────────────┘
```

Position Description

Dancers use body movement to express ideas and tell stories. They move to sound, music, and rhythm with their bodies. Individuals may use traditional moves or improvised ones. Professional Dancers may perform ballet, classical, folk, ethnic, jazz, or modern dance. Most individuals specialize in one or two forms.

Professional Dancers working in theater may work in ballets, musicals, comedies, other plays and productions. They may also perform in stage shows. Dancers also might work in other entertainment fields including television, films, or music videos.

Competition among professional Dancers is great. Many individuals who aspire to become professional Dancers take on other related jobs and/or responsibilities, including singing and/or acting. Many Dancers also teach to supplement their income.

To become a successful Dancer, an individual needs a great deal of training in the form of classes, private lessons, or watching others perform. Dancers practice many hours a day to perfect their movements and keep their bodies in shape.

It is important for the Dancer to say in top physical condition and in good health. A Dancer not only practices and exercises but eats well too. The lifestyle of a professional Dancer requires self-discipline.

Dancers must audition for jobs. They may have an agent or manager who obtains auditions for them or they may go to open auditions and casting calls. Before going to an audition, the dancer prepares a résumé, listing the individual's name, address, phone number, education, training, and jobs he or she has had dancing or in the performing arts. The résumé also includes any special skills. For example, the Dancer may also be a choreographer or singer. Dancers also bring 8×10 color or black-and-white photographs of themselves in a few different poses, including a head shot.

Hundreds of Dancers audition for each job. Even if a Dancer does well at an audition, he or she still may not get the job. Many individuals feel rejected or develop low self-esteem. The difference between a successful dancer and a less successful one is that the former keeps auditioning in spite of the rejections.

Once a Dancer obtains a job, he or she must attend rehearsals. Rehearsals are long and grueling, but are necessary to the success of a performance. At the rehearsal, a choreographer will explain the steps to the Dancers. The individuals will then learn the steps and routines perfecting them as they go.

Dancers will perform at every show. Depending on when performances are scheduled, individuals may work in the afternoon, evening, and/or on weekends. If the individual is hired to dance in a road show, he or she must also be prepared to travel.

There can be a lot of stress in this type of job. Most Dancers do not have steady employment. Individuals must also worry about constantly doing their best or someone else may get their job.

Salaries

Due to the nature of the job, it is impossible to estimate earnings. Many variables affect salaries, such as experience, expertise, and reputation of the Dancer. Other factors affecting income include the type of dance production the individual is involved in and the amount of time he or she works annually. Many Dancers supplement earnings with other related jobs such as choreography and teaching.

Minimum earnings for those working in unionized situations are set by the unions. Minimum weekly salaries for individuals working in ballet companies or modern productions for the 2004–05 season began around $700. Dancers who travel will also receive a per diem for room and board. Dancers who are in demand can command much higher earnings. Minimums will be dependent on the specific union.

Salaries for Dancers who are working in nonunion situations can vary greatly from $100 a performance and up.

Employment Prospects

Employment prospects for Dancers are poor. There are not a lot of opportunities, and there are a great many people who want to fill them. Competition is tremendous.

Individuals may work in major opera, ballet, or classical ballet companies. They may also work in stage shows, musical reviews, musicals, comedies, and other productions. Other options not involved in theater include television, movies, and music videos.

Those aspiring to become professional dancers might find success entering the field through dance groups affiliated with colleges and universities.

Advancement Prospects

Competition is keen in this field and advancement prospects for Dancers are poor. This is not to say that advancement cannot occur, just that it is difficult.

Some Dancers get to the next rung on the career ladder by finding a position with a more prestigious production. Others may advance by becoming better known. This in turn helps them obtain more jobs and demand higher pay.

Education and Training

Educational and training requirements will vary depending on the type of Dancer an individual aspires to become. Ballet Dancers usually start their training early in life. By the time most Ballet Dancers are in their late teens, they have gone through extensive training and lessons in the art of ballet. Many individuals take intensive lessons and attend workshops and training programs with ballet companies and at ballet schools.

Those who aspire to be other types of Dancers must also go through extensive training and constant classes. Individuals may also obtain training through summer programs.

There are colleges offering degrees in dance. A degree can be helpful to the individual by offering training, background, and experience.

Experience, Skills, and Personality Traits

Dancers must be very dedicated and have a great love for the art of dance. They must have had extensive training in the art form. Individuals need to be creative and graceful in their movements.

Dancers should be physically fit with a great deal of stamina. They need to be flexible, agile, and coordinated. Individuals also have a feeling for music.

Dancers should be able to work well with others. They need the ability to learn steps and routines quickly. It is important for individuals to be able to deal with the constant rejection which comes with the various aspects of this type of job.

Unions and Associations

Dancers may belong to a number of different unions. Individuals working with musicals, comedies, or other theatrical performances may be members of Actors' Equity. Those performing in ballets, operas, or modern dance companies will belong to the American Guild of Musical Artists (AGMA). Dancers working on television or in movies may be members of the American Federation of Television and Radio Artists (AFTRA), the Screen Actors Guild (SAG), or the Screen Extras Guild (SEG).

Individuals may belong to one or a number of unions depending on the type of work they find. They may also be members of trade associations specific to the type of dance they perform including the American Dance Guild (ADG).

Tips for Entry

1. Get as much training as possible. Take classes and workshops from a variety of professional instructors and dancers who teach. This will help you learn additional styles and techniques.
2. Try to perform whenever you can, in school productions, community theater shows, etc.
3. Put together a professional looking résumé and photographs.
4. Send your résumé, glossies and a letter to professional dance companies requesting information about any training programs that they might offer.
5. If you believe in yourself, do not give up. Your big break will eventually come.

OPERA SINGER

CAREER PROFILE

Duties: Singing and performing in operas

Alternate Title(s): Classical Singer

Salary Range: $10,000 to $150,000+

Employment Prospects: Fair

Advancement Prospects: Fair

Best Geographical Location(s): New York City is the opera capital of the country; culturally active cities worldwide hosting opera companies will offer other opportunities.

Prerequisites:

Education or Training—Graduate of music conservatory, college, or university

Experience—Experience singing opera and other classical music necessary

Special Skills and Personality Traits—Familiarity with operas; physical, mental, and emotional stamina; perseverance; drive; determination

CAREER LADDER

```
┌─────────────────────────────────┐
│ Opera Singer in More Prestigious │
│     Production or Soloist        │
└─────────────────────────────────┘

┌─────────────────────────────────┐
│        Opera Singer             │
└─────────────────────────────────┘

┌─────────────────────────────────┐
│ Student in Music Conservatory,  │
│     College, or University       │
└─────────────────────────────────┘
```

Position Description

Operas are theatrical productions which are set to music. Most, if not all of the dialogue in an opera is sung instead of spoken. Those who perform in operas are called Opera Singers. These singers are highly trained in classical music. Individuals may be principal singers in the opera singing lead, feature, or support roles. Singers may also sing in opera choruses.

Each opera is a story. The story is written in a book called the libretto, which means little book. Operas, like many other theatrical plays, can be elaborate productions. They rely on extensive costuming, scenery, and lighting.

Individuals go through many years of training to become Opera Singers. Many participate in apprenticeship programs with regional or national opera companies before becoming full-fledged Opera Singers.

In order to get jobs in opera productions, Opera Singers usually have to audition. Individuals may have agents or managers who obtain auditions for them. Others find out about openings in shows through word of mouth, the union, or reading about them in the trade papers.

When an Opera Singer does get a part, he or she is required to attend show rehearsals. During this time, the individual will become familiar with the opera and learn the staging of his or her parts. The Opera Singer will also be fitted with costumes. Hairstyle and makeup is also decided.

Many traditional operas are written and performed in other languages, and Opera Singers learn their roles in the particular foreign language. In some situations, the Opera Singer learns the part without being able to speak or understand the meaning of the words. Modern operas by American and British composers are usually written and performed in English. Opera Singers need some acting ability to interpret the story of the opera effectively and dramatically.

Opera Singers are responsible for performing their parts at the actual show. Work hours vary depending on the schedule of performances. He or she may work in the afternoon, evening, and/or on weekends.

Salaries

Salaries vary for Opera Singers. Individuals may be paid by the performance or on a weekly basis. Factors affecting earnings include the prestige of the company the individual is singing in, the geographic location, and the size and budget of the opera company. Other variables include the reputation and experience of the individual and the role he or she is singing.

Aspiring Opera Singers, taking part in an apprentice program, earn a weekly salary of approximately $250 to $550 or more, plus housing. Individuals with additional experience such as those involved in a young singer program may earn between $550 and $750 or more a week.

Opera Singers working in unionized halls have their minimum salaries set by the American Guild of Musical Artists (AGMA). Earnings are based on whether the individual is a principal soloist or a chorus singer; minimum earnings are also based on the specific opera company, its size, budget, and location. Opera Singers working in unionized situations are paid extra for rehearsal time. In addition to salaries, AGMA has negotiated required employer contributions to a medical plan for working opera singers.

Opera Singers who are in demand earn $150,000 or more a year. In addition to earnings for live performances, many singers are asked to record certain roles and they receive royalties from recordings.

Employment Prospects

Employment prospects are fair for talented Opera Singers who are determined and driven to be in this profession. The opera capital of the country is New York City. Opera companies do exist, though, in other culturally active cities throughout the world. Individuals with talent who do start their careers as soloists at the Metropolitan Opera in New York can find jobs singing in the choruses of opera companies throughout the country and in other countries.

Many Opera Singers find employment with the help of a manager or talent agent. There are a number of talent agencies specializing in classical music. Most of them are located in New York City.

Advancement Prospects

Advancement prospects are fair for Opera Singers once they get their first role. Individuals advance their career in a number of ways, by practicing, by singing with more prestigious opera companies, and by winning lead or solo roles in a production.

Education and Training

Education and training are extremely important for the aspiring Opera Singer. Individuals must be trained in classical singing. Most Opera Singers are either graduates of a music conservatory or a college or university with a major

in classical music. Conservatories and universities offering classical music training are very valuable to Opera Singers. They offer not only training and education but opportunities to perform that the individual may not find elsewhere. Individuals may also take classes from private vocal coaches and teachers to supplement their training.

Experience, Skills, and Personality Traits

Opera Singers must have a great deal of experience singing classical music. Many obtain this experience by taking part in young singer and apprenticeship programs sponsored by opera companies.

An individual in this field must have an extraordinary voice. In addition, the Opera Singer must have acting skills. Familiarity with operas is helpful. As noted previously, the majority of operas currently written in this country are in English. However, many of the classic operas are in various foreign languages. It is therefore useful for the Singer to be fluent in other languages.

Individuals must practice their art. To be successful, the Opera Singer should have physical, mental, and emotional stamina. Drive, determination, and patience are also necessary.

Unions and Associations

Opera Singers working in unionized concert halls, theaters, and other venues must be members of the American Guild of Musical Artists (AGMA). This union negotiates minimum earnings for its members as well as minimum working conditions and standards.

Tips for Entry

1. Look for an internship or apprenticeship program. These can often be located through various opera companies. These programs are a good way to get your foot in the door and help you to obtain necessary experience.
2. Training is essential to this type of career. Get the best training you can.
3. Look for summer workshops and programs with opera companies. They offer excellent training experience.
4. Many communities now have local opera companies. Get involved with these groups and take part in their productions.
5. Look into grants and competitions in opera. These will give you opportunities to make contacts.
6. Attend as many operas as you can to learn from other singers.

CHORUS SINGER

CAREER PROFILE

Duties: Singing in the chorus of a theatrical production

Alternate Title(s): Chorus Vocalist; Chorus Member; Vocalist

Salary Range: Impossible to determine earnings due to nature of job

Employment Prospects: Fair

Advancement Prospects: Poor

Best Geographical Location(s): Culturally active cities will offer more opportunities.

Prerequisites:

Education or Training—No formal educational requirement

Experience—Experience singing in public helpful

Special Skills and Personality Traits—Ability to read music, harmonize, and deal with rejections; perseverance; drive; determination

CAREER LADDER

```
┌─────────────────────────────────┐
│  Chorus Singer in More Prestigious │
│   Production or Solo Singer       │
└─────────────────────────────────┘

┌─────────────────────────────────┐
│         Chorus Singer            │
└─────────────────────────────────┘

┌─────────────────────────────────┐
│     Singer or Actor/Actress      │
└─────────────────────────────────┘
```

Position Description

Chorus Singers sing in the chorus of musical productions. The Chorus Singer backs up the lead singers and other performers. He or she acts and/or dances depending on the requirements of the production.

In order to get jobs in theatrical productions, Chorus Singers usually audition. Many individual have agents or managers who obtain auditions for them. Others learn about openings in shows through word of mouth, their union, or reading about it in the trade papers, such as *Variety* and *Backstage*.

Chorus Singers audition at open casting calls, so called because any singer can try out. Before going to any audition, the singer prints up a résumé listing the individual's name, address and phone number, education and training. It should also include all of the artist's singing, dancing, and acting experience, as Chorus Singers may also be required to dance and/or act.

The Chorus Singer also brings professional photographs. In the performing arts industry, these photos are called 8 × 10 glossies and show the performer in different poses, including a head shot. Photographs are in color or black and

white. Each photograph includes the singer's name and phone number stamped on the back of it.

When singers audition for the chorus, they usually bring a piece of sheet music with them. In most cases, the singer gives the sheet music to the accompanist who is hired by the producers. In some cases, the singer brings his or her own accompanist. In smaller shows, the Chorus Singer may also bring a cassette tape of the accompanying music and sing along with the tape.

Depending on the specific production, there may be hundreds of other singers auditioning for the same job. Singers may not get the part even though they performed well at the audition because they don't have the right "look" for the show or do not sing in the style the production requires. The director determines if the singer fills the dancing or acting requirements that might accompany the job. The important thing is that the individual must keep trying. Singers may be called back to audition a number of times for the same part.

Once a Chorus Singer gets a job, he or she will be required to attend rehearsals. The individual will receive a copy of the script and music. The singer learns all the words, parts, and music, and any movement that will be necessary on stage. During the rehearsal period, he or she is fitted for costumes, and hairstyles and makeup are set.

The Chorus Singer performs at every show. The individual's work hours vary depending on the schedule of performances. He or she may work in the afternoon, evening, and/or on weekends. If the singer is hired for a touring company, he or she must also be prepared to travel.

There is a great deal of competition in all fields of the performing arts, including the chorus of a theatrical production. In order to make a living while waiting for a big break, many singers take on related jobs and/or responsibilities, such as acting or dancing in productions without singing. Others may freelance as background singers on recordings, jingles, or television commercials. Some may sing backup for performing artists in nightclubs, in concerts, or in recording studios.

There is no job security in this type of career. The individual may land a job as a Chorus Singer for a show, go through the rehearsal period and then have the production close in previews. He or she then has to start the job search process all over again. Lack of job security does not seem to deter individuals in the field. Instead, it provides them with the drive and determination necessary for success in this type of career.

Salaries

Due to the nature of the job, it is impossible to determine the annual earnings of Chorus Singers in theatrical productions. Earnings vary greatly depending on a number of factors. These factors include the individual's talent and responsibilities as well as the amount of work they secure annually and the type of productions in which they perform.

Individuals singing in choruses in Broadway productions will have their minimum earnings set by Actors' Equity. As of May 2005 the minimum weekly salary for a Chorus Singer was $1,381.

Employment Prospects

Employment prospects are fair for Chorus Singers in theatrical productions. Competition for these positions is such that hundreds or even thousands of singers can audition for the same spot.

The most difficult position to land is one in a Broadway show. Individuals have better prospects working in dinner theaters, regional theaters, and stock productions. Those who can act and dance well increase their marketability.

Advancement Prospects

Advancement prospects are poor for Chorus Singers in theatrical productions. Individuals may climb the career ladder in a number of ways. The most difficult path is to become the featured singer in a production. Another method of

career advancement is finding similar work in choruses of larger, more prestigious productions.

Many Chorus Singers advance to work as solo or background singers in television, recordings, or the live performing arts.

Education and Training

There is no formal educational requirement for Chorus Singers in theatrical productions. Individuals should, however, have a broad background in all styles of singing, music, and the performing arts. Some individuals are trained in music conservatories. Others go to vocal coaches and private teachers. Many Chorus Singers are self-taught.

Experience, Skills, and Personality Traits

Chorus Singers need a good voice and the ability to sing in front of others. The ability to sing harmony and in all styles of music is helpful in obtaining employment. A good vocal range is necessary. Chorus Singers should also be able to read music.

Individuals should be able to deal with rejection without letting it bother them. Perseverance, drive, and determination will help the Singer attain success.

Unions and Associations

Chorus Singers working in theatrical productions may be members of the American Guild of Musical Artists (AGMA) or Actors' Equity Association, commonly referred to as Equity.

As many individuals in this field work in other mediums, they may also belong to other unions. These include the American Federation of Television and Radio Artists (AFTRA) and the Screen Actors Guild (SAG).

Tips for Entry

1. When including your phone number on your résumé and photograph, remember to use a number where someone can reach you easily or where a message can be left. If you are using a service or an answering machine, check your messages frequently. Directors and casting agents will not wait long for you to call back.
2. Make sure your résumé and photographs are neat and professional.
3. The local union offices are full of information on openings. Visit there and become friendly with the people who run the office. You might learn about some good leads.
4. Get as much singing, acting, and dancing experience as possible. Take part in school and other amateur productions to gain such experience.
5. Local community theater productions offer valuable experience.

BACKGROUND SINGER

Duties: Backing up the singing of other vocalists and musicians in live performances or on recordings

Alternate Title(s): Vocalist; Studio Singer; Chorus Singer

Salary Range: Impossible to determine due to nature of the job

Employment Prospects: Fair

Advancement Prospects: Poor

Best Geographical Location(s): Positions may be located throughout the country; more opportunities may be located in culturally active cities.

Prerequisites:

Education or Training—No formal educational requirement; vocal training may be useful

Experience—Singing or performing

Special Skills and Personality Traits—Ability to sing in front of others; wide vocal range; ability to harmonize; versatility; reliability; dependability

```
┌─────────────────────────────────────┐
│  Background Singer for Prestigious   │
│   Singers and Projects or Soloist    │
└─────────────────────────────────────┘

┌─────────────────────────────────────┐
│         Background Singer            │
└─────────────────────────────────────┘

┌─────────────────────────────────────┐
│              Singer                  │
└─────────────────────────────────────┘
```

Position Description

Background Singers provide background, color, and harmony to the performances of other vocalists and musicians. Individuals work in varied professional and theatrical media, at live performances, or in recording sessions.

Background Singers work with show groups, single performing artists, lounge acts, touring recording artists, instrumentalists, or any other type of musical performers.

The Background Singer sings background vocals for the act's show. If the act tours, he or she will be required to travel and work at all performances.

The singer attends all necessary rehearsals. He or she learns the act's repertoire. The individual learns exactly when to begin singing his or her part. Background Singers harmonize and learn to blend voices with any other Background Singer in the group.

In certain situations, the Background Singer may be required to have dancing skills. Background Singers who perform may be required to wear costumes provided by the act in order to present a uniform or complementary appearance.

Background Singers, who work in theatrical productions are known as chorus singers. They must learn parts, attend rehearsals, and sing in all productions.

Other employment opportunities for Background Singers in the performing arts are in recording sessions. These individuals are called session or studio singers. Singing for recording sessions is a difficult area to break into until the Background Singer builds a reputation. The individual must be a great singer with a flexible voice and style, and must also be responsible and available when needed.

Background Singers who work in the recording industry often must perform without any rehearsal. They must be able to walk into a studio, pick up the music, go over it quickly, and be ready to record without a mistake. This type of work requires the singer to be able to harmonize with other vocalists with whom he or she has never sung.

In some cases the Background Singer must sing the part exactly as instructed. On other occasions, the individual may be asked to improvise. No matter what type of work the Background Singer is doing, he or she must be versatile. The individual who has a broad vocal range and can sing a variety of styles, including show tunes, pop, R & B, country, etc, will find more opportunities for employment.

The individual singing backup for a live act may be employed on a full-time basis or may just be hired for shows when the act performs. Background Singers working in the recording industry usually freelance, although there are a small number of full-time jobs available with record companies. Many Background Singers may work for live acts and in the studio doing session work too.

Background Singers do not usually work regular hours. Those who are employed singing backup with live acts will usually rehearse in the afternoon and work in the evenings and on weekends. Individuals who are involved in theatrical productions will have similar hours. Background Singers doing studio work may have very irregular hours because studio time is often less expensive after midnight.

Salaries

Due to the nature of the job, it is impossible to determine the annual earnings of Background Singers. There are some Background Singers who earn a few hundred dollars a year. There are others who are successful and may earn up to $100,000 and more annually.

A number of factors affect the salary of the individual, including prior success and how much in demand a Background Singer is. Other factors include the amount and type of work the singer gets and his or her geographic location.

Background Singers working with performing artists in live performances or theatrical productions are either paid by the show or employed on a weekly basis. These individuals may earn between $100 and $1,500 and more a week.

Individuals working as Background Singers in the recording industry usually, but not always, have minimum salaries set by the union. Variables in salaries for those singing backup on recordings include the length of the finished product, how many songs are recorded, what day and time the individual works, how long he or she is in the studio, and how many vocalists are singing on the recording.

Employment Prospects

Employment prospects are fair for ambitious Background Singers who are versatile and talented. The best way to enter this field is either in the chorus of a small theatrical production or by singing background for performing artists who are rising to the top of their professions.

Prospects are more limited for those aspiring to work in choruses of Broadway musicals, singing backup for top acts in the performing arts, and in recording studios.

Advancement Prospects

Advancement prospects are limited for Background Singers. Many individuals aspire to climb the career ladder by becoming a soloist in the theater, the performing arts, and/or on recordings, although advancement in these areas is also limited.

Background Singers may have more luck advancing their career by finding similar work with more prestigious performing arts projects. They can, for example, become Background Singers with a more established act or work in a larger theatrical production.

Those individuals who can get their foot in the door singing backup on recordings, who are talented, can pick up music and learn it quickly, and are reliable will be called on a more constant basis and earn more money as a result.

Education and Training

There are no formal educational requirements for a Background Singer. Some Background Singers are graduates of music conservatories. Others have degrees in music or theater arts from colleges and universities. Many individuals take private lessons from vocal coaches and private teachers or are self-taught.

Experience, Skills, and Personality Traits

The most important qualification for a Background Singer is a good voice. He or she should also be comfortable singing in front of others.

Background Singers must be versatile in their craft. The ability to sing a variety of styles of music ensures more employment opportunities.

Individuals must be able to harmonize with other singers. The ability to sight-read is essential. Drive and determination and perseverance are necessary for success, as are dependability and reliability.

Unions and Associations

Background Singers are members of various unions depending on the type of work they are doing, and may belong to more than one union. Individuals singing in a theatrical job may belong to the American Guild of Musical Artists (AGMA) or Actors' Equity Association (AEA) also referred to as Equity. Those working in recording studios may belong to the American Federation of Television and Radio Artists (AFTRA). Background Singers working with live entertainment may not have to belong to a union.

Tips for Entry

1. Local performing artists may advertise for a Background Singer in a newspaper's display or classified section. Look under heading classifications of "Background Singer," "Singer," "Vocalist," "Music," "Entertainment," etc.
2. Theatrical productions may hold auditions or casting calls. Find out where these calls are advertised in your area.
3. Read the trades on a regular basis. They will provide you with information on what is happening in the industry as well as where there might be openings.
4. Visit a recording studio. Get to know people who book studio time, producers, engineers, etc. These individuals are often helpful in finding work for you. Make sure you tell them what you do and leave your card with a phone number.
5. The telephone is your lifeline. Make sure that someone always answers your phone or get a beeper or voice mail. If this is not possible, get an answering machine or use an answering service and check in frequently.

CONDUCTOR—SYMPHONY ORCHESTRA

CAREER PROFILE

Duties: Preparing the orchestra for the performance; conducting the orchestra; choosing the orchestra's repertoire

Alternate Title(s): Musical Director

Salary Range: $18,000 to $275,000+; individuals working in small orchestras may earn $75 to $500+ per service

Employment Prospects: Poor

Advancement Prospects: Fair

Best Geographical Location(s): Culturally active cities will offer the most opportunities.

Prerequisites:

Education or Training—Training in conducting; musical study

Experience—Practical experience conducting different types of orchestras and/or chamber ensembles is useful.

Special Skills and Personality Traits—Ability to communicate musical thoughts; proficiency at piano and at least one other instrument; thorough knowledge of symphonic repertoire

CAREER LADDER

```
┌─────────────────────────────────┐
│  Conductor of Major Orchestra   │
└─────────────────────────────────┘

┌─────────────────────────────────┐
│           Conductor             │
└─────────────────────────────────┘

┌─────────────────────────────────┐
│       Assistant Conductor       │
└─────────────────────────────────┘
```

Position Description

The Conductor holds the top musical position in an orchestra. His or her main duty is preparing the orchestra for the finest performances they are capable of presenting.

The job is stressful as well as demanding. Hours are long. The Conductor must often put many hours into rehearsals before a performance. When the orchestra is on tour in cities throughout the country or the world, he or she must travel, too.

Top Conductors possess dynamic, charismatic stage personalities and immense musical talent.

A Conductor must be proficient in at least one musical instrument in addition to the piano. He or she must have the ability to sight-read. Most important, the Conductor must know how to communicate musical thoughts and ideas not only verbally during rehearsals, but also through his or her body movements while involved in a performance.

The Conductor in a symphony is responsible for choosing the orchestra's repertoire. He or she studies the orchestral scores and decides how the works will be played. The same piece of music might sound different depending on

who conducts the orchestra. Each Conductor possesses his or her own style.

A good Conductor with a unique technique is often sought out to make appearances as a guest Conductor with other orchestras. As a guest Conductor, the individual's only responsibility is to prepare the program for that particular performance.

While with his or her own orchestra, the Conductor has many other responsibilities. In addition to numerous rehearsals preparing the orchestra for individual performances, the Conductor must plan an entire musical season. He or she is responsible for choosing guest soloists, artists, and other conductors to "guest" or fill in with the orchestra.

The Conductor's job includes advising various section leaders and assisting them when auditions are held for section members. The Conductor of an orchestra is also called on for public and private appearances at fund-raising events on behalf of the orchestra. During summers, many leading Conductors teach at seminars, assisting aspiring Conductors to reach their goals, as well as conducting special summer concert series.

The Conductor of a symphony orchestra is usually responsible to the board of directors of that orchestra.

Salaries

Conductors' salaries vary widely. In major orchestras the Conductor may earn $275,000 or more. In smaller orchestras, the individual may earn between $75 and $500 per service. In between there are orchestras where Conductors' salaries range from $18,000 to $85,000 or more. As a rule, Conductors negotiate their salaries with the boards or management of individual orchestras.

Employment Prospects

Jobs are not plentiful for Conductors. The field is very limited. To get a job as a Conductor or even as an assistant Conductor one must have the opportunity to audition. Competition is fierce. Most Conductors work for years as musicians while studying to become Conductors.

Work possibilities for a Conductor include all varieties of orchestras. Not all positions are full-time jobs. Many successful Conductors have agents or managers who seek positions for them. Individuals may also conduct orchestras for theatrical performances or opera or ballet companies.

Advancement Prospects

The Conductor has the top position in an orchestra. Conductors can, however, advance from one type of orchestra to another. For instance, one might obtain a job as a Conductor in a community orchestra and move up to the position of assistant conductor in a larger urban orchestra. In this profession advancement occurs as a result of both great talent and a degree of luck.

Education and Training

Even with a doctoral degree in conducting, a talented musician is still not assured of a job as a Conductor. A conservatory or college degree in conducting is not usually required, but may be helpful. Training similar to that received in an educational setting is required, whether it be through seminars or private study.

Summer seminars in conducting are extremely useful to an individual aspiring to be a Conductor. Through these seminars, one can find out if he or she has the talent to be in this field. The best seminars are led by world renowned Conductors. A seminar given by a skilled Conductor can help an individual bring out his or her own personal style of conducting.

Experience, Skills, and Personality Traits

Any practical experience is useful in becoming a Conductor. Conducting chamber ensembles, small community orchestras, and youth orchestras gives the individual needed experience. Most conservatories and schools with strong music departments also offer assistant programs where the student is given an opportunity to conduct.

Summer seminars, such as those held in Tanglewood, Massachusetts, also offer individuals a chance to acquire conducting experience.

Unions and Associations

Conductors belong to the American Federation of Musicians (AFM) or the American Guild of Musical Artists (AGMA) depending on their situation. For example, if the Conductor plays or played an instrument, he or she probably belongs to the AFM. If the individual was a soloist, he or she might also belong to AGMA. However many Conductors do not belong to either union.

Tips for Entry

1. Try to attend a summer seminar that has world renowned Conductors associated with it. Aside from the excellent experience gained at these seminars, you can often make important contacts. If you show exceptional talent in the art of conducting, a well-known Conductor may help you and guide you up the ladder of success.

2. There are a number of orchestras that offer internships and fellowships in conducting. Check with orchestras in your area to see what programs they offer and whether you qualify.

3. Positions are advertised in many music-oriented publications, including *The International Musician.*

4. Positions may also be advertised in the newspaper classified or display section. Look under heading classifications of "Music," "Orchestra," "Symphony" or "Conductor."

SECTION MEMBER

CAREER PROFILE

Duties: Playing an instrument in an orchestra of a musical production, symphony, ballet, or opera company

Alternate Title(s): Section Player; Musician

Salary Range: Weekly earnings in major orchestra of musical production, symphony, ballet, or opera company: $750 to $2,500+; weekly earnings in smaller or less prestigious orchestra of musical production, symphony, ballet, or opera company: $300 to $750+

Employment Prospects: Poor

Advancement Prospects: Poor

Best Geographical Location(s): Culturally active cities will offer the most opportunities.

Prerequisites:

Education or Training—No formal educational requirement; extensive musical training necessary

Experience—Experience playing in orchestral situations

Special Skills and Personality Traits—Musical proficiency; a love of performing in front of audience; dedication to music; perseverance

CAREER LADDER

```
┌─────────────────────────────────┐
│  Section Member in Larger or     │
│  More Prestigious Orchestra or   │
│  Section Leader                  │
└─────────────────────────────────┘

┌─────────────────────────────────┐
│       Section Member             │
└─────────────────────────────────┘

┌─────────────────────────────────┐
│   Musician in School or          │
│   Community Orchestra            │
└─────────────────────────────────┘
```

Position Description

Every orchestra, whether functioning as a symphony, performing for a ballet or opera company, or playing as an orchestra for a music production is composed of players known as Section Members. It is the responsibility of Section Members to play the various musical instruments that make up the orchestra. As the size of every orchestra varies, there is no set number of Section Members in an orchestra.

In order to become a Section Member, an individual must be extremely talented at playing his or her musical instrument. A Section Member must audition for the job.

The Section Member auditions in front of a number of people including the conductor, section leaders, concertmaster/concertmistress, personnel director, and/or orchestra manager. The individual may be called back a number of times to audition.

Every orchestra does not play the same type of music. Some orchestras play symphonic music. Others may perform classical or operatic pieces. There are orchestras that play the music for ballet, modern, or other dance-related performances. Still others play the music for Broadway musicals and other musical productions.

Once an individual becomes part of an orchestra, it is his or her responsibility to become knowledgeable about the orchestral repertoire. The repertoire is the music that the orchestra performs. The Section Member must know and be able to play the music perfectly before going into a scheduled rehearsal.

During rehearsals, the Section Members practice with other members of the orchestra. It is important that the music of the various instruments blend together so that the music is pleasing to the ear.

Section Members may be required to travel to other cities in the country or to foreign lands. When individuals tour, their travel expenses are paid by the orchestra that employs them.

A Section Member with a major orchestra is usually under contract to perform a specific number of concerts and rehearsals per week. The number of performances and rehearsals will vary with the job. The individual is paid extra for any rehearsal or concert over the number specified in the contract.

The Section Member is responsible to the section leader, who determines correct bowings or phrasing in the string section, the correct breathing in the brass section, and who will play what parts.

Salaries

Salaries for Section Members vary from job to job depending on the size, budget, geographic location, and type of orchestra that employs the musician. Earnings also depend on the musician's experience, seniority, and reputation.

Section Members playing in a major orchestra of a symphony, ballet, or opera company earn more than an individual playing in metropolitan or urban companies. The same applies to Section Members playing in musical theater productions, with those performing in Broadway musicals earning more than those playing in regional productions.

Section Members working in unionized orchestras will have their minimum salaries negotiated by the local affiliation of the American Federation of Musicians (AFM). Section Members working in major orchestras of symphonies, ballet or opera companies, or Broadway productions earn between $750 and $2,500 or more weekly.

Annual salaries depend on how many weeks per year the company is in session, or how many weeks a musical production runs. In addition to salaries, Section Members receive vacation pay and other benefits. They also receive extra income for playing at recording sessions.

Section Members working in smaller orchestras of symphonies, ballet or opera companies, and less prestigious musical productions usually earn considerably less than those playing in major orchestras and music productions. Individuals in these situations earn between $300 and $750 or more weekly.

Some Section Members working in orchestras of smaller companies are paid on a per service basis, that is, Section Members are paid for each rehearsal and concert in which they perform instead of by the week.

Employment Prospects

Employment prospects for Section Members are poor but not hopeless. While competition is keen, talented musicians with drive, determination, and perseverance can find a job. The chances of obtaining a position as a Section Member in a major orchestra or a symphony, ballet or opera company, or Broadway musical are limited. However, prospects are brighter for those interested in joining smaller, less prestigious orchestras and musical productions.

Advancement Prospects

Advancement prospects are limited. Once a Section Member obtains a position in an orchestra of a symphony, ballet or opera company, or a musical production, he or she has a chance to advance to section leader. The individual must be very talented to advance to this position.

Another way the Section Member can advance his or her career is by joining a more prestigious orchestra. Some individuals work as a Section Member in a musical production that closes and then find a position as a Section Member in an orchestra of a symphony, ballet, or opera company. As many of these orchestras have longer seasons, work is more consistent and secure.

Education and Training

There is no formal educational requirement to become a Section Member in an orchestra. However, extensive musical training is essential. This training is often acquired by studying at music conservatories, colleges and universities, and through intensive private study.

Experience, Skills, and Personality Traits

Section Members must have experience playing in orchestral settings. Many Section Members play in school and community orchestras and musical productions in order to obtain this experience.

Section Members are excellent musicians, proficient with their instrument. Section Members enjoy performing in front of an audience. There are many excellent musicians who cannot stand playing in front of others and do not work as Section Members.

Section Members are dedicated to their music; they must also have a great deal of drive, determination, and perseverance in order to become successful in this career. The ability to deal with rejection is necessary.

Unions and Associations

Section Members working in unionized orchestras must be members of the American Federation of Musicians (AFM). The local affiliation of the AFM negotiates minimum wages and working conditions for its members.

Individuals may also be members of the American Symphony Orchestra League (ASOL) or the National Orchestral Association (NOA).

Tips for Entry

1. Openings for Section Members are listed in music-oriented trade journals and newsletters.
2. Try to locate internships sponsored by orchestra companies of symphonies, opera, and ballet companies as well as colleges, universities, and trade associations.
3. There are a number of summer programs that aspiring Section Members can participate in. These are also sponsored by orchestra companies of symphonies, opera, and ballet companies as well as colleges, universities, and trade associations. One such program is offered by the National Orchestral Association (NOA).
4. Play in as many orchestras as possible. Offer to play in school and local theatrical productions, ballets, operas, and symphonies.
5. This position is obtained through application and auditions. Become the best possible musician you can. Practice and play in orchestras. Persevere. You will eventually become a Section Member.

STUDIO MUSICIAN

CAREER PROFILE

Duties: Playing instruments to back up the music and/or singing of performing artists on recordings

Alternate Title(s): Session Player

Salary Range: Impossible to determine due to nature of job

Employment Prospects: Fair

Advancement Prospects: Poor

Best Geographical Location(s): Culturally active cities hosting large numbers of recording studios; New York City, Los Angeles, and Nashville are the recording capitals of the country.

Prerequisites:

Education or Training—No formal educational requirement; training in the form of private study helpful

Experience—Experience playing instrument in groups, bands, orchestras, etc.

Special Skills and Personality Traits—Ability to sight-read and get along with others; dependability; reliability; versatility; talented musician

CAREER LADDER

```
┌─────────────────────────────┐
│  Successful Studio Musician  │
│      Who Is in Demand        │
└─────────────────────────────┘

┌─────────────────────────────┐
│      Studio Musician         │
└─────────────────────────────┘

┌─────────────────────────────┐
│  Musician in Group, Band, or │
│         Orchestra            │
└─────────────────────────────┘
```

Position Description

When a performing artist goes into a recording studio, he or she usually requires the services of Studio Musicians. These individuals are responsible for playing the instruments that accompany the sounds created by the singer or group.

Studio Musicians are responsible for the sounds heard on the music played on radio, records, and CDs. Even if a group plays the majority of its own instruments in performance it uses Studio Musicians to augment the music on a recording.

Studio Musicians are experts in their field. Those who are flexible and can play a variety of styles and instruments find a lot of work. Studio Musicians are used on all types of recordings from pop, rock, and folk to orchestral, operatic, and Broadway musicals.

Studio Musicians obtain jobs in a number of ways. They may be hired by a contractor. The contractor is called when musicians are needed for a recording session by a performing artist, the artist's management team, or a recording studio. The contractor is told how many musicians are required and what instruments and style they must play.

The contractor then calls musicians who fit the bill. In most instances, the contractor will often call individuals he or she knows and has worked with before. The Studio Musician then either accepts or rejects the job. If the individual rejects too many jobs, no matter what the reason, the contractor stops calling.

Studio Musicians also obtain jobs through requests by the performing artist, group members, or their management team. The recording studio and record producers also recommend various Studio Musicians who have a good reputation.

Once the Studio Musician accepts a job, he or she is told exactly when and where the recording session takes place. The individual may be provided with music to learn ahead of time or may see the music for the first time when he or she arrives at the studio.

It is imperative that the Studio Musician be able to sight-read music. Recording studio time and personnel are expensive. There is usually not a great deal of time for rehearsals and mistakes are not often tolerated.

Studio Musicians do not usually have the opportunity to improvise. At the recording session, the individual is required to play what he or she is told, in the manner and style requested.

In addition to being an excellent musician, the individual must be reliable, dependable, and responsible. A Studio Musician who shows up for a session late, or worse, not at all, can cost the recording artist a tremendous amount of money. If it happens more than once, such behavior will cost the Studio Musician his or her professional reputation. As there is a great deal of competition in this field, the Studio Musician must also be easy to work with.

Studio Musicians are paid by the hour. Their minimum fees are negotiated by the local affiliation of the American Federation of Musicians (AFM). If individuals are in great demand, they can negotiate and receive higher fees. Successful Studio Musicians can make a good living.

As most artists do not record on a constant basis, Studio Musicians must work for a number of different performing artists. There is not a great deal of job security in this field. Some individuals back up other acts in live concerts on a freelance basis. Others stay in the studio, performing background music for television and radio commercials.

One of the most difficult aspects of being a Studio Musician is that the individual does not have an opportunity to express his particular musical creativity. As mentioned above, he or she is told what to play and how to play it. Some Studio Musicians find it difficult not to get credit for their work and to work in the shadow of other musicians.

Successful Studio Musicians have highly irregular working hours. As studio time is often less expensive in the evening, the individual may work through the night at a recording session.

Salaries

Salaries can vary greatly for Studio Musicians. Factors affecting earnings include the amount of work they get and their geographic location. Other important variables include how often the individual is requested and his or her musical reputation.

The American Federation of Musicians (AFM) sets the minimum fees Studio Musicians receive. Individuals who are in demand can negotiate for more than the minimum rates. Individuals who play more than one instrument during a session will usually receive additional earnings.

Successful, talented Studio Musicians who are in constant demand and are well known in the field earn $100,000 or more annually. Those who are not in that position earn considerably less.

Employment Prospects

Employment prospects for Studio Musicians are fair. The individual must be extremely talented and very aggressive. Contacts are important. Living in a culturally active city which hosts a large number of recording studios helps too. The majority of studio work is located in New York City,

Los Angeles, and Nashville, although there are studios located throughout the country.

Once a Studio Musician makes contacts or is hired by a contractor who trusts him or her, he or she is usually called continually for jobs. Individuals who can play more than one instrument, are versatile, dependable, and reliable have good prospects in this field.

Advancement Prospects

Advancement prospects are poor for Studio Musicians. Individuals may climb the career ladder by being in greater demand, obtaining more jobs, and earning higher fees. Other Studio Musicians advance their careers by becoming top recording musicians and performing artists in their own right.

Education and Training

There are no formal educational requirements for Studio Musicians. Individuals must, however, be highly trained on their instruments. This training is obtained through private study or musicians can be self-taught. There are also Studio Musicians who are graduates of conservatories, colleges, and universities, and have music degrees.

Experience, Skills, and Personality Traits

Studio Musicians usually have a great deal of experience playing their instruments. Some have performed in school or local bands and orchestras. Many worked as sidemen or sidewomen with other performing artists in concerts.

Studio Musicians excel at their craft. The ability to play more than one instrument well is helpful. Most Studio Musicians are able to sight-read.

Studio Musicians must be aggressive in order to make the contacts that result in job recommendations. They must also be easy to work with, dependable, responsible, and reliable.

Unions and Associations

Studio Musicians are represented by the American Federation of Musicians (AFM). This union negotiates the minimum earnings and working conditions for their members.

Tips for Entry

1. Visit recording studios. Talk to the people who work there and let them know what instrument you play and your past experience. Leave a business card with your name, instrument, and phone number.
2. Join the union. There you will hear of job possibilities.
3. Make as many contacts as possible in the performing arts and recording industries. Pass your business cards out regularly.
4. Consider working as a sideman or sidewoman backing up a performing artist or group in concert. This performing experience will give you additional important contacts.

SHOW GROUP

CAREER PROFILE

Duties: Singing, dancing, playing instruments, performing comedy or theatrical skits at theaters, nightclubs, concert halls, etc.; developing and putting together creative shows

Alternate Title(s): Show Act; Floor Show Group

Salary Range: $500 to $20,000+ per show

Employment Prospects: Fair

Advancement Prospects: Difficult to determine

Best Geographical Location(s): Employment opportunities may be located throughout the country; large, culturally active cities will offer more opportunities.

Prerequisites:

Education or Training—No formal educational requirement

Experience—Experience performing in public necessary

Special Skills and Personality Traits—Singing, dancing, acting, and/or musical skills necessary; charismatic stage presence; ability to entertain; dependability; reliability; ability to travel

CAREER LADDER

```
┌─────────────────────────────────────┐
│   More Popular Show Group or         │
│ Show Group Performing at Larger,     │
│     More Prestigious Venues          │
└─────────────────────────────────────┘

┌─────────────────────────────────────┐
│            Show Group                │
└─────────────────────────────────────┘

┌─────────────────────────────────────┐
│   Nightclub Band or Singers,         │
│ Dancers, Musicians, Actors, Performing│
│        in Other Situations           │
└─────────────────────────────────────┘
```

Position Description

Show Groups are performing artists who entertain in floor shows at theaters, nightclubs, and concert halls. Many of these groups work in hotels and on board cruise ships. Individuals entertain patrons with a variety of forms of entertainment during their act. They may sing, dance, play instruments, perform dramatic skits, and/or comedy. Many Show Groups also use extensive light shows, sound, and other special effects.

Show Groups must have pizzazz in order to become and stay successful. This act does not merely stand up on stage and play instruments or sing; rather it is creatively developed to suit the setting and the audience. Show sets are planned quite extensively. Ad-libs may sound like ad-libs to the audience but they have usually been rehearsed over and over again. In some situations, the group will hire outside talent such as choreographers or writers to develop a show for them. In others, the group's members create the show themselves.

Patrons will not come back to see the same show time after time. The Show Group must, therefore, have a number of different shows or sets prepared. Some sets may have the same middle portion but a different opening and closing.

Others will be entirely different. The finale of a Show Group's act is usually planned to be rather exciting and leave the audience wanting more.

Many Show Groups have themes for their act. They may do revues of certain eras such as the roaring twenties, the musical fifties, the turbulent sixties, etc. Most Show Groups wear costumes on stage. These will reflect the type of show the act does. Members may often change costumes a number of times during each set.

Some Show Groups perform in a club for one or two nights and then go on to the next club. Other Show Groups may work in the same place for a number of weeks before moving on to another engagement. There is quite a bit of travel involved in this type of career. Individuals must like to live out of a suitcase for months at a time.

The Show Group must continually try to build up its following. One way of accomplishing this is for the club manager to like the show and book the group back again. Another way is to advertise in the newspaper spotlighting the group's performance. Some groups who appear at the same location time after time develop a fan club of patrons who always come to their show. Show Groups also may acquire a bit of stardom on their circuit where they perform.

Show Groups must appear professional at all times. They must arrive at the correct times for their sets, dressed appropriately, and be ready to work. Members must also be available for any rehearsals or sound checks that are necessary.

Individuals in Show Groups are usually responsible to the club, theater, hall manager, or owner. Working hours will be mostly at night and on weekends.

Salaries

Show Groups are usually paid a fee for each engagement or group of engagements. They may earn between $500 to $20,000 or more per show.

Variables regarding earnings include the popularity of the act, whether they work under a union contract, the number of members in the group, the type of establishment where they work, and geographic location.

Earnings of Show Group Members can vary even within groups. Some acts split the money between members equally and some do not. If the act is working under a union contract, the leader of the group earns more than the other members. Earnings also are dependent on how often the group works.

Individuals working for one or more weeks at the same location may be paid weekly or semiweekly. They may also receive lodging and/or food as part of their fee.

Employment Prospects

Employment prospects for Show Groups are fair. Individuals may work in concert halls, theaters, or clubs. They may also find employment on cruise ships and in hotels.

Groups book themselves or may work with agents. Obtaining jobs without an agent is often difficult, especially if the group has not yet built a steady following. Show Groups may find it profitable to work with agents who have contracts with various venues around the country.

There are some Show Groups who work a specific area of the country such as the upper portion of the East Coast, the Midwest, etc. Others zigzag around the country wherever they can find employment.

Advancement Prospects

Advancement prospects for Show Groups are determined by a number of factors, including the talent, charisma, drive, and determination of the act. Luck also plays a part.

In order for Show Groups to advance their careers and increase earnings they must find similar employment at more prestigious theaters, halls, and clubs. Show Groups who build a following and become more popular will be booked on a more frequent basis.

Education and Training

There are no formal educational requirements for members of Show Groups. Individuals must, however, be trained in music, dance, singing, and/or acting. This training may be accomplished by attending schools, colleges, private lessons, or it may be self-taught.

Experience, Skills, and Personality Traits

In order to be successful, members of Show Groups should be extremely talented. There are some members of Show Groups who can sing better than the rest. Others excel at dancing, acting, or playing musical instruments.

Show Groups must be exciting. Members need to have good stage presence and a lot of charisma. Show Groups must be able to entertain. Their creativity is key in putting shows together.

Individuals in groups should be articulate. They must also be dependable and reliable. Missing a show or being late will not usually be tolerated by theater club owners or managers.

Unions and Associations

Individuals in Show Groups may belong to the American Federation of Musicians (AFM), Actors' Equity, and/or the American Guild of Musical Artists (AGMA). These unions negotiate minimum salaries and working conditions for their members.

Tips for Entry

1. Consider developing brochures to secure new business. Include the group's picture, name, and contact phone number. It is also important to include your specialties. Does your act do musical revues? show tunes? comedy? dance? Some groups include an insert with the names of places where they have performed.

2. Videotaped highlights of your show are also good selling pieces.

3. Have a professional photographer take photos of your group. Be sure to include the group's name and your manager or agent's name and phone number. If your group does not have a manager or agent yet, use a phone number where you know someone will be available to answer the phone most of the time.

4. Be professional. If you have an interview with a talent agent or club manager, show up on time. If you cannot get to an interview on time, managers and agents may be afraid you will also be late for your shows.

5. When you do get bookings, place an advertisement in the newspaper to let people know where you will be appearing. Ads help get your name around.

6. Remember to get commitments in writing in the form of contracts. Make sure dates, times, monies, and all other pertinent information is included. The contract must be signed by both parties to be valid.

7. Contact casinos and casino hotels; they often hire Show Groups for production shows.

8. You may want to get experience by performing in school or community productions.

COMEDIAN

Duties: Attempting to make an audience laugh by telling jokes, delivering comic lines, singing humorous songs, using movements and facial contortions

Alternate Title(s): Comic

Salary Range: Impossible to determine earnings due to nature of the job

Employment Prospects: Fair

Advancement Prospects: Fair

Best Geographical Location(s): Positions located throughout the country.

Prerequisites:

Education or Training—No formal educational requirements

Experience—Experience performing in front of audience necessary

Special Skills and Personality Traits—Ability to see everyday occurrences in life in a humorous manner; ease in performing in front of audiences; articulation; determination; ambition

```
┌─────────────────────────────┐
│     Successful Comedian      │
└─────────────────────────────┘

┌─────────────────────────────┐
│          Comedian           │
└─────────────────────────────┘

┌─────────────────────────────┐
│      Aspiring Comedian       │
└─────────────────────────────┘
```

Position Description

A Comedian is a performing artist who attempts to make an audience laugh. The individual uses many methods to amuse an audience.

The Comedian tells jokes, delivers comic lines, or sings humorous songs, although some Comedians never say a word to make people laugh. These individuals perform funny renditions of dances, walks, and other movements. They sometimes wear funny costumes or make facial contortions. An example of a famous Comedian who did not speak on stage was Harpo Marx of the Marx Brothers.

Comedians who use movements and facial contortions without speaking are called mimes. There are mimes, however, who are not Comedians.

Comedians have a range of employment opportunities. A stand-up Comedian works in front of a microphone in clubs, halls, and on television shows and performs a monologue. He or she may tell stories or jokes or sing songs.

Some Comedians work alone. Others work in pairs with one Comedian feeding off the other's lines. One individual is known as the "straight man" (or woman). Examples of the type of Comedians who worked like this would be George

Burns and Gracie Allen and Amos and Andy. One would say something in a serious fashion and the other would react in a humorous fashion.

There are Comedians who work in comedy troupes. These individuals perform in nightclubs, theaters, arenas, halls, and on television. Their performance usually contains one or more comedy skits.

Up-and-coming Comedians must usually do what is known in the performing arts and entertainment industry as "paying their dues." Paying dues may mean different things to different entertainers. For some Comedians it might mean performing in small clubs, going on stage late at night, and not being paid or being paid a minimal fee.

Many Comedians get experience performing in front of audiences at showcase comedy clubs. At these shows, they hone their skills and work on their act. This is a good way to determine the audience's reaction to new material. It is usually done solely for experience. As a rule, these individuals are not compensated at all or paid only a small fee.

Comedians may write their own material or may use the services of a comedy writer. Individuals who are starting out usually write their own for a number of reasons. To start with, purchasing material is often expensive. It can run from $100 a minute and up. Another reason is that it is often easier to perform material that comes from personal experience.

Comedians obtain work in a number of ways. They audition live for club owners, managers, or promoters. They submit audition tapes to club owners, managers, and promoters. People who hire Comedians often visit comedy clubs seeking out new promising talent. Many professional Comedians also seek out agents who obtain work for them.

The length of a Comedian's show varies. Some individuals perform for 10 or 15 minutes. Others have shows ranging from 30 minutes to an hour. Individuals are responsible to the club owner, manager, or promoter who hires them.

Salaries

Salaries for Comedians vary greatly depending on a number of factors, including the experience and reputation of the individual and the venue in which he or she is working. Comedians just starting out work in clubs merely for the experience of performing in front of an audience. Other individuals "work for the door," meaning the performer receives a portion or the full amount of the admission paid by patrons of the club.

Comedians who have more experience may earn between $100 and $1,000 or more for a show depending on their reputation and the venue in which they are working.

Very successful Comedians who are well known earn $25,000 or more per show.

Employment Prospects

Employment prospects for Comedians are fair. There are more and more comedy clubs springing up around the country. Talented Comedians work in comedy clubs, hotels, lounges, nightclubs, and on cruise ships. Individuals also perform on the college circuit. Some Comedians work as opening acts for singers, musicians, and recording artists.

Advancement Prospects

Advancement prospects are determined by the Comedian's talent, ambition, determination, and drive. Advancement for a Comedian is based on luck, contacts, and being in the right place at the right time.

Comedians advance their careers by performing in more prestigious clubs, halls, and arenas. Success for Comedians means they demand higher fees for their performances.

There are performers such as Robin Williams who begin as stand-up Comedians and go on to star in a comedy series on television and then have a successful movie career. Eddie Murphy began as a stand-up and went on to a successful television and film career.

Other paths of advancement for Comedians include writing television scripts or movie screenplays and/or directing or recording a successful comedy album.

Education and Training

There are no formal educational requirements for Comedians. Some individuals have high school diplomas; others have advanced degrees.

Courses, seminars, and workshops in comedy writing and performing are offered throughout the country and are useful to individuals pursuing this type of career.

Experience, Skills, and Personality Traits

Most professional Comedians obtain experience trying out their act in comedy clubs and talent showcases. Many Comedians say that their careers really started when they were in school acting as the class clown.

Comedians see life and most things occurring in life in a humorous manner. They must be funny people and be comfortable performing in front of audiences. The ability to write comic material is helpful.

Comedians are articulate with good communications skills. Drive, determination, perseverance, and ambition are useful in attaining success. The ability to deal with rejection is useful.

Unions and Associations

Comedians may be members of a number of unions and other organizations depending on the type of work they are doing. Individuals may belong to the American Guild of Variety Artists (AGVA), the Actors' Equity Association (AEA) (better known as Equity), the American Federation of Television and Radio Artists (AFTRA), or the National Mime Association (NMA).

Tips for Entry

1. Get as much experience performing as you can. Volunteer to M.C. school and community variety shows and take part in local talent shows.
2. Find out where in your area the many nightclubs and comedy clubs are. They have talent showcases and open mike nights where new performers can try out material.
3. Practice your act and hone your skills. Do not try to get a paying job in comedy until you are ready.
4. Find an agent who specializes in booking comedy acts.
5. If you know any singers or bands that are performing, talk to them about opening for their act.
6. Watch other Comedians perform live and in different entertainment media and determine what factors—timing, content, costume, gestures—make their acts successful.
7. Videotape your act so that you can see what "works" and what doesn't work with the audience.

WRITING AND COMPOSING FOR THE PERFORMING ARTS

PLAYWRIGHT

CAREER PROFILE

Duties: Writing scripts for comedies, tragedies, thrillers, mysteries, dramas, or musicals

Alternate Title(s): Writer; Scriptwriter

Salary Range: Impossible to determine due to nature of job

Employment Prospects: Poor

Advancement Prospects: Poor

Best Geographical Location(s): Positions located throughout the country; more opportunities may be available in culturally active cities.

Prerequisites:

Education or Training—College background or degree helpful, but not required

Experience—Experience writing useful

Special Skills and Personality Traits—Excellent writing skills; creativity; resiliency

CAREER LADDER

```
┌─────────────────────────────────┐
│      Playwright for Larger,      │
│  More Prestigious Production or  │
│        Hit Broadway Play         │
└─────────────────────────────────┘

┌─────────────────────────────────┐
│           Playwright             │
└─────────────────────────────────┘

┌─────────────────────────────────┐
│        Writer or Student         │
└─────────────────────────────────┘
```

Position Description

A Playwright is the individual responsible for writing the story for a theatrical production. The story is known as a script. Scripts are written in a special manner. The words that the characters speak are written next to or under each character's name. Some parts of the script explain the setting of particular scenes. The Playwright writes both dialogue and setting descriptions.

Playwrights can write a variety of scripts, such as comedies, tragedies, thrillers, mysteries, dramas, or musicals. Playwrights write original shows or may adapt themes from fictional, historical, or narrative sources.

When working on the script, the Playwright involves the characters in actions that have conflict, purpose, and a resolution to the events in the story. The story includes the actors' and actresses' dialogue and directions for actions during the production of the script.

In some instances, a producer requests changes in the script. The Playwright is responsible for revisions. He or she might be required to be present at rehearsals to tighten up lines or make changes from producer or director notes.

Playwrights have an extremely difficult job. They must not only write a good script, but also may have to find a producer willing to finance the production.

In some instances a producer has an idea that he or she wants developed into a script. The producer and writer meet and discuss the idea. The Playwright will then try to write a suitable script.

The life of a Playwright is a solitary one. Most of their work is done alone. Once a script is developed and written, the Playwright shows the script to people until it is accepted for production. This existence leads to a great deal of stress. However, most Playwrights feel that seeing their play produced on the stage is worth the stress and strain.

Salaries

Earnings for Playwrights are difficult to assess. Some individuals never make a cent from their work while others, such as Neil Simon, earn millions.

Playwrights earn money in a number of ways. They may sell their script outright for a specific sum. Others accept option payments on their script. Options allow a producer to "own" the script for a set period of time to see if financing for the production can be obtained. If the producer does find financing, he or she will negotiate with the Playwright or his or her representative for the use of the script. The Playwright then earns money by receiving a royalty each time his or her script is performed.

Employment Prospects

Anyone who has the technical knowledge and means to write a script can write a play. To become a successful Playwright, however, one must find producers willing to use the script and produce the show.

Prospects for production range from poor to fair. It is extremely difficult to get a major producer to use the script of an unknown Playwright because there is a great deal of competition for producers even among those Playwrights who are successful. Sales do occur, however, it is difficult.

Individuals aspiring to be Playwrights have better luck submitting their scripts to experimental theaters, community theaters, college theaters, and to producers who are also trying to make a name for themselves.

Another form of possible employment for an individual is to become a Playwright-in-residence for a community, school, or repertory theater.

Many aspiring Playwrights have other jobs both in and out of the theatrical world. They write in their spare time until their big break comes along.

Advancement Prospects

Advancement prospects are poor for Playwrights. Career advancement can take a number of different paths. Some Playwrights advance their career by writing for television or movies. Others climb the career ladder by having their scripts produced by a major producer on Broadway.

Education and Training

A college degree gives the Playwright a background that may prove useful but will not guarantee a Playwright's script will be produced and turned into a major production. Majors that an aspiring Playwright might consider include theater, playwrighting, theater arts, acting, journalism, English, communications, or liberal arts. Courses, seminars, and workshops in scriptwriting, English, writing, theater, stage, and acting would also be helpful.

Colleges with degrees in theater, theater arts, playwrighting, and acting offer programs where the individual can write or work on a play and have it read aloud or produced within the school. This experience gives the aspiring Playwright an edge over others.

Experience, Skills, and Personality Traits

Successful Playwrights have had a great deal of experience writing. Many have written and published short stories, novels, nonfiction articles, and poetry before attaining success in theater.

Playwrights have excellent writing skills and a good command of the English language. They are not only able to write well, but have the ability to write dialogue. They have a story to tell and the ability to script it for the stage.

Playwrights are creative people. They can take an idea and make it exciting for others. Writing can often be lonely. Even if the Playwright is collaborating with another author, he or she will be doing a lot of work on his or her own.

Those aspiring to become Playwrights must be thick-skinned and resilient. There is a great deal of rejection in this industry. Scripts are constantly turned down. The individual must have the ability to deal with these rejections without taking them personally and getting depressed.

While there are Playwrights who do not type, typing skills and knowledge of word processing are extremely useful.

An ability to research is imperative for Playwrights. With research, an individual can learn about the language, problems, and life of certain time periods that he or she develops in the course of writing.

Unions and Associations

Playwrights are often members of the Dramatist Guild (DG). The Guild offers members assistance in a number of areas including business advice, internships, opportunities to have plays read, contracts, and royalties. Playwrights may also be members of the New Dramatist, a service organization for scriptwriters.

Tips for Entry

1. Write as much as you can in all areas of the writing field. The writing experience is invaluable.
2. Look for seminars, courses, and workshops in scriptwriting. These will provide you with an opportunity to learn, write, and be reviewed.
3. Considering entering playwrighting contests, which are often sponsored by play publishers, regional and community theaters, local and national theater organizations, and colleges.
4. Read a variety of scripts. These will give you inspiration as well as help teach you how scripts are developed.
5. See as many different productions and shows as you can. Include productions put on by school and church theater groups, colleges, community theater, regional theater, summer stock, and, if possible, Broadway.
6. Join dramatists' associations and other professional groups. These organizations will help put you in touch with others interested in the same field as well as giving you an opportunity to make important contacts.
7. Search the Internet for Web sites for Playwrights. Many have helpful tips and techniques for writing scripts.

LIBRETTIST

CAREER PROFILE

Duties: Developing a story for an opera; writing the libretto

Alternate Title(s): None

Salary Range: $10,000 to $100,000+ per opera

Employment Prospects: Poor

Advancement Prospects: Poor

Best Geographical Location(s): New York City is the opera capital of the country; culturally active cities worldwide hosting opera companies will offer other opportunities.

Prerequisites:

Education or Training—No educational requirement necessary; college background may be helpful

Experience—Experience writing scripts useful

Special Skills and Personality Traits—Creativity; understanding of opera; good writing skills; sense of the stage; ability to develop a story; perseverance; determination

CAREER LADDER

```
┌─────────────────────────────────┐
│  Librettist for More Prestigious │
│       Opera Production           │
└─────────────────────────────────┘

┌─────────────────────────────────┐
│           Librettist            │
└─────────────────────────────────┘

┌─────────────────────────────────┐
│ Amateur Librettist, Playwright, or │
│            Student              │
└─────────────────────────────────┘
```

Position Description

Every opera has a story. The story is written in a book called the libretto, which translated means "little book." The person who writes the libretto is called a Librettist.

Operas are theatrical productions which are set to music. Most, if not all the dialogue in an opera is sung instead of spoken.

The Librettist writes the words, which are set to music by a composer. In some instances, the individual will also be the musical composer.

A Librettist may have different responsibilities depending on production requirements. Some individuals develop the entire story. They first come up with an idea for an opera, then write the dialogue, which will be sung and/or spoken by the singers in the production.

Other Librettists are given a basic story to work with. They are then responsible for writing the dialogue of the opera. These individuals are required to write the dialogue for all the singers in the production, including the principal singers who perform the lead, feature, and support roles and the chorus singers.

The librettos in operas are really musical scripts, and Librettists are comparable to playwrights or screenwriters.

One of the differences between a screenplay or theatrical production script and the libretto is its length. As the majority of the dialogue in an opera is sung instead of spoken, the libretto is about one-third the length of a theatrical play.

Opera has changed over the years. Once, Librettists needed to write like poets using rhyming words. Rhyme is no longer necessary in modern opera.

Another change in the technique of writing modern operas is that they no longer must be written in foreign languages. Modern operas are usually sung in the native language of the composer. If an individual is commissioned to write the libretto of an opera composed in America, he or she will write it in English.

Librettists are hired to write the libretto by either a composer or a producer. He or she may work with others including the composers, and the producers, or may work alone. Librettists write original librettos or adapt themes from other sources.

The Librettist reports either to the producer or to the composer, depending on who commissioned the piece. Librettists do not have normal business hours. They work long hours until the piece is finished. The completion of a libretto can take weeks, months, or even years.

Salaries

Librettists may earn between $10,000 and $100,000 or more for writing a full-length opera. Factors affecting earnings include the nature of the specific piece that is commissioned as well as the experience, responsibilities, and reputation of the writer and the funding available to produce the work.

Employment Prospects

Employment prospects are very limited for a Librettist. He or she is hired by either a producer or recommended by a composer, and these individuals prefer to work with others who have a track record or whose work they know.

The opera capital of the country is New York City, and it is one of the best cities in which to make contacts in this field. Other cities that support opera companies offer opportunities as well.

Advancement Prospects

Advancement prospects for the Librettist are limited. In order to climb the career ladder, the individual must write a libretto for a more prestigious production.

Education and Training

There are no formal educational requirements necessary to become a Librettist. A college background helps develop skills and contacts and provides experiences the individual might not otherwise have.

Classes, workshops, and seminars in all areas of theater arts, opera, script writing, English, music, and literature are useful.

Experience, Skills, and Personality Traits

Librettists are very creative people with excellent writing skills. An understanding and knowledge of opera is a must.

The ability to develop a good story is mandatory, as is a sense of staging and drama. Librettists write dialogue that sounds good when sung. A good command of the English language is necessary.

Librettists must be very determined. It is often difficult to find a composer or producer willing to take a chance on a new talent. Perseverance is essential.

Typing, computer, and word processor skills are helpful to the individual in this profession.

Unions and Associations

There is no specific trade association for Librettists. Opera America (OA), an organization of professional opera companies, is helpful for individuals interested in careers in opera.

Tips for Entry

1. Attend a variety of writers' workshops, as they provide inspiration and education as well as the opportunity to make contacts.
2. Try to meet and get to know a composer. Tell this person of your aspirations. Sometimes a successful composer will provide contacts or the chance to collaborate.
3. Find internships that allow you to work on operatic productions. They are an excellent source of contacts in the field.
4. Go to the library and review librettos from other operas.
5. Attend live operas and watch them on television. Learn as much as you can about the subject.
6. Contact Opera America, an association for professional opera companies. This group sponsors seminars and workshops.

COMPOSER—MUSICAL THEATER/OPERA

Duties: Writing the music for a theatrical musical production or opera; collaborating with lyricist, librettist, and/or playwright

Alternate Title(s): Songwriter

Salary Range: Impossible to determine due to the nature of the job

Employment Prospects: Fair

Advancement Prospects: Fair

Best Geographical Location(s): Culturally active cities provide the best opportunities.

Prerequisites:

Education or Training—No formal educational requirements; musical training necessary

Experience—Experience in writing music helpful

Special Skills and Personality Traits—Ability to play piano and to read and write music; understanding of theater; creativity; aggressiveness; determination; ability to work under pressure; ability to work well with others

```
┌─────────────────────────────────────┐
│ Composer for More Prestigious Musical │
│   Theater Productions and/or Operas   │
└─────────────────────────────────────┘

┌─────────────────────────────────────┐
│   Composer—Musical Theater/Opera     │
└─────────────────────────────────────┘

┌─────────────────────────────────────┐
│    Songwriter or Amateur Composer    │
└─────────────────────────────────────┘
```

Position Description

Composers in musical theater and/or opera write the music for the production. The Composer works alone or collaborates with others on the musical score of a production. The Composer also collaborates with the playwright, lyricists, and librettists of the production.

The Composer for musical theater and/or opera is a special type of songwriter. Composing music for a show is not a simple job. It may take weeks, months, or even years to complete. Then, as rehearsals demand, a composer turns out songs in a matter of days.

The music of a show is perhaps the one element that audiences remember most. Many songs that become standards have emerged from Broadway musicals. While not everyone has the opportunity to see a production, anyone can turn on the radio or listen to a record or tape of the music from one of these shows.

The Composer of a musical production or opera begins work when given a script and/or the libretto for the show and after consultations with the producer, director, and writers; with this information, the composer gets the "feel" of the show and begins to develop ideas for the music. Tunes must fit in with the theme of the play. At times, the Composer adjusts music to fit the talents of various actors or actresses who will be singing the parts. Sometimes the Composer works directly with the lyricist; sometimes the two work independently.

The Composer may put a great deal of time into writing the music only to find out the words will not fit in properly or the director does not like it. He or she will then have to start again. In some instances, the Composer can spend months writing the music for a show that opens and closes quickly.

While composing for musical theater is difficult, it is a thrill to hear one's songs on stage and on recordings.

Salaries

Earnings vary for the Composer working in musical theater and/or opera. Some composers are paid a flat fee for their composition and some receive a percentage of the show and royalties for music and sheet music. Successful Composers earn millions of dollars for the music they write for shows that become popular.

Employment Prospects

Employment prospects are fair for Composers aspiring to work in musical theater and opera. Almost anyone who has talent can become a Composer for a musical production or opera. Talent alone does not ensure success in this field. Composers need to team up with someone to finance the project. Even after composers work with a lyricist and a playwright to come up with an idea for a production, they must then attract the interest of a producer who will fund the project. While finding a producer is difficult, it is not impossible. Composers must be very aggressive, talented, determined, and driven.

Another employment prospect is locating smaller theaters and production companies that offer opportunities for new talented composers.

Composers also get involved in projects through producers who have heard their work.

Advancement Prospects

Advancement prospects are impossible to determine for a Composer. Advancement in this field, like employment, depends on the drive, determination, and talent of the individual. It also depends to a great extent on having good contacts, being in the right place at the right time, and a generous amount of luck.

Composers climb the career ladder by writing music for more prestigious productions and shows that turn into hits, and receiving good notices of their work. Good reviews lead to more work.

Education and Training

There are no formal educational requirements to become a Composer. Composers are knowledgeable about music. Some are self-trained; most have a musical background, even if it has come exclusively from private teachers.

Many that are interested in pursuing a career in composing for musical theater attend colleges and universities offering majors in music and/or theater arts. Others attend music conservatories.

Experience, Skills, and Personality Traits

Composers are very creative people. They see a script, look at some dialogue, and develop the music that will fit the script. They can also turn their ideas into music. They then develop that music to suit the lyrics or a libretto.

A complete knowledge of music and music theory is needed. Composers must know how to read music and be able to play the piano. Composers in this field have an understanding of theater as well.

Composers must have the ability to work well with others, as they will collaborate with lyricists, librettists, or other composers. They will also have to deal with directors, playwrights and others who create musicals.

Composers work under pressure. Getting a piece of music completed by a set time is often necessary. Composers have the ability to deal with rejection. Aggressiveness is helpful in making contacts and obtaining auditions with producers. In order to become successful, the Composer must usually have a great deal of drive and determination.

Unions and Associations

Composers are members of a number of associations and organizations. These include the American Society of Composers, Authors and Publishers (ASCAP), Broadcast Music, Inc. (BMI), and the Society of European Stage Authors and Composers (SESAC). These performing rights organizations pay composers royalties for public performances of their songs.

Composers might also be members of the Dramatists Guild (DG) or the American Guild of Authors and Composers (AGAC). Composers who are also musicians may be members of the American Federation of Musicians (AFM). Those who have written show tunes which are recorded may also belong to the National Academy of Recording Arts and Sciences (NARAS).

Tips for Entry

1. Attend musical productions and operas. Go to all types of productions, such as stock, amateur, and regional in addition to Broadway shows and performances by major companies. Listen to the music of a variety of Broadway musicals and operas on CDs and tapes. This exposure provides you with an insight into what kind of music has been successful.
2. If you are attending school, begin writing for college productions.
3. Compose music for local community productions.
4. Find an internship in musical theater. If nothing else, you will be making good contacts in the industry.
5. Work in summer stock, dinner, or regional theaters to become more familiar with the theatrical world and give you the opportunity to make additional contacts.
6. Contact opera companies to see if they offer any training, guidance, or internship programs in composing.

SONGWRITER

CAREER PROFILE

Duties: Writing the music, lyrics, or both for a song

Alternate Title(s): Lyricist; Composer; Writer

Salary Range: 0 to millions

Employment Prospects: Fair

Advancement Prospects: Fair

Best Geographical Location(s): Culturally active cities may offer more opportunities to make contacts; any location is suitable for writing songs.

Prerequisites:

Education or Training—No formal educational requirements; workshops, seminars, and classes in songwriting are helpful

Experience—Writing of lyrics, music, and poetry is helpful.

Special Skills and Personality Traits—Creativity; knowledge of music and performing arts industry; ambition; drive; determination; ability to deal with rejection; persistence

CAREER LADDER

```
┌─────────────────────────────────────────┐
│  Successful Songwriter with Hit Songs    │
└─────────────────────────────────────────┘

┌─────────────────────────────────────────┐
│              Songwriter                   │
└─────────────────────────────────────────┘

┌─────────────────────────────────────────┐
│          Aspiring Songwriter              │
└─────────────────────────────────────────┘
```

Position Description

Songwriters write songs for any style of music, including pop, rock, folk, easy listening, country, and rhythm and blues. Individuals also write songs for Broadway plays, other musical productions, and operas. Songwriters are also called composers, writers, or lyricists.

Many Songwriters write the lyrics, the melody, or both. Some have an inspiration about a thought, a person, a feeling, and write song about it. Others have a time each day when they sit and write. Others write the music first and then attempt to fit lyrics to it. Others work on the lyrics and try to find the perfect music. In some cases, the Songwriter is talented in one area, either lyrics or music. In those cases, the Songwriter will collaborate with someone who is talented in the other area.

The goal of most Songwriters is to write a song that becomes a hit, then a standard. A standard is a song that becomes popular in all markets and stays that way for a long time. An example of a standard is the song, "Yesterday." After becoming a hit for the Beatles in the pop market, it was recorded and/or performed by many artists for other markets. The song, recorded in the 1960s, is still popular today. After finishing a song, the Songwriter makes sure it is protected by copyrighting it. Some individuals also use another method of protecting their song: putting the finished music and words into an envelope, sealing it with wax, addressing it and sending it to themselves via registered mail. When the Songwriter receives the envelope from the post office, he or she puts it away without opening it. The official postmark is a type of protection, although industry professionals say the only real protection for a song is a copyright.

Once a song is protected, the Songwriter's next job is to find a music publisher or recording artist to use the song. The Songwriter writes query letters, makes phone calls, sends tapes, or knocks on the doors of music publishers, recording acts, producers, artists and repertoire people, and managers in order to drum up interest.

When a Songwriter can perform his or her song for any of these people, a more effective way to seek interest is to make a demo record or cassette. Demos do not need to be elaborate but should be as professional as possible and be an accurate showcase of the song.

Once a demo tape is made, the Songwriter makes copies to send out. Each tape is labeled with the Songwriter's name, address, and phone number as well as the names and times of each song on the tape.

Once a song is accepted by a music publisher, recording group, record company, or an A & R person, the Songwriter retains a lawyer to go over the details of the contract. The individual may sell the song outright or may sell the rights to it.

The Songwriter receives credit for the song on the record, tape, or sheet music but does not receive a lot of attention for writing the song unless he or she also performs it.

Salaries

Salaries for Songwriters can vary greatly. There are some individuals who write songs and never sell them or the rights to the song and do not make a dime. There are others who write the music or lyrics for a Broadway musical or a stream of hit songs that top the music charts and earn millions of dollars.

Earnings for Songwriters depend on a number of factors. These include the number of songs he or she has published and/or sold; the number of times each song is played, used, or performed; the general popularity of the song; and the type of agreement made for each song.

There are different ways to make money from writing a song. Some Songwriters sell the song outright, some get paid royalties upon performance. If the song or songs are written for a Broadway play, the Songwriter may receive a percentage of the show as well as royalties from the recorded music and the sheet music.

Songwriters who collaborate on the music, lyrics, or both will share the earnings of these songs. Splits will differ depending on the individuals and the tunes.

One of the wonderful things about writing a song is that once it is published, the Songwriter may receive royalties from it for the rest of his or her life. A hit or a successful Broadway musical can mean millions of dollars to the Songwriter in his or her lifetime.

Employment Prospects

Employment prospects for Songwriters are fair. Almost anyone with musical talent can write a song. Selling it or publishing it is the key to success in this field.

Individuals may write songs for a performing artist to sing in concert or on a record. They may also write radio or television jingles and music for plays, operas, films, or television.

Some Songwriters work full time. Others work part time. A great many Songwriters are also performing artists themselves. Individuals may work for themselves or work with a collaborator. Songwriters can also work for record companies, performing artists, producers, or recording groups as staff Songwriters.

Advancement Prospects

Advancement prospects are difficult to determine for Songwriters. Individuals may climb the career ladder by writing a song that turns into a hit. They also advance their career by writing the songs (words or music) for a successful Broadway musical.

Advancement depends as much on luck as it does on talent in songwriting. A song can turn into a hit at any time just as a Broadway musical can become a box office bonanza.

Education and Training

There are no formal educational requirements for Songwriters. For individuals aspiring to write the music of a song, it is helpful to study music theory, harmony, orchestration, and/or ear training. Being able to play an instrument is useful. Those who aspire to write the words may benefit from courses in lyric and songwriting.

Courses, workshops, seminars, and private lessons are helpful to the Songwriter for their educational value, inspiration, and introductions to individuals interested in the same goals.

Experience, Skills, and Personality Traits

Songwriters are creative and talented individuals who have songwriting skills. The ability to play one or more instruments is useful for those who write music.

A knowledge of music and the performing arts industry is helpful in marketing, selling, and publishing songs. Ambition, drive, and determination are essential to success.

Songwriters must be able to handle rejection. They may play their songs for hundreds of people before one likes it enough to record it.

As in many of the careers related to the performing arts, contacts and luck are important factors in one's success.

Unions and Associations

Songwriters may belong to a number of associations and organizations. These include Broadcast Music, Inc. (BMI), the American Society of Composers, Authors and Publishers (ASCAP), and/or the Society of European Stage Authors and Composers (SESAC). These three groups are the performing rights organizations that pay Songwriters royalties for public performances of their songs.

Individuals may also be members of the Songwriters Guild of America (SGA), the National Academy of Recording Arts and Sciences (NARAS), the Nashville Songwriters Association International (NSAI), the Country Music Association (CMA), or the Gospel Music Association (GMA).

Tips for Entry

1. Remember to protect your songs! If you don't, you might write the best song in the world and have it turn into a megahit with someone else's name as the writer. Copyright your songs or send them to yourself by registered, certified mail. Copyrighting is best.
2. Avoid anyone who wants you to pay to publish your songs. Reputable publishers pay you for the right to publish your song, not the other way around.
3. Write as much as you can. Practice does not always make perfect, but it helps develop your craft.
4. Try to find songwriting courses and workshops. These offer helpful advice, tips, and inspiration.
5. Join music organizations and associations. These groups will also give you helpful advice.
6. If you are interested in writing music for the theater, look for internships with theater groups, schools, and theatrical organizations.
7. Learn as much as you can about every aspect of the music industry and the performing arts. Such exposure helps you become a success as a Songwriter.
8. You may have already written a hit song. Be persistent and persevere.

ARRANGER

CAREER PROFILE

Duties: Determining voice, instrument, harmonic structure, rhythm, tempo, etc., of a song; arranging songs for musical artist

Alternate Title(s): Adapter; Transcriber; Transcripter

Salary Range: $25,000 to $200,000+

Employment Prospects: Fair

Advancement Prospects: Fair

Best Geographical Location(s): Culturally active cities will offer the most opportunities.

Prerequisites:

Education or Training—Training in music theory, orchestration, composition, and harmony required

Experience—Writing music; playing one or more instruments; copying charts

Special Skills and Personality Traits—Ability to read music; possession of a good musical ear; proficiency as a musician

CAREER LADDER

```
┌─────────────────────────────────────────┐
│  Arranger or Composer of Music for       │
│  Broadway Show or Successful Arranger     │
└─────────────────────────────────────────┘

┌─────────────────────────────────────────┐
│             Arranger                      │
└─────────────────────────────────────────┘

┌─────────────────────────────────────────┐
│   Writer, Composer, or Musician          │
└─────────────────────────────────────────┘
```

Position Description

An Arranger's primary function is to arrange the various parts of a musical composition. An Arranger determines voice, instrument, harmonic structure, rhythm, tempo, and tone balance to achieve the desired effect.

A talented Arranger can take a song and, through creative arranging, turn it into a hit. Often, it is the Arrangers who transform songs of theatrical musicals into hits. A good Arranger is aware of current musical trends, and reworks a song to fit them.

One of the functions of the Arranger is to transcribe a musical composition for an orchestra, band, choral group, or individual artist in order to adapt the tune to different musical styles.

The Arranger, in addition to working on new songs, works on new arrangements of old hits or classics. Arranged well, these songs often outsell the original versions.

The Arranger works in a variety of situations in the performing arts including recording and performing artists, theatrical productions, and music services such as Muzak.

Music Arrangers also work for music publishers. They develop new and/or different ways to write and play music.

Arrangers also work in television, putting together music for skits or musical guests on comedy or variety shows.

Arrangers also work in the motion picture industry, scoring, and/or arranging music for the title theme and the music used throughout the film. Job opportunities are plentiful once an Arranger is established in the field.

Most Arrangers work freelance. The more jobs they obtain, the greater their earnings. Hours for Arrangers are extremely irregular. Staff Arrangers—those who are on the payroll of recording or entertainment production teams—have a more regulated workday.

Arrangers are musicians first. Many Arrangers are performers and also write music as well as arrange it.

Salaries

Arrangers who are not yet established may earn so little from their arranging jobs that they must work other jobs to make a living. Once an Arranger starts to get more work in the field, he or she can expect to make from $25,000 to $35,000 annually.

Others who have attained more success in arranging may earn up to $40,000 or more annually. Salaries depend, of course, on how much work one gets. Minimum fees for Arrangers of movies, television, or recordings are paid according to the scale set by the American Federation of Musicians (AFM).

In some instances, Arrangers are paid a royalty for each sale of a recording to which they have contributed, in addition to their fee.

Top Arrangers who demand and receive fees well over scale payments as well as royalties, may earn between $75,000 and $200,000 or more yearly.

Employment Prospects

It is not difficult for an Arranger to break into the profession on a small scale. Arranging music for local theatrical companies and other regional groups is an example of the work available to Arrangers. These jobs don't pay much, but they give the aspiring Arranger credits in the profession.

Arrangers have opportunities to work for the recording industry, television, theater, motion pictures, music publishers, or for print-music licensees. Other opportunities include working for an individual artist or group of artists, arranging materials for recordings or concerts.

Advancement Prospects

Advancement as an Arranger depends on being hired for more prestigious projects. As the Arranger's talent is recognized, more job opportunities will materialize. Composing and arranging one's own material for a Broadway show or a top group is the professional goal of most Arrangers.

Education and Training

No formal education is required to become an Arranger. Some type of musical training—at a conservatory or college or through private study, however, is necessary.

The Arranger must be knowledgeable of and be able to implement all phases of orchestration. Either formally or informally. Arrangers study and are competent in composition, harmony, and theory.

Most people aspiring to be Arrangers have studied at least one instrument, either privately, at a conservatory or through college classes, or a combination of both.

Experience, Skills, and Personality Traits

Arrangers begin as musicians. They need to play at least one instrument well, and the ability to play and understand the ranges and ability of more than one is a plus.

Most Arrangers compose music either professionally or as a hobby. The Arranger must be able to read and write music. Talented Arrangers—those who become most successful—are creative individuals who can develop their ideas into musical arrangements.

A good musical ear is a necessity, as are versatility and familiarity with current musical trends.

Unions and Associations

Arrangers may belong to the American Federation of Musicians (AFM), a bargaining union that sets payment scales for arrangements.

Arrangers may also be members of the National Academy of Recording Arts and Sciences (NARAS). This organization gives out the Grammy awards each year.

Many Arrangers additionally belong to the American Society of Music Arrangers.

Tips for Entry

1. Join the American Federation of Musicians (AFM). Members receive the organization's publication, *The International Musician.* This newspaper has a number of job opportunities and openings listed in it.
2. Spend spare time around recording studios to learn about the profession and develop contacts.
3. Write as much music as you can. Write for up-and-coming groups, productions, and even yourself.
4. Arrange songs and send them to publishers to see what kind of reaction you get.
5. Any type of experience in this field helps. Consider donating your talent (writing and arranging) to a local production or school or college musical. Offer to arrange for a local community theater group.

ORCHESTRATOR

CAREER PROFILE

Duties: Transposing music from one instrument or voice to another in order to accommodate a particular musician or group; writing scores for an orchestra, band, choral group, individual instrumentalist, or vocalist

Alternate Title(s): None

Salary Range: Earnings depend on how much orchestrating is done; impossible to estimate earnings

Employment Prospects: Fair

Advancement Prospects: Fair

Best Geographical Location(s): New York City, Los Angeles, Boston, Philadelphia, Chicago, and other culturally active cities offer opportunities.

Prerequisites:

Education or Training—Training in music theory and notation

Experience—Experience copying music and/or arranging

Special Skills and Personality Traits—Knowledge of music theory; ability to transpose music; accuracy; reliability; neatness; understanding of music

CAREER LADDER

```
┌─────────────────────────────────────┐
│   Successful Composer or Musician or │
│     Orchestrator Who Is in           │
│        Constant Demand               │
└─────────────────────────────────────┘

┌─────────────────────────────────────┐
│            Orchestrator              │
└─────────────────────────────────────┘

┌─────────────────────────────────────┐
│     Arranger, Writer, or Musician    │
└─────────────────────────────────────┘
```

Position Description

The prime function of an Orchestrator is to write the scores for an orchestra, band, choral group, individual instrumentalist, or vocalist. In this position, the individual transposes the music from one instrument or voice to another to accommodate a particular musician or musical group. For example, an Orchestrator might be asked to transpose a score for a song into a key more suited to a vocalist.

When accomplishing this function, the individual does not usually alter the musical quality, harmony, or rhythm. He or she just scores the composition so that it is consistent with the instrumental and vocal capabilities of the artists.

Although many Orchestrators work with the compositions of composers and arrangers, sometimes the individual is asked to work as the arranger. For instance, the Orchestrator may be asked to transcribe a composition while adapting it to another style of music. An example of this is when the individual changes the style of a pop song to an easy listening, instrumental version. This type of work often requires additional knowledge or training.

The Orchestrator may also function in the capacity of a copyist, transcribing musical parts onto staff or manuscript paper from a score written by an arranger. The individual performing as an Orchestrator can work full time or part time. He or she may be responsible for orchestrating, arranging, and/or copying as part of a job.

Salaries

Salaries for Orchestrators will vary depending on how much work they do and under what conditions. Orchestrators may be paid according to fees set by the American Federation of Musicians (AFM). In certain situations, the individual may be paid by the hour. These situations include work where the Orchestrator must do adjustments, alterations, additions, or takedowns of the score. Time rates are also used when page rates are not practical.

Individuals are urged to contact the AFM for specific rates.

Rates will vary for work done by the page depending on the type of arrangement orchestrated and what needs to be done. Rates also vary depending on whether the orchestration is done for live performances or recordings.

Employment Prospects

Employment prospects are fair for Orchestrators. They may work for orchestras, bands, choral groups, individual instrumentalists, or vocalists. Individuals may work for, with, or as arrangers in the recording field. They may also do orchestration for theater, films, and television.

Advancement Prospects

Advancement for an Orchestrator occurs when he or she is constantly kept busy with jobs. The professional goal of some Orchestrators is to become successful composers and musicians in their own right. They may also go on to work in the music publishing field as music editors.

Education and Training

There are no formal educational requirements for Orchestrators. The individual must know all the qualities of voice and the different instruments. He or she must know how to write scores for orchestras, bands, choral groups, etc., and how to transpose them from one instrument to another. This knowledge might be acquired at a conservatory, college or university, through private study, or may be self-taught.

Experience, Skills, and Personality Traits

An Orchestrator must have a thorough knowledge of music and music theory. He or she needs the ability to transpose music and must be accurate and have neat handwriting. Reliability and dependability are essential for success in this job.

Unions and Associations

Orchestrators may belong to the American Federation of Musicians (AFM). This union sets the minimum rate scale for Orchestrators.

Tips for Entry

1. Check the classified section of newspapers in major cultural centers for listings for Orchestrators.
2. Make up flyers and business cards. Put them up in music and instrument repair shops.
3. Talk to the orchestra(s), theaters, amateur acting, and music groups in your area to see if they have part- or full-time work.
4. If you are just beginning, volunteer to orchestrate for a production of a local theater group putting on a musical. It will give you valuable experience and will add strength to your résumé.

COPYIST

CAREER PROFILE

Duties: Transcribing musical parts onto staff or manuscript paper from a score

Alternate Title(s): None

Salary Range: Impossible to determine earnings due to nature of the job

Employment Prospects: Good

Advancement Prospects: Fair

Best Geographical Location(s): Positions are located through the country; large, culturally active cities will offer the most opportunities.

Prerequisites:

Education or Training—No formal educational requirement; training in music notation and theory necessary

Experience—Music background helpful; writing music useful

Special Skills and Personality Traits—Knowledge of musical notation; knowledge of music theory; neatness; accuracy; dependability; reliability

CAREER LADDER

```
┌─────────────────────────────────────────┐
│   Well-known Writer, Arranger,           │
│   Composer, or Orchestrator or           │
│   Copyist with Large Following or Music  │
│   Editor in Music Publishing Company     │
└─────────────────────────────────────────┘

┌─────────────────────────────────────────┐
│               Copyist                    │
└─────────────────────────────────────────┘

┌─────────────────────────────────────────┐
│   Aspiring Writer, Arranger, or          │
│               Composer                   │
└─────────────────────────────────────────┘
```

Position Description

A Copyist works in theater, music, and other performing arts settings. His or her job is to transcribe the musical parts of a song or arrangement onto staff or manuscript paper. The song is called the score. This score may have been done by an arranger, composer, or orchestrator. The individual reproduces the various parts for instruments and/or voices. Writing sheet music is one example of the work of a Copyist.

The Copyist must have a complete knowledge of music notation as well as experience and background in music to do his or her work. Part of the job of the Copyist is to make it easier for the musician or vocalist to play or sing his or her part. It is essential that the individual copy the music in a neat and accurate manner. If not, it will be extremely difficult for the artist to perform well.

The Copyist may be asked to do a number of different things. He or she may, for example, have to copy the various parts of a score for different instruments. Or, the individual may be asked to copy a corrected or changed score.

One of the major tasks a Copyist may have to accomplish in his or her work is to write out the music on paper from hearing a record or tape. Individuals who can do this are always in demand. It is very difficult and requires a knowledge of music theory, notations, harmony, composition, and orchestration.

Many individuals now also do electronic or computer music transcribing. This is often done with a computer, electronic instruments capable of MIDI (music instrument digital interface), and software. Transcribing electronically makes it easier and quicker to copy music. As a result, it can be done less expensively. Just a few years ago, equipment to do this was too expensive for most people to buy. Currently, prices on computers, software, and electronic MIDI instruments have gone down making this type of transcribing and copying affordable.

The Copyist may work full time or part time. He or she may work either independently or for a music publisher. The individual is responsible to the person or organization utilizing his or her services. As the world of music and theater in any given area is small, the Copyist must do his or her work neatly, legibly, accurately, and on time. Otherwise, the word will go out and he or she will not be hired again.

Salaries

Earnings for Copyists will vary depending on how much work they handle in a year and what type of work is done.

The American Federation of Musicians (AFM) sets the minimum fees and wages for Copyists. There are different fee schedules depending on the type of work the Copyist does.

Generally, Copyists are paid by the page copied in relation to the score page. Individuals are usually remunerated per page and a half produced. Rates will vary depending on the parts copied.

In some situations, the Copyist may also be paid by the hour. Rates vary depending on the hour and day the individual works. As there are multiple variables affecting rates, individuals are urged to contact the AFM for specifics.

Employment Prospects

Employment prospects are good for Copyists. There are opportunities for individuals who can perform this function in most of the major music, theater, and other cultural centers as well as some of the smaller ones.

There are many writers, composers, arrangers, and orchestrators who require the services of Copyists. Individuals who can do both manual and electronic copying will be more in demand.

Many Copyists work part time while pursuing a career in music, theater, and other performing arts as a composer, singer, or musician.

Advancement Prospects

Advancement prospects for Copyists will vary from person to person. Many Copyists become very successful by building up a big client following. Other individuals may advance their careers by becoming well-known arrangers, composers, orchestrators, or singers. There are also some Copyists who climb the career ladder by becoming music editors for music publishing companies.

Education and Training

There are no formal educational requirements necessary to become a Copyist. Individuals must, however, know how to transcribe musical parts onto manuscript paper. They should also have a complete knowledge of music notation, music theory, and orchestration. This training may be obtained in high school, college, through private music lessons, or may be self-taught.

Experience, Skills, and Personality Traits

Individuals usually begin their careers with some type of background in music. Many are aspiring writers, composers, arrangers, or orchestrators. Most individuals develop a reputation for doing good work and as a result are given references to others who need their services.

Copyists must know how to transcribe musical parts onto manuscript paper. Individuals should have the ability to do this work neatly, accurately, and legibly. Copyists must be dependable and reliable always finishing work when promised.

Individuals must have a complete knowledge of music theory, notation, and orchestration. A great interest in music is necessary.

Computer skills are necessary for those interested in performing electronic and/or computer copying.

Unions and Associations

Copyists may be members of the American Federation of Musicians (AFM). This union sets the minimum wages and fees that Copyists should be paid. It also sets standards for working conditions for individuals.

Copyists may also belong to the American Society of Music Copyists (ASMC). This organization provides professional guidance and support to members.

Tips for Entry

1. Send your résumé and a short cover letter to music publishers. If they don't have any openings, request that they keep your résumé on file.
2. Positions may be advertised in the display or classified section of the newspaper. Look under heading classifications of "Copyist," "Music," or "Music Publishing."
3. Consider taking classes or seminars in computer and electronic copying and transcribing. These classes are often offered by computer companies.
4. If you are still in school, take courses in transcribing, notation, orchestration, and music theory. The better prepared you are, the more opportunities you will have.
5. Advertise your skills in the newspaper or entertainment magazine in your area.
6. If you are living near a college or university that offers majors in theater arts or music, post signs explaining your talent on the bulletin boards in the school. You may find people who need your services.

PRODUCTION, DIRECTING, AND DESIGN

PRODUCER—THEATRICAL PRODUCTION

CAREER PROFILE

Duties: Finding scripts for productions; locating investors; hiring support staff; making major decisions necessary to producing plays

Alternate Title(s): None

Salary Range: Impossible to determine due to nature of job

Employment Prospects: Poor

Advancement Prospects: Fair

Best Geographical Location(s): New York City is the theatrical capital of the country; other culturally active cities may offer additional opportunities.

Prerequisites:

Education or Training—No formal educational requirement; college background or degree may be helpful

Experience—Experience in theater and business useful

Special Skills and Personality Traits—Good business sense; knowledge of theater industry and production; negotiation skills; articulateness; creativity; flair for putting projects together; reliability

CAREER LADDER

```
┌─────────────────────────────────────┐
│   Producer of More Prestigious       │
│           Productions                │
└─────────────────────────────────────┘

┌─────────────────────────────────────┐
│   Producer—Theatrical Production     │
└─────────────────────────────────────┘

┌─────────────────────────────────────┐
│  Director or Individual Working in   │
│   Some Capacity in Theater or        │
│ Businessperson Interested in Theater │
└─────────────────────────────────────┘
```

Position Description

The Producer of a theatrical production is an important person in the theatrical support team. He or she is ultimately responsible for everything that happens in a production from its inception throughout its run.

Commercial Producers working in legitimate theater are self-employed. If they can find a good script and locate financing, they can put on a production.

Responsibilities and functions of the Producer will vary depending on the specific job. A Producer for a theatrical production for a not-for-profit company, for example, will have different responsibilities than a commercial Producer working with a major Broadway show. No matter what type of show he or she is working with, however, the individual will be responsible for making all the important decisions regarding the production.

A great many of the responsibilities of the Producer are related to the amount the individual knows about the theater. In some instances, the Producer may be a businessperson who is fascinated with the theater. In these cases, individuals often surround themselves with knowledgeable people who can handle specific jobs and limit their production functions to major decision making.

Without a good script, there will usually not be a successful play. One of the initial functions of the Producer is to find the right script or story. If a story has not been scripted, the Producer is responsible for finding a playwright and commissioning that person to write a script. After it is written, the producer pays the playwright for the option of using the script for a certain period of time. During this period, the producer tries to find financing for the production. If, at the end of the option period the Producer has not found financing, the Producer may drop the play altogether or negotiate another option on it.

Before a play opens, a great deal of money is spent getting it ready for the public. Scripts are written and revised, directors, choreographers, general managers, actors, and actresses are hired, sets are designed and built, and rent is paid on the theater. One of the major functions of the Producer is to locate money to finance these start-up costs.

Producers seek investors or "angels" as they are often called. These people invest money in the production and hope to make a profit once the play opens. There are no set terms for investors. The Producer is responsible for developing and negotiating terms. After opening, a production may become self-sustaining and earn money or may not be well received and lose money. The Producer is responsible for locating people willing to take that financial risk. In some instances, the Producer is one of the individuals investing money in the show.

Once the Producer has secured financing, he or she locates and hires other important production personnel including the director. The Producer also hires a general manager, press agent, choreographer, and set designer. The Producer may also hire a casting director or work with the director on this aspect of the production.

The Producer, the director, and the casting director are responsible for choosing actors and actresses for the production. The Producer may have actors and actresses in mind to play specific parts, may sit in on auditions, or may just oversee the selections made by the director and the casting director.

As previously noted, the Producer is self-employed and works extra hard because the success or failure of a production rests on how skillfully and quickly he or she puts together all the elements of a theatrical production. The Producer puts in long hours and is ultimately responsible to other investors in the show.

Salaries

Producers are not usually paid a salary. Instead they make their money by either receiving a finder's fee for putting together the group of people willing to invest in the show or receive a percentage of the profits earned if the show is successful. Those who produce a hit production such as *The Lion King, The Producers,* or *Phantom of the Opera* stand to earn millions of dollars during the show's run. Those who produce shows that don't make it commercially lose money as well as the time they have invested in getting the show ready.

Producers working for other types of theaters such as not-for-profit and community theaters may be paid a salary. These individuals may earn between $17,000 and $40,000 or more annually. Variables include the length of the season; location, size, and prestige of the theater; and the responsibilities, duties, and expertise of the individual.

Employment Prospects

Any person with either money, contacts with people who have money to invest in theatrical productions, or business skills, combined with an interest in theater, can become a Producer. However, not everyone who attempts to be a Producer will be successful.

Prospects are poor for those seeking success as a Broadway Producer, because productions on Broadway are very expensive and risky. The Producer may find success producing shows for regional theaters.

Advancement Prospects

Advancement prospects are difficult to determine for Producers. Those producing in smaller regional theaters might advance their careers by doing the same type of work at a larger, more prestigious theater. The top rung of the career ladder for Producers is having a successful show on Broadway while working on another potentially successful show.

A great deal of the success in this job is built on an individual's reputation. If he or she has a success, it enhances the opportunities to produce another show.

Education and Training

Although a college degree is not mandatory to become a Producer, it is helpful. Good choices for majors for aspiring Producers include theater arts, arts management, communications, business, English, or liberal arts.

Experience, Skills, and Personality Traits

Producers who have a good business sense are more likely to be successful at this job. Business, administrative, and math skills are necessary. Producers must also know enough about the theater industry to be able to speak knowledgeably about advantages and risks in investing in a particular production. Negotiation skills are a must.

Producers should be extremely articulate and able to write clearly. They should be exciting, creative people who have a flair for putting projects together.

Unions and Associations

Individuals may belong to such organizations as the Producers Group (PG), the League of Off-Broadway Theatres and Producers (LOBTP), or the League of American Theatres and Producers (LAPT). These groups offer professional guidance and support to their members.

Tips for Entry

1. Become involved in your local community theater. Work in a variety of positions to get experience and learn the different aspects of theater.
2. Volunteer to do fund-raising for a community theater, arts council, or not-for-profit theater group. You will be gaining valuable on-the-job training and making contacts that will help you as you advance in your career.
3. Try to locate an internship with a theatrical company. It is another way to become involved in the theatrical world.
4. Look for courses and seminars in theater, business, and fund-raising. These will help you in your quest to become a producer.
5. Consider any job in the theater. The more contacts you make and experience you have, the better qualified you become.

DIRECTOR—THEATRICAL PRODUCTION

Duties: Visually interpreting the script; guiding the actors and actresses in their speech patterns and physical movement; coordinating all creative aspects of production; preparing the show for opening

Alternate Title(s): None

Salary Range: $22,000 to $200,000+

Employment Prospects: Poor

Advancement Prospects: Poor

Best Geographical Location(s): Positions are located throughout the country; culturally active cities may have more opportunities.

Prerequisites:

Education or Training—Four-year college degree helpful but not always necessary

Experience—Experience working in theater in some capacity from actor to assistant director to stage manager or director

Special Skills and Personality Traits—Knowledge of theater and stage; creativity; ability to coordinate; detail oriented; patience

```
┌─────────────────────────────────────┐
│   Director for More Prestigious      │
│      Theatrical Productions          │
└─────────────────────────────────────┘

┌─────────────────────────────────────┐
│   Director—Theatrical Productions    │
└─────────────────────────────────────┘

┌─────────────────────────────────────┐
│ Assistant Director, Stage Director, or│
│           Actor/Actress              │
└─────────────────────────────────────┘
```

Position Description

The Director in a theatrical production is the individual who brings the play to life. He or she takes the words in the script that the playwright has written and helps the actors interpret them visually for the audience. A good Director adds the spark to a production that turns it into a megahit. The Director's job can be compared to that of a sports coach. The coach tells the team members what to do and how to do it. The Director does the same sort of thing with actors and actresses. He or she does a combination of guiding, teaching, and telling actors and actresses how their lines should be spoken, where they should stand on the stage, and the movements they should make.

The Director has input with virtually every creative aspect of the play. He or she will work with the producer and the casting director, if there is one, to choose actors and actresses whose talents will enable the Director's vision of the play to be realized.

The Director coordinates all aspects of the production, from the set, costume, and lighting designers to soundmen, production hands, and even ushers to give the play a unified look.

The Director works very hard during rehearsals, determining what lines, actions, and moves best convey his vision of the script. A Director spends many hours in pre-production, getting the show ready for opening night.

Once the play is rehearsed and ready, it opens. After the opening, the Director's job is essentially done. He or she moves on to another project, although he or she may be called back to rehearse new cast members if the play runs for an extended period.

Salaries

Due to the nature of job, it is impossible to determine the earnings of Directors. They may negotiate a salary for weeks worked or may be offered a set fee to direct a particular show. Some Directors negotiate a deal where they are paid a fee plus royalties derived from each production.

This is not the type of job where individuals are guaranteed work year-round. Once the Director has brought the production to its opening, he or she looks for another job. A successful director who is in demand may obtain employment directing the same play in another location or may quickly be hired to direct an entirely new production. Directors are also hired to work for theaters or production companies for an entire season. These Directors are paid a salary.

Aspiring Directors may not earn any income in their profession all year. Others may work consistently. Some Directors whose productions become hits are able to negotiate not only a salary but also a royalty for each production or seat sold. Average earnings for Directors can range between $22,000 and $75,000 or more annually with the majority of individuals earning between $25,000 and $50,000 for their directing efforts in one year. There are some very successful individuals who earn $200,000 or more.

Employment Prospects

Employment prospects for Directors are poor. A lot of people want to be Directors and competition is keen.

Employment is dependent on a number of factors including talent and experience of the individual. Other important factors include contacts an individual has developed, being at the right place at the right time, and luck.

Advancement Prospects

Advancement prospects are poor. Most producers would rather hire a known Director or one who has some experience than one who has little background in the field.

Directors advance their careers in a number of ways, by directing more prestigious productions or a show in a more prestigious theater. Individuals might also direct a production which turns into a hit. As success follows success, the Director is usually in greater demand.

Education and Training

While it is not absolutely necessary to have a college degree to become a Director, it is helpful. It gives the Director a certain amount of credibility and better prepares the Director to face both the competition in the industry, and the opportunities that open up.

There are some Directors who have no college background and others who hold bachelor's and master's degrees. Good choices for majors include theater arts, acting, and arts management.

In addition to the college education, many Directors get their training watching other Directors do their job.

Experience, Skills, and Personality Traits

Directors have some type of theater experience, although there is no one career path. Many individuals work as assistant directors. Others begin their careers as actors, actresses, stage directors, or managers.

Directors must be creative people. They need to have the ability to guide actors and actresses in their speech and physical movements. A knowledge of theater, staging, and acting is imperative. Knowing stage jargon is also necessary.

Directors must be good at coordinating the various aspects of preparing a production, since much of their job is spent doing that. They need to be detail oriented and have the ability to manage many aspects of a production at one time.

Directors need to have a lot of patience as they must constantly explain their creative vision to those interpreting it. They must also be good working with people.

Unions and Associations

Directors in the theater may be members of the Society of Stage Directors and Choreographers (SSDC). This organization brings together individuals interested in the same field as well as setting guidelines and rules for negotiations and working conditions.

Depending on the specific job, individuals may also be members of Actors' Equity Association and the American Guild of Musical Artists (AGMA).

Tips for Entry

1. Make as many contacts in the theater as possible. You cannot audition to be a Director. Networking is required in this field.
2. When you land jobs, do your best and make a good impression on your coworkers. The theater world is small and a good reputation will follow you everywhere.
3. Get involved with school plays and other theatrical productions.
4. Volunteer to work in your local community theater as an assistant to the director, if possible. If not, work in the theater in any capacity.
5. Try to find an internship working in the theater. Contact schools, colleges, arts councils, theater groups, organizations, and associations about availabilities. Once you locate an internship, get involved. Do more than you are asked to and learn as much as possible.
6. Many summer theaters offer part-time or summer jobs to students learning their craft. Send your résumé with a short cover letter asking for an interview.

PRODUCTION ASSISTANT

CAREER PROFILE

Duties: Handling production-related secretarial duties; typing production notes and casting lists; typing, duplicating, and distributing script revisions

Alternate Title(s): Production Secretary

Salary Range: $350 to $600+ weekly; $28,000 to $34,000+ annually

Employment Prospects: Fair

Advancement Prospects: Good

Best Geographical Location(s): Positions are located throughout the country. More opportunities are available in culturally active cities.

Prerequisites:

Education or Training—Minimum of high school diploma; college background or degree helpful to advance in the field

Experience—Secretarial experience useful but not always necessary

Special Skills and Personality Traits—Knowledge of theater industry; typing skills; shorthand or speed writing skills; ability to communicate; reliability; organized

CAREER LADDER

```
┌─────────────────────────────────────┐
│  Production Assistant for More       │
│  Prestigious Production or for Larger│
│  Number of Productions or Various    │
│  Positions in Production, Directing, │
│  Writing, or Acting                  │
└─────────────────────────────────────┘

┌─────────────────────────────────────┐
│       Production Assistant           │
└─────────────────────────────────────┘

┌─────────────────────────────────────┐
│  Entry-level Assistant, Student, or  │
│  Assistant or Secretary in Other Field│
└─────────────────────────────────────┘
```

Position Description

A Production Assistant working in theater is responsible for handling production-related secretarial duties. While a Production Assistant works for the producer, the immediate supervisor is usually the director. The Production Assistant has varied responsibilities and functions depending on the specific production or job.

The Production Assistant is in a unique position to learn about all aspects of the theater. A Production Assistant is involved in every aspect of a production from its inception until the show opens and beyond.

During rehearsals, changes occur quite frequently in scripts. Sometimes, the playwright or director does not like the way certain words or phrases sound. In other situations, there may be creative changes. The Production Assistant takes every change that is made and revises the script. In addition, the Production Assistant may be required to type everything from cast lists to contracts. He or she will also be responsible for typing production notes.

After the Production Assistant types and revises the script, the individual makes duplicate copies and distributes them to the cast and crew. Every rehearsal means additional changes and more revisions. Sometimes the changes don't work and the director decides to go back to the previous script and the entire process starts again. Nothing is final until the production opens.

The Production Assistant is responsible for typing the blocking directions and cues for the production into the director's book, a task that may also be done by the stage manager. Blocking, in the theater, refers to the places where actors and actresses are to stand at various times in the production. It also indicates where props and other equipment are located. The director's book is a record of everything that occurs in a production. It is used by the stage manager to adjust props and the lighting manager to ensure proper lighting. It is used to produce revivals of the same play.

The Production Assistant helps the director in every way possible to get the show ready. Other duties besides typing include making or answering phone calls, contacting individuals who are needed for the production, and taking notes.

Part of the job entails acting as a sounding board for the director as he or she comes up with possibilities for creative changes. In some instances, the Production Assistant may be asked to offer suggestions.

The Production Assistant is likely to work irregular hours to ensure that script changes are ready for the next rehearsal. The Production Assistant may work during the day, evening, or at night.

Salaries

Salaries for Production Assistants vary greatly depending on the number of weeks a year the individual works, the specific production, and experience and responsibilities.

Weekly earnings can range from $250 to $550 or more. Those who work steadily earn from $28,000 to $34,000 or more annually.

Employment Prospects

Employment prospects are fair for Production Assistants. Individuals may work for various types of theatrical productions. While jobs are located throughout the country, there are many more opportunities available in culturally active cities.

Individuals who have made a lot of contacts in the industry increase their chances of employment.

Advancement Prospects

Advancement prospects for Production Assistants are determined by the skills and drive of the individual. Luck and being in the right place at the right time are also helpful.

Many individuals take jobs as Production Assistants as entry level opportunities in theater and move up the career ladder depending on specific interests. Production Assistants have advanced to positions of directors, stage managers, playwrights, and producers.

Another path a Production Assistant takes up the career ladder is to locate a similar position in a television station or film production company. These jobs may offer steadier work resulting in increased earnings.

Education and Training

There are no formal education requirements for Production Assistants, although individuals should have a minimum of a high school diploma. Typing and other secretarial skills are essential and can be learned in high school, by attending a secretarial school, or through work experience.

A college degree or background can be very valuable to anyone using this position as an entrée into theater and who wants to advance from there.

Majors to consider depend on the specific area the individual wants to specialize in. Production Assistants may have degrees in theater arts, drama, or arts management.

Experience, Skills, and Personality Traits

This is an entry-level position. Contacts in the industry are helpful. A knowledge of theater is useful.

Good typing and word processing skills are essential. The Production Assistant should be able to type quickly and accurately. Good spelling is also necessary. Shorthand or speed writing skills are also important in order to be able to take down what is said rapidly. A Production Assistant should be familiar with other office equipment including dictating machines, photocopy machines, and faxes.

The Production Assistant should have good verbal and written communication skills. The ability to speak well on the phone is necessary. A good memory is essential.

Production Assistants must have the ability to get along well with others. They must be personable, compassionate, and flexible. Part of the job includes delivering the new scripts and changes to each actor and actress as well as other cast and crew members. In some instances, when a script is changed, an actor or actress may personally lose what they consider to be important lines. The Production Assistant has the ability to deal with frustrating situations like this without getting upset.

Individuals must be dependable and reliable. They should also be organized and have the ability to handle many details at once.

Unions and Associations

Production Assistants in unionized theaters are members of the International Association of Theatrical Stage Employees (IATSE). This organization negotiates minimum wages and working conditions.

Individuals working in nonunionized theaters are not members.

Tips for Entry

1. Learn basic office skills. Practice typing, word processing, and shorthand until you work quickly and accurately.
2. Volunteer to act as the Production Assistant for your school or local community theater production.
3. Use any contacts you have in theater to secure jobs.
4. Try to find an internship in any phase of theater production. This will give you valuable experience and help you make more contacts.

STAGE MANAGER

Duties: Acting as the director's representative; scheduling rehearsals; updating scripts; blocking shows; calling cues; handling paperwork

Alternate Title(s): Production Stage Manager; Assistant Stage Manager

Salary Range: $450 to $1,951+ per week

Employment Prospects: Fair

Advancement Prospects: Good

Best Geographical Location(s): Culturally active cities offer more job possibilities.

Prerequisites:

Education or Training—No formal educational requirement; college degree useful; practical training necessary

Experience—Experience working in theater required

Special Skills and Personality Traits—Knowledge of all aspects of theater; personableness; compassion; diplomacy; calmness; detail oriented

Stage Manager for More Prestigious Production or Director

Stage Manager

Assistant Stage Manager

Position Description

The Stage Manager is the individual who takes over the responsibilities of the director when his or her job is completed. The Stage Manager's job usually formally begins two weeks before the production's first rehearsal. His or her main function will then be acting as the representative of the director.

Every production has a Stage Manager. Very elaborate shows may also have assistants. As a Stage Manager, the individual acts as a liaison between the cast and crew, and the management. He or she also coordinates what occurs on stage.

The Stage Manager has many responsibilities. The individual may attend auditions to provide input into casting decisions. He or she will also keep records of the actors, actresses, singers, and dancers who have auditioned.

The Stage Manager is required to schedule and plan rehearsals and make sure that actors and actresses are there on time. To do this the individual may prepare a written schedule or might instead verbally inform cast members. The Stage Manager is required to be present at rehearsals.

The individual is responsible for updating the script as changes are made and then making sure that cast members are given the new script.

Another of the functions of the Stage Manager is to block the show. This means he or she will verbally tell or physi-

cally tape the stage to illustrate where actors or actresses should be at certain times and where props and scenery should be placed.

Part of the responsibility of the Stage Manager is making sure that the show goes on the way the director intended it to. If, during rehearsals or the actual production, the Stage Manager sees that an actor or actress is performing his or her part differently than agreed upon, he or she will talk to the individual to get things back on track.

The Stage Manager also must be on hand to make sure that things are running smoothly among the cast and crew members. He or she may be required to settle both professional and personal disputes.

The Stage Manager has a great many responsibilities during a performance. The individual does what is referred to as "calling the show." He or she will call cues for the sound, lighting, and scenic technicians. If actors or actresses need a line, he or she will give it to them. The Stage Manager will make absolutely sure that everything goes according to the script and schedule.

During the performance, the Stage Manager is responsible for everything that goes on backstage. He or she will make sure that everybody does their job and does it properly.

After each performance the Stage Manager will write a report regarding the show. In this report, he or she will document activities and discuss things that went well, things that went wrong and other occurrences. Any accidents or injuries must also be reported. The Stage Manager's job ends about one week after closing. In the time period between the last performance and the final day of work, he or she will do all required paperwork, get necessary files in order, and load the show out of the theater.

The Stage Manager works many hours in his or her job. When finished, the only people who know if the Stage Manager performed well or not are the cast, crew, and director.

Salaries

Salaries can vary greatly for Stage Managers depending on a number of variables. These include the individual's experience, responsibilities, and reputation. Salaries are also dependent on the type of theater and production the individual is working for. Minimum earnings are higher for those involved in Broadway musicals than those working in summer stock.

For example, a Stage Manager working in a Broadway musical can earn a minimum salary of approximately $1,951 a week. Stage Managers who work in resident theater will earn minimums of approximately $893 to $1,179 weekly. Individuals employed by Off-Broadway shows or by nonunionized theater productions may work for $450 weekly or less depending on how much they want the job.

It is important to note that if a Stage Manager is in demand or highly regarded in the profession, the individual can earn a great deal more. The figures given are just minimums.

Employment Prospects

Employment prospects are fair for Stage Managers who are willing to work in a variety of theaters in various locations. These venues might include summer stock, regional theaters, Off Broadway, and Off-Off-Broadway. Prospects become more difficult for individuals when they aspire to work as Stage Managers in Broadway productions.

While New York City is the major theatrical capital, there is so much competition that it may be easier to find work in other culturally active cities.

Advancement Prospects

Advancement prospects are good for Stage Managers who are proficient at their jobs. Individuals may take a number of paths to advancement.

Stage Managers who want to stay in their profession may advance their careers by obtaining similar jobs with more prestigious productions. They may also find a steady stream of employment possibilities resulting in higher annual earnings.

Another method for Stage Managers to climb the career ladder is by becoming a director. There are also a number of former Stage Managers, who, after obtaining experience, went on to become producers.

Education and Training

There is no formal educational requirement for a Stage Manager. A college degree is not mandatory, but may be helpful in the individual's career. A degree offers a basic background, opportunities for experience and making contacts, and a degree of credibility. Good choices for majors include theater arts or arts management.

Training, in the form of practical experience, is necessary to get a job and be successful at it. This experience can be obtained by working as an intern, assistant, or in almost any area of the theater. School, summer stock, and regional theaters are all good training grounds.

Experience, Skills, and Personality Traits

Stage Managers must have a great deal of experience working in the theater. Individuals may gain this by working in various capacities. Most, but not all, have acted as assistant Stage Managers before obtaining their first position.

Stage Managers must know at least a little about everything in the theater. They must know something about acting, directing, set design, lighting, and costuming. The more knowledgeable the Stage Manager is, the more successful he or she will be in the job.

Individuals must be personable and get along well with people. In many circumstances, the Stage Manager must deal with others who are tense, worried, and/or nervous about openings. The individual must be compassionate and have the ability to calm people down and make them feel comfortable. He or she must be diplomatic in all situations.

The Stage Manager should be detail oriented and have the ability to work on many projects at once. He or she should be able to remain calm in the eye of a storm.

Unions and Associations

Stage Managers working in unionized settings must belong to Actors' Equity. This union negotiates minimum salaries and working conditions for their members.

Tips for Entry

1. Learn as much as you can about all aspects of theater. This knowledge will be useful in obtaining a job and being successful.
2. Look for internships to obtain on-the-job training.
3. Try to locate a job in summer stock. It doesn't matter what type of position you get. The experience will help you learn as well as provide an opportunity to make important contacts that may help you during the rest of your career.
4. Become involved in your school's theater production.
5. Volunteer at your local community theater. This is another way to learn more about the theater industry.

CASTING DIRECTOR

CAREER PROFILE

Duties: Casting the roles in a theatrical production; auditioning actors and actresses

Alternate Title(s): Casting Agent

Salary Range: $2,500 to $25,000 plus per production for consulting Casting Directors; staff salaries vary widely

Employment Prospects: Poor

Advancement Prospects: Fair

Best Geographical Location(s): Culturally active cities offer the most opportunities.

Prerequisites:

Education or Training—No formal educational requirement

Experience—Experience working in theater required

Special Skills and Personality Traits—Ability to match an actor or actress with the right part; organized; detail oriented; knowledge of theater industry; communication skills

CAREER LADDER

```
┌─────────────────────────────────┐
│   Casting Director for More      │
│     Prestigious Productions      │
└─────────────────────────────────┘

┌─────────────────────────────────┐
│        Casting Director          │
└─────────────────────────────────┘

┌─────────────────────────────────┐
│  Apprentice to Casting Director or │
│    Assistant Casting Director    │
└─────────────────────────────────┘
```

Position Description

The Casting Director is responsible for casting actors for the roles in a theatrical production. Good casting can mean the difference between a great production and a mediocre one. Without the proper characters acting out the script, the power of a play can be diminished.

The Casting Director works with the producer, the playwright, and the director of the production. He or she first reads the script. In this way, the Casting Director determines the characters that are needed for the play.

Once the Casting Director finds actors and actresses to fill the parts, he or she brings them to the attention of the producer, director, and playwright who then make the final decisions.

In order to begin casting, the Casting Director must understand the character's personality and physical appearance. The Casting Director chooses actors and actresses who look like the characters the playwright describes and who can make particular characters come to life on stage.

Depending on the situation, the Casting Director is responsible for creating, mailing, or delivering display or classified advertisements for newspapers or the trades announcing casting requirements for specific productions.

The Casting Director keeps records on file cards or in a computers of all talent who audition as well as actors and actresses who merely sent in résumés with photographs. This information includes an actress's or actor's name, address, phone number, agent affiliation, and professional acting credits. It also contains data about the individual's hair and eye color, height, weight, age, personality type, and skills. If the actor auditioned or was interviewed, the date is indicated with any comments made by the Casting Director. This information is useful when searching for a certain type of face, look, personality, or talent.

The Casting Director is responsible for arranging preliminary casting calls or auditions. Casting calls are events where many actors and actresses come in with their résumés and photographs (commonly known in the business as 8 × 10 glossies). During a preliminary casting call, the Casting Director or an assistant eliminates those who do not fit the look or talent type of the specific role. Actors and actresses are found not to be suitable for a particular part for any number of reasons, from being the wrong age, to having the wrong hair color, body type, or even accent, or because they do not sing or dance as well as they can act.

The Casting Directors or an assistant takes résumés and photos from all applicants. After reviewing them and deciding who he or she wants to see, the Casting Director or the assistant is responsible for calling the actors, actresses, or their talent agents back for another audition or interview.

In some cases, the Casting Director has a specific actor in mind to play a part and approaches that actor or his agent.

Sometimes established actors hear that productions are being cast and have their agents call the Casting Director to inquire about the possibility of a role. If these individuals are right for a part, they often get the job without auditioning for it.

Sometimes the Casting Director holds open auditions. He or she will advertise the parts that are available for a production and the types of actors or actresses needed to fill each part. The Casting Directors may see hundreds or even thousands of people in this manner.

The Casting Director may be hired to handle the casting for just the major stars of the show or for all the parts. If the production also has a road company production, the Casting Director may be required to fill the parts in those shows too.

Casting Directors are responsible to the production company or theater that hires them. In some instances, Casting Directors may handle the casting requirements for television, film, and commercials as well as for theatrical productions.

Salaries

Salaries for Casting Directors vary depending on the specific production to be cast as well as the Casting Director's experience and reputation in the field. Earnings also depend on whether the Casting Director is on staff at a theater or is acting as a consultant.

Casting Directors working on a consulting basis are paid a fee for their services ranging from $2,500 to $25,000 or more per production. Some Casting Directors receive a fee plus royalties on the show and earn $200,000 or more per year.

Employment Prospects

Employment prospects are poor for Casting Directors seeking consulting positions. Every production does not employ a Casting Director, because casting sometimes falls on the shoulders of the director, the producer, or both. Usually only larger, more prestigious productions use Casting Directors. However, individuals aspiring to have a career in this field can join the production staffs of regional or dinner theaters and concentrate on casting the shows.

Advancement Prospects

Casting Directors advance in their field by their own drive, determination, contacts, and reputation. Individuals take a number of different paths to climb the career ladder, by finding similar positions in a greater number of productions, or by becoming Casting Director of more prestigious productions. Still other Casting Directors advance their careers by becoming directors.

In some cases individuals find similar jobs casting parts for television or films.

Education and Training

There is no formal education requirement for Casting Directors. While it is not necessary to have a college degree, it is helpful. Good choices for majors include theater arts, drama, and arts management. A degree gives the individual a certain amount of credibility while the education offers experiences he or she may not otherwise have. There are some Casting Directors who have no college background at all.

Many individuals obtain training by assisting other Casting Directors, directors, and producers who handle the job.

Experience, Skills, and Personality Traits

Casting Directors usually need some experience working in theater, working as assistant casting directors, apprentices, stage managers, or assistant directors. There are also Casting Directors who worked as actors or actresses before landing their job. There is no one way to obtain experience.

Casting Directors must have good communication skills and must be good listeners. In some situations, the producer or director may tell the Casting Director what type of actor or actress he or she is looking for. The Casting Director must have the ability to match up the actor or actress with the right part and the contacts to be able to supply the right actors.

A knowledge of the workings of theater—stage and acting—is imperative. Casting Directors are very organized and detail oriented. They have the ability to do many things at one time. A good memory is essential.

Unions and Associations

Casting Directors may belong to the Casting Society of America, a trade association for those working in the field. Trade associations such as this one often hold seminars and conferences and offer valuable information for individuals in the field.

Tips for Entry

1. Volunteer to cast a school or community theater production.
2. Find an apprenticeship or intern program in this field. It will offer an excellent way to obtain on-the-job training and important contacts.
3. Get involved in your community theater. Learn all you can about the industry.
4. Consider a job as an assistant at an advertising agency handling accounts that produce television commercials, then get involved in learning the casting process for those commercials.
5. Attend casting calls. Facing the rejection that most actors routinely face gives you valuable insight into the demands of the job of Casting Director.

ASSISTANT CASTING DIRECTOR

CAREER PROFILE

Duties: Helping the casting director cast parts in a theatrical production; clerical work; running preliminary auditions; keeping records of auditioning talent

Alternate Title(s): Assistant Casting Agent

Salary Range: $18,000 to $40,000+

Employment Prospects: Fair

Advancement Prospects: Fair

Best Geographical Location(s): Culturally active cities will offer the most opportunities.

Prerequisites:

Education or Training—No formal educational requirement; college degree in theater arts, drama, or arts management helpful

Experience—Experience working in theater useful but not always necessary

Special Skills and Personality Traits—Energetic; enthusiastic; organized; detail oriented; knowledge of theater industry; communication skills; ability to perform clerical tasks

CAREER LADDER

```
┌─────────────────────────────────┐
│        Casting Director          │
└─────────────────────────────────┘

┌─────────────────────────────────┐
│    Assistant Casting Director    │
└─────────────────────────────────┘

┌─────────────────────────────────┐
│  Apprentice to Casting Director, │
│      Intern, or Clerk or         │
│   Secretary in Casting Office    │
└─────────────────────────────────┘
```

Position Description

The Assistant Casting Director works with the casting director selecting the talent for theatrical productions, for movies, television shows, and commercials.

Responsibilities vary for people in this position depending on the experience of the assistant as well as the specific casting director the individual is working with.

Assistant Casting Directors with little experience are often responsible for clerical duties. They are required to write and type memos and letters to talent agents and managers regarding casting for specific parts. They phone agents about casting calls and auditions or to arrange to have talent come back for additional interviews.

The Assistant Casting Director attends casting calls and auditions with the casting director. Being present at the auditions helps the assistant learn more about choosing the correct actor or actress for a particular part. The assistant usually is asked his or her opinion of a particular actor or actress's work.

The assistant is required to keep records on all the talent who audition for parts. The individual is also required to keep records of actors and actresses who send résumés with photographs to the casting director. The assistant keeps information such as the actor's name, address, phone number, agent affili-

ation, and professional acting credits on file cards or enters the data into a computer. The data includes the individual's hair color, eye color, height, weight, age, personality type, and skills. If the talent was auditioned or interviewed, the date is indicated with any comments offered by the casting director. This information is useful when the casting director is searching for a certain look in an actor or actress.

In some instances, the assistant is responsible for creating display or classified advertisements for newspapers or the trades announcing casting requirements for specific parts. Sometimes the assistant is required to mail or deliver finished advertisements.

The Casting Assistant is responsible for arranging or running preliminary casting calls or auditions where many actors and actresses come with their résumés and photographs (commonly known in the business as 8 × 10 glossies). During a preliminary casting call, the assistant is required by the casting director to eliminate people who do not fit the part to be filled. For example, the casting director will instruct the assistant to look for actresses who can sing and dance. When the assistant talks to potential actresses or reviews their résumé, he or she will eliminate those who do not sing and dance.

The assistant takes résumés and photos from all suitable applicants and gives them to the casting director. After the casting director reviews them and decides who he or she wants to see, the assistant is responsible for calling the actors, actresses, or talent agents representing these people back for another audition or interview.

When the casting director finds an actor or actress that looks promising for a part, the assistant is responsible for calling or notifying the producer, the director, and the playwright. He or she will also be responsible for setting up further auditions for the people involved.

Once the talent is chosen, the Assistant Casting Director is responsible for booking it through the proper agent or agency. The assistant is required to type contracts. He or she may be responsible for delivering the finished contracts and any other material to the talent or the talent agent and then getting the contracts signed and returned. If the actors or actresses are union employees, the assistant obtains union membership numbers and takes care of any other union-related business.

The Assistant Casting Director handles a great deal of telephone work for the casting director. He or she is required to make calls on behalf of the individual as well as answer the phone. The individual is required to buffer calls from talent agents, directors, and producers when the casting director has not decided on the casting of a particular project.

The Assistant Casting Director is responsible to the casting director and usually works long hours. The Assistant regularly attends new and nonunion productions to report on new talent.

Salaries

Salaries for Assistant Casting Directors can range from $18,000 to $40,000 or more annually depending on a number of factors, such as his or her responsibilities, experience, and geographic location. Earnings also depend on whether the Assistant Casting Director is on staff at a theater or working as a consultant.

Assistant Casting Directors working in New York City and Los Angeles earn more than individuals employed in other cities.

Employment Prospects

Employment prospects are fair for Assistant Casting Directors. While every production does not employ a casting director, Assistants land jobs with those who are handling the casting responsibilities in those productions.

Assistant Casting Directors work for consultants or on the staffs of regional or dinner theaters. More opportunities for Assistant Casting Directors are available in major cultural centers.

Advancement Prospects

Although Assistant Casting Directors may have difficulty finding their first job, once they do, advancement prospects are good. Individuals may advance their careers by taking a number of different paths. Some Assistant Casting Directors

move up the career ladder by becoming casting directors in theater. Others become casting consultants for either theater, television, or film. In order to advance, the assistant must have a great deal of determination, drive, and ambition.

Education and Training

There are no formal educational requirements for Assistant Casting Directors. A college degree for this position is helpful but not necessary. Previous experience in theater arts, drama, or arts management offers an opportunity to make contacts and obtain hands-on experience.

Experience, Skills, and Personality Traits

Assistant Casting Directors should be energetic, enthusiastic people with a great deal of personality.

Depending on their experience level and duties, assistants may be required to perform a number of clerical tasks and should have typing and word processing skills and be able to file and keep records. Assistants should be detail oriented and highly organized.

A knowledge of theater and acting is helpful. Good communications skills are necessary. A pleasant phone manner is essential. The assistant will be both making and taking calls from agents, actors and actresses, and managers. The ability to take instructions and follow them is a must.

The ability to match up the actor and actress with the right parts is a plus. Some individuals have an innate sense of this skill, while others can learn it by watching professionals in the field select actors and actresses for various parts.

Assistant Casting Directors obtain jobs in this field by working in clerical jobs for casting directors or consultants. Others work as interns or apprentices.

Unions and Associations

Assistant Casting Directors belong to the Casting Society of America, a trade association for those working in the casting field.

Tips for Entry

1. If you are still choosing your college, try to locate one with a theater arts or broadcast department. In addition to the courses, participate in extracurricular activities that will help prepare you for this job.
2. Participate in school plays and productions.
3. Volunteer your services to a nonprofit or local theater group to gain hands-on experience.
4. Try out for a few casting calls yourself. This experience enables you to see the casting process from the other end and brings you into contact with actors.
5. Seek a part-time or summer job as a clerk, secretary, or assistant in a theatrical agent's office. You'll gain valuable experience and make important contacts.
6. Try to locate an internship or training program in a theater. This position will help you get established on this career path.

SCENIC DESIGNER

Duties: Creating the set design for a theatrical production; conceptualizing the ideas necessary for sets

Alternate Title(s): Set Designer

Salary Range: Impossible to determine earnings due to nature of job

Employment Prospects: Fair

Advancement Prospects: Poor

Best Geographical Location(s): Culturally active cities such as New York, Los Angeles, Chicago, Atlanta, and Philadelphia

Prerequisites:

Education or Training—No formal educational requirement; undergraduate or postgraduate degree helpful; on-the-job training necessary

Experience—Experience working in theater helpful

Special Skills and Personality Traits—Creativity; ability to conceptualize; knowledge of theater, staging, and color; drawing and painting skills; reliability; ability to work well with others

```
┌─────────────────────────────┐
│   Scenic Designer for More   │
│    Prestigious Production     │
└─────────────────────────────┘

┌─────────────────────────────┐
│       Scenic Designer        │
└─────────────────────────────┘

┌─────────────────────────────┐
│  Assistant Scenic Designer or │
│      Apprentice or Intern     │
└─────────────────────────────┘
```

Position Description

Scenic Designers working in theater and the performing arts are responsible for creating stage sets. The Scenic Designer works with the director, lighting designer, and one or more assistants.

The word "set" in theater means the physical look of the stage. Stage settings are very important to a production. They help create the mood for a show and visually explain to the audience where a specific scene is taking place. The Scenic Designer produces a variety of effects using different backdrops, props, and lighting.

In many productions, the Scenic Designer creates more than one set depending on the requirements of the play. For example, an individual may develop an opening set for a scene in a living room. The next set may have to illustrate a backyard. The Scenic Designer determines how each set will be changed. When using multiple sets, it is important that the scenery and props are designed so that they can be moved easily and replaced quickly with new sets.

One of the major responsibilities of the Scenic Designer is to formulate the look of the show. He or she meets with the director to get a sense of the director's thinking. The

Scenic Designer also researches a specific time period to make sure props are appropriate.

The Scenic Designer determines what equipment, props, and backdrops are needed to produce the desired effects, working with a lighting designer to achieve the necessary effects. Once the Scenic Designer has some ideas, he or she may produce sketches or create models to illustrate them to the director.

Once the director has agreed to the set designs, the Scenic Designer is responsible for writing all the information on paper including plans, ideas, and necessary equipment. He or she may also create models of each set. After the documentation and models are completed, the Scenic Designer is responsible for soliciting bids on building the sets from scenery shops. After the production's general manager approves the bid, the scenery shop builds the sets under the Scenic Designer's direction.

When a shop is chosen and the price has been agreed upon, it is the responsibility of the Scenic Designer to check on the progress of the scenery shop to make sure that everything is on schedule. If there are any problems with the scenery, or if the costs are escalating, the Scenic Designer must sometimes change his designs to keep costs within the production's budget.

Sometimes, a Scenic Designer of a Broadway production designs sets for a number of theaters because the show may go into previews in other theaters before it actually opens in New York. The scenery must be adaptable to every theater, as all stages are not the same. The Scenic Designer finds a way to make every set fit in every theater.

Once built, the sets are checked on stage. The Scenic Designer makes sure that the sets change smoothly, and that the lighting is right. Once the play opens, the Scenic Designer's job is usually over. He or she may, however, be contracted to handle the scenic design for any road shows. The Scenic Designer is responsible to the director of the production.

Salaries

Scenic Designers working in the theater are usually paid a fee for each production they work on. Individuals may also receive a percentage of the profits in addition to or instead of a fee.

Salaries for Scenic Designer vary greatly depending on the individual's experience, expertise, and reputation. Earnings also depend on the specific production the individual is working with, the type of theater, and its location.

Individuals working in unionized theaters have minimum fees set by the United Scenic Artists. The minimum fee in 2005 for designing the sets for a Broadway multi-set musical was $31,858.93 A portion of this is a guaranteed advance. Which is paid in case the show does not open or closes quickly. In addition, the individual receives 13% for pension and welfare.

Those working in nonunionized settings may receive fees ranging from $750 to $30,000 or more for designing the sets for a production. Established Scenic Designers who are in demand for Broadway shows may earn $150,000 plus if their compensation includes a large percentage of the box office gross.

Employment Prospects

Employment prospects are fair for Scenic Designers who are willing to work on a variety of smaller, less prestigious productions in different types of theaters. Prospects are difficult for those aspiring to be Scenic Designers for Broadway productions.

Advancement Prospects

Advancement is difficult for Scenic Designers. It takes ambition, talent, and determination.

A beginner in the field works with a Scenic Designer which can keep him employed on a regular basis. The young Scenic Designer advances his career by taking on more responsibility in more prestigious productions. Creating the set design for a major Broadway show is a giant career step on the ladder of success.

Education and Training

A college degree or background is not always necessary to become a Scenic Designer but is helpful in obtaining training. Most individuals who are professionals in this field have at least a bachelor's degree in theater arts, design, or a related field. Many Scenic Designer also hold graduate degrees. There are colleges located throughout the country which offer degrees or courses in theater arts, scenic design, art, lighting, and architecture. These schools usually offer hands-on-training and experience.

Courses and/or seminars in art history, drawing, mechanical drawing, painting, architecture, lighting, and stagecraft are useful.

Experience, Skills, and Personality Traits

Scenic Designers need to be extremely creative, artistic people. They should have the ability to take an idea from its inception and turn into a reality on stage.

Experience working on sets for school plays and community theater is helpful for aspiring Scenic Designer. Work in any aspect of theater is useful to obtain experience and help make important contacts. Some individuals intern or apprentice with other Scenic Designers in order to get additional valuable experience.

Scenic Designers should be able to work well with others, for the job demands good working relationships with the producer, director, lighting designer, carpenters, electricians, engineers, and assistants.

Scenic Designers should be reliable and be able to complete work in a timely fashion. The ability to work under pressure is necessary.

Unions and Associations

Scenic Designers working in unionized theaters must be members of the United Scenic Artist union. In order to become a member of this group, an individual must go through an interview process and pass an examination. United Scenic Artists negotiates and sets the minimum fees and working conditions for their members.

Tips for Entry

1. Get involved with school plays and other theatrical productions.
2. Volunteer to work with your local community theater. Get experience designing sets, painting, constructing, and working with the theater lighting.
3. Try to locate an internship working in a theater in the scenic design department. If a position isn't open in that department, take any available internship you can find. Ask questions and keep your eyes and ears open.
4. Many summer theaters offer part-time or summer jobs to students learning their craft. Send your résumé with a short cover letter asking for an interview.
5. Contact the local affiliation of the United Scenic Artists to learn more about membership requirements.

ASSISTANT SCENIC DESIGNER

CAREER PROFILE	CAREER LADDER

Duties: Helping the scenic designer create the set design for a theatrical production; locating props; drafting plans to build a prop; doing research

Alternate Title(s): Assistant Set Designer

Salary Range: $350 to $1,200+ per week

Employment Prospects: Fair

Advancement Prospects: Fair

Best Geographical Location(s): Culturally active cities offer more opportunities.

Prerequisites:

Education or Training—No formal educational requirement; undergraduate or postgraduate degree helpful

Experience—Experience working in theater helpful

Special Skills and Personality Traits—Creativity; research skills; ability to develop ideas for props; knowledge of theater and staging; drawing and drafting skills; reliability; ability to work well with others; organized

CAREER LADDER

```
┌─────────────────────────────┐
│       Scenic Designer        │
└─────────────────────────────┘

┌─────────────────────────────┐
│   Assistant Scenic Designer  │
└─────────────────────────────┘

┌─────────────────────────────┐
│ Student, Apprentice, or Intern │
└─────────────────────────────┘
```

Position Description

Every theatrical production has at least one set. The word "set" in theater means the physical look of the stage. Stage settings are very important to a production as they visually explain to the audience where a specific scene is taking place on stage. The Assistant Scenic Designer in a theatrical production helps the designer create the sets that the audience sees onstage. Individuals will have varied responsibilities depending on the specific job.

One of the responsibilities of the Assistant Scenic Designer will be to find props that are necessary to complete the look of sets in a play. This task is sometimes passed onto a propman or propwoman.

Props, or properties, are the articles used on stage by the actors and actresses. They are used to decorate a set in order to make it look more realistic. Examples of props might be sofas, chairs, telephones, pens, fruits, flowers, etc. Props may also include costume props for the cast members such as umbrellas. Props are not always easy to find. In some instances, needed items are antiques or other items from bygone eras. One of the interesting parts of the job of an Assistant Scenic Designer is looking for a prop or coming up with solutions for finding props that are easily located.

Sometimes, props can be purchased. Other times, props are rented from warehouses, museums, or rental companies. The Assistant Scenic Designer must know where to go to find needed items. A great deal of the individual's job is looking, shopping, and calling around to find just the right piece that will complete a stage set. Experienced individuals in this line of work develop lists over the years of where specific items can be located. In some cases, the scenic designer cannot buy or rent a certain prop and must design it personally.

In some situations, the Assistant Scenic Designer will be responsible for drafting the plans to build a prop. He or she will then give the plans to a propmaker or carpenter to build. At other times, the individual may be responsible for building models of sets or scenery at the request of his or her superior.

Once the scenic designer has come up with some ideas, he or she may give them to the assistant to sketch or make models of so that the ideas can be illustrated for the director.

The Assistant Scenic Designer may sit in on meetings with the scenic designer and the director. He or she may be asked to help develop ideas when the scenic designer is conceptualizing thoughts for show sets.

The Assistant Scenic Designer will be expected to do a lot of the legwork for the scenic designer. He or she may be required to do research about specific time periods to determine what types of items might be used in a production from a certain time period. The individual may do this research in libraries, through books and magazines, or by visiting museums.

The Assistant Scenic Designer will help the scenic designer and lighting designer work on ideas that can be used for props, backdrops, and other scenery. He or she may be required to locate equipment that is needed to produce certain effects.

The assistant will also be required to do a great deal of the necessary paperwork. This may include documentation of set designs or detailing plans. The Assistant Scenic Designer will be responsible for helping the scenic designer check the props and set designs on the actual stage. He or she will work with the individual making sure that scenery moves smoothly off and on the stage and that each set design is as perfect and problem-free as is possible.

The Assistant Scenic Designer is responsible to the scenic designer of the production.

Salaries

Earnings for Assistant Scenic Designers can range greatly depending on a number of factors including the type of production the individual is working in, his or her experience, responsibilities, and reputation. Assistants are usually paid by the week in contrast to their superiors who are paid fees for projects. Assistant Scenic Designers working in unionized theaters will have their minimum earnings set by the United Scenic Artists union. Minimum weekly salaries for those working on Broadway in 2005 were $1,198.92 plus 13.58% pension and welfare for a five-day week. Assistant Scenic Designers working in nonunionized theaters may earn between $350 and $1,000 or more per week.

Employment Prospects

Employment prospects for Assistant Scenic Designers are fair. Most productions have at least one if not more people in this position. Individuals may work in any type of theatrical production using sets including operas and ballets. There are opportunities in dinner theaters, stock theaters, and resident theaters.

Advancement Prospects

Advancement prospects for Assistant Scenic Designers are determined to a great extent by the determination, ambition, skills, and luck of the individual. The path most individuals take toward career advancement is becoming a full-fledged scenic designer.

Other Assistant Scenic Designers may advance their careers by locating similar positions in more prestigious theatrical productions. Some individuals climb the career ladder by doing similar work in television or films.

Education and Training

While there is no formal educational requirement for Assistant Scenic Designers, most individuals in this profession do have a college background or degree. Many hold postgraduate degrees. A major in theater arts or scenic design is helpful in obtaining experience, honing skills, and making contacts necessary for success.

Experience, Skills, and Personality Traits

Individuals interested in becoming Assistant Scenic Designers should get experience working in theater. A good way to do this is to work in community or school theatrical productions doing such things as building scenery or finding props. Additional experience can also be obtained by working as an apprentice or intern.

Assistant Scenic Designers should be creative. They must possess the ability to develop ideas and to locate solutions. Individuals should have the ability to take an idea from its inception and know how to make it into an onstage reality. Drafting and drawing skills are needed.

Knowing how to fix and build props and scenery is helpful. Knowledge of the theater and stage are necessary.

Assistant Scenic Designers should be highly organized with good record-keeping skills. Individuals should also enjoy searching through shops, warehouses, factories, and antique stores for props.

Unions and Associations

Assistant Scenic Designers working in unionized theaters must belong to the local affiliation of the United Scenic Artists. This union sets the minimum salaries and working conditions for its members.

Tips for Entry

1. Get involved in your school and community theater. Offer to build sets, create scenery, or find props.
2. Attend as many productions of all types that you can and study their set designs. If possible, try to go backstage to see up close what is entailed in each set.
3. Try to locate an internship working in a theater in the prop or scenic design department. If one isn't open in that department, take any internship you can find that is available. Ask questions and keep your eyes and ears open.
4. Many theater, opera, and ballet companies offer part-time or summer jobs to students learning their craft. Send your résumé with a short cover letter asking for an interview.

LIGHTING DESIGNER

CAREER PROFILE

Duties: Creating the stage lighting for a theatrical production; conceptualizing the ideas necessary for lighting; determining necessary equipment; charting light boards; mapping out light placement

Alternate Title(s): Lighting Director

Salary Range: Impossible to determine earnings due to nature of job

Employment Prospects: Poor

Advancement Prospects: Poor

Best Geographical Location(s): Culturally active cities such as New York, Los Angeles, Chicago, Atlanta, Boston, and Philadelphia

Prerequisites:

Education or Training—No formal educational requirement; undergraduate or postgraduate degree helpful; on-the-job-training necessary

Experience—Experience working as electrician

Special Skills and Personality Traits—Creativity; ability to conceptualize; knowledge of theater, staging and color; electrician skills; communications skills; ability to work under pressure

CAREER LADDER

```
┌─────────────────────────────────┐
│   Lighting Designer for More     │
│      Prestigious Production       │
└─────────────────────────────────┘

┌─────────────────────────────────┐
│        Lighting Designer         │
└─────────────────────────────────┘

┌─────────────────────────────────┐
│          Electrician             │
└─────────────────────────────────┘
```

Position Description

The Lighting Designer is responsible for creating the onstage lighting and lighting effects for a theatrical production. This work is extremely important in creating the mood of the show. With proper lighting, a Lighting Designer can create sunrise, a cloudy day, a moonlit night, or the lighting of the interior of a house, all on the same set. Lighting is also necessary in theaters so that the audience can see the actors' and actresses' faces and movements.

The Lighting Designer produces a variety of effects by using different lights, filters, and colors and by placing lights in certain positions in the theater. In some circumstances, the Lighting Designer is also required to spotlight certain actors or actresses on stage.

One of the major responsibilities of the Lighting Designer is to create the lighting that conveys the mood of the show. He or she then determines what equipment—spotlights, floodlights, colored filters—will be needed to produce the desired effects.

The Lighting Designer meets with the director of the show to determine what type of lighting ideas he or she has. The individual meets with the scenic designer to learn more about the sets to be used.

The Lighting Designer writes down all lighting information, including details of plans, ideas, and equipment. He or she also documents the methods that must be used to obtain the proper lighting. A schedule is prepared so that people manning the lighting boards will know when to turn on the proper lights. A chart illustrating which knobs on the light board relate to which lights is also prepared. The Lighting Designer also draws a map of where each light is placed and lists the wattage of every light.

Once everything is documented, the Lighting Designer works with a master electrician to put the plan into action. During this period, the designer will instruct the electrician on how lights are to be focused, what colors are to be used, and where lights are to be located. In some productions, the Lighting Designer acts as his or her own electrician performing these tasks.

The lighting is then checked with the scenery and costumes. Lighting often looks fine until it hits a different color costume. The designer adjusts the lighting until it is as perfect as possible.

After everything is set up, the Lighting Designer is responsible for checking the system again during the dress rehearsal. If problems develop, he or she must take care of them. Once the play opens, the Lighting Designer's job is over. The lighting of each performance of the show is then the responsibility of the person working the light board and an electrician.

Salaries

Lighting Designers working in the theater are usually paid a fee for each production they work on. Individuals may also receive a percentage of the profits in addition to or instead of a fee.

Salaries for Lighting Designers vary greatly depending on the individual's experience, expertise, and reputation. Earnings also depend on the specific production the individual is working with, the type of theater, and its location.

The United Scenic Artists sets minimum fees for Lighting Designers working in union shops. The minimum fee in 2005 for designing the lighting for a single set dramatic production on Broadway was $7,089.49.

Lighting Designers working in nonunionized settings receive fees ranging from $500 to $4,500 or more per production. The few Lighting Designers who are in demand for Broadway shows may earn $200,000 plus, because they receive a fee plus a percentage of the box office gross.

Employment Prospects

The job of Lighting Director is usually a freelance position. Employment prospects are poor for Lighting Designers aspiring to work in theatrical productions. Some productions do not have a Lighting Designer and instead use a production assistant to handle the responsibilities of the Lighting Designer as well as other positions.

Those seeking employment can find opportunities in universities, colleges, Off Broadway or Off-Off-Broadway, or theaters that belong to LORT (League of Regional Theaters).

Advancement Prospects

Advancement prospects are poor for Lighting Designers. As noted previously, there are limited opportunities for work. Producers and directors usually would rather work with a Lighting Designer who they have worked with before and who has performed satisfactorily. Because of this, openings do not occur frequently.

Lighting Designers may advance in their profession by broadening their experience, working on different kinds of productions. The Lighting Designer might also advance his

or her career by handling the lighting for a more prestigious production. Creating the lighting for a major Broadway show would be a career pinnacle.

Education and Training

There are no formal educational requirements to become a Lighting Designer. There are some Lighting Designers who have no college background at all and others who have undergraduate and graduate degrees. Good choices for majors include theater arts and design.

Other training can be obtained by watching Lighting Designers and electricians at work or becoming an apprentice, assistant, or intern.

Experience, Skills, and Personality Traits

Lighting Designers working in theater must have a great deal of creativity. They must also have the ability to conceptualize what a particular scene should look like to achieve the desired effect. Individuals must have the capability and expertise to turn ideas into reality.

Lighting Designers should have a thorough knowledge of theater, staging, and color, as well as the skills of an electrician. They need the ability to communicate their ideas to others.

Lighting Designers should work well with people, such as directors, scenic designers, and electricians. Individuals should be detail oriented and able to work under pressure.

Unions and Associations

Lighting Designers working in unionized theaters are members of the United Scenic Artist local. Some individuals are also members of the International Brotherhood of Electrical Workers (IBEW) and/or the International Alliance of Theatrical Stage Employees (IATSE). These groups set minimum fees and working conditions for their members.

Tips for Entry

1. Internships are a great way to learn as well as to make contacts. Try to locate them through schools, theater groups, and organizations. You might also ask a Lighting Designer if he or she will let you intern.
2. Apprenticeships are another method of learning the trade. Contact appropriate unions for information.
3. Go to as many plays and productions as possible and study the lighting techniques.
4. Read the numerous books that are published on the subject. These will help you understand and learn more about lighting design.
5. Offer to act as the Lighting Designer or his or her assistant for your school or local community theater production. This position will give you good hands-on experience.

COSTUME DESIGNER

CAREER PROFILE

Duties: Developing and creating costume designs for clothing worn in theatrical productions

Alternate Title(s): Designer

Salary Range: Impossible to determine earnings due to nature of job

Employment Prospects: Poor

Advancement Prospects: Poor

Best Geographical Location(s): Culturally active cities such as New York, Los Angeles, Chicago, Atlanta, and Philadelphia

Prerequisites:

Education or Training—College degree or background in theater, fashion, or costume design helpful, but not always required.

Experience—Experience in designing clothing necessary

Special Skills and Personality Traits—Knowledge of fashion, colors, and fabrics; expertise in designing; sketching skills; fashion drawing skills; creativity; ability to work under pressure

CAREER LADDER

```
┌─────────────────────────────┐
│  Costume Designer for More   │
│    Prestigious Production     │
└─────────────────────────────┘

┌─────────────────────────────┐
│      Costume Designer        │
└─────────────────────────────┘

┌─────────────────────────────┐
│ Clothing Designer or Apprentice │
└─────────────────────────────┘
```

Position Description

The Costume Designer in a theatrical production is responsible for developing and creating the costumes worn in the show. Depending on the size and type of the production, the Costume Designer has varied responsibilities. The Costume Designer is usually hired by the producer at the request of the director.

The Costume Designer is an important part of the production. Costumes help the characters come to life on stage. Without them, a great deal of the allure of the performance is not present.

In some productions the Costume Designer creates and executes elaborate designs. In others, he or she is responsible for locating clothing "off the rack" that fits into the production.

A Costume Designer first becomes familiar with the script. He or she then discusses costuming ideas with the director. Together they will determine how elaborate a production will be. For example, the Costume Designer determines the number of times the actors and actresses change costumes and the number of costumes needed. The Costume Designer also meets with the scenic and lighting designers to learn more about their ideas for the production.

If the production is set in a certain time period, the Costume Designer researches clothing, fabrics, and styles of the era by reading, by watching television or movies, by checking museums, and by looking through periodicals. He or she then begins developing ideas for costumes by sketching them and bringing them to the director for approval.

A lot of thought goes into developing costumes for productions. If, for instance, an actor must make quick changes, costumes are designed so that they are easy to get in and out of. Costumes are designed so that they look as good from the back of a theater as they do from the front. As the same costumes are used for every performance, fabrics and designs must be made to withstand heavy wear.

The responsibilities of the Costume Designer depends on the production. In some productions, the costumes are sent out to companies for construction. Other productions hire workers to make the costumes under the direction of the Designer. In other instances, the Costume Designer makes the costumes either alone or with the help of one or two assistants.

In most productions, when all the costumes are ready, there is what is known as a "dress parade," a dress rehearsal for actors and actresses in costume. Each person walks across the stage in their costume to see how it looks under the lights and with the sets. If the actors have problems with the costumes such as a button that doesn't remain closed or a seam that inhibits movement, the designer fixes it.

In addition to designing the actual costumes that the actors and actresses wear in a production, the Costume Designer is also responsible for designing, selecting, or finding accessories to go with each outfit. These include items such as shoes, stockings, socks, jewelry, hats, and purses. He or she is also responsible for undergarments to be worn by the actors and actresses with their costumes. Nothing is left to chance.

The Costume Designer is responsible for handling all the details related to costuming. He or she must make sure that all costumes are complete and ready for the production. The designer also discusses care and maintenance of costumes with actors and actresses and with members of the wardrobe department.

Once costumes are turned over to the wardrobe department, the clothing becomes their responsibility and the job is completed.

Salaries

Earnings for Costume Designers can range greatly depending on a number of factors, including how often the individual works and the location and type of production with which he or she is working. Other factors include the individual's expertise, experience, reputation, and responsibilities.

Costume Designers working in nonunionized settings may negotiate any type of fee. Those that are working in unionized theaters will have their minimum fee set by the United Scenic Artists. In 2005, the minimum fee for a Costume Designer designing costumes for a large Broadway production with a cast of 36 or more people was $15,023.58. Individuals also receive a 13.5% pension and welfare fund.

Employment Prospects

Employment prospects are poor for a Costume Designer in the theater. There are a large number of people seeking positions and competition is great. Many producers and directors feel more comfortable hiring people who have proven themselves in the field.

Most Costume Designers work on a per project basis, that is, after they finish one project they must find another one to stay employed. Some theaters have designers who work on staff.

Aspiring Costume Designers often break into the profession by designing the costumes for productions at dinner and regional theaters.

Advancement Prospects

Advancement prospects are poor for Costume Designers. Those working with smaller productions may advance their careers by finding similar jobs with more prestigious productions. A major accomplishment for a Costume Designer is designing the costumes for a Broadway musical.

Others may climb the career ladder by designing costumes for television shows or films.

Education and Training

A college degree does not guarantee an individual a position as a Costume Designer, but it may help in getting work in the theater.

There are colleges that offer degrees in costume design. Aspiring Costume Designers may also major in theater or fashion. Classes in drawing, art history, sewing, history, theater, costuming, fashion, sketching, and design are also useful.

Experience, Skills, and Personality Traits

Costume Designers must have a great deal of knowledge about fashion, colors, and fabrics, and expertise in all facets of designing. They must be able to sketch and do fashion drawing. A sense of style is necessary to success. While it is not imperative to be an expert seamstress or tailor, it helps to have the ability.

Creativity is a must. A knowledge of art history and costuming is useful.

The Costume Designer works with a great many different people from directors and producers to actors and actresses to seamstresses, assistants, and scenic and lighting designers. He or she must be personable and easy to work with.

Costume Designers should have the ability to work on a number of different projects at one time without getting flustered. He or she should be reliable and be able to finish projects within budgets and on time. The Costume Designer must have the ability to work under pressure.

Unions and Associations

Costume Designers belong to a number of organizations and unions. Individuals working in unionized situations must be members of the United Scenic Artists. This group negotiates minimum fees and working conditions for its members. Costume Designers may also be members of the Costume Designers Guild.

Tips for Entry

1. Many museums have costume exhibits from different eras. Visit these exhibits often.
2. Learn how to sew well. While you might not have to sew garments as a Costume Designer, knowing how will give you an edge over others and over pressured situations once productions are under way.
3. Take as many classes as you can in art history, fashion design, theater, and costuming. They will be useful in bringing you together with others interested in the field.
4. Offer to act as the Costume Designer for a school production or a local community theater. This work will give you good hands-on experience.
5. Try to find an internship in costume design, fashion design, or costuming within the theater, another opportunity for hands-on experience and for developing important contacts.

SOUND DESIGNER

Duties: Handling sound requirements for theatrical productions; determining sound mix; blending and amplifying sound; designing sound effects

Alternate Title(s): Master Sound Technician

Salary Range: Impossible to determine earnings due to nature of the job

Employment Prospects: Poor

Advancement Prospects: Poor

Best Geographical Location(s): More opportunities can be found in culturally active cities.

Prerequisites:

Education or Training—No formal educational requirement; training in electronics and sound

Experience—Experience as apprentice necessary in many positions.

Special Skills and Personality Traits—Understanding of acoustics; complete knowledge of electronics; creativity; supervisory skills; communication skills; ability to work under pressure

```
┌─────────────────────────────────┐
│   Sound Designer for More        │
│   Prestigious Production         │
└─────────────────────────────────┘

┌─────────────────────────────────┐
│      Sound Designer              │
└─────────────────────────────────┘

┌─────────────────────────────────┐
│      Apprentice                  │
└─────────────────────────────────┘
```

Position Description

The Sound Designer is responsible for the acoustics for a theatrical production. He or she makes sure that everyone can hear what is going on and that the sound is pleasing to the ears of the audience.

Sound Designers work in Broadway theaters as well as dinner and summer stock theaters. They also work in concert halls, arenas or other venues. Their job is to design the sound for the production before the show opens. Sound requirements and responsibilities are then passed on to other sound technicians. Many theaters, however, give the responsibilities of the Sound Designer to a soundman or soundwoman who will stay with the show once it opens and also handle the soundboard.

Sound Designers do with sound what lighting designers do with lights. The sound of a show, like the lighting, helps create the mood of a production. With proper sound, a scene can include a thunderstorm, a quiet night, or a noisy dance hall. Without good sound control, the playwright's words

may not be heard and sound effects may not create the mood the director wants.

As each theater has different acoustics, obtaining good sound with the proper effects is difficult. The sound for each production is examined, thought out, developed, and executed in a unique way for each theater.

The Sound Designer has varied responsibilities depending on the specific production. In some instances, he or she will be supervising other sound specialists. In others, the Sound Designer handles all sound-related tasks personally.

The Sound Designer meets with the director to determine what type of sound and effects are needed and then works toward achieving these effects. For example, if the sound of thunder is required, the Sound Designer must find something that can imitate the sound. He or she then decides if the effect will be used live for each performance or if a recording will work as well.

The Sound Designer also determines if the production requires any recorded music. If it does, he or she is responsible for recording it or assigning the task to a sound technician.

The Sound Designer produces a variety of sound effects with different equipment and is responsible for determining what equipment is needed and making sure it is available. He or she must also decide where equipment, such as microphones and amplifiers are placed to obtain optimum sound.

The Sound Designer makes the sound the audience hears appear normal and lifelike. This is accomplished by mixing and blending the various sounds that come from all the microphones used on stage and backstage. The designer decides what amplification each microphone should have. When music is playing, for instance, the Sound Designer will want to make sure the audience can still hear on-stage voices.

A great deal of this work is accomplished by determining how the controls should be adjusted at the soundboard. The Sound Designer will try various levels until he or she comes up with the perfect mix.

The Sound Designer documents all sound information on paper, including all equipment used and its placement. He or she also prepares the schedule that will be used by technicians operating the soundboard during a performance. From the schedule, the sound technician knows how to adjust controls to appropriate levels.

The Sound Designer reports to the director of the production.

Salaries

Sound Designers working in the theater are paid a fee for each production, or on a weekly salary. Earnings vary depending on the individual's experience, expertise, and reputation. The earnings also depend on the specific production, the type of theater, and its location.

Those working in unionized settings have minimum earnings set and negotiated by the local affiliation of the International Alliance of Theatrical Stage Employees (IATSE).

Earnings for Sound Designer can range from $350 to $1,000 or more per week on a salary basis, or they may be paid a fee for the production ranging from $1,000 to $25,000 or more. Some individuals who are in demand for Broadway shows earn $100,000 or more if they have worked out deals where they receive a fee plus a percentage of the gross at the box office. There are, however, not many people in the field earning this type of money.

Employment Prospects

Employment prospects are poor for individual aspiring to work as Sound Designers in theatrical productions. Job prospects increase for those who do the technical work as well as the sound design.

All productions do not have a Sound Designer. Some use other sound technicians to handle the responsibilities of Sound Designer.

Advancement Prospects

Advancement prospects are limited for Sound Designers. Individuals may climb the career ladder by finding a greater number of productions to design the sound for or by doing similar work for more prestigious productions. Another method of career advancement is to do similar work for major popular music acts, which in turn may lead to more a permanent position and increased earnings.

Many producers and directors hire Sound Designers they have worked with before and who have performed satisfactorily. Openings in this field do not occur that frequently.

Education and Training

There are no formal educational requirements for becoming a Sound Designer. Training in electronics and sound techniques is necessary. There are vocational schools that teach this. Some Sound Designers pick up necessary skills by watching others.

A college background is not required, but it gives the individual a well-rounded education, opportunities to gain experience in the field, and a way to make important contacts. Majors for those interested in sound design include theater arts or design.

Sound Designers who work in unionized settings must be members of the local affiliation of the International Alliance of Theatrical Stage Employees (IATSE). In order to become a member of this union, individuals must go through an apprenticeship program.

Experience, Skills, and Personality Traits

Sound Designers for theatrical productions obtain experience by taking part in apprenticeship programs. Others get experience by handling the sound requirements for school and community productions. Still others work in the music industry doing sound design for groups and singers.

Sound Designers working in theater must have an understanding of acoustics plus a full knowledge of electronics and the use of all sound equipment.

Sound Designers are creative. While to the layperson "sound is sound," the Designer uses it to create a mood in the theater. Designers need the ability to understand how to produce a desired sound effect and then make it happen.

Sound Designers also need supervisory skills. The ability to communicate is necessary. Individuals should be able to work under pressure without getting flustered.

Unions and Associations

Sound Designers working in unionized theaters are members of the International Alliance of Theatrical Stage Employees (IATSE). Some individuals may also be members of the International Brotherhood of Electrical Workers

(IBEW). These organizations negotiate and set minimum fees and working conditions for their members.

Tips for Entry

1. Internships are a great way to learn, as well as to make contacts. Try to locate them through schools, theater groups, and other organizations.

2. Apprenticeships are another method of learning the trade. Contact the appropriate unions for information.

3. Offer to act as the Sound Technician or assistant for your school or local community theater production. This will give you good hands-on experience.

4. Work with a local music group that needs a Sound Technician.

THEATRICAL ADMINISTRATION AND BUSINESS

COMPANY MANAGER

CAREER PROFILE

Duties: Overseeing the day-to-day activities and operations of a theatrical production; record keeping; keeping production moving smoothly; setting up and dispersing payroll funds; overseeing ticket sales; documenting sales of tickets and cash flow after each performance

Alternate Title(s): None

Salary Range: $400 to $3,000+ per week

Employment Prospects: Fair

Advancement Prospects: Fair

Best Geographical Location(s): Culturally active cities offer the most opportunities.

Prerequisites:

Education or Training—College background or degree useful but not always required; apprenticeship usually necessary

Experience—Experience as assistant or apprentice

Special Skills and Personality Traits—Detail oriented; reliable; personable; knowledge of theater business; book-keeping, payroll and math skills; articulate

CAREER LADDER

```
┌─────────────────────────────────────┐
│  Company Manager for More Prestigious │
│  Production or General Manager        │
└─────────────────────────────────────┘

┌─────────────────────────────────────┐
│        Company Manager               │
└─────────────────────────────────────┘

┌─────────────────────────────────────┐
│  Assistant to Company Manager or      │
│  Apprentice                           │
└─────────────────────────────────────┘
```

Position Description

The Company Manager of a production represents the show's producer and oversees day-to-day business operations. Company Managers supervise everything that relates to the business of running the show, including record keeping, documentation, and the negotiation of contracts.

The Company Manager's job begins when rehearsals for the production start, although some managers start a short time prior to rehearsals. He or she attends every rehearsal and performance.

The Company Manager makes sure that the production proceeds on schedule. If things have stalled, the manager talks to the director about getting the schedule back on track.

The Company Manager is required to check on the progress of sets, costumes, and lighting design to make sure that production is moving along smoothly and on schedule. When there is a problem, the Company Manager determines where and what it is and then fixes it quickly.

One of the major responsibilities of a Company Manager is to set up the payroll. To do this, the manager goes over

each contract and determines salaries while the show is in rehearsal as well as when it is in production. The manager also determines the daily allowances for room and board if they are included. He or she is then responsible for dispersing funds to each member of the production. The manager also requires each performer to file the proper tax forms.

Another function of the Company Manager is to oversee production expenses. The manager keeps tabs on expenses to make sure that the production does not go over budget. If expenses are running over budget, the manager notifies the general manager and tries to find ways to cut costs.

Ticket sales are vital to a production and it is the Company Manager who oversees ticket sales and finds ways to increase both single and groups sales. The Company Manager works directly with the ticket office or with the assistance of a theatrical press agent. The manager is responsible for keeping a number of seats available for reviewers and other members of the press and media.

After each performance, the Company Manager determines how much money was taken in for each performance, checking the number of tickets sold, the price category, and the number of discounted and free tickets. A report is then written to document this information.

The Company Manager is required to be with the production for each performance and travels with the company if it goes on a road tour. He or she is also responsible at the close of a show for taking care of any necessary last minute details, including the return of rental equipment and storing scenery.

The Company Manager works long, hard hours at his or her job and is responsible to the general manager of the production company.

Salaries

Salaries for Company Managers vary depending on the size of the theater, its geographic location, and the experience and specific responsibilities of the Manager. Weekly earnings of Company Managers range from $400 to $3,000 or more.

Company Managers working in unionized settings have minimum salaries that are set by the Association of Theatrical Press Agents and Managers (ATPAM). The minimum base weekly earnings for a Company Manager working in a Broadway production as of September 2004 was $1,731.27 inclusive of vacation pay. Company Managers also receive a welfare fund, pension, and annuity.

Employment Prospects

Employment prospects are fair for Company Managers. Once a manager gets the proper training by acting as an assistant or going through an apprenticeship program, he may work in any unionized theatrical setting.

Advancement Prospects

Advancement prospects are fair for Company Managers and are determined by the individual's expertise, experience, and reputation. Drive and determination are crucial to advancement in this field.

There are two different paths a Company Manager can take in career advancement, either as a Company Manager for a more prestigious production or becoming a general manager of a production.

Education and Training

A college degree does not guarantee a job as a Company Manager, but it does give the individual good background, experience, and credibility. Good choices for college majors include theater arts or arts management.

Classes in all areas of theater, theater management, lighting, sound, and scenic design are useful. Courses in bookkeeping, math, entertainment law, business, and payroll are also useful.

Company Managers working in unionized theaters go through an internship program.

Experience, Skills, and Personality Traits

Company Managers working in unionized theaters get job experience by entering an internship program run by the Association of Theatrical Press Agents and Managers (ATPAM). These programs provide on-the-job training by requiring an intern to work as an assistant to a Company Manager or general manager.

Company Managers must be detail oriented and able to work on a great many projects at once without getting flustered. They should be honest and reliable, and have a great deal of knowledge about the theater and its workings. They need to know and enforce union rules and regulations.

Bookkeeping, math, and payroll skills are necessary, as are negotiations skills. Company Managers must work well with a variety of people and should be articulate and have good communications skills.

Unions and Associations

Company Managers are members of the Association of Theatrical Press Agents and Managers (ATPAM). This union sets minimum fees, working conditions, and standards for their members. It also regulates and runs an apprenticeship program that Company Managers take part in.

Tips for Entry

1. Work in as many areas of theater as possible. The more experience you have, the better prepared you are for this career.
2. Volunteer to work in your local community theater to get experience in production.
3. Get involved with your school productions to learn every aspect of theater.
4. Find an internship with a Company Manager or general manager of a theatrical company. Internships provide excellent hands-on experience as well as helping you make contacts.
5. Contacts are extremely important in this job. The more people you make a good impression on, the more job opportunities you will have.
6. Apprenticeships are available through the Association of Theatrical Press Agents and Managers (ATPAM) as well as a number of other theater groups.

BOX OFFICE TREASURER

Duties: Managing box office operations; selling tickets; filling requests for mail order tickets; determining seating arrangements; counting money after performance; preparing statements detailing tickets sold and money received

Alternate Title(s): Box Office Manager

Salary Range: $22,000 to $50,000+

Employment Prospects: Fair

Advancement Prospects: Fair

Best Geographical Location(s): Culturally active cities offer the most opportunities.

Prerequisites:

Education or Training—Educational requirements vary from high school diploma to college background or bachelor's degree.

Experience—Experience working in box office necessary

Special Skills and Personality Traits—Organizational and communication skills; detail oriented; ability to keep accurate records; bookkeeping skills; supervisory skills

```
┌─────────────────────────────────┐
│   Box Office Treasurer in More   │
│    Prestigious Theater or        │
│        House Manager             │
└─────────────────────────────────┘

┌─────────────────────────────────┐
│      Box Office Treasurer        │
└─────────────────────────────────┘

┌─────────────────────────────────┐
│  Assistant Box Office Treasurer or │
│           Apprentice             │
└─────────────────────────────────┘
```

Position Description

The Box Office Treasurer or box office manager is responsible for managing the box office that sells tickets that in turn makes money for the production. The Box Office Treasurer is employed by the theater and schedules hours when patrons can purchase show tickets. The Box Office Treasurer handles everything that occurs in the ticket office. He or she oversees the entire office and staff. If the theater is small and hires only one person for the ticket office, the Box Office Treasurer sells tickets. If the theater is larger, the Box Office Treasurer assigns sales duties to staff members who sell the tickets, obtain payment, and assign seats.

The treasurer or staff who is responsible for selling tickets at the theater's box office window puts credit card purchases through the system and authorizes ticket sales made by check. The treasurer learns how to spot counterfeit tickets and counterfeit money.

The treasurer is responsible for selling tickets in advance of the performance for the night or day of the event. Even if the Box Office Treasurer is not selling tickets, he or she must be at the theater for each performance.

The Box Office Treasurer is responsible for ordering the printing of the tickets, although sometimes the producer of the show may handle this task. When tickets arrive, the director examines them to be sure they have been printed correctly.

There is no room for error in the box office. All tickets must be accounted for. The Box Office Treasurer counts the tickets to make sure that the same number that were ordered are received. It is important that the Box Office Treasurer keep track of each ticket sold by number and the payment received. In some theaters the use of computerized ticket machines makes this task easier.

The Box Office Treasurer is aware of the various sections of seating in the theater and the prices for tickets in each of these sections. In most theaters, the Box Office Treasurer has a chart of the seats and marks off seats as they are purchased by patrons. This chart, on computers in some theaters, helps the Box Office Treasurer see at a glance which seats are available and their locations. The Box Office Treasurer is responsible for fulfilling telephone requests for tickets, giving callers information regarding the various price breakdowns, availability of seats, and the times of performances.

Many patrons purchase tickets well in advance of the opening of a production. The Box Office Treasurer is responsible for handling and filling all requests for advance ticket sales. He or she must make sure that all tickets are mailed in time for patrons to receive them or hold the tickets at the box office for pickup.

Handling group ticket sales is another function of the Box Office Treasurer, who is responsible for informing theater parties and school groups about discounts for tickets purchased in blocks. He or she makes the necessary arrangements for the blocks of seats to be sold sometimes working through an agency that solicits orders from theater parties.

The treasurer is busy before the opening of a production. During this time, he or she is responsible for handling requests for tickets for friends of the cast, critics, and reviewers. One of the more difficult jobs of the Box Office Treasurer is juggling the seating arrangements for opening nights among celebrities, dignitaries, critics, and reviewers.

The treasurer is responsible for holding and dispersing tickets to patrons who have ordered tickets prior to a performance but have not picked them up. The treasurer also gives out complimentary tickets or passes issued by the producers, cast, and press agents.

After each performance, the Box Office Treasurer prepares a statement detailing the number of tickets sold and the prices they were sold at. He or she must also count the money, checks, credit card slips, and money owed by ticket agents and computer ticket sales. Each ticket not sold must be counted. When the entire process is completed, the treasurer can account for every ticket in the house for that night and at the end of the week document in a financial statement, the amount of money the production earned in any time period.

Salaries

Earnings of Box Office Treasurers vary according to the responsibilities and experience of the individual and the size and prestige of the theater. Treasurers working in unionized theaters earn a minimum salary set by the union.

Box Office Treasurers working in nonunionized theaters earn from $22,000 a year for those working smaller theaters to $50,000 or more a year for those handling a lot of responsibilities in the box offices of larger theaters.

Employment Prospects

Employment prospects are fair for Box Office Treasurers, who can look to theaters, performing arts centers, orchestra, ballet, or opera company box offices for employment.

While positions are located throughout the country, prospects are better in culturally active cities that support a large number of theaters.

Advancement Prospects

Box Office Treasurers advance by finding similar positions in more prestigious theaters that result in increased earnings and responsibilities. Treasurers also climb the career ladder by becoming house managers.

Education and Training

Educational requirements vary for Box Office Treasurers. Some theaters offer the position to an individual with a high school diploma and prior experience working in a box or ticket office. Other theaters require that the individual have a college degree or background.

A major in theater arts management is helpful. Useful courses, seminars, and workshops include arts management, box office management, accounting, math, bookkeeping, and computer science.

Experience, Skills, and Personality Traits

Box Office Treasurers must be highly organized and able to deal with many details at the same time. The ability to keep accurate records is essential.

Bookkeeping and math skills are mandatory. A good memory is necessary, as well as the ability to supervise and work well with others.

Treasurers need both verbal and written communications skills and must be very patient and diplomatic, since box office patrons sometimes express displeasure with their seats or the prices. The treasurer must remain cool and calm to resolve disputes.

As many box offices are now computerized, computer skills are essential.

Unions and Associations

Box Office Treasurers working in a Broadway theater must be members of the International Alliance of Theatrical Stage Employees (IATSE). This organization offers on-the-job training in the form of an internship. The union also negotiates minimum earnings and working conditions for its members. Those working in nonunionized theaters need not be members of a union.

Tips for Entry

1. Work in the box office of your college's activity department selling tickets to entertainment or sporting events or doing clerical work in the activities office.
2. Consider a summer or part-time job in a movie or theater ticket office to gain on-the-job experience.
3. Make sure that you have computer training and know how to work and feel comfortable with these systems. Many offices are automated. Computer literacy gives you an extra edge in the job market.
4. Volunteer to help sell tickets and run the box office for a community theater. It's a good way to gain experience.
5. Look in the classified ads under headings for "Box Office," "Tickets," "Theater," or "Sales" for jobs working in the box office of theaters.
6. Contact the local affiliation of the appropriate unions to determine specific membership requirements.
7. Try to locate an internship program with the help of your school or by contacting theaters directly.

THEATRICAL PRESS AGENT

CAREER PROFILE

Duties: Publicizing theater productions such as Broadway and off Broadway shows, regional theater groups; compiling press kits; writing press releases; arranging press conferences; developing publicity and promotional campaigns

Alternate Title(s): Press Agent

Salary Range: Minimum salary for individuals working on Broadway shows is $1,801.44 per week plus benefits.

Employment Prospects: Poor

Advancement Prospects: Fair

Best Geographical Location(s): New York City, Hollywood, and Los Angeles offer the most opportunities; Chicago, Atlanta, Philadelphia, Washington, D.C., or any large and culturally active city may hold additional possibilities.

Prerequisites:

Education or Training—Three-year apprentice program required

Experience—Experience in publicity or public relations a plus

Special Skills and Personality Traits—Creativity; innovation; good writing skills; communications skills; ability to work under pressure; knowledge of entertainment industry

CAREER LADDER

```
┌─────────────────────────────────────┐
│  Theatrical Press Agent Working with │
│       More Prestigious Projects      │
└─────────────────────────────────────┘

┌─────────────────────────────────────┐
│        Theatrical Press Agent        │
└─────────────────────────────────────┘

┌─────────────────────────────────────┐
│    Theatrical Press Agent Apprentice │
└─────────────────────────────────────┘
```

Position Description

A Theatrical Press Agent works with theater productions such as Broadway plays, off Broadway shows, and regional theater groups. His or her main function is to publicize the production in order to get as much exposure as possible. Such exposure makes people aware of the show and generates audiences. A press agent develops various forms of publicity and promotion to keep the production in the public eye as much as possible.

Much of the Theatrical Press Agent's work is done before a show opens. During this time, agents work on creating ideas, putting programs and concepts together, and developing preopening publicity.

The Theatrical Press Agent has many responsibilities. Once he or she is hired to work on a production, they develop a publicity and promotional campaign that includes writing and producing a press kit, getting information about and photographs of the talent for fact sheets, and planning press releases, interviews, and feature articles.

The agent deals with media, arranging press conferences, press parties, opening night parties, and media events. He or she does this by setting up television and radio interviews

with the stars to help publicize the production locally, regionally and nationally.

The Theatrical Press Agent calls editors and reporters with feature stories and article ideas. With luck and a good idea, the Agent can convince a writer or producer to cover the show on television and radio, as well as in magazines and newspapers.

A press agent uses every avenue possible to obtain press coverage for a show. The Agent calls theater critics and reporters of newspapers, magazines, radio, and television. He or she may also contact cooking editors, fashion editors, or financial editors to offer interesting tie-in possibilities with the show and its stars. For example, the agent may place an actress on a television talk show during the cooking segment. The Theatrical Press Agent may arrange an interview with a financial reporter of a newspaper and the financial backer of a successful play. The idea is to get as much publicity reaching as many different people as possible.

If the show features well-known stars, the Theatrical Press Agent arranges for a photographer to take pictures of the stars attending a media event, party, or fund-raiser. He or she may also pass information along to a television, radio, or publication columnist about the celebrity.

The Theatrical Press Agent contacts critics and other members of the media to invite them to show openings, prepares a guest list ahead of time, and then arranges for tickets, assigns seats, and distributes appropriate press material prior to the opening.

The Theatrical Press Agent puts in long hours. They often start in the morning, contacting media people, writing press releases, developing and implementing publicity and promotional strategies, and attending performances.

Theatrical Press Agents work under a lot of pressure and stress. There are constant deadlines to meet and new, clever, creative, and innovative ideas to develop that will result in publicity for the show.

Salaries

Theatrical Press Agents belong to the Association of Theatrical Press Agents and Managers, AFL-CIO (ATPAM), a union that negotiates salaries and working conditions with theatrical producers.

As of November 2004, the minimum salaries allowed for Theatrical Press Agents working on Broadway shows were $1,801.44 per week plus 85% vacation pay, and 8% pension and welfare fund. Minimum salaries for individuals working on Off-Broadway productions are determined by the seating capacity of the theater.

It is difficult to estimate earnings of Theatrical Press Agents because these individuals may not work every week of the year. They are usually hired for a specific project and there is no way to tell how long each production will last.

Individuals who are in demand command weekly salaries that are higher.

Employment Prospects

Employment prospects are poor for Theatrical Press Agents. To get into this profession, an individual must first apprentice with a press agent who is a member of the Association of Theatrical Press Agents and Managers (ATPAM). This apprenticeship takes three years to complete. During this time, the Theatrical Press Agent must show talent, creativity, and an aptitude for the profession.

After becoming a member of ATPAM, the individual will have to build a good reputation in order to find work.

Advancement Prospects

Advancement prospects are fair for agents who are good at their job, create a lot of excitement for theatrical productions in the media, and have built up their professional reputation.

Theatrical Press Agents move up the career ladder by obtaining more prestigious projects to work on. These could include shows that are produced, directed, or written by famous producers, well-known directors, and established authors, as well as shows that spotlight major stars.

Education and Training

There are no educational requirements for the position of Theatrical Press Agent. Individuals must, however, go through a three-year apprenticeship working with an ATPAM member.

Those who are considering college should take courses in writing, communications, journalism, public relations, advertising, marketing, English, theater arts, and business. Seminars and courses in publicity and promotion are also useful in honing skills.

Experience, Skills, and Personality Traits

Theatrical Press Agents need to be creative, innovative people who write well. A good command of the English language, word usage, and spelling is necessary in order to produce factual, accurate press releases, feature stories, and other materials with unique angles or "hooks" to catch an editor's eye.

Theatrical Press Agents should be articulate and possess excellent communications skills. A good phone manner is essential, as much of the press agent's work is done on the telephone.

The ability to create excitement through unique publicity and promotional campaigns is imperative to a Theatrical Press Agent's success, so a good working relationship with the press and media is helpful.

Unions and Associations

As noted previously, the bargaining union of Theatrical Press Agents is the Association of Theatrical Press Agents and Managers, AFL-CIO (ATPAM). This organization negotiates and sets the minimum salary that can be paid to Theatrical Press Agents. It also set standards for the profession and provides a welfare fund for members.

Theatrical Press Agents might also belong to trade associations, including the Public Relations Society of America (PRSA). This organization offers seminars, booklets, periodicals, and other helpful information to those in the industry.

Tips for Entry

1. Publicize and promote productions for school or local theater groups.
2. Take courses in all facets of writing. Honing your skills now will help in the future.
3. Become a member of Public Relations Society of America (PRSA). The organization offers student memberships. You will have the opportunity to attend seminars and conferences which will be helpful in learning skills.
4. Find an ATPAM member who will sponsor you through a three-year apprentice program. Contact the appropriate union if you have any questions or want to find the closest branch office.

THEATRICAL PRESS AGENT APPRENTICE

CAREER PROFILE

Duties: Assisting senior press agent in publicizing and promoting theatrical productions; learning techniques of the trade

Alternate Title(s): Press Agent Apprentice

Salary Range: $350 per week, first year of apprenticeship

Employment Prospects: Poor

Advancement Prospects: Good

Best Geographical Location(s): New York City, Hollywood, and Los Angeles offer most opportunities; Chicago, Atlanta, Philadelphia, Washington, D.C., or any large and culturally active city may hold additional possibilities.

Prerequisites:

Education or Training—No educational requirement

Experience—Experience with publicity helpful

Special Skills and Personality Traits—Good verbal communications skills; good writing skills; ability to handle details; innovation; creativity; personable

CAREER LADDER

```
┌─────────────────────────────────────┐
│      Theatrical Press Agent          │
└─────────────────────────────────────┘

┌─────────────────────────────────────┐
│  Theatrical Press Agent Apprentice   │
└─────────────────────────────────────┘

┌─────────────────────────────────────┐
│  Entry-level or Publicity Assistant in │
│          Other Industry              │
└─────────────────────────────────────┘
```

Position Description

The Theatrical Press Agent Apprentice is a full-time paid assistant who works in the office of a senior theatrical press agent, and who helps publicize and promote theatrical productions.

The apprentice works as an assistant for a three-year period. During this time, he or she will work with one specific press agent at a time, although he or she may change employers during their apprenticeship. The employer, however, must be a certified, union member of the Association of Theatrical Press Agents and Managers (ATPAM).

When an individual decides to enter the profession of theatrical press agents, he or she will apply to work with a senior theatrical press agent who is a member of ATPAM. If the senior press agent feels that the applicant is dedicated to the profession, he or she will sponsor the individual who can them become an apprentice.

The individual will be a Theatrical Press Agent Apprentice for the next three years. He or she will take this time to learn everything possible from the senior press agent about publicizing and promoting theatrical productions.

The Theatrical Press Agent Apprentice will learn the techniques of the profession. Everything he or she does will be under the strict supervision of the senior press agent. It is important for the apprentice to work with an individual he or she both likes and respects professionally. The two will be spending many hours together. A lot of the future success of the apprentice will be the result of the training received from his or her superior.

A great amount of the apprentice's time will be spent watching the senior press agent do his or her job. As the apprentice monitors the mentor's techniques, he or she will find that many of the techniques used in publicity are similar. For example, every time the press agent arranges and runs a press conference, he or she will follow the same basic steps. The press agent may create new promotions but a location must always be chosen for the program, the media must be invited, and there has to be a reason to hold an event.

The Theatrical Press Agent Apprentice will learn how to write a press release, put together a press or media kit, and prepare biographies. At this point in the educational process, the individual will just be learning. He or she might gather information for the senior press agent or check the accuracy of facts, but probably would not do much of the actual writing. As time goes by in the apprenticeship, the individual will begin by writing simple press releases or bio copy.

The individual will also learn how to stage media events. This might include the development of ideas which attract media attention as well as the implementation of the actual event. The apprentice will assist with many of the details involved in the running of these events. He or she may do a lot of the legwork including reviewing the media guest list, checking to make sure that press kits are compiled and brought to the event location, or helping to greet media people. The Theatrical Press Agent Apprentice will learn to put press lists together and may be responsible for making sure that names, addresses, and phone numbers are kept accurate. He or she may make calls on behalf of the senior press agent to the media and others.

The Theatrical Press Agent Apprentice will do a lot of running around. He or she may deliver press kits, press releases, or photographs. The individual might accompany one of the stars of the production to a press interview or television appearance.

On opening nights, the Theatrical Press Agent Apprentice will help the senior press agent with his or her duties. The individual may call critics or reviewers to make sure that they will be attending, put names on seats so that the reviewers will know where to sit, or pass out press kits and media information.

The Theatrical Press Agent Apprentice's main function is to assist the senior press agent in every way while learning everything the individual knows about publicizing and promoting theatrical productions.

The Theatrical Press Agent Apprentice is responsible directly to the senior press agent. He or she will work long hours. This is not a 9-to-5 job. After the apprenticeship, the individual will be ready to strike out on his or her own and become a full-fledged theatrical press agent.

Salaries

Minimum salaries for Theatrical Press Agent Apprentices are set by the Association of Theatrical Press Agents and Managers, AFL-CIO (ATPAM).

In 1998, the minimum salary was $350 per week for the first year of their apprenticeship.

Employment Prospects

Employment prospects are extremely limited for a Theatrical Press Agent Apprentice. To obtain this position, an individual must first locate an Association of Theatrical Press Agents and Managers union member who is willing to sponsor him or her. He or she will then work with the senior Theatrical Press Agent learning the ropes.

Advancement Prospects

Advancement prospects are good for individuals who become Theatrical Press Agent Apprentices. The apprentice will go through a three-year program where he or she learns as much as possible about performing the functions of the job. Those who make it through the program and are creative, innovative, and aggressive will likely become successful theatrical press agents.

Education and Training

There is no educational requirement for a Theatrical Press Agent Apprentice. The individual must go through a three-year apprentice program learning the skills of the trade.

Those who are considering college first, may want to take courses in public relations, writing, communications, journalism, advertising, marketing, English, theater arts, and business.

Experience, Skills, and Personality Traits

Individuals have to possess good communications skills to excel in this position. They should be able to verbalize clearly, intelligently, and articulately. The ability to make and take phone calls and to obtain the correct information is essential.

The Theatrical Press Agent Apprentice must have excellent writing skills.

In order for the individual to succeed, he or she should be an innovative, creative person; someone who can "brainstorm" and come up with unique ideas and concepts for publicity and promotion. They should be aggressive, persuasive, and able to get along well with others.

Unions and Associations

Theatrical Press Agent Apprentices are members of the Association of Theatrical Press Agents and Managers, AFL-CIO (ATPAM). This a bargaining union which negotiates and sets minimum salaries for members, sets standards for the profession, and provides a welfare fund for members.

Individuals may also belong to trade associations which offer professional and educational guidance and other information. The most prominent trade association for those working in publicity is the Public Relations Society of America (PRSA). This organization also offers a student membership.

Tips for Entry

1. Contact the Association of Theatrical Press Agents and Managers (ATPAM) to get information regarding the union, branch offices, members who might sponsor you, and specifics about Apprentice applications.
2. Get as much experience as you can ahead of time doing publicity and promotion. If you're in school, work on

your school theater productions. If you aren't, you might consider doing publicity for a local theater group.

3. You might also want to take seminars in publicity, promotion, and writing. These will help you learn the basics.

4. Join the Public Relations Society of America (PRSA) or their student chapter to take advantage of their seminars, courses, literature, and professional guidance. Look in the appendix for their address and phone number.

5. You might consider getting a summer or part-time job working in the administrative end of local theater groups or summer stock to give you a partial understanding of the theater industry.

ORCHESTRA, OPERA, AND BALLET COMPANY ADMINISTRATION

BUSINESS MANAGER—ORCHESTRA, OPERA, OR BALLET COMPANY

CAREER PROFILE

Duties: Supervising the financial affairs of an orchestra, opera or ballet company; preparing and distributing payroll

Alternate Title(s): Comptroller

Salary Range: $23,000 to $75,000+

Employment Prospects: Fair

Advancement Prospects: Poor

Best Geographical Location(s): Culturally active cities offer the most opportunities.

Prerequisites:

Education or Training—Educational requirements vary; four-year college degree preferred, but not required for all positions

Experience—Bookkeeping or accounting experience helpful

Special Skills and Personality Traits—Ability to work well with figures; accuracy; accounting and bookkeeping skills; detail oriented; communications skills

CAREER LADDER

```
┌─────────────────────────────────────┐
│  Business Manager of Larger, More    │
│        Prestigious Company           │
└─────────────────────────────────────┘

┌─────────────────────────────────────┐
│          Business Manager            │
└─────────────────────────────────────┘

┌─────────────────────────────────────┐
│      Bookkeeper or Accountant        │
└─────────────────────────────────────┘
```

Position Description

The Business Manager of a symphony orchestra, opera, or ballet company is in charge of supervising its financial affairs. Depending on the size and budget of the organization, the Business Manager may work alone or have an assistant and a staff.

The Business Manager is responsible for checking all bills the organization receives. If they are correct, he or she issues checks to pay the bills on time. If they are wrong or if there is any discrepancy, the Business Manager or comptroller rectifies the problem.

The Business Manager looks at prices of various items—for example, the prices of music stands—to establish the best price. The Business Manager works out deals with airlines and with hotel or motel chains for transporting and housing the singers, orchestra, or ballet members while on tour. As the budgets for most organizations are extremely tight, the Business Manager continually tries to find ways to save money.

Accurate records are kept on all expenditures paid out for the organization and include payment dates, check numbers, and lists of items purchased.

The Business Manager is responsible for preparing and distributing the payroll both for staff members and visiting artists. These payments are disbursed in accordance with any applicable union regulations. The Business Manager makes sure that the proper deductions are taken from everyone's salary and that these monies are correctly deposited and reported to the government.

The Business Manager works closely with the organization's director of development, keeping account of money raised by donations. The Business Manager oversees the bookkeeping for the fund-raising department.

The Business Manager also works with the managing director in putting together an annual budget for the organization. After the budget is approved by the board of directors, the Business Manager is responsible for keeping costs within bounds.

The Business Manager works fairly regular hours. Depending on the specific job structure of the organization, he or she may report to the orchestra, opera, or ballet's general manager or to a board of directors.

Salaries

Salaries of Business Managers of orchestra, opera, and ballet companies vary depending on a number of factors including the classification, size, and budget of the organization, as well as the candidate's responsibilities, expertise, experience, and qualifications. Earnings of full-time Business Managers may range from $23,000 to $75,000 or more annually.

Employment Prospects

Employment prospects are fair for Business Managers. In major cultural centers, full-time work is available. In other regions the jobs may consist of part-time work.

Advancement Prospects

Advancement prospects for Business Managers working in orchestra, ballet, or opera companies are limited. Candidates climb the career ladder by moving to similar positions with more prestigious organizations that offer increased responsibilities and increased earnings. A Business Manager may also be promoted to the position of company manager.

Education and Training

Educational requirements vary from position to position. A four-year college degree is recommended and preferred, but not always necessary. College majors include business, accounting, finance, theater arts, or arts management.

Experience, Skills, and Personality Traits

Business Managers working in the performing arts should have a good sense of business. The primary skills a Business Manager needs is an ability to work with numbers and to keep immaculate records. Accuracy is essential.

The ability to set up a payroll and disperse funds is necessary. Bookkeeping skills and/or accounting experience are helpful.

The Business Manager must be able to handle many details at once without becoming flustered. The ability to communicate well is necessary.

Unions and Associations

The Business Manager belongs to different organizations depending on the specific job. The candidate may be a member of local arts councils, the American Symphony Orchestra League (ASOL), Metropolitan Opera Association (MOA), Metropolitan Opera Guild (MOG), National Opera Association (NOA), Opera America (OA), or the Ballet Theater Foundation (BTF). These organizations offer professional guidance and support to their members.

Tips for Entry

1. Check for jobs in the classified ads sections of newspapers. Most of these jobs open at the end of a season. Organization and trade association newsletters also list job openings.
2. Find an internship in the business department of a performing arts company.
3. Send a résumé and a cover letter to orchestra, ballet and opera companies. Ask that they keep your résumé on file if there is no current opening.
4. Check out opportunities on-line. Many orchestra, opera, and ballet companies post openings on their Web site.

DIRECTOR OF FUND-RAISING AND DEVELOPMENT—ORCHESTRA, OPERA, BALLET COMPANY, OR NOT-FOR-PROFIT THEATER

CAREER PROFILE

Duties: Raising funds for not-for-profit theater, orchestra, opera, or ballet company to sustain organization; creating and developing fund-raising programs; implementing programs; cultivating potential donors

Alternate Title(s): Fund-Raising and Development Director; Fund-Raising Director; Development Director; Director of Development

Salary Range: $19,000 to $85,000+

Employment Prospects: Good

Advancement Prospects: Good

Best Geographical Location(s): Positions may be located throughout the country; large, culturally active cities offer more possibilities.

Prerequisites:

Education or Training—Requirements vary from high school diploma through bachelor's degree.

Experience—Experience in fund-raising, public relations, and marketing may be preferred.

Special Skills and Personality Traits—Communication skills, interpersonal skills; enthusiasm; aggressiveness; persuasiveness; organizational skills; creativity

CAREER LADDER

```
┌─────────────────────────────────┐
│   Director of Fund-Raising       │
│   and Development for            │
│   More Prestigious Company       │
└─────────────────────────────────┘

┌─────────────────────────────────┐
│   Director of Fund-Raising and   │
│   Development                    │
└─────────────────────────────────┘

┌─────────────────────────────────┐
│ Assistant to Fund-Raising Director or │
│ Fund-Raising and Development     │
│ Department Staff Member          │
└─────────────────────────────────┘
```

Position Description

Running a not-for-profit theater, orchestra, ballet, or opera company is expensive. Ticket sales usually do not cover the costs of running such an organization. Most not-for-profit organizations augment the monies earned from ticket sales with fund-raising activities. The person responsible for directing these efforts is called the Director of Fund-Raising and Development or the development director.

Director of Fund-Raising and Development is an important administrative position in an orchestra, opera, or ballet company or a not-for-profit theater. The individual's main responsibility is to raise money to run the company.

Finding donations is not easy, especially when the country is in a recession. Many organizations and causes vie for funds donated by the public. However, many people take a special interest in their community's cultural and performing arts organizations, and it is the director's job to find ways to urge these people to donate money.

The fund-raising director is responsible for developing programs to raise funds to keep the company solvent. The candidate is expected to find ways to raise money not only for large capital campaigns to pay for new buildings or performing arts centers, but also for other sustaining programs of the organization.

The director creates and develops these programs and is then responsible for their implementation. The individual coordinates the annual giving activities, sustaining campaigns, capital campaigns, and deferred giving opportunities for donors and potential donors. These programs may increase attendance and result in increased revenue from ticket sales. They may also help develop direct financial support for the organization.

Some Directors of Fund-Raising and Development run special events or create huge annual fund-raising dinners, auctions, and dances to raise money. Other activities launched by the Director of Fund-Raising and Development include direct mail campaigns, telephone fund-raisers, telethons, galas, and cocktail parties. Many fund-raising and development directors will also look for benefactors or grants to raise needed funds.

The fund-raising and development director is responsible for cultivating potential donors. To do this, he or she might attend luncheons, dinners, meetings, parties, and other affairs on behalf of the performing arts organization. The director also speaks to groups of people about the theater, orchestra, ballet, or opera.

A large amount of money for not-for-profit theaters, orchestras, operas, and ballet companies is raised through grants, foundations, corporations, and endowments for the arts. The fund-raising and development director keeps up with the latest information on these programs and applies for grants, writes proposals, and follows up in order to receive the largest possible gifts.

The director handles a great deal of paperwork, including reports describing the progress of fund-raising projects, press releases, and publicity programs to promote specific fund-raising events. Other writing responsibilities include direct mail pieces, advertising copy, fliers, fund-raising letters, invitations, speeches, and brochures about the company.

The director is responsible for keeping accurate records of donor activities and resource development. He or she also develops and writes newsletters advising patrons of the organization's programs, new artists performing with the company, and other highlights of the season.

In addition to regular job requirements, the director attends community meetings, volunteer meetings, and special events. The director reports to either the company's manager, managing director, or the board of directors.

Salaries
Annual earnings range from $19,000 to $85,000+ or more. Salaries for fund-raising and development directors can vary greatly depending on a number of factors, including the size, prestige, budget, and geographic location of the company. Variables also include the individual's experience, duties, and record.

Employment Prospects
Employment prospects for fund-raising and development directors in the performing arts are good, as there is always a demand for individuals who can produce results. Candidates may find positions in not-for-profit theaters, performing arts centers, orchestras, or ballet or opera companies.

Advancement Prospects
Advancement prospects for fund-raising and development directors are good for those who are good at their jobs. An individual who is knowledgeable in the field and gets results can move on to positions with more prestigious theater, orchestra, ballet, or opera companies.

Education and Training
Educational requirements vary for Directors of Fund-Raising and Development. Some positions require a high school diploma; others a college degree or background. A college degree is useful both for its educational value and for the experience and the opportunities to make contacts.

Good choices for majors include arts administration, arts management, marketing, business, public relations, and liberal arts. Courses, workshops, for seminars in fund-raising, public relations, marketing, business, arts administration, and arts management are also helpful.

Experience, Skills, and Personality Traits
Experience is helpful in attaining a job as the Director of Fund-Raising and Development for a performing arts company. Many individuals work as assistants or staff members in a fund-raising department before obtaining their current jobs. Other individuals get experience volunteering to chair an organization's fund-raising drive. Other candidates work in public relations, fund-raising, development, or marketing in either the performing arts or in another industry.

The director must be articulate with excellent verbal and written communication skills. He or she also should have good organizational and interpersonal skills and the ability to work well with volunteers.

Fund-raising directors have an interest and an understanding of the performing arts. Success in raising funds comes from talking to others interested in the same areas.

Unions and Associations
Directors of Fund-Raising and Development working for not-for-profit theaters, orchestras, or operas or ballet companies may belong to the Associated Council of the Arts and local arts councils. Depending on the specific performing art the individual is working in, he or she may also be involved with the American Symphony Orchestra League (ASOL), Metropolitan Opera Association (MOA), Metropolitan Opera Guild (MOG), National Opera Association (NOA), Opera America (OA), or the Ballet Theater Foundation (BTF).

Tips for Entry
1. Send your résumé and a short cover letter to not-for-profit theaters, orchestras, or ballet or opera companies. These organizations often have assistant or trainee positions open.
2. Find an internship program in the fund-raising and development office of a performing arts company.
3. Check newspaper classified ads for positions for fund-raising and development directors under headings of "Fund-Raising," "Development," "Performing Arts," "Not-For-Profit," "Theater," "Orchestra," "Ballet," and "Opera."
4. Look for lists of jobs in the various newsletters and publications put out by arts councils and trade associations.

DIRECTOR OF AUDIENCE DEVELOPMENT—ORCHESTRA, OPERA, BALLET COMPANY, OR NOT-FOR-PROFIT THEATER

CAREER PROFILE

Duties: Finding ways to increase the size of a company or theater's audience through single-ticket and annual subscription sales

Alternate Title(s): Subscription and Ticket Service Director

Salary Range: $18,000 to $50,000+

Employment Prospects: Fair

Advancement Prospects: Fair

Best Geographical Location(s): Cities hosting symphonies, operas, ballets, and not-for-profit theaters

Prerequisites:

Education or Training—High school diploma, minimum requirement. Some positions may prefer or require college degree.

Experience—Experience working in the administrative end of theater or performing arts helpful

Special Skills and Personality Traits—Detail oriented; creativity; administrative ability; communication skills; writing skills; basic understanding of theater and performing arts; organized

CAREER LADDER

```
┌─────────────────────────────────────┐
│  Director of Audience Development    │
│  in Larger, More Prestigious Company │
│  or Theater or Director of           │
│  Funding and Development             │
└─────────────────────────────────────┘

┌─────────────────────────────────────┐
│  Director of Audience Development    │
└─────────────────────────────────────┘

┌─────────────────────────────────────┐
│  Assistant Director of Audience      │
│  Development or Student              │
└─────────────────────────────────────┘
```

Position Description

The Director of Audience Development finds ways to increase the size of a company's or theater's audience through single-ticket and annual subscription sales. This position is found in nonprofit theaters, orchestras, and opera and ballet companies. The candidate is also called a subscription and ticket service director.

The director develops a variety of programs in an effort to increase the number of tickets sold, seeking new subscribers and new markets to sell tickets. The director also works with schools, theater groups, and other organizations to develop group sales.

The director runs a variety of campaigns to find potential subscribers. These programs include telemarketing, mailing, and telethons. The individual also works with the company's advertising department in designing and running advertisements and brochures to obtain new subscribers. He or she works with the public relations department sending out press releases and feature articles about upcoming events.

The Director of Audience Development tries to target specific audiences. If the theater is presenting children's plays, he or she develops sales letters, brochures, and fliers targeted to schools and parents' groups. The individual might also develop mailings and special pricing schedules for senior citizens groups and theater clubs.

The Director of Audience Development may be required to do research to find out what types of people have come to the theater or performing arts center previously. The individual may also need to determine the demographics of annual subscribers to the theater. With this in mind, he or she can develop strategies to bring in more of the same types of people and find ways to open markets of new audiences.

The Director of Audience Development often works with other departments in the organization. These include public relations, advertising, and the box office. In some situations, the Director of Audience Development is responsible for the box office and all its activities.

The Director of Audience Development is responsible for keeping track of current subscribers. The individual may personally send out renewal forms to current subscribers or pass the duty on to an assistant, secretary, or volunteer.

Depending on the situation, the Director of Audience Development may be responsible for handling the coordination of individual theater tickets sales. Tickets for theatrical events are often sold on location at the box office, at schools, stores, or through a ticket service such as Ticketron, and the director may be required to keep records of how many tickets are sold at each location. In many instances, especially when the theater is a small one operating with a skeleton staff, the director will be responsible for making sure they receive monies owed to them for ticket sales.

The Director of Audience Development must keep clear, concise records of everything that is done in the department. This includes records of subscribers, logistics, new markets, phone calls, letters, renewals, and promotions.

As a rule, the Director of Audience Development will work fairly regular hours. He or she may, however, also be required to be in attendance at theatrical performances. The Director of Audience Development knows he or she has been successful when the majority of seats for all performances are sold out ahead of time.

Salaries

Salaries for Directors of Audience Development will vary greatly depending on the specific job, including the size, budget, and prestige of the theater or company and its geographic location, as well as the responsibilities and experience of the individual.

Earnings may range from $18,000 a year for an individual working in a small theater, orchestra, opera, or ballet company to $50,000 or more a year for someone working in a larger, more prestigious setting in a major city.

Employment Prospects

Employment prospects for positions as the Director of Audience Development are fair, as the duties of this position may be handled by the director of fund-raising and development. The great majority of the available jobs are with smaller theatrical companies, orchestras, or ballets or opera companies.

Advancement Prospects

Advancement prospects are fair for the Director of Audience Development. Directors climb the career ladder by finding a position in a larger more prestigious theater or by becoming the director of funding and development.

Education and Training

Educational requirements differ from job to job. Some positions require only a high school diploma while others require or prefer a college degree or background. Good choices for college majors include theater arts, communications, marketing, business, and liberal arts.

Courses and seminars in theatrical development, audience development, bookkeeping, computers, and marketing are also useful.

Experience, Skills, and Personality Traits

In some cases, the Director of Audience Development is an entry-level position someone fills after performing similar duties in a voluntary capacity or in an internship. Some people also enter this position after earning a degree in theater arts in college. Some people obtain experience working as an assistant director of audience development.

The Director of Audience Development should be detail oriented and organized. An ability to keep accurate records is a must.

The director should be a creative individual who has the ability to come up with unique ways to market the theater to potential audiences. The Director of Audience Development requires good verbal communications skills as well as written ones. A basic understanding of the theater and performing arts is necessary.

Unions and Associations

The Director of Audience Development belongs to any number of associations depending on the type of theater with which he or she is working. The director may be a member of local arts councils. The director working in orchestra, ballet, or opera companies may belong to the American Symphony Orchestra League (ASOL), Metropolitan Opera Association (MOA), Metropolitan Opera Guild (MOG), National Opera Association (NOA), Opera America (OA), and the Ballet Theater Foundation (BTF). These organizations offer professional guidance and support to their members.

Tips for Entry

1. Find an internship with a symphony, ballet, opera, or nonprofit theater group.
2. Volunteer with a local community theater group or symphony in the development or ticket services department. This job provides good hands-on experience and helps you make useful contacts.
3. Look in the classified ads under heading such as "Theater," "Community Theater," "Symphony," "Orchestra," "Opera," "Dance," "Arts Council," or "Audience Development." Openings may also be listed in arts council newsletters, theater group newsletters, and the American Symphony Orchestra League (ASOL) newsletter.
4. Send your résumé and a short cover letter to community and other nonprofit theater groups, orchestras, ballets, or opera companies.
5. Check out openings online. Many theaters and companies post job opportunities on their Web sites.

PUBLIC RELATIONS DIRECTOR— ORCHESTRA, OPERA, OR BALLET COMPANY

CAREER PROFILE

Duties: Handling the promotion and public relations activities for an orchestra, opera, or ballet company; writing press releases

Alternate Title(s): P.R. Director; Director of Public Relations

Salary Range: $21,000 to $60,000+

Employment Prospects: Fair

Advancement Prospects: Poor

Best Geographical Location(s): Positions located throughout the country; culturally active cities will offer more opportunities.

Prerequisites:

Education or Training—Educational requirements vary; smaller companies may prefer, but not require, a college degree; bachelor's degree may be required in larger companies.

Experience—Experience in public relations, publicity or as a journalist

Special Skills and Personality Traits—Creativity; good writing skills; articulate; verbal communication skills; organized; supervisory skills; interest in and knowledge of orchestra, ballet, or opera

CAREER LADDER

```
┌─────────────────────────────────────────┐
│  Public Relations Director at Larger,     │
│  More Prestigious Orchestra, Opera, or    │
│  Ballet Company                           │
└─────────────────────────────────────────┘

┌─────────────────────────────────────────┐
│  Public Relations Director                │
└─────────────────────────────────────────┘

┌─────────────────────────────────────────┐
│  Assistant Public Relations Director,     │
│  Publicist, or Journalist                 │
└─────────────────────────────────────────┘
```

Position Description

The Public Relations Director handles the promotion and public relations activities of a performing arts organization. Specific responsibilities depend on the size and prestige of the company.

If the orchestra, ballet, or opera company is large and prestigious, it supports a large public relations department. The director of the department is responsible for supervising the staff, the size of which varies. In very small organizations, the Public Relations Director works alone.

All orchestras, operas, and ballet companies have specific seasons, during which they put on performances. One of the duties of the Public Relations Director is to make sure that the community knows about the performances during any given season. The director does so by notifying the press and other media so that they can publicize the company's activities. The Public Relations Director writes press releases about the performers and the performances. He or she also invites the press to press conferences or press parties. During these events, the media learns about the various activities that the organization has planned for the season. The press, in turn, writes about the events and activities in their newspapers and magazines and talks about them on radio and television programs.

The Public Relations Director obtains additional publicity by promoting special activities that the company has planned for the season including children's performances, educational activities, and holiday shows.

The Public Relations Director is responsible for building up a media contact list. This list consists of names, addresses, and phone numbers of newspapers, magazines, television and radio stations, along with contact names of editors and reporters.

In order to obtain the maximum amount of publicity for the organization, the Public Relations Director writes press releases with a variety of slants about the organization, including the hiring of new members of the company, interesting stories about the organization, performance schedules, guest soloists, dancers, or conductors.

After writing and sending out press releases, the Public Relations Director follows up by calling individual editors to find out if they need more information or photographs.

The director is required to set up interviews with members of the company and various media on a regular basis to coincide with special events. It is the director's job to call radio or television stations to set up dates for guest appearances of members of the company on various shows.

The Public Relations Director works with other departments in the organization, such as the fund-raising and development department during a fund-raising drive.

The Public Relations Director is also responsible for placing advertising about the company in the various media, working with the organization's advertising director or an outside agency.

The Public Relations Director is responsible for developing, writing, and printing the publications used for promotion, education, or fund-raising. The Director assigns these tasks to others and supervises the project.

Although the Public Relations Director has a relatively normal work schedule, he or she sometimes works long hours, since his or her attendance at press parties, functions, and affairs after hours is required. The Public Relations Director is responsible to the company manager, managing director, or the organization's board of directors.

Salaries

Salaries of Public Relations Directors working in orchestras, operas, or ballet companies vary depending on the size, prestige, geographic location, and budget of the company. Other factors affecting earnings include the responsibilities and experience level of the individual.

Public Relations Directors earn between $21,000 and $60,000 or more annually with the lower salaries going to those with less experience and those working in smaller companies.

Employment Prospects

Employment prospects are fair for Public Relations Directors who aspire to work with orchestras, operas, or ballet companies. Individuals may, however, work in smaller organizations or relocate to find positions. Jobs are located throughout the country. However, culturally active cities offer more opportunities.

Advancement Prospects

Advancement prospects are poor for Public Relations Directors in orchestras, operas, or ballet companies. The career path many individuals attempt is to find similar positions with more prestigious companies, although there are not a lot of openings in the more prestigious companies. When someone does leave a position, it is usually filled from within the ranks of the organization. Another route up the career ladder for a Public Relations Director is to become the director of development.

Education and Training

Educational requirements vary for Public Relations Directors in orchestra, ballet, or opera companies. In very small companies, the Public Relations Director is not required to hold a college degree although one may be preferred. In larger companies, however, a bachelor's degree is often required. Good college majors for this type of job include public relations, communications, liberal arts, English, marketing, and music or theater arts management.

Courses, workshops, or seminars in journalism, theater and music arts, communications, public relations, publicity, and marketing are also helpful.

Experience, Skills, and Personality Traits

Public Relations Directors in orchestra, opera, and ballet companies are required to have some promotion experience, either as publicists in a similar organization or in an unrelated field, or as an assistant in the marketing or development department. Some PR Directors work as assistant public relations directors prior to their current jobs; others work as journalists in either the print media, television, or radio.

Public Relations Directors must be creative. A significant part of their job involves writing, and they should be able to write clearly and concisely.

Public Relations Directors must be articulate and have good communications skills, as they speak on a one-to-one basis and in front of large groups regularly.

Supervisory skills are often necessary. The Director learns to work under pressure without becoming flustered. Public Relations Directors must be very organized and have the ability to work on many projects at one time.

Unions and Associations

Public Relations Directors working in orchestra, opera, or ballet companies belong to a number of organizations related to the specific performing art they are working with. These organizations include the American Symphony Orchestra League (ASOL), Metropolitan Opera Association (MOA), Metropolitan Opera Guild (MOG), National Opera Association (NOA), Opera America (OA), and the Ballet Theater Foundation (BTF). They offer professional guidance and support to their members.

Directors also belong to the Public Relations Society of America (PRSA).

Tips for Entry

1. Find an internship program where you gain valuable on-the-job training as well as opportunities to make valuable contacts. Internships are offered through organizations, associations, colleges, orchestras, operas, ballet companies.
2. Look for openings in the newspaper classified or display section under the headings "Public Relations," "PR," "Orchestras," "Music," "Ballet," "Dance," "Opera," or "Publicity." Jobs are also advertised in the trade journals of the various organizations and associations.
3. Check the newsletters of regional arts councils for lists of job openings.
4. Send your résumé and a short cover letter to the personnel directors of orchestra, opera, and ballet companies. Request that your résumé be kept on file if there are no current openings.
5. Openings are often listed on theater company Web sites.

ORCHESTRA MANAGER

CAREER PROFILE

Duties: Assisting orchestra's managing director in various management duties; negotiating contracts with musical orchestra personnel

Alternate Title(s): Assistant Manager; Operations Manager

Salary Range: $21,000 to $70,000+

Employment Prospects: Poor

Advancement Prospects: Fair

Best Geographical Location(s): Culturally active cities hosting orchestras offer more opportunities.

Prerequisites:
Education or Training—College degree preferred or recommended for most positions
Experience—Positions in supervisory capacities useful
Special Skills and Personality Traits—Management, supervisory, and negotiating skills

CAREER LADDER

```
┌─────────────────────────────┐
│     Managing Director        │
└─────────────────────────────┘

┌─────────────────────────────┐
│     Orchestra Manager        │
└─────────────────────────────┘

┌─────────────────────────────┐
│ Director of Development or   │
│ Publicity or Public          │
│ Relations Position           │
└─────────────────────────────┘
```

Position Description

The Orchestra Manager is the assistant to the orchestra's managing director. A primary duty of the individual is negotiating with the musician's union on behalf of the orchestra's management. An Orchestra Manager tries to get the best deal for the orchestra management from the union while keeping the players happy.

The Orchestra Manager also arranges any concert tours for the orchestra, arranging the details to make it easy for the orchestra. The manager is responsible for handling the problems that are not directly music-related: from a musician's instrument that arrives late to an auditorium with bad acoustics or a musician who becomes ill in the middle of a tour to a dispute caused by hot tempers erupting on the road.

The Orchestra Manager also oversees the orchestra's administrative employees including the director of development, director of public relations, music administrator, business manager, director of educational activities, and director of ticket subscriptions. He or she is knowledgeable about these positions and the problems that might occur. The manager also understands the needs of the community or area in which the orchestra is based. As Orchestra Manager, he or she negotiates contracts for guest soloists and guest conductors.

The Orchestra Manager is responsible to the managing director of the orchestra and works very long hours. Enjoyment of symphonic music makes the long hours and hard work worthwhile.

Salaries

Symphony orchestras are classified into different groups depending on size, budget, and other factors. There are major orchestras, such as the Boston Symphony or the Cleveland Orchestra; regional orchestras, for example, the Birmingham Symphony Orchestra or the Memphis Symphony Orchestra; and metropolitan, urban, community, college, and youth orchestras. Salaries of Orchestra Managers vary according to the classification and location of the orchestra. Salaries range from $21,000 to $70,000 or more annually. Orchestra Managers of urban, community, college, or youth orchestras often donate services or work on a per-service basis.

Employment Prospects

There are a limited number of major and regional orchestras in the country. Therefore, employment prospects at this level are poor. Positions are sometimes available at the metropolitan, urban, and community levels. However, these jobs are not always full time.

Advancement Prospects

The position of an Orchestra Manager is not an entry-level job. Positions that contribute to the Orchestra Manager's experience include public relations director, fund-raising director, business manager, or assistant in one of these fields. Once an individual has proven himself or herself in the position of Orchestra Manager, he or she is a valuable commodity to the orchestra and has the opportunity to move up to the position of managing director or to a position as Orchestra Manager in a more prestigious orchestra.

Education and Training

A college degree is preferred or recommended for most positions as Orchestra Manager. Individuals may find a few positions without this requirement, usually with smaller orchestras.

Courses in music management, administration, and/or business are helpful. Classes in publicity, labor negotiations, fund-raising, and psychology are useful too. There are also seminars given around the country in arts administration. These seminars put the individual in touch with others already in the field and help develop contacts.

Experience, Skills, and Personality Traits

A good sense of business is important to the Orchestra Manager. An understanding of and sensitivity to musicians and their problems and pressures are equally important. To do the job well, a manager must be able to deal effectively with problems and people under pressure. Hands-on experience is helpful. Many conservatories and universities have internship programs that provide practical experience. Enjoying music makes it all worthwhile.

Unions and Associations

The Orchestra Manager belongs to the American Symphony Orchestra League (ASOL) and may also belong to a local arts council.

Tips for Entry

1. Find an orchestra or school that has an internship in orchestral management. The American Symphony Orchestra League (ASOL) sponsors a variety of intern programs.
2. Attend seminars on orchestra management. Seminars are sponsored by various universities and orchestras in addition to the ASOL.
3. Check openings listed in the ASOL newsletter, the Associated Council of the Arts newsletter, and many regional arts organization publications.
4. Look for job openings in the classified or display section of the newspaper under the headings of "Performing Arts," "Orchestra," "Symphony," or "Music."
5. Job openings may also be located on the Internet. Look for orchestra Web sites, which often list employment opportunities.

DIRECTOR OF EDUCATIONAL ACTIVITIES— ORCHESTRA, OPERA, BALLET COMPANY, OR NOT-FOR-PROFIT THEATER

CAREER PROFILE

Duties: Developing young people's concert series, ballets, and/or plays; coordinating activities for students; planning learning activities related to the theater and performing arts

Alternate Title(s): Director of Education; Manager of Educational Activities; Education Director

Salary Range: $18,000 to $42,000+

Employment Prospects: Poor

Advancement Prospects: Fair

Best Geographical Location(s): Major cultural centers offer more opportunities.

Prerequisites:

    Education or Training—High School diploma is the minimum requirement; some positions may require or prefer a college degree.

    Experience—Experience working in a theater, orchestra, ballet, or opera company in some capacity helpful; administrative and business experience useful

    Special Skills and Personality Traits—Good writing and communications skills; ability to get along with young people; basic knowledge of the workings of theater, ballet, opera, and orchestra companies

CAREER LADDER

```
┌──────────────────────────────────────┐
│  Director of Educational Activities at │
│  Larger, More Prestigious Company or   │
│  Theater or Director of Public Relations, │
│  Funding and Development               │
└──────────────────────────────────────┘

┌──────────────────────────────────────┐
│   Director of Educational Activities   │
└──────────────────────────────────────┘

┌──────────────────────────────────────┐
│   Assistant Director of Educational    │
│   Activities, Publicist, or Student    │
└──────────────────────────────────────┘
```

Position Description

The Director of Educational Activities in a performing arts setting is responsible for coordinating activities for students and other young people in the community where the company performs. As a rule, this position is found in the not-for-profit performing arts sector.

The Director of Educational Activities is responsible for coordinating programs with the schools in the area surrounding the theater, orchestra, ballet, or opera company's base of operations. The director meets with school district personnel as well as music supervisors or teachers, dance or physical education teachers or supervisors, and English teachers regarding programs that are available for students.

The Director of Educational Activities offers various programs to the schools. For example, the director might bring the entire orchestra or just parts of it directly into the school to perform. The director might offer actors, actresses, directors, playwrights, dancers, and musicians as guest speakers at a school assembly. He or she might also gather various members of an ensemble for a theater and the performing arts career day.

The Director of Educational Activities works closely with other departments in the theatrical organization. If the director is working with an orchestra, he or she works with the music administrator, managing director, and/or orchestra manager designing young people's concerts. If the director is working with a ballet company, he or she works closely with the managing director, dance company manager, and other administrators designing programs for young people. After these performances, the director sets up question-and-answer periods for the performers and students.

The director recommends reduced prices for student tickets and makes sure that students, parents, and school administrators are aware of the special activities and ticket prices by designing and sending brochures or posters to the schools, placing them in the surrounding areas, sending out press releases to newspapers, and mailing notices to current subscribers of the performing, arts company.

Other activities the director plans include coordinating tours for students of their performing arts center, including backstage and/or business offices. The Director of Educational Activities is also responsible for the development and preparation of booklets and pamphlets explaining the different career opportunities in the field. He or she may be asked to counsel students about educational and training requirements of various positions.

The Director of Educational Activities works long hours that include regular business hours as well as the performances at schools and meetings with administrators to develop programs.

Salaries

Salaries for the Director of Educational Activities working in a theatrical or performing arts setting vary depending on a number of factors, including the size, prestige, budget, and geographic location of the company as well as the individual's responsibilities and experience. Earnings can range from $18,000 a year for a person with little or no experience working in a small theatrical situation to $42,000 or more a year for an experienced director working for a more prestigious theater group, orchestra, ballet, or opera company.

Employment Prospects

Employment prospects are poor for those seeking positions as Director of Educational Activities. As the majority of these jobs are found with nonprofit companies, budgets often can not be stretched to include this position. Many times, the duties of the Director of Educational Activities are absorbed by the director of public relations, director of audience development, or director of subscriptions and ticket services.

Advancement Prospects

Advancement prospects are fair for those who get their first job in this position. The Director of Educational Activities climbs the career ladder in a number of ways—finding a similar position in a larger, more prestigious theater group, orchestra, ballet, or opera company or by becoming the director of public relations, development, or fund-raising for a similar organization.

Education and Training

Educational requirements vary from job to job. Some positions require a high school diploma; others a college degree. Good choices for college majors include theater arts, liberal arts, communications, education, or public relations.

Experience, Skills, and Personality Traits

Directors of Educational Activities should have a working knowledge of the organization that employs them. If working for an orchestra, the director should understand the workings of the orchestra and have a knowledge of music in general. If the person works with a theatrical group, he or she should have a basic knowledge of theatrical arts and business.

Some directors obtain their jobs without a lot of experience, although they probably have worked for a theater, orchestra, or ballet company in another capacity—such as administrative assistant, publicist, journalist, musician, dancer, or actor—prior to their appointment as director.

The Director of Educational Activities should be articulate and well groomed. He or she should have the ability to develop and write clear, concise, and creative copy, letters, and brochures. The director needs good verbal communications skills both in person and on the telephone.

An ability to get along well with young people is necessary. A basic understanding and ability to describe the specific type of performance group is essential.

Unions and Associations

There are no unions or associations to which the Director of Educational Activities must belong. The director of the company may be a member of various arts councils, the American Symphony Orchestra League (ASOL), Metropolitan Opera Association (MOA), Metropolitan Opera Guild (MOG), National Opera Association (NOA), Opera America (OA), the Ballet Theater Foundation (BTF), or the Public Relations Society of America (PRSA).

Tips for Entry

1. Find an internship with an orchestra, ballet, opera, or theatrical company. This job gives you hands-on experience working with a group as well as leads you to important contacts. Find these positions by contacting the companies themselves, through colleges and universities, or local arts councils.
2. Look for jobs advertised in the classified or display section of newspapers under headings of "Educational Activities," "Arts," "Theater," "Orchestra," "Symphony," "Ballet," "Opera," or "Music." Openings are

also listed in various arts council newsletters. For those interested in working with an orchestra, the American Symphony Orchestra League's (ASOL) newsletter also lists openings.

3. Call the theatrical department of your local college or university, arts councils, or ballet, opera, orchestra, or theatrical companies to find seminars, workshops, and courses on management and administration of a theater or other performing arts that will be useful in obtaining information and making contacts.

4. Send your résumé with a short cover letter to the personnel director of symphony orchestras, opera, ballet, and theatrical companies.

5. Visit the Web sites of orchestras, operas, ballet companies, and other theaters. Many post their job openings and opportunities.

PERSONNEL MANAGER—ORCHESTRA, OPERA, OR BALLET COMPANY

CAREER PROFILE

Duties: Hiring all employees on both the business and the artistic side of the company; sending out notices of job openings; placing advertisements; interviewing applicants

Alternate Title(s): Personnel Director

Salary Range: $21,000 to $55,000+

Employment Prospects: Poor

Advancement Opportunities: Poor

Best Geographical Location(s): Culturally active cities hosting orchestra, ballet, and opera companies offer more possibilities.

Prerequisites:

Education or Training—Requirements vary from high school diploma to bachelor's degree.

Experience—Experience working in personnel useful

Special Skills and Personality Traits—Ability to put the right person in the right job; interviewing skills; organized; detail oriented; communication skills

CAREER LADDER

```
┌─────────────────────────────────────┐
│     Personnel Manager for            │
│ More Prestigious Orchestra, Opera, or│
│         Ballet Company               │
└─────────────────────────────────────┘

┌─────────────────────────────────────┐
│ Orchestra, Ballet, or Opera Company  │
│         Personnel Manager            │
└─────────────────────────────────────┘

┌─────────────────────────────────────┐
│        Personnel Staff Member        │
└─────────────────────────────────────┘
```

Position Description

Many often wonder how people are chosen to work in an orchestra, opera, or ballet company. The individual responsible for hiring staff is the company's Personnel Manager, who has a variety of duties depending on the specific position.

The Personnel Manager is responsible for all the hiring and firing decisions in the organization. In some situations the Personnel Manager supervises a staff and, if so, delegates many of these responsibilities.

One of the main functions of the Personnel Manager is to send out notices whenever there are openings in either the business or the artistic end of the organization. These notices are sent to a number of places, including schools, colleges, conservatories, newsletters, associations, organizations, and unions.

The Personnel Manager is also responsible for writing and placing classified advertisements in the print media for job openings and for determining which magazines and newspapers will bring responses from the most qualified candidates for the jobs.

Once people respond to notices or advertisements, the Personnel Manager is responsible for screening their appli-

cations and setting up preliminary interviews with applicants. The Personnel Manager then calls back the best candidates for further interviews with others in the company. The Personnel Manager has ability to put people into the jobs for which they are best suited.

When there are openings for dancers, musicians, or singers, the Personnel Manager works with others who handle the auditions. For example, in an orchestra, the Personnel Manager works with the conductor or concertmaster; in a ballet company, with the balletmaster or mistress.

In addition to looking for applicants and holding interviews for full-time artists, the Personnel Manager is often responsible for finding substitutes often needed on the spur of the moment. The Personnel Manager develops and maintains a list of backup people in all performance areas, knows exactly how they perform, what they are capable of, and where they are at all times. Names, addresses, and phone numbers are updated constantly. A substitute performer who cannot be located is of no value to a company.

The Personnel Manager makes sure that all those who are hired understand the orchestra, ballet, or opera company's policies, rules, and regulations. He or she negotiates or assists in the negotiation of salaries and working conditions. While not given a free hand regarding salaries, the Personnel Manager is given a range within which to work and finds the most competent, talented person to fill the position at the lowest price.

Another responsibility of the Personnel Manager is to make sure that all necessary forms are filled out, since many of the jobs are filled by members of various unions. These organizations have very strict rules and regulations that must be adhered to with proper documentation. The Personnel Manager also makes sure all contracts are signed, dated, and filed in the appropriate place.

The Personnel Manager of an opera, orchestra, or ballet company is responsible for keeping track of employee attendance and punctuality.

One of the more difficult responsibilities of the Personnel Manager is handling the firing of employees.

Salaries
Salaries for Personnel Managers working in ballet, orchestra, or opera companies vary depending on the size of the company, its budget, and the geographical location. Other variables affecting salaries include the Personnel Manager's experience, responsibilities, and qualifications.

Annual earnings for Personnel Managers range from $21,000 to $55,000 or more, with the higher salaries going to those with more experience and responsibilities working in larger ballet, opera, or orchestra companies.

Employment Prospects
Employment prospects are poor for those aspiring to be Personnel Managers in orchestra, ballet, or opera companies, as there are a limited number of companies large enough to hire Personnel Managers. Smaller companies that tour assign the duties of the Personnel Manager to another staff member in the organization.

Advancement Prospects
Advancement prospects are limited for Personnel Managers due to the limited availability of jobs. When people secure these positions, they tend to keep them.

Though difficult, advancement is not impossible. Individuals climb the career ladder in a number of ways, such as finding a similar position with a larger, more prestigious company. Personnel Managers also advance to other departments in the company if they are qualified, or some move into labor relations in either the performing arts or an unrelated field.

Education and Training
Educational requirements vary for Personnel Managers in orchestra, opera, and ballet companies. A few positions require a high school diploma; others require a four-year college degree.

While some Personnel Managers have degrees in any subject matter, major orchestra, ballet, and opera companies prefer or require degrees in personnel administration or human resources.

Experience, Skills, and Personality Traits
Personnel Managers may have experience working in personnel in either the performing arts or an unrelated field. It is usually necessary for the Personnel Director to have a background in or basic knowledge of music, dance, and the performing arts.

One of the most important skills Personnel Managers can have is the ability to match the right people with the right jobs. The Personnel Manager must be skilled at interviewing techniques, screening applications, and reading between the lines.

Personnel Managers must be very organized and detail oriented and have an ability to keep records. A good memory is helpful. Personnel Managers should have good verbal and written communication skills.

Unions and Associations
Personnel Managers working in orchestra, opera, or ballet companies are members of various organizations depending on their specific job, including the Associated Council of the Arts, the American Symphony Orchestra League (ASOL), Metropolitan Opera Association (MOA), Metropolitan Opera Guild (MOG), National Opera Association (NOA), Opera America (OA), or the Ballet Theater Foundation (BTF). Individuals may also be members of local arts and councils.

Tips for Entry
1. Look for an internship program through schools, organizations, associations, orchestras, operas, or ballet companies. Once you are working with a company, you have an easier time finding or creating this position.
2. Look for openings for Personnel Manager in the various association and organization newsletters and trade journals.
3. Look for other job possibilities in the classified ads or display section of the newspaper under the headings of "Arts," "Personnel," "Opera," "Symphony," "Orchestra," "Ballet," "Dance," "Theater Arts," "Performing Arts," or "Human Resources."
4. Stay in school to get the highest degree you can. The more qualified you are the better. Education gives you the edge in securing and keeping this position.
5. Send your résumé and a short cover letter to orchestra, opera, and ballet companies. Request that they keep your résumé on file if there are no current openings.
6. Job openings may also be located on the Internet. Look for orchestra, opera, or ballet Web sites that list employment opportunities.

MUSIC LIBRARIAN—ORCHESTRA, OPERA, OR BALLET COMPANY

CAREER PROFILE

Duties: Cataloging and ordering music for an orchestra, ballet, or opera company; assisting conductor in copying scores and parts; handing out and collecting music before and after performances

Alternate Title(s): None

Salary Range: $19,000 to $42,000+

Employment Prospects: Poor

Advancement Prospects: Poor

Best Geographical Location(s): Culturally active cities hosting larger orchestra, ballet, or opera companies

Prerequisites:

Education or Training—Bachelor's degree in music history or theater and library sciences; master's degree in music or library science often required

Experience—Experience as assistant to music librarian helpful; internship useful

Special Skills and Personality Traits—Organized; detail oriented; ability to copy conductor's markings; interest in music and the performing arts

CAREER LADDER

```
┌─────────────────────────────────────────┐
│ Music Librarian for More Prestigious     │
│ Orchestra, Opera, or Ballet Company      │
└─────────────────────────────────────────┘

┌─────────────────────────────────────────┐
│ Orchestra, Opera, or Ballet Company      │
│ Music Librarian                          │
└─────────────────────────────────────────┘

┌─────────────────────────────────────────┐
│ Music Librarian's Assistant              │
└─────────────────────────────────────────┘
```

Position Description

Music Librarians involved in the performing arts work with orchestra, opera, and ballet companies and have varied responsibilities depending on their specific job.

Working with orchestra, opera, and ballet companies, Music Librarians combine their skills as librarians with their love for and comprehensive knowledge of music and the performing arts. The responsibilities of the Music Librarian include cataloging the organization's printed music and ordering new music when needed. In cases where the company decides not to purchase certain pieces of music, the librarian locates the sheet music, rents it, and returns it when the company has finished with it.

The Music Librarian needs to be able to copy musical markings, as he or she often assists the conductor of the orchestra in this task. The Music Librarian copies parts for the different section members, makes the necessary corrections, and adds bowings or phrasing where indicated.

Another function of the Music Librarian working with orchestra, opera, or ballet companies is to organize and then hand out the music. He or she is responsible for collecting the music after the rehearsal or the performance has concluded.

The Music Librarian travels with the company when it goes on tour or has special performances. On the road, the Librarian is responsible for all of the sheet music.

The Music Librarian is also responsible for contacting guest conductors or soloists to find out about the music needed for the artist's performance.

A Music Librarian working at a school or a library has some of the same responsibilities as a company Music Librarian but usually less involvement with the performer and performance and more contact with students. One of the big differences between a company Music Librarian and those working other settings is the working hours. Music Librarians working with orchestra, ballet, or opera companies do not work regular hours. Instead, they are required to do routine tasks in the morning and afternoon and attend rehearsal or performance at night or on weekends. Music Librarians for performance troupes are responsible to the orchestra conductor.

This job can be quite enjoyable for those who have the skills and enjoy being in a performing arts setting. Music Librarians attend every rehearsal and performance and thus have the opportunity to see a production evolve from its beginning to the final performance.

Salaries

Salaries vary for Music Librarians as they do for most jobs in the performing arts. Factors affecting earnings include the experience and responsibilities of the individual as well as the specific company, its size, prestige, and geographic location.

A Music Librarian working for a major orchestra, ballet, or opera company earns between $30,000 and $42,000 or more annually.

An individual working for a regional or metropolitan orchestra, opera, or ballet company earns an annual salary between $19,000 and $30,000. In smaller orchestras, ballet and opera companies, duties of the Music Librarian are often assumed by a section member of the orchestra, and thus there is no paid position with these organizations.

Employment Prospects

Employment prospects for Music Librarians working in orchestras, ballet, or opera companies are poor. There are a limited number of these companies in the country, and as previously noted, some companies do not employ paid Music Librarians. In very small opera or ballet companies, they often do not even use an orchestra, relying instead on recorded music.

Advancement Prospects

Advancement prospects are limited for Music Librarians working in orchestra, ballet, or opera companies. Because jobs are so hard to find, once an individual does land a position, he or she usually does not leave it. Those who do advance find similar jobs in larger, more prestigious companies. Others move into positions in other settings such as universities, colleges, or libraries.

Education and Training

The educational requirements for Music Librarians vary from job to job. Some positions require an undergraduate degree in music theory or history. Others require a dual major in music and library sciences. Still others require a master's degree in either music or library sciences.

Music Librarians also have training in copying musical parts and scores.

Experience, Skills, and Personality Traits

Music Librarians working in orchestra, opera, or ballet companies often get experience prior to obtaining their current job by working as assistants to music librarians. These jobs are usually available only in larger orchestra, opera, and ballet companies. Individuals may also get experience through internship programs.

Music Librarians should be very organized, detail oriented, dependable, and reliable.

Music Librarians working in these settings must have the ability to copy conductor's markings on scores in neat, legible handwriting.

Music Librarians must have the ability to get along well with others and should have a great interest in music and a love for the performing arts.

Unions and Associations

Music Librarians belong to a number of associations depending on their specific job. These organizations provide professional guidance and support to their members. They offer seminars, newsletters, and other valuable information.

Organizations include the American Library Association (ALA), the Special Libraries Association (SLA), the American Federation of Musicians (AFM), the American Symphony Orchestra League (ASOL), Metropolitan Opera Association (MOA), Metropolitan Opera Guild (MOG), National Opera Association (NOA), Opera America (OA), and the Ballet Theater Foundation (BTF).

Tips for Entry

1. Find an internship as a Music Librarian with a major orchestra, ballet, or opera company.
2. Volunteer to act as the Music Librarian of your college or school orchestra or band. This position will provide you with good hands-on experience.
3. Write to orchestra, ballet, and opera companies to find out if they employ music librarian assistants. If they do, send your résumé and a short cover letter.
4. Work as a Music Librarian in a radio station. While the duties vary from performance work, the experience is useful.
5. Job openings may be located on the Internet. Look for orchestra, ballet, and opera company Web sites; they often list employment opportunities.

TOUR COORDINATOR—ORCHESTRA, OPERA, OR BALLET COMPANY

CAREER PROFILE

Duties: Coordinating all facets of the company's appearances when away from home city; overseeing everything that is done on the road; organizing schedules

Alternate Title(s): Tour Coordinator; Road Coordinator

Salary Range: $32,000 to $80,000+

Employment Prospects: Poor

Advancement Prospects: Poor

Best Geographical Location(s): Culturally active cities hosting orchestra, ballet, and opera companies offer more possibilities for employment.

Prerequisites:

Education or Training—Requirements vary from high school diploma to preference for college degree.

Experience—Experience working with orchestra, opera or ballet company useful; experience on the road helpful

Special Skills and Personality Traits—Coordination skills; ability to work under pressure; understanding of performing arts industry; organized; detail oriented; communication skills; supervisory skills; dependability; reliability

CAREER LADDER

```
┌─────────────────────────────────────┐
│         Tour Coordinator for         │
│ More Prestigious Orchestra, Ballet, or│
│            Opera Company             │
└─────────────────────────────────────┘

┌─────────────────────────────────────┐
│ Orchestra, Ballet, or Opera Company  │
│           Tour Coordinator           │
└─────────────────────────────────────┘

┌─────────────────────────────────────┐
│   Assistant Tour Coordinator or      │
│        Orchestra, Ballet, or         │
│      Opera Company Staff Member       │
└─────────────────────────────────────┘
```

Position Description

Orchestra, ballet, and opera companies have a home city where they perform during their regular season. Most companies also schedule appearances in other cities. These performances take the form of a tour that lasts from one day to a few months or more depending on the specific company. The person in charge of arranging the tour and handling all details while the company is on the road is called the company Tour Coordinator.

The coordinator is responsible for all facets of the touring company's appearances and for overseeing everything that is done while the company is on the road. The coordinator handles details for the performers as well as for all staff members, crew, and equipment.

In some situations, the company Tour Coordinator works with a road manager. In others, he or she is the road man-

ager. He or she must coordinate the efforts of every person on the road to make sure that the tour and all appearances are successful.

The company Tour Coordinator begins his or her job before the company leaves its home city. He or she works with the company manager, production manager, booking agents, publicists, and public relations people to determine the locations, date, and time of each performance.

Many times, when symphony orchestra, ballet, or opera companies are performing in other cities, receptions, galas, or charity events are scheduled to coincide with the performances. Members of the company are invited and expected to be on hand for these events. The company Tour Coordinator also determines what additional appearances are made in radio interviews, television spots, print media interviews, and special events promoting the tour.

When the Tour Coordinator has compiled all this information, he or she makes up a schedule of appearances, rehearsals, and performances. Most Coordinators prepare schedules for each member of the company and crew and hands them out before a tour begins.

The company Tour Coordinator is also responsible for arranging transportation. Depending on the number of people traveling and the distance, the individual may rent buses, vans, or cars or use train service. If the company is traveling a great distance, the Tour Coordinator arranges air travel.

The company Tour Coordinator is responsible for making reservations for accommodations or for contacting a travel agent to handle the task. He or she also arranges for meals for the company. In some cases meals are catered at the hall or at a restaurant or hotel. In others, company members receive a per diem allotment for food.

While on the road, the company Tour Coordinator has a great deal of responsibility and must coordinate all the activities of the company. In this job, everybody else's problems become the problems of the company Tour Coordinator.

The coordinator maintains close contact with the company's main office and advises it about the schedule or any problems that develop.

Before a performance, the Tour Coordinator makes sure all the equipment has arrived and is in place. The company Tour Coordinator is in charge of getting everybody to rehearsals and performances on time. After a performance, he or she is responsible for making sure all the equipment is packed up and loaded to go to the next destination.

In some situations, the company Tour Coordinator is responsible for handing out per diems and paychecks. He or she is also required to keep expense sheets.

The company Tour Coordinator is present at all performances on the road. If something goes wrong, he or she takes care of it on the spot. The coordinator stays with the company until it returns home.

Salaries

Salaries for company Tour Coordinators vary depending on the size and prestige of the company. The coordinator's responsibilities and previous experience influence earnings as well.

Earnings for company Tour Coordinators range from $600 to $1,500 or more per week. Coordinators also receive a per diem or are reimbursed for expenses.

In some instances, when the company Tour Coordinator is not on the road, he or she may receive a reduced salary.

Employment Prospects

Employment prospects are poor for company Tour Coordinators. While there are orchestra, opera, and ballet companies throughout the country, they do not all go on the road. Even the ones that do tour do not always hire a company Tour Coordinator.

Advancement Prospects

Advancement prospects are limited for company Tour Coordinators, as there are more people looking for these positions than there are openings.

A company Tour Coordinator advances his or her career by finding a similar position with a larger or more prestigious company.

Education and Training

Educational requirements vary for company Tour Coordinators depending on the specific position. Some jobs require a high school diploma; others require a college background or diploma.

As competition is stiff for these jobs, those aspiring to work with major orchestra, ballet, or opera companies should have a four-year degree. Good choices for college majors include arts management, theater arts, music, business administration, communications, or liberal arts.

Experience, Skills, and Personality Traits

Company Tour Coordinators usually have experience working with orchestra, ballet, or opera companies in other capacities. Some have worked on the road with music groups or on road tours for theatrical productions.

Company Tour Coordinators should have a background and understanding of the particular performing art they are working with. Coordinators must enjoy traveling, as they are away from home for sometimes extended periods of time.

Company Tour Coordinators should be extremely organized and detail oriented. Supervisory skills are needed and coordination skills are a must. Individuals must be articulate and able to communicate effectively. Dependability and reliability are essential to this position.

Coordinators should be personable and easy to talk to, since people come to them with problems that need to be solved. Coordinators must be able to deal with crises effectively without panicking. Individuals must also be able to work under a great deal of pressure and related stress.

Unions and Associations

Company Tour Coordinators belong to a number of organizations related to the specific performing art they are working with, including the American Symphony Orchestra League (ASOL), Metropolitan Opera Association (MOA), Metropolitan Opera Guild (MOG), National Opera Association (NOA), Opera America (OA), or the Ballet Theater Foundation (BTF).

Tips for Entry

1. Contact associations and organizations to find out if they offer any training programs. This is a good

way to get your foot in the door and make valuable contacts.

2. Look for an internship program through schools, organizations, associations, orchestras, or ballet or opera companies.

3. Try to get some experience on the road even if it is not with an orchestra, opera, or ballet company. Consider touring music groups, musical revues, and theatrical road tours.

4. Send your résumé with a short cover letter to orchestra, opera, and ballet companies that you know tour and perform in other cities.

5. Check out orchestra, opera, and ballet company Web sites. Many post job openings.

BEHIND THE SCENES

SOUND PERSON

CAREER PROFILE

Duties: Making sure the theater audience can hear the dialogue and sound effects during a production; mixing and blending sound; amplifying sound; playing sound effects

Alternate Title(s): Soundman/Soundwoman; Master Sound Technician; Sound Operator; Sound Mixer

Salary Range: $400 to $2500+ a week

Employment Prospects: Fair

Advancement Prospects: Fair

Best Geographical Location(s): Positions located throughout the country; more opportunities can be found in culturally active cities.

Prerequisites:

Education or Training—No formal educational requirement; training in electronics and sound

Experience—Experience as apprentice necessary in many positions

Special Skills and Personality Traits—Complete knowledge of electronics; skill at using soundboard; ability to work well with others and follow written and verbal directions; reliability

CAREER LADDER

```
┌─────────────────────────────────────┐
│  Sound Designer or Sound Person for  │
│     Larger Number of Productions     │
└─────────────────────────────────────┘

┌─────────────────────────────────────┐
│            Sound Person              │
└─────────────────────────────────────┘

┌─────────────────────────────────────┐
│   Apprentice or Amateur Sound Person │
└─────────────────────────────────────┘
```

Position Description

The main function of a Sound Person working in a theater setting is to make sure that everyone in the house can hear what is going on. This is not always an easy job because of the acoustics of a theater.

Sound People may also be referred to as master sound technicians, sound operators, or sound mixers and may work in a variety of situations ranging from Broadway theaters to dinner and summer stock theaters. They may also work in concert halls, arenas, or other venues. Duties will vary depending on the specific job.

Individuals working in situations where there are a number of Sound People have more specialized duties. Those working in jobs where they are the only Sound Person will perform more general duties.

If actors and actresses had to yell out every line in a play, it would take away from the production and would not be pleasing to the ear. Part of the job of a Sound Person working in a theater is to make the sound lifelike to those listening in the audience. To accomplish this, the Sound Person will do what is called mixing or blending the sound. He or she must put the sounds from all the sources together. These sources might include microphones used to amplify the voices of actors or actresses, background noises, special effects, and music.

The Sound Person uses various machines and equipment to mix the sound and amplify it. He or she may also be responsible for doing the mixing for the "house" or the "stage." (The house refers to the audience and the stage to the area where the actors, actresses, and musicians are situated.)

The Sound Person strives to obtain the type of sound effect that the director indicates. In large productions, the Sound Person is told what to do and how to do it by a sound designer. In smaller productions, the Sound Person may be the sound designer.

The Sound Person is responsible for making sure that microphones and speakers are placed in a way that will produce the best sound. He or she may be required to physically install them or may have someone else perform this task.

During a performance, the Sound Person is required to work at a control board, where he or she adjusts the sound. In most instances, they remain in contact with the stage manager who alerts them to cues for using various sound effects or playing recorded music.

The Sound Person will work varied hours depending on performance times. He or she will also be responsible for readying and placing equipment, and in some instances performing sound checks before a performance.

The Sound Person is responsible to either the sound designer, stage manager, or director, depending on the specific show.

Salaries

Salaries for Sound People vary depending on a number of factors, including experience and responsibilities. Other factors include the size, type, and location of the theater in which the individual is working. Weekly earnings for Sound People can range from $400 to $2,500 or more per week.

Those working in unionized situations have their minimum salary dictated by the International Alliance of Theatrical Stage Employees (IATSE).

Employment Prospects

Employment prospects are fair for qualified Sound People. Work in this area can be found in a variety of situations including dinner theater, stock, Broadway, Off Broadway, Off-Off-Broadway, experimental theater, or university theater. Work can also be found on road tours or with orchestra, opera, or ballet companies.

Jobs can be located throughout the country. However, more opportunities exist in culturally active cities.

Advancement Prospects

Sound People can advance their careers in a number of ways. These include becoming sound designers for theatrical productions, doing a satisfactory job, and being recommended for additional positions with increased annual earnings and by locating similar positions for more prestigious productions.

Education and Training

There are no formal educational requirements for Sound People. Individuals must, however, be trained in electronics and sound technology. Those who plan on working in unionized settings, which include most professional theaters, must be members of the International Alliance of Theatrical Stage Employees (IATSE). In order to become a member of this union, individuals must go through an apprenticeship.

Other training may be obtained by attending a college or university with classes in sound, electronics, and staging. There are also many vocational schools offering training in sound and electronics throughout the country.

Experience, Skills, and Personality Traits

Sound People need a complete knowledge of electronics, the soundboard, and other sound equipment. Most people get this experience handling the sound requirements for school productions or community theater productions. Others get this experience from watching technicians at work.

Sound People must be able to work well with people. At one time or another, they will have to work with lighting designers, sound designers, actors, actresses, directors, stage managers, and a variety of other technicians. They must have the ability to follow written or verbal directions supplied by a lighting designer or stage manager.

Sound People must be responsible; they must be at the job when they are supposed to be there. A show cannot wait for them to show up.

Unions and Associations

Sound People working in unionized situations must be members of the International Alliance of Theatrical Stage Employees (IATSE). This is a bargaining union for individuals working in theater that negotiates and sets the minimum salary and working conditions for its members. Sound People working in nonunion facilities, obviously, do not have to be members of this group.

Tips for Entry

1. Contact IATSE to find out how you can become an apprentice. Involvement in this union will help you make valuable contacts.
2. Get experience by volunteering to do the sound for your local community theater production.
3. Obtain additional experience by working for musical acts handling their sound.
4. Contact clubs in your area to see if they need a resident sound technician.
5. Take classes, courses, seminars, and workshops in all areas of theater, staging, sound, and lighting. These will be useful for the educational value and for making contacts.

LIGHTING PERSON

CAREER PROFILE

Duties: Working the lighting control board during a theatrical performance; checking to see that lighting equipment is in working order

Alternate Title(s): Lightman/Lightwoman

Salary Range: $400 to $3,500+ per week

Employment Prospects: Fair

Advancement Prospects: Fair

Best Geographical Location(s): Culturally active cities offer more employment opportunities.

Prerequisites:

Education or Training—No formal educational requirement; training in lighting and electronics

Experience—Experience working with lighting in theatrical situations

Special Skills and Personality Traits—Knowledge of lighting and electronics; background in theater; ability to follow written instructions; reliability; dependability

CAREER LADDER

```
┌─────────────────────────────────────┐
│   Lighting Designer or Lighting Person │
│   for Larger Number of Productions or  │
│      More Prestigious Productions      │
└─────────────────────────────────────┘

┌─────────────────────────────────────┐
│          Lighting Person             │
└─────────────────────────────────────┘

┌─────────────────────────────────────┐
│    Apprentice or Amateur Lighting    │
│                Person                │
└─────────────────────────────────────┘
```

Position Description

The Lighting Person is responsible for the lighting of a theatrical stage. While the lighting designer creates the lighting for the production, the Lighting Person will be the one working at the lighting control board.

The Lighting Person is required to be at the theater for all performances. His or her duties usually start an hour or so before the show begins. At that time, the Lighting Person is responsible for checking that all lights and lighting equipment are in proper working order. He or she must make sure that every bulb is ready, that filters are in place as well as making other lighting checks. The individual also sees that every light is in the correct position.

The Lighting Person works from the documentation prepared in the preproduction period by the lighting designer. In smaller productions, the individual may have done the documentation of lighting instructions him or herself.

Documentation includes all lighting information necessary to duplicate the lighting effects that the designer created. A written schedule is used by the Lighting Person during the production so he or she will be able to man the lighting board. The schedule contains cues so that the person working the lighting or control board will know which lights should be used and at what time during the production.

By following the schedule, the Lighting Person produces a variety of effects with different lights, filters, and colors. He or she may, for example, turn the spotlight on an actor or actress at a specific time or make the light on the stage fade to darkness.

Depending on the specific production, the Lighting Person is responsible to the stage manager or to a head lighting technician.

Salaries

Earnings for Lighting People can range from approximately $400 to $3,500 or more per week. Variables include the individual's experience, expertise, and reputation. Earnings will also depend on the specific production, type of theater, and its location. Lighting People working in unionized theaters will have minimum earnings set by the union. Those working in nonunionized settings must negotiate their own salaries.

Employment Prospects

Employment prospects are fair for Lighting People working in theatrical productions. Almost every production uses the services of a professional in this field. Jobs may be found handling the lighting requirements in any type of production or theater including dinner theaters, Broadway, Off Broadway, Off-Off-Broadway, regional theaters, or resident theaters.

Advancement Prospects

Advancement prospects are fair for Lighting People. Individuals can climb the career ladder in a number of ways including finding more frequent work, finding similar work for more prestigious productions, or becoming a lighting designer.

Education and Training

There are no formal educational requirements for becoming a Lighting Person. There are some who do not have a college background and others who have undergraduate and graduate degrees. Good choices for college majors include theater arts or design.

A lot of the necessary training can be learned watching other Lighting People, lighting designers, and electricians at work. Interested individuals should consider becoming an apprentice or assistant or finding an internship.

Experience, Skills, and Personality Traits

Lighting People working in theater should have a background in theater and a complete knowledge of lighting, staging, and electronics. Experience handling the lighting for school plays or community theater productions is useful.

Individuals must know how to follow written instructions for the lighting requirements developed by the lighting designer. They must also be able to follow the directions of the stage manager who may call lighting cues. They should be reliable and dependable. A Lighting Person who does not show up for a production can ruin a show.

Unions and Associations

Lighting People working in unionized theaters must be members of the local affiliation of the International Alliance of Theatrical Stage Employees (IATSE). If they also assume duties of the lighting designer they may be members of the United Scenic Artists. Some may also be members of the International Brotherhood of Electrical Workers (IBEW). These groups set minimum fees and working conditions for their members.

Lighting People working in nonunionized theaters may or may not be members of these organizations.

Tips for Entry

1. Learn as much as you can about lighting and electronics. Take classes in school or find courses offered through vocational programs.
2. Workshops in theatrical lighting, staging, and other related subjects will also be useful for their educational value and to help make contacts.
3. Internships are another good way to learn, make important contacts, and obtain hands-on experience. Locate them through schools or theater groups.
4. Apprenticeships are another method of learning the trade. Contact the appropriate union for information.
5. Offer to handle the lighting at your school or local community theater production.
6. Attend a variety of productions to see how the lighting requirements are handled.

PROPERTY PERSON

CAREER PROFILE

Duties: Locating the necessary props for stage sets; moving props; handing props to actors or actresses; making minor repairs on prop

Alternate Title(s): Property Man/Property Woman; Stagehand

Salary Range: $350 to $2,000+ per week

Employment Prospects: Fair

Advancement Prospects: Fair

Best Geographical Location(s): Culturally active cities offer more opportunities.

Prerequisites:

Education or Training—No formal educational requirement; on-the-job training helpful

Experience—Internship or apprenticeship useful

Special Skills and Personality Traits—Creativity; handiness with tools; knowledge of building props; good memory; organizational skills; knowledge of theater

CAREER LADDER

```
┌─────────────────────────────────────────┐
│ Property Master or Property Person for    │
│       More Prestigious Production         │
└─────────────────────────────────────────┘

┌─────────────────────────────────────────┐
│             Property Person               │
└─────────────────────────────────────────┘

┌─────────────────────────────────────────┐
│       Student, Apprentice, or Intern      │
└─────────────────────────────────────────┘
```

Position Description

The Property Person working in a theatrical production is a stagehand and has varied responsibilities depending on the specific job. One of these responsibilities is to assist the scenic designer or the assistant scenic designer to locate props for a stage setting. Props, or properties, are the articles used on stage sets to make a setting appear more authentic. Examples of props might be furniture, telephones, or dishes. Props also include costume props for the cast members. Some props are not easy to find and in some instances may be antiques or other items from different eras. One of the interesting parts of the job of a Property Person is finding difficult to locate props.

Sometimes props can be purchased and other times they are rented from warehouses, museums, or rental companies. The Property Person must know where to find needed items. A lot of the job involves shopping and calling around to find just the right piece that will complete a stage set. Part of the art of doing this is knowing where to find needed items. Sometimes, a scenic designer will be looking for an antique chair which might cost $1,000 in an antique store, while the

Property Person may have seen a chair that would fit the bill in a Goodwill store for $5. Those experienced in this field develop lists over the years of where specific items can be located. The Property Person must keep accurate records of everything he or she rents or purchases and will be required to submit bills to the scenic designer in a timely manner.

In some cases, the Property Person cannot buy or rent a certain prop that a scenic designer requests and must construct it or have it made. In some instances he or she may be responsible for actually building a prop or may just be responsible for assembling the pieces of props to get them ready for the stage.

One of the major functions of a Property Person is to make sure props are in the correct place on stage. To accomplish this, they must know exactly which scenes use which specific props. After a scene takes place, they may also be required to remove the props from the stage and replace them with the new props for the following scene.

Another function the Property Person will be responsible for is physically handing props to actors and actresses during a performance. For example, they may hand an actor or actress an umbrella or bouquet of flowers before he or she walks on stage for a scene.

When actors or actresses appear to be drinking alcoholic beverages on stage, it is the Property Person who is responsible for mixing liquids that resemble these drinks. He or she is also responsible for cooking any food that the actors or actresses will be using as props during a scene.

All props must be kept clean and in good condition. The Property Person, depending on the production, may be responsible for handling minor repairs on props. For example, he or she may fix the leg of a table that is unsteady. Or hammer a picture frame back together. If the repair is a major one, the Property Person will be required to have it fixed or must obtain a duplicate prop.

In the event that the Property Person is working on a road tour, he or she will be responsible for packing and unpacking all props and arranging them where they belong.

Salaries

Earnings for Property People can range greatly depending on a number of factors. Weekly salaries can run from $350 to $2,000 or more. Factors affecting earnings include the type of production an individual is working in, his or her experience, responsibilities, and reputation. Property People working in unionized theaters have their minimum earnings set by the local affiliation of the International Alliance of Theatrical Stage Employees (IATSE).

Employment Prospects

Employment prospects for Property People are fair. Most productions have more than one person in this position. Work can be found in any type of theatrical production that uses sets including operas and ballets. There are opportunities in dinner and resident theaters as well as stock productions.

Advancement Prospects

Advancement prospects for Property People are determined to a great extent by the determination, ambition, skills, and luck of the individual. The next step up the career ladder for many individuals is to become property masters.

Careers may be advanced by locating similar positions in more prestigious theatrical productions such as Broadway musicals. Other Property People climb the career ladder by doing prop work in television or films.

Education and Training

While there is no formal educational requirement for Property People, individuals with college degrees are not uncommon in this field. A college education may be helpful in obtaining experience, honing skills, and making contacts necessary for success.

Experience, Skills, and Personality Traits

Individuals interested in becoming Property People should get experience working backstage in theater. Many people obtain experience in community or school theatrical productions building scenery and finding props. Additional experience can also be obtained by working as an apprentice or intern.

Property People should be creative individuals. They must possess the ability to develop ideas for solutions to finding props that are difficult to locate. Individuals who are handy with tools will be more employable. Knowing how to fix and build props is helpful. Knowledge of the theater and stagecraft is important.

Property People should have a good memory. Individuals should also enjoy searching through shops, warehouses, factories, and antique stores for props. The ability to get along well with others is necessary.

Unions and Associations

Property People working in unionized theaters must belong to the local affiliation of the International Alliance of Theatrical Stage Employees (IATSE). This union sets the minimum salaries and working conditions for its members. It also provides apprenticeship programs for those seeking memberships.

Tips for Entry

1. Get involved in your school and community theater. Offer to build sets, create scenery, and find props.
2. Try to locate an internship working in a theater in the prop or scenic design department. If one isn't open in that department, take any internship you can find that is available. Ask questions and keep your eyes and ears open.
3. Many theaters offer part-time or summer jobs to students learning their craft. Send your résumé with a short cover letter asking for an interview.
4. Don't forget to contact opera and ballet companies about jobs in the prop or scenic design department.

WARDROBE DRESSER

CAREER PROFILE

Duties: Keeping costumes used in theatrical productions in good condition; assisting actors and actresses into costume; making minor repairs on costumes

Alternate Title(s): Dresser; Day Worker

Salary Range: $35,000 to $55,000+ for full-time employment

Employment Prospects: Fair

Advancement Prospects: Fair

Best Geographical Location(s): Culturally active cities, including New York City and Los Angeles

Prerequisites:

Education or Training—No formal educational requirement

Experience—Prior experience in theater in some capacity necessary

Special Skills and Personality Traits—Basic sewing skills; knowledge of laundering and pressing; personableness; dependability; reliability

CAREER LADDER

```
┌─────────────────────────────────┐
│      Personal Dresser or         │
│      Wardrobe Supervisor         │
└─────────────────────────────────┘

┌─────────────────────────────────┐
│       Wardrobe Dresser           │
└─────────────────────────────────┘

┌─────────────────────────────────┐
│ Actor/Actress or Individual      │
│ Working in Theater Behind the    │
│ Scenes                           │
└─────────────────────────────────┘
```

Position Description

A Wardrobe Dresser working in the theater is responsible for making sure that the costumes used in a production are in good condition. The dresser has varied duties depending on the specific situation and works under the supervision of a wardrobe supervisor. As a rule, he or she is assigned one or more actors or actresses to help costume during a production.

If the dresser works in the daytime before a performance, he or she is called a day worker. Wardrobe Dressers may work during the day and/or immediately before and during a theatrical performance. Many dressers work both shifts, increasing their earnings considerably. The dresser is responsible for maintaining the complete wardrobe that the actors and actresses wear in the production including dresses, pants, blouses, shirts, suits, hats, glasses, shoes, underwear, and jewelry.

Before a performance, the dresser makes sure that every piece of the costume is available and in good condition. He or she is responsible for attending to any minor repairs such as sewing on buttons, sequins or beads, fixing a hem, or repairing a seam. In the event that a costume is in need of a major repair, he or she reports this situation to the wardrobe supervisor. The dresser then makes sure that the repairs are made and the costume is available for the next performance.

In addition to other duties, dressers are required to help actors and actresses into their costumes during performances. In elaborate productions, the actors and actresses change costumes frequently, and the dresser makes sure they change quickly and helps them dress properly. The dresser also checks that the actor or actress is wearing the correct hat, shoes, jewelry, and other accessories.

After a performance, the dresser is required to check the condition of the costume. He or she makes repairs, cleans a costume at that time, or makes note of a problem for the attention of the day worker.

A career as a dresser allows an individual to work behind the scenes. Dressers have the satisfaction of knowing that they have performed an important function in making a performance aesthetically pleasing to patrons. In addition, many dressers have a unique relationship with the actors and actresses who they help costume and work with.

Salaries

Minimum salaries are set for dressers working in unionized theaters by the local affiliation of the International Alliance of Theatrical Stage Employees (IATSE). Salaries for dressers vary depending on the amount of work the individual performs, his or her responsibilities and experience level, and the specific local he or she is affiliated with.

As of August 30, 2004, the minimum salaries set by the IATSE Local 764 for dressers working eight performances was $717.76 per week. If the dresser works by the hour, he or she receives a minimum of $25.59 per hour for a minimum of a four-hour call. Individuals who are paid by performance receive a minimum of $89.72. In addition, union members receive 8% vacation pay, 11% welfare fund, 9% annuity, and 6% pension.

Dressers working full time earn between $35,000 and $55,000 or more a year. It is important to remember, however, that not all dressers work all 52 weeks a year.

Employment Prospects

Employment prospects are fair for dressers who are ambitious and good at their jobs. While opportunities are found throughout the country, major cultural centers such as New York and Los Angeles that have a great number of theaters provide the most jobs.

Advancement Prospects

A Dresser climbs the career ladder in a number of ways, including landing a position with the star of the show. He or she may also rise to the position of wardrobe supervisor. Others move up the career ladder by becoming dressers in television, commercials, or films.

Advancement prospects depend on the skills, personality, and qualifications of the dresser. As in other facets of the entertainment industry, advancement also depends on luck, being in the right place at the right time, and contacts.

Education and Training

There are no formal educational requirements for becoming a Wardrobe Dresser. In order to be successful, however, individuals should have basic sewing, pressing, and laundering skills.

Experience, Skills, and Personality Traits

Most dressers have prior experience working in the theater in some capacity. Some have been actors or actresses in theater or have worked in other capacities behind the scenes.

Dressers must have basic sewing skills. They must know how to make costume repairs including fixing hems and seams and sewing on buttons, sequins, and beads. Individuals must also know how to launder and press costumes.

Successful dressers are personable and get along with everyone. They are good listeners and know how to make the actors and actresses comfortable in their costumes. Dressers learn to keep all conversations between themselves and the actors and actresses they dress confidential.

Dressers see actors and actresses in situations that other people do not. Dressers must be careful not to make negative comments on costumes or the way the actor or actress looks in them.

It is imperative that dressers be dependable and reliable.

Unions and Associations

The union responsible for Wardrobe Dresser is the International Alliance of Theatrical Stage Employees (IATSE). The local affiliation of this union negotiates minimum salaries and working conditions. In order to work in a unionized theater, dressers must be either a member of the union or in the process of becoming a member.

Tips for Entry

1. Volunteer your services as a dresser in a local community or school play. This position give you hands-on experience.
2. Take classes in basic sewing skills.
3. If you are near a college or university that offers a major in theater arts, take courses or seminars in theater and theatrical costuming.
4. Contact IATSE to find out what the membership requirements are in your area.
5. Contacts are important. If you know anybody in this field, ask for their help.

STAR DRESSER

CAREER PROFILE

Duties: Checking costumes of production's star to make sure the costumes are ready and in good condition; laying out costumes; assisting star to dress and change

Alternate Title(s): Dresser; Personal Wardrobe Dresser; Personal Dresser

Salary Range: $40,000 to $75,000+

Employment Prospects: Poor

Advancement Prospects: Fair

Best Geographical Location(s): New York City

Prerequisites:

Education or Training—No formal educational requirements

Experience—Experience as wardrobe dresser usually necessary

Special Skills and Personality Traits—Easy to get along with; basic sewing skills; knowledge of laundering; ability to work under pressure; organized; dependable; reliable

CAREER LADDER

```
┌─────────────────────────────────────┐
│ Star Dresser for More Prestigious    │
│ Stars or Wardrobe Supervisor         │
└─────────────────────────────────────┘

┌─────────────────────────────────────┐
│           Star Dresser               │
└─────────────────────────────────────┘

┌─────────────────────────────────────┐
│         Wardrobe Dresser             │
└─────────────────────────────────────┘
```

Position Description

A Star Dresser works with a featured star in a major production and has a number of responsibilities, primarily overseeing the star's costumes to make sure that they are in good condition and ready for the actor or actress to wear at show time and assisting with costume changes.

To do this, the Star Dresser must be completely familiar with the script of a show and may be required to attend rehearsals to determine when, where, how quickly, and in what order the star will have to change costumes. A quick change may not always take place in the star's dressing room but, depending on the requirements of the script, may occur in the wings, backstage, or in another dressing room. The Star Dresser must make sure that the correct costume and any accessories are available wherever the changes occur and be there, ready to assist. As a featured star is generally onstage through much of a show, a Star Dresser must be well organized and prepared to help the star make each change smoothly and—in most instances—rapidly.

The Star Dresser is responsible for maintaining all the star's costumes for each production, from dresses, pants, blouses, shirts, suits, and underwear to hats, shoes, glasses, and jewelry.

The Star Dresser must check costumes before and after each performance and do what is necessary to keep each costume piece clean, pressed and in good condition. He or she will be responsible for attending to minor repairs such as sewing on buttons, sequins, or beads or fixing hems or seams. When necessary, the Star Dresser will report major repairs to the costume or wardrobe supervisor. The Star Dresser must then follow up to make sure that repairs are completed before the next performance.

To keep costumes clean, the Star Dresser will spot clean or launder some items and take others to a dry cleaner or Laundromat to have them cleaned, washed, and pressed. The Star Dresser may also be responsible for polishing or repairing the dye on the star's shoes, checking stockings or socks for holes, and buying replacements or spares as necessary.

Many Star Dressers are also required to put the star's makeup on the dressing table in the order in which it will be used. Some may also put out wigs, hairpieces, or hair ornaments that are to be worn in the production though this is more often the function of a wigmaster or hairdresser.

Before each show, the Star Dresser will help the star put on the first costume and check to make sure the star looks right and that all costume pieces are on.

After each change or at the end of the show, the Star Dresser will check the costumes for any repairs that are required and make notes on what the repairs are. He or she will then hang up each costume. The Star Dresser may repair and launder costumes after final curtain or the next day.

The Star Dresser may have additional duties that other dressers do not. A star often requires special attention and may have a variety of more personal needs that their dresser must attend to such as keeping the star's dressing room neat and comfortable, providing a favored beverage, seeing that flowers received from friends and fans are put in water and arranged around the dressing room, writing thank-you notes to people who send the star gifts, flowers, or correspondence, or passing this task on to the star's personal assistant or secretary.

Becoming a dresser to a Broadway star can be exciting and glamorous. It is also demanding. A Star Dresser who fulfills his or her wardrobe duties and develops a personal rapport with the actor or actress with whom they are working may establish a bond that will last for years.

Salaries

Minimum salaries for individuals working in unionized theaters are set by the local affiliate of the International Alliance of Theatrical Stage Employees (IATSE). Salary ranges for Star Dressers are determined by their level of responsibility and experience. If a star requests the services of a particular dresser, he or she may be paid more.

Star Dressers negotiate their earnings over the scale of wardrobe dressers. It is important to note that Star Dressers usually receive more than the minimum. Individuals working full time may earn between $40,000 and $75,000 plus annually.

Employment Prospects

Employment prospects are poor for Star Dressers. Many productions do not use Star Dressers, relying instead on the services of wardrobe dressers who handle the costuming needs of the general cast.

Obtaining employment as a Star Dresser depends on many things including their experience and expertise. Other factors include the Star Dresser's personality, luck, and being in the right place at the right time. Contacts also help.

The best location for an individual seeking this type of position is New York City.

Advancement Prospects

Advancement prospects are fair for Star Dressers who have determination, drive, and ambition. Those who make the stars most comfortable, are good at their jobs, and have developed pleasant business relationships will be requested again and again. This factor can lead to increased earnings.

Individuals may also advance their careers doing similar work for stars in television and film. Those who prefer to stay in theater may become wardrobe supervisors. As previously noted, advancement, like employment, is dependent on luck, being in the right place at the right time, and contacts.

Education and Training

There are no formal educational requirements necessary to become a Star Dresser. In order to be successful, however, individuals should have at least basic sewing, pressing, and laundering skills.

Experience, Skills, and Personality Traits

Star Dressers usually have prior experience working as wardrobe dressers. Many have had exposure to other kinds of theater craft as well.

To be successful, Star Dressers need to be easy to get along with because they work closely with the star. If the star is not happy and comfortable with the Star Dresser, he or she will either be replaced or not requested again.

Star Dressers must have basic sewing skills and be able to make basic costume repairs including fixing hems and seams and sewing on buttons, sequins, and beads. They should also have a knowledge of how to launder and press costumes.

The ability to work quickly and well under pressure is essential, as is dependability and reliability. Star Dressers must be organized and able to perform a number of tasks at one time without getting flustered.

Unions and Associations

To work in a unionized theater, Star Dressers must be either a member of the union or in the process of becoming a member of the local. The union to which Star Dressers belong is International Alliance of Theatrical Stage Employees (IATSE) whose local affiliate negotiates minimum salaries, working conditions, etc.

Tips for Entry

1. Contacts are important for Star Dressers. If you have any, use them.
2. You might consider having business cards printed to give to people who might either hire you or know someone who is in a position to help you.
3. A résumé is another important tool that may help you find employment. Put all theater-related experience on your résumé and list any references. Make sure your résumé is neatly typed and duplicated.
4. Send actors and actresses your résumé with a cover letter requesting that they consider you for the Star Dresser position. It won't cost you anything, and you might even obtain an interview or, better yet, the job.
5. Courses in basic sewing, theatrical costuming, wardrobe, etc. will be useful.
6. Contact the union to find out what the membership requirements are in your area.

MAKEUP ARTIST

CAREER PROFILE

Duties: Creating or changing the appearance of actors and actresses through the use of makeup

Alternate Title(s): Makeup Designer

Salary Range: $18,000 to $100,000+

Employment Prospects: Fair

Advancement Prospects: Fair

Best Geographical Location(s): Culturally active cities offer more employment opportunities.

Prerequisites:

Education or Training—Requirements vary from position to position; some require an ability to handle theatrical makeup, others proficiency in theatrical hairstyling and makeup; some positions may require completion of a cosmetology course.

Experience—Experience doing theatrical makeup useful

Special Skills and Personality Traits—Cosmetology skills; knowledge of lighting, staging, and costume design; creativity; ability to get along well with others

CAREER LADDER

```
┌─────────────────────────────────┐
│   Makeup Artist for Larger,      │
│   More Prestigious Production     │
└─────────────────────────────────┘

┌─────────────────────────────────┐
│        Makeup Artist             │
└─────────────────────────────────┘

┌─────────────────────────────────┐
│   Makeup Artist Apprentice,      │
│    Assistant, or Student         │
└─────────────────────────────────┘
```

Position Description

A Makeup Artist working in a theatrical situation is responsible for the physical appearance of actors and actresses in a production. Makeup Artists use makeup as their medium and an actor's or actress's face as their canvas.

The Makeup Artist is responsible for helping to convey the persona of a character in a play. He or she applies makeup so that the performer looks the part and their faces and expressions can be seen by the audience. When doing this, the Makeup Artist takes into account the lighting in the theater as well as the lighting used for the various scenes.

In some productions, the Makeup Artist may be required to design a look. For example, Makeup Artists in the popular production of *CATS* had to make actors and actresses look like cats. Along with the costumes, the makeup created the feline look. Makeup also gave each "cat" a distinct personality.

In other productions, the Makeup Artist is responsible for taking a beautiful young actress and turning her into an old hag through the magic of makeup. Makeup Artists also use makeup to age actors to show the passage of time.

The Makeup Artist works with the costume designer and the hairstylist. Together, they determine the type of look for each actor and actress, then the Makeup Artist coordinates the colors of makeup with the individual's costumes, hair color, and style. In some instances, the Makeup Artist is also the production hairstylist.

Depending on the production, the Makeup Artist is responsible to either the costume designer or to the director.

Salaries

Minimum salaries for Makeup Artists working in theatrical settings vary depending on a number of factors, including the specific production and the experience, responsibilities, and reputation of the individual. Annual earnings range from $18,000 to $100,000 or more.

Individuals working in Broadway productions must be members of the local affiliation of the International Alliance of Theatrical Stage Employees (IATSE). In New York the local is 798. This union sets minimum salaries and working conditions for its members. The minimum weekly earnings through August 1, 2005 for individuals was $1,000.17. Those who work as assistants had minimum weekly earnings of $909.27. Individuals can, of course, negotiate higher salaries.

Makeup Artists working in other theatrical settings set their own salaries. They may be paid by the performance or by the week depending on the type of production. Earnings can range from $350 to $700 or more per week.

Employment Prospects

Employment prospects are fair for individuals seeking employment as theatrical Makeup Artists. They may find work in Off Broadway, Off-Off-Broadway, stock productions, and dinner theaters. Prospects are more difficult for individuals aspiring to work in major theatrical productions such as Broadway plays.

Some Makeup Artists work in the cosmetics and hairstyling industries in fields other than theater and the performing arts to augment their earnings.

Advancement Prospects

Advancement prospects are difficult to determine in this profession since so much depends on the reputation that the Makeup Artist builds for himself or herself. Makeup Artists who are good at their jobs become a commodity and are requested. They advance their careers by being sought out to work in larger, more prestigious productions. Depending on their aspirations, Makeup Artists also advance their careers by doing the same work in television and films.

Education and Training

There are no formal educational requirements for theatrical Makeup Artists. Requirements will vary depending on the specific position. Some productions want the Makeup Artist to have previous experience working with theatrical makeup and techniques. Others prefer the Makeup Artist to have had courses, workshops, or seminars in theatrical makeup.

Those who attend college with a major in theater arts find courses in theatrical makeup, hairstyling, costuming, staging, and lighting useful.

In many areas, Makeup Artists hold a state cosmetology or hairstyling license. To obtain this, individuals attend a licensed school of cosmetology and hair styling for a specified number of hours. They then take a state examination that usually consists of a written section and a practical portion.

Individuals who want to become members of the International Alliance of Theatrical Stage Employees local take a practical exam in order to be admitted. During this examination, Makeup Artists must show that they can perform certain makeup techniques such as applying scars and bruises and laying mustaches.

Experience, Skills, and Personality Traits

Makeup Artists must have the ability to get along well with others and make them feel comfortable. Makeup Artists should be creative, artistic people, skilled in cosmetology and theatrical makeup and hairstyling. They should also have a knowledge of theater, lighting, staging, and costume design.

Unions and Associations

The local affiliation of the International Alliance of Theatrical Stage Employees (IATSE) is the major bargaining union for Makeup Artists working in Broadway theater. In the East, it is local 798. This union negotiates minimum salaries and working conditions. Individuals may also be members of a number of trade associations including the National Hair-dressers and Cosmetologists Association (NHCA). Groups such as this provide professional guidance, support, and educational opportunities to their members.

Tips for Entry

1. Try to find an internship as a Makeup Artist in a theater. Look into community, regional, stock, and dinner theaters.
2. Volunteer as a Makeup Artist for school or college productions.
3. Find an apprenticeship with a theatrical Makeup Artist as a method of entering the field.
4. Contact the local affiliation of the appropriate union to determine membership requirements.
5. Take classes, workshops, and seminars in theatrical makeup staging, lighting, and costume design.

PRODUCTION HAIRSTYLIST

CAREER PROFILE

Duties: Creating hairstyles for actors and actresses in the-atrical productions; washing, cutting, styling, and color-ing hair and wigs for cast members

Alternate Title(s): Hairstylist; Hairdresser

Salary Range: $18,000 to $100,000+

Employment Prospects: Fair

Advancement Prospects: Poor

Best Geographical Location(s): Culturally active cities will offer more job possibilities.

Prerequisites:

Education or Training—Requirements vary from posi-tion to position; some may require an ability to work well with hair; others may require completion of a cosmetol-ogy/hairstyling course and still others may prefer classes in theatrical hairstyling and makeup; many states require a license in hairstyling or cosmetology.

Experience—Experience in hairstyling necessary; expe-rience in theatrical hairstyling helpful

Special Skills and Personality Traits—Hairstyling skills; ability to research; personableness; knowledge of theatrical lighting, makeup, and costuming

CAREER LADDER

```
┌─────────────────────────────────┐
│ Production Hairstylist for Larger,│
│   More Prestigious Production      │
└─────────────────────────────────┘

┌─────────────────────────────────┐
│      Production Hairstylist        │
└─────────────────────────────────┘

┌─────────────────────────────────┐
│ Hairstylist Apprentice or Assistant or│
│   Hairstylist in Unrelated Field   │
└─────────────────────────────────┘
```

Position Description

A Production Hairstylist working in a theatrical setting is responsible for the appearance of the hair of the actors and actresses in a production. The hairstylist works with the actual hair of the cast members or with wigs. He or she is also responsible for the styling of facial hair.

The Production Hairstylist works with the costume designer and the makeup artist. Together they are responsi-ble for creating the look of the characters in the production. In many instances, the Production Hairstylist also acts as the makeup artist.

The hairstylist determines many things before creating a hairstyle for an actor or actress, such as the time period of the production. If, for example, the hairstylist is working on a production that was supposed to have taken place 50 years ago, he or she researches the hairstyles from that period. This research is conducted by visiting museums or libraries or by looking through books and magazines, or by watching movies.

In some productions, the hairstylist is required to design special looks for cast members that also require research. The hairstylist has to handle various hairstyling situations within a production. For instance, the production may have characters who age as the scenes change. The hairstylist develops styles that can change as quickly as scenes do.

The hairstylist knows how to wash, style, cut, and color hair to fit the look of characters created by the playwright and the director. He or she must also be familiar with work-ing with wigs. Through the use of wigs, a character can change his or her hairstyle within minutes. Wigs allow the actor or actress to have perfectly styled hair at all times.

Depending on the budget of the production, wigs are pur-chased or are custom made by a wigmaker. In instances where they are custom made, the hairstylist is responsible for making appointments for fittings for cast members with the wigmaker. After the fitting, the hairstylist is required to cut and style the wig appropriately for the actors or actresses.

The Production Hairstylist may be responsible for all the cast members' hair or for only a few. In some situations, he or she is the hairstylist for the star of the show only.

Other responsibilities of the hairstylist include determining what equipment and supplies are required and ordering or purchasing them. Expenses are reimbursed if the Production Hairstylist pays for these items.

The hairstylist works in the preproduction period of the show designing hairstyles. He or she may also work before, during or after performances styling the hair and wigs of cast members.

Depending on the production, the Production Hairstylist is responsible to either the costume designer or the director.

Salaries

Minimum salaries for Production Hairstylists working in theatrical settings vary with the specific production and the experience, responsibilities, and reputation of the individual. Annual salaries for Production Hairstylists working fairly frequently can range from $18,000 to $100,000 or more. Individuals augment earnings by styling hair outside the theater industry.

Production Hairstylists working in Broadway productions are members of the local affiliation of the International Alliance of Theatrical Stage Employees (IATSE) for Makeup Artists and Hairstylists. On the East Coast, the local for this group is local 798.

This union sets minimum salaries and working conditions for its members. The minimum weekly earnings for individuals through August 1, 2005 were $1,000.17. Those who work as assistants earned a minimum salary of $909.27. Many individuals negotiate higher salaries.

Production Hairstylists working in Off Broadway or regional theatrical productions negotiate their own salaries. They are paid by the performance or by the week depending on the demands and budget of the job. Earnings range from $350 to $700 or more per week.

Employment Prospects

Employment prospects are fair for Production Hairstylists. They find work in Off Broadway, Off-Off-Broadway, stock productions, and dinner theaters. Prospects are more difficult for individuals aspiring to work in major theatrical productions such as Broadway plays.

Advancement Prospects

Advancement prospects are poor for Production Hairstylists and most select a couple of different career paths. One way to climb the career ladder is by doing similar work for more prestigious productions. Another method is to perform similar work in television, commercials, or films.

Advancement prospects depend to a great extent on the reputation the hairstylist builds for himself or herself. Those who are reliable, are qualified to do a great job, and make people feel comfortable are consistently requested.

Education and Training

Educational requirements vary for Production Hairstylists depending on the state in which they work. Some positions require that an individual know how to work well with hair and wigs. In may areas, Production Hairstylists are required to hold a state cosmetology or hairstyling license and they obtain this by attending and graduating from a licensed school of cosmetology and hairstyling. They are then required to take a state examination which usually consists of a written section and a practical portion.

Individuals who want to become members of the International Alliance of Theatrical Stage Employees local also take a practical exam in order to be admitted. During this examination, Production Hairstylists illustrate that they can perform certain hair techniques and do styling for various eras in time.

Courses, workshops, and seminars in theatrical hairstyling, makeup, costuming, staging, and lighting are useful. A college degree with a major in theater arts gives the individual a well-rounded background and the opportunity to obtain experience in theatrical hairstyling and makeup procedures.

Experience, Skills, and Personality Traits

Production Hairstylists need to have a flair for working with hair. Individuals must be able to wash, style, cut, and color hair and wigs. They must have the ability to create hairstyles for all types of hair and wigs that might be used on stage. Those who are also skilled at theatrical makeup techniques will be more marketable.

Production Hairstylists need to get along well with others and make them feel comfortable.

Production Hairstylists should have an interest in and knowledge of the theater. An understanding of lighting, staging and costume design is helpful in their work, and an ability to research is useful.

Unions and Associations

Production Hairstylists working on Broadway must be members of the local affiliation of the International Alliance of Theatrical Stage Employees (IATSE). This union negotiates minimum salaries and working conditions for its members. The East Coast affiliation for Broadway's Production Hairstylist is local 798.

Individuals may also be members of a number of trade associations including the National Hairdressers and Cosmetologists Association (NHCA).

Tips for Entry

1. Get experience in theatrical hairstyling by offering to be the Production Hairstylist for your local school or community theater group.
2. Consider an internship in theatrical hairstyling. Contact associations, schools, or theatrical groups for information.
3. Consider an apprenticeship with a Production Hairstylist. It is a good way to learn the trade and make contacts.
4. Take as many classes, workshops, and seminars in theatrical hairstyling and makeup as possible. Participation in these groups is important for learning techniques as well as for making important contacts.
5. Become a licensed hairstylist. While it isn't always necessary to have a license, it gives you the opportunity to earn extra money outside the theater while waiting for your big break in the industry.

SUPPORT SERVICES FOR PERFORMING ARTISTS

PERSONAL MANAGER

Duties: Representing a client; overseeing and guiding all aspects of his or her career

Alternate Title(s): Manager; Artist's Representative

Salary Range: 10% to 50% of a client's earnings; impossible to determine exact salary due to nature of the job

Employment Prospects: Good

Advancement Prospects: Fair

Best Geographical Location(s): Positions located throughout the country; culturally active cities will offer more opportunities.

Prerequisites:

Education or Training—No educational requirement; college background useful

Experience—Experience in entertainment industry preferred

Special Skills and Personality Traits—Knowledge of and contacts in entertainment industry; aggressiveness; creativity; ability to work under pressure

```
┌─────────────────────────────────────┐
│  Personal Manager for Large Roster of │
│       Prestigious Clients             │
└─────────────────────────────────────┘

┌─────────────────────────────────────┐
│         Personal Manager              │
└─────────────────────────────────────┘

┌─────────────────────────────────────┐
│  Assistant to Personal Manager or     │
│  Entertainer or Performing Artist     │
└─────────────────────────────────────┘
```

Position Description

A Personal Manager can represent one or more clients. His or her main function is to oversee all aspects of a client's career. Managers may represent actors and actresses, dancers, or singers in theater, film, television, music, dance, or a combination of these arts. Some entertainments prefer a manager who specializes in one type of client area such as theater or dance. Others prefer that their Manager represent entertainers in a different field to eliminate the possibility of conflicts.

In his or her job, the Personal Manager deals with and advises the client on all business decisions and many of the creative decisions that must be made. While doing this, the manager attempts to guide the artist to the top of his or her profession.

Some managers develop a plan for an entertainer's career. Others plan as they go. The manager can be the single most important person assisting an artist.

Part of the manager's job is surrounding the client with people who can help him or her become successful. The manager will advise the client on the hiring or firing of important support personnel such as agents, public relations firms, publicists, photographers, accountants, business managers, record companies, or choreographers.

The manager must oversee all the support personnel and their jobs in relation to the client. The manager might feel,

for instance, that the finances of a project do not sound right. He or she would make sure that the business manager or accountant look into the potential problem.

Managers must work hard on behalf of their clients. However, a hard working manager does not ensure that the client will become a superstar. It is extremely helpful for the Personal Manager to have a variety of industry contacts that can make a major difference in a client's success.

When an actor or actress is rehearsing for the reading of a part, or a client is polishing an act, many managers help in a creative sense. Individuals, for example, may help their clients choose songs when auditioning for a musical.

Personal Managers may be given what is called power of attorney by their clients. This may be a complete power of attorney or a limited one. Whatever the case, the manager usually is given authority to approve dates and monies for employment and publicity materials.

The manager and the actor, actress, or other entertainer being represented should be compatible. He or she must be available on a day-to-day basis to discuss any problems the client has or develops. In addition, the two must meet on a regular basis to discuss new methods to advance the career of the client.

In some instances, the manager will put up money to finance some of the expenses of a client in hopes of making the money back later. In other cases, he or she may search for a financial backer.

The manager must be in constant communication with all the people working with the client. He or she must call agents to see what type of work is available and when casting calls and auditions are being held. The manager may also work closely with the client's public relations firm or publicist in an attempt to promote the individual.

Managers are responsible directly to the client. Although the terms of each contract are different, most run for a specified number of years. Some have option clauses that the manager can pick up if he or she desires.

Salaries

Earnings for Personal Managers are impossible to determine due to the nature of the job. Managers receive a percentage of the client's earnings. This percentage varies with the individual and the manager. It can range from 10% to 50%, although the usual amount is 15% to 20%. In some situations, the manager may earn a higher percentage as his or her client attains greater success or makes more money.

Managers receive their earnings, also called a fee, off the top. Fees can be received from all personal appearances, theatrical engagements, television shows, films, concerts, performances, recordings, merchandising, commercials, and endorsements.

For a manager representing a major star, 20% of all the star's earnings can add up to a great deal of money. As managers can represent more than one client, they can earn $1 million or more annually. However, most managers do not represent major clients and receive only a fraction of this sum.

Employment Prospects

There are thousands of people who aspire to be actors and actresses in the theater, television, and films. Countless others want to be dancers, singers, or musicians. Some think that they can do it by themselves. Others feel that a manager will make the quest quicker and more successful.

Employment prospects are good for Personal Managers. Almost anyone who wants to be a Personal Manager can be one if they find one or more clients to represent. However, not everyone can be a successful manager. In order to be successful, they must have important contacts and the ability to guide a client's career.

Advancement Prospects

Advancement prospects are difficult to determine for Personal Managers. A great deal of the advancement has to do with the experience and expertise of the individual as well as luck, contacts, and being in the right place at the right time.

Personal Managers attain advancement in a number of ways, by developing a roster of more prestigious clients that results in increased earnings; by starting with a relatively unknown actor or actress and successfully guiding their rise to stardom; by working for a management firm and taking on more management responsibilities for more prestigious clients.

Education and Training

There are no formal educational requirements for Personal Managers. A college degree or background often is helpful to lend credibility to the individual and for contacts.

Good choices for college degrees include theater, theater arts, arts management, business, communications, liberal arts, or law. Courses, seminars, and workshops in publicity, theater, promotion, public relations, arts management, music, marketing, negotiation, psychology, business, writing, and law are also useful in the manager's career.

Experience, Skills, and Personality Traits

Managers must have a broad knowledge of the entertainment industry. Many learn as they go. Some have been entertainers and find they are more successful in the business end of the industry.

Business skills are a must for Personal Managers. Contacts are especially important. The more prestigious contacts a manager has, the better the opportunities are for his or her clients.

Personal Managers must be extremely aggressive on behalf of the people that they represent. Individuals need good communications skills and should be very articulate.

The ability to negotiate is essential. Creativity is helpful in building a client's image. Individuals must be able to offer their clients constructive advice in a positive manner.

Successful Managers are hard working people who are confident enough in their abilities to surround themselves with a good team. They offer advice to their clients on the retention of attorneys, agents, and publicists. Managers must also have the ability to see the raw talent of a performer and develop that talent in ways that enhance their career.

Unions and Associations

Managers of actors are familiar with the rules and regulations of Actor's Equity as well as any other union that their clients come under the auspices of. Those working with musicians are familiar with the American Federation of Musicians (AFM).

Managers may be members of the Conference of Personal Managers (CPM), an organization that sets the standards for the conduct of Personal Managers.

Tips for Entry

1. Find an internship in any facet of the theater gives you a good background in the industry.
2. Consider working for a management agency in an entry-level position to learn the ropes.
3. Go to the library and find books on entertainers who have made it. Read all you can on their struggle to the top to get an insight into the business.
4. If you are interested in becoming a manager of a singer, dancer, or musician, try to break in on a local level. There are many acts that need guidance from someone willing to help.

PRESS AGENT

CAREER PROFILE

Duties: Getting the name or project of a performing artist better known and more familiar to the public; compiling press kits; writing press releases; arranging press conferences; plotting publicity campaigns

Alternate Title(s): Publicist

Salary Range: $21,000 to $200,000+

Employment Prospects: Fair

Advancement Prospects: Fair

Best Geographical Location(s): New York City, Los Angeles, Hollywood, Chicago, Atlanta, Philadelphia, Washington, D.C., or any large and culturally active city will offer opportunities.

Prerequisites:

　Education or Training—College degree in communications, journalism, English, advertising, marketing, or public relations preferred

　Experience—Experience as journalist or critic for newspaper or magazine helpful; experience in publicity or public relations a plus

　Special Skills and Personality Traits—Creativity; good writing skills; persuasiveness; ability to work under pressure; knowledge of entertainment industry; aggressiveness

CAREER LADDER

```
┌─────────────────────────────────────┐
│    Independent Press Agent or        │
│  Press Agent with Large Roster of    │
│        Prestigious Clients           │
└─────────────────────────────────────┘

┌─────────────────────────────────────┐
│            Press Agent               │
└─────────────────────────────────────┘

┌─────────────────────────────────────┐
│         Press Agent Trainee          │
└─────────────────────────────────────┘
```

Position Description

The basic duty of a Press Agent or publicist working in the performing arts field is to create methods of making an entertainer's name or their project better known. The best way to do this is to keep the entertainer or the project in the public eye as much as possible. The more popular and well-known personalities and projects in show business are, the more successful they will be.

Press Agents work with many types of entertainers, including performing artists, movie stars, television stars, actors, disc jockeys, radio commentators, models, comedians, singers, musicians, or magicians. They also work with theatrical revues.

The Press Agent must not have a big ego and must be willing to accept the fact that if a client is successful, the client will take and get the credit, and if he or she is unsuccessful, the Press Agent will often be blamed.

The Press Agent must be able to come up with creative campaigns for placing their clients in the public eye. This is

accomplished in any number of ways, including inducing magazine and newspaper editors to do feature stories and articles on their client or scheduling television or radio appearances. The Press Agent sometimes uses some type of advertising campaign featuring their client. Press Agents often create something called "hype" to gain notoriety for their client. Hype is a supersaturation of publicity in the media which is used to promote people and projects in the entertainment business. While publicity should be true, hype sometimes exaggerates facts.

Press Agents write creative press releases for the press to use. The successful Press Agent has the ability to come up with a good hook or angle for a press release. The hook is what will draw attention to that particular press release as it sits on a desk with dozens of others. Press kits, consisting of press releases, biographies, pictures, and reprints or reviews and articles are also compiled by the agent. The Press Agent is responsible for sending the press kits or media kits, as they are sometimes known, to editors, TV and radio producers, talent coordinators, and column planters. The individual knows how to get through to these people in order to place their client on television, radio, or to have feature articles written. The Press Agent also has the ability to work under the constant pressure of deadlines.

Press Agents are responsible for calling and arranging press conferences for their client. He or she knows what type of event is important enough to call a press conference for, how to put one together, and how to have the right people attend.

Often the media isn't really interested in a client until he or she is so well known that publicity will be self-generating. In these types of cases, the Press Agent has the ability to come up with unique ideas and angles to gain attention from the media.

Some acts are so well known that every editor, television and radio show, journalist and reporter wants an interview and appearance. In these cases, the Press Agent must be selective and decide which opportunities are in the best interest of the client. For example, a well-known entertainer would gain more media attention from an appearance on the *The Tonight Show* than from a local morning talk show.

The Press Agent also has to act as a shield to keep the press away from a client if he or she feels it would harm a client's image to give interviews. The Press Agent might also not allow an interview if he or she feels it would over-expose the client in the media.

Press Agents often attend press parties, dinners, luncheons, and other social events on a client's behalf or to make important contacts. These contacts are important for a number of reasons including helping to promote the client and helping to build a client list for either the individual Press Agent or the company he or she works for.

As a Press Agent the individual is usually responsible directly to the client. He or she may also be responsible to the client's management representative. If the Press Agent is working for a company, he or she will be answerable to his or her supervisor, or the owner or president of the company.

Salaries

Salaries for Press Agents are dependent on a number of variables including experience, the type of client, whether the agent is self-employed or working for a radio station, television station or for an agency. The individual may also be working part time for one or more clients.

A Press Agent may earn anywhere from approximately $21,000 to $80,000 a year. Press Agents working with major stars or projects in the performing arts industry might make $200,000 or more a year.

Employment Prospects

Press Agents in this field can work for theatrical companies, public relations firms, television stations, radio stations, record companies, film companies, publicity firms, or other press agents. There are a fair amount of jobs available for qualified individuals at public relations firms and publicity organizations. Positions at major television and radio stations and film companies and record companies are harder to come by. A Press Agent can also work as an independent, which means that he or she must get their own clients. Press Agents working as independents usually have to have a proven track record with clients in order to get other clients and to be successful.

Advancement Prospects

Press Agents can advance their careers in a number of ways. As one example, they can advance at the firm or organization they are working at by seeking opportunities to work with better, more established clients. The interesting thing about advancement in this field is that it really can happen at any time. For example, a Press Agent might move up the ladder of success by working with a relatively unknown client, like a new actor on a television pilot which hits it big, or he or she might be working with a client who lands a part in a big Broadway musical production. Anything can happen.

Education and Training

Although there are exceptions, the most qualified person applying for the job will usually get it. While a Press Agent doesn't really need a college degree, it helps. Courses in communications, journalism, public relations, advertising, marketing, English, or business are helpful in honing the skills necessary for the job. Seminars and courses in publicity and promotion are also useful.

Experience, Skills, and Personality Traits

A Press Agent must come up with creative angles for a client's press releases, media events and feature stories. He or she must be articulate and able to write enticing press releases to persuade the media to use his or her ideas for articles and appearances.

The Press Agent must also be able to work under the constant pressure of not only deadlines, but also of clients who feel that they are not getting the exposure they deserve.

In order for Press Agents to gain a good reputation with reporters, journalists, producers, and TV and radio people, they must be credible or they will lose their contacts.

Press Agents often have prior experience as journalists, producers, reviewers, or talent coordinators.

Unions and Associations

Press Agents may belong to the Association of Theatrical Press Agents and Managers (ATPAM), the National Entertainment Journalists Association (NEJA), or the Public Relations Society of America (PRSA). These organizations offer seminars, booklets, periodicals, and other helpful information to those in the industry.

Tips for Entry

1. Try and get an internship with one of the larger entertainment public relations firms, record labels, or television stations. Most internships it should be noted are very low-paying or unpaid positions.
2. Send your résumé, a short cover letter, and samples of your writing to entertainment-oriented public relations companies in areas where you are interested in working.
3. Work with a local theater, television station, or entertainer as an independent publicist to get some experience for yourself and for your résumé. At this level you probably will have to work at a nominal fee.
4. Work as a reviewer for your local newspaper or magazine entertainment section. This will help you build contacts.

PRESS AGENT TRAINEE

CAREER PROFILE

Duties: Assisting a senior press agent in getting the name or project of an entertainer into the media and before the public; compiling press kits; writing press releases; assisting press agents in arranging press conferences; handling detail work for press agent

Alternate Title(s): Junior Publicist; Junior Press Agent; Assistant Publicist; Assistant Press Agent

Salary Range: $18,000 to $24,000+

Employment Prospects: Fair

Advancement Prospects: Good

Best Geographical Location(s): New York City, Los Angeles, Chicago, Atlanta, Philadelphia, Washington, D.C., or any large and culturally active city will offer opportunities.

Prerequisites:

Education or Training—College degree in communications, journalism, English, advertising, marketing, or public relations preferred

Experience—Writing experience helpful; knowledge of entertainment business useful but not always necessary; experience in publicity or public relations a plus

Special Skills and Personality Traits—Creativity; good writing skills; articulateness; ability to work under pressure; aggressiveness

CAREER LADDER

```
┌─────────────────────────────────┐
│       Senior Press Agent        │
└─────────────────────────────────┘

┌─────────────────────────────────┐
│       Press Agent Trainee       │
└─────────────────────────────────┘

┌─────────────────────────────────┐
│  Intern, Newspaper or Magazine  │
│  Reporter, or Entry-level Position │
└─────────────────────────────────┘
```

Position Description

The Press Agent Trainee or junior publicist assists the senior press agent in making an entertainer's name or entertainment project better known. This entry-level position is a good way to break into the entertainment business.

The Press Agent Trainee may work with any type of entertainer or performing artist, including actors, actresses, movie stars, television stars, disc jockeys, models, comedians, singers, musicians, or magicians. He or she might also work with theatrical productions, television shows, movies, or other types of special programs.

The Press Agent Trainee might sit in on a creative meeting with a client but will usually not contribute any campaign ideas to the client directly. If he or she does come up with some concept, it is discussed with the senior press agent in a private meeting.

The Press Agent Trainee does a lot of the detail work for the press agent. He or she might types releases, calendar event sheets, and prepare envelopes for the press. The trainee is the one who puts together the various parts of the press kits—stapling, compiling, and placing information into folders.

The Press Agent Trainee spends a lot of time on the phone calling important members of the press on behalf of the senior press agent and answering routine calls from the media.

As the trainee gets more experience, he or she begins writing press releases or bio sheets of the client. Most of this writing however, will have to be checked with the senior press agent before it goes out to the media. With more experience, the Press Agent Trainee will begin to find hooks or angles for press releases. These are the ideas that make a press release exciting and capture the attention of editors or talent coordinators.

The Press Agent Trainee learns how to plan press conferences. He or she addresses envelopes for invitations, makes calls, learns who is to be invited, and decides on the correct time to hold a conference. During the press conference, he or she will give press or media kits to the people attending, mingle, and make sure that everything is going according to schedule.

At times, the Press Agent Trainee will act as a buffer for the press agent. For example, when the press agent is preparing to break a big story that he or she isn't ready to let the media in on, the Trainee might answer the phones and keep the media at bay.

The Press Agent Trainee usually has opportunities to attend press parties, dinners, luncheons, and other social events with the press agent. These events are necessary to attend in order to make important contacts that will help the Press Agent Trainee meet people in the media and in the industry. Contacts will not only help the trainee do a better job at this stage in his or her career, they will be of assistance in finding better jobs or potential clients down the road.

The Press Agent Trainee often seems like a glorified secretary. There is a lot of typing, stuffing envelopes, answering phones, tracking bills, and running around involved. Eventually, trainees begin writing releases, talking to the clients, and handling more and more work without supervision.

The Press Agent Trainee will get little recognition and he or she must accept this fact, much as a senior press agent does. The Press Agent Trainee is getting paid to help keep someone else's name, image, or product in the public eye. When and if a press or publicity campaign works, the press agent won't get much credit; the Press Agent Trainee will get even less. If the trainee does come up with a good campaign idea, in many cases the senior press agent may take full credit. Ego cannot play a big part in the Press Agent Trainee's career.

Salaries
Salaries for a Press Agent Trainee are relatively low. It is important to remember, though, that as the individual gains experience, salaries will go up. Press Agent Trainees may begin their careers earning as little as $18,000 a year. This figure could go up to $24,000 or more annually.

Employment Prospects
Press Agent Trainees may find work in public relations firms, television stations, radio stations, record companies, film companies, publicity firms, or with independent press agents. An individual who is willing to work in any of the above mediums and is also willing to work in a major city will have a fair chance at finding employment.

Advancement Prospects
As mentioned previously, a Press Agent Trainee's position at times seems like a glorified secretary. Fortunately, though, the trainee phase does not last forever. If the individual is lucky, he or she will soon gain the experience necessary to become a full-fledged publicist.

Advancement can move in many directions for the Press Agent Trainee. It can mean becoming a senior press agent for a company or going out and locating clients for working on a freelance basis; both of which usually means a dramatic rise in salary.

Press Agent Trainees who show a flair for publicity and who are aggressive will move up the career ladder.

Education and Training
Although there are some successful press agents who haven't even finished high school, a college degree in business, marketing, advertising, English, journalism, or liberal arts is usually required to get a job as a trainee. Any type of course or seminar in public relations, publicity, or marketing will also be useful.

Experience, Skills, and Personality Traits
A Press Agent Trainee must be creative, articulate, and able to develop persuasive press releases to entice the media to use his or her ideas for articles.

The Press Agent Trainee must have the ability to work under the constant pressure not only from deadlines but from the senior press agent who is in turn being put under pressure by his or her clients.

The Press Agent Trainee must be credible or the individual will not have the ability to build a list of contacts. In order to advance his or her career, it is important for the Press Agent Trainee to be aggressive in a nonthreatening way. Press agents are often concerned that the trainee will become too capable and take their list of clients when they establish their own practice.

Unions and Associations
Press Agent Trainees do not have to belong to any union. They may belong to trade associations which put them in contact with others in their field as well as providing professional guidance and support. These could include the Association of Theatrical Press Agents and Managers (ATPAM), the Public Relations Society of America (PRSA) or its student chapter, or the National Entertainment Journalists Association (NEJA).

Tips for Entry
1. Try to find an internship program. While most of these internships are very low-paying or even nonpaying positions, getting involved in one is a good idea. Once someone invests time in your training, you are likely to remain with the company. Internships can be found at many of the larger entertainment public relations firms, record labels, and television stations.
2. Work at a local theater, performing arts center, television, or radio station during the summer to gain some type of experience in the entertainment industry.
3. Work as a reviewer for a local or school newspaper or magazine entertainment section. This will give you needed experience and help build contacts.

THEATRICAL AGENT

CAREER PROFILE

Duties: Finding parts for actors and actresses in theatrical productions; contacting producers and casting directors to fill openings; setting up auditions for clients; negotiating contracts

Alternate Title(s): Agent

Salary Range: $23,000 to $1,000,000+

Employment Prospects: Poor

Advancement Prospects: Fair

Best Geographical Location(s): New York City offers the most employment prospects; other culturally active cities offer additional opportunities.

Prerequisites:

Education or Training—Educational requirements vary from high school diploma to college background or bachelor's degree.

Experience—Experience working in theatrical or other booking agency necessary

Special Skills and Personality Traits—Knowledgeable about theatrical industry; good phone skills; articulateness; selling skills; aggressive; organization; negotiation skills; ability to work under pressure; determination; drive

CAREER LADDER

```
┌─────────────────────────────────┐
│   Theatrical Agent with Large    │
│  Roster of Clients or Working for│
│     More Prestigious Agency      │
└─────────────────────────────────┘

┌─────────────────────────────────┐
│        Theatrical Agent          │
└─────────────────────────────────┘

┌─────────────────────────────────┐
│        Assistant to Agent        │
└─────────────────────────────────┘
```

Position Description

Theatrical Agents specialize in finding jobs for actors and actresses in theatrical productions.

Theatrical Agents representing well-known clients are called often by producers to determine if a specific actor or actress is interested in playing a part in an upcoming Broadway show. In some cases, the actor or actress learns about a certain production and asks his or her agent to find out if the lead part has been cast. If it has not been cast yet, the Theatrical Agent determines if his or her client might be considered.

Theatrical Agents representing less well-known clients work hard finding parts and obtaining auditions. To accomplish this, the Theatrical Agent researches the productions that are being planned by reading about them in trade papers or by talking to productions, casting directors, and others in the industry.

Theatrical Agents socialize with others in the theatrical world in hopes of hearing news about new productions, auditions, and casting calls. They also spend a lot of time talking on the telephone in the hopes of making contacts, locating possible parts, and setting up auditions.

Contacts are essential to the Theatrical Agent. The more contacts he or she has, the better. Agents also must have good working relationships with producers and casting directors. When an opening for a part occurs, he or she places a call and requests an audition for a client.

The Theatrical Agent is careful to send only actors and actresses that fit the part. The Agent knows the strong points and limitations of the clients he or she represents.

The agent's duties also include helping the actor or actress put together a portfolio or press kit to bring to auditions, developing or writing their résumé, and suggesting professional photographers to take the necessary pictures.

At open auditions, thousands of actors and actresses may try out the same part. Those who are represented by an agent often receive more attention from the casting director or producer, especially if the agent has contacted the producer or casting director about a particular client.

Theatrical Agents act as the intermediary between actors and actresses and producers. If the producer is interested in an actor, he or she calls the Theatrical Agent to set up another audition. The Theatrical Agent then calls the actor or actress with the good news about the callback.

Once a producer or casting director has decided to hire an actor or actress, the Theatrical Agent handles the financial negotiations.

Negotiations for theatrical artists include areas other than money. A big point of negotiation for many actors and actresses is billing, that is, where the actor's or actress's name is placed on the marquee, in advertisements, and on the program. Other negotiating points include length of the contract, dressing room size, and extra perks.

Once everything is successfully negotiated and a deal is struck, the Theatrical Agent is responsible for preparing contracts and seeing that they are signed and returned.

Theatrical Agents can be self-employed or may work for an agency. Some agencies employ many agents who represent all types of clients. Other agencies represent only theatrical artists.

Theatrical Agents working for an agency are assigned clients and are responsible for bringing in new clients. To accomplish this, the agent attends talent showcases and small theatrical productions.

Theatrical Agents have a difficult job and work under a great deal of pressure. They must constantly produce auditions, parts and jobs for the actors and actresses they represent. Theatrical Agents are responsible either to the actor or actress who employs them or to the manager of the agency.

Salaries

Earnings for Theatrical Agents vary greatly. Annual salaries range from approximately $23,000 to $1 million or more. Individuals starting out or those handling clients who are not yet well known will be paid at the lower end of the scale. Successful agents handling well-known actors earn more.

Factors affecting earnings include the number and prestige of clients that the agent represents as well as the fees clients receive for performances. Other factors include whether the agent is self-employed or works for an agency. Theatrical Agents are paid in a number of ways. If they work for an agency, they earn a salary or a salary plus a commission on business brought in. In some agencies, Theatrical Agents are paid a bonus plus a commission on new clients signed up.

Theatrical Agents are paid on a commission or percentage basis, that is, a percentage off the top of the fee that the actor or actress is paid. Commissions vary from agent to agent, ranging from 10% to 25% of a client's gross earnings.

Depending on the situation, the agent may receive a percentage of earnings from the client's participation in productions, personal appearances, engagements, commercial endorsements, or recordings.

Employment Prospects

Employment prospects are poor for Theatrical Agents. While Theatrical Agents who produce results are in demand, there is a great deal of competition for these jobs and too few top performers to sustain high earnings for all those who seek to be agents.

Advancement Prospects

Advancement prospects for Theatrical Agents vary with the specific agency an agent works for, as well as their aggressiveness, ambition, drive, and determination.

Theatrical Agents climb the career ladder by building up a large client roster of successful actors and actresses. Other agents advance by locating similar positions in more prestigious agencies or starting their own agency.

Theatrical Agents also climb the career ladder by handling a relatively unknown actor or actress who zooms to the top of their profession in a relatively short time.

Education and Training

Educational requirements vary for Theatrical Agents.

A number of colleges around the country offer majors in arts management. Classes, workshops, and seminars in all areas of arts management, business, contract negotiation, contract law, theater, theater arts, and booking entertainment are also useful.

In some states, Theatrical Agents, like other booking agents, must be licensed. These licenses are similar to those required at other employment agencies. They are usually obtained through the state's department of licensing.

Experience, Skills, and Personality Traits

Theatrical Agents should have some experience working in a theatrical or other talent agency, either as an assistant, secretary, or intern to other agents.

Theatrical Agents should be knowledgeable about the theatrical industry and all its components. They should have extensive contacts in the industry, well-practiced negotiation skills, and an understanding of the rules and regulations of the various unions involved in theater.

Theatrical Agents should be articulate and have the ability to communicate well on the phone. They should be very organized as they frequently work on a variety of projects at one time.

Successful Theatrical Agents are very determined, ambitious, and hard working.

Unions and Associations

Theatrical Agents may work with a number of unions. The union for actors working in theater is Actors' Equity, which sets minimum earnings and working conditions for its members. Agents must adhere to all union rules and regulations when representing their clients.

Tips for Entry

1. Try to find a training program with one of the larger booking agencies. Even if the agency does not special- ize in theatrical clients, the job gives you an opportunity to make important contacts and learn the trade.
2. Consider an entry-level position in a theatrical agency as an assistant, secretary, receptionist, or mail room clerk. These jobs are often advertised in the classified or display section of the newspaper under the headings of "Entertainment," "Theatrical," "Theater," "Talent," "Agent," "Administrative Assistant," or "Secretary."
3. Look for an internship program in a theatrical booking agency through the agency itself or with the help of a school offering a degree in arts management.

BOOKING AGENT

CAREER PROFILE

Duties: Securing work for performing artists; negotiating contracts; locating and signing up new talent

Alternate Title(s): Agent; Booking Manager; Booker; Booking Representative

Salary Range: $24,000 to $1,000,000+

Employment Prospects: Fair

Advancement Prospects: Fair

Best Geographical Location(s): Major booking agencies are located in New York City and Los Angeles; other culturally active cities offer the most opportunities; smaller cities offer other opportunities.

Prerequisites:

Education or Training—Educational requirements vary from high school diploma to college background or bachelor's degree.

Experience—Experience working in performing arts or entertainment industry helpful

Special Skills and Personality Traits—Marketing ability; communications skills; aggressiveness; organization; good phone manner; negotiation skills; understanding of performing arts and entertainment industry

CAREER LADDER

```
┌─────────────────────────────────────┐
│  Booking Agent for Large Roster of   │
│       Prestigious Clients            │
└─────────────────────────────────────┘

┌─────────────────────────────────────┐
│           Booking Agent              │
└─────────────────────────────────────┘

┌─────────────────────────────────────┐
│ Assistant to Booking Agent, Intern, or│
│       Agent for Local Talent         │
└─────────────────────────────────────┘
```

Position Description

Booking Agents help performers find jobs. Agents represent a variety of performing artists, including musicians, singers, dancers, actors, actresses, and comedians.

Booking Agents may be self-employed or may work for an agency. There are a variety of agencies that employ Booking Agents, including theatrical and various types of talent agencies. Talent agencies work with a number of different clients in the performing arts or may specialize in one or two areas. For example, an agency may handle only classical artists. Very large talent agencies such as the William Morris Agency handle all types of entertainers and performing artists. Some agencies handling a variety of performing artists separate their agents into categories, assigning one to the classical singers and musicians, another to the comics, and a third to dancers.

Booking Agents are assigned clients by their agency. They may also be responsible for bringing in new clients, both established and new. The agent accomplishes this by attending showcases, clubs, concerts, and recitals. Booking Agents also receive audiotapes and videotapes of performing artists seeking representation. Depending on the specific job, the agent may be responsible for reviewing these tapes

and contacting the performing artists or their management to let them know if the agency is interested in booking them.

The Booking Agent obtains engagements or jobs for his or her clients in a number of ways. If the client is a well-known performing artist such as Itzhak Perlman, the world-famous violinist, concert halls and arena booking managers and promoters often seek out and contact the agent to determine booking information such as dates the performing artist is available and fees for an appearance.

In some situations the Booking Agent actively seeks places for a performing artist to be booked. This is done by sending out literature, brochures, and photographs of the performing artists represented by the agency to a mailing list of clubs, concert halls, arenas, and theaters.

The telephone is the lifeline of the Booking Agent, who also spends most of the working day calling promoters, negotiating, and talking to the performing artist's management.

The Booking Agent is responsible for negotiating prices for client appearances. Sometimes the performer takes less for an appearance if it coincides with another appearance in the area or if the appearance provides good exposure. Fees are not the only negotiating point. Other items the agent must negotiate include the type of accommodations, instrumental augmentation, background singers, food, and expenses.

Once a deal has been struck, the Booking Agent is responsible for preparing and sending copies of contracts to the promoter or buyer. These contracts include all the information required by both parties. The Booking Agent sees to it that contracts are signed and returned.

The contract also includes riders, which are the parts of contracts that stipulate the extras the act is supposed to receive. Depending on what is negotiated, the riders may stipulate limousines, first-class air travel to and from a particular city, refreshments in the dressing rooms, extra background singers, or instrumental augmentation.

The performing artist is often paid a percentage of the fees when the contract is signed and the rest at the performance. The Booking Agent is responsible for collecting the money, taking the agency percentage, and paying the act.

The Booking Agent may book appearances individually across the country or may set up an entire tour, such as a summer tour or an East Coast tour.

Booking Agents usually represent more than one client. They can represent clients either exclusively or non-exclusively. Agents may also represent clients exclusively in one field, such as concerts and non-exclusively in another such as personal appearances.

Booking Agents usually work long hours. They must constantly try to sell the services of their clients to talent buyers, booking managers, and promoters. The agent is responsible to either the performing artist or his or her management team.

Salaries

Salaries for Booking Agents can vary greatly depending on the number and prestige of clients the agent handles as well as the fees clients receive for performances and other appearances. Very successful agents can earn between $200,000 and $1 million or more a year. Individuals just starting out, or those working with clients who are not well known, may earn considerably less. Some earn as little as $24,000 a year.

Booking Agents are paid on a commission basis. That means that they receive a percentage off the top of the fee that the performing artist is paid. Commissions vary from agent to agent, ranging from 10% to 25% of a client's gross earnings. Depending on the situation, the agent may receive a percentage of earnings from personal appearances, engagements, commercial endorsements, or recordings. Booking Agents who work in agencies may be paid a salary plus a percentage of the money that they bring in.

Employment Prospects

Employment prospects are fair for Booking Agents if they are willing to work in smaller, regional agencies with less well-known clients. Booking agencies are located throughout the country in culturally active cities.

Prospects are more competitive for agents aspiring to work in large well-known booking agencies in New York and Los Angeles.

Advancement Prospects

Advancement prospects are fair for aggressive and ambitious Booking Agents, who climb the career ladder by building up a large client roster of more prestigious performing artists or by starting their own booking agencies.

Booking Agents also move to similar positions in more prestigious agencies.

Education and Training

Some agencies require their agents to be high school graduates and have the ability to perform the job well. Other agencies prefer that their agents have college backgrounds or degrees. There are degree programs offered in performing arts management that are helpful in this field. Classes, seminars, or workshops in booking entertainment, arts management, performing arts, business, contracts, and contract law are also useful.

In some states, Booking Agents must be licensed. These licenses are similar to those required at other employment agencies and are obtained through the state's department of licensing.

Experience, Skills, and Personality Traits

Many Booking Agents get experience by working as assistants or secretaries to other Agents. Some work as interns; others book local talent into clubs, work with arts councils, or place talent in other regional projects.

Booking Agents must have a good understanding of the performing arts and entertainment industry and a basic knowledge of contracts.

Booking Agents must be excellent sales people and have a well-practiced ability to negotiate. Communications skills are also mandatory. Agents must be aggressive without being obnoxious.

Unions and Associations

Booking Agents work with various unions and must adhere to their rules and regulations; depending on their clients' fields, these unions include Actors' Equity, the American Federation of Musicians (AFM), the American Federation of Television and Radio Artists (AFTRA), the American Guild of Variety Artists (AGVA), the American Guild of Musical Artists (AGMA), and the Screen Actors Guild (SAG).

Tips for Entry

1. Volunteer to work with your local arts council, booking acts for the organization.
2. If you are still in school, get involved with the student activities department.
3. Investigate training programs offered by many of the larger booking agencies. These are a good way to get your foot in the door, make important contacts, and learn the trade.
4. Check out opportunities online. Start with job sites like monster.com and hotjobs.com. Booking agencies may also post openings on their Web sites.

LITERARY AGENT

CAREER PROFILE

Duties: Marketing playwrights' scripts to producers; reading scripts; suggesting revisions; negotiating contracts

Alternate Title(s): Writers' Agent; Agent

Salary Range: $23,000 to $850,000+

Employment Prospects: Fair

Advancement Prospects: Fair

Best Geographical Location(s): New York City offers the most opportunities; other culturally active cities may offer other opportunities.

Prerequisites:

Education or Training—Educational requirements vary from high school diploma to bachelor's degree.

Experience—Experience working in publishing, theater, or the entertainment industry helpful

Special Skills and Personality Traits—Ability to see raw talent; communication skills; aggressiveness; marketing skills; organizational skills; contacts in theatrical industry

CAREER LADDER

```
┌─────────────────────────────────────┐
│   Literary Agent with More Prestigious │
│   Clients in Larger, More Prestigious  │
│      Agency or Self-Employed          │
└─────────────────────────────────────┘

┌─────────────────────────────────────┐
│           Literary Agent              │
└─────────────────────────────────────┘

┌─────────────────────────────────────┐
│  Assistant Literary, Theatrical, or   │
│     Talent Agent; Editor; or          │
│     Playwright or Producer            │
└─────────────────────────────────────┘
```

Position Description

The text of a play—the script—is written by a playwright and contains the story of the production, the words the characters speak, the settings where the scenes take place, and the stage directions. When playwrights finish writing their scripts, they must find someone to either buy them or buy the rights to use them. Literary Agents are used by many playwrights to find buyers for their works.

Literary Agents are either self-employed or they work for an agency. There are a variety of agencies that employ Literary Agents. These include theatrical, talent, and literary agencies and they may work with a number of different types of clients ranging from performing artists to authors and playwrights.

Agents usually specialize in one or two types of clients. Literary Agents may also handle authors, and theatrical agents may assume the responsibilities of Literary Agents.

The duties of Literary Agents vary depending on whether they are working alone or are employed by an agency. Their primary function, however, remains the same: the Literary Agent must market as many scripts or other literary works as possible for the greatest amount of money.

Selling a work outright means that the playwright is paid a one-time fee for his or her script. Limited rights, called options, may also be sold, meaning the buyer has the exclusive right to use the script for a specified amount of time.

Sometimes agents actively pursue authors or playwrights. Writers may also send scripts to a Literary Agent to review, and if the agent thinks the script or the writer has talent, he or she attempts to acquire the client.

Successful Literary Agents read hundreds of scripts, often finding it difficult to tell if they show promise. Agents must have the ability to read a script and envision an entire production. In some instances, the agent reads a script and suggests that the playwright make revisions before trying to market it.

In order for agents or agencies to make money, they must sell their client's work. Literary Agents working with playwrights must have a great many contacts in the theatrical world. It is the responsibility of the Literary Agent to bring the work of his or her client to the attention of the proper people. In this business, theatrical producers are the lifeline of agents.

Playwrights are constantly urging producers to read their scripts. Many producers do not have time to read every script. Because of possible legal problems, some producers will not read scripts unless they come through an agent. It is the responsibility of the Literary Agent to contact producers about clients' scripts. In some cases, the agent first needs to peak the interest of the producer. If the producer is interested, the agent then sends the script to the producer.

Sometimes a producer is looking for a certain type of script and will contact a number of agents to see if any of their clients have suitable scripts. The producer may also be looking for a playwright to write a specific script he or she has in mind. In some cases, a producer may contact the agent of a playwright to see if the author is willing to sell the rights of the play for a movie production.

Another responsibility of the Literary Agent is to negotiate contracts. The agent must try to get the best possible terms for his or her client. Money is not always the only consideration in a contract. Other things that must be considered include length of time for which a script is under option, the billing of the author if the play is produced and the control the playwright has over changes to the script.

Literary Agents representing playwrights spend a lot of time on their job. While they may work regular hours, they may also have to entertain and socialize with producers, clients, and others in the theatrical industry.

Salaries
Earnings for Literary Agents representing playwrights can vary tremendously. Individuals may earn between $23,000 and $850,000 or more a year.

Literary Agents usually receive a percentage of the monies earned by their clients. If agents are working for an agency, they may earn a salary plus a commission for each new client brought in. They may also receive a percentage of all deals negotiated.

Employment Prospects
Employment prospects are fair for Literary Agents. They may work for large literary, theatrical or talent agencies or be self-employed. Being self-employed, however, means that they must obtain all their own clients.

The best location for a Literary Agent in the theatrical field is New York City. However, other culturally active cities also offer opportunities.

Advancement Prospects
Advancement prospects for Literary Agents in the theatrical field depend to a great extent on the drive, determination, and luck of the individual. Literary Agents advance their careers by obtaining a position with a larger, more prestigious agency or by being assigned more prestigious clients in the agency for which they currently work. Some Literary

Agents climb the career ladder by becoming sufficiently well known to open their own literary agency.

If an agent sells the work, or the rights to the work, of a client to a producer who turns it into a success, that Agent will earn more money and will be sought out by more prestigious clients.

Education and Training
Educational requirements vary for Literary Agents. Some individuals hold high school diplomas. Others have college degrees with majors in arts management, theater arts, English, or business.

Experience, Skills, and Personality Traits
Literary Agents may start their careers as assistants to other agents, although many obtain experience in other fields prior to becoming Literary Agents. Agents sometimes work in publishing as editors or writers. Others gain experience working in the theatrical field as playwrights, producers, theatrical or talent agents, or assistants.

Literary Agents must have the ability to see raw talent. They must be able to read a script and envision the play.

Literary Agents must be aggressive without being so pushy that producers will not want to talk to them. Marketing skills are necessary, as it is an agent's job to sell his or her client's work to other individuals.

Agents should be organized and detail oriented. They must be able to work on many different projects at once without becoming confused.

Contacts in the theatrical world are essential. If the Agent does not have contacts, he or she must be able to make them.

Unions and Associations
Literary Agents may be members of the Authors Guild (AG) or the Association of Authors' Representatives (AAR). These organizations bring others in the same field together, provide educational guidance and professional support.

Tips for Entry
1. Find an internship in one of the larger literary or theatrical agencies. This is a good way to obtain experience and make important contacts.
2. Take classes, workshops, or seminars in playwriting and other aspects of theater.
3. Try to find a job as an assistant or secretary to a producer. In this position, you make contacts with others in the theatrical world as well as with Literary Agents who are attempting to contact the producer you are working with.
4. Look for a job as an editor or assistant editor with a book publishing company. You will be able to make contact with Literary Agents trying to sell their clients' work.

PLACEMENT SPECIALIST

Duties: Placing clients on radio and television shows; scheduling media tours; preparing clients for interviews; arranging for clients to be interviewed for print media

Alternate Title(s): Placement Professional

Salary Range: $24,000 to $200,000+

Employment Prospects: Fair

Advancement Prospects: Fair

Best Geographical Location(s): Positions are located throughout the country.

Prerequisites:

Education or Training—College background is useful but not always required.

Experience—Experience in publicity, public relations, advertising, or selling helpful

Special Skills and Personality Traits—Good phone manner; persuasiveness; articulateness; good communications skills; excellent writing skills

---

Placement Specialist for Prestigious Clients or Press Agent or Publicist in Large Agency

---

Placement Specialist

Publicity Assistant or Press Agent Trainee

Position Description

A Placement Specialist places people as guests on television and radio shows and also arranges for clients to be interviewed for print media. There are many television and radio stations throughout the country with scheduled talk, news, and variety shows and programs. These shows must have guests booked on a constant basis.

The Placement Specialist or placement professional, as he or she is frequently called, may work for a variety of clients. He or she may work for celebrities such as theatrical actors and actresses, movie or television stars, singers, dancers, musicians, or other show business personalities. These performers or their management team often use the services of a Placement Specialist to promote the opening of a new play, concert tour, or recital.

The Placement Specialist decides whether the client will be placed on a local, syndicated, national, or cable show. While most clients want to get on *The Tonight Show* or the *Late Show with David Letterman,* this is not always feasible. The Placement Specialist must decide on the most effective booking.

Local shows are television or radio shows which have a local listening or viewing audience. There is a difference,

however, between small-market local and major-market local. New York City would be an example of a local major broadcast market. Middletown, New York, would be an example of a local small broadcast market. The Placement Specialist usually finds it easier to place guests on shows in small local markets than larger local markets.

Placement Specialists often find that syndicated shows are good avenues to place clients. Syndicated shows are bought by local stations and may be shown at different times in a number of different locations. There can be small syndicated shows which only go to two or three areas, or large ones, such as *The Oprah Winfrey Show,* which is bought by local stations throughout the country.

The Placement Specialist frequently uses cable shows when arranging interviews for clients because they are plentiful and have specialized audiences.

National shows broadcast throughout the country on the affiliate stations of networks such as ABC, CBS, or NBC. Placing guests on national shows is difficult unless the guest is a very well-known celebrity or personality.

To do their job, Placement Specialists must obtain a biography of the client, press kits, news releases, photographs, and any other pertinent information. In some cases, the Placement Specialist will put these together for an additional fee. In others, the information is supplied by a publicist or manager. The Placement Specialist must also find out if the client wants to do a media tour or just one or two placement shots.

The Placement Specialist then goes to work by looking at specific cities and making a list of potential shows. Placement Specialists know what radio and television stations are in an area as well as what type of programming is available. They then write cover letters and send them with press information to either the program producer or guest coordinator. If the Placement Specialist does not hear from a program within a reasonable amount of time, he or she may call the producer or guest coordinator asking about the possibilities of an interview for the client.

If the Placement Specialist is booking a media tour, he or she must make sure that the scheduling is both cost and time efficient. With new technology, the client can, however, do phone interviews for radio or satellite hookups for television without leaving the house. In some instances, the Placement Specialist accompanies clients to shows or arranges for someone else to accompany them. In other situations, the Placement Specialist prepares a list of shows, the dates and times of appearances, contact names at the stations, and phone numbers and addresses and then gives the list to the client. The Placement Specialist also sends confirmation letters to the program personnel.

The specialist may work with clients to prepare them for interviews. He or she sets up mock interviews to make sure that the individual can answer questions easily and feel comfortable in front of a microphone or television camera.

Placement Specialists work long hours. If they have many clients or are placing people in different time zones, they may stay on the phone for hours. The Placement Specialist who is consulting or freelancing will usually be responsible to the client who has done the hiring.

Salaries

Earnings are almost impossible to estimate for Placement Specialists. The individual may work on a per-project or freelance basis. He or she may also be retained for weeks, months or longer by clients. Individuals working full time may have annual earnings ranging from approximately $24,000 to $200,000 or more.

Placement Specialists earn from $25 to $7,500 or more per placement on a show depending on the specific program and whether it is local, syndicated, or national. Individuals might receive a flat fee per week, month, or city at a flat rate that can range from $50 to $20,000 or more.

Earnings increase if the Placement Specialist performs other services such as writing press releases, compiling press kits, preparing clients for interviews, or accompanying them to shows. Successful Placement Specialists can earn up to $200,000 or more annually.

Employment Prospects

Individuals who are interested in becoming Placement Specialists on a consulting or freelance level will have to find clients. There are performing artists, singers, dancers, actors and actresses, as well as people in other fields who want media exposure. Aspiring Placement Specialists may have to advertise or do publicity and promotions in order to make people aware of their business, but they can usually find clients to get started.

This job can be accomplished successfully by seasoned pros and those just entering the field. Success depends on persistence, perseverance, persuasiveness, and personality.

Advancement Prospects

Anyone can become a Placement Specialist, but everyone will not be successful. Those who enlist clients and get them booked on shows will have little problem finding additional clients.

Placement Specialists who climb the career ladder advance by obtaining a larger client list and more prestigious clients.

Education and Training

While there are no educational requirements for Placement Specialists working on a freelance or consulting level, some training helps. If the individual is in college, a major in public relations, communications, journalism, English, liberal arts, marketing, or advertising is useful.

Seminars and courses in publicity and media placement are also helpful in honing skills and making contacts.

Experience, Skills, and Personality Traits

The Placement Specialist must be persuasive and persistent. He or she needs to be articulate and have good communications skills and an excellent phone personality.

The Placement Specialist should know how to write press releases, compile press kits, and prepare effective letters.

A good working relationship with the media is important to the Placement Specialist's success.

Unions and Associations

There are no unions that the Placement Specialist must belong to. He or she may become a member of the Public Relations Society of America (PRSA). This organization provides useful seminars, educational materials, and guidance to those working in publicity of public relations.

Tips for Entry

1. Begin by volunteering to place people from a local nonprofit theater group on television or radio shows to publicize an event that the group is holding. This will give you hands-on experience.

2. Place a small display ad in a local publication. Keep it running regularly. When people need your service, they will remember seeing your advertisement.

3. Use your skills to get yourself on television or radio to publicize your own business.

4. You may not find performing artists, celebrities, and other entertainers to work with right away, so try to place people in other fields on television or radio. Send out a brochure or letter to corporations and trade associations in your area letting them know about your service.

5. Get experience at a company specializing in client placement. Even if you have to take a position as an administrative assistant for a short time, the experience will be valuable.

CELEBRITY PERSONAL ASSISTANT

CAREER PROFILE

Duties: Assisting actors, actresses, singers, dancers, and other celebrities to manage, coordinate, and organize their day-to-day activities; screening fan mail; answering phones; coordinating activities of other support personnel; planning parties or events; answering e-mails; assisting in maintaining household

Alternate Title(s): Assistant; CPA

Salary Range: $25,000 to $100,000+

Employment Prospects: Fair

Advancement Prospects: Fair

Best Geographic Location(s): The greatest number of opportunities will be located in culturally active cities such as New York, Los Angeles, Chicago, Washington, D.C., Philadelphia, Nashville, etc.

Prerequisites:

Education or Training—Educational requirements vary by position.

Experience—Experience requirements vary.

Special Skills and Personality Traits—Excellent communication skills; persuasiveness; energetic; dependability; reliability; creativity; ability to multitask

CAREER LADDER

```
┌─────────────────────────────────────┐
│  Celebrity Personal Assistant to More │
│  Prestigious Celebrities or Position in│
│  Other Area of Entertainment Industry │
└─────────────────────────────────────┘

┌─────────────────────────────────────┐
│     Celebrity Personal Assistant      │
└─────────────────────────────────────┘

┌─────────────────────────────────────┐
│ Production Assistant, College Student,│
│      or Other Entry-level Position    │
└─────────────────────────────────────┘
```

Position Description

Actors, actresses, singers, dancers, musicians, comedians, and others in the entertainment business work hard toward getting to the top. Once they make it, their lives are often so busy with commitments that there just isn't time to do everything themselves. Top actors and actresses working in theater have a very hectic schedule, often working eight performances a week. Others in the performing arts have similar schedules. In order to help promote shows, many stars also are expected to do publicity and promotion. Being a celebrity can be more than a full-time job. Consequently, many working in theater and the other performing arts, as well as other areas of entertainment, hire personal assistants to help them handle their day-to-day activities.

Celebrity Personal Assistants are professionals who help manage the lives of celebrities. Their ultimate responsibility is making the life of the celebrity they work for easier and more efficient. This might include helping them in their professional, personal, or family life.

The duties and responsibilities of Celebrity Personal Assistants can vary greatly depending on the specific celebrities for whom they work. In some cases, the job is much like that of an executive secretary. In others, the job can be much more involved, with the assistant traveling with the celebrity, helping the individual learn lines, and in many cases, becoming a confidant.

One of the main functions of the Celebrity Personal Assistant is to help the celebrity organize and manage his or her life. In general, the assistant tries to make things easier by handling a lot of the grunt work.

This might mean anything from going grocery shopping to picking out gifts for family, friends, colleagues, or business associates. It might mean picking up the dry cleaning, making medical appointments, or making travel arrangements. It often means walking the dog, picking up the children from school, coordinating schedules with the celebrity's nanny, and checking to see that maintenance is done on the car or that the cable is fixed.

Those tasks are often just the tip of the iceberg for Celebrity Personal Assistants. They may be responsible for sorting through a celebrity's mail and e-mail, answering fan mail, sending out photos and autographs, and responding when necessary. The personal assistant must be aware of what mail is important and what needs to be brought to the attention of the celebrity.

Bills, invitations, and media inquiries, must be attended to as well. In some cases, the personal assistant will handle bill paying. In others, he or she will just be responsible for making sure that the celebrity or his or her bookkeeper, accountant, or manager handles the task. Depending on the specific situation, he or she may work in conjunction with the celebrity's manager, business manager, or publicist coordinating activities and tasks.

Celebrities generally receive lots of phone calls from business associates, the media, family, and fans. Often turning into the gatekeeper, the personal assistant is responsible for screening phone calls so the celebrity is not unnecessarily bothered. As the personal assistant becomes more familiar with the celebrity, he or she will begin to know how specific situations need to be handled. The personal assistant helps coordinate the celebrity's calendar, reminding the individual when appointments are scheduled.

Often celebrities expect their personal assistant to handle tasks which seem almost impossible to complete. This can be anything from planning a party in 12 hours to making a plane reservation when there isn't an available seat. It might be finding a way to help the celebrity sneak out of a location when the paparazzi is stalking him or her. It might even be something like persuading someone to not say the celebrity was there when he or she was. Those who are quick thinking, resourceful, and persuasive will find ways to accomplish their tasks successfully.

In many cases the celebrity will treat his or her assistant as a confidant. In this position an individual might be asked advice on anything from fashion to acting to relationships. The assistant may be responsible for packing for the celebrity's trip, helping pick out the right clothes for media interviews, ordering room service, or doing a million other things that might make the celebrity's life easier. The Celebrity Personal Assistant may be expected to plan, coordinate, and execute events for the celebrity in both his or her personal and professional life.

It should be noted that one of the things some people don't enjoy about being a Celebrity Personal Assistant is that in many instances, there is not a lot of personal recognition. Some are not comfortable being in the background.

With that said, the life of a Celebrity Personal Assistant can also be glamorous and exciting. In this position, individuals often will go to opening night parties, premieres, and press parties with the star. When the celebrity travels, the personal assistant will frequently travel with him or her. As the individual is in the inner circle, he or she will meet a lot of other celebrities and have the opportunity to make contacts within the industry.

The Celebrity Personal Assistant often works long, irregular hours. While the "job" may be from 9 to 5 or 10 to 6, frequently when the celebrity gets off stage at night, he or she thinks about something which needs to be done the next day and gives the personal assistant a call. The individual may also be required to travel.

The personal assistant is generally responsible to the celebrity who has hired the individual.

Salaries

Earnings for personal assistants can vary greatly. There are some personal assistants who earn only $350 per week. Others individuals earn $100,000 or more a year plus very liberal fringe benefits. Some Celebrity Personal Assistants, for example, travel with the celebrity, going first class all the way. Others may enjoy the luxurious lifestyles of the celebrity—staying in the top hotels, eating at the best restaurants, and attending premieres and other events.

Variables affecting earnings include the specific celebrity for which the individual works as well as his or her popularity and success. Other factors include the experience, responsibilities, and reputation of the personal assistant. Earnings will also be dependent on whether the individual is working directly for a celebrity or for an agency.

Employment Prospects

Employment prospects for Celebrity Personal Assistants aspiring to work in the theater and performing arts area are fair and getting better all the time. Individuals may either work directly for a celebrity or may be employed by an agency handling personal assistants.

While positions may be located throughout the country, culturally active cities such as New York City, Chicago, Los Angeles, Philadelphia, and Boston will have the most opportunities for those interested in working for celebrities in the theatrical area. Opportunities working for others in the performing arts may be located in other areas as well.

Possibilities for employment opportunities include actors, actresses, playwrights, singers, dancers, musicians, songwriters, producers, directors, choreographers, comedians, etc.

Advancement Prospects

Advancement prospects are fair for personal assistants who are good at their job. Advancement is dependent to a great extent on the long-term goals of the Celebrity Personal Assistant as well as the path he or she wants to pursue.

One of the perks of a job as a Celebrity Personal Assistant is the opportunity to make contacts in the industry. Depending on the career direction the personal assistant is interested in going toward, these contacts can be very valuable. They may lead to better jobs either working in the same field for a bigger celebrity or moving into a totally different position in the entertainment industry. Some personal assistants use their job as a springboard for learning the business and moving into other areas of the entertainment industry.

Education and Training

Educational requirements for personal assistants depend on the specific job. While a college degree isn't required in every position, it will often give applicants the edge over other individuals with similar skills.

Degree or not, the broader the training an individual has in this career, the better. Classes, seminars, or workshops in project management, organization, party planning, etiquette, and computer software may be useful. Courses in psychology may also be helpful in understanding the way people think and act.

There are also a number of seminars offered throughout the country specifically geared toward succeeding as Celebrity Personal Assistants.

Experience, Skills, and Personality Traits

Experience requirements for Celebrity Personal Assistants vary from job to job. In some cases, it's an entry-level job. In others, the individual is expected to have some experience in the field.

Generally, the personality and skills of the personal assistant are more important than experience. Often, for example, a celebrity may meet someone who is working in another field, make a connection and/or feel that they are savvy, and offer them a job.

Successful Celebrity Personal Assistants are well-rounded, proactive individuals with broad knowledge in a variety of areas and a wide range of skills. This is the type of job where the individual needs to be very well organized with the ability to multitask. Computer skills are essential. Proficiency in a variety of computer software programs is useful.

Superior written and verbal communications skills are needed. As the personal assistant is generally in the inner circle of the celebrity's life, he or she often sees or hears things that the celebrity does not necessarily want out in the public. Therefore the ability to be discrete is vital.

It's also essential that the personal assistant have the ability to fit in no matter the situation. He or she should have a neat, polished, professional, and classy appearance that won't outshine the star. Excellent etiquette is also crucial.

Unions and Associations

Celebrity Personal Assistants may belong to the National Celebrity Personal Assistants Association (NCPAA) or the Association of Celebrity Personal Assistants (ACPA). These groups offer career guidance and support to members.

Tips for Entry

1. Get some experience as a noncelebrity personal assistant. This will help you hone your skills and get some experience for your résumé.
2. Openings in this field are often advertised in the classified section of trades such as *Backstage* and *Billboard.*
3. Openings may also be advertised in the classified section of newspapers in culturally active areas.
4. Network, network, network! Tell everyone you are looking for a job as a Celebrity Personal Assistant. You would be surprise how many people know celebrities. If these people know you are looking for a job, they might give you a personal referral.
5. Send your résumé and a short cover letter to celebrities with whom you are interested in working. While you might not be able to get through directly to the celebrity, you can usually make contact with their publicist, manager, or agent.
6. A short stint as a production assistant often gives you experience helpful in this type of job as well as the opportunity to make important contacts.
7. Once you get the job, always be professional and discrete.

HALLS, ARENAS, AND OTHER VENUES

HALL MANAGER

CAREER PROFILE

Duties: Managing theater, concert hall, arena, or other facility; overseeing all activities in venue; supervising employees

Alternate Title(s): Theater Manager; Concert Hall Manager; Arena Director; Facility Director; Director of Hall Operations

Salary Range: $25,000 to $85,000+

Employment Prospects: Fair

Advancement Prospects: Fair

Best Geographical Location(s): Positions may be located throughout the country; culturally active cities offer more opportunities.

Prerequisites:

    Education or Training—High school diploma minimum; some positions may require additional education.

    Experience—Working in concert halls, clubs, theaters, or arenas in various positions helpful; experience as assistant hall manager useful

    Special Skills and Personality Traits—Knowledge of theater, entertainment, or music business; responsible; ability to handle crises

CAREER LADDER

```
┌─────────────────────────────┐
│   Hall Manager in Larger,   │
│   More Prestigious Venue    │
└─────────────────────────────┘

┌─────────────────────────────┐
│        Hall Manager         │
└─────────────────────────────┘

┌─────────────────────────────┐
│    Assistant Hall Manager   │
└─────────────────────────────┘
```

Position Description

A Hall Manager is in charge of managing the hall and overseeing all activities occurring in the facility. The individual has diverse duties to perform depending on the facility and the position held. He or she may work in large concert halls hosting major symphonies or smaller halls hosting concerts, ballets, plays, and other types of theatrical entertainment.

The individual is also called an arena manager, arena director, or concert hall manager. One of the functions of the Hall Manager is to supervise all employees of the facility. These workers include electricians, sound technicians, lighting technicians, ticket sellers, ushers, security, maintenance personnel, and a host of others. In some situations, the manager also hires a publicist, public relations firm, or advertising agency to handle promotion. In other circumstances, the hall owner might handle this portion of the project. As a rule, the Hall Manager has the authority to hire and fire employees. In directing the activities of all these workers,

the manager tries to ensure the most efficient operations possible for theater management.

Another function of the Hall Manager is to oversee the financial business of the hall. The manager tries to keep the hall or theater booked; sometimes buying the talent, sometimes renting out the hall to various promoters. Whatever system is used, the manager must negotiate to get the best price. When promoters rent the hall, the Hall Manager obtains the best rental fee, giving away the least possible extras.

The Hall Manager may also be responsible for payroll. In some cases if a union is involved (and they frequently are), the manager sees that all union regulations are enforced at the hall. Unions involved might include the musicians union, the electricians union, and others.

After an event has been planned, the manager is in charge of advertising and publicizing the program in order to maximize attendance. This might be accomplished with the assistance of an advertising agency or a public relations firm, or the hall may have its own in-house advertising agency or publicist. The Hall Manager ideally must obtain the most exposure for an event at a minimum cost.

It is the responsibility of the Hall Manager to make sure that the facility is in good condition and clean at all times. If there are items requiring repair, he or she oversees the work. On occasion, the hall may be refurbished. The Hall Manager, once again, is in charge of these projects.

The Hall Manager handles all types of crises effectively and without panicking. Potential problems include an act not showing up for a performance, union workers going on strike before a show, inclement weather on the night of a performance when tickets are being sold at the door, or a patron getting unruly during a show.

The Hall Manager sees to it that the money paid to the acts is available on the night of a show. He or she must also be sure to fulfill any contract riders exactly as they are written.

The Hall Manager works closely with all the media in the immediate area. Most of the time the press is offered press or backstage passes. Maintaining a good relationship with the press and other media goes a long way toward helping the theater become successful.

The Hall Manager works long irregular hours and is responsible to the owner of the theater, hall, or arena.

Salaries

The salary of a hall or arena manager or director varies greatly depending on the size of the venue, the location, the prestige of the hall, qualifications of the individual, and the duties.

Someone managing a small concert theater in a small city will not earn as much as one who is managing a large, prestigious hall in a major metropolitan area. Those managing small theaters might earn from $25,000 to $40,000 yearly. Those who manage larger, more prestigious halls in major metropolitan areas earn from $36,000 to $85,000 or more annually.

Employment Prospects

Employment prospects for a Hall Manager are fair. There are different types of theaters and halls that vary in size and location. Major cities have the greatest number of concert halls, theaters, and arenas. However, it may be more difficult to obtain a job in these locations.

Smaller cities have fewer opportunities, but jobs are usually easier to obtain due to less competition.

Advancement Prospects

Advancement prospects are fair for Hall Managers. In order to move up the career ladder, individuals must find positions in larger or more prestigious facilities.

While there is usually a correlation between the size and prestige of a hall and the difficulty in obtaining jobs at these larger facilities, individuals who do move into better positions, as a rule, continue advancing their careers.

Education and Training

Most positions as Hall Manager require a high school diploma. Many people who hold these positions have degrees in music, theater, or business. A large number of these individuals originally aspired to be musicians, actors, or actresses. When the opportunities fell through, these individuals went into managing concert halls as a way of maintaining contact with the theater industry.

Courses that may prove useful include theater management, business, bookkeeping, accounting, communications, marketing, and public relations.

Experience, Skills, and Personality Traits

Hall Managers need previous experience. Usually the individuals have worked in a theater, entertainment, or music business in some capacity for a period of time. A job as assistant manager of a concert hall is often extremely helpful to the individual.

In managing a hall, one must be adept at reading entertainment contracts and the long riders that sometimes accompany them. One must have the ability to handle crises effectively and have considerable knowledge about the theater, entertainment, or music industries, as well as concert hall and arena affairs.

Supervisory skills and responsibility are imperative for this position as well.

Unions and Associations

Hall Managers may belong to the International Association of Auditorium Managers (IAAM). They may also have to deal with a variety of performing arts unions, including the American Federation of Musicians (AFM).

Tips for Entry

1. Look for a job at a smaller facility or in a smaller city, if you are not experienced.
2. Look for jobs for theater or concert Hall Managers in the classified or display section of newspapers under the heading classifications of "Theater," "Concert Hall," "Arena," or "Venue."
3. Try to find a job as an assistant manager in a small venue. The employee turnover is higher in these halls and you will have a better chance of promotion in a shorter span of time.
4. Seek out Hall Managers in other facilities. Many openings are advertised in a word-of-mouth fashion.
5. Find an internship through your college or other theatrical program in hall management.
6. Surf the World Wide Web for job openings. Check major job and career sites under key words including "entertainment," "venue," "arena," or "concert hall management."

RESIDENT SOUND TECHNICIAN—
THEATERS, HALLS, ARENAS, OR CLUBS

CAREER PROFILE

Duties: Overseeing the sound requirements of a facility; providing the sound for performances at concert halls, arenas, theaters, and clubs; working the soundboard; keeping sound equipment in good working condition

Alternate Title(s): Sound Technician; Sound Tech; Audio Technician; Sound Man/Sound Woman; Sound Engineer

Salary Range: $22,000 to $44,000+

Employment Prospects: Fair

Advancement Prospects: Poor

Best Geographical Location(s): Employment prospects are located throughout the country; culturally active cities may offer more opportunities.

Prerequisites:

Education or Training—No formal educational requirement; some positions may require formal or self-taught electronic or sound training.

Experience—Experience working soundboards, sound equipment and electronic equipment necessary

Special Skills and Personality Traits—Knowledge of electronics; knowledge of soundboard; ability to work well with others; dependability; reliability

CAREER LADDER

```
┌─────────────────────────────────────┐
│  Resident Sound Technician in Larger,│
│  More Prestigious Theater, Club, Arena,│
│  or Hall or Resident Stage Manager   │
└─────────────────────────────────────┘

┌─────────────────────────────────────┐
│     Resident Sound Technician        │
└─────────────────────────────────────┘

┌─────────────────────────────────────┐
│   Sound Technician Apprentice or     │
│             Student                  │
└─────────────────────────────────────┘
```

Position Description

The main function of a Resident Sound Technician is to attend to the sound requirements of a facility. He or she is responsible for making sure that everything sounds as good as possible. Individuals may work in a variety of facilities, including theaters, clubs, concert halls, arenas, and schools.

The technician must fully understand the sound in the facility. He or she must be aware of any acoustical problems that occur and then be able to resolve these difficulties, often by moving certain pieces of equipment or adjusting controls on the soundboard to compensate for problems.

The Resident Sound Technician is responsible for overseeing the setup of the facility's sound equipment. In some situations, such as when performing artists bring their own sound equipment, the technician is responsible for advising and assisting them with this task. He or she also oversees their sound setup.

The Resident Sound Technician works closely with the resident lighting technician and stage manager. He or she also works closely with the performing artist or group and their sound, lighting, and road crews.

Sound requirements change depending on the type of act that is appearing in the facility. A theatrical production, for example has different sound requirements than a rock concert; a ballet requires different sound than a comedian.

The Resident Sound Technician is required to attend all rehearsals and sound checks. During these times, the technician talks to the performing artists themselves, their manager, road manager, or sound technician to determine what type of sound they require and if the show has any special sound effects.

In certain locations, sound is not allowed to exceed a certain level. If the performing artist or group is handling its own sound, the technician is responsible for letting the artist or group know what the volume requirements of the facility are. If he or she is responsible for the sound and the performers have planned to use louder sound than permitted, the technician must regulate it.

Sound Technicians are required to check all sound equipment and make sure it is in good working condition. If something is missing or not working properly, they are responsible for locating a replacement.

One of the major functions of the Resident Sound Technician is to run the sound or control board during the performance. The soundboard is usually set up in the middle of the front of the stage, although this depends on the specific facility. From this location, the individual can best hear the sound and make the proper adjustments. He or she must be sure that the sound is properly balanced and regulated. If special effects are required, the Technician adjusts the soundboard for them. If, during the performance, there are any sound problems, the individual must attend to them immediately.

After each performance, the Resident Sound Technician is responsible for checking each piece of equipment for any problems. If repairs are required, the technician either makes them or arranges for others to take care of them immediately.

The Resident Sound Technician is responsible to either the stage manager or the manager or owner of the facility. Individuals in this job work afternoons, evenings, and on weekends.

Salaries

Salaries for Resident Sound Technicians vary greatly. Individuals may work on either a full-time or part-time basis. Those who are working part time are usually paid by the hour or by the show. Rates can range from a minimum wage up to $85 per hour.

Resident Sound Technicians working full time may earn between $22,000 and $44,000 or more annually. Factors affecting salaries include the size, prestige, and location of the theater, club, arena, or hall. Other factors include the experience and responsibilities of the individual. Resident Sound Technicians working in a unionized facility have minimum earnings set by their union.

Employment Prospects

Employment prospects are fair for Resident Sound Technicians. Individuals may find opportunities throughout the country. Culturally active cities usually have more prospects.

Virtually any facility that hosts performing artists uses the services of a Resident Sound Technician. Technicians are hired by all types of theaters, clubs, arenas, and concert halls. Positions are also found on cruise ships and in hotels.

Advancement Prospects

Advancement prospects are limited for Resident Sound Technicians. Individuals may climb the career ladder by locating similar positions in larger, more prestigious theaters, halls, arenas, clubs, or other facilities.

Some individuals advance their career by becoming the facility's resident stage manager. Others are hired by major touring artists seeking qualified sound technicians.

Education and Training

There are no formal educational requirements for Resident Sound Technicians. Various positions may require, however, that applicants have some sort of training, formal or informal, in electronics and sound.

There are vocational and technical schools that teach electronics throughout the country. Most individuals pick up the basics of sound engineering by watching and listening to others.

Experience, Skills, and Personality Traits

Resident Sound Technicians must be able to work well with a variety of people. As noted, the individual may work with the facility's lighting technicians and stage managers as well as the performing artist or group and their sound technicians, lighting people, management, and road crew.

The technician must be responsible and dependable. Without proper sound a show can be ruined. He or she must attend all sound checks, rehearsals, and performances on time.

The Resident Sound Technician needs a knowledge of electronics, the soundboard, and sound equipment. As the individual must be at every performance, he or she should enjoy music, dance, theater, and all aspects of the performing arts.

Unions and Associations

Resident Sound Technicians may be members of the International Alliance of Theatrical Stage Employees (IATSE). This union negotiates minimum salaries and working conditions for its members.

Individuals working in nonunionized facilities do not have to belong to a union.

Tips for Entry

1. Check the classified or display section of the newspaper for ads for Resident Sound Technicians. Look under "Resident Sound Technician," "Sound Technician," "Sound Engineer," "Audio Technician," "Facility," "Hall," or "Club" for this position.
2. Find an apprenticeship with a Resident Sound Technician as a good way to obtain on-the-job experience.
3. Don't be afraid to ask other Resident Sound Technicians if they know of any openings.
4. Send your résumé and a short cover letter to clubs, theaters, arenas, and concert halls inquiring about openings. Request that your résumé be kept on file if there are no current openings.

RESIDENT STAGE MANAGER—CONCERT HALLS, CLUBS, OR ARENAS

CAREER PROFILE

Duties: Supervising activities that occur on stage and backstage during a performance at a concert hall, club, or arena

Alternate Title(s): Stage Manager

Salary Range: $22,000 to $55,000+

Employment Prospects: Fair

Advancement Prospects: Poor

Best Geographical Location(s): Jobs located throughout the country; culturally active cities offer more employment possibilities.

Prerequisites:

Education or Training—No formal educational requirement; training in lighting, sound, and electronics helpful

Experience—Experience as a fighting or sound technician or assistant stage manager useful

Special Skills and Personality Traits—Knowledge of lighting and sound technology; ability to get along well with people; organized; supervisory skills; dependability

CAREER LADDER

```
┌─────────────────────────────────────┐
│   Resident Stage Manager at Larger,  │
│    More Prestigious Facility or      │
│         Facility Manager             │
└─────────────────────────────────────┘

┌─────────────────────────────────────┐
│   Resident Stage Manager at Concert  │
│        Halls, Clubs, or Arenas       │
└─────────────────────────────────────┘

┌─────────────────────────────────────┐
│ Sound Technician, Lighting Technician,│
│    Assistant Stage Manager, or       │
│           College Student            │
└─────────────────────────────────────┘
```

Position Description

The Resident Stage Manager works in concert halls, clubs, or arenas. He or she is responsible for supervising everything that happens both on stage and backstage during a performance.

This job is not always easy. Concert halls, arenas, and clubs do not book the same entertainment every night. As a result, the stage manager has to work with new people every few days. The Resident Stage Manager may work with a classical soloist one night, a modern dance troupe the next, and a rock band the day after. He or she must be able to deal well with individuals in every aspect of the performing arts.

The Resident Stage Manager has a lot of responsibility. Depending on the size of the facility, he or she may work alone or may supervise a large staff. The stage manager must attend all rehearsals. At this time, he or she will inquire about sound and lighting requirements.

In some cases, the performing artist travels with his or her own lighting and sound technicians. The stage manager is responsible for helping and advising them about the requirements of the hall. In other situations, the facility has its own resident sound and lighting technicians whom the stage manager supervises. In facilities that are very small, stage managers themselves may be responsible for handling the sound

and lighting requirements. They must also check to see that all the equipment that is required is available and working properly. If the facility is unionized, the stage manager must be sure that all union rules and regulations are adhered to.

In some jobs, the Resident Stage Manager is also responsible for assigning dressing rooms to the performers. He or she must find out how many dressing rooms and what amenities are needed.

One of the duties of the stage manager is to keep the backstage area as clear as possible. Some time before the performance, the stage manager obtains a list of people allowed backstage, including the performers as well as any backup singers, musicians, and crew members. The stage manager will then issue backstage passes to each individual who is permitted there during and after the performance. The stage manager also obtains the names of business associates, journalists, and family members who will also be allowed backstage. The stage manager is responsible for checking that everyone who is backstage is authorized to be there. If not, he or she must clear the area as quickly as possible.

During the performance, the stage manager is responsible for almost everything that occurs backstage and must make sure that everybody does his or her job properly. The stage manager is responsible for telling the performers how long they have before show time and indicating when it is actually time to go on stage.

Stage managers are in charge of curtain changes. They must find out exactly how long the show will last and when intermissions will be held. In order to do this, he or she must discuss the length of the show with the performer or the road crew. During the show, the stage manager is responsible for opening the curtains at the proper times and cueing the performers when there is an intermission or when the show has ended.

If there are any problems during the show, the stage manager handles them. He or she may cue the sound and lighting technicians or the curtain operators. The manager is also responsible for documenting any accidents, injuries, or other mishaps that occur before or during the performance.

Resident Stage Managers are usually responsible to the facility manager or owner. They do not usually work regular hours. They may work split shifts attending rehearsals in the morning or afternoon and the performances in the evening or on weekends.

While Resident Stage Managers do work hard, they have the opportunity of seeing a variety of performing artists. Individuals also have the opportunity of making important contacts in the industry.

Salaries

Salaries vary greatly for Resident Stage Managers depending on a number of factors including experience, responsibilities, and qualifications. Salaries are also dependent on the size, type, and prestige of the facility as well as its geographic location.

Individuals can earn between $22,000 and $55,000 or more annually. As a rule, the larger and more prestigious the facility, the higher the stage manager's earnings are.

Employment Prospects

Employment prospects are fair for Resident Stage Managers. Individuals can work almost anywhere in the country. There will, however, be more opportunities in larger, more culturally active cities.

Resident Stage Managers can work in a variety of locations from large arenas to concert halls and clubs.

Advancement Prospects

Advancement prospects are limited for Resident Stage Managers. Individuals may advance their career by locating a similar position at a larger, more prestigious facility. There are also some stage managers who go on to become facility managers.

Education and Training

There is no formal educational requirement for Resident Stage Managers. Some positions may require training in sound, lighting, and electronics. This training is often secured working as an apprentice or intern or by watching others working in the position.

Experience, Skills, and Personality Traits

Resident Stage Managers should have a basic knowledge of lighting, sound equipment, and electronics. They either have to handle the lighting and sound requirements or advise technicians.

The Resident Stage Manager should be dependable and reliable. The ability to get along well with people is helpful. Supervisory skills are often necessary if the individual is working with an assistant or crew.

The Resident Stage Manager must be detail oriented and have the ability to work on many projects at once. He or she should be able to remain calm in situations where others might panic.

Many Resident Stage Managers get experience as sound or lighting technicians, while others work as Resident Stage Managers. Some learn the ropes while participating in theater, music, and other performing arts productions in school.

Unions and Associations

Resident Stage Managers in arenas, concert halls, and clubs may belong to the International Alliance of Theatrical Stage Employees (IATSE), a bargaining union which negotiates minimum salaries and working conditions. If the individual is working in a theatrical setting, he or she may belong to Actors' Equity. The Resident Stage Manager might also belong to the American Guild of Musical Artists (AGMA) under certain conditions. Individuals not working in unionized facilities might not belong to any union.

Tips for Entry

1. Volunteer to act as the stage manager in a community, school, or church concert or a theatrical production. This will provide you with good hands-on experience.

2. Learn all you can about lighting, sound, electronics, and stage techniques. Take any relevant courses, workshops, or seminars. These will provide you will skills and help you make important contacts.

3. Look under heading classifications of "Resident Stage Manager," "Stage Manager," "Concert Hall," "Arena," and "Clubs" in the display or classified sections of newspapers and jobs as Resident Stage Manager.

4. Send your résumé and a short cover letter to the personnel director, owner, or manager of clubs, arenas, and concert halls. Request that your résumé be kept on file if there are no current openings.

5. Find an internship that will give you on-the-job training and help you get your foot in the door for a job.

USHER

CAREER PROFILE

Duties: Helping patrons to get to their seats in a theater, hall, arena, or performing arts center; handing out programs; directing patrons to restrooms, telephones, and refreshments; settling disputes between patrons; handling complaints

Alternate Title(s): Usherette

Salary Range: $250 to $500+ weekly

Employment Prospects: Excellent

Advancement Prospects: Fair

Best Geographical Location(s): Positions may be located throughout the country; culturally active cities offer more prospects.

Prerequisites:

Education or Training—No formal educational requirements; high school diploma preferred

Experience—Experience as usher in school or community theaters helpful, but not required

Special Skills and Personality Traits—Pleasant; friendly; outgoing; good verbal communication skills; ability to remain on feet for long hours; ability to remain calm

CAREER LADDER

```
┌─────────────────────────────────────┐
│  Head Usher; Usher in More Prestigious│
│     Theater, Hall, or Arena; or       │
│      Other Position in Theater        │
└─────────────────────────────────────┘

┌─────────────────────────────────────┐
│                 Usher                 │
└─────────────────────────────────────┘

┌─────────────────────────────────────┐
│   Usher in Amateur Theater or         │
│    Aspiring Actor or Actress          │
└─────────────────────────────────────┘
```

Position Description

Ushers in theaters, halls, or performing arts centers help patrons locate their seats for performances. The number of Ushers in a venue depends on the size of the facility. Very small theaters may have only two or three Ushers, larger theaters often have 10 or more, and halls, arenas, and large performing arts centers may have more than 30.

Seating in theaters and other venues is often separated into sections designating the various price categories of tickets. Ushers are usually assigned a certain section of the theater in which to work.

Ushers stand in their section of the theater or other facility waiting for patrons to enter. The Usher may be assigned a position at the entrance of the theater. If this is the case, he or she may be responsible for looking at the patron's tickets and directing them toward the proper section.

Ushers determine where patrons' seating is by looking at their ticket stub. The stub contains information such as a

seat number, letter, or symbol, or may be color coded. The Usher matches the information on the ticket stub with the proper number or letter of a seat.

Ushers responsible for specific sections look at patrons' tickets and guide them to their seats. While doing this, they may be required to hand out programs to the patrons. The Usher may be responsible for walking patrons directly to their seats or may indicate where the seats are.

Ushers are responsible for directing patrons to restrooms, refreshment stands, telephones, and other areas within the theater. If a patron gets up and leaves his or her seat during a performance, the Usher will also direct the individual back to the proper seat.

The Usher is required to enforce any rules and regulations of the theater, hall, or facility. For example, in some theaters, the patrons are not allowed to go to their seats after the curtain goes up until there is a pause in the performance or until intermission.

After the performance, the Usher is required to help people locate the most convenient exits. The Usher is also responsible for assisting patrons looking for lost articles or items that were left in their seats after the performance such as purses, glasses, packages, wallets, or umbrellas.

Other functions of the Usher include resolving the complaints of patrons. In some instances, patrons might not like their seats and want to change them. In others, two people may insist that they are both supposed to be sitting in the same seat. The Usher must solve the problem calmly, quietly, and quickly.

In the event of a fire, accident, or emergency, the Usher is responsible for coordinating the exit of patrons. He or she is also required to help break up fights that might occur in the theater.

Salaries

Earnings vary for Ushers depending on their responsibilities and the type of theater they are working in. Salaries can range from minimum wage to $10 per hour or more. Individuals working full time may earn between $250 and $500 or more a week. In some situations, Ushers are volunteers and not paid anything.

Ushers working in unionized theaters have their minimum salaries set by the union.

Employment Prospects

Employment prospects for Ushers are excellent. Individuals may work in a variety of settings, including theaters, performing arts centers, concert halls, and arenas.

Jobs for Ushers are located throughout the country. However, larger, culturally active cities offer more prospects.

Individuals interested in becoming Ushers for theatrical productions on Broadway may have a more difficult time finding employment.

Advancement Prospects

Advancement prospects for Ushers depend to great extent on what career direction an individual wants to take.

Those that want to continue working as Ushers can find similar positions in more prestigious theaters and facilities. Individuals may also seek the position of head usher.

Ushers aspiring to work in theatrical situations may advance to a job working in a Broadway theater. Ushers who take the job as a means of getting their foot in the door of a theater or performing arts career may take varied paths when climbing the career ladder. Advancement depends on the drive, determination, ambition, and skills of the individual.

Education and Training

As a rule, there are no formal educational requirements for Ushers, although many theaters prefer their employees have at least a high school diploma. There are a great many people who become Ushers as a way of getting their foot in the door of a career in theater and the performing arts. There are, therefore, Ushers who have college degrees in everything from theater arts to liberal arts.

Experience, Skills, and Personality Traits

In most instances, the job of an Usher is an entry-level position. Ushers should be pleasant and friendly people with outgoing personalities. An ability to deal with others is necessary. Individuals should be articulate.

Ushers need to have the physical stamina to be on their feet for many hours. They will either be standing or walking for a good portion of their work time.

Ushers should also have the ability to remain calm in a crisis. They must be able to deal with occasional irate patrons who are too loud or do not like the location of their seats.

Unions and Associations

Ushers working in Broadway theaters must be members of the International Alliance of Theatrical Stage Employees (IATSE). This organization sets the minimum salaries and working conditions for its members.

Individuals working in nonunionized situations need not belong to a union.

Tips for Entry

1. Volunteer to act as an Usher for your school or local community theater production.
2. Look in the newspaper classified or display section under heading classification of "Theater," "Performing Arts," "Arenas," "Halls," or "Ushers."
3. Send your résumé with a short cover letter to the personnel director of theaters, concert halls, performing arts centers, or arenas. Inquire about openings and ask for an interview. Request that your résumé be kept on file if there are no current openings.
4. Find a summer or part-time job as an Usher in a movie theater. It provides good hands-on experience.

PERFORMING ARTS
EDUCATION

THEATER ARTS PROFESSOR— COLLEGE/UNIVERSITY

CAREER PROFILE

Duties: Teaching courses in theater and the performing arts, including drama, acting, staging, scenic design, scriptwriting, dance, and music

Alternate Title(s): Instructor; Educator

Salary Range: $24,000 to $65,000+

Employment Prospects: Fair

Advancement Prospects: Fair

Best Geographical Location(s): Positions may be located throughout the country.

Prerequisites:

Education or Training—Minimum of master's degree; some positions require doctoral degree.

Experience—Teaching experience helpful; experience in theater or the performing arts

Special Skills and Personality Traits—Knowledge of theater and performing arts industry; teaching skills; good communications skills; enthusiasm

CAREER LADDER

```
┌─────────────────────────────────────────┐
│  Tenured Theater Arts Professor or       │
│  Professor at More Prestigious College or│
│  University                              │
└─────────────────────────────────────────┘

┌─────────────────────────────────────────┐
│        Theater Arts Professor            │
└─────────────────────────────────────────┘

┌─────────────────────────────────────────┐
│  Theater Arts Teacher in Lower Level of  │
│  Education or Private School or          │
│  Performing Artist, Director             │
└─────────────────────────────────────────┘
```

Position Description

College or university Theater Arts Professors are hired for a variety of different positions. They may be brought into a school as a general theater educator or may teach in specialized areas of theater arts management, theater history, acting, staging, lighting, scenic design, drama, or playwriting. Some educators are also responsible for teaching dance or music. Individuals may work in colleges and universities with majors in theater and the various performing arts or they may work in a school that doesn't. They may teach undergraduate classes, postgraduate classes, or a combination.

Professors are also called educators or instructors. Those teaching in institutions of higher learning, especially those schools specializing in theater degrees, generally teach students hungry to learn all they can and who are seriously considering professional careers in theater.

It is the duty of the professor to be as knowledgeable and informed about his or her subject matter as possible, and to help the students learn all they can.

Many professors in theater-related subjects have worked in theater and the performing arts in some capacity. Some were actors, actresses, dancers, or singers, while others worked in production, direction, and a variety of behind-the-scenes careers. A great many of the educators are still active in various theatrical projects.

Professors working in a college setting usually participate in the cultural programs of the school. A great deal of this responsibility depends on the demands of the school. Those teaching in educational institutions with theater arts, drama, dance, and music degrees may have duties relating to their specialty. For example, those teaching theater-related courses may be required to guide students in putting on campus productions.

An educator cannot walk into a classroom or lecture hall and begin teaching without preparation. Preparation for each class takes a great deal of time especially for the beginning instructor or for someone who is teaching a particular course for the first time.

In addition to teaching courses, professors set aside specific hours each week to meet with students. The individual's other duties might require reading students' papers and grading exams.

The professor, working in a community college setting, probably teaches about 18 hours a week. An individual working at a four-year college or university spends fewer hours teaching, usually from nine to 12 hours per week. Additional hours are spent in preparation, student meetings, grading, and evaluation. Those working on productions may put in extra time. The total working time may end up considerably over 40 hours per week.

The professor is responsible to the head of his or her department or to the administrator of the school.

Salaries

Earnings for professors working in colleges and universities can vary greatly depending on a number of factors, including the specific school, its reputation, and geographic location. Salaries also depend on the professional status of the instructor and his or her experience and responsibilities.

Salaries for assistant professors can begin at $24,000 annually. Full professors earn $65,000 plus a year.

Individuals who have achieved acclaim in theater and other performing arts may earn more than other professors. Educators teaching at more prestigious universities will also earn larger salaries than those with similar duties at a smaller college.

Employment Prospects

Employment prospects are fair for those aspiring to teach theater or the performing arts in colleges and universities. Applicants, however, must be willing to relocate to areas that have openings.

There may also be more opportunities for those willing to teach in smaller schools. Those who are qualified in a number of different subject areas increase their employment prospects.

Advancement Prospects

Advancement prospects are fair for college or university Theater Arts Professors. Individuals may climb the career ladder by finding similar positions in larger, more prestigious schools.

An educator starting out as an assistant professor may teach for a few years and be promoted to an associate professor. Associate professors advance their careers through promotion to a full professor position. Individuals working in a school for a number of years may also be granted tenure, assuring them of security in that position.

Education and Training

Most college and university professors are usually required to hold a master's degree. Many positions may require a doctoral degree.

The educational requirement is sometimes waived if an individual has achieved acclaim in the theatrical world. An example of this might be a famous actor or actress teaching a drama course or an accomplished playwright teaching a playwriting course.

Experience, Skills, and Personality Traits

Experience for college and university professors teaching theater and other performing arts classes can vary. Most but not all individuals have had some experience teaching on some level prior to their appointment at a college or university. Others have had actual experience working in the theater in various capacities.

Professors must have a tremendous knowledge of the performing arts or theater industry as well as his or her own specialization. A genuine love of the performing arts is important.

Individuals should be good communicators and should be enthusiastic about the subject matter with an ability to teach others.

Unions and Associations

Instructors in the theater arts at colleges and universities may belong to a number of associations depending on their specialization. Those teaching dance may be members of the Congress on Research in Dance (CORD), World Congress of Teachers of Dancing (WCTD), or Dance Educators of America (DEA).

Individuals involved in theater may be members of the Organization of Professional Acting Coaches and Teachers (OPACT) or the American Alliance for Theatre and Education (AATE). Their schools can be members of the University Resident Theatre Association (URTA).

Those teaching music-related subjects may be members of the College Music Society (CMS) or the American Musicological Society (AMS).

Tips for Entry

1. Obtain experience teaching theater and other performing arts subjects to local community youth groups.
2. Look in the display or classified sections of newspapers under headings of "Education," "Educators," "Instructors," "Professors," "Theater Arts," "Performing Arts," "Music," or "Dance."
3. Check with your school's placement office. They often know of openings.
4. Send your résumé with a short cover letter to a college or university personnel office. Request that your résumé be kept on file if there are no current openings.
5. Many colleges and universities have Web sites advertising job openings.

PRIVATE DANCE TEACHER

CAREER PROFILE

Duties: Instructing students in the techniques of various forms of dance

Alternate Title(s): Instructor

Salary Range: $10 to $500+ per class

Employment Prospects: Good

Advancement Prospects: Fair

Best Geographical Location(s): Positions located throughout the country; culturally active cities may offer more opportunities.

Prerequisites:

Education or Training—No formal educational requirement; training in dance necessary

Experience—Experience as a dancer

Special Skills and Personality Traits—Knowledge of dance techniques; excellent teaching skills; patience; good communication skills; reliability

CAREER LADDER

```
┌─────────────────────────────────────┐
│  Dance Teacher with Large Roster of  │
│             Students                 │
└─────────────────────────────────────┘

┌─────────────────────────────────────┐
│            Dance Teacher             │
└─────────────────────────────────────┘

┌─────────────────────────────────────┐
│               Dancer                 │
└─────────────────────────────────────┘
```

Position Description

A Private Dance Teacher, as the name implies, teaches students how to dance. Individuals teach the fundamentals as well as advanced techniques and a variety of dancing styles. Some students are eager to learn, while others may have been forced to take lessons by parents. Students who take classes under these circumstances can be quite frustrating for a teacher.

Many of the students of private instructors already know how to dance and want to learn additional dance skills and techniques. Instructors may teach beginners or advanced students. One of the opportunities for expert instructors is the chance to teach professionals.

Teachers may provide instruction in all forms of dance, including ballet, folk, ethnic, modern, jazz, and ballroom. Most individuals specialize in one or two forms of dance and become recognized in the field for classes in these specialties.

Private instructors work in a variety of settings. Some teach in private studios, while others work for organizations or schools offering private lessons. Some instructors have studios in their home.

Good dance teachers have the ability to make a lesson exciting, an important skill when teaching a youngster who is being forced to take lessons. It is also important for those who are experienced dancers seeking knowledge about another's style and technique.

Private Dance Teachers may teach small groups of students at one time or may offer private lessons to individual students. Lessons can run from 45 minutes to an hour or more. Students may take one lesson a week or two or three. Some serious dance students take lessons six days a week.

Private Dance Teachers may be self-employed or may work on staff for a studio or school. Those who are self-employed must not only be very knowledgeable about dance techniques and be good teachers but must also know how to run a business. He or she must make such decisions as how much to charge for lessons, how and when the fee will be paid, and how to run the classes.

Other responsibilities for Private Dance Teachers include putting on dance programs and recitals with their students. These activities give students confidence as well as the opportunity to showcase their talents.

Private Dance Teachers, working with professional dancers, often help them prepare for auditions. Individuals may also work with dancers in productions, providing assistance in perfecting their techniques and styles.

Private Dance Teachers may be responsible to a number of different people depending on the specific situation. If he or she is self-employed, the individual is responsible to the student or, in the case of children, to the parents. Those working for private studios, schools, or organizations are responsible to the director or supervisor of the program.

Salaries

Salaries for Private Dance Teachers vary greatly depending on a number of factors, including the skills, experience, and expertise of the teacher. Another factor is whether the individual is self-employed, in which case earnings will depend on the fees charged and the number of students receiving lessons, or whether the individual works for schools, studios, or organizations. In that case, fees are paid by the class, by the number of students, on a weekly basis, or a combination of these factors.

Fees for Private Dance Teachers can range from $10 per class up to $500 or more depending on the instructor. Fees are higher for teachers who have achieved fame and are well known in the field.

Those working for studios, schools, or organizations may charge a flat fee ranging from $25 per hour up to $250 or more. Private Dance Teachers working on a weekly salary may earn $250 to $1,000 or more.

Employment Prospects

Employment prospects are good for Private Dance Teachers. Individuals may work freelance, be self-employed, or work for private schools, organizations, or studios.

Private teachers may instruct students in any age bracket and in all forms of dance. While employment can be found throughout the country, culturally active cities offer more opportunities.

Advancement Prospects

Advancement prospects are fair for Private Dance Teachers. Advancement is determined to a great extent by the determination and drive of the individual as well as by his or her expertise and experience.

Private Dance Teachers may advance their careers in a number of ways. They may work for a studio or school and decide to open their own studio. Another path for career advancement is to increase the number of students and collect more earnings. Dance teachers who have a good reputation and are sought out will also be able to increase their fees for lessons.

Education and Training

There is no formal educational requirement for Private Dance Teachers. Individuals must, however, have training in the various forms of dance that they teach. This training may be in the form of professional training from a school of dance, private lessons, self-taught skills, or a combination.

Experience, Skills, and Personality Traits

While Private Dance Teachers need to know how to dance well, they do not have to be excellent dancers themselves. They must, however, be excellent teachers.

Teachers must know the basic techniques and styles and be able to perform them. They must also have the capability to communicate instructions so that others can fully understand. They must also be able to see areas where students need improvement and know how to correct technical flaws.

Private Dance Teachers must be dependable. Forgetting a lesson or habitually canceling a class is not tolerated.

One of the most important traits a Private Dance Teacher can have is patience. It often takes a while for a student to grasp a step or a concept. The teacher should also be enthusiastic and excited about the craft of dance whether the student is an amateur or professional.

Unions and Associations

There is no union for Private Dance Teachers. Individuals may belong to a number of associations with others interested in the same goals and subjects. Some of these organizations provide educational support and professional guidance and include the Dance Educators of America (DEA), Ceccetti Council of America (CCA), Dance Masters of America (DMA), World Congress of Teachers of Dancing (WCTD), the National Dance Council of America (NDCA), and the Professional Dance Teachers Association (PDTA).

Tips for Entry

1. Volunteer to teach dance for your local community youth organization. This will give you good hands-on experience and help you make local contacts.
2. Make up business cards, fliers, and posters. Distribute these on store bulletin boards, community centers, and to local civic organizations. Include information such as your name, phone number, any accomplishments in your field of dance, and other pertinent information.
3. Contact local dance studios to see if they need a teacher. You may call or write. Either way, send your résumé with a short cover letter. Ask that it be kept on file if there are no current openings.
4. Continue taking classes, courses, and workshops. Just because you are teaching does not mean you should stop learning yourself.
5. Join trade associations. These will put you in touch with others interested in your field and offer a variety of other opportunities.

DRAMA COACH

CAREER PROFILE

Duties: Coaching actors and actresses in acting techniques; instructing performers in stage movements; evaluating the performance of an actor or actress

Alternate Title(s): Drama Teacher; Theater Coach

Salary Range: $24,000 to $85,000+

Employment Prospects: Fair

Advancement Prospects: Fair

Best Geographical Location(s): New York City, Los Angeles, or other culturally active cities offer the most opportunities.

Prerequisites:

Education or Training—No formal educational requirement; college degree or background in theater is helpful

Experience—Acting or directing experience necessary

Special Skills and Personality Traits—Knowledge of acting skills and techniques; good communication skills; ability to teach; ability to critique students; enthusiasm

CAREER LADDER

```
┌─────────────────────────────────────┐
│   Drama Coach with Large Roster of   │
│ Students or More Prestigious Students │
└─────────────────────────────────────┘

┌─────────────────────────────────────┐
│             Drama Coach              │
└─────────────────────────────────────┘

┌─────────────────────────────────────┐
│    Actor, Actress, or Director       │
└─────────────────────────────────────┘
```

Position Description

Drama Coaches are individuals who coach actors and actresses in their acting techniques. Coaches teach students how to better interpret scripts and place themselves in character roles. They also instruct performers in stage techniques that may help their performances. Sometimes a Drama Coach teaches a student how to project his or her voice differently or use other accents.

Drama Coaches may work in a variety of situations, including colleges, universities, and schools that supplement the teaching of instructors and professors. Coaches may also work with theatrical groups and movie and television production companies. Many Drama Coaches are self-employed. They have workshops or studios where they coach either groups of students or one actor or actress at a time.

A Drama Coach has varied responsibilities depending on the situation he or she is working in. His or her major function is to develop the acting skills of the performer. This may be accomplished in a number of ways.

The Drama Coach first evaluates the abilities of the actor or actress by asking the individual to read a portion of a script. Some coaches have students do readings while other students evaluate and comment on their performance. Other coaches do the evaluation of performances themselves. With camcorders, many coaches film the performance and have the students themselves do the evaluation.

After the evaluation process is completed, the coach works on training techniques. He or she may read the script him- or herself, illustrating changes that can be made in inflection, vocalization, and movement. The coach may also instruct the student on changes that may improve the reading.

Another function of the Drama Coach is to teach the students stage presence and techniques. Stage presence is the way an actor or actress stands and moves while on stage. If the individual is working in television or film, he or she must also coach the students about where to stand and how to look to take advantage of various camera angles.

A Drama Coach may work with an actor or actress who is auditioning for a part. If this is the case, the Drama Coach works on the audition script with the student.

After the actor or actress reads the script, the coach evaluates the student's performance. He or she then suggests techniques and methods that the student can incorporate into the performance. The coach works with the actor or actress until the audition script is mastered.

Many well-known actors and actresses who appear in theatrical productions, television shows, or movies also use the services of a Drama Coach. The two may work with the script, perfecting the performance before rehearsals begin.

Another function of the Drama Coach is to prepare students for their professional careers as actors or actresses. This preparation may include advice on wardrobe, hairstyle, and makeup for auditions for acting jobs. Some Drama Coaches prepare audition tapes for their students to send to casting directors and producers.

Drama Coaches work varied hours depending on the times that their classes and workshops are scheduled. The Drama Coach working in a school, university, or college is responsible to the department chairperson. The coach who is self-employed is responsible to his or her students.

Salaries

Earnings can vary greatly for Drama Coaches depending on a number of factors, including the specific situations the individual is working in as well as his or her responsibilities, experience, and reputation.

Drama Coaches working in schools, colleges, or universities may earn between $24,000 and $45,000 or more annually. Those who are self-employed may have annual earnings of $85,000 or more.

Individuals who are self-employed may charge students a monthly fee for group lessons. The fees can run between $100 and $500 or more a month. Drama Coaches teaching individual students may charge the student on an hourly, daily, weekly, or per-project basis. Fees can range from $25 to $500 or more.

Many Drama Coaches are actors, actresses, or directors who augment their earnings by teaching.

Employment Prospects

Employment prospects are fair for Drama Coaches. Individuals may work in schools, universities, colleges, or for theater groups. Coaches may also open up their own drama or acting workshops and be self-employed.

Some Drama Coaches specialize in working with children, while others work with actors or actresses of any age. Opportunities for Drama Coaches in theatrical situations are greater in New York City, Los Angeles, and other culturally active areas. However, individuals may find opportunities for self-employment throughout the country.

Advancement Prospects

Drama Coaches advance their careers in a number of ways. If they are working in a school, college, or university, they find a similar position in a larger or more prestigious facility. This move usually results in increased earnings.

Drama Coaches may also climb the career ladder by building either a larger roster of students or of more prestigious students. Some individuals start out as theatrical Drama Coaches and advance their careers by coaching actors and actresses in movies or television.

Education and Training

There are no formal educational requirements for self-employed Drama Coaches. Schools, universities, and colleges may require a bachelor's or master's degree in theater arts or drama.

While a college degree or background may not always be required, it may be helpful for the educational value, experience, and contacts.

Drama Coaches should be trained in acting through the formal education offered by a college, private acting classes, or on-the-job experience.

Experience, Skills, and Personality Traits

Drama Coaches should possess a full range of acting skills and techniques. While it is not imperative that they be excellent actors or actresses themselves, they must have the ability to teach others the craft. Good communication skills are helpful in this profession.

Acting experience is essential for the Drama Coach. Without it, he or she will have a difficult time explaining concepts and techniques. There is no substitute for on-the-job training. Many Drama Coaches are currently or were previously actors, actresses, or directors.

Drama Coaches should have a great deal of integrity, they must have the ability to critique students honestly and gently. Enthusiasm toward a student's progress is helpful.

Unions and Associations

There is no union for Drama Coaches. There is, however, a group called the Organization of Professional Acting Coaches and Teachers (OPACT), which provides guidelines of professional conduct for those in this profession.

Tips for Entry

1. Volunteer to coach actors and actresses taking part in your school or community theater productions.
2. Work as a drama counselor in a children's camp.
3. Develop contacts. If you have a good working relationship with casting directors, producers, and directors, let them know what you do.
4. Offer to teach a minicourse at the local community college on drama, acting, or theater. This will help you obtain hands-on experience.
5. Get as much performance and directing experience as you can.
6. Take classes, workshops, and seminars from others. This will help you learn new techniques.

VOCAL COACH

CAREER PROFILE

Duties: Coaching singers, actors, and actresses on methods to improve their voices; instructing on better singing techniques; evaluating the performance of singers; instructing individuals on how to modulate their voice

Alternate Title(s): Coach; Singing Coach; Voice Coach

Salary Range: $23,000 to $100,000+

Employment Prospects: Fair

Advancement Prospects: Fair

Best Geographic Location(s): Culturally active areas such as New York City, Los Angeles, Boston, Philadelphia, Boston, and Washington, D.C., will offer the largest number of opportunities; other areas will offer additional possibilities.

Prerequisites:

Education or Training—Educational requirements vary; conservatory, college degree, or professional music background may be helpful.

Experience—Experience in acting, singing, and/or professional speaking

Special Skills and Personality Traits—Knowledge of vocal techniques; good communication skills; good ear for music; ability to teach; ability to critique students; enthusiasm; motivating ability

CAREER LADDER

```
┌─────────────────────────────────┐
│  Vocal Coach with Large Roster of │
│     Clients or Roster of More     │
│       Prestigious Students        │
└─────────────────────────────────┘

┌─────────────────────────────────┐
│           Vocal Coach             │
└─────────────────────────────────┘

┌─────────────────────────────────┐
│    Singer, Actor, Actress, or     │
│       Professional Speaker        │
└─────────────────────────────────┘
```

Position Description

There is an adage that says you never get a second chance to make a good first impression. While the first impression for many is an individual's appearance, often the first impression of singers, actors, actresses, television, and radio on-air talent, and the like, is their voice.

No matter how talented an actor, actress, or singer is, if his or her voice is dull or flat, that is what people will remember. This can be a disaster for auditions as well as a professional career in the performing arts. The good news is, in many cases, the voice can be trained. The person who helps people do this is called a Vocal Coach.

Vocal Coaches, who are also know as voice coaches help individuals in a variety of career areas improve their vocal techniques. Depending on this situation, they may work with singers, actors and actresses, or others who use their voice as a tool in their career.

Vocal Coaches may be on staff at colleges, universities, or schools, theatrical companies, opera companies, record labels, and corporations. Some coaches may be self-employed or consultants working with clients including singers, actors, actresses, movie and television production companies, and recording artists. Other Vocal Coaches work with on-air personalities such as radio news, talk show, and variety show hosts or announcers. There are also Vocal Coaches who work with corporate clients and others who want to improve the quality of their voice.

Responsibilities of a Vocal Coach will vary depending on the specific situation in which he or she is working. Generally, the major function of the Vocal Coach is finding ways to develop the vocal skills of clients and teaching them how to train and modulate their voice to perform and sound better.

The coach may accomplish this task in a number of ways. He or she usually begins by exploring the ultimate goal of the individual. For example, does a singer need to improve his or her range? Does he or she want to find ways to reach the notes without straining his or her vocal cords?

Is the goal of an actor to learn to project more effectively in a theater? Does the actress need to learn a new accent for a part? Is the goal of the television or radio personality to lose his or her regional accent? Does a corporate client want to learn how to give his or her voice power and authority? It is the responsibility of the Vocal Coach to determine exactly what the individual's goals are, both long and short term, so that a plan to accomplish them can be developed.

Within the scope of the job, the Vocal Coach is expected to evaluate the abilities of the individual with whom he or she is working. The coach may, for example, ask the individual to sing one or more pieces of music or do a reading. The coach then has the responsibility of evaluating the performance. Is it too pitchy? Does the singer need to improve his or her range? Does he or she need to practice breathing techniques? Does the speaker need to improve the tone or modulation of the voice? Is the individual talking too quickly or slurring words. While the coach needs to be honest, he or she also needs to be sensitive to the feelings of the client.

After the individual's performance has been evaluated, the coach develops a plan of action. This might include suggestions and training techniques which will help the individual improve his or her performance.

Sometimes it is as simple as utilizing a different breathing technique. Other times the individual may need to do vocal exercises. The coach is expected to explain various techniques and exercises designed to improve the vocal quality of the individual. At times, the coach may give the individual exercises to practice between sessions.

Vocal Coaches may also teach individuals how to sing correctly so that they protect and strengthen their voice or maximize their vocal talent. Coaches may teach individuals warm-up exercises to use before performance or give them the edge by helping them to gain confidence in their performance.

In many cases, actors and actresses, although not trained as professional singers, will be expected to sing. Vocal Coaches can help them learn how to strengthen their voice, project their singing, and add power to their performance.

A great deal of the success of Vocal Coaches comes from their ability to motivate and inspire their clients. Individuals who are really good at their job in this field help give their clients confidence. They know how to push their clients to the next step, helping them realize that they can exceed their own expectations.

Well-known professionals, up-and-coming performers, and those at various stages in between may work with Vocal Coaches at different times in their career. Some may want to learn good vocal techniques in order to keep their voice in tip-top shape. Others may be preparing for a tour, show, recital, concert, recording, or even an audition. A good Vocal Coach can help individuals just starting out to look and sound like polished professionals and help professionals sound even better.

Vocal Coaches must be versed in the various techniques utilized to help individuals improve their vocal performance. Many coaches who work with singers accompany the singer on the piano or other instrument during sessions to help them hear exactly what something should sound like. The coach must also be able to demonstrate vocal or breathing techniques to individuals. While coaches need to be encouraging, it's essential that they be realistic—pointing out the singer's strong points while finding ways to focus on improving the individual's weak points. To chart progress, many coaches make recordings of clients so that they can see their progress as time goes on in the process.

Vocal Coaches often have niches in which they specialize. For example, there are Vocal Coaches who focus in teaching singers how to sing in other languages. This is especially useful to those singing opera. Others coaches may work with helping individuals sing in a specific style. Some Vocal Coaches specialize in working with actors and actresses or television or radio on-air talent in helping them hone their vocal skills. It's important to realize that every Vocal Coach does not necessarily specialize in all areas.

Vocal Coaches have become popular outside of the entertainment area as well. Today, many coach corporate leaders, motivational speakers, and others who want to project a better vocal style utilize the services of Vocal Coaches to help make them achieve a powerful, smooth speaking voice.

Vocal Coaches may work with clients on a one-to-one basis or in a group. Work hours may vary depending on the times individuals schedule classes or workshops.

This is a good career choice for those who are talented in the vocal area and love to teach and motivate others. Many find it very gratifying to see students not only progress but get the parts of their dreams.

Salaries

Earnings can vary greatly for Vocal Coaches depending on a variety of factors. These include the specific situation in which the individual is working as well as his or her responsibilities, experience, and professional reputation.

Vocal Coaches working in schools, colleges, or universities may earn between $23,000 and $45,000 or more. Those who are self-employed as consultants may have annual earnings between $25,000 and $100,000 or more.

Self-employed Vocal Coaches may charge clients on an hourly, daily, weekly, monthly, or per project basis. Fees can range from $25 to $500 or more per hour.

Employment Prospects

Employment prospects are fair for Vocal Coaches. Individuals may work in school, college, or university settings as well as theatrical, opera, or other music companies. Many Vocal Coaches are self-employed consultants. Clients can include singers, actors, actresses, television and radio on-air personalities, motivational speakers, corporate clients, and others interested in improving the quality of the speaking or singing voice.

The greatest number of opportunities exist in culturally active cities such as New York City, Los Angeles, Atlanta, Philadelphia, Washington, D.C., Boston, and Chicago, among others.

Advancement Prospects

Advancement prospects are fair for talented Vocal Coaches. Those employed by schools, colleges, theaters, musical companies, or other institutions can climb the career ladder by finding similar positions with larger or more prestigious facilities. Individuals who are self-employed consultants advance their careers by developing a good reputation and attracting either a larger roster of clients or a more prestigious clients.

Education and Training

Educational requirements vary for Vocal Coaches depending on their employment situation. Successful Vocal Coaches are usually trained in either singing, vocal performance, or acting through formal education offered by a college or conservatory or less formal education, including private singing, vocal, or acting lessons, as well as on-the-job experiences.

Those employed by schools, colleges, theaters, or musical companies often are required to have a college degree, conservatory training, or some other background in music.

While a college degree or background may not always be required, it is often helpful for both the educational value, experiences, and contacts it offers. Courses, workshops, and seminars in music, vocal instruction, and voice techniques will be helpful.

Experience, Skills, and Personality Traits

Most Vocal Coaches have been involved in the performing arts area in some manner. Many either are or were professional singers, actors, or actresses themselves. To be successful in this area, individuals should possess a full range of vocal and singing skills and techniques. The ability to communicate and teach others is essential.

Vocal Coaches should be motivating, enthusiastic individuals with the ability to critique others. An understanding of the performing arts industry is helpful. A knowledge of various vocal techniques is essential.

Unions and Associations

There is no major association specific to Vocal Coaches. Individuals may, however, be members of the Organization of Professional Acting Coaches and Teachers (OPACT), which provides guidelines of professional conduct.

Tips for Entry

1. Get experience working as a Vocal Coach at a children's summer camp.
2. Offer to teach a minicourse or seminar at your local community college on learning to sing better, vocal techniques, or improving your voice. This will not only give you experience but also get your name out to the public on your specialty.
3. Take classes, workshops, and seminars from other Vocal Coaches to learn new techniques.
4. Make sure you make business cards noting your specialty. Go to places where you might meet potential clients, such as concerts, theatrical performances, and even charity events.
5. Volunteer to coach singers, actors, or actresses taking part in your school or community theater production.

PERFORMING ARTS JOURNALISM

CRITIC—BROADCASTING

Duties: Viewing plays, theatrical productions, movies, and television shows; writing, preparing, and broadcasting reviews for on-air execution

Alternate Title(s): Journalist; Reviewer; Reporter; Cultural or Entertainment Editor

Salary Range: $23,000 to $1,000,000+

Employment Prospects: Poor

Advancement Prospects: Fair

Best Geographical Location(s): Positions may be located throughout the country; large, culturally active cities offer more possibilities.

Prerequisites:

Education or Training—Four-year college degree required for most positions

Experience—Journalism or broadcasting experience necessary

Special Skills and Personality Traits—Excellent writing skills; comfortable in front of a microphone or a camera; articulate; clear, pleasant speaking voice; pleasing appearance; ability to work under pressure; objectivity; interest in and knowledge about theater and the performing arts

```
┌─────────────────────────────────────┐
│  Critic for Larger, More Prestigious │
│     Television or Radio Station      │
└─────────────────────────────────────┘

┌─────────────────────────────────────┐
│               Critic                 │
└─────────────────────────────────────┘

┌─────────────────────────────────────┐
│  Television, Radio Journalist, or    │
│          Print Journalist            │
└─────────────────────────────────────┘
```

Position Description

A Critic working in the broadcasting media reviews plays, theatrical productions, movies, and TV shows for broadcast on television or radio. As is true in print media, a good review by an objective, respected Critic can mean success or failure for a production.

Critics working in the broadcasting field may work in either television, radio or, both. Most radio stations, however, do not have their own Critics. Instead they rely on an entertainment reporter or purchase a series of reviews from a syndicate. Depending on the size of the television station, the Critic may also function as an entertainment reporter or be responsible for reporting on nonentertainment, but related, feature stories.

Critics in major television markets such as New York, Los Angeles, Chicago, Washington, D.C., and Boston attend plays, operas, symphonies, concerts, or movies and review the shows. In some cases, they may also review new television shows.

In smaller television markets, the Critic reviews productions that come through the area. He or she is also responsible for reviewing local theatrical productions, including summer stock, community theater, concerts by local artists, and school and college productions.

The Critic may be responsible for nightly entertainment news or may be assigned three or four shows a week to review. As individuals move into positions in larger markets, their jobs usually become more specialized. Critics may review plays, operas, or symphonies or may review only movies or television shows.

Examples of well-known broadcast Critics are Ebert and Roeper. They present movie reviews in different media, including television shows, radio reports, and in syndicated newspapers and magazines.

After watching a show, Critics write their own copy for the review. When doing this, the individual has to be objective, honest, and fair. The review gives the viewers or listeners an idea of how well the production was done. It may include information on the specific show, story, production, actors, and actresses. Many Critics may also give the play or production a rating such as one star, two stars, etc.

The next step in the Critic's job is reading the review on air. They may do this live on a broadcast or may tape the review. Critics are also responsible for obtaining a clip or short piece of film of the production. While reading the review, the clip is often shown on air.

The more the Critic knows about the medium to be reviewed, the better the review will be. For example, it may be difficult for a Critic to review a production of *Romeo and Juliet* unless he or she is familiar with other productions of the play and with all of Shakespeare's work.

Critics must watch and review all shows without bias. They cannot let their personal opinions of certain actors or actresses or specific shows get in the way of honestly critiquing a particular production.

One of the perks Critics enjoy is getting invited to openings of theatrical productions or screenings of new movies or television shows. Those working for television stations in New York and Los Angeles may also be invited to opening night parties and galas to meet and mingle with the stars.

It may appear that all a Critic does is go to a play or movie and then show up to broadcast his or her review, but that is not the way it happens. A Critic's working hours may vary depending on the specific shift they are working, on-air schedules, and the times productions and shows have to be viewed.

Salaries

Earnings for Critics working in the broadcasting field will vary greatly. Factors affecting salaries include the size, market, and prestige of the television or radio station at which an individual works. The Critic's salary will also depend on his or her experience level, responsibilities, and fame.

Individuals working for national or major-market television or radio stations can earn $1 million more annually. Critics working in smaller and medium markets may earn between $23,000 and $65,000 or more.

Employment Prospects

Employment prospects for Critics working in broadcasting are generally poor. There are a great many people who want this type of job and competition is keen. The larger and more prestigious a station or market is, the harder it is to find employment. Prospects are slightly better in smaller markets.

Jobs are located throughout the country. Major markets are located in large cities such as New York, Chicago, and Los Angeles.

Advancement Prospects

Advancement prospects are fair for Critics in broadcasting once they get their foot in the door. Most people who aspire to be Critics move from station to station, trying each time to find similar jobs at larger, more prestigious stations.

As in most broadcasting jobs, advancement prospects are more difficult as individuals obtain positions working at larger and more prestigious stations.

Education and Training

Critics working in broadcasting are usually required to have a minimum of a four-year college degree. Good choices for a major include journalism, English, liberal arts, broadcasting, mass media, theater and the performing arts, and communications. Any additional writing and broadcasting courses and seminars are useful.

Experience, Skills, and Personality Traits

Most Critics working in television have experience in broadcasting. Often, they have come up through the ranks in college serving as interns and reporters covering nonentertainment subjects. Most have some type of journalism background either in college or writing for a newspaper, magazine, or for broadcast news.

Critics usually have a great interest and a basic knowledge and understanding of different forms of entertainment, theater, and the performing arts before becoming involved in this career.

Individuals should have excellent writing skills, with a good command of the English language, and should be comfortable in front of a microphone and cameras. The broadcast Critic must be articulate and have a clear, pleasant speaking voice. Those aspiring to be Critics on television should be well groomed and have a pleasing appearance.

The Critics must be objective and interesting when presenting a review. The ability to perform well under pressure is necessary for those working on a deadline.

Unions and Associations

Critics working in television or radio may belong to a number of unions, organizations, and trade associations. Some of these include the Writers Guild of America (WGA), American Federation of Television and Radio Artists (AFTRA), the National Critics Institute (NCI), and the American Theatre Critics Association (ATCA).

Tips for Entry

1. Join your school's radio or television station. Get as much experience as possible in all aspects of broadcasting.
2. Find an internship in a television station. This will be a good learning experience and will help you make important contacts.

3. Learn to write well. Obtain experience critiquing performances of all types by reviewing plays, music events, concerts, records, movies, and television shows for your school paper.

4. Look for and take seminars in journalism, broadcasting, and writing. These programs will help prepare you for your career in addition to putting you in touch with others interested in the same field.

CRITIC—PRINT MEDIA

CAREER PROFILE

Duties: Viewing plays, theatrical productions, movies, and television shows and then writing reviews for publication in newspapers and magazines

Alternate Title(s): Journalist; Reviewer; Performing Arts Critic

Salary Range: $23,000 to $1 million+

Employment Prospects: Fair

Advancement Prospects: Fair

Best Geographical Location(s): Positions may be located throughout the country; culturally active cities offer more possibilities.

Prerequisites:

Education or Training—Bachelor's degree required or preferred for most positions

Experience—Journalistic experience helpful

Special Skills and Personality Traits—Excellent writing skills; ability to work under pressure; objectivity; interest and knowledge in theater and performing arts

CAREER LADDER

```
┌─────────────────────────────────────────┐
│  Critic for More Prestigious Publication  │
└─────────────────────────────────────────┘

┌─────────────────────────────────────────┐
│                  Critic                   │
└─────────────────────────────────────────┘

┌─────────────────────────────────────────┐
│                 Reporter                  │
└─────────────────────────────────────────┘
```

Position Description

Critics in the print media are responsible for reviewing plays and other theatrical productions, movies, and television shows for a newspaper or magazine. A good review by a respected Critic can mean financial success to a show. A bad review can close it quickly.

Critics work in many different outlets from small weekly publications to large, prestigious daily newspapers and weekly or monthly magazines. Depending on the situation, a Critic might be responsible for writing reviews on any plays, shows, concerts, and theatrical productions in the area. The Critic might also write a weekly, biweekly, or monthly column on the performing arts. In some small circulation papers, the Critic might also be responsible for writing and reporting on nonentertainment subjects.

As individuals move into positions with larger newspapers and magazines, their jobs typically become more specialized. The Critic may review plays, operas, or symphonies, or may review only movies or television shows.

The more specialized the job, the more the Critic must know about the subject being covered. For example, Critics reviewing plays must have a good working knowledge of theater in general as well as a familiarity with similar productions, actors, actresses, halls, lighting, and set designs. The more he or she knows about the subject area being covered, the better the Critic will be able to review a show.

Critics must review a show without any bias. They cannot let their personal opinions of certain actors or actresses or specific shows get in the way of honestly critiquing a particular production.

After attending a play or show the Critic will be required to write a review, in which he or she will give an idea of how well the production was done. The review includes things such as whether the show, story, production, actors, or actresses were good or bad and why the Critic thinks so. In some instances, the Critic might think the production was bad but the acting of one or two actors was excellent.

Critics may be invited to openings of theatrical productions or screenings of new movies or television shows before the general public has the opportunity to view it. Those working for newspapers and magazines with large circulations in cities such as New York and Los Angeles may also be invited to opening parties and galas to meet the stars.

Critics work irregular hours; many work a full day at the office writing and researching and then in the evening go to the theater to review a play or the movies to critique a film. Critics are usually responsible to the entertainment editor of their publication.

Salaries

Salaries for Critics vary greatly depending on a number of factors including the type of production employing the Critic, and the individual's experience level and responsibilities.

Individuals working full time may earn between $23,000 and $65,000 or more a year. There are a few nationally known Critics who earn $1 million or more annually.

There are also some Critics who work for smaller local publications on a review-by-review basis. Earnings for these reviews may range from a few cents a word to a flat fee of $100 or more.

Employment Prospects

Employment prospects for Critics working in the print media are fair for those who don't mind starting at the bottom of the career ladder. Prospects become more limited as individuals seek positions with larger newspapers and publications.

Jobs are located throughout the country, although those aspiring to review Broadway and other major theatrical productions must move to New York City or other large, culturally active cities.

Almost every newspaper and a great many magazines have entertainment sections. Local newspapers and magazines are no exception and provide those entering the field with a good place to find employment.

Advancement Prospects

Advancement prospects are fair for Critics who start out at smaller, local newspapers and publications. The next rung up the career ladder for these individuals is a similar position at a larger, more prestigious publication. Individuals may also advance their careers by becoming specialists in one area of the arts such as plays, movies, or television.

Advancement prospects become more difficult for individuals working at larger and more prestigious publications. At this point, there is a great deal of competition for each job.

Education and Training

Most larger publications now require at least a bachelor's degree in order to be considered for employment. There are, however, smaller, local newspapers which may hire individuals who do not have a college education. Advancement in these cases is usually difficult.

Good college majors for aspiring Critics include journalism, English, liberal arts, theater and the performing arts, or communications. Writing courses are helpful.

Experience, Skills, and Personality Traits

Most Critics have journalistic experience in either high school, college, or on a small local newspaper. Many individuals have written on a variety of subjects before becoming involved in entertainment, theater, and the performing arts.

Critics must have excellent writing skills with a good command of the English language. They should be able to turn out clear, concise, objective and interesting reviews in a timely fashion. The ability to type or use a computer or word processor is necessary. The ability to work well under pressure is essential for those working on a deadline.

An interest and knowledge of the type work being reviewed is needed whether it be theater, television, or films. In order to become successful in this field, the Critic's views must be respected for their honesty and objectivity over a long period of time.

Unions and Associations

Many newspapers and magazines are unionized. Individuals working as Critics may therefore be members of the specific union the publication is affiliated with.

Critics may also be members of a number of trade associations and other organizations. These might include the Music Critics Association (MCA), the New York Drama Critics Circle (NYDCC), and the Outer Critics Circle (OCC).

Tips for Entry

1. Obtain experience by reviewing plays, concerts, records, movies, and television shows for your school paper.
2. Call the entertainment editor at your local newspaper and see if you can review a play or concert on spec, which means that if the editor likes the review he may run it. If not, you have gained some experience writing a review as well as making an important contact.
3. Find an internship in a newspaper or magazine in the entertainment department. If this is not possible, find an internship in any area of journalism.
4. If you are in college, try to get on the school newspaper. Every bit of experience is important: The more you obtain, the better journalist and Critic you will be in the long run.
5. Send your résumé, a short cover letter, and samples of your writing to the editors of publications for which you are interested in working. Names and addresses of daily newspapers are available in the *Editor and Publisher International Year Book*. This publication is available in many libraries and larger newspaper offices around the country.

MISCELLANEOUS CAREERS IN THEATER AND THE PERFORMING ARTS

ARTS COUNCIL DIRECTOR

CAREER PROFILE

Duties: Managing the affairs of an arts council; fund-raising; auditioning, reviewing, and selecting talent for performances; writing grants; performing public relations duties; working with volunteer committees

Alternate Title(s): Executive Director; Chief Executive Officer

Salary Range: $24,000 to $65,000+

Employment Prospects: Fair

Advancement Prospects: Poor

Best Geographical Location(s): Culturally active cities offer more opportunities.

Prerequisites:

Education or Training—Requirements vary from high school diploma to bachelor's degree; some positions require a master's degree.

Experience—Experience working in the performing arts, public relations, fund-raising, or marketing

Special Skills and Personality Traits—Knowledge of the performing arts industry; business skills; fund-raising, organizational coordination and communications skills

CAREER LADDER

```
┌─────────────────────────────────┐
│   Arts Council Director for Larger, │
│      More Prestigious Council       │
└─────────────────────────────────┘

┌─────────────────────────────────┐
│        Arts Council Director        │
└─────────────────────────────────┘

┌─────────────────────────────────┐
│  Assistant Arts Council Director or │
│  Individual Involved in Fund-Raising, │
│ Publicity, Public Relations, Marketing, │
│      or the Performing Arts          │
└─────────────────────────────────┘
```

Position Description

Arts councils are usually private, not-for-profit agencies established by people interested in the arts. In very small organizations all work is handled by volunteers from the membership. Other arts councils employ a number of people to run the organization. The person who coordinates the activities of the arts council is called the Arts Council Director. He or she may also be called the executive director or chief executive officer.

The main function of the Arts Council Director is to manage the affairs of the organization. Responsibilities will vary depending on the job. In smaller organizations, the director may handle everything with the help of committees of volunteers. In larger arts councils, the director may have assistants and a staff to work with who handle the various duties. In these councils, the director serves as a coordinator.

Arts councils bring a variety of events in the performing arts to the community, including a full range of performers, singers, dancers, musicians, theatrical, ballet or opera productions, symphonies, mimes, lecture or concert series, and comedians.

The director, sometimes in conjunction with a committee from the council, determines the type of events the council wants to schedule for the coming year.

Once the type of shows are decided upon, the Arts Council Director finds the talent for these performances. One of the primary responsibilities of the director is to audition, review, and select the talent. The director may travel to various locations or may simply obtain audiotapes or videotapes from booking agents, managers, or directly from performing artists.

When making a decision on booking any performance, Arts Council Directors must keep a number of things in mind, including the potential community audience and the policies and preferences of the council. They must also work within the budget of the organization.

The Arts Council Director also handles contract negotiations with the performers or their booking agents. The individual arranges the terms of the contract, schedules the dates, and determines fees to be paid for each engagement. He or she is responsible for seeing that all contracts are signed by all parties concerned. The director may also be required to make sure that checks are made out for deposits or fees and paid to the proper people at the correct times.

The Arts Council Director is heavily involved in the budget and finances of the organization. One of the responsibilities of the individual may be the preparation of an annual budget. This is generally difficult because many arts councils work with limited funds.

In order to help increase the funds of an organization, the Arts Council Director is responsible for fund-raising. The individual develops, implements, and runs a number of special events during the year to raise needed money. These events may include annual dinner dances, membership drives, auctions, galas, or special performances.

Grants are another source of money that many arts councils depend on. The Arts Council Director is responsible for locating grants from federal, state, or local agencies and from private industry. They must then write and prepare the grant application. If the council receives grant money, the Arts Council Director makes sure that all rules and regulations of the grant are adhered to.

The director is also responsible for handling the council's public relations and advertising for activities and performances, as well as internal publicity within the organization.

The director is also responsible for handling the council's public relations and advertising for activities and performances, as well as internal publicity within the organization.

The director is required to write and prepare press releases, calendar schedules, and newsletters and is responsible for developing, writing, and producing all brochures, leaflets, and booklets.

Most not-for-profit groups, such as arts councils, depend on the help of volunteers. The Arts Council Director is responsible for coordinating the efforts of all the volunteer groups and committees in the council.

The Arts Council Director usually works regular hours. He or she may work overtime, however, to finish a project, audition talent, or attend a performance. The individual is responsible to the council's board of directors or trustees.

Salaries

Earnings for Arts Council Directors vary greatly depending on the geographic location, size, prestige, and budget of the arts council. Other variables include the experience and responsibilities of the individual.

Salaries for full-time Arts Council Directors can range from $24,000 to $65,000 or more annually. Salaries on the lower end of the scale go to individuals with little experience working in smaller organizations with limited budgets. Those with more experience and working in larger organizations in culturally active cities earn salaries on the higher end of the scale.

Employment Prospects

Employment prospects are fair for Arts Council Directors. While there are arts councils located through the country, individuals may have to relocate to find a position. Culturally active cities offer more opportunities.

It should be mentioned that all arts councils do not employ full-time directors. Some use the services of a volunteer to handle the tasks of the director.

Advancement Prospects

Advancement prospects are limited for Arts Council Directors. In order to climb the career ladder individuals must find a similar position in a more prestigious arts council with a larger budget. This may be difficult.

Some Arts Council Directors advance their careers by becoming booking agents or managers for performers, arenas, halls, or theaters.

Education and Training

Educational requirements vary for Arts Council Directors. Some positions require a high school diploma while others require a bachelor's or a master's degree.

Good choices for college majors include arts management, public relations, communications, theater arts, business, and liberal arts. Any courses, seminars, or workshops in fund raising, grant writing, public relations, business, or arts management are also useful.

Experience, Skills, and Personality Traits

Arts Council Directors come from different types of backgrounds. Many have had experience in some facet of the performing arts, public relations, or marketing. Others have worked in fund raising, or in other not-for-profit organizations. There are some who were promoted to Arts Council Director from an assistant's position.

Most people in this job have a genuine love for the performing arts. They enjoy ballets, orchestras, dancers, chamber music, theatrical productions, and operas. They also enjoy being around others who have the same interests.

Arts Council Directors should be very organized and detail oriented. Individuals must handle many different tasks at the same time. They need to be able to coordinate the activities of both staff members and volunteers.

Verbal and written communications skills are essential. The ability to research and write grants is helpful. Fund-raising skills are a must. The director should also have the ability to carry out the full spectrum of public relations skills.

A knowledge of the performing arts industry is necessary, as are a variety of business skills, including the ability to negotiate and understand performers' contracts.

Unions and Associations

Arts Council Directors may be members of their specific state's council of the arts or the National Endowment for the Arts. Individuals may also belong to other associations.

Tips for Entry

1. Look for jobs under such heading classifications as "Arts Council," "Performing Arts," and "Executive Director" in the display or classified section of the newspaper. Openings may also be listed in local arts council newsletters.
2. Become a member of your local arts council. Volunteer to work on a number of committees. This work will provide you with experience and help you make contacts.
3. Offer to do the publicity or fund-raising for a local not-for-profit organization. It does not matter if the organization is related to the performing arts or not. If you can do publicity or fund-raising for one organization, you can do it for any type of group.
4. Check out the Web sites of various arts councils. Many post openings.

ADVANCE PERSON

CAREER PROFILE

Duties: Arriving ahead of the performance of a theatrical or performing arts show to prepare for the program; assisting road manager or show coordinator with details prior to performance

Alternate Title(s): Advance Agent; Advance Man/Advance Woman

Salary Range: $23,000 to $50,000+

Employment Prospects: Fair

Advancement Prospects: Fair

Best Geographical Location(s): Positions are located in culturally active cities.

Prerequisites:

Education or Training—No formal educational requirement

Experience—Publicity or promotion experience helpful but not required

Special Skills and Personality Traits—Ability to travel alone; organizational skills; dependability; good communication skills

CAREER LADDER

```
┌─────────────────────────────────────┐
│  Tour Manager, Company Tour          │
│  Coordinator, or Advance Person for  │
│  More Prestigious Productions        │
└─────────────────────────────────────┘

┌─────────────────────────────────────┐
│          Advance Person              │
└─────────────────────────────────────┘

┌─────────────────────────────────────┐
│  Publicist, Promotional Staff        │
│  Person, or Other Entry-level Position│
└─────────────────────────────────────┘
```

Position Description

Many theatrical productions, including plays, concerts, ballets, opera, and circuses, travel from city to city. The Advance Person is the individual who goes out on the road from the home city before the rest of the entourage departs to set up before a theatrical or performing arts production takes place. As a rule, the Advance Person leaves a town before the performance and moves on to the next location.

The main function of the Advance Person is to make sure that everything is set up as planned in the city and venue where a performance is scheduled to occur. The individual checks to see that posters and billboards are put up in the area. If they are not, he or she might either put them up personally or hire a crew. The individual also sees that fliers and other promotional material are distributed throughout the area.

The Advance Person is responsible for checking advance ticket sales to determine how they are selling. With smaller events, the Advance Person is responsible for physically bringing the tickets for the event to ticket sellers. Larger concerts, plays, and ballets, however, generally use the services of a computerized ticket agency such as Ticketron.

The Advance Person, who is also referred to as the advance man or advance woman, may be responsible for delivering press passes or press lists issued by the publicist, public relations company, or organization sponsoring the event. Other promotional responsibilities may include delivering press packages, photographs, and programs to sponsors or promoters in each city.

The Advance Person is responsible for checking out the venue, hall, or auditorium where the theatrical event is scheduled to take place. The individual looks into the seating, exits, entrances, and loading docks of each hall and reports all information to the tour manager handling the event. The Advance Person is expected to measure mileage and check routes between cities on the tour. He or she might see what options are available for transportation as well as hotels, motels, and restaurants in each city. All of this information is relayed back to the tour manager or road coordinator of the show.

The Advance Person is responsible for bringing camera-ready advertisements to local newspapers, video advertisements to television stations, and copy for radio ads to stations.

In most instances, the Advance Person is expected to visit the local promoter or director of the organization sponsoring the event to go over last minute details which must be taken care of before a show.

In order to be successful as an Advance Person, the individual must be very dependable and responsible. He or she must be able to structure his or her own day in order to get everything accomplished.

The amount of traveling the Advance Person does depends to a great extent on the specific job. Some theatrical Advance People travel from coast to coast while others stay within a 100- or 200-mile radius of the home city.

Salaries

Salaries for Advance People vary depending on the specific job. Earnings may start out at approximately $400 per week. Those with experience may earn $1,000 a week or more. Advance People generally receive either a per diem or reimbursement for their traveling expenses.

Individuals are usually paid by the week for the time that they work. For weeks that they are not on the road, they might receive a reduction in salary, no salary, or a retainer.

Employment Prospects

Employment prospects for Advance People are fair. They may find work with theater, ballet, concert, or opera companies, or they may be employed by circuses, musical acts, management companies, or promoters.

Advancement Prospects

Advance People may become road or tour managers or coordinators for any type of performing artist or company.

Other individuals advance their careers by finding more prestigious types of shows to work with.

Education and Training

There is no formal education requirement for this position; however, a valid driver's license is usually required.

Experience, Skills, and Personality Traits

Many Advance People obtain their job having no prior experience. Others have worked as publicity or promotional assistants.

The Advance Person must like to travel and not mind traveling alone. He or she must be extremely organized and detail oriented and should be responsible and dependable.

Successful Advance People are personable and articulate.

Unions and Associations

There is no union or trade association specifically geared towards Advance People working in theater or other performing arts.

Tips for Entry

1. Send your résumé and a short cover letter to the head offices of theatrical, ballet, symphony, and opera companies. You might also send résumés to circuses and touring rock, country, and easy listening acts.
2. Advertise your availability in a small display or classified ad in any of the trade magazines.
3. Check ads for this position in the classified or display section of newspapers in larger culturally active cities.
4. Prepare your résumé, listing all skills and experience that might interest a potential employer.
5. Openings for this type of position may be located online. Check out Web sites of ballets, symphonies, and touring companies.

DANCE THERAPIST

Duties: Using dance and movement activities to treat physical, mental, and emotional disabilities in patients

Alternate Title(s): Dance/Movement Therapist

Salary Range: $24,000 to $70,000+

Employment Prospects: Excellent

Advancement Prospects: Good

Best Geographical Location(s): Positions are located throughout the country.

Prerequisites:

Education or Training—Master's degree required

Experience—Internship required

Special Skills and Personality Traits—Dancing and movement skills; researching skills; emotional stability; ability to work with the handicapped and disabled; compassion; patience; empathy

```
┌─────────────────────────────────────┐
│     Supervisory Position or          │
│  Dance Therapist in Private Practice │
└─────────────────────────────────────┘

┌─────────────────────────────────────┐
│          Dance Therapist             │
└─────────────────────────────────────┘

┌─────────────────────────────────────┐
│          Intern or Dancer            │
└─────────────────────────────────────┘
```

Position Description

A rewarding way to work in the performing arts is to do so while helping others. Dance Therapists use dance, movement, and related activities to treat disabilities in patients. The function of a Dance Therapist is to provide a patient with a means of expression. A patient may be referred to a Dance Therapist for a variety of reasons, including physical, mental, or emotional disabilities or illness. Victims of various diseases, accidents, or handicaps may also become patients of Dance Therapists.

Dance Therapists are registered with the American Dance Therapy Association (ADTA) and must go through a program of training. There are two levels of Dance Therapists. The first is called DTR (Dance Therapist Registered) and is for those who have completed the training and education for the basic level of competency in the job. Individuals who complete additional requirements go to the next level called ADTR (Academy of Dance Therapists Registered).

The Dance Therapist's main function is to help restore a patient's health. This is accomplished with the help of other professionals, including doctors, nurses, teachers, physical therapists, music therapists, psychologists, and psychiatrists. Together this team determines what course of action to take for a patient's therapy. Dance therapy, along with other expressive arts therapies, can often provide a breakthrough with a patient who cannot be reached in any other manner. The Dance Therapist uses various forms of dance and movement to help the patient regain his or her health. The therapist must have a complete knowledge and understanding of body movement and what it can accomplish.

The responsibilities of the Dance Therapist vary depending on the specific job and the specific patient. He or she must observe, assess, and evaluate each patient before developing the best course of treatment.

The Dance Therapist plans dance and other movement activities based on the knowledge and experience gained while training for the job. In some instances, the Dance Therapist works with one patient at a time. In other instances, he or she works with a group of patients. Dance Therapists use dance and movement to accomplish their goals in treatment of the patient. They may teach a variety of forms of dance to a patient or may have the patient move freely and observe his or her movements, facial expressions, and other body language. It is important for the Dance Therapist to realize that what works for one patient will not always work with another.

Dance therapy may be used to soothe patients who are angry or irritated. It may also be used to evoke various reactions. Sometimes when a patient uses a great deal of energy moving around, he or she loses inhibitions or gains the ability to talk about a problem. Dance and movement may also make people feel less self-conscious. In some cases, patients are able to express emotions through movement.

Conferences are often held with other members of the professional team as well as with the patient's family to discuss the individual's needs and progress.

This job can be very fulfilling. Seeing a patient with an unhealthy emotional or physical condition change and become healthier through dance and movement is very rewarding.

Salaries

Earnings for Dance Therapists vary greatly depending on a number of factors, including the specific facility an individual is working for, its size, prestige, and geographic location. Other factors affecting salary include the individual's experience, responsibilities, and educational level.

Dance Therapists earn between $24,000 and $70,000 or more annually. The average yearly salary is between $35,000 and $50,000.

Employment Prospects

Employment prospects are excellent for Dance Therapists. They can work full or part time in a variety of health-care situations including hospitals, other health-care facilities, psychiatric hospitals, mental health centers, rehabilitation centers, nursing homes, extended care facilities, schools, correctional facilities, or independent expressive arts therapy centers. Opportunities are located throughout the country.

Advancement Prospects

Dance Therapists have good advancement prospects. With drive and determination, individuals can move into supervisory positions, including that of director of recreation therapy or expressive arts therapy.

An individual may also advance by locating a similar position at a more prestigious facility, with increased responsibilities and earnings.

Another path many individuals take is to go into private practice. In order to go into private practice or to teach, Dance Therapists may need to fulfill additional requirements.

Education and Training

Dance Therapists must hold a master's degree. The American Dance Therapy Association has approved the programs of a number of colleges throughout the country offering graduate degrees in dance therapy. They also allow alternative education requirements for individuals who do not attend one of the schools participating in approved programs.

Dance Therapists may have undergraduate degrees in any area, including liberal arts, dance, psychology, or physical education. As most aspiring Dance Therapists are extremely interested in dance, they usually take a large number of classes in that area. Other helpful undergraduate classes include those in kinesiology and dance education.

Experience, Skills, and Personality Traits

In order to be registered by the American Dance Therapy Association, the registering agency for this profession, Dance Therapists must fulfill certain requirements. They also need the experience received through internship programs.

Dance Therapists must have the ability to work with ill, handicapped, and disabled patients. They must have a great deal of patience as it often takes a long time for a patient to make any progress.

The Dance Therapist must be compassionate, empathetic, and emotionally stable. He or she must have training in a variety of forms of dance. The ability to do research is helpful.

Unions and Associations

Dance Therapists may belong to the American Dance Therapy Association (ADTA). This organization offers education, professional support, and guidance to their members as well as bringing individuals interested in the field together. It is also the registering agency for Dance Therapists.

Tips for Entry

1. Check the college job placement office for schools offering degrees in dance therapy. These schools often have listings of job openings. Many facilities send employment opportunities to these schools in hopes of locating qualified applicants.
2. Look under heading classifications of "Dance Therapy," "Health Care," "Therapists," "Recreation Therapy," and "Expressive Arts Therapists" in the display or classified section of the newspaper.
3. Contact the American Dance Therapy Association (ADTA) for the requirements for becoming a registered Dance Therapist.
4. Send your résumé and a short cover letter to the personnel director of facilities, schools, or independent expressive arts therapies centers. Request that they keep your résumé on file if there is not a current opening.
5. There are positions for Dance Therapists available through the state and federal government. These civil service positions can be located by contacting your state and federal employment service.
6. Check the Internet for job possibilities. Search the major job and employment sites and sites related to dance or dance therapy.

MUSIC THERAPIST

CAREER PROFILE

Duties: Using music or musical activities to treat physical, mental, or emotional disabilities in patients

Alternate Title(s): None

Salary Range: $24,000 to $55,000+

Employment Prospects: Excellent

Advancement Prospects: Good

Best Geographical Location(s): Positions are located throughout the country.

Prerequisites:

Education or Training—Minimum requirement is a bachelor's degree in music therapy; some positions may require a master's degree.

Experience—Internship in music therapy usually required; experience working with the handicapped or disabled helpful

Special Skills and Personality Traits—Ability to play a musical instrument; ability to sing in front of others; emotional stability; ability to work with the handicapped and disabled; compassion; patience; empathy

CAREER LADDER

```
┌─────────────────────────────────┐
│   Music Therapist in Larger or   │
│   More Prestigious Facility or   │
│      Supervisory Position        │
└─────────────────────────────────┘

┌─────────────────────────────────┐
│        Music Therapist           │
└─────────────────────────────────┘

┌─────────────────────────────────┐
│        Intern or Student         │
└─────────────────────────────────┘
```

Position Description

One of the more rewarding ways to work in the performing arts is to do so while helping others. Music Therapists use music and musical activities to treat physical, mental, or emotional disabilities in patients. They attempt to restore an individual's health, working with a number of other professionals. These professionals include physicians, nurses, teachers, physical therapists, dance therapists, psychologists, and psychiatrists.

The Music Therapist will use various forms of music as therapy for individuals who have physical, mental, or emotional disabilities or illness. The therapist can often make a breakthrough in a patient's therapy when all else has failed.

Music Therapists have varied duties depending on the specific job and patient. They may be responsible for choosing pieces of music to be used as background in certain rooms in a facility. Background music may be used to either soothe patients or to evoke various reactions.

Music Therapists who work in a hospital, nursing home, or extended-care facility may be responsible for bringing together a group of patients to sing or play instruments for the facility staff and other patients. This type of therapy is

used to bring people out of their shells, to build self-confidence, and to express memories and emotions when verbal attempts have failed.

The Music Therapist is responsible for planning musical activities for one person at a time or for a group. He or she may teach a group of patients in a nursing home a new song or play a tape of songs that were popular when the patients were younger. This type of therapy often helps to engage a withdrawn patient.

In some cases, Music Therapists work with handicapped children. For example, they may be responsible for teaching a blind child how to play a musical instrument. This activity gives the child a tremendous sense of accomplishment that he or she might not have had before.

Through the use of all these therapies, the therapist can often accomplish a degree of healing by giving a patient a sense of accomplishment, helping another patient express a long suppressed emotion, or simply making patients feel more secure.

The therapist works with a patient on a one-to-one basis or in a group, depending on the patient and his or her needs. Conferences are often held with other members of the professional team as well as with the patient's family, where the therapist discusses the individual's needs and progress.

As in most therapy, Music Therapists realize that progress may be slow, but even the slightest progress can mean a great deal to the patient. The reward some Music Therapists receive when they see a patient acting or feeling better is often as exciting to the therapist as a recital would be to a performance artist.

The object of music therapy is not to make a patient an accomplished musician or vocalist. It is, rather, through the medium of music, to improve the emotional, mental, and physical stability of the patient.

Salaries

Salaries for Music Therapists vary from job to job. Factors affecting salaries include experience, responsibilities, and education of the therapist. Other factors include the specific job and the size, prestige, and geographic location of the facility.

Therapists entering the field can expect to earn from $24,000 to $29,000 annually. Those working at larger facilities and who have more experience may command yearly salaries ranging from $27,000 to $50,000. Supervisory positions in the field of music therapy may offer annual earnings of $55,000 and up.

Employment Prospects

Employment prospects for Music Therapists are excellent. There are currently more positions than there are qualified individuals. Music Therapists work in a variety of settings, including hospitals, other health-care facilities, rehabilitation centers, nursing homes, extended-care facilities, schools, or independent expressive arts therapy centers. Opportunities are located throughout the country.

Advancement Prospects

Advancement prospects are good for Music Therapists who have the education, drive, and determination. Individuals climb the career ladder by locating a similar position in a more prestigious facility with increased responsibilities and earnings.

Another method of career advancement is for the Music Therapist to assume a supervisory or administrative position. One of the drawbacks of this career path for many is that it limits the contact the therapist has with patients.

The Music Therapist can also climb the career ladder by finding a position in research or by teaching at a university. There are some individuals who advance their careers by going into private practice or consulting.

Education and Training

The minimum educational requirement for a Music Therapist is a bachelor's degree in music therapy. Courses usually include music theory, voice studies, instrument lessons, psychology, sociology, and biology in addition to general liberal arts courses. Music Therapists who aspire to work in the public school system must also have a teaching degree.

Many positions require a master's degree. There are a great many colleges throughout the country that offer both an undergraduate and a postgraduate degree program in music therapy.

Music Therapists in most situations must be licensed in order to obtain employment.

Experience, Skills, and Personality Traits

Music Therapists obtain experience in a number of ways. In order to be licensed, individuals go through a six-month internship program. Many Music Therapists have also worked at health-care facilities or schools in part-time jobs or in voluntary positions to gain additional experience.

One of the most important personality traits a good Music Therapist must have is the ability to work with the handicapped and disabled. He or she must also have a great deal of patience. As noted previously, it often takes the Music Therapist a long time to see results. The Music Therapist must also be compassionate, empathetic, and emotionally stable to be successful.

Music Therapists must have the ability to play a musical instrument. Knowing how to play more than one is a plus as is the ability to sing in front of others. They must be able to teach others to play an instrument or sing. A good knowledge of all forms of music is essential.

Unions and Associations

Music Therapists may belong to the American Association for Music Therapy (AAMT). This organization provides valuable assistance to those in the field. It helps place qualified Music Therapists, does research and acts as liaison for colleges that offer music therapy programs.

Tips for Entry

1. Check with the college placement office for openings for Music Therapists. Many facilities or schools looking for people to fill positions send a list of openings to colleges and universities granting degrees in music therapy.
2. Contact both the National Association for Music Therapy, Inc. (NAMT) and the American Association for Music Therapy (AAMT) for registration and placement services.
3. Many positions for Music Therapists are available through the federal government. These civil service positions can be located through federal and state employment services.
4. Look under heading classifications of "Music Therapist," "Therapist," "Health Care," or "Expressive Arts Therapist" in the classified or display sections of newspapers.
5. Search the major job and employment sites on the Internet for job openings. Also, look for sites related to music or music therapy.

APPENDIXES

APPENDIX I
DEGREE AND NONDEGEE PROGRAMS

A. COLLEGES AND UNIVERSITIES OFFERING DRAMA AND THEATER ARTS PROGRAMS

Although a college degree does not guarantee a job in the theatrical field, many people feel that it is in their best interest to pursue an education beyond high school to gain knowledge, learn new skills, and make important contacts. As the theatrical and performing arts industries are competitive, a higher education may often give one person a competitive edge.

The following is a listing of some of the four-year schools granting majors and/or degrees in drama and theater arts. They are grouped by state. School names, addresses, phone numbers, Web addresses, and admissions e-mail addresses are included when available.

Inclusion or exclusion in this listing does not indicate the author endorses any one school or program over another. Use this list as a beginning. As colleges frequently change programs, be sure to check the newest copy of *Lovejoy's College Guide* (usually located in the reference section of libraries or in guidance or counseling centers) for current schools offering courses or giving degrees in this field.

Remember that there are also numerous two-year schools offering study in theater arts as well as four-year schools which have courses in theater but do not offer a degree or major in the field.

ALABAMA

Alabama State University
915 South Jackson Street
Montgomery, AL 36104
Phone: (334) 229-4291
http://www.alasu.edu

Auburn University
Auburn, AL 36849
Phone: (334) 844-4080
E-mail: admissions@auburn.edu
http://www.auburn.edu

Birmingham–Southern College
Box 549008
900 Arkadelphia Road
Birmingham, AL 35254
Phone: (205) 226-4696
E-mail: admission@bsc.edu
http://www.bsc.edu

Faulkner University
5345 Atlanta Highway
Montgomery, AL 36109
Phone: (334) 386-7200
Fax: (334) 386-7137
E-mail: admissions@faulkner.edu
http://www.faulkner.edu

Huntingdon College
1500 East Fairview Avenue
Montgomery, AL 36106
Phone: (334) 833-4497

Fax: (334) 833-4347
E-mail: admiss@huntingdon.edu
http://www.huntingdon.edu

Jacksonville State University
700 Pelham Road North
Jacksonville, AL 36265
Phone: (256) 782-5363
Fax: (256) 782-5291
E-mail: info@jsucc.jsu.edu
http://www.jsu.edu

Samford University
Birmingham, AL 35229
Phone: (205) 726-3673
http://www.samford.edu

Spring Hill College
4000 Dauphin Street
Mobile, AL 36608
Phone: (251) 380-3030
Fax: (251) 460-2186
E-mail: admit@shc.edu
http://www.shc.edu

Troy University
111 Adams Administration Building
Troy, AL 36082
Phone: (334) 670-3179
http://www.troy.edu

University of Alabama
Box 870132
Tuscaloosa, AL 35487

Phone: (205) 348-5666
E-mail: uaadmit@enroll.ua.edu
http://www.ua.edu

University of Alabama–Birmingham
1530 3rd Avenue South
Birmingham, AL 35294
Phone: (205) 934-8221
E-mail: undergradadmit@uab.edu
http://www.uab.edu

University of Mobile
P.O. Box 13220
Mobile, AL 36663
Phone: (251) 442-2287
Fax: (251) 442-2498
E-mail: adminfo@umobile.edu
http://www.umobile.edu

University of Montevallo
Montevallo, AL 35115
Phone: (205) 665-6030
E-mail: admissions@montevallo.edu
http://www.montevallo.edu

University of South Alabama
307 University Boulevard
Mobile, AL 36688
Phone: (251) 460-6141

ALASKA

University of Alaska Anchorage
P.O. Box 141629

Anchorage, AK 99514
Phone: (907) 786-1480
http://www.uaa.alaska.edu

University of Alaska Fairbanks
P.O. Box 757480
Fairbanks, AK 99775
Phone: (907) 474-7500
http://www.uaf.edu

ARKANSAS

Arkansas State University
P.O. Box 1630
State University, AR 72467
Phone: (870) 972-3024
Fax: (870) 910-8094
E-mail: admissions@astate.edu
http://www.astate.edu

Harding University
Box 12255
Searcy, AR 72149
Phone: (501) 279-4407
Fax: (501) 279-4129
E-mail: admissions@harding.edu
http://www.harding.edu

Henderson State University
1100 Henderson Street
P.O. Box 7560
Arkadelphia, AR 71999
Phone: (870) 230-5028
Fax: (870) 230-5066
E-mail: hardwrv@hsu.edu
http://www.hsu.edu

Hendrix College
1600 Washington Avenue
Conway, AR 72032
Phone: (501) 450-1362
Fax: (501) 450-3843
E-mail: adm@hendrix.edu
http://www.hendrix.edu

Lyon College
P.O. Box 2317
Batesville, AR 72503
Phone: (870) 698-4250
Fax: (870) 793-1791
E-mail: admissions@lyon.edu
http://www.lyon.edu

Ouachita Baptist University
Arkadelphia, AR 71998
Phone: (870) 245-5110
Fax: (870) 245-5500
E-mail: goodmand@obu.edu
http://www.obu.edu

**Southern Arkansas
    University–Magnolia**
P.O. Box 9382
Magnolia, AR 71754
Phone: (870) 235-4040
Fax: (870) 235-5005
E-mail: addanne@saumag.edu
http://www.saumag.edu

University of Arkansas
Fayetteville, AR 72701
Phone: (479) 575-5346
Fax: (479) 575-7515
E-mail: uofa@uark.edu
http://www.uark.edu

University of Arkansas at Fort Smith
5210 Grand Avenue
P.O. Box 3649
Fort Smith, AR 72913
Phone: (479) 788-7405
Fax: (479) 788-7016
E-mail: information@uafortsmith.edu
http://www.uafortsmith.edu

University of Arkansas at Little Rock
2801 South University Avenue
Little Rock, AR 72204
Phone: (501) 569-3127
Fax: (501) 569-8915
http://www.ualr.edu

University of Arkansas at Pine Bluff
Mail Slot 4981
1200 North University Drive
Pine Bluff, AR 71611
Phone: (870) 575-8487
Fax: (870) 543-8014
E-mail: fulton_e@uapb.edu
http://www.uapb.edu

University of the Ozarks
415 North College Avenue
Clarksville, AR 72830
Phone: (479) 979-1421
Fax: (479) 979-1355
E-mail: admiss@ozarks.edu
http://www.ozarks.edu

CALIFORNIA

California Baptist University
8432 Magnolia Avenue
Riverside, CA 92504
Phone: (951) 343-4212
Fax: (951) 343-4525
E-mail: admissions@calbaptist.edu
http://www.calbaptist.edu

California Institute of the Arts
24700 McBean Parkway
Valencia, CA 91355
Phone: (661) 255-1050
E-mail: admiss@calarts.edu
http://www.calarts.edu

California Lutheran
60 West Olsen Road #1350
Thousand Oaks, CA 91360
Phone: (805) 493-3135
Fax: (805) 493-3114
E-mail: admissions@callutheran.edu
http://www.callutheran.edu

**California State Polytechnic
    University–Pomona**
3801 West Temple Avenue
Pomona, CA 91768
Phone: (909) 869-3210
http://www.csupomona.edu

California State University–Bakersfield
9001 Stockdale Highway
Bakersfield, CA 93311
Phone: (805) 664-2160
E-mail: admissions@csub.edu
http://www.csub.edu

California State University–Chico
400 West First Street
Chico, CA 95929
Phone: (530) 898-4879
Fax: (530) 898-6456
E-mail: info@csuchico.edu
http://www.csuchico.edu

**California State University–Dominguez
    Hills**
1000 East Victoria Street
Carson, CA 90747
Phone: (800) 344-5484
Fax: (310) 217-6800
http://www.csudh.edu/soh

California State University–East Bay
25800 Carlos Bee Boulevard
Hayward, CA 94542
Phone: (510) 885-3248
Fax: (510) 885-3816
E-mail: adminfo@csuhayward.edu
http://www.csuhayward.edu

California State University–Fresno
5150 North Maple Avenue
Fresno, CA 93740
Phone: (559) 278-6115
Fax: (559) 278-4812
E-mail: donna_mills@csufresno.edu
http://www.csufresno.edu

California State University–Fullerton
P.O. Box 6900
800 North State College Boulevard
Fullerton, CA 92834
Phone: (714) 278-2350
http://www.fullerton.edu

**California State University–Long
  Beach**
1250 Bellflower Boulevard
Long Beach, CA 90840
Phone: (562) 985-4641
http://www.csulb.edu

**California State University–Los
  Angeles**
5151 State University Drive
Los Angeles, CA 90032
Phone: (323) 343-3839
E-mail: admission@calstatela.edu
http://www.calstatela.edu

**California State University–Monterey
  Bay**
Seaside, CA 93955
Phone: (831) 582-4093
Fax: (831) 582-3087
E-mail: moreinfo-
  prospective@csumb.edu

California State University–Northridge
18111 Nordhoff Street
Northridge, CA 91330
Phone: (818) 677-3777
Fax: (818) 677-3766
E-mail: admissions.records@csun.edu
http://www.csun.edu

California State University–Sacramento
6000 J Street
Sacramento, CA 95819
Phone: (916) 278-7362
Fax: (916) 278-5603
E-mail: admissions@csus.edu
http://www.csus.edu

Chapman University
One University Drive
Orange, CA 92866
Phone: (714) 997-6711
Fax: (714) 997-6713
E-mail: admit@chapman.edu
http://www.chapman.edu

Claremont McKenna College
890 Columbia Avenue
Claremont, CA 91711
Phone: (909) 621-8088
http://www.clarmontmckenna.edu

Concordia University
1530 Concordia West
Irvine, CA 92612
Phone: (949) 854-8002
Fax: (949) 854-6894
E-mail: admission@cui.edu
http://www.cui.edu

Humboldt State University
1 Harpst Street
Arcata, CA 95521
Phone: (707) 826-4402
Fax: (707) 826-6194
E-mail: hsuinfo@humboldt.edu
http://www.humboldt.edu

Loyola Marymount University
One LMU Drive
Los Angeles, CA 90045
Phone: (310) 338-2750
Fax: (310) 338-2797
http://www.lmu.edu

Notre Dame de Namur University
1500 Ralston Avenue
Belmont, CA 94002
Phone: (650) 508-3600
E-mail: admiss@ndnu.edu
http://www.ndnu.edu

Occidental College
1600 Campus Road
Los Angeles, CA 90041
Phone: (323) 259-2700
Fax: (323) 341-4875
E-mail: admission@oxy.edu
http://www.oxy.edu

Pepperdine University
24255 Pacific Coast Highway
Malibu, CA 90263
Phone: (310) 506-4392
Fax: (310) 506-4861
http://www.pepperdine.edu

Pitzer College
1050 North Mills Avenue
Claremont, CA 91711
Phone: (909) 621-8129
Fax: (909) 621-8770
E-mail: admission@pitzer.edu
http://www.pitzer.edu

Saint Mary's College of California
Moraga, CA 94575
Phone: (925) 631-4224
Fax: (925) 376-7193
E-mail: smcadmit@stmarys-ca.edu
http://www.stmarys-ca.edu

San Diego State University
5500 Campanile Drive
San Diego, CA 92182
Phone: (619) 594-6336
E-mail: admissions@sdsu.edu
http://www.sdsu.edu

San Francisco State University
1600 Holloway Avenue
San Francisco, CA 94132
Phone: (415) 338-1113
Fax: (415) 338-7196
E-mail: ugadmit@sfsu.edu
http://www.sfsu.edu

San Jose State University
One Washington Square
San Jose, CA 95192
Phone: (408) 283-7500
Fax: (408) 924-2050
E-mail: contact@sjsu.edu
http://www.sjsu.edu

Scripps College
1030 Columbia Avenue, P.B. 1265
Claremont, CA 91711
Phone: (909) 621-8149
Fax: (909) 607-7508
E-mail: admission@scrippscollege.edu
http://www.scrippscollege.edu

Sonoma State University
1801 East Cotati Avenue
Rohnert Park, CA 94928
Phone: (707) 664-2074
Fax: (707) 664-2060
E-mail: csumentor@sonoma.edu
http://www.sonoma.edu

Stanford University
520 Lasuen Mall
Stanford, CA 94305
Phone: (650) 723-2091
Fax: (650) 723-6050
E-mail: admission@stanford.edu
http://admission.stanford.edu

University of California–Berkeley
Berkeley, CA 94720
Phone: (510) 642-3175
Fax: (510) 642-7333
E-mail: ouars@uclink.berkeley.edu
http://www.berkeley.edu

University of California–Davis
Davis, CA 95616
Phone: (530) 752-2971
Fax: (530) 752-1280
E-mail: freshmanadmissions@ucdavis.edu
http://www.ucdavis.edu

University of California–Irvine
204 Administration
Irvine, CA 92697
Phone: (949) 824-6703
http://www.uci.edu

University of California–Los Angeles
405 Hilgard Avenue
Box 951436
Los Angeles, CA 90095
Phone: (310) 825-3101
E-mail: ugadm@saonet.ucla.edu
http://www.ucla.edu

University of California–Riverside
900 University Avenue
Riverside, CA 92521
Phone: (951) 827-4531
Fax: (951) 827-6344
E-mail: discover@ucr.edu
http://www.ucr.edu

University of California–San Diego
9500 Gilman Drive
La Jolla, CA 92093
Phone: (858) 534-4831
E-mail: admissionsinfo@ucsd.edu
http://www.ucsd.edu

University of California–Santa Barbara
Santa Barbara, CA 93106
Phone: (805) 893-2485
Fax: (805) 893-2676
E-mail: appinfo@sa.ucsb.edu
http://www.ucsb.edu

University of California–Santa Cruz
Santa Cruz, CA 95064
Phone: (831) 459-5779
Fax: (831) 459-4452
E-mail: admissions@ucsc.edu
http://www.ucsc.edu

University of La Verne
1950 Third Street
La Verne, CA 91750
Phone: (909) 392-2800
Fax: (909) 392-2714
E-mail: admissions@ulv.edu
http://www.ulv.edu

University of San Francisco
2130 Fulton Street
San Francisco, CA 94117
Phone: (415) 422-6563
Fax: (415) 422-2217
E-mail: admission@usfca.edu
http://www.usfca.edu

University of Southern California
Los Angeles, CA 90089
Phone: (213) 740-1111
E-mail: admitusc@usc.edu
http://www.usc.edu

University of the Pacific
Stockton, CA 95211
Phone: (209) 946-2211
E-mail: admissions@uop.edu
http://www.pacific.edu

Vanguard University of Southern California
55 Fair Drive
Costa Mesa, CA 92626
Phone: (714) 556-3610
Fax: (714) 966-5471
E-mail: admissions@vanguard.edu
http://www.vanguard.edu

Westmont College
955 La Paz Road
Santa Barbara, CA 93108
http://www.westmont.edu

Whittier College
P.O. Box 634
Whittier, CA 90608
Phone: (562) 907-4238
Fax: (562) 907-4870
E-mail: admission@whittier.edu
http://www.whittier.edu

Woodbury University
7500 Glenoaks Boulevard
Burbank, CA 91510
Phone: (818) 767-0888
E-mail: info@woodbury.edu
http://www.woodbury.edu

COLORADO

Adams State College
Alamosa, CO 81102
Phone: (719) 587-7712
Fax: (719) 587-7522
E-mail: ascadmit@adams.edu
http://www.adams.edu

Colorado Christian University
8787 West Alameda Avenue
Lakewood, CO 80226
Phone: (303) 963-3200
Fax: (303) 963-3201
E-mail: admission@ccu.edu
http://www.ccu.edu

Colorado State University
8020 Campus Delivery
Fort Collins, CO 80523
Phone: (970) 491-6909
http://admissions.colostate.edu

Fort Lewis College
1000 Rim Drive
Durango, CO 81301
Phone: (970) 247-7184
Fax: (970) 247-7179
E-mail: admission@fortlewis.edu
http://www.fortlewis.edu

Mesa State College
1100 North Avenue
Grand Junction, CO 81501
Phone: (970) 248-1875
Fax: (970) 248-1973
E-mail: admissions@mesastate.edu
http://www.mesastate.edu

Naropa University
2130 Arapahoe Avenue
Boulder, CO 80302
Phone: (303) 546-3572
Fax: (303) 546-3583
E-mail: admissions@naropa.edu
http://www.naropa.edu

University of Colorado at Boulder
Boulder, CO 80309
Phone: (303) 492-6301
http://www.colorado.edu

University of Colorado at Denver
Denver, CO 80217
Phone: (303) 556-2704
Fax: (303) 556-4838
E-mail: admissions@cudenver.edu
http://www.cudenver.edu

University of Denver
University Park
Denver, CO 80208
Phone: (303) 871-3125
Fax: (303) 871-3301
E-mail: admission@du.edu
http://www.du.edu

University of Northern Colorado
Greeley, CO 80639
Phone: (970) 351-2881
Fax: (970) 351-2984
E-mail: unc@mail.unco.edu
http://www.unco.edu

Western State College of Colorado
Gunnison, CO 81231
Phone: (800) 876-5309

E-mail: admiss@western.edu
http://www.western.edu

CONNECTICUT

Albertus Magnus College
700 Prospect Street
New Haven, CT 06511
Phone: (203) 773-8501
Fax: (203) 773-5248
E-mail: admissions@alburtus.edu
http://www.albertus.edu

Central Connecticut State University
1615 Stanley Street
New Britain, CT 06050
Phone: (860) 832-CCSU
E-mail: admissions@ccsu.edu
http://www.ccsu.edu

Connecticut College
270 Mohegan Avenue
New London, CT 06320
Phone: (860) 439-2200
Fax: (860) 439-4301
E-mail: admission@conncoll.edu
http://www.connecticutcollege.edu

Sacred Heart University
5151 Park Avenue
Fairfield, CT 06825
Phone: (203) 371-7880
E-mail: guastellek@sacredheart.edu
http://www.sacredheart.edu

Southern Connecticut State University
131 Farnham Avenue
New Haven, CT 06515
Phone: (203) 392-SCSU
http://www.southernCT.edu

Trinity College
Hartford, CT 06106-3100
Phone: (860) 297-2180
Fax: (860) 297-2287
E-mail: admissions.office@trincoll.edu
http://www.trincoll.edu

University of Connecticut
2131 Hillside Road, Box Unit 3088
Storrs, CT 06269
Phone: (860) 486-3137
E-mail: beahusky@uconn.edu
http://www.uconn.edu

University of Hartford
West Hartford, CT 06117
Phone: (860) 768-4296
Fax: (860) 768-4961

E-mail: admission@hartford.edu
http://admission.hartford.edu

Wesleyan University
70 Wyllys Avenue
Middletown, CT 06459
Phone: (860) 685-3000
Fax: (860) 685-3001
E-mail: admissions@wesleyan.edu
http://www.wesleyan.edu

Western Connecticut State University
181 White Street
Danbury, CT 06810
Phone: (203) 837-9000
E-mail: hallla@wcsu.edu
http://www.wcsu.edu

Yale University
New Haven, CT 06520
Phone: (203) 432-9316
E-mail: student.questions@yale.edu
http://www.yale.edu

DELAWARE

University of Delaware
Newark, DE 19716
Phone: (302) 831-8123
Fax: (302) 831-6905
E-mail: admissions@udel.edu
http://www.udel.edu

DISTRICT OF COLOMBIA

American University
4400 Massachusetts Avenue NW
Washington, D.C. 20016
Phone: (202) 885-6000
Fax: (202) 885-1025
E-mail: admissions@american.edu
http://admissions.american.edu

Catholic University of America
Washington, D.C. 20064
Phone: (202) 319-5305
Fax: (202) 319-6533
E-mail: cua-admissions@cua.edu
http://www.cua.edu

Gallaudet University
800 Florida Avenue NE
Washington, DC 20002
Phone: (202) 651-5750
Fax: (202) 651-5744
E-mail: admissions.studentvisits@
    gallaudet.edu
http://www.gallaudet.edu

George Washington University
2121 I Street NW
Suite 201
Washington, DC 20052
Phone: (202) 994-6040
E-mail: gwadm@gwu.edu
http://www.gwu.edu

Howard University
2400 Sixth Street NW
Washington, DC 20059
Phone: (202) 806-2763
E-mail: admission@howard.edu
http://www.howard.edu

University of the District of Columbia
4200 Connecticut Avenue NW
Washington, DC 20008
Phone: (202) 274-6200
http://www.udc.edu

FLORIDA

Barry University
11300 Northeast Second Avenue
Miami Shores, FL 33161
Phone: (305) 899-3100
Fax: (305) 899-2971
E-mail: admissions@mail.barry.edu
http://www.barry.edu

Eckerd College
4200 54th Avenue South
St. Petersburg, FL 33711
Phone: (727) 864-8331
Fax: (727)866-2304
E-mail: admissions@eckerd.edu
http://www.eckerd.edu

Flagler College
74 King Street
St. Augustine, FL 32084
Phone: (800) 304-4208
E-mail: admiss@flagler.edu
http://www.flagler.edu

**Florida Agricultural and Mechanical
    University**
Tallahassee, FL 32307
Phone: (850) 599-3796
E-mail: admissions@famu.edu
http://www.famu.edu

Florida Atlantic University
777 Glades Road
P.O. Box 3091
Boca Raton, FL 33431
Phone: (603) 535-2237
http://www.fau.edu

Florida International University
Miami, FL 33265
Phone: (305) 348-2363
Fax: (305) 348-3648
http://www.fiu.edu

Florida Southern College
111 Lake Hollingsworth Drive
Lakeland, FL 33801
Phone: (800) 274-4131
E-mail: fscadm@flsouthern.edu
http://www.flsouthern.edu

Florida State University
Tallahassee, FL 32306
Phone: (850) 644-6200
Fax: (850) 644-0197
E-mail: admissions@admin.fsu.edu
http://admissions.fsu.edu

Jacksonville University
2800 University Boulevard North
Jacksonville, FL 32211
Phone: (904) 256-7000
E-mail: admissions@ju.edu
http://www.ju.edu

Palm Beach Atlantic University
P.O. Box 24708
West Palm Beach, FL 33416
Phone: (561) 803-2000
E-mail: admit@pba.edu
http://www.pba.edu

Rollins College
1000 Holt Avenue
Winter Park, FL 32789
Phone: (407) 646-2161
Fax: (407) 646-1502
E-mail: admission@rollins.edu
http://www.rollins.edu

Stetson University
421 North Woodland Boulevard
DeLand, FL 32723
Phone: (386) 822-7100
Fax: (386) 822-7112
E-mail: admissions@stetson.edu
http://www.stetson.edu

University of Central Florida
Orlando, FL 32816
Phone: (407) 823-3000
E-mail: admission@mail.ucf.edu
http://www.ucf.edu

University of Florida
P.O. Box 114000
Gainesville, FL 32611

Phone: (352) 392-1365
E-mail: freshmen@ufl.edu
http://www.ufl.edu

University of Miami
P.O. Box 248025
1252 Memorial Drive
Coral Gables, FL 33146
Phone: (305) 284-4323
Fax: (305) 284-2507
E-mail: admission@miami.edu
http://www.miami.edu

University of South Florida
4202 East Fowler Avenue
Tampa, FL 33620
Phone: (813) 974-3350
Fax: (813) 974-9689
E-mail: http://www.usf.edu/askrocky
http://www.usf.edu

University of Tampa
401 West Kennedy Boulevard
Tampa, FL 33606
Phone: (813) 253-6211
Fax: (813) 254-4955
E-mail: admissions@ut.edu
http://www.ut.edu

University of West Florida
11000 University Parkway
Pensacola, FL 32514
Phone: (850) 474-2230
E-mail: admissions@uwf.edu
http://www.uwf.edu

GEORGIA

Agnes Scott College
141 East College Avenue
Decatur, GA 30030
Phone: (404) 471-6285
Fax: (404) 471-6414
E-mail: admission@agnesscott.edu
http://www.agnesscott.edu

Armstrong Atlantic State University
Savannah, GA 31419
Phone: (912) 925-5275
Fax: (912) 921-5462

Brenau University
The Women's College
One Centennial Circle
Gainesville, GA 30501
Phone: (770) 534-6100
E-mail: wcadmissions@lib.brenau.edu
http://www.brenau.edu

Clark Atlanta University
223 James P. Brawley Drive SW
Atlanta, GA 30314
Phone: (404) 880-6605
E-mail: admissions@panthernet.cau.edu
http://www.cau.edu

Clayton State University
5900 North Lee Street
Morrow, GA 30260
Phone: (770) 961-3500
Fax: (770) 961-3752
E-mail: csc-info@mail.clayton.edu
http://www.clayton.edu

Columbus State University
4225 University Avenue
Columbus, GA 31907
Phone: (706) 568-2035
Fax: (706) 568-5272
http://www.colstate.edu

Emory University
Atlanta, GA 30322
Phone: (404) 727-6036
E-mail: admiss@learnlink.emory.edu
http://www.emory.edu

Georgia College & State University
Milledgeville, GA 31061
Phone: (478) 445-1284
Fax: (478) 445-1914
E-mail: info@gcsu.edu
http://www.gcsu.edu

Georgia Southern University
Statesboro, GA 30460
Phone: (912) 681-5391
Fax: (912) 486-7240
E-mail: admissions@georgiasouthern.
edu
http://www.georgiasouthern.edu

Kennesaw State University
1000 Chastain Road
Kennesaw, GA 30144
Phone: (770) 423-6300
Fax: (770) 423-6541
E-mail: ksuadmit@kennesaw.edu
http://www.kennesaw.edu

LaGrange College
601 Broad Street
LaGrange, GA 30240
Phone: (706) 880-8005
Fax: (706) 880-8010
E-mail: admission@lagrange.edu
http://www.lagrange.edu

Macon State College
Macon, GA 31206
Phone: (478) 471-2800
Fax: (478) 471-5343

Mercer University
1400 Coleman Avenue
Macon, GA 31207
Phone: (478) 301-2650
E-mail: admissions@mercer.edu
http://www.mercer.edu

Morehouse College
830 Westview Drive SW
Atlanta, GA 30314
Phone: (404) 215-2632
E-mail: admissions@morehouse.edu
http://www.morehouse.edu

Paine College
1235 Fifteenth Street
Augusta, GA 30901
Phone: (706) 821-8320
http://www.paine.edu

Piedmont College
P.O. Box 10
165 Central Avenue
Demorest, GA 30535
Phone: (706) 776-0103
Fax: (706) 776-6635
http://www.piedmont.edu

Savannah College of Art and Design
P.O. Box 2072
Savannah, GA 31402
Phone: (912) 525-5100
Fax: (912) 525-5986
E-mail: admission@scad.edu
http://www.scad.edu

Shorter College
315 Shorter Avenue
Rome, GA 30165
Phone: (706) 233-7319
http://www.shorter.edu

Spelman College
Atlanta, GA 30314
Phone: (404) 681-3643
E-mail: admiss@spelman.edu
http://www.spelman.edu

University of West Georgia
Carrollton, GA 30118
Phone: (678) 839-4000
E-mail: admiss@westga.edu
http://www.westga.edu

University of Georgia
Athens, GA 30602
Phone: (706) 542-8776
Fax: (706) 542-1466
E-mail: undergrad@admissions.uga.edu
http://www.admissions.uga.edu

HAWAII

Brigham Young University–Hawaii
55-220 Kulanui Street
Laie, Oahu, HI 96762
Phone: (808) 293-3731
Fax: (808) 293-3741
E-mail: admissions@byuh.edu
http://www.byuh.edu

University of Hawaii at Manoa
2600 Campus Road
Honolulu, HI 96822
Phone: (808) 956-8975
Fax: (808) 956-4148
E-mail: ar-info@hawaii.edu
http://www.hawaii.edu

IDAHO

Boise State University
Boise, ID 83725
Phone: (208) 426-1177
E-mail: bsuinfo@boisestate.edu
http://www.boisestate.edu

College of Idaho
2112 Cleveland Boulevard
Caldwell, ID 83605
Phone: (208) 459-5305
Fax: (208) 459-5151
E-mail: admission@albertson.edu
http://www.albertson.edu

Idaho State University
741 South 7th
Pocatello, ID 83209
Phone: (208) 282-2477
Fax: (208) 282-4511
E-mail: info@isu.edu
http://www.isu.edu

University of Idaho
Moscow, ID 83844
Phone: (208) 885-6326
Fax: (208) 885-9119
http://www.uidaho.edu

ILLINOIS

Augustana College
639 38th Street
Rock Island, IL 61201

Phone: (309) 794-7341
Fax: (309) 794-7422
E-mail: admissions@augustana.edu
http://www.augustana.edu

Bradley University
1501 West Bradley Avenue
Peoria, IL 61625
Phone: (309) 677-1000
http://www.bradley.edu

Columbia College Chicago
600 South Michigan Avenue
Chicago, IL 60605
Phone: (312) 344-7130
Fax: (312) 344-8024
E-mail: admissions@colum.edu
http://www.colum.edu

Concordia University
7400 Augusta Street
River Forest, IL 60305
Phone: (708) 209-3100
Fax: (708) 209-3473
E-mail: crfadmis@curf.edu
http://www.curf.edu

DePaul University
1 East Tackson
Chicago, IL 60604
Phone: (312) 362-8000
E-mail: admitpu@depaul.edu
http://www.depaul.edu

Dominican University
7900 West Division
River Forest, IL 60305
Phone: (708) 524-6800
Fax: (708) 524-5990
E-mail: domadis@dom.edu
http://www.dom.edu

Eastern Illinois University
600 Lincoln Avenue
Charleston, IL 61920
Phone: (217) 581-2223
Fax: (217) 581-7060
E-mail: admissns@eiu.edu
http://www.eiu.edu

Elmhurst College
190 Prospect Avenue
Elmhurst, IL 60126
Phone: (630) 617-3400
Fax: (630) 617-5501
E-mail: admit@elmhurst.edu
http://www.elmhurst.edu

Eureka College
300 East College Avenue
Eureka, IL 61530

Phone: (309) 467-6530
E-mail: admissions@eureka.edu
http://www.eureka.edu

Greenville College
315 East College Avenue
Greenville, IL 62246
Phone: (618) 664-7100
Fax: (618) 664-9841
E-mail: admissions@greenville.edu
http://www.greenville.edu

Illinois College
1101 West College
Jacksonville, IL 62650
Phone: (217) 245-3030
Fax: (217) 245-3034
E-mail: admissions@ic.edu
http://www.ic.edu

Judson College
1151 North State Street
Elgin, IL 60123
Phone: (847) 695-2500
Fax: (847) 628-2526
E-mail: admission@judsoncollege.edu
http://www.judsoncollege.edu

Knox College
2 East South Street
Galesburg, IL 61401
Phone: (309) 341-7000
Fax: (309) 341-7070
E-mail: admission@knox.edu
http://www.knox.edu

Lewis University
One University Parkway
Romeoville, IL 60446
Phone: (800) 897-9000
E-mail: admissions@lewisu.edu
http://www.lewisu.edu

Loyola University Chicago
820 North Michigan Avenue
Chicago, IL 60611
Phone: (312) 915-6500
E-mail: admission@luc.edu
http://www.luc.edu

MacMurray College
447 East College Avenue
Jacksonville, IL 62650
Phone: (217) 479-7056
Fax: (217) 291-0702
http://www.mac.edu

Monmouth College
700 East Broadway
Monmouth, IL 61462

Phone: (309) 457-2136
Fax: (309) 457-2141
E-mail: admit@monm.edu
http://www.monm.edu

National-Louis University
122 South Michigan Avenue
Chicago, IL 60603
Phone: (888) NLU-TODAY
http://www.nl.edu

North Central College
30 North Brainard Street
Naperville, IL 60540
Phone: (630) 637-5800
Fax: (630) 637-5819
E-mail: ncadm@noctrl.edu
http://www.northcentralcollege.edu

North Park University
3225 West Foster Avenue
Chicago, IL 60625
Phone: (773) 244-5500
http://www.northpark.edu

Olivet Nazarene University
One University Avenue
Bourbonnais, IL 60914
Phone: (800) 648-1463
E-mail: admission@olivet.edu
http://www.olivet.edu

Principia College
One Maybeck Place
Elsah, IL 62028
Phone: (618) 374-5180
Fax: (618) 374-4000
E-mail: collegeadmissions@prin.edu
http://www.prin.edu

Rockford College
5050 East State Street
Rockford, IL 61108
Phone: (815) 226-4050
Fax: (815) 226-2822
E-mail: rcadmissions@rockford.edu
http://www.rockford.edu

Roosevelt University
430 South Michigan Avenue
Chicago, IL 60605
Phone: (877) APPLY-RU
Fax: (312) 341-3523
E-mail: applyRU@roosevelt.edu
http://www.roosevelt.edu

Southern Illinois University Carbondale
Carbondale, IL 62901
Phone: (618) 536-4405

Fax: (618) 453-3250
E-mail: joinsiuc@siu.edu
http://www.siuc.edu

University of Illinois at Chicago
Box 5220
Chicago, IL 60680
Phone: (312) 996-4350
Fax: (312) 413-7628
E-mail: uic.admit@uic.edu
http://www.uic.edu

University of Illinois at Urbana–Champaign
901 West Illinois
Urbana, IL 61801
Phone: (217) 333-0302
E-mail: admissions@oar.uiuc.edu
http://www.uiuc.edu

Western Illinois University
1 University Circle
Macomb, IL 61455
Phone: (309) 298-3157
http://www.wiu.edu

INDIANA

Anderson University
1100 East 5th Street
Anderson, IN 46012
Phone: (765) 641-4080
Fax: (765) 641-3851
E-mail: info@anderson.edu
http://www.anderson.edu

Ball State University
Muncie, IN 47306
Phone: (765) 285-8300
E-mail: askus@absu.edu
http://www.bsu.edu

Bethel College
1001 West McKinley Avenue
Mishawaka, IN 46545
Phone: (574) 257-3319
Fax: (574) 257-3335
E-mail: admissions@bethelcollege.edu
http://www.bethelcollege.edu

Butler University
4600 Sunset Avenue
Indianapolis, IN 46208
Phone: (317) 940-8100
Fax: (317) 940-8150
E-mail: admission@butler.edu
http://www.butler.edu

DePauw University
Greencastle, IN 46135

Phone: (765) 658-4006
Fax: (765) 658-4007
E-mail: admission@depauw.edu
http://www.depauw.edu

Earlham College
801 National Road West
Richmond, IN 47374
Phone: (765) 983-1600
Fax: (765) 983-1560
E-mail: admission@earlham.edu
http://www.earlham.edu

Goshen College
1700 South Main Street
Goshen, IN 46526
Phone: (574) 535-7535
Fax: (574) 535-7609
E-mail: admissions@goshen.edu
http://www.goshen.edu

Huntington College
2303 College Avenue
Huntington, IN 46750
Phone: (260) 356-6000
Fax: (260) 356-9448
E-mail: admissions@huntington.edu
http://www.huntington.edu

Indiana State University
Terre Haute, IN 47809
Phone: (812) 237-2121
E-mail: admisu@amber.indstate.edu
http://www.indstate.edu

Indiana University Bloomington
300 North Jordan Avenue
Bloomington, IN 47405
Phone: (812) 855-0661
Fax: (812) 855-5102
E-mail: iuadmit@indiana.edu
http://www.indiana.edu

Indiana University Northwest
3400 Broadway
Gary, IN 46408
Phone: (219) 980-6767
Fax: (219) 981-4219
E-mail: admit@iun.edu
http://www.iun.edu

Indiana University–Purdue University Fort Wayne
2101 East Coliseum Boulevard
Fort Wayne, IN 46805
Phone: (260) 481-6812
Fax: (260) 481-6880
E-mail: ipfwadms@ipfw.edu
http://www.ipfw.edu

Indiana University South Bend
1700 Mishawaka Avenue
P.O. Box 7111
South Bend, IN 46634
Phone: (574) 237-4480
Fax: (574) 237-4834
E-mail: admissio@iusb.edu
http://www.iusb.edu

Manchester College
North Manchester, IN 46962
Phone: (800) 852-3648
E-mail: admitinfo@manchester.edu
http://www.manchester.edu

Saint Mary's College
Notre Dame, IN 46556
Phone: (574) 284-4587
Fax: (574) 284-4841
E-mail: admission@saintmarys.edu
http://www.saintmarys.edu

Taylor University
236 West Reade Avenue
Upland, IN 46989
Phone: (765) 998-5511
E-mail: admissions_u@taylor.edu
http://www.taylor.edu

University of Evansville
1800 Lincoln Avenue
Evansville, IN 47722
Phone: (812) 479-2468
E-mail: admission@evansville.edu
http://www.evansville.edu

University of Indianapolis
1400 East Hanna Avenue
Indianapolis, IN 46227
Phone: (317) 788-3216
Fax: (317) 788-3300
E-mail: admission@uindy.edu
http://uindy.edu

Valparaiso University
Valparaiso, IN 46383
Phone: (219) 464-5011
Fax: (219) 464-6898
E-mail: undergrad.admissions@valpo.edu
http://www.valpo.edu

Wabash College
P.O. Box 352
Crawfordsville, IN 47933
Phone: (765) 361-6225
http://www.wabash.edu

IOWA

Briar Cliff University
3303 Rebecca Street

Sioux City, IA 51104
Phone: (712) 279-5200
Fax: (712) 279-1632
E-mail: admissions@briarcliff.edu
http://www.briarcliff.edu

Central College
812 University Street
Pella, IA 50219
Phone: (641) 628-7600
Fax: (641) 628-5316
E-mail: admissions@central.edu
http://www.central.edu

Clarke College
1550 Clarke Drive
Dubuque, IA 52001
Phone: (563) 588-6316
Fax: (319) 588-6789
E-mail: admissions@clarke.edu
http://www.clarke.edu

Coe College
1220 First Avenue NE
Cedar Rapids, IA 52402
Phone: (319) 399-8500
Fax: (319) 399-8816
E-mail: admission@coe.edu
http://www.coe.edu

Cornell College
600 First Street West
Mount Vernon, IA 52314
Phone: (319) 895-4477
E-mail: admissions@cornellcollege.edu
http://www.cornellcollege.edu

Dordt College
498 4th Avenue NE
Sioux Center, IA 51250
Phone: (712) 722-6080
Fax: (712) 722-1967
E-mail: admissions@dordt.edu
http://www.dordt.edu

Drake University
2507 University Avenue
Des Moines, IA 50311
Phone: (515) 271-3181
Fax: (515) 271-2831
http://www.choose.drake.edu

Franklin College
501 East Monroe Street
Franklin, IA 46131
Phone: (317) 738-806
Fax: (317) 738-8274
E-mail: admissions@franklincollege.edu
http://www.franklincollege.edu

Graceland University
1 University Place
Lamoni, IA 50140
Phone: (641) 784-5196
Fax: (641) 784-5480
E-mail: admissions@graceland.edu
http://www.graceland.edu

Grand View College
1200 Grandview Avenue
Des Moines, IA 50316
Phone: (515) 263-2810
Fax: (515) 263-2974
E-mail: admiss@gvc.edu
http://www.gvc.edu

Grinnell College
1103 Park Street
Grinnell, IA 50112
Phone: (641) 269-3600
E-mail: askgrin@grinnell.edu
http://www.grinnell.edu

Hanover College
P.O. Box 108
Hanover, IA 47243
Phone: (800) 213-2178
Fax: (812) 866-2164
E-mail: admission@hanover.edu
http://www.hanover.edu

Iowa State University of Science and Technology
Ames, IA 50011
Phone: (515) 294-3094
Fax: (515) 294-2592
E-mail: admissions@iastate.edu
http://www.iastate.edu

Morningside College
1501 Morningside Avenue
Sioux City, IA 51106
Phone: (712) 274-5111
E-mail: mscadm@morningside.edu
http://www.morningside.edu

Mount Mercy College
1330 Elmhurst Drive NE
Cedar Rapids, IA 52402
Phone: (319) 368-6460
E-mail: admission@mtmercy.edu
http://www.mtmercy.edu

St. Ambrose University
518 West Locust Street
Davenport, IA 52803
Phone: (563) 333-6300
E-mail: admit@sau.edu
http://www.sau.edu

Waldorf College
106 South 6th Street
Forest City, IA 50436
Phone: (641) 585-8119
Fax: (641) 585-8125
E-mail: admissions@waldorf.edu
http://www.waldorf.edu

KANSAS

Baker University
P.O. Box 65
Baldwin City, KS 66006
Phone: (800) 873-4282
E-mail: admission@bakeru.edu
http://www.bakeru.edu

Benedictine College
1020 North Second Street
Atchison, KS 66002
Phone: (913) 367-5340
E-mail: bcadmiss@benedictine.edu
http://www.benedictine.edu

Bethel College
300 East 27th Street
North Newton, KS 67117
Phone: (316) 283-2500
Fax: (316) 284-5870
E-mail: admissions@bethelks.edu
http://www.bethelks.edu

Emporia State University
1200 Commercial Street
Emporia, KS 66801
Phone: (620) 341-5465
Fax: (620) 341-5599
E-mail: go2esu@emporia.edu
http://www.emporia.edu

Kansas State University
119 Anderson Hall
Manhattan, KS 66506
Phone: (785) 532-6250
E-mail: kstate@k-state.edu
http://k-state.edu

Kansas Wesleyan University
100 East Claflin Avenue
Salina, KS 67401
Phone: (785) 829-5541
Fax: (785) 827-0927
E-mail: admissions@kwu.edu
http://www.kwu.edu

Ottawa University
1001 South Cedar #17
Ottawa, KS 66067
Phone: (785) 242-5200

Fax: (785) 242-7429
E-mail: admiss@ottawa.edu
http://www.ottawa.edu

Sterling College
125 West Cooper
P.O. Box 98
Sterling, KS 67579
Phone: (620) 278-4364
Fax: (620) 278-4416
E-mail: admissions@sterling.edu
http://www.sterling.edu

Washburn University
1700 SW College Avenue
Topeka, KS 66621
Phone: (785) 231-1010
Fax: (785) 231-1089
http://www.washburn.edu

Wichita State University
1845 North Fairmount
Wichita, KS 67260
Phone: (316) 978-3085
Fax: (316) 978-3174
E-mail: admissions@wichita.edu
http://www.wichita.edu

KENTUCKY

Berea College
Berea, KY 40404
Phone: (859) 985-3500
E-mail: admissions@berea.edu
http://www.berea.edu

Centre College
600 West Walnut Street
Danville, KY 40422
Phone: (859) 238-5350
Fax: (859) 238-5373
E-mail: admission@centre.edu
http://www.centre.edu

Cumberland College
6191 College Station Drive
Williamsburg, KY 40769
Phone: (606) 539-4241
E-mail: admiss@cumberlandcollege.edu
http://www.cumberlandcollege.edu

Eastern Kentucky University
521 Lancaster Avenue
Richmond, KY 40475
Phone: (859) 622-2106
Fax: (859) 622-8024
E-mail: admissions@eku.edu
http://www.eku.edu

Georgetown College
400 East College Street
Georgetown, KY 40324
Phone: (502) 863-8009
E-mail: admissions@georgetowncollege.
    edu
http://www.georgetowncollege.edu

Northern Kentucky University
Nunn Drive
Highland Heights, KY 41099
Phone: (859) 572-5220
E-mail: admitnku@nku.edu
http://www.nku.edu

Spalding University
851 South Fourth Street
Louisville, KY 40203
Phone: (502) 585-9911
Fax: (502) 992-2418
E-mail: admissions@spalding.edu
http://www.spalding.edu

Thomas More College
333 Thomas More Parkway
Crestview Hills, KY 41017
Phone: (859) 344-3332
E-mail: enroll@thomasmore.edu
http://www.thomasmore.edu

Transylvania University
300 North Broadway
Lexington, KY 40508
Phone: (859) 233-8242
E-mail: admissions@transy.edu
http://www.transy.edu

University of Kentucky
Lexington, KY 40506
Phone: (859) 257-2000
E-mail: admissio@uky.edu
http://www.uky.edu

University of Louisville
2211 South Brook
Louisville, KY 40292
Phone: (502) 852-6531
Fax: (502) 852-4776
E-mail: admitme@gwise.louisville.edu
http://www.louisville.edu

Western Kentucky University
1 Big Red Way
Bowling Green, KY 42101
Phone: (270) 745-2551
Fax: (270) 745-6133
E-mail: admission@wku.edu
http://www.wku.edu

LOUISIANA

Centenary College of Louisiana
2911 Centenary Boulevard
P.O. Box 41188
Shreveport, LA 71134
Phone: (318) 869-5134
Fax: (318) 869-5005
E-mail: egregory@centenary.edu
http://www.centenary.edu

Dillard University
2601 Gentilly Boulevard
New Orleans, LA 70122
Phone: (504) 816-4670
Fax: (504) 816-4895
E-mail: admissions@dillard.edu
http://www.dillard.edu

Grambling State University
100 Main Street
Grambling, LA 71245
Phone: (318) 274-6183
E-mail: admissions@gram.edu
http://www.gram.edu

Louisiana College
1140 College Drive
Pineville, LA 71359
Phone: (318) 487-7439
Fax: (318) 487-7550
E-mail: admissions@lacollege.edu
http://www.lacollege.edu

**Louisiana State University and
    Agricultural and Mechanical College**
Baton Rouge, LA 70803
Phone: (225) 578-1175
E-mail: admissions@lsu.edu
http://www.lsu.edu

Loyola University
6363 Saint Charles Avenue
New Orleans, LA 70118
Phone: (504) 865-3240
Fax: (504) 865-3383
E-mail: admit@loyno.edu
http://www.loyno.edu

McNeese State University
P.O. Box 92895
Lake Charles, LA 70609
Phone: (337) 475-5238
E-mail: info@mail.mcneese.edu
http://www.mcneese.edu

**Southern University and Agricultural
    and Mechanical College**
P.O. Box 9901
Baton Rouge, LA 70813

Phone: (225) 771-2430
Fax: (225) 771-2500

University of Louisiana at Lafayette
P.O. Box 44652
Lafayette, LA 70504
Phone: (800) 752-6553
E-mail: enroll@louisiana.edu
http://www.louisiana.edu

Tulane University
6823 Saint Charles Avenue
New Orleans, LA 70118
Phone: (504) 865-5731
Fax: (504) 862-8715
E-mail: undergrad.admission@tulane.edu
http://www.tulane.edu

MAINE

Bates College
Lewiston, ME 04240
Phone: (207) 786-6000
Fax: (207) 786-6025
E-mail: admissions@bates.edu
http://www.bates.edu

Bowdoin College
5000 College Station
Brunswick, ME 04011
Phone: (207) 725-3100
Fax: (207) 725-3101
E-mail: admissions@bowdoin.edu
http://www.bowdoin.edu

Colby College
4800 Mayflower Hill
Waterville, ME
Phone: (800) 723-3032
Fax: (207) 872-3474
E-mail: admissions@colby.edu
http://www.colby.edu

University of Maine
Orono, ME 04469
Phone: (207) 581-1561
Fax: (207) 581-1213
E-mail: um-admit@maine. edu
http://www.maine.edu

University of Maine at Farmington
246 Main Street
Farmington, ME 04938
Phone: (207) 778-7050
E-mail: umfadmit@mmaine.edu
http://www.umaine.farmington.edu

University of Maine at Machias
Machias, ME 04654
Phone (207) 255-1318

Fax: (207) 255-1363
E-mail: ummadmissions@maine.edu
http://www.maine.edu

MARYLAND

Frostburg State University
101 Braddock Road
Frostburg, MD 21532
Phone: (301) 687-4201
Fax: (301) 687-7074
E-mail: fsuadmission@frostburg.edu
http://www.frostburg.edu

Goucher College
1021 Dulaney Valley Road
Baltimore, MD 21204
Phone: (410) 337-6100
E-mail: admissions@goucher.edu
http://www.goucher. edu

McDaniel College
2 College Hill
Westminster, MD 21157
Phone: (410) 857-2230
E-mail: admissions@mcdaniel.edu
http://www.mcdaniel.edu

Morgan State University
1700 East Cold Spring Lane
Baltimore, MD 21251
Phone: (443) 885-3333
E-mail: admissions@morgan.edu
http://www.morgan.edu

Salisbury University
1200 Camden Avenue
Salisbury, MD 21801
Phone: (410) 543-6161
Fax: (410) 546-6016
E-mail: admissions@salisbury.edu
http://www.salisbury.edu

Towson University
8000 York Road
Towson, MD 21252
Phone: (410) 704-2113
http://www.townson.edu

University of Maryland
College Park, MD 20742
Phone: (301) 314-8385
Fax: (301) 314-9693
http://www.maryland.edu

Villa Julie College
1525 Greenspring Valley Road
Stevenson, MD 21153
Phone: (410) 486-7001
Fax: (443) 334-2600

E-mail: admissions@mail.vjc.edu
http://www.vjc.edu

Washington College
300 Washington Avenue
Chestertown, MD 21620
Phone: (410) 778-7700
http://www.washcoll.edu

MASSACHUSETTS

Amherst College
P.O. Box 5000
Amherst, MA 01002
Phone: (413) 542-2328
Fax: (413) 542-2040
E-mail: admission@amherst.edu
http://www.amherst.edu

Boston College
140 Commonwealth Avenue
Chestnut Hill, MA 02467
Phone: (617) 552-3100
Fax: (617) 552-0798
http://www.bc.edu

Boston Conservatory
8 The Fenway
Boston, MA 02215
Phone: (617) 912-9153
Fax: (617) 536-3176
E-mail: admissions@bostonconservatory.
   edu
http://www.bostonconservatory.edu

Boston University
121 Bay State Road
Boston, MA 02215
Phone: (617) 353-2300
E-mail: admissions@bu.edu
http://www.bu.edu

Brandeis University
415 South Street
Waltham, MA 02454
Phone: (781) 736-3500
E-mail: sendinfo@brandeis.edu
http://www.brandeis.edu

Bridgewater State College
131 Summer Street
Bridgewater, MA 02325
Phone: (508) 531-1237
Fax: (508) 531-1746
E-mail: admission@bridgew.edu
http://www.bridgew.edu

Eastern Nazarene College
23 East Elm Avenue
Quincy, MA 02170
Phone: (617) 745-3711

E-mail: admissions@enc.edu
http://www.enc.edu

Emerson College
120 Bolyston Street
Boston, MA 02116
Phone: (617) 824-8600
Fax: (617) 824-8609
E-mail: admission@emerson.edu
http://www.emerson.edu

Framingham State College
100 State Street
P.O. Box 9101
Framingham, MA 01701-9101
Phone: (508) 626-4500
E-mail: admiss@frc.mass.edu
http://www.frc.edu

Hampshire College
893 West Street
Amherst, MA 01002
Phone: (413) 559-5471
E-mail: admissions@hampshire.edu
http://www.hampshire.edu

Harvard University
8 Garden Street
Cambridge, MA 02138
Phone: (617) 495-1551
E-mail: college@fas.harvard.edu
http://www.harvard.edu

Massachusetts College of Liberal Arts
375 Church Street
North Adams, MA 01247
Phone: (413) 662-5410
Fax: (413) 662-5179
E-mail: admissions@mcla.edu
http://www.mcla.edu

Mount Holyoke College
50 College Street
South Hadley, MA 01075
Phone: (413) 538-2023
Fax: (413) 538-2409
E-mail: admission@mtholyoke.edu
http://www.mtholyoke.edu

Northeastern University
150 Richards Hall
360 Huntington Avenue
Boston, MA 02115
Phone: (617) 373-2200
E-mail: admissions@neu.edu
http://www.neu.edu

Regis College
235 Wellesley Street
Weston, MA 02493
Phone: (781) 768-7100

E-mail: admission@regiscollege.edu
http://www.regiscollege.edu

Salem State College
352 Lafayette Street
Salem, MA 01970
Phone: (978) 542-6200
Fax: (978) 542-6893
E-mail: admissions@salemstate.edu
http://www.salemstate.edu

Simon's Rock College of Bard
84 Alford Road
Great Barrington, MA 01230
Phone: (413) 528-7312
Fax: (413) 528-7334
http://www.simons-rock.edu

Smith College
Northampton, MA 01063
Phone: (413) 585-2500
Fax: (413) 585-2527
http://www.smith.edu

Suffolk University
8 Ashburton Place
Boston, MA 02108
Phone: (617) 573-8749
Fax: (617) 742-4291
E-mail: admission@suffolk.edu
http://www.suffolk.edu

Tufts University
Medford, MA 02155
Phone: (617) 627-3170
Fax: (617) 627-3860
http://www.tufts.edu

University of Massachusetts–Amherst
37 Mather Drive
Amherst, MA 01003
Phone: (413) 545-0222
Fax: (413) 545-4312
http://www.umass.edu

University of Massachusetts–Boston
100 Morrissey Boulevard
Boston, MA 02125
Phone: (617) 287-6000
Fax: (617) 287-5999
http://www.umb.edu

Wellesley College
106 Central Street
Wellesley, MA 02481
Phone: (781) 283-2270
Fax: (781) 283-3678
http://www.wellesley.edu

Wheaton College
Norton, MA 02766
Phone: (508) 286-8251
E-mail: admission@wheatoncollege.edu
http://www.wheatoncollege.edu

MICHIGAN

Adrian College
110 South Madison Street
Adrian, MI 49221
Phone: (517) 265-5161
E-mail: admissions@adrian.edu
http://www.adrian.edu

Albion College
611 East Porter Street
Albion, MI 49224
Phone: (800) 858-6770
Fax: (517) 629-0569
E-mail: admissions@albion.edu
http://www.albion.edu

Alma College
614 West Superior Street
Alma, MI 48801
Phone: (800) 321-ALMA
E-mail: admissions@alma.edu
http://www.alma.edu

Calvin College
3201 Burton Street SE
Grand Rapids, MI 49546
Phone: (616) 526-6106
Fax: (616) 526-6777
E-mail: admissions@calvin.edu
http://www.calvin.edu

Central Michigan University
Mt. Pleasant, MI 48859
Phone: (989) 774-3076
Fax: (989) 774-7267
E-mail: cmuadmit@cmich.edu
http://www.cmich.edu

Eastern Michigan University
401 Pierce Hall
Ypsilanti, MI 48197
Phone: (734) 487-3060
Fax: (734) 487-6559
E-mail: admissions@emich.edu
http://www.emich.edu

Grand Valley State University
1 Campus Drive
Allendale, MI 49401
Phone: (616) 331-2025
E-mail: go2gvsu@gvsu.edu
http://www.gvsu.edu

Hillsdale College
33 East College Street
Hillsdale, MI 49242
Phone: (517) 607-2327
E-mail: admissions@hillsdale.edu
http://www.hillsdale.edu

Hope College
69 East 10th Street
P.O. Box 9000
Holland, MI 49422
Phone: (616) 395-7850
E-mail: admissions@hope.edu
http://www.hope.edu

Kalamazoo College
1200 Academy Street
Kalamazoo, MI 49006
Phone: (269) 337-7166
E-mail: admission@kzoo.edu
http://www.kzoo.edu

Michigan State University
250 Administration Building
East Lansing, MI 48824
Phone: (517) 355-8332
Fax: (517) 353-1647
E-mail: admis@msu.edu
http://www.msu.edu

Northern Michigan University
1401 Presque Isle Avenue
Marquette, MI 49855
Phone: (906) 227-2650
Fax: (906) 227-1747
E-mail: admiss@nmu.edu
http://www.nmu.edu

Oakland University
2200 North Squirrel Road
Rochester, MI 48309
Phone: (248) 370-3360
E-mail: ouinfo@oakland.edu
http://www.oakland.edu

Saginaw Valley State University
7400 Bay Road
University Center, MI 48710
Phone: (989) 964-4200
Fax: (517) 790-0180
E-mail: admissions@svsu.edu
http://www.svsu.edu

Siena Heights University
1247 East Siena Heights Drive
Adrian, MI 49221
Phone: (517) 264-7180
Fax: (517) 264-7745
E-mail: admissions@sienahts.edu
http://www.sienahts.edu

University of Detroit–Mercy
P.O. Box 19900
Detroit, MI 48219
Phone: (313) 993-1245
Fax: (313) 993-3326
E-mail: admissions@udmercy.edu
http://www.udmercy.edu

University of Michigan
515 East Jefferson
Ann Arbor, MI 48109
Phone: (734) 764-7433
Fax: (734) 936-0740
E-mail: ugadmiss@umich.edu
http://www.umich.edu

University of Michigan–Flint
303 East Kearsley Street
Flint, MI 48502
Phone: (810) 762-3434
Fax: (810) 762-3272
E-mail: admissions@umflint.edu
http://www.umflint.edu

Western Michigan University
1903 West Michigan Avenue
Kalamazoo, MI 49008
Phone: (269) 387-2000

MINNESOTA

Augsburg College
2211 Riverside Avenue
Minneapolis, MN 55454
Phone: (612) 330-1001
Fax: (612) 330-1590
E-mail: admissions@augsburg.edu
http://www.augsburg.edu

Bemidji State University
1500 Birchmont Drive NE
Bemidji, MN 56601
Phone: (218) 755-2040
Fax: (218) 755-2074
E-mail: admissions@bemidjistate.edu
http://www.bemidjistate.edu

Bethel University
3900 Bethel Drive
St. Paul, MN 55112
Phone: (651) 638-6242
Fax: (651) 635-1490
E-mail: BUadmissions-cas@bethel.edu
http://www.bethel.edu

Concordia College
901 8th Street South
Moorhead, MN 56562
Phone: (218) 299-3004

Fax: (218) 299-3947
E-mail: admissions@cord.edu
http://www.cord.edu

Concordia University–St. Paul
275 Syndicate North
St. Paul, MN 55104
Phone: (651) 641-8230
Fax: (651) 659-0207
E-mail: admiss@csp.edu
http://www.csp.edu

Gustavus Adolphus College
800 West College Avenue
Saint Peter, MN 56082
Phone: (507) 933-7676
Fax: (507) 933-7474
E-mail: admission@gustavus.edu
http://www.gustavus.edu

Hamline University
1536 Hewitt
St. Paul, MN 55104
Phone: (651) 523-2207
Fax: (651) 523-2458
E-mail: cla-admis@gw.hamline.edu
http://www.hamline.edu

Macalester College
1600 Grand Avenue
St. Paul, MN 55105
Phone: (651) 696-6357
Fax: (651) 696-6724
E-mail: admissions@macalester.edu
http://www.macalaster.edu

Metropolitan State University
700 East 7th Street
St. Paul, MN 55106
Phone: (651) 793-1303
Fax: (651) 793-1310
E-mail: admissionsmetro@metrostate.
   edu
http://www.metrostate.edu

Minnesota State University–Mankato
122 Taylor Center
Mankato, MN 56001
Phone: (507) 389-6670
Fax: (507) 389-1511
E-mail: admissions@mnsu.edu
http://www.mnsu.edu

Minnesota State University–Moorhead
Moorhead, MN 56563
Phone: (218) 477-2161
Fax: (218) 236-2168
http://www.mnstate.edu

North Central University
910 Elliot Avenue
Minneapolis, MN 55404
Phone: (612) 343-4460
Fax: (612) 343-4146
E-mail: admissions@northcentral.edu
http://www.northcentral.edu

Northwestern College
3003 Snelling Avenue North
St. Paul, MN 55113
Phone: (651) 631-5209
Fax: (651) 631-5680
E-mail: admissions@nwc.edu
http://www.nwc.edu

St. Cloud State University
720 4th Avenue South
St. Cloud, MN 56301
Phone: (320) 308-2244
Fax: (320) 308-2243
E-mail: scsu4u@stcloudstate.edu
http://www.stcloudstate.edu

Saint Mary's University of Minnesota
700 Terrace Heights
Winona, MN 55987
Phone: (507) 457-1700
Fax: (507) 457-1722
E-mail: admissions@smumn.edu
http://www.smumn.edu

Southwest Minnesota State University
1501 State Street
Marshall, MN 56258
Phone: (507) 537-6286
Fax: (507) 537-7154
E-mail: shearerr@southwest.msus.edu
http://www.southwest.msus.edu

University of Minnesota–Duluth
1117 University Drive
Duluth, MN 55812
Phone: (218) 726-7171
Fax: (218) 726-7040
E-mail: umdadmis@d.umn.edu
http://www.d.umn.edu

University of Minnesota–Morris
600 East 4th Street
Morris, MN 56267
Phone: (320) 539-6035
Fax: (320) 589-1673
E-mail: admissions@mrs.umn.edu
http://www.mrs.umn.edu

University of Minnesota–Twin Cities Campus
240 Williamson Hall
Minneapolis, MN 55455

Phone: (612) 625-2008
Fax: (612) 626-1693
E-mail: admissions@tc.umn.edu
http://www.tc.umn.edu

Winona State University
P.O. Box 5838
Winona, MN 55987
Phone: (507) 457-5100
Fax: (507) 457-5620
E-mail: admissions@winona.edu
http://www.winona.edu

MISSISSIPPI

Belhaven College
150 Peachtree Street
Jackson, MS 39202
Phone: (601) 968-5940
Fax: (601) 968-8946
E-mail: admissions@belhaven.edu
http://www.belhaven.edu

Blue Mountain College
P.O. Box 160
Blue Mountain, MS 38610
Phone: (662) 685-4161 Ext. 176
E-mail: admissions@bmc.edu
http://www.bmc.edu

Delta State University
1003 West Sunflower
Cleveland, MS 38733
Phone: (662) 846-4658
Fax: (662) 846-4684
E-mail: admissions@deltastate.edu
http://www.deltastate.edu

Mississippi State University
P.O. Box 6305
Mississippi State, MS 39762
Phone: (662) 325-2224
Fax: (662) 325-7360
E-mail: admit@admissions.msstate.edu
http://www.msstate.edu

Mississippi University for Women
P.O. Box 1613
Columbus, MS 39701
Phone: (601) 329-7106
Fax: (601) 241-7481
E-mail: admissions@muw.edu
http://www.muw.edu

William Carey College
498 Tuscan Avenue
Hattiesburg, MS 39401
Phone: (601) 318-6051
E-mail: admissions@wmcarey.edu
http://www.wmcarey.edu

MISSOURI

Central Missouri State University
1401 Ward Edwards
Warrensburg, MO 64093
Phone: (660) 543-4170
E-mail: admit@cmsuvmb.cmsu.edu
http://www.cmsu.edu

College of the Ozarks
P.O. Box 1
Point Lookout, MO 65726
Phone: (417) 334-6411
Fax: (417) 335-2618
E-mail: admiss4@cofo.edu
http://www.cofo.edu

Culver-Stockton College
One College Hill
Canton, MO 63435
Phone: (800) 537-1883
E-mail: enrollment@culver.edu
http://www.culver.edu

Drury University
900 North Benton
Springfield, MO 65802
Phone: (417) 873-7205
Fax: (417) 866-3873
E-mail: druryad@drury.edu
http://www.drury.edu

Fontbonne University
6800 Wydown Boulevard
St. Louis, MO 63105
Phone: (314) 889-1400
Fax: (314) 719-8021
E-mail: pmusen@fontbonne.edu
http://www.fontbonne.edu

Lindenwood University
209 South Kingshighway
St. Charles, MO 63301
Phone: (636) 949-4949
Fax: (636) 949-4989
http://www.lindenwood.edu

Missouri Southern State University
3950 East Newman Road
Joplin, MO 64801
Phone: (417) 781-6778
Fax: (417) 659-4429
E-mail: admissions@mssu.edu
http://www.mssu.edu

Missouri Valley College
500 East College Street
Marshall, MO 65340
Phone: (660) 831-4000
E-mail: admissions@moval.edu
http://www.moval.edu

Northwest Missouri State University
800 University Drive
Maryville, MO 64468
Phone: (660) 562-1146
Fax: (660) 562-1121
E-mail: admissions@acad.nwmissouri.edu
http://www.nwmissouri.edu

Rockhurst University
1100 Rockhurst Road
Kansas City, MO 64110
Phone: (816) 501-4100
Fax: (816) 501-4241
E-mail: admission@rockhurst.edu
http://www.rockhurst.edu

Southwest Missouri State University
901 South National
Springfield, MO 65804
Phone: (417) 836-5517
E-mail: smuinfo@smsu.edu
http://www.smsu.edu

Stephens College
1200 East Broadway
Columbia, MO 65215
Phone: (573) 876-7207
Fax: (573) 876-7237
E-mail: apply@stephens.edu
http://www.stephens.edu

Truman State University
100 East Normal
Kirksville, MO 63501
Phone: (660) 785-4114
Fax: (660) 785-7456
E-mail: admissions@truman.edu
http://www.truman.edu

University of Missouri–Kansas City
5100 Rockhill Road
Kansas City, MO 64110
Phone: (816) 235-1111
Fax: (816) 235-5544
E-mail: admit@umkc.edu
http://www.umkc.edu

William Jewell College
500 College Hill
Liberty, MO 64068
Phone: (816) 781-7700
Fax: (816) 415-5040
E-mail: admission@william.jewell.edu
http://www.william.jewell.edu

William Woods University
1 University Avenue
Fulton, MO 65251
Phone: (573) 592-4221
http://www.williamwoods.edu

MONTANA

Carroll College
1601 North Benton Avenue
Helena, MT 59625
Phone: (406) 447-4384
E-mail: admit@carroll.edu
http://www.carroll.edu

Montana State University–Billings
1500 University Drive
Billings, MT 59101
Phone: (406) 657-2158
Fax: (406) 657-2302
E-mail: admissions@msubillings.edu
http://www.msubillings.edu

Rocky Mountain College
1511 Poly Drive
Billings, MT 59102
Phone: (406) 657-1026
Fax: (406) 259-9751
E-mail: admissions@rocky.edu
http://www.rocky.edu

University of Montana–Missoula
32 Campus Drive
Missoula, MT 59812
Phone: (406) 243-6266
Fax: (406) 243-5711
http://www.umt.edu

University of Montana–Western
710 South Atlantic Street
Dillon, MT 59725
Phone: (406) 683-7331
Fax: (406) 683-7493
E-mail: admissions@umwestern.edu
http://www.umwestern.edu

NEBRASKA

Chadron State College
1000 Main Street
Chadron, NE 69337
E-mail: inquire@csc.edu
http://www.csc.edu

Concordia University
800 North Columbia Avenue
Seward, NE 68434
Phone: (402) 643-7233
Fax: (402) 643-4073
E-mail: admiss@cune.edu
http://www.cune.edu

Creighton University
2500 California Plaza
Omaha, NE 68178

Phone: (402) 280-2703
Fax: (402) 280-2685
E-mail: admissions@creighton.edu
http://www.creighton.edu

Hastings College
710 North Turner Avenue
Hastings, NE 68901
Phone: (402) 461-7320
Fax: (402) 461-7490
http://www.hasting.edu

Midland Lutheran College
Fremont, NE 68025
Phone: (402) 941-6504
Fax: (402) 941-6513
E-mail: admissions@admin.mlc.edu
http://www.mlc.edu

Nebraska Wesleyan University
5000 Saint Paul Avenue
Lincoln, NE 68504
Phone: (402) 465-2218
Fax: (402) 465-2177
E-mail: admissions@nebrwesleyan.edu
http://www.nebrwesleyan.edu

University of Nebraska at Kearney
905 West 25th Street
Kearney, NE 68849
Phone: (308) 865-8702
Fax: (308) 865-8987
E-mail: admissionsug@unk.edu
http://www.unk.edu

University of Nebraska–Lincoln
313 North 13th Street
Lincoln, NE 68588
Phone: (402) 472-2023
Fax: (402) 472-0670
E-mail: admissions@unl.edu
http://www.unl.edu

University of Nebraska at Omaha
6001 Dodge Street
Omaha, NE 68182
Phone: (402) 554-2416
Fax: (402) 554-3472
http://www.unomaha.edu

Wayne State College
1111 Main Street
Wayne, NE 68787
Phone: (402) 375-7234
Fax: (402) 375-7204
E-mail: admit1@wsc.edu
http://www.wsc.edu

NEW HAMPSHIRE

Dartmouth College
Hanover, NH 03755
Phone: (603) 646-2875
E-mail: admissions.office@dartmouth.edu
http://www.dartmouth.edu

Franklin Pierce College
20 College Road
Rindge, NH 03461
Phone: (603) 899-4050
Fax: (603) 899-4394
E-mail: admissions@fpc.edu
http://www.fpc.edu

Keene State College
229 Main Street
Keene, NH 03435
Phone: (603) 358-2276
Fax: (603) 358-2767
E-mail: admissions@keene.edu
http://www.keene.edu

New England College
26 Bridge Street
Henniker, NH 03242
Phone: (800) 521-7642
Fax: (603) 428-3155
E-mail: admission@nec.edu
http://www.nec.edu

Plymouth State University
17 High Street
Plymouth, NH 03264
Phone: (603) 535-2237
Fax: (603) 535-2714
http://www.plymouth.edu

University of New Hampshire
4 Garrison Avenue
Durham, NH 03801
Phone: (603) 862-1360
Fax: (603) 862-0077
http://www.unh.edu

NEW JERSEY

Bloomfield College
467 Franklin Street
Bloomfield, NJ 07003
Phone: (973) 748-9000
Fax: (973) 748-0916
E-mail: admission@bloomfield.edu
http://www.bloomfield.edu

Drew University
36 Madison Avenue
Madison, NJ 07940

Phone: (973) 408-3739
Fax: (973) 408-3068
http://www.drew.edu

Fairleigh Dickinson University
1000 River Road
Teaneck, NJ 07666
Phone: (800) FDU-8803
http://www.fdu.edu

Kean University
1000 Morris Avenue
Union, NJ 07083
Phone: (908) 737-7100
Fax: (908) 737-7105
E-mail: admitme@kean.edu
http://www.kean.edu

Montclair State University
Upper Montclair, NJ 07043
Phone: (800) 331-9205
http://www.montclair.edu

Ramapo College of New Jersey
505 Ramapo Valley Road
Mahwah, NJ 07430
Phone: (201) 684-7300
E-mail: admissions@ramapo.edu
http://www.ramapo.edu

Rowan University
201 Mullica Hill Road
Glassboro, NJ 08028
Phone: (856) 256-4200
E-mail: admissions@rowan.edu
http://www.rowan.edu

Rutgers–Camden Branch
406 Penn Street
Camden, NJ 08102
Phone: (856) 225-6133
E-mail: camden@ugadm.rutgers.edu
http://www.camden.rutgers.edu

Rutgers–Newark Branch
249 University Avenue
Newark, NJ 07102
Phone: (973) 353-5205
E-mail: newarkadmission@ugadm.
    rutgers.edu
http://www.newark.rutgers.edu

Rutgers–New Brunswick Branch
65 Davidson Road
Piscataway, NJ 08854
Phone: (732) 932-INFO
E-mail: admissions@ugadm.rutgers.edu
http://nbp.rutgers.edu

Seton Hall University
400 South Orange Avenue
South Orange, NJ 07079
Phone: (800) THE-HALL
E-mail: thehall@shu.edu
http://www.shu.edu

Thomas Edison State College
101 West State Street
Trenton, NJ 08608
Phone: (888) 442-8372
Fax: (609) 984-8447
E-mail: info@tesc.edu
http://www.tesc.edu

**William Paterson University of New
    Jersey**
Wayne, NJ 07470
Phone: (973) 720-2125
E-mail: admissions@wpunj.edu
http://www.wpunj.edu

NEW MEXICO

College of Santa Fe
1600 St. Michael's Drive
Santa Fe, NM 87505
Phone: (505) 473-6133
Fax: (505) 473-6127
http://www.csf.edu

College of the Southwest
6610 Lovington Highway
Hobbs, NM 88240
Phone: (505) 392-6563
Fax: (505) 392-6006
http://www.csw.edu

New Mexico State University
Box 30001
Las Cruces, NM 88003
Phone: (505) 646-3121
E-mail: admission@nmsu.edu
http://www.nmsu.edu

University of New Mexico
P.O. Box 4895
Albuquerque, NM 87196
Phone: (505) 277-2446
Fax: (505) 277-6686
E-mail: apply@unm.edu
http://www.unm.edu

NEW YORK

Adelphi University
P.O. Box 701
Garden City, NY 11530
Phone: (800) ADELPHI

E-mail: admissions@adelphi.edu
http://www.adelphi.edu

Alfred University
1 Saxon Drive
Alfred, NY 14802
Phone: (607) 871-2115
Fax: (607) 871-2198
E-mail: admwww@alfred.edu
http://www.alfred.edu

Barnard College
3009 Broadway
New York, NY 10027
Phone: (212) 854-2014
Fax: (212) 854-6220
E-mail: admissions@barnard.edu
http://www.barnard.edu

Binghamton University
P.O. Box 6000
Binghamton, NY 13902
Phone: (607) 777-2171
E-mail: admit@binghamton.edu
http://www.binghamton.edu

Briarcliffe College
10 Lake Street
Patchogue, NY 11772
Phone: (866) 235-5207
Fax: (631) 654-5082
E-mail: info@bcl.edu
http://www.briarcliffe.edu

Buffalo State College
1300 Elmwood Avenue
Buffalo, NY 14222
Phone: (716) 878-4017
Fax: (716) 878-6100
E-mail: admissions@buffalostate.edu
http://www.buffalostate.edu

Cazenovia College
22 Sullivan Street
Cazenovia, NY 13035
Phone: (315) 655-7208
Fax: (315) 655-4860
E-mail: admission@cazenovia.edu
http://www.cazenovia.edu

Colgate University
13 Oak Drive
Hamilton, NY 13346
Phone: (315) 228-7401
E-mail: admission@mail.colgate.edu
http://www.colgate.edu

College at Oneonta
State University of New York
Ravine Parkway

Oneonta, NY 13820
Phone: (607) 436-2524
Fax: (607) 436-3074
E-mail: admissions@oneonta.edu
http://www.oneonta.edu

College of Staten Island
City University of New York
2800 Victory Boulevard
Staten Island, NY 10314
Phone: (718) 982-2010
E-mail: admissions@mail.csi.cuny.edu
http://www.csi.cuny.edu

Columbia University
1130 Amsterdam Avenue
New York, NY 10027
Phone: (212) 854-2522
Fax: (212) 854-1209
http://www.columbia.edu

**The Cooper Union for the
    Advancement of Science and Art**
30 Cooper Square
New York, NY 10003
Phone: (212) 353-4120
Fax: (212) 353-4342
E-mail: admission@cooper.edu
http://www.cooper.edu

Cornell University
410 Thurston Avenue
Ithaca, NY 14850
Phone: (607) 255-5241
E-mail: admissions@cornell.edu
http://www.cornell.edu

Elmira College
One Park Place
Elmira, NY 14901
Phone: (800) 935-6472
E-mail: admissions@elmira.edu
http://www.elmira.edu

Five Towns College
305 North Service Road
Dix Hills, NY 11746
Phone: (631) 424-7000
Fax: (631) 656-2172
E-mail: admissions@ftc.edu
http://www.ftc.edu

Fordham University
441 East Fordham Road
New York, NY 10458
Phone: (800) 367-3426
E-mail: enroll@fordham.edu
http://www.fordham.edu

Fredonia
State University of New York
280 Central Avenue
Fredonia, NY 14063
Phone: (716) 673-3251
http://www.fredonia.edu

Geneseo
State University of New York College
1 College Circle
Geneseo, NY 14454
Phone: (585) 245-5571
Fax: (585) 245-5550
E-mail: admissions@geneseo.edu
http://www.geneseo.edu

Hamilton College
198 College Hill Road
Clinton, NY 13323
Phone: (315) 859-4421
Fax: (315) 859-4457
http://www.hamilton.edu

Hartwick College
One Hartwick Drive
Oneonta, NY 13820
Phone: (607) 431-4150
E-mail: admissions@hartwick.edu
http://www.hartwick.edu

Hobart and William Smith Colleges
629 South Main Street
Geneva, NY 14456
Phone: (800) 245-0100
E-mail: admissions@hws.edu
http://www.hws.edu

Hofstra University
Hempstead, NY 11549
Phone: (516) 463-6700
Fax: (516) 463-5100
http://www.hofstra.edu

Hunter College
City University of New York
695 Park Avenue
New York, NY 10021
Phone: (212) 772-4490
Fax: (212) 650-3336
E-mail: admission@hunter.cuny.edu
http://www.hunter.cuny.edu

Iona College
715 North Avenue
New Rochelle, NY 10801
Phone: (914) 633-2502
Fax: (914) 637-2778
E-mail: admission@iona.edu
http://www.iona.edu

Ithaca College
100 Job Hall
Ithaca, NY 14850
Phone: (607) 274-3124
Fax: (607) 274-1900
E-mail: admission@ithaca.edu
http://www.ithaca.edu

Le Moyne College
1419 Salt Springs Road
Syracuse, NY 13214
Phone: (315) 445-4300
E-mail: admission@lemoyne.edu
http://www.lemoyne.edu

**Long Island University–C.W. Post
    Campus**
720 Northern Boulevard
Brookville, NY 11548
Phone: (516) 299-2900
Fax: (516) 299-2137
E-mail: enroll@cwpost.liu.edu
http://www.cwpost.liu.edu

Marist College
3399 North Road
Poughkeepsie, NY 12601
Phone: (845) 575-3226
E-mail: admission@marist.edu
http://www.marist.edu

**Marymount College of Fordham
    University**
100 Marymount Avenue
Tarrytown, NY 10591
Phone: (914) 332-8295
Fax: (914) 332-7442
E-mail: mcenroll@fordham.edu
http://www.marymt.edu

The New School
65 West 12th Street
New York, NY 10011
Phone: (212) 229-5600
Fax: (212) 229-5355
http://www.newschool.edu

New York University
22 Washington Square North
New York, NY 10011
Phone: (212) 998-4500
http://www.nyu.edu

Oswego
State University of New York
7060 Route 104
Oswego, NY 13126
Phone: (315) 312-2250
Fax: (315) 312-3260
http://www.oswego.edu

Plattsburgh State University
101 Broad Street
Plattsburgh, NY 12901
Phone: (518) 564-2040
E-mail: admissions@plattsburgh.edu
http://www.plattsburgh.edu

Potsdam
State University of New York College
44 Pierrepont Avenue
Potsdam, NY 13676
Phone: (315) 267-2180
E-mail: admissions@potsdam.edu
http://www.potsdam.edu

Purchase College
State University of New York
735 Anderson Hill Road
Purchase, NY 10577
Phone: (914) 251-6300
Fax: (914) 251-6314
E-mail: admissn@purchase.edu
http://www.purchase.edu

Queens College
City University of New York
65-30 Kissena Boulevard
Flushing, NY 11367
Phone: (718) 997-5600
E-mail: admissions@qc.edu
http://www.qc.edu

Russell Sage College
45 Ferry Street
Troy, NY 12180
Phone: (518) 244-2444
Fax: (518) 244-6880
E-mail: rscadm@sage.edu

St. Bonaventure University
3261 West State Road
St. Bonaventure, NY 14778
Phone: (716) 375-2400
E-mail: admission@sbu.edu
http://www.sbu.edu

St. Lawrence University
23 Romoda Drive
Canton, NY 13617
Phone: (315) 229-5261
E-mail: admission@stlawu.edu
http://www.stlawu.edu

Sarah Lawrence College
1 Mead Way
Bronxville, NY 10708
Phone: (914) 395-2510
Fax: (914) 395-2515
E-mail: slcadmit@sarahlawrence.edu
http://www.sarahlawrence.edu

Skidmore College
815 North Broadway
Saratoga Springs, NY 12866
Phone: (518) 580-5570
E-mail: admission@skidmore.edu
http://www.skidmore.edu

Stony Brook University
Stony Brook, NY 11794
Phone: (631) 632-6868
Fax: (631) 632-9898
E-mail: enroll@stonybrook.edu
http://www.stonybrook.edu

Syracuse University
Syracuse, NY 13244
Phone: (315) 443-3611
http://www.syracuse.edu

University at Albany
State University of New York
1400 Washington Avenue
Albany, NY 12222
Phone: (518) 442-5435
E-mail: ugadmissions@albany.edu
http://www.albany.edu

University at Buffalo
State University of New York
17 Capen Hall
Buffalo, NY 14260
Phone: (716) 645-6900
E-mail: ub-admissions@buffalo.edu
http://www.buffalo.edu

Vassar College
124 Raymond Avenue
Poughkeepsie, NY 12604
Phone: (845) 437-7300
Fax: (845) 437-7063
E-mail: admissions@vassar.edu
http://www.vassar.edu

Wells College
Aurora, NY 13026
Phone: (800) 952-9355
E-mail: admissions@wells.edu
http://www.wells.edu

NORTH CAROLINA

Appalachian State University
Boone, NC 28608
Phone: (828) 262-2120
Fax: (828) 262-3296
E-mail: admissions@appstate.edu
http://www.appstate.edu

Barton College
Box 5000
Wilson, NC 27893

Phone: (252) 399-6317
Fax: (252) 399-6572
E-mail: enroll@barton.edu
http://www.barton.edu

Brevard College
400 North Broad Street
Brevard, NC 28712
Phone: (800) 527-9090
E-mail: admission@brevard.edu
http://www.brevard.edu

Catawba College
2300 West Inness Street
Salisbury, NC 28144
Phone: (704) 637-4402
E-mail: admissions@catawba.edu
http://www.catawba.edu

Campbell University
P.O. Box 546
Buies Creek, NC 27506
Phone: (910) 893-1320
E-mail: adm@mailcenter.campbell.edu
http://www.campbell.edu

Davidson College
Box 7156
Davidson, NC 28035
Phone: (704) 894-2230
E-mail: admission@davidson.edu
http://www.davidson.edu

Duke University
Durham, NC 27708
Phone: (919) 684-3214
Fax: (919) 681-8941
http://www.duke.edu

East Carolina University
200 Prospect Street
Greenville, NC 27858
Phone: (252) 328-6640
Fax: (252) 328-6945
E-mail: admis@mail.ecu.edu
http://www.ecu.edu

Elon University
Elon, NC 27244
Phone: (336) 278-3566
E-mail: admissions@elon.edu
http://www.elon.edu

Fayetteville State University
1200 Murchison Road
Fayetteville, NC 28301
Phone: (910) 486-1371
http://www.uncfsu.edu

Gardner-Webb University
Boiling Springs, NC 28017
Phone: (704) 406-4GWU
http://www.gardner-webb.edu

Greensboro College
815 West Market Street
Greensboro, NC 27401
Phone: (800) 346-8226
E-mail: admissions@gborocollege.edu
http://www.gborocollege.edu

Guilford College
5800 West Friendly Avenue
Greensboro, NC 27410
Phone: (336) 316-2100
E-mail: admission@guilford.edu
http://www.guilford.edu

High Point University
833 Montlieu Avenue
High Point, NC 27262
Phone: (336) 841-9216
E-mail: admiss@highpoint.edu
http://www.highpoint.edu

Lees-McRae College
P.O. Box 128
Banner Elk, NC 28604
Phone: (828) 898-3432
Fax: (828) 898-8707
E-mail: admissions@lmc.edu
http://www.lmc.edu

Lenoir-Rhyne College
P.O. Box 7227
Hickory, NC 28603
Phone: (828) 328-7300
Fax: (828) 328-7378
E-mail: admission@lrc.edu
http://www.lrc.edu

Mars Hill College
100 Athletic Street
Mars Hill, NC 28754
Phone: (828) 689-1201
Fax: (828) 689-1473
E-mail: admissions@mhc.edu
http://www.mhc.edu

Meredith College
3800 Hillsborough Street
Raleigh, NC 27607
Phone: (919) 760-8581
Fax: (919) 760-2348
E-mail: admissions@meredith.edu
http://www.meredith.edu

North Carolina Agricultural and Technical State University
1601 East Market Street
Greensboro, NC 27411
Phone: (336) 334-7946
http://www.ncat.edu

North Carolina Central University
P.O. Box 19717
Durham, NC 27707
Phone: (919) 530-6298
Fax: (919) 530-7625
E-mail: admissions@nccu.edu
http://www.nccu.edu

North Carolina School of the Arts
1533 South Main Street
P.O. Box 12189
Winston-Salem, NC 27127
Phone: (336) 770-3290
Fax: (336) 770-3370
E-mail: admissions@ncarts.edu
http://www.ncarts.edu

Saint Augustine's College
1315 Oakwood Avenue
Raleigh, NC 27610
Phone: (919) 516-4016
E-mail: admissions@st-aug.edu

University of North Carolina at Asheville
One University Heights
Asheville, NC 28804
Phone: (828) 251-6481
Fax: (828) 251-6482
E-mail: admissions@unca.edu
http://www.unca.edu

University of North Carolina at Chapel Hill
Chapel Hill, NC 27599
Phone: (919) 966-3621
Fax: (919) 962-3045
E-mail: uadm@email.unc.edu
http://www.unc.edu

University of North Carolina at Greensboro
123 Mossman
P.O. Box 26170
Greensboro, NC 27402
Phone: (336) 334-5243
Fax: (336) 334-5036
E-mail: undergrad_admissions@ uncg.edu
http://www.uncg.edu

University of North Carolina at Pembroke
One University Drive
Pembroke, NC 28372
Phone: (910) 521-6262
Fax: (910) 521-6497
E-mail: admissions@uncp.edu
http://www.uncp.edu

University of North Carolina at Wilmington
601 South College Road
Wilmington, NC 28403
Phone: (910) 962-4198
Fax: (910) 962-3038
E-mail: admissions@uncwil.edu
http://www.uncwil.edu

Western Carolina University
Cullowhee, NC 28723
Phone: (828) 227-7317
Fax: (828) 227-7319
E-mail: admiss@wcu.edu
http://www.poweryourmind.com

NEW HAMPSHIRE

Franklin Pierce College
20 College Road
Rindge, NH 03461
Phone: (603) 899-4050
Fax: (603) 899-4394
E-mail: admissions@fpc.edu
http://www.fpc.edu

New England College
26 Bridge Street
Henniker, NH 03242
Phone: (800) 521-7642
Fax: (603) 428-3155
E-mail: admission@nec.edu
http://www.nec.edu

University of New Hampshire
4 Garrison Avenue
Durham, NH 03801
Phone: (603) 862-1360
Fax: (603) 862-0077
http://www.unh.edu

NEVADA

University of Nevada–Las Vegas
4505 Maryland Parkway
Las Vegas, NV 89154
Phone: (702) 895-3011
Fax: (702) 774-8008
http://www.unlv.edu

University of Nevada–Reno
Reno, Nevada 89557
Phone: (775) 784-4700
E-mail: asknevada@unr.edu
http://www.unr.edu

NORTH DAKOTA

Dickinson State University
21 Campus Drive
Dickinson, ND 58601
Phone: (701) 483-2175
E-mail: dsu.hawks@dickinsonstate.edu
http://www.dickinsonstate.edu

Jamestown College
6081 College Lane
Jamestown, ND 58405
Phone: (701) 252-3467
Fax: (701) 253-4318
E-mail: admissions@jc.edu
http://www.jc.edu

North Dakota State University
P.O. Box 5454
Fargo, ND 58105
Phone: (701) 231-8643
Fax: (701) 231-8802
E-mail: ndsu.admission@ndsu.edu
http://www.ndsu.edu

University of North Dakota
P.O. Box 8135
Grand Forks, ND 58202
Phone: (701) 777-3821
Fax: (701) 777-2721
E-mail: enrollment_services@mail.und.
    nodak.edu
http://www.und.edu

OHIO

Antioch College
795 Livermore Street
Yellow Springs, OH 45387
Phone: (937) 769-1100
Fax: (937) 769-1111
E-mail: admissions@antioch-college.edu
http://www.antioch-college.edu

Ashland University
401 College Avenue
Ashland, OH 44805
Phone: (419) 289-5052
Fax: (419) 289-5999
E-mail: enrollme@ashland.edu
http://www.ashland.edu

Baldwin-Wallace College
275 Eastland Road
Berea, OH 44017
Phone: (440) 826-2222
Fax: (440) 826-3830
E-mail: info@bw.edu
http://www.bw.edu

Bowling Green State University
110 Mcfall Center
Bowling Green, OH 43403
Phone: (419) 372-BGSU
E-mail: choosebgsu@bgnet.bgsu.edu
http://www.bgsu.edu

Capital University
1 College and Main
Columbus, OH 43209
Phone: (614) 236-6101
Fax: (614) 236-6926
E-mail: admissions@capital.edu
http://www.capital.edu

Case Western Reserve University
10900 Euclid Avenue
Cleveland, OH 44106
Phone: (216) 368-4450
E-mail: admission@case.edu
http://www.case.edu

Cedarville University
251 North Main Street
Cedarville, OH 45314
Phone: (800) 233-2784
E-mail: admissions@cedarville.edu
http://www.cedarville.edu

Cleveland State University
1983 East 24th Street
Cleveland, OH 44115
Phone: (216) 523-5139
Fax: (216) 687-9210
E-mail: admissions@csuohio.edu
http://www.csuohio.edu

College of Wooster
1189 Beall Avenue
Wooster, OH 44691
Phone: (330) 263-2000
Fax: (330) 263-2621
E-mail: admissions@wooster.edu
http://www.wooster.edu

Denison University
100 South Road
Granville, OH 43023
Phone: (740) 587-6276
E-mail: admissions@denison.edu
http://www.denison.edu

Heidelberg College
310 East Market Street
Tiffin, OH 44883
Phone: (419) 448-2330
Fax: (419) 448-2334
E-mail: adminfo@heidelberg.edu
http://www.heidelberg.edu

Kent State University
P.O. Box 5190
Kent, OH 44242
Phone: (330) 672-2444
E-mail: kentadm@kent.edu
http://www.kent.edu

Lake Erie College
391 West Washington Street
Painesville, OH 44077
Phone: (440) 375-7050
E-mail: admissions@lcc.cdu
http://www.lec.edu

Marietta College
215 Fifth Street
Marietta, OH 45750
Phone: (800) 331-7896
E-mail: admit@marietta.edu
http://www.marietta.edu

Mount Union College
1972 Clark Avenue
Alliance, OH 44601
Phone: (330) 823-2590
E-mail: admissn@muc.edu
http://www.muc.edu

Oberlin College
173 West Lorain Street
Oberlin, OH 44074
Phone: (440) 775-8411
E-mail: college.admissions@oberlin.
    edu
http://www.osu.edu

Ohio State University
154 West 12th Avenue
Columbus, OH 43210
Phone: (614) 247-6281
Fax: (614) 292-4818
E-mail: askabuckeye@osu.edu
http://www.osu.edu

Ohio University
618 Sandosky Street
Athens, OH 45701
Phone: (740) 593-4100
E-mail: admissions.freshmen@ohiou.
    edu
http://www.ohiou.edu

Ohio Wesleyan University
618 Sandosky Street
Delaware, OH 43015
Phone: (800) 922-8953
Fax: (740) 368-3314
E-mail: owadmit@owu.edu
http://www.owu.edu

Shawnee State University
940 Second Street
Portsmouth, OH 45662
Phone: (740) 351-4-SSU
Fax: (740) 351-3111
E-mail: to_ssu@shawnee.edu
http://www.shawnee.edu

University of Akron
277 East Buchtel Avenue
Akron, OH 44325
Phone: (330) 972-6425
Fax: (330) 972-7022
E-mail: admissions@uakron.edu
http://www.uakron.edu

University of Cincinnati
P.O. Box 210091
Cincinnati, OH 45221
Phone: (513) 556-1100
Fax: (513) 556-1105
E-mail: admissions@uc.edu
http://www.uc.edu

University of Dayton
300 College Park
Dayton, OH 45469
Phone: (937) 229-4411
E-mail: admission@udayton.edu
http://www.udayton.edu

University of Findlay
1000 North Main Street
Findlay, OH 45840
Phone: (419) 434-4732
E-mail: admissions@findlay.edu
http://www.findlay.edu

University of Rio Grande
Rio Grande, OH 45674
Phone: (740) 245-7208
Fax: (740) 245-7260
http://www.rio.edu

University of Toledo
2801 West Bancroft
Toledo, OH 43606
Phone: (419) 530-5728
Fax: (419) 530-5872
E-mail: enroll@utnet.utoledo.edu
http://www.utoledo.edu

Wilmington College
251 Ludovic Street
Wilmington, OH 45177
Phone: (937) 382-6661
Fax: (937) 382-7077
E-mail: admission@wilmington.edu
http://www.wilmington.edu

Wittenberg University
Springfield, OH 45501
Phone: (937) 327-6314
E-mail: admission@wittenberg.edu
http://www.wittenberg.edu

Wright State University
Dayton, OH 45435
Phone: (937) 775-5700
E-mail: admission@wright.edu
http://www.wright.edu

OKLAHOMA

Bacone College
2299 Old Bacone Road
Muskogee, OK 74403
Phone: (918) 781-7340
Fax: (918) 781-7416
E-mail: admissions@bacone.edu
http://www.bacone.edu

Langston University
P.O. Box 728
Langston, OK 73120
Phone: (405) 466-2984
http://www.lunet.edu

Northeastern State University
601 North Grand
Tahlequah, OK 74464
Phone: (918) 456-5511
Fax: (918) 458-2342
E-mail: nsuadmis@nsuok.edu
http://www.nsuok.edu

Oklahoma City University
2501 North Blackwelder
Oklahoma City, OK 73106
Phone: (405) 521-5050
E-mail: uadmissions@okcu.edu
http://www.okcu.edu

Oklahoma State University
Stillwater, OK 74078
Phone: (405) 744-6858
Fax: (405) 744-5285
E-mail: admit@okstate.edu
http://www.okstate.edu

Oral Roberts University
7777 South Lewis Avenue
Tulsa, OK 74171
Phone: (918) 495-6518
Fax: (918) 495-6222
E-mail: admissions@oru.edu
http://www.oru.edu

Southeastern Oklahoma State University
1405 North 4th Avenue
Durant, OK 74701
Phone: (580) 745-2060
Fax: (580) 745-7502
E-mail: admissions@sosu.edu
http://www.sosu.edu

University of Oklahoma
1000 Asp Avenue
Norman, OK 73019
Phone: (405) 325-2151
Fax: (405) 325-7124
E-mail: admrec@ou.edu
http://www.ou.edu

University of Science and Arts of Oklahoma
1727 West Alabama
Chickasha, OK 73018
Phone: (405) 574-1212
Fax: (405) 574-1220
http://www.usao.edu

University of Tulsa
600 South College Avenue
Tulsa, OK 74104
Phone: (918) 631-2307
Fax: (918) 631-5003
E-mail: admission@utulsa.edu
http://www.utulsa.edu

OREGON

Concordia University
2811 Northeast Holman Street
Portland, OR 97211
Phone: (503) 280-8501
Fax: (503) 280-8531
E-mail: admissions@cu-portland.edu
http://www.cu-portland.edu

Eastern Oregon University
One University Boulevard
La Grande, OR 97850
Phone: (800) 452-8639
Fax: (541) 962-3418
E-mail: admission@eou.edu
http://www.eou.edu

Lewis & Clark College
0615 Southwest Palatine Hill Road
Portland, OR 97219
Phone: (503) 768-7040
Fax: (503) 768-7055
E-mail: admissions@lclark.edu
http://www.lclark.edu

Linfield College
900 Southeast Baker Street
McMinnville, OR 97128
Phone: (503) 883-2213
Fax: (503) 883-2472
E-mail: admission@linfield.edu
http://www.linfield.edu

Oregon State University
104 Kerr Administration Building
Corvallis, OR 97331
Phone: (800) 291-4192
Fax: (541) 737-2482
E-mail: osuadmit@oregonstate.edu
http://www.oregonstate.edu

Pacific University
2043 College Way
Forest Grove, OR 97116
Phone: (503) 352-2218
E-mail: admissions@pacificu.edu
http://www.pacificu.edu

Portland State University
P.O. Box 751
Portland, OR 97207
Phone: (503) 725-3511
Fax: (503) 725-5525
E-mail: admissions@pdx.edu
http://www.pdx.edu

Reed College
3203 Southeast Woodstock Boulevard
Portland, OR 97202
Phone: (503) 777-7511
Fax: (503) 777-7553
E-mail: admission@reed.edu
http://www.reed.edu

Southern Oregon University
1250 Siskiyou Boulevard
Ashland, OR 97520
Phone: (541) 552-6411
E-mail: admission@sou.edu
http://www.sou.edu

University of Oregon
Eugene, OR 97403
Phone: (541) 346-3201
http://www.uoregon.edu

University of Portland
5000 North Willamette Boulevard
Portland, OR 97203
Phone: (503) 943-7147
Fax: (503) 943-7315
E-mail: admissio@up.edu
http://www.up.edu

Willamette University
900 State Street
Salem, OR 97301
Phone: (877) LIB-ARTS
Fax: (503) 375-5363
E-mail: libarts@willamette.edu
http://www.willamette.edu

PENNSYLVANIA

Albright College
13th and Bern Streets
P.O. Box 15234
Reading, PA 19612
Phone: (610) 921-7512
E-mail: albright@alb.edu
http://www.alb.edu

Allegheny College
520 North Main Street
Meadville, PA 16335
Phone: (814) 332-4351
E-mail: admissions@allegheny.edu
http://www.allegheny.edu

Arcadia University
450 South Easton Road
Glenside, PA 19038
Phone: (215) 572-2910
E-mail: admisadmiss@arcadia.edu
http://www.arcadia.edu

Bloomsburg University of Pennsylvania
104 Student Services Center
Bloomsburg, PA 17815
Phone: (570) 389-4316
E-mail: buadmiss@bloomu.edu
http://www.bloomu.edu

Bucknell University
Moore Avenue
Lewisburg, PA 17837
Phone: (570) 577-1101
Fax: (570) 577-3538
E-mail: admissions@bucknell.edu
http://www.bucknell.edu

California University of Pennsylvania
250 University Avenue
California, PA 15419
Phone: (724) 938-4404

E-mail: inquiry@cup.edu
http://www.cup.edu

Carnegie Mellon University
5000 Forbes Avenue
Pittsburgh, PA 15213
Phone: (412) 268-2082
Fax: (412) 268-7838
E-mail: rgraduate-
    admissions@andrew.cmu.edu
http://www.andrew.cmu.edu

Cedar Crest College
100 College Drive
Allentown, PA 18104
Phone: (800) 360-1222
Fax: (610) 606-4647
E-mail: cccadmis@cedarcrest.edu
http://www.cedarcrest.edu

Chatham College
Woodland Road
Pittsburgh, PA 15232
Phone: (412) 365-1290
Fax: (412) 365-1609
E-mail: admissions@chatham.edu
http://www.chatham.edu

Cheyney University of Pennsylvania
1837 University Circle
P.O. Box 200
Cheyney, PA 19319
Phone: (610) 399-2275
http://www.cheyney.edu

Clarion University of Pennsylvania
840 Wood Street
Clarion, PA 16214
Phone: (814) 393-2306
E-mail: admissions@clarion.edu
http://www.clarion.edu

Drexel University
3141 Chestnut Streets
Philadelphia, PA 19104
Phone: (800) 2-DREXEL
http://www.drexel.edu

Duquesne University
600 Forbes Avenue
Pittsburgh, PA 15282
Phone: (412) 396-5000
Fax: (412) 396-5644
E-mail: admissions@duq.edu
http://www.duq.edu

Edinboro University of Pennsylvania
Edinboro, PA 16444
Phone: (814) 732-2761

Fax: (814) 732-2420
http://www.edinboro.edu

Gannon University
109 University Square
Erie, PA 16541
Phone: (814) 871-7240
Fax: (814) 871-5803
E-mail: admissions@gannon.edu
http://www.gannon.edu

Indiana University of Pennsylvania
1011 South Drive
Indiana, PA 15705
Phone: (724) 357-2230
Fax: (724) 357-6281
E-mail: admissions-inquiry@iup.edu
http://www.iup.edu

King's College
133 North River Street
Wilkes-Barre, PA 18711
Phone: (570) 208-5858
E-mail: admissions@kings.edu
http://www.kings.edu

Kutztown University of Pennsylvania
P.O. Box 730
Kutztown, PA 19530
Phone: (610) 683-4000
E-mail: admission@kutztown.edu
http://www.kutztown.edu

Lehigh University
27 Memorial Drive West
Bethlehem, PA 18015
Phone: (610) 758-3100
Fax: (610) 758-4361
E-mail: admissions@lehigh.edu
http://www.lehigh.edu

Lock Haven University of Pennsylvania
Lock Haven, PA 17745
Phone: (570) 893-2027
E-mail: admissions@lhup.edu
http://www.lhup.edu

Messiah College
One College Avenue
Grantham, PA 17027
Phone: (717) 691-6000
Fax: (717) 796-5374
E-mail: admiss@messiah.edu
http://www.messiah.edu

Penn State Abington
1600 Woodland Road
Abington, PA 19001
Phone: (215) 881-7600

Fax: (215) 881-7655
http://www.abington.psu.edu

**Penn State–Berks and Lehigh Valley
    Campuses**
Tulpehocken Road
P.O. Box 7009
Reading, PA 19610
Phone: (814) 865-5471
Fax: (610) 396-6077
E-mail: admissionsbk@psu.edu
http://www.bklv.psu.edu

**Penn State Erie–The Behrend
    College**
5091 Station Road
Erie, PA 16563
Phone: (814) 898-6100
E-mail: behrend.admissions@psu.edu
http://www.pserie.psu.edu

Penn State–University Park Campus
201 Shields Building
Box 3000
University Park, PA 16804
Phone: (814) 865-5471
Fax: (814) 863-7590
E-mail: admissions@psu.edu
http://www.psu.edu

Point Park University
201 Wood Street
Pittsburgh, PA 15222
Phone: (412) 392-3430
Fax: (412) 392-3902
http://www.ppc.edu

Seton Hill University
Seton Hill Drive
Greensburg, PA 15601
Phone: (724) 838-4255
Fax: (724) 830-1294
E-mail: admit@setonhill.edu
http://www.setonhill.edu

Slippery Rock University
1 Morrow Way
Slippery Rock, PA 16057
Phone: (724) 738-2015
E-mail: asktherock@sru.edu
http://www.sru.edu

Susquehanna University
514 University Avenue
Selinsgrove, PA 17870
Phone: (570) 372-4260
Fax: (570) 372-2722
E-mail: suadmiss@susqu.edu
http://www.susqu.edu

Temple University
1801 North Broad Street
Philadelphia, PA 19122
Phone: (215) 204-7200
E-mail: tuadm@temple.edu
http://www.temple.edu

University of Pennsylvania
3451 Walnut Street
Philadelphia, PA 19104
Phone: (215) 898-7507
http://www.upenn.edu

University of Pittsburgh
4227 Fifth Avenue
Pittsburgh, PA 15260
Phone: (412) 624-7488
Fax: (412) 648-8815
http://www.pitt.edu

University of Scranton
800 Linden Street
Scranton, PA 18510
Phone: (570) 941-7540
Fax: (570) 941-5928
E-mail: admissions@scranton.edu
http://www.scranton.edu

University of the Arts
320 South Broad Street
Philadelphia, PA 19102
Phone: (215) 717-6030
Fax: (215) 717-6045
http://www.uarts.edu

RHODE ISLAND

Brown University
Providence, RI 02912
Phone: (401) 863-2378
E-mail: admission_undergraduate@
    brown.edu
http://www.brown.edu

Providence College
549 River Avenue
Providence, RI 02918
Phone: (401) 865-2535
Fax: (401) 865-2826
E-mail: pcadmiss@providence.edu
http://www.providence.edu

Roger Williams University
One Old Ferry Road
Bristol, RI 02809
Phone: (401) 254-3500
E-mail: admit@rwu.edu
http://www.rwu.edu

Salve Regina University
100 Ochre Point Avenue
Newport, RI 02840
Phone: (401) 341-2908
Fax: (401) 848-2823
E-mail: sruadmis@salve.edu
http://www.salve.edu

SOUTH CAROLINA

Anderson College
316 Boulevard
Anderson, SC 29621
Phone: (864) 231-2030
Fax: (864) 231-2033
http://www.anderson-college.edu

Charleston Southern University
9200 University Boulevard
P.O. Box 118087
Charleston, SC 29423
Phone: (843) 863-7050
http://www.charlestonsouthern.edu

Coastal Carolina University
P.O. Box 261954
Conway, SC 29528
Phone: (843) 349-2037
Fax: (843) 349-2127
E-mail: admissions@coastal.edu
http://www.coastal.edu

Coker College
300 East College Avenue
Hartsville, SC 29550
Phone: (843) 383-8050
Fax: (843) 383-8056
E-mail: admissions@coker.edu
http://www.coker.edu

College of Charleston
66 George Street
Charleston, SC 29424
Phone: (843) 953-5670
Fax: (843) 953-6322
E-mail: admissions@cofc.edu
http://www.cofc.edu

Converse College
580 East Main Street
Spartanburg, SC 29302
Phone: (864) 596-9040
E-mail: admissions@converse.edu
http://www.converse.edu

Francis Marion University
P.O. Box 100547
Florence, SC 29501
Phone: (843) 661-1231
Fax: (843) 661-4635

E-mail: admissions@fmarion.edu
http://www.fmarion.edu

Furman University
3300 Poinsett Highway
Greenville, SC 29613
Phone: (864) 294-2034
Fax: (864) 294-3127
E-mail: admission@furman.edu
http://www.furman.edu

Limestone College
1115 College Drive
Gaffney, SC 29340
Phone: (864) 488-4554
Fax: (864) 488-8206
E-mall: admiss@limestone.edu
http://www.limestone.edu

South Carolina State University
300 College Street Northeast
Orangeburg, SC 29117
Phone: (803) 536-8408
Fax: (803) 536-8990
E-mail: admissions@scsu.edu
http://www.scsu.edu

University of South Carolina
Columbia, SC 29208
Phone: (803) 777-7700
E-mail: admissions-ugrad@sc.edu
http://www.sc.edu

Winthrop University
Rock Hill, SC 29733
Phone: (803) 323-2191
E-mail: admissions@winthrop.edu
http://www.winthrop.edu

Wofford College
429 North Church Street
Spartanburg, SC 29303
Phone: (864) 597-4130
Fax: (864) 597-4147
E-mail: admissions@wofford.edu
http://www.wofford.edu

SOUTH DAKOTA

Augustana College
2001 South Summit Avenue
Sioux Falls, SD 57197
Phone: (605) 274-5516
Fax: (605) 274-5518
E-mail: admission@augie.edu
http://www.audie.edu

Dakota Wesleyan University
1200 West University Avenue
Mitchell, SD 57301

Phone: (605) 995-2650
Fax: (605) 995-2699
E-mail: admissions@dwu.edu
http://www.dwu.edu

Northern State University
1200 South Jay Street
Aberdeen, SD 57401
Phone: (605) 626-2544
Fax: (605) 626-2587
E-mail: admissions1@northern.edu
http://www.northern.edu

South Dakota State University
P.O. Box 2201
Brookings, SD 57007
Phone: (605) 688-4121
Fax: (605) 688-6891
E-mail: sdsu_admissions@sdstate.edu
http://www.sdstate.edu

University of Sioux Falls
1101 West 22nd Street
Sioux Falls, SD 57105
Phone: (605) 331-6600
Fax: (605) 331-6615
E-mail: admissions@usiouxfalls.edu
http://www.usiouxfalls.edu

University of South Dakota
414 East Clark Street
Vermillion, SD 57069
Phone: (605) 677-5434
Fax: (605) 677-6753
E-mail: admiss@usd.edu
http://www.usd.edu

TENNESSEE

Belmont University
1900 Belmont Boulevard
Nashville, TN 37212
Phone: (615) 460-6785
Fax: (615) 460-5434
E-mail: buadmission@mail.belmont.edu
http://www.belmont.edu

Bethel College
325 Cherry Avenue
McKenzie, TN 38201
Phone: (731) 352-4030
Fax: (731) 352-4069
E-mail: admissions@bethel-college.edu
http://www.bethel-college.edu

Carson-Newman College
2130 Branner Avenue
Jefferson City, TN 37760
Phone: (865) 471-3223

E-mail: thuebner@cn.edu
http://www.cn.edu

Cumberland University
One Cumberland Square
Lebanon, TN 37087
Phone: (615) 444-2562
Fax: (615) 444-2569
http://www.cumberland.edu

Fisk University
1000 17th Avenue North
Nashville, TN 37208
Phone: (615) 329-8666
Fax: (615) 329-8774
E-mail: admit@fisk.edu
http://www.fisk.edu

Lambuth University
705 Lambuth Boulevard
Jackson, TN 38301
Phone: (731) 425-3223
E-mail: admit@lambuth.edu
http://www.lambuth.edu

Maryville College
502 East Lamar Alexander Parkway
Maryville, TN 37804
Phone: (865) 981-8092
Fax: (865) 981-8005
E-mail: admissions@
    maryvillecollege.edu
http://www.maryvillecollege.edu

Middle Tennessee State University
1301 East Main Street
Murfreesboro, TN 37132
Phone: (615) 898-2111
Fax: (615) 898-5478
E-mail: admissions@mtsu.edu
http://www.mtsu.edu

Rhodes College
2000 North Parkway
Memphis, TN 38112
Phone: (901) 843-3700
E-mail: adminfo@rhodes.edu
http://www.rhodes.edu

Union University
1050 Union University Drive
Jackson, TN 38305
Phone: (800) 33-UNION
E-mail: info@uu.edu
http://www.uu.edu

University of Memphis
101 John Wilder Tower
Memphis, TN 38152

Phone: (901) 678-2169
http://www.memphis.edu

University of Tennessee
Knoxville, TN 37996
Phone: (865) 974-2184
Fax: (865) 974-6341
E-mail: admissions@tennessee.edu
http://www.tennessee.edu

Vanderbilt University
2305 West End Avenue
Nashville, TN 37203
Phone: (615) 322-2561
E-mail: admissions@vanderbilt.edu
http://www.vanderbilt.edu

TEXAS

Abilene Christian University
ACU Box 29000
Abilene, TX 79699
Phone: (325) 674-2650
E-mail: info@admissions.acu.edu
http://www.acu.edu

Angelo State University
2601 West Avenue North
San Angelo, TX 76909
Phone: (325) 942-2041
http://www.angelo.edu

Baylor University
One Bear Place #97056
Waco, TX 76798
Phone: (254) 710-3435
http://www.baylor.edu

Howard Payne University
1000 Fisk Avenue
Brownwood, TX 76801
Phone: (325) 649-8027
Fax: (325) 649-8901
E-mail: enroll@hputx.edu
http://www.hputx.edu

Lamar University
4400 MLK Boulevard
P.O. Box 10009
Beaumont, TX 77710
Phone: (409) 880-8888
Fax: (409) 880-8463
E-mail: admissions@lamar.edu
http://www.lamar.edu

McMurry University
South 14th Sayles Boulevard
Abilene, TX 79697
Phone: (325) 793-4700

Fax: (325) 793-4701
http://www.mcm.edu

Midwestern State University
3410 Taft Boulevard
Wichita Falls, TX 76308
Phone: (940) 397-4334
Fax: (940) 397-4672
E-mail: admissions@mwsu.edu
http://www.mwsu.edu

Our Lady of the Lake University
411 SW 24th Street
San Antonio, TX 78207
Phone: (210) 431-3961
E-mail: admission@lake.ollusa.edu
http://www.ollusa.edu

Prairie View A&M University
P.O. Box 3089
Prairie View, TX 77446
Phone: (936) 857-2626
Fax: (936) 857-2699
E-mail: admissions@pvamu.edu
http://www.pvamu.edu

Sam Houston State University
P.O. Box 2418
Huntsville, TX 77341
Phone: (936) 294-1828
Fax: (936) 294-3758
http://www.shsu.edu

Schreiner University
2100 Memorial Boulevard
Kerrville, TX 78028
Phone: (830) 792-7277
Fax: (830) 792-7226
E-mail: admissions@schreiner.edu
http://www.schreiner.edu

Southwestern University
1001 East University
Georgetown, TX 78626
Phone: (512) 863-1200
Fax: (512) 863-9601
E-mail: admission@southwestern.edu
http://www.southwestern.edu

Stephen F. Austin State University
Nacogdoches, TX 75962
Phone: (936) 468-2504
E-mail: admissions@sfasu.edu
http://www.sfasu.edu

Sul Ross State University
P.O. Box C-114
Alpine, TX 79832
Phone: (915) 837-8050

Fax: (915) 837-8431
E-mail: rcullins@sulross.edu
http://www.sulross.edu

Tarleton State University
Box T-0001
Tarleton Station, TX 76402
Phone: (254) 968-9125
Fax: (254) 968-9951
E-mail: uadm@tarleton.edu
http://www.tarleton.edu

Texas A&M University
College Station, TX 77843
Phone: (979) 845-3741
Fax: (979) 845-8737
E-mail: admissions@tamu.edu
http://www.tamu.edu

Texas A&M University–Commerce
P.O. Box 3011
Commerce, TX 75429
Phone: (903) 886-5103
Fax: (903) 886-5888
E-mail: admissions@tamu-
    commerce.edu
http://www.tamu-commerce.edu

Texas A&M University–Kingsville
700 University Boulevard
Kingsville, TX 78363
Phone: (361) 593-2811
Fax: (361) 593-2195
http://www.tamuk.edu

Texas Southern University
3100 Cleburne Street
Houston, TX 77004
Phone: (713) 313-7472
http://www.tsu.edu

Texas State University–San Marcos
601 University Drive
San Marcos, TX 78666
Phone: (512) 245-2364
Fax: (512) 245-8044
E-mail: admissions@txstate.edu
http://www.txstate.edu

Texas Tech University
P.O. Box 45005
Lubbock, TX 79409
Phone: (806) 742-1480
Fax: (806) 742-0062
E-mail: admissions@ttu.edu
http://www.ttu.edu

Texas Woman's University
P.O. Box 425589
Denton, TX 76204

Phone: (940) 898-3188
E-mail: admissions@twu.edu
http://www.twu.edu

Trinity University
One Trinity Place
San Antonio, TX 78212
Phone: (210) 999-7207
E-mail: admissions@trinity.edu
http://www.trinity.edu

University of Dallas
1845 East Northgate Drive
Irving, TX 75062
Phone: (972) 721-5266
http://www.udallas.edu

University of Houston
122 East Cullen Building
Houston, TX 77204
Phone: (713) 743-9595
http://www.uh.edu

University of North Texas
P.O. Box 311277
Denton, TX 76203
Phone: (940) 565-3190
Fax: (940) 565-2408
E-mail: undergrad@unt.edu
http://www.unt.edu

University of Texas at Arlington
P.O. Box 19111
701 South Nedderman Drive
Arlington, TX 76019
Phone: (817) 272-6287
Fax: (817) 272-3435
E-mail: admissions@uta.edu
http://www.uta.edu

University of Texas at Austin
P.O. Box 8058
Austin, TX 78713
Phone: (512) 475-7440
Fax: (512) 475-7475
http://www.utexas.edu

University of Texas at Dallas
P.O. Box 830688
Richardson, TX 75083
Phone: (972) 883-2270
E-mail: interest@utdallas.edu
http://www.utdallas.edu

University of Texas at El Paso
500 West University Avenue
El Paso, TX 79968
Phone: (915) 747-5588
Fax: (915) 747-8893

E-mail: futureminer@utep.edu
http://www.utep.edu

University of Texas at Tyler
3900 University Boulevard
Tyler, TX 75799
Phone: (903) 566-7195
Fax: (903) 566-7068
E-mail: admissions@uttyler.edu
http://www.uttyler.edu

University of Texas–Pan American
1201 West University Drive
Edinburg, TX 78541
Phone: (956) 381-2201
Fax: (956) 381-2212
E-mail: admissions@utpa.edu
http://www.utpa.edu

West Texas A&M University
Canyon, TX 79016
Phone: (806) 651-2020
Fax: (806) 651-5285
E-mail: lvars@mail.wtamu.edu
http://www.wtamu.edu

UTAH

Brigham Young University
A-153 ASB
Provo, UT 84602
Phone: (801) 422-2507
Fax: (801) 422-0005
E-mail: admissions@byu.edu
http://www.byu.edu

Southern Utah University
351 West Center Street
Cedar City, UT 84720
Phone: (801) 586-7740
Fax: (435) 865-8223
E-mail: adminfo@suu.edu
http://www.suu.edu

University of Utah
201 S1460 East
Salt Lake City, UT 84112
Phone: (801) 581-8761
Fax: (801) 585-7864
E-mail: admissions@sa.utah.edu
http://www.sa.utah.edu

Utah State University
0160 Old Main Hill
Logan, UT 84322
Phone: (435) 797-1079
Fax: (435) 797-3708
E-mail: admit@cc.usu.edu
http://www.usu.edu

Weber State University
1137 University Circle
3750 Harrison Boulevard
Ogden, UT 84408
Phone: (801) 626-6050
Fax: (801) 626-6744
E-mail: admissions@weber.edu
http://www.weber.edu

VERMONT

Bennington College
One College Drive
Bennington, VT 05201
Phone: (802) 440-4312
Fax: (802) 440-4320
E-mail: admissions@bennington.edu
http://www.bennington.edu

Castleton State College
86 Seminary Street
Castleton, VT 05735
Phone: (802) 468-1213
Fax; (802) 468-1476
E-mail: info@castleton.edu
http://www.castleton.edu

Johnson State College
337 College Hill
Johnson, VT 05656
Phone: (802) 635-1219
Fax: (802) 635-1230
E-mail: jscadmissions@jsc.vsc.edu

Saint Michael's College
One Winooski Park
Colchester, VT 05439
Phone: (800) 762-8000
Fax: (802) 654-2906
E-mail: admission@smcvt.edu
http://www.smcvt.edu

University of Vermont
194 South Prospect Street
Burlington, VT 05401-3596
Phone: (802) 656-3370
Fax: (802) 656-8611
E-mail: admissions@uvm.edu
http://www.uvm.edu

VIRGINIA

Averett University
420 West Main Street
Danville, VA 24541
Phone: (434) 791-4996
E-mail: admit@averett.edu
http://www.averett.edu

Bluefield College
3000 College Drive
Bluefield, VA 24605
Phone: (276) 326-4214
Fax: (276) 326-4288
E-mail: admissions@mail.bluefield.edu
http://www.bluefield.edu

Christopher Newport University
1 University Place
Newport News, VA 23606
Phone: (757) 594-7015
E-mail: admit@cnu.edu
http://www.cnu.edu

College of William and Mary
P.O. Box 8795
Williamsburg, VA 23187
Phone: (757) 221-4223
Fax: (757) 221-1242
E-mail: admiss@wm.edu
http://www.wm.edu

Ferrum College
P.O. Box 1000
Ferrum, VA 24088
Phone: (540) 365-4290
http://www.ferrum.edu

George Mason University
4400 University Drive
Fairfax, VA 22030
Phone: (703) 993-2398
Fax: (703) 993-2392
E-mail: admissions@gmu.edu
http://www.gmu.edu

Hampton University
Hampton, VA 23668
Phone: (757) 727-5328
Fax: (757) 727-5095
E-mail: admit@hamptonu.edu
http://www.hamptonu.edu

Hollins University
P.O. Box 9707
Roanoke, VA 24020
Phone: (540) 362-6401
E-mail: huadm@hollins.edu
http://www.hollins.edu

James Madison University
Harrisonburg, VA 22807
Phone: (540) 568-5681
Fax: (540) 568-3332
E-mail: gotojmu@jmu.edu
http://www.jmu.edu

Longwood University
201 High Street
Farmville, VA 23909
Phone: (434) 395-2060
Fax: (434) 395-2332
E-mail: admit@longwood.edu
http://www.longwood.edu

Lynchburg College
1501 Lakeside Drive
Lynchburg, VA 24501
Phone: (434) 544-8300
Fax: (434) 544-8653
E-mail: admissions@lynchburg.edu
http://www.lynchburg.edu

Mary Baldwin College
Staunton, VA 24401
Phone: (540) 887-7287
Fax: (540) 887-7292
E-mail: admit@mbc.edu
http://www.mbc.edu

Old Dominion University
108 Rollins Hall
Norfolk, VA 23529
Phone: (757) 683-3685
E-mail: admit@odu.edu
http://www.odu.edu

Radford University
East Main Street
Radford, VA 24142
Phone: (540) 831-5371
Fax: (540) 831-5038
E-mail: ruadmiss@radford.edu
http://www.radford.edu

Randolph-Macon Woman's College
2500 Rivermont Avenue
Lynchburg, VA 24503
Phone: (434) 947-8100
E-mail: admissions@rmwc.edu
http://www.rmwc.edu

Roanoke College
221 College Lane
Salem, VA 24153
Phone: (540) 375-2270
Fax: (540) 375-2267
E-mail: admissions@roanoke.edu
http://www.roanoke.edu

Shenandoah University
1460 University Drive
Winchester, VA 22601
Phone: (540) 665-4581
Fax: (540) 665-4627
E-mail: admit@su.edu
http://www.su.edu

Southern Virginia University
One University Hill Drive
Buena Vista, VA 24416
Phone: (540) 261-8421
Fax: (540) 261-8559
E-mail: admissions@southernvirginia.edu
http://www.southernvirginia.edu

Sweet Briar College
P.O. Box 400160
Sweet Briar, VA 24595
Phone: (434) 381-6142
Fax: (434) 381-6152
E-mail: admissions@sbc.edu
http://www.sbc.edu

University of Mary Washington
1301 College Avenue
Fredericksburg, VA 22401
Phone: (540) 654-2000
Fax: (540) 654-1857
E-mail: admit@umw.edu
http://www.umw.edu

University of Virginia
P.O. Box 400160
Charlottesville, VA 22904
Phone: (434) 982-3200
Fax: (434) 924-3587
E-mail: undergradadmission@virginia.edu
http://www.virginia.edu

The University of Virginia's College at Wise
1 College Avenue
Wise, VA 24293
Phone: (276) 328-0322
Fax: (276) 328-0251
E-mail: admissions@uvawise.edu
http://www.uvawise.edu

Virginia Commonwealth University
821 West Franklin Street
P.O. Box 842526
Richmond, VA 23284
Phone: (804) 828-1222
E-mail: ugrad@vcu.edu
http://www.vcu.edu

Virginia State University
20708 Fourth Avenue
Petersburg, VA 23806
Phone: (804) 524-5901
E-mail: admiss@vsu.edu
http://www.vsu.edu

Virginia Wesleyan College
1584 Wesleyan Drive
Norfolk, VA 23502

Phone: (757) 455-3208
Fax: (757) 461-5238
E-mail: admissions@vwc.edu
http://www.vwc.edu

Washington and Lee University
Lexington, VA 24450
Phone: (540) 458-8710
Fax: (540) 458-8062
E-mail: admissions@wlu.edu
http://www.wlu.edu

WASHINGTON

Central Washington University
400 East University Way
Ellensburg, WA 98926
Phone: (509) 963-1211
Fax: (509) 963-3022
E-mail: cwuadmis@cwu.edu
http://www.cwu.edu

Cornish College of the Arts
1000 Lenora Street
Seattle, WA 98121
Phone: (206) 726-5017
Fax: (206) 720-1011
E-mail: admissions@cornish.edu
http://www.cornish.edu

Eastern Washington University
101 Sutton Hall
Cheney, WA 99004
Phone: (509) 359-2397
Fax: (509) 359-6692
E-mail: admission@mail.ewu.edu
http://www.ewu.edu

The Evergreen State College
2700 Evergreen Parkway NW
Olympia, WA 98505
Phone: (360) 867-6170
E-mail: admissions@evergreen.edu
http://www.evergreen.edu

Gonzaga University
502 East Boone
Spokane, Washington 99258
Phone: (800) 322-2584
E-mail: admissions@gu.gonzaga.edu
http://www.gonzaga.edu

Northwest University
P.O. Box 579
Kirkland, WA 98083
Phone: (425) 889-5598
Fax: (425) 889-5224
E-mail: admissions@northwestu.edu
http://www.northwestu.edu

Seattle Pacific University
3307 Third Avenue West
Suite 115
Seattle, WA 98119
Phone: (206) 281-2021
E-mail: admissions@spu.edu
http://www.spu.edu

Seattle University
901 12th Avenue
Seattle, WA 98122
Phone: (206) 296-2000
E-mail: admissions@seattleu.edu
http://www.seattleu.edu

University of Puget Sound
1500 North Warner Street, #1062
Tacoma, WA 98416
Phone: (253) 879-3211
E-mail: admission@ups.edu
http://www.ups.edu

Western Washington University
516 High Street
Bellingham, WA 98225
Phone: (360) 650-3440
Fax: (360) 650-7369
E-mail: admit@awwu.edu
http://www.wwu.edu

Whitman College
515 Boyer Avenue
Walla Walla, WA 99362
Phone: (509) 527-5176; (877) 462-9448
Fax: (509) 527-4967
E-mail: admission@whitman.edu
http://www.whitman.edu

Whitworth College
West 300 Hawthorne Road
Spokane, WA 99251
Phone: (509) 777-3212
E-mail: admission@whitworth.edu
http://www.whitworth.edu

WEST VIRGINIA

Alderson-Broaddus College
College Hill Road
Philippi, WV 26416
Phone: (800) 263-1549
E-mail: admissions@ab.edu
http://www.ab.edu

Bethany College
Bethany, WV 26032
Phone: (304) 829-7611
Fax: (304) 829-7142
E-mail: admission@bethanywv.edu
http://www.bethanywv.edu

Davis & Elkins College
100 Campus Drive
Elkins, WV 26241
Phone: (304) 637-1230
E-mail: admiss@davisandelkins.edu
http://www.davisandelkins.edu

Fairmont State University
1201 Locust Avenue
Fairmont, WV 26554
Phone: (304) 367-4892
E-mail: admit@fairmontstate.edu
http://www.fairmontstate.edu

West Virginia University
P.O. Box 6009
Morgantown, WV 26506
Phone: (304) 293-2124
Fax: (304) 293-3080
E-mail: go2wvu@mail.wvu.edu
http://www.wvu.edu

West Virginia Wesleyan College
59 College Avenue
Buckhannon, WV 26201
Phone: (304) 473-8510
E-mail: admission@wvwc.edu
http://www.wvwc.edu

WISCONSIN

Beloit College
700 College Street
Beloit, WI 53511
Phone: (608) 363-2500
Fax: (608) 363-2075
E-mail: admiss@beloit.edu
http://www.beloit.edu

Cardinal Stritch University
6801 North Yates Road
Milwaukee, WI 53217
Phone: (414) 410-4040
E-mail: admityou@stritch.edu
http://www.stritch.edu

Carroll College
100 North East Avenue
Waukesha, WI 53186
Phone: (262) 524-7220
E-mail: ccinfo@cc.edu
http://www.cc.edu

Carthage College
2001 Alford Park Drive
Kenosha, WI 53140
Phone: (262) 551-6000

E-mail: admissions@carthage.edu
http://www.carthage.edu

Lawrence University
P.O. Box 599
Appleton, WI 54912
Phone: (920) 832-6500
E-mail: excel@lawrence.edu
http://www.lawrence.edu

Marquette University
P.O. Box 1881
Milwaukee, WI 53201
Phone: (414) 288-7004
Fax: (414) 288-3764
E-mail: admissions@marquette.edu
http://www.marquette.edu

Ripon College
300 Seward Street
P.O. Box 248
Ripon, WI 54971
Phone: (800) 94RIPON
E-mail: adminfo@ripon.edu
http://www.ripon.edu

University of Wisconsin–Green Bay
2420 Nicolet Drive
Green Bay, WI 54311
Phone: (920) 465-2111
Fax: (920) 465-5754
E-mail: uwgb@uwgb.edu
http://www.uwgb.edu

University of Wisconsin–Madison
716 Langdon Street
Madison, WI 53706
Phone: (608) 262-3961
Fax: (608) 262-7706
E-mail: onwisconsin@
   admissions.wisc.edu
http://www.wisc.edu

University of Wisconsin–Milwaukee
P.O. Box 749
Milwaukee, WI 53201
Phone: (414) 229-4397
Fax: (414) 229-6940
E-mail: uwmlook@uwm.edu
http://www.uwm.edu

University of Wisconsin–Oshkosh
Oshkosh, WI 54901
Phone: (920) 424-0202
E-mail: oshadmuw@uwosh.edu
http://www.uwosh.edu

University of Wisconsin–River Falls
410 South Third Street
River Falls, WI 54022
Phone: (715) 425-3500
Fax: (715) 425-0676
E-mail: admit@uwrf.edu
http://www.uwrf.edu

University of Wisconsin–Stevens Point
2100 Main Street
Stevens Point, WI 54481
Phone: (715) 346-2441
Fax: (715) 346-3296
E-mail: admiss@uwsp.edu
http://www.uwsp.edu

**University of Wisconsin–Superior,
   Belknap, and Catlin**
P.O. Box 2000
Superior, WI 54880
Phone: (715) 394-8217
Fax: (715) 394-8407
E-mail: admissions@uwsuper.edu
http://www.uwsuper.edu

University of Wisconsin–Whitewater
800 West Main Street
Whitewater, WI 53190
Phone: (262) 472-1440
Fax: (262) 472-1515
http://www.uww.edu

Viterbo University
900 Viterbo Drive
LaCrosse, WI 54601
Phone: (608) 796-3010
Fax: (608) 796-3020
E-mail: admission@viterbo.edu
http://www.viterbo.edu

Wisconsin Lutheran College
8800 West Bluemound Road
Milwaukee, WI 53226
Phone: (414) 443-8811
Fax: (414) 443-8514
E-mail: admissions@wlc.edu
http://www.wlc.edu

WYOMING

Middlebury College
Middlebury, VT 05753
Phone: (802) 443-3000
Fax: (802) 443-2056
E-mail: admissions@middlebury.edu
http://www.middlebury.edu

B. COLLEGES AND UNIVERSITIES OFFERING ARTS MANAGEMENT AND ADMINISTRATION PROGRAMS

The following is a listing of four-year schools offering majors and/or granting degrees in arts management and administration in the visual and performing arts fields. They are grouped by state. School names, addresses, phone numbers, Web addresses, and admissions e-mail addresses are included when available.

While possession of a college degree does not guarantee a job, many feel that it is in their best interest to continue their education after high school to gain knowledge, learn new skills, and make important contacts. A higher education may also provide a competitive edge.

Inclusion or exclusion in this listing does not indicate the author endorses any one school or program over another. Use this list as a beginning. As colleges frequently add or change programs, be sure to check the newest copy of *Lovejoy's College Guide* (usually located in the reference section of libraries or in guidance or counseling centers) for current schools offering courses or giving degrees in this field.

ALABAMA

Spring Hill College
4000 Dauphin Street
Mobile, AL 36608
Phone: (251) 380-3030
Fax: (251) 460-2186
E-mail: admit@shc.edu
http://www.shc.edu

ARIZONA

Northern Arizona University
P.O. Box 4084
Flagstaff, AZ 86011
Phone: (205) 348-5666
Fax: (205) 348-9046
E-mail: admissions@ua.edu
http://www.nau.edu

CALIFORNIA

California State University, Hayward
25800 Carlos Bee Boulevard
Hayward, CA 94542
Phone: (510) 885-3248
Fax: (510) 885-3816
E-mail: adminfo@csuhayward.edu
http://www.csuhayward.edu

University of San Francisco
2130 Fulton Street
San Francisco, CA 94117
Phone: (415) 422-6563
Fax: (415) 422-2217
E-mail: admission@usfca.edu
http://www.usfca.edu

DELAWARE

Delaware State University
1200 North Dupont Highway
Dover, DE 19901
Phone: (302) 857-6344
Fax: (302) 857-6352
E-mail: dadmiss@dsc.edu
http://www.dsc.cdu

GEORGIA

Brenau University
One Centennial Circle
Gainesville, GA 30501
Phone: (770) 534-6100
E-mail: wcadmissions@lib.brenau.edu
http://www.brenau.edu

Georgia College & State University
Milledgeville, GA 31061
Phone: (478) 445-1284
Fax: (478) 445-1914
E-mail: info@gcsu.edu
http://www.gcsu.edu

ILLINOIS

Benedictine University
5700 College Road
Lisle, IL 60532
Telephone: (630) 829-6300
Fax: (630) 829-6301
E-mail: admissions@ben.edu
http://www.ben.edu

Columbia College Chicago
600 South Michigan Avenue
Chicago, IL 60605
Phone: (312) 344-7130
Fax: (312) 344-8024
E-mail: admissions@colum.edu
http://www.colum.edu

DePaul University
1 East Jackson
Chicago, IL 60604
Phone: (312) 362-8300
E-mail: admitpu@depaul.edu
http://www.depaul.edu

Illinois Wesleyan University
P.O. Box 2900
Bloomington, IL 61702
Phone: (309) 556-3031
Fax: (309) 556-3820
E-mail: iwuadmit@iwu.edu
http://www.iwu.edu

Millikin University
1184 West Main Street
Decatur, IL 62522
Phone: (217) 424-6210
Fax: (217) 425-4669
E-mail: admis@millikin.edu
http://www.millikin.edu

Quincy University
1800 College Avenue
Quincy, IL 62301
Phone: (217) 228-5210
E-mail: admissions@quincy.edu
http://www.quincy.edu

INDIANA

Butler University
4600 Sunset Avenue
Indianapolis, IN 46208
Phone: (317) 940-8100
Fax: (317) 940-8150
E-mail: admission@butler.edu
http://www.butler.edu

University of Evansville
1800 Lincoln Avenue
Evansville, IN 47722
Phone: (812) 479-2468
E-mail: admission@evansville.edu
http://www.evansville.edu

IOWA

Buena Vista University
610 West Fourth Street
Storm Lake, IA 50588

Phone: (712) 749-2235
E-mail: admissions@bvu.edu
http://www.bvu.edu

Luther College
700 College Drive
Decorah, IA 52101
Phone: (563) 387-1287
Fax: (563) 387-2159
E-mail: admissions@luther.edu
http://www.luther.edu

University of Iowa
Iowa City, IA 52242
Phone: (319) 335-3847
Fax: (319) 335-1535
E-mail: admissions@uiowa.edu
http://www.uiowa.edu

Upper Iowa University
P.O. Box 1859
605 Washington Street
Fayette, IA 52142
Phone: (563) 425-5281
Fax: (563) 425-5323
E-mail: admission@uiu.edu
http://www.uiu.edu

Wartburg College
100 Wartburg Boulevard
P.O. Box 1003
Waverly, IA 50677
Phone: (319) 352-8264
Fax: (319) 352-8579
http://www.wartburg.edu

KANSAS

Aquinas College
1607 Robinson Road SE
Grand Rapids, MI 49506
Phone: (616) 732-4460
E-mail: admission@aquinas.edu
http://www.aquinas.edu

Kansas Wesleyan University
100 East Claflin Avenue
Salina, KS 67401
Phone: (785) 829-5541
Fax: (785) 827-0927
E-mail: admissions@kwu.edu
http://www.kwu.edu

KENTUCKY

Bellarmine University
2001 Newburg Road
Louisville, KY 40205
Phone: (502) 452-8131

Fax: (502) 452-8002
E-mail: admissions@bellarmine.edu
http://www.bellarmine.edu

University of Kentucky
Lexington, KY 40506
Phone: (859) 257-2000
E-mail: admissio@uky.edu
http://www.uky.edu

LOUISIANA

Southeastern Louisiana University
Hammond, LA 70402
Phone: (985) 549-2066
Fax: (985) 549-5632
E-mail: admissions@selu.edu
http://www.selu.edu

MASSACHUSSETS

Simmons College
300 The Fenway
Boston, MA 02115
Phone: (800) 345-8468
Fax: (617) 521-3190
http://www.simmons.edu

MICHIGAN

Adrian College
110 South Madison Street
Adrian, MI 49221
Phone: (517) 265-5161
E-mail: admissions@adrian.edu
http://www.adrian.edu

Eastern Michigan University
401 Pierce Hall
Ypsilanti, MI 48197
Phone: (734) 487-3060
Fax: (734) 487-6559
E-mail: admissions@emich.edu
http://www.emich.edu

University of Michigan–Dearborn
4901 Evergreen Road
Dearborn, MI 48128
Phone: (313) 593-5100
Fax: (313) 436-9167
E-mail: admissions@umd.umich.edu
http://www.umd.umich.edu

MISSOURI

Culver-Stockton College
Canton, MO 63435
Phone: (800) 537-1883
E-mail: enrollment@culver.edu
http://www.culver.edu

Drury University
900 North Benton
Springfield, MO 65802
Phone: (417) 873-7205
Fax: (417) 866-3873
E-mail: druryad@drury.edu
http://www.drury.edu

Fontbonne University
6800 Wydown Boulevard
St. Louis, MO 63105
Phone: (314) 889-1400
Fax: (314) 719-8021
E-mail: pmusen@fontbonne.edu
http://www.fontbonne.edu

NEW MEXICO

College of Santa Fe
1600 St. Michael's Drive
Santa Fe, NM 87505
Phone: (505) 473-6133
Fax: (505) 473-6127
http://www.csf.edu

NEW YORK

Baruch College
City University of New York
One Bernard Baruch Way
New York, NY 10010
Phone: (646) 312-1400
Fax: (646) 312-1363
E-mail: admissions@baruch.cuny.edu
http://www.baruch.cuny.edu

Concordia College
171 White Plains Road
Bronxville, NY 10708
Phone: (914) 337-9300
Fax: (914) 395-4636
E-mail: admission@concordia-ny.edu
http://www.concordia-ny.edu

Fredonia
State University of New York
280 Central Avenue
Fredonia, NY 14063
Phone: (716) 673-3251
E-mail: admissions.office@fredonia.edu
http://www.fredonia.edu

Ithaca College
100 Job Hall
Ithaca, NY 14850
Phone: (607) 274-3124
Fax: (607) 274-1900
E-mail: admission@ithaca.edu
http://www.ithaca.edu

Long Island University, C.W. Post Campus
720 Northern Boulevard
Brookville, NY 11548
Phone: (516) 299-2900
Fax: (516) 299-2137
E-mail: enroll@cwpost.liu.edu
http://www.liu.edu

Wagner College
Staten Island, NY 10301
Phone: (718) 390-3411
Fax: (718) 390-3105
E-mail: admissions@wagner.edu
http://www.wagner.edu

NORTH CAROLINA

Appalachian State University
Boone, NC 28608
Phone: (828) 262-2120
Fax: (828) 262-3296
E-mail: admissions@appstate.edu
http://www.appstate.edu

Bennett College
Campus Box H
Greensboro, NC 27401
Phone: (336) 517-8624
E-mail: admiss@bennett.edu
http://www.bennett.edu

North Carolina State University
P.O. Box 7103
Raleigh, NC 27695
Phone: (919) 515-2434
Fax: (919) 515-5039
E-mail: undergrad_admissions@ncsu.edu
http://www.ncsu.edu

Pfeiffer University
P.O. Box 960
Highway 52 North
Misenheimer, NC 28109
Phone: (704) 463-1360
Fax: (704) 463-1363
E-mail: admiss@pfeiffer.edu
http://www.pfeiffer.edu

Salem College
601 South Church Street
Winston-Salem, NC 2718
Phone: (336) 721-2621
E-mail: admission@salem.edu
http://www.salem.edu

OHIO

Ohio University
Athens, OH 45701
Phone: (740) 593-4100

E-mail: admissions.freshmen@ohiou.edu
http://www.ohiou.edu

Wright State University
3640 Colonel Glen Highway
Dayton, OH 45435
Phone: (937) 775-5700
E-mail: admission@wright.edu
http://www.wright.edu

OKLAHOMA

Oklahoma City University
2501 North Blackwelder
Oklahoma City, OK 73106
Phone: (405) 521-5050
E-mail: uadmissions@okcu.edu
http://www.okcu.edu

University of Tulsa
600 South College Avenue
Tulsa, OK 74104
Phone: (918) 631-2307
Fax: (918) 631-5003
E-mail: admission@tulsa.edu
http://www.tulsa.edu

OREGON

University of Portland
5000 North Willamette Boulevard
Portland, OR 97203
Phone: (503) 943-7147
Fax: (503) 943-7315
E-mail: admissio@up.edu
http://www.up.edu

PENNSYLVANIA

Chatham College
Woodland Road
Pittsburgh, PA 15232
Phone: (412) 365-1290
Fax: (412) 365-1609
E-mail: admissions@chatham.edu
http://www.chatham.edu

Marywood University
2300 Adams Avenue
Scranton, PA 18509
Phone: (570) 348-6211
E-mail: ugadm@ac.marywood.edu
http://www.marywood.edu

Mercyhurst College
501 East 38th Street
Erie, PA 16546
Phone: (814) 824-2202
E-mail: admissions@mercyhurst.edu
http://www.mercyhurst.edu

Point Park College
201 Wood Street
Pittsburgh, PA 15222
Phone: (800) 321-0129
E-mail: enroll@ppc.edu
http://www.ppc.edu

Seton Hill University
One Seton Hill Drive
Greensburg, PA 15601
Phone: (724) 838-4255
Fax: (724) 830-1294
E-mail: admit@setonhill.edu
http://www.setonhill.edu

Waynesburg College
51 West College Street
Waynesburg, PA
Phone: (724) 852-3248
E-mail: admissions@waynesburg.edu
http://www.waynesburg.edu

SOUTH CAROLINA

College of Charleston
66 George Street
Charleston, SC 29424
Phone: (843) 953-5670
Fax: (843) 953-6322
E-mail: admissions@cofc.edu
http://www.cofc.edu

SOUTH DAKOTA

Dakota State University
820 North Washington
Madison, SD 57042
Phone: (605) 256-5139
Fax: (605) 256-5316
E-mail: yourfuture@dsu.edu
http://www.dsu.edu

VERMONT

Green Mountain College
One College Circle
Poultney, VT 05764
Phone: (802) 287-8207
Fax: (802) 287-8099
E-mail: admiss@greenmtn.edu
http://www.greenmtn.edu

VIRGINIA

Mary Baldwin College
Staunton, VA 24401
Phone: (540) 887-7287
Fax: (540) 887-7292
E-mail: admit@mbc.edu
http://www.mbc.edu

Randolph-Macon College
P.O. Box 5005
Ashland, VA 23005
Phone: (804) 752-7305
E-mail: admissions@rmc.edu
http://www.rmc.edu

Shenandoah University
1460 University Drive
Winchester, VA 22601
Phone: (540) 665-4581
Fax: (540) 665-4627
E-mail: admit@su.edu
http://www.su.edu

WASHINGTON

Whitworth College
West 300 Hawthorne Road
Spokane, WA 99251
Phone: (509) 777-3212
E-mail: admission@whitworth.edu
http://www.whitworth.edu

WISCONSIN

University of Wisconsin–Stevens Point
2100 Main Street
Stevens Point, WI 54481

Phone: (715) 346-2441
Fax: (715) 346-3296
E-mail: admiss@uwsp.edu
http://www.uwsp.edu

Viterbo University
900 Viterbo Drive
LaCrosse, WI 54601
Phone: (608) 796-3010
Fax: (608) 796-3020
E-mail: admission@viterbo.edu
http://www.viterbo.edu

C. COLLEGES, UNIVERSITIES, AND SCHOOLS OFFERING DANCE PROGRAMS

The following is a listing of schools offering programs and/or granting degrees in dance.

They are grouped by state. School names, addresses, phone numbers, Web addresses, and admissions e-mail addresses are included when available.

Inclusion or exclusion in this listing does not indicate the author endorses any one school or program over another. Use this list as a beginning. As colleges frequently change programs, be sure to check the newest copy of *Lovejoy's College Guide* (usually located in the reference section of libraries or in guidance or counseling centers) for current schools offering courses or giving degrees in this field.

ALABAMA

Birmingham-Southern College
P.O. Box 549008
900 Arkadelphia Road
Birmingham, AL 35254
Phone: (205) 226-4696
E-mail: admission@bsc.edu
http://www.bsc.edu

University of Alabama–Tuscaloosa
Tuscaloosa, AL 35487
Phone: (205) 348-8185
Fax: (205) 348-9046
http://www.ua.edu

ARIZONA

University of Arizona
P.O. Box 210011
Tucson, AZ 85721
Phone: (520) 621-3237
Fax: (520) 621-9799
http://www.arizona.edu

CALIFORNIA

California Institute of the Arts
24700 McBean Parkway
Valencia, CA 91355
Phone: (661) 255-1050
E-mail: admiss@calarts.edu
http://www.calarts.edu

California State University–Fresno
5150 North Maple Avenue
Fresno, CA 93740
Phone: (559) 278-6115
Fax: (559) 278-4812
http://www.csufresno.edu

California State University–Fullerton
Fullerton, CA 92834
Phone: (714) 278-2350
http://www.fullerton.edu

California State University–Hayward
25800 Carlos Bec Boulevard
Hayward, CA 94542
Phone: (510) 885-3248
Fax: (510) 885-3816
http://www.csuhayward.edu

California State University–Long Beach
1250 Bellflower Boulevard
Long Beach, CA 90840
Phone: (562) 985-4641
http://www.csulb.edu

California State University–Los Angeles
5151 State University Drive
Los Angeles, CA 90032
Phone: (323) 343-3839
E-mail: admission@calstatela.edu
http://www.calstatela.edu

California State University–Northridge
18111 Nordhoff Street
Northridge, CA 91330
Phone: (818) 677-3777
Fax: (818) 677-3766
E-mail: admissions.records@csun.edu
http://www.csun.edu

California State University–Sacramento
6000 J Street
Sacramento, CA 95819
Phone: (916) 278-7362
Fax: (916) 278-5603
E-mail: admissions@csus.edu
http://www.csus.edu

Chapman University
One University Drive
Orange, CA 92866
Phone: (714) 997-6711
Fax: (714) 997-6713
E-mail: admit@chapman.edu
http://www.chapman.edu

Claremont McKenna College
890 Columbia Avenue
Claremont, CA 91711
Phone: (909) 621-8088
http://www.claremontmckenna.edu

Loyola Marymount University
One LMU Drive
Los Angeles, CA 90045

Phone: (310) 338-2750
Fax: (310) 338-2797
http://www.lmu.edu

Mills College
5000 MacArthur Boulevard
Oakland, CA 94613
Phone: (510) 430-2135
Fax: (510) 430-3314
E-mail: admission@mills.edu
http://www.mills.edu

San Diego State University
5500 Campanile Drive
San Diego, CA 92182
Phone: (619) 594-6336
E-mail: admissions@sdsu.edu
http://www.sdsu.edu

San Francisco State University
1600 Holloway Avenue
San Francisco, CA 94132
Phone: (415) 338-1113
Fax: (415) 338-7196
E-mail: ugadmit@sfsu.edu
http://www.sfsu.edu

San Jose State University
One Washington Square
San Jose, CA 95192
Phone: (408) 283-7500
Fax: (408) 924-2050
E-mail: contact@sjsu.edu
http://www.sjsu.edu

Scripps College
1030 Columbia Avenue, P. B. 1265
Claremont, CA 91711
Phone: (909) 621-8149
Fax: (909) 607-7508
E-mail: admission@scrippscollege.edu
http://www.scrippscollege.edu

University of California
Berkeley, CA 94720
Phone: (510) 642-3175
Fax: (510) 642-7333
E-mail: ouars@uclink.berkeley.edu
http://www.berkeley.edu

University of California–Irvine
204 Administration
Irvine,CA 92697
Phone: (949) 824-6703
http://www.uci.edu

University of California–Los Angeles
405 Hilgard Avenue
Box 951436
Los Angeles, CA 90095

Phone: (310) 825-3101
E-mail: ugadm@saonet.ucla.edu
http://www.ucla.edu

University of California–Riverside
900 University Avenue
Riverside, CA 92521
Phone: (951) 827-4531
Fax: (951) 827-6344
E-mail: discover@ucr.edu
http://www.ucr.edu

University of California–San Diego
9500 Gilman Drive
La Jolla, CA 92093
Phone: (858) 534 4831
E-mail: admissionsinfo@ucsd.edu
http://www.ucsd.edu

University of California–Santa Barbara
Santa Barbara, CA 93106
Phone: (805) 893-2485
Fax: (805) 893-2676
E-mail: appinfo@sa.ucsb.edu
http://www.ucsb.edu

University of California–Santa Cruz
1156 High Street
Santa Cruz, CA 95064
Phone: (831) 459-5779
Fax: (831) 459-4452
E-mail: admissions@ucsc.edu
http://www.ucsc.edu

Westmont College
955 La Paz Road
Santa Barbara, CA 93108
http://www.westmont.edu

COLORADO

Colorado College
14 East Cache La Poudre Street
Colorado Springs, CO
Phone: (719) 389-6344
Fax: (719) 228-1482
E-mail: admission@coloradocollege.edu
http://www.coloradocollege.edu

Colorado State University
8020 Campus Delivery
Fort Collins, CO 80523
Phone: (970) 491-6909
http://www.colostate.edu

Naropa University
2130 Arapahoe Avenue
Boulder, CO 80302

Phone: (303) 546-3572
Fax: (303) 546-3583
E-mail: admissions@naropa.edu
http://www.naropa.edu

University of Colorado at Boulder
Boulder, CO 80309
Phone: (303) 492-6301
http://www.colorado.edu

CONNECTICUT

Connecticut College
270 Mohegan Avenue
New London, CT 06320
Phone: (860) 439 2200
Fax: (860) 439-4301
E-mail: admission@conncoll.edu
http://www.connecticutcollege.edu

Trinity College
300 Summit Street
Hartford, CT 06106-3100
Phone: (860) 297-2180
Fax: (860) 297-2287
E-mail: admissions.office@trincoll.edu
http://www.trincoll.edu

University of Hartford
200 Bloom Field Avenue
West Hartford, CT 06117
Phone: (860) 768-4296
Fax: (860) 768-4961
E-mail: admission@hartford.edu
http://www.hartford.edu

DISTRICT OF COLUMBIA

George Washington University
2121 I Street NW
Suite 201
Washington, DC 20052
Phone: (202) 994-6040
E-mail: gwadm@gwu.edu
http://www.gwu.edu

FLORIDA

Florida State University
Tallahassee, FL 32306
Phone: (850) 644-6200
Fax: (850) 644-0197
E-mail: admissions@admin.fsu.edu
http://www.fsu.edu

Jacksonville University
2800 University Boulevard North
Jacksonville, Florida 32211
Phone: (904) 256-7000

E-mail: admissions@ju.edu
http://www.ju.edu

University of Miami
P.O. Box 248025
1252 Memorial Drive
Coral Gables, FL 33146
Phone: (305) 284-4323
Fax: (305) 284-2507
E-mail: admission@miami.edu
http://www.miami.edu

University of Florida
P.O. Box 114000
Gainesville, FL 32611
Phone: (352) 392-1365
E-mail: freshmen@ufl.edu
http://www.ufl.edu

University of South Florida
4202 East Fowler Avenue
Tampa, FL 33620
Phone: (813) 974-3350
Fax: (813) 974-9689
http://www.usf.edu

GEORGIA

Brenau University
One Centennial Circle
Gainesville, GA 30501
Phone: (770) 534-6100
E-mail: wcadmissions@lib.brenau.edu
http://www.brenau.edu

Emory University
201 Downtown Drive
Atlanta, GA 30322
Phone: (404) 727-6036
E-mail: admiss@learnlink.emory.edu
http://www.emory.edu

HAWAII

University of Hawaii at Manoa
2600 Campus Road
Honolulu, HI 96822
Phone: (808) 956-8975
Fax: (808) 956-4148
E-mail: ar-info@hawaii.edu
http://www.uhm.hawaii.edu

IDAHO

University of Idaho
Moscow, ID 83844
Phone: (208) 885-6326
Fax: (208) 885-9119
http://www.uidaho.edu

ILLINOIS

Columbia College Chicago
600 South Michigan Avenue
Chicago, IL 60605
Phone: (312) 344-7130
Fax: (312) 344-8024
E-mail: admissions@colum.edu
http://www.colum.edu

**University of Illinois at
   Urbana–Champaign**
901 West Illinois
Urbana, IL 61801
Phone: (217) 333-0302
E-mail: admissions@oar.uiuc.edu
http://www.uiuc.edu

INDIANA

Ball State University
2000 West University Avenue
Muncie, IN 47306
Phone: (765) 285-8300
E-mail: askus@bsu.edu
http://www.bsu.edu

Butler University
4600 Sunset Avenue
Indianapolis, IN 46208
Phone: (317) 940-8100
Fax: (317) 940-8150
E-mail: admission@butler.edu
http://www.butler.edu

Indiana University–Bloomington
300 North Jordan Avenue
Bloomington, IN 47405
Phone: (812) 855-0661
Fax: (812) 855-5102
E-mail: iuadmit@indiana.edu
http://www.indiana.edu

IOWA

University of Iowa
107 Calvin Hall
Iowa City, IA 52242
Phone: (319) 335-3847
Fax: (319) 335-1535
E-mail: admissions@uiowa.edu
http://www.uiowa.edu

KANSAS

Friends University
2100 West University Street
Wichita, KS 67213
Phone: (316) 295-5100

Fax: (316) 262-5027
http://www.friends.edu

University of Kansas
1502 Iowa Street
Lawrence, KS 66045
Phone: (785) 864-3911
Fax: (785) 864-5006
E-mail: adm@ku.edu
http://www.ku.edu

LOUISIANA

Centenary College of Louisiana
2911 Centenary Boulevard
P.O. Box 41188
Shreveport, LA 71134
Phone: (318) 869-5134
Fax: (318) 869-5005
E-mail: egregory@centenary.edu
http://www.centenary.edu

MARYLAND

Frostburg State University
101 Braddock Road
Frostburg, MD 21532
Phone: (301) 687-4201
Fax: (301) 687-7074
E-mail: fsuadmission@frostburg.edu
http://www.frostburg.edu

Goucher College
1021 Dulaney Valley Road
Baltimore, MD 21204
Phone: (410) 337-6100
E-mail: admissions@goucher.edu
http://www.goucher.edu

Towson University
8000 York Road
Towson, MD 21252
Phone: (410) 704-2113
http://www.towson.edu

University of Maryland
College Park, MD 20742
Phone: (301) 314-8385
Fax: (301) 314-9693
http://www.umd.edu

**University of Maryland–Baltimore
   County**
1000 Hilltop Circle
Baltimore, MD 21250
Phone: (410) 455-2291
Fax: (410) 455-1094
http://www.umbc.edu

MASSACHUSETTS

Hampshire College
893 West Street
Amherst, MA 01002
Phone: (413) 559-5471
E-mail: admissions@hampshire.edu
http://www.hampshire.edu

Mount Holyoke College
50 College Street
South Hadley, MA 01075
Phone: (413) 538-2023
Fax: (413) 538-2409
E-mail: admission@mtholyoke.edu
http://www.mtholyoke.edu

Simon's Rock College of Bard
84 Alford Road
Great Barrington, MA 01230
Phone: (413) 528-7312
Fax: (413) 528-7334
http://www.simons-rock.edu

Smith College
Northampton, MA 01063
Phone: (413) 585-2500
Fax: (413) 585-2527
http://www.smith.edu

University of Massachusetts–Amherst
37 Mather Drive
Amherst, MA 01003
Phone: (413) 545-0222
Fax: (413) 545-4312
http://www.umass.edu

MICHIGAN

Alma College
614 West Superior Street
Alma, MI 48801
Phone: (800) 321-ALMA
E-mail: admissions@alma.edu
http://www.alma.edu

Eastern Michigan University
401 Pierce Hall
Ypsilanti, MI 48197
Phone: (734) 487-3060
Fax: (734) 487-6559
E-mail: admissions@emich.edu
http://www.emich.edu

Marygrove College
8425 West McNichols Road
Detroit, MI 48221
Phone: (313) 927-1240
Fax: (313) 927-1399
E-mail: info@marygrove.edu
http://www.marygrove.edu

Oakland University
Rochester, MI 48309
Phone: (248) 370-3360
E-mail: ouinfo@oakland.edu
http://www.oakland.edu

University of Michigan
515 East Jefferson
Ann Arbor, MI 48109
Phone: (734) 764-7433
Fax: (734) 936-0740
E-mail: ugadmiss@umich.edu
http://www.umich.edu

Wayne State University
Detroit, MI 48202
Phone: (313) 577-9753
Fax: (313) 577-7536
E-mail: admissions@wayne.edu
http://www.wayne.edu

Western Michigan University
1903 West Michigan Avenue
Kalamazoo, MI 49008
Phone: (269) 387-2000
http://www.wmich.edu

MINNESOTA

Gustavus Adolphus College
800 West College Avenue
Saint Peter, MN 56082
Phone: (507) 933-7676
Fax: (507) 933-7474
E-mail: admission@gustavus.edu
http://www.gustavus.edu

University of Minnesota–Twin Cities
Minneapolis, MN 55455-0115
Phone: (612) 625-2008
Fax: (612) 626-1693
E-mail: admissions@tc.umn.edu
http://www.tu.umn.edu

MISSISSIPPI

University of Southern Mississippi
118 College Drive
Hattiesburg, MS 39406
Phone: (601) 266-5000
Fax: (601) 266-5148
E-mail: admission@usm.edu
http://www.usm.edu

MISSOURI

Lindenwood University
209 South Kingshighway
St. Charles, MO 63301
Phone: (636) 949-4949

Fax: (636) 949-4989
http://www.lindenwood.edu

Southwest Missouri State University
901 South National Avenue
Springfield, MO 65804
Phone: (417) 836-5517
E-mail: admissions@smsu.edu
http://www.smsu.edu

Stephens College
1200 East Broadway
Columbia, MO 65215
Phone: (573) 876-7207
Fax: (573) 876-7237
E-mail: apply@stephens.edu
http://www.stephens.edu

University of Missouri–Kansas City
5100 Rockhill Road
Kansas City, MO 64110
Phone: (816) 235-1111
Fax: (816) 235-5544
E-mail: admit@umkc.edu
http://www.umkc.edu

MONTANA

University of Montana–Missoula
32 Campus Drive
Missoula, MT 59812
Phone: (406) 243-6266
Fax: (406) 243-5711
E-mail: admiss@umt.edu
http://www.umt.edu

NEBRASKA

University of Nebraska–Lincoln
313 North 13th Street
Lincoln, NE 68588
Phone: (402) 472-2023
Fax: (402) 472-0670
E-mail: admissions@unl.edu
http://www.unl.edu

NEVADA

University of Nevada, Las Vegas
4505 Maryland Parkway
Las Vegas, NV 89154
Phone: (702) 895-3011
Fax: (702) 774-8008
http://www.unlv.edu

NEW JERSEY

Montclair State University
Upper Montclair, NJ 07043

Phone: (800) 331-9205
http://www.montclair.edu

Rutgers, The State University of New Jersey
65 Davidson Road
Piscataway, NJ 08854
Phone: (732) 932-INFO
http://www.rutgers.edu

Thomas Edison State College
101 West State Street
Trenton, NJ 08608
Phone: (888) 442-8372
Fax: 609-984-8447
E-mail: info@tesc.edu
http://www.tesc.edu

NEW MEXICO

New Mexico State University
Box 30001
Las Cruces, NM 88003
Phone: (505) 646-3121
E-mail: admission@nmsu.edu
http://www.nmsu.edu

University of New Mexico
P.O. Box 4895
Albuquerque, NM 87196
Phone: (505) 277-2446
Fax: (505) 277-6686
E-mail: apply@unm.edu
http://www.umn.edu

NEW YORK

Adelphi University
P.O. Box 701
Garden City, NY 11530
Phone: (800) ADELPHI
E-mail: admissions@adelphi.edu
http://www.adelphi.edu

Barnard College
3009 Broadway
New York, NY 10027
Phone: (212) 854-2014
Fax: (212) 854-6220
E-mail: admissions@barnard.edu
http://www.barnard.edu

Columbia University–School of General Studies
2970 Broadway
New York, NY 10027
Phone: (212) 854-2772
http://www.gs.columbia.edu

Cornell University
410 Thurston Avenue
Ithaca, NY 14850
Phone: (607) 255-5241
E-mail: admissions@cornell.edu
http://www.cornell.edu

Hamilton College
198 College Hill Road
Clinton, NY 13323
Phone: (315) 859-4421
Fax: (315) 859-4457
http://www.hamilton.edu

Hobart and William Smith Colleges
629 South Main Street
Geneva, NY 14456
Phone: (800) 245-0100
E-mail: admissions@hws.edu
http://www.hws.edu

Hofstra University
Hempstead, NY 11549
Phone: (516) 463-6700
Fax: (516) 463-5100
http://www.hofstra.edu

Hunter College
695 Park Avenue
New York, NY 10021
Phone: (212) 772-4490
Fax: (212) 650-3336
E-mail: admission@hunter.cuny.edu
http://www.hunter.cuny.edu

Ithaca College
953 Danby Road
Ithaca, NY 14850
Phone: (607) 274-3124
Fax: (607) 274-1900
E-mail: admission@ithaca.edu
http://www.ithaca.edu

Juilliard School
60 Lincoln Center Plaza
New York, NY 10023
Phone: (212) 799-5000
Fax: (212) 724-0263
E-mail: admissions@juilliard.edu
http://www.juilliard.edu

Lehman College
250 Bedford Park Boulevard West
Bronx, NY 10468
Phone: (718) 960-8713
E-mail: enroll@lehman.cuny.edu
http://www.lehman.cuny.edu

Long Island University, C.W. Post Campus
720 Northern Boulevard
Brookville, NY 11548

Phone: (516) 299-2900
Fax: (516) 299-2137
E-mail: enroll@cwpost.liu.edu
http://www.liu.edu

Manhattanville College
2900 Purchase Street
Purchase, NY 10577
Phone: (914) 323-5464
http://www.mville.edu

Marymount Manhattan College
221 East 71st Street
New York, NY 10021
Phone: (212) 517-0430
E-mail: admissions@mmm.edu
http://www.mmm.edu

New York University
22 Washington Square North
New York, NY 10011
Phone: (212) 998-4500
http://www.nyn.edu

Sarah Lawrence College
1 Mead Way
Bronxville, NY 10708
Phone: (914) 395-2510
Fax: (914) 395-2515
E-mail: slcadmit@sarahlawrence.edu
http://www.sarahlawrence.edu

Skidmore College
815 North Broadway
Saratoga Springs, NY 12866
Phone: (518) 580-5570
E-mail: admission@skidmore.edu
http://www.skidmore.edu

Brockport
State University of New York
350 New Campus Drive
Brockport, NY 14420
Phone: (585) 395-2751
Fax: (585) 395-5452
E-mail: admit@brockport.edu
http://www.brockport.edu

University at Buffalo
State University of New York
Buffalo, NY 14260
Phone: (716) 645-6900
E-mail: ub-admissions@buffalo.edu
http://www.buffalo.edu

Fredonia
State University of New York
280 Central Avenue
Fredonia, NY 14063
Phone: (716) 673-3251

E-mail: admission.office@fredonia.edu
http://www.fredonia.edu

Potsdam
State University of New York College
44 Pierrepont Avenue
Potsdam, NY 13676
Phone: (315) 267-2180
E-mail: admissions@potsdam.edu
http://www.potsdam.edu

Wells College
Aurora, NY 13026
Phone: (800) 952-9355
E-mail: admissions@wells.edu
http://www.wells.edu

NORTH CAROLINA

East Carolina University
Greenville, NC 27858
Phone: (252) 328-6640
Fax: (252) 328-6945
E-mail: admis@mail.ecu.edu
http://www.ecu.edu

Meredith College
3800 Hillsborough Street
Raleigh, NC 27607
Phone: (919) 760-8581
Fax: (919) 760-2348
E-mail: admissions@meredith.edu
http://www.meredith.edu

North Carolina School of the Arts
1533 South Main Street
P.O. Box 12189
Winston-Salem, NC 27127
Phone: (336) 770-3290
Fax: (336) 770-3370
E-mail: admissions@ncarts.edu
http://www.ncarts.edu

University of North Carolina at Charlotte
9201 University City Boulevard
Charlotte, NC 28223
Phone: (704) 687-2213
Fax: (704) 687-6483
http://www.uncc.edu

University of North Carolina at Greensboro
123 Mossman
P.O. Box 26170
Greensboro, NC 27402
Phone: (336) 334-5243
Fax: (336) 334-5036
E-mail: undergrad_admissions@uncg.edu
http://www.uncg.edu

OHIO

Baldwin-Wallace College
275 Eastland Road
Berea, OH 44017
Phone: (440) 826-2222
Fax: (440) 826-3830
E-mail: info@bw.edu
http://www.bw.edu

Bowling Green State University
110 McFall Center
Bowling Green, OH 43403
Phone: (419) 372-BGSU
Fax: (419) 372-6955
E-mail: chosebgsu@bgnet.bgsu.edu
http://www.bgsu.edu

Denison University
100 Chapel Drive
Granville, OH 43023
Phone: (740) 587-6276
E-mail: admissions@denison.edu
http://www.denison.edu

Kent State University
P.O. Box 5190
Kent, OH 44242
Phone: (330) 672-2444
E-mail: kentadm@kent.edu
http://www.kent.edu

Kenyon College
Gambier, OH 43022
Phone: (740) 427-5776
Fax: (740) 427-5770
E-mail: admissions@kenyon.edu
http://www.kenyon.edu

Lake Erie College
391 West Washington Street
Painesville, OH 44077
Phone: (440) 375-7050
E-mail: admissions@lec.edu
http://www.lec.edu

Oberlin College
173 West Lorain Street
Oberlin, OH 44074
Phone: (440) 775-8411
E-mail: college.admissions@
    oberlin.edu
http://www.oberlin.edu

Ohio State University
154 West 12th Avenue
Columbus, OH 43210
Phone: (614) 247-6281
Fax: (614) 292-4818

E-mail: askabuckeye@osu.edu
http://www.osu.edu

Ohio University
Athens, OH 45701
Phone: (740) 593-4100
E-mail: admissions.freshmen@ohiou.edu
http://www.ohiou.edu

University of Akron
277 East Buchtel Avenue
Akron, OH 44325
Phone: (330) 972-6425
Fax: (330) 972-7022
E-mail: admissions@uakron.edu
http://www.uakron.edu

University of Cincinnati
P.O. Box 210091
Cincinnati, OH 45221
Phone: (513) 556-1100
Fax: (513) 556-1105
E-mail: admissions@uc.edu
http://www.uc.edu

OKLOHAMA

Oklahoma City University
2501 North Blackwelder
Oklahoma City, OK 73106
Phone: (405) 521-5050
E-mail: uadmissions@okcu.edu
http://www.okcu.edu

University of Central Oklahoma
100 North University Drive
Edmond, OK 73034
Phone: (405) 974-2338
Fax: (405) 341-4964
E-mail: admituco@ucok.edu
http://www.ucok.edu

University of Oklahoma
1000 Asp Avenue
Norman, OK 73019
Phone: (405) 325-2151
Fax: (405) 325-7124
E-mail: admrec@ou.edu
http://www.ou.edu

OREGON

Reed College
3203 Southeast Woodstock Boulevard
Portland, OR 97202
Phone: (503) 777-7511
Fax: (503) 777-7553
E-mail: admission@reed.edu
http://www.reed.edu

University of Oregon
Eugene, OR 97403
Phone: (541) 346-3201
http://www.uoregon.edu

PENNSYLVANIA

Cedar Crest College
100 College Drive
Allentown, PA 18104
Phone: (800) 360-1222
Fax: (610) 606-4647
E-mail: cccadmis@cedarcrest.edu
http://www.cedarcrest.edu

DeSales University
2755 Station Avenue
Center Valley, PA 18034
Phone: (610) 282-1100
Fax: (610) 282-2254
http://www.desales.edu

Dickinson College
P.O. Box 1773
Carlisle, PA 17013
Phone: (800) 644-1773
Fax: (717) 245-1442
E-mail: admit@dickinson.edu
http://www.dickinson.edu

La Roche College
9000 Babcock Boulevard
Pittsburgh, PA 15237
Phone: (412) 536-1272
E-mail: admission@laroche.edu
http://www.laroche.edu

Mercyhurst College
501 East 38th Street
Erie, PA 16546
Phone: (814) 824-2202
E-mail: admissions@mercyhurst.edu
http://www.mercyhurst.edu

Muhlenberg College
2400 Chew Street
Allentown, PA 18104
Phone: (484) 664-3200
E-mail: admissions@muhlenberg.edu
http://www.muhlenberg.edu

Slippery Rock University
1 Morrow Way
Slippery Rock, PA 16057
Phone: (724) 738-2015
E-mail: asktherock@sru.edu
http://www.sru.edu

Swarthmore College
500 College Avenue
Swarthmore, PA 19081

Phone: (610) 328-8300
E-mail: admissions@swarthmore.edu
http://www.swarthmore.edu

Temple University
1801 North Broad Street
Philadelphia, PA 19122
Phone: (215) 204-7200
E-mail: tuadm@temple.edu
http://www.temple.edu

University of the Arts
320 South Broad Street
Philadelphia, PA 19102
Phone: (215) 717-6030
Fax: (215) 717-6045
http://www.uarts.edu

RHODE ISLAND

Rhode Island College
600 Mount Pleasant Avenue
Providence, RI 02908
Phone: (401) 456-8234
Fax: (401) 456-8817
E-mail: admission@ric.edu
http://www.ric.edu

Roger Williams University
One Old Ferry Road
Bristol, RI 02809
Phone: (401) 254-3500
E-mail: admit@rwu.edu
http://www.rwu.edu

SOUTH CAROLINA

Coker College
300 East College Avenue
Hartsville, SC 29550
Phone: (843) 383-8050
Fax: (843) 383-8056
E-mail: admissions@coker.edu
http://www.coker.edu

Columbia College
1301 Columbia College Drive
Columbia, SC 29203
Phone: (803) 786-3765
Fax: (803) 786-3674
E-mail: admission@colacoll.edu
http://www.columbiacollegesc.edu

TEXAS

Lamar University
P.O. Box 10009
Beaumont, TX 77710
Phone: (409) 880-8888

Fax: (409) 880-8463
E-mail: admissions@lamar.edu
http://www.lamar.edu

Sam Houston State University
P.O. Box 2418
Huntsville, TX 77341
Phone: (936) 294-1828
Fax: (936) 294-3758
http://www.shsu.edu

Stephen F. Austin State University
SFA Box 13051
Nacogdoches, TX 75962
Phone: (936) 468-2504
E-mail: admissions@sfasu.edu
http://www.sfasu.edu

Texas State University–San Marcos
601 University Drive
San Marcos, TX 78666
Phone: (512) 245-2364
Fax: (512) 245-8044
E-mail: admissions@txstate.edu
http://www.txstate.edu

Texas Tech University
Box 45005
Lubbock, TX 79409
Phone: (806) 742-1480
Fax: (806) 742-0062
E-mail: admissions@ttu.edu
http://www.ttu.edu

Texas Woman's University
P.O. Box 425589
Denton, TX 76204
Phone: (940) 898-3188
E-mail: admissions@twu.edu
http://www.twu.edu

University of North Texas
Box 311277
Denton, TX 76203
Phone: (940) 565-3190
Fax: (940) 565-2408
E-mail: undergrad@unt.edu
http://www.unt.edu

University of Texas at Austin
P.O. Box 8058
Austin, TX 78713
Phone: (512) 475-7440
Fax: (512) 475-7475
http://www.utexas.edu

West Texas A&M University
2501 4th Avenue
Canyon, TX 79016

Phone: (806) 651-2020
Fax: (806) 651-5285
E-mail: lvars@mail.wtamu.edu
http://www.wtamu.edu

UTAH

Southern Utah University
351 West Center Street
Cedar City, UT 84720
Phone: (801) 586-7740
Fax: (435) 865-8223
E-mail: adminfo@suu.edu
http://www.suu.edu

University of Utah
Salt Lake City, UT 84112
Phone: (801) 581-8761
Fax: (801) 585-7864
E-mail: admissions@utah.edu
http://www.utah.edu

Weber State University
Ogden, UT 84408
Phone: (801) 626-6050
Fax: (801) 626-6744
E-mail: admissions@weber.edu
http://www.weber.edu

VERMONT

Bennington College
One College Drive
Bennington, VT 05201
Phone: (802) 440-4312
Fax: (802) 440-4320
E-mail: admissions@bennington.edu
http://www.bennington.edu

Johnson State College
337 College Hill
Johnson, VT 05656
Phone: (802) 635-1219
Fax: (802) 635-1230
E-mail: iscadmissions@jsc.vsc.edu
http://www.jsc.vsc.edu

Marlboro College
P.O. Box A, South Road
Marlboro, VT 05344
Phone: (802) 257-4333
Fax: (802) 451-7555
E-mail: admissions@marlboro.edu
http://www.marlboro.edu

VIRGINIA

George Mason University
4400 University Drive
Fairfax, VA 22030
Phone: (703) 993-2398
Fax: (703) 993-2392
E-mail: admissions@gmu.edu
http://www.gmu.edu

Old Dominion University
108 Rollins Hall
Norfolk, VA 23529
Phone: (757) 683-3685
E-mail: admit@odu.edu
http://www.odu.edu

Randolph-Macon Woman's College
2500 Rivermont Avenue
Lynchburg, VA 24503
Phone: (434) 947-8100
E-mail: admissions@rmwc.edu
http://www.rmwc.edu

Shenandoah University
1460 University Drive
Winchester, VA 22601
Phone: (540) 665-4581
Fax: (540) 665-4627
E-mail: admit@su.edu
http://www.su.edu

Sweet Briar College
Sweet Briar, VA 24595
Phone: (434) 381-6142
Fax: (434) 381-6152
E-mail: admissions@sbc.edu
http://www.sbc.edu

Virginia Commonwealth University
821 West Franklin Street
P.O. Box 842526
Richmond, VA 23284
Phone: (804) 828-1222
E-mail: ugrad@vcu.edu
http://www.vcu.edu

WASHINGTON

Cornish College of the Arts
1000 Lenora Street
Seattle, WA 98121
Phone: (206) 726-5017
Fax: (206) 720-1011
E-mail: admissions@cornish.edu
http://www.cornish.edu

Eastern Washington University
101 Sutton Hall
Cheney, WA 99004
Phone: (509) 359-2397
Fax: (509) 359-6692
E-mail: admission@mail.ewu.edu
http://www.ewu.edu

University of Washington
Seattle, WA 98195
Phone: (206) 543-9686
http://www.washington.edu

WISCONSIN

University of Wisconsin–Milwaukee
P.O. Box 749
Milwaukee, WI 53201
Phone: (414) 229-4397
Fax: (414) 229-6940
E-mail: uwmlook@uwm.edu
http://www.uwm.edu

University of Wisconsin–Stevens Point
2100 Main Street
Stevens Point, WI 54481
Phone: (715) 346-2441
Fax: (715) 346-3296
E-mail: admiss@uwsp.edu
http://www.uwsp.edu

D. COLLEGES AND UNIVERSITIES OFFERING DEGREES IN MUSIC THERAPY

The following is a listing of colleges and universities granting degrees in music therapy. They are grouped by state. School names, addresses, phone numbers, Web addresses, and admissions e-mail addresses are included when available.

Inclusion or exclusion in this listing does not indicate the author endorses any one school or program over another. Use this list as a beginning. As colleges frequently change programs, be sure to check the newest copy of *Lovejoy's College Guide* (usually located in the reference section of libraries or in guidance or counseling centers) for current schools offering courses or giving degrees in this field.

ARIZONA

Arizona State University
Box 870112
Tempe, AZ 85287
Phone: (480) 965-7788
Fax: (480) 965-3610
http://www.asu.edu

CALIFORNIA

Chapman University
One University Drive
Orange, CA 92866
Phone: (714) 997-6711
Fax: (714) 997-6713
E-mail: admit@chapman.edu
http://www.chapman.edu

University of the Pacific
3601 Pacific Avenue
Stockton, California 95211
Phone: (209) 946-2211
E-mail: admissions@uop.edu
http://www.pacific.edu

COLORADO

Colorado State University
8020 Campus Delivery
Fort Collins, CO 80523
Phone: (970) 491-6909
http://www.colostate.edu

FLORIDA

Florida State University
Tallahassee, FL 32306
Phone: (850) 644-6200
Fax: (850) 644-0197
E-mail: admissions@admin.fsu.edu
http://www.fsu.edu

University of Miami
P.O. Box 248025
1252 Memorial Drive
Coral Gables, FL 33146
Phone: (305) 284-4323
Fax: (305) 284-2507
E-mail: admission@miami.edu
http://www.miami.edu

GEORGIA

Georgia College & State University
Milledgeville, GA 31061
Phone: (478) 445-1284
Fax: (478) 445-1914
E-mail: info@gcsu.edu
http://www.gcsu.edu

University of Georgia
Athens, GA 30602
Phone: (706) 542-8776
Fax: (706) 542-1466
E-mail: undergrad@admissions.uga.edu
http://www.uga.edu

INDIANA

**Indiana University–Purdue University
  Fort Wayne**
2101 East Coliseum Boulevard
Fort Wayne, IN 46805
Phone: (260) 481-6812
Fax: (260) 481-6880
E-mail: ipfwadms@ipfw.edu
http://www.ipfw.edu

Saint Mary-of-the-Woods College
Saint Mary-of-the-Woods, IN 47876
Phone: (812) 535-5106
Fax: (812) 535-5010
E-mail: swcadms@smwc.edu
http://www.smwc.edu

University of Evansville
1800 Lincoln Avenue
Evansville, IN 47722
Phone: (812) 479-2468
E-mail: admission@evansville.edu
http://www.evansville.edu

IOWA

University of Iowa
Iowa City, IA 52242
Phone: (319) 335-3847
Fax: (319) 335-1535
E-mail: admissions@uiowa.edu
http://www.uiowa.edu

Wartburg College
100 Wartburg Boulevard
P.O. Box 1003
Waverly, IA 50677
Phone: (319) 352-8264
Fax: (319) 352-8579
http://www.wartburg.edu

KANSAS

University of Kansas
1502 Iowa Street
Lawrence, KS 66045
Phone: (785) 864-3911
Fax: (785) 864-5006
http://www.kn.edu

KENTUCKY

University of Louisville
2211 South Brook
Louisville, KY 40292
Phone: (502) 852-6531
Fax: (502) 852-4776
E-mail: admitme@gwise.louisville.edu
http://www.louisville.edu

LOUISIANA

Dillard University
2601 Gentilly Boulevard
New Orleans, LA 70122
Phone: (504) 816-4670
Fax: (504) 816-4895
E-mail: admissions@dillard.edu
http://www.dillard.edu

MASSACHUSETTS

Anna Maria College
50 Sunset Lane
Paxton, MA 01612
Phone: (508) 849-3360
Fax: (508) 849-3362
E-mail: admission@annamaria.edu
http://www.annamaria.edu

Berklee College of Music
1140 Boylston Street
Boston, MA 02215
Phone: (617) 266-1400
Fax: (617) 747-2047
E-mail: admissions@berklee.edu
http://www.berklee.edu

MICHIGAN

Eastern Michigan University
401 Pierce Hall
Ypsilanti, MI 48197
Phone: (734) 487-3060
Fax: (734) 487-6559
E-mail: admissions@emich.edu
http://www.emich.edu

Michigan State University
250 Administration Building
East Lansing, MI 48824
Phone: (517) 355-8332
Fax: (517) 353-1647
E-mail: admis@msu.edu
http://www.msu.edu

Western Michigan University
1903 West Michigan Avenue
Kalamazoo, MI 49008

Phone: (269) 387-2000
http://www.wmich.edu

MINNESOTA

Augsburg College
2211 Riverside Avenue
Minneapolis, MN 55454
Phone: (612) 330-1001
Fax: (612) 330-1590
E-mail: admissions@augsburg.edu
http://www.augsburg.edu

University of Minnesota–Twin Cities Campus
240 Williamson Hall
Minneapolis, MN 55455
Phone: (612) 625-2008
Fax: (612) 626 1693
E-mail: admissions@tc.umn.edu
http://www.tc.umn.edu

MISSISSIPPI

William Carey College
498 Tuscan Avenue
Hattiesburg, MS 39401
Phone: (601) 318-6051
E-mail: admissions@wmcarey.edu
http://www.wmcarey.edu

MISSOURI

University of Missouri–Kansas City
5100 Rockhill Road
Kansas City, MO 64110
Phone: (816) 235-1111
Fax: (816) 235-5544
E-mail: admit@umkc.edu
http://www.umkc.edu

NEW JERSEY

Montclair State University
1 Normal Avenue
Upper Montclair, NJ 07043
Phone: (800) 331-9205
http://www.montclair.edu

NEW YORK

Molloy College
1000 Hempstead Avenue
P.O. Box 5002
Rockville Centre, NY 11570
Phone: (888) 4-MOLLOY
http://www.molloy.edu

Nazareth College
4245 East Avenue
Rochester, NY 14618
Phone: (585) 389-2860
http://www.haz.edu

Fredonia
State University of New York
Fredonia, NY 14063
Phone: 800-252-1212
E-mail: admissions.office@fredonia.edu
http://www.fredonia.edu

New Paltz
State University of New York
75 South Manhcim Boulcvard
New Paltz, NY 12561
Phone: (845) 257-3200
Fax: (845) 257-3209
E-mail: admissions@newpaltz.edu
http://www.newpaltz.edu

NORTH CAROLINA

Appalachian State University
Boone, NC 28608
Phone: (828) 262-2120
Fax: (828) 262-3296
E-mail: admissions@appstate.edu
http://www.appstate.edu

East Carolina University
East Fifth Street
Greenville, NC 27858
Phone: (252) 328-6640
Fax: (252) 328-6945
E-mail: admis@mail.ecu.edu
http://www.ecu.edu

Livingstone College
701 West Monroe Street
Salisbury, NC 28144
Phone: (704) 216-6001
E-mail: admissions@livingstone.edu
http://www.livingstone.edu

Queens University of Charlotte
1900 Selwyn Avenue
Charlotte, NC 28274
Phone: (704) 337-2212
Fax: (704) 337-2403
E-mail: admissions@queens.edu
http://www.queens.edu

OHIO

Baldwin-Wallace College
275 Eastland Road
Berea, OH 44017

Phone: (440) 826-2222
Fax: (440) 826-3830
E-mail: info@bw.edu
http://www.bw.edu

College of Wooster
1189 Beall Avenue
Wooster, OH 44691
Phone: (330) 263-2000
Fax: (330) 263-2621
E-mail: admission@wooster.edu
http://www.wooster.edu

University of Dayton
300 College Park
Dayton, OH 45469
Phone: (937) 229-4411
E-mail: admission@udayton.edu
http://www.udayton.edu

OKLAHOMA

Southwestern Oklahoma State University
100 Campus Drive
Weatherford, OK 73096
Phone: (580) 774-3009
Fax: (580) 774-3795
http://www.swosu.edu

PENNSYLVANIA

Duquesne University
600 Forbes Avenue
Pittsburgh, PA 15282
Phone: (412) 396-5000
Fax: (412) 396-5644
E-mail: admissions@duq.edu
http://www.duq.edu

Elizabethtown College
One Alpha Drive
Elizabethtown, PA 17022
Phone: (717) 361-1400
Fax: (717) 361-1365
http://www.etown.edu

Immaculata University
1145 King Road
Immaculata, PA 19345
Phone: (610) 647-4400
Fax: (610) 640-0836
E-mail: admis@immaculata.edu
http://www.immaculata.edu

Mansfield University of Pennsylvania
1801 North Broad Street
Mansfield, PA 16933
Phone: (570) 662-4813
Fax: (570) 662-4121

E-mail: admissions@mansfield.edu
http://www.mansfield.edu

Marywood University
2300 Adams Avenue
Scranton, PA 18509
Phone: (570) 348-6211
E-mail: ugadm@ac.marywood.edu
http://www.marywood.edu

Slippery Rock University
1 Morrow Way
Slippery Rock, PA 16057
Phone: (724) 738-2015
E-mail: asktherock@sru.edu
http://www.sru.edu

Temple University
1801 North Broad Street
Philadelphia, PA 19122
Phone: (215) 204-7200
E-mail: tuadm@temple.edu
http://www.temple.edu

SOUTH CAROLINA

Charleston Southern University
9200 University Boulevard
P.O. Box 118087
Charleston, SC 29423
Phone: (843) 863-7050
http://www.charlestonsouthern.edu

TEXAS

Sam Houston State University
P.O. Box 2418
Huntsville, TX 77341
Phone: (936) 294-1828
Fax: (936) 294-3758
http://www.shsu.edu

Southern Methodist University
P.O. Box 425589
Dallas, TX 75275
Phone: (214) 768-2058
E-mail: ugadmission@smu.edu
http://www.smu.edu

Texas Woman's University
P.O. Box 425589
Denton, TX 76204
Phone: (940) 898-3188
E-mail: admissions@twu.edu
http://www.twu.edu

University of the Incarnate Word
4301 Broadway
San Antonio, TX 78209
Phone: (210) 829-6005
Fax: (210) 829-3921
http://www.uiw.edu

West Texas A&M University
2501 4th Avenue
Canyon, TX 79016
Phone: (806) 651-2020
Fax: (806) 651-5285
E-mail: lvars@mail.wtamu.edu
http://www.wtamu.edu

UTAH

University of Utah
201 South Presidents Circle
Salt Lake City, UT 84112
Phone: (801) 581-8761
Fax: (801) 585-7864
E-mail: admissions@utah.edu
http://www.utah.edu

VIRGINIA

Shenandoah University
1460 University Drive
Winchester, VA 22601
Phone: (540) 665-4581
Fax: (540) 665-4627
E-mail: admit@su.edu
http://www.su.edu

WISCONSIN

Alverno College
3400 South 43rd Street
P.O. Box 343922
Milwaukee, WI 53234
Phone: (414) 382-6100
E-mail: admissions@alverno.edu
http://www.alverno.edu

University of Wisconsin–Eau Claire
P.O. Box 4004
Eau Claire, WI 54702
Phone: (715) 836-5415
Fax: (715) 836-2409
http://www.uwec.edu

University of Wisconsin–Milwaukee
P.O. Box 749
Milwaukee, WI 53201
Phone: (414) 229-4397
Fax: (414) 229-6940
E-mail: uwmlook@uwm.edu
http://www.uwm.edu

University of Wisconsin–Oshkosh
800 Algoma Boulevard
Oshkosh, WI 54901
Phone: (920) 424-0202
E-mail: oshadmuw@uwosh.edu
http://www.uwosh.edu

E. COLLEGES AND UNIVERSITIES OFFERING DEGREES IN DANCE THERAPY

The following colleges and universities grant graduate degrees in dance/movement therapy. All schools listed are approved by the American Dance Therapy Association. Graduates from approved programs meet professional requirements necessary for membership in DTR (Dance Therapy Registry). This list is provided by the American Dance Therapy Association. Check out the ADTA Web site, http://www.adta.org, for more information.

COLORADO

Naropa University
2130 Arapahoe Avenue
Boulder, CO 80302
Phone: (303) 245-4545
Fax: (303) 245-4827
http://www.naropa.edu

ILLINOIS

Columbia College Chicago
600 South Michigan
Chicago, IL 60605
Phone: (312) 344-7697
E-mail: simus@popmail.colum.edu
http://www.colum.edu/graduate/
    graddance.html

NEW HAMPSHIRE

Antioch/New England Graduate School
40 Avon Street
Keene, NH 03431
Phone: (603) 357-3122
Fax: (603) 357-0718
E-mail: sloman@antiochne.edu

http://apdept.antiochne.edu/APDegrees/
   dance

NEW YORK

Pratt Institute
200 Willoughby Avenue
Brooklyn, NY 11205

Phone: (718) 636-2428
E-mail: lthompso@pratt.edu
http://www.pratt.edu/ad/ather

PENNSYLVANIA

Drexel University
Mail Stop 905

1505 Race Street
Philadelphia, PA 19102
Phone: (215) 762-7851
Fax: (215) 762-6933
E-mail: es42@drexel.edu
http://www.cnhp.drexel.edu/GradProgs/
   CreativeArts

APPENDIX II
WORKSHOPS, SEMINARS, AND SYMPOSIA

The following is a list of workshops, seminars, courses, and symposia and the general subject matter covered in each. You may want to contact associations related to your area of interest for additional information on programs not listed here.

This list is offered to help you find programs of interest. The author does not endorse one program over another and is not responsible for subject content.

Actors Studio, Inc.
8341 DeLongpre Avenue
West Hollywood, CA 90060
Phone: (323) 654-7125
Fax: (323) 654-8266
http://www.actors-studio.com/policies
The Actors Studio offers workshops of interest to professional actors, directors, and playwrights.

Alliance of Resident Theaters/New York (A.R.T./New York)
575 Eighth Avenue
Suite 17S
New York, NY 10018
Phone: (212) 244-6667
E-mail: artnewyork@aol.com
http://www.offbroadwayonline.com
A.R.T./New York offers seminars, roundtables, and workshops for members in a variety of areas.

American Association of Community Theatre (AACT)
8402 Briarwood Center
Lago Vista, TX 78645
http://www.aact.org
Phone: (512) 267-0711
Fax: (512) 267-0712
http://www.aact.org
The AACT sponsors workshops and conferences to promote excellence in community theater.

American Conservatory Theater Foundation (ACTF)
30 Grant Avenue
San Francisco, CA 94109
Phone: (415) 834-3200
Fax: (415) 834-3360
E-mail: sfjimmy@aol.com
http://www.act-sfbay.org
The ACTF offers an array of programs, workshops, and courses to those interested in acting.

The American Mime Theatre
American Mime, Inc.
61 Fourth Avenue
New York, NY 10003
Phone: (212) 777-1710
E-mail: mime@americanmime.org
http://www.americanmime.org
The American Mime Theatre offers classes, courses, workshops, and lectures in the art of mime.

American Place Theatre (APT)
266 West 37th Street
New York, NY 10018
Phone: (212) 594-4482
Fax: (212) 594-4208
E-mail: contact@americanplacetheatre. org
http://www.americanplacetheatre.org
The APT offers a large number of workshops each year to those interested in learning more about developing and presenting plays.

American Society of Composers and Publishers (ASCAP)
One Lincoln Plaza
New York, NY 10023
Phone: (212) 621-6000
Fax: (212) 724-9064
E-mail: info@ascap.com
http://www.ascap.com
The ASCAP offers an array of workshops and seminars for songwriters.

American Society of Music Arrangers and Composers (ASMAC)
P.O. Box 17840
Encino, CA 91416
Phone: (818) 994-4661
Fax: (818) 994-6181
E-mail: properimage2000@earthlink.net
http://www.asmac.org

ASMAC conducts workshops on new techniques in music for orchestras.

American Symphony Orchestra League (ASOL)
33 West 60th Street
New York, NY 10023
Phone: (212) 262-5161
Fax: (212) 262-5198
E-mail: league@symphony.org
http://www.symphony.org
ASOL offers regional workshops, seminars, and symposia in various phases of orchestra business and craft, including orchestra management, marketing, fundraising, and conducting.

American Theatre Critics Association (ATCA)
P.O. Box 15282
Evansville, IN 47716
Phone: (812) 474-0549
Fax: (812) 476-4168
E-mail: ts@evansville.edu
http://www.americantheatrecritics.org
The ATCA hosts conferences open to members and nonmembers on the subject of the art and craft of critical writing.

Artistic New Directions
c/o Larry Rosen
160 Claremont Avenue
New York, NY 10027
Phone: (212) 665-7000
E-mail: info@artisticnewdirections.org
http://www.artisticnewdirections.org
Artistic New Directions offers a number of workshops, seminars, and retreats on acting and theatrical production.

Broadcast Music Inc. (BMI)
320 West 57th Street
New York, NY 10019

Phone: (212) 586-2000
Fax: (212) 956-2059
E-mail: newyork@bmi.com
http://www.bmi.com
BMI conducts seminars and workshops throughout the country on various aspects of the music business.

Career Opportunities Seminars and Speakers
P.O. Box 711
Monticello, NY 12701
Phone: (845) 794-7312
http://www.shellyfield.com
Career Opportunities Seminars and Speakers offers seminars and workshops throughout the country on a broad variety of careers and career-oriented subjects.

Circle in the Square Theatre
1633 Broadway
New York, NY 10019
Phone: (212) 307-0388
http://www.circlesquare.org
The Circle in the Square Theatre offers acting classes for those interested in working in theater.

Cleveland Playhouse
8500 Euclid Avenue
Cleveland, OH 44106
Phone: (216) 795-7000
Fax: (216) 795-7005
http://www.clevelandplayhouse.com
The Cleveland Playhouse conducts classes in the professional side of theater as well as in acting and writing.

Dallas Theater Center
3636 Turtle Creek Boulevard
Dallas, TX 75219
Phone: (214) 526-8210
http://www.dallastheatercenter.org
The Dallas Theater Center conducts classes in various facets of acting.

Drama League
165 West 46th Street
New York, NY 10036
Phone: (212) 302-2100
E-mail: diny@econyc.com
The Drama League offers seminars and workshops in a variety of areas to those interested in theatre.

Dramatists Guild of America
1501 Broadway
New York, NY 10036
Phone: (212) 398-9366

Fax: (212) 944-0420
E-mail: igor@dramatistsguild.com
http://www.dramatistsguild.com
The Dramatists Guild of America sponsors symposia and other educational programs in a variety of areas of interest to playwrights, lyricists, and composers.

The Eugene O'Neill Theater Center
305 Great Neck Road
Waterford, CT 06385
Phone: (860) 443-5378
Fax: (860) 443-9653
E-mail: info@theONEILL.org
http://www.oneilltheatercenter.org
The Eugene O'Neill Theater Center offers an array of conferences, seminars, and workshops in various areas for those involved in the theatrical industry.

Glitter, Glamour & Gold Seminars
P.O. Box 711
Monticello, NY 12701
Phone: (845) 794-7312
http://www.shellyfield.com
Glitter, Glamour & Gold Seminars offer various seminars throughout the country in entering and succeeding in various facets of the entertainment industry.

IDEA Health and Fitness Association
6190 Cornerstone Court
San Diego, CA 92121
Phone: (800) 999-IDEA
Fax: (858) 535-8234
E-mail: member@ideafit.com
http://www.ideafit.com
IDEA offers continuing education credits for professionals, studio and club owners, and trainers.

Lee Strasberg Theatre and Film Institute
115 Lee Strasberg Way
New York, NY 10003
Phone: (212) 533-5500
http://www.newyork-strasberg.com
The Lee Strasberg Theater and Film Institute offers classes and other programs for those interested in acting.

Making It in Theater Seminars and Speakers
P.O. Box 711
Monticello, NY 12701
Phone: (845) 794-7312
http://www.shellyfield.com
Making It in Theater conducts seminars and workshops throughout the country in

a broad variety of subjects related to careers in theater and the performing arts.

National Association of Dramatic and Speech Arts (NADSA)
P.O. Box 561
Grambling, LA 71245
Phone: (225) 216-6803
Fax: (225) 216-6801
E-mail: info@nadsa.com
http://www.nadsa.com
NADSA offers educational programs for those interested in educational, community, children's, and professional theater.

O'Neill Critics Institute
c/o Dan Sullivan
Eugene O'Neill Theater Center
305 Great Neck Road
Waterford, CT 06385
Phone: (860) 443-5378
Fax: (860) 443-9653
E-mail: sulli008@umn.edu
http://www.oneilltheatercenter.org/prog/
   critic/critprog.htm
The O'Neill Critics Institute holds annual boot camps for critics and workshops on critical writing.

National Music Publishers Association (NMPA)
475 Park Avenue South
New York, NY 10016
Phone: (646) 742-1651
Fax: (646) 742-1779
E-mail: pr@nmpa.org
http://www.nmpa.org
The NMPA holds periodic forums for people involved in music publishing.

National Theatre Workshop of the Handicapped (NTWH)
535 Greenwich Street
New York, NY 10013
Phone: (212) 206-7789
Fax: (212) 206-0200
E-mail: ntwhny@ntwh.org
http://www.ntwh.org
The NTWH offers training in the theater arts to physically challenged adults interested in preparing for professional acting careers.

New Dramatists (ND)
424 West 44th Street
New York, NY 10036
Phone: (212) 757-6960
Fax: (212) 265-4738
E-mail: newdramatists@
   newdramatists.org

http://newdramatists.org
New Dramatists conducts classes in play-writing on a regular basis.

Non-Traditional Casting Project (NTCP)
1560 Broadway
New York, NY 10036
Phone: (212) 730-4750
Fax: (212) 730-4820
E-mail: info@ntcp.org
http://www.ntcp.org
The NTCP sponsors forums and roundtables in a variety of areas for artists interested in learning more about increasing employment for artists of color, women, and those with disabilities.

Opera America
1156 15th Street NW
Washington, DC 20005

Phone: (202) 293-4466
Fax: (202) 393-0735
E-mail: frontdesk@operaamerica.org
http://www.operaam.org
Opera America conducts seminars and workshops in various opera-related subject areas.

Public Relations Society of America (PRSA)
33 Maiden Lane
New York, NY 10038
Phone: (212) 460-1400
Fax: (212) 995-0757
http://www.prsa.org
The PRSA offers a multitude of seminars and workshops in public relations and publicity.

Songwriters Guild of America (SGA)
1500 Harbor Boulevard

Weehawken, NJ 07086
Phone: (201) 867-7603
Fax: (201) 867-7535
E-mail: songwritersnj@aol.com
http://www.songwriters.org
The Songwriters Guild of America conducts regional and national workshops, seminars, and critiques for those interested in both the business and craft of songwriting.

Theater Communications Group (TCG)
520 Eighth Avenue
New York, NY 10018
Phone: (212) 609-5900
Fax: (212) 609-5901
E-mail: tcg@tcg.org
http://www.tcg.org
The TCG conducts workshops and seminars in a variety of areas related to theater.

APPENDIX III
INTERNSHIPS IN THEATER AND THE PERFORMING ARTS

The following is a list of agencies and associations offering internships in theater and the performing arts. Many associations, school, nonprofit organizations, arts councils, theatrical groups, and dance companies throughout the country offer programs of this type.

This is by no means a complete listing but will serve as a starting point. Inclusion or exclusion from this list does not indicate endorsement of any one program over another. The author is not responsible for program content.

Keep in mind that some internships are paid positions while others are not. Some of these programs offer credits toward a college degree. Write or call to inquire about eligibility requirements and application procedures for internships.

ACT Theatre
Kreielsheimer Place
700 Union Street
Seattle, WA 98101-4037
Phone: (206) 292-7660
http://www.acttheatre.org
ACT sponsors a number of internship training programs on the technical side as well as on the administrative end of theater.

Alliance of Resident Theaters/New
    York (A.R.T./New York)
575 Eighth Avenue
Suite 17S
New York, NY 10018
Phone: (212) 244-6667
E-mail: artnewyork@aol.com
http://www.offbroadwayonline.com
A.R.T./New York offers internship opportunities in theater and arts management and production.

American Symphony Orchestra
    League (ASOL)
33 West 60th Street
New York, NY 10023
Phone: (212) 262-5161
Fax: (212) 262-5198
E-mail: league@symphony.org
http://www.symphony.org
ASOL offers intern programs in orchestra management.

Berkshire Theatre Festival
P.O. Box 797
Stockbridge, MA 01262
Phone: (413) 298-5536
Fax: (413) 298-3368
E-mail: info@berkshiretheatre.org
http://www.berkshiretheatre.org

The Berkshire Theatre Festival offers internships in areas ranging from acting to the business of theater.

Center Stage
700 North Calvert Street
Baltimore, MD 21202
Phone: (410) 986-4000
http://www.centerstage.org
Center Stage offers internship programs in production, costuming, business, and theatrical administration.

Cincinnati Playhouse in the Park
P.O. Box 6537
Cincinnati, OH 45206
Phone: (513) 345-2242
http://www.cincyplay.com
Cincinnati Playhouse in the Park offers internship programs in acting, directing, playwriting, and production.

Circle in the Square Theatre
1633 Broadway
New York, NY 10019
Phone: (212) 307-0388
http://www.circlesquare.org
Circle in the Square Theatre has internship opportunities in a range of theatrical disciplines.

Cleveland Playhouse
8500 Euclid Avenue
Cleveland, OH 44106
Phone: (216) 795-7000
Fax: (216) 795-7005
http://www.clevelandplayhouse.com
The Cleveland Playhouse offers internship programs in administrative, artistic, and technical fields of theater.

College Light Opera Company
c/o Robert Haslun
162 South Cedar Street
Oberlin, OH 44074
http://www.collegelightopera.com
The College Light Opera Company has programs in a variety of summer stock theater specialties.

Dallas Theater Center
3636 Turtle Creek Boulevard
Dallas, TX 75219
Phone: (214) 522-8499
http://www.dallastheatercenter.org
The Dallas Theater Center has internship programs in theater production, arts administration, management, and technical fields.

District of Columbia Commission on
    the Arts and Humanities
410 Eighth Street NW
Washington, DC 20004
Phone: (202) 724-5613
Fax: (202) 727-4135
http://dcarts.dc.gov
The DC Commission on the Arts and Humanities offers internships in arts management. Interns have the opportunity to gain job experience, build professional skills, and network with arts professionals throughout Washington, D.C.

Drama League
520 8th Avenue
New York, NY 10018
Phone: (212) 244-9494
Fax: (212) 244-9494

E-mail: audienceproject@dramaleague.org
http://www.dramaleague.org
The Drama League offers a variety of internships in theater production, marketing development, business, and administration.

Guthrie Theater
725 Vineland Place
Minneapolis, MN 55403
Phone: (612) 347-1133
Fax: (612) 347-1188
E-mail: joh@guthrietheater.org
http://www.guthrietheater.org
The Guthrie Theater offers internships in a variety of theater disciplines.

John F. Kennedy Center for the Performing Arts
2700 F Street NW
Washington, DC 20566
Phone: (202) 416-8000
http://www.kennedy-center.org
The National Institute for Music Theater at the Kennedy Center offers internships in a variety of areas to individuals interested in working in musical theater. These include administration, production management, stage direction, design, and music.

Juilliard School Stage Department
144 West 66th Street
New York, NY 10023
Phone: (212) 799-5000
http://www.juilliard.edu
Juilliard offers intern programs in a range of theater and the performing arts disciplines.

Lincoln Center for the Performing Arts
70 Lincoln Center Place
New York, NY 10023
Phone: (212) 875-5000
http://www.lincolncenter.org
Lincoln Center for the Performing Arts offers internships in theater administration.

Maine State Music Theatre
22 Elm Street
Brunswick, ME 04011
Phone: (207) 725-8760
Fax: (207) 725-1199
E-mail: info@msmt.org
http://www.msmt.org
The Maine State Music Theatre offers programs for performers, theater technicians, stage managers, and others in the fields of theater.

New Dramatists
424 West 44th Street
New York, NY 10036
Phone: (212) 757-6960
Fax: (212) 265-4738
E-mail: newdramatists@newdramatists. org
http://newdramatists.org
New Dramatists offers a number of internships for those interested in various aspects of theater business and craft.

The Eugene O'Neill Theater Center
305 Great Neck Road
Waterford, CT 06385
Phone: (860) 443-5378
Fax: (860) 443-9653
E-mail: info@theONEILL.org
http://www.oneilltheatercenter.org
The Eugene O'Neill Theater Center offers a variety of internships in the business and craft of theater.

Pearl Theatre Company, Inc.
80 Saint Marks Place
New York, NY 10003
Phone: (212) 505-3401
http://www.pearltheatre.org
The Pearl Theatre Company offers intern programs in stage management, costume design, and theater administration.

Roundabout Theatre Company
231 West 39th Street
New York, NY 10018
Phone: (212) 719-9393
http://www.roundabouttheatre.org
The Roundabout Theatre Company has internships available in marketing, fund-raising, business management, and production.

San Jose Repertory Company
1010 Paseo De San Antonio
San Jose, CA 95113
Phone: (408) 367-7262
http://www.sjrep.com
The San Jose Repertory Company has internships in production, artistic management, and marketing.

Steppenwolf Theatre Company
1650 North Halsted Street
Chicago, IL 60614
Phone: (312) 335-1650
http://www.steppenwolf.org
The Steppenwolf Theatre Company offers internships in stage management, front house management, public relations, and technical production.

Theatre Communications Group
520 8th Avenue
New York, NY 10018
Phone: (212) 609-5900
Theatre Communications Group has internships available in arts administration, management services and publications, artist services, and literacy services.

Theatre Development Fund/The Costume Collection
1501 Broadway
New York, NY 10036
Phone: (212) 221-0013
The Theatre Development Fund offers internships in costuming.

Walnut Street Theatre
825 Walnut Street
Philadelphia, PA 19107
Phone: (215) 574-3550
http://www.wstonline.org
The Walnut Street Theatre offers internships in acting, marketing, stage management, and various aspects of production.

APPENDIX IV
TRADE ASSOCIATIONS AND UNIONS

The following is a listing of associations and unions discussed in this book, as well as other associations that might be useful to you. Names, addresses, phone numbers, e-mail addresses, and Web sites (when available) are included so that you can contact organizations for information about membership, career guidance, scholarships, or internships.

Academy of Country Music
4100 West Alemeda
Burbank, CA 91505
Phone: (818) 842-8400
Fax: (818) 842-8535
E-mail: info@acmcountry.com
http://www.acmcountry.com

Academy of Television Arts and Sciences (ATAS)
5220 Lankershim Boulevard
North Hollywood, CA 91601
Phone: (818) 754-2800
Fax: (818) 761-2827
E-mail: todd@emmys.org
http://www.emmys.org

Acoustical Society of America
2 Huntington Quadrangle
Melville, NY 11747
Phone: (516) 576-2360
Fax: (516) 576-2377
E-mail: asa@aip.org
http://asa.aip.org

Actors' Equity Association (AEA)
165 West 46th Street
New York, NY 10036
Phone: (212) 869-8530
Fax: (212) 719-9815
E-mail: equityjobsny@actorsequity.org
http://www.actorsequity.org

Actors Studio
432 West 44th Street
New York, NY 10036
Phone: (212) 757-0870
Fax: (212) 757-7638
http://www.actors-studio.com

Alliance of Resident Theatres/New York (A.R.T./New York)
575 8th Avenue
New York, NY 10018
Phone: (212) 244-6667
Fax: (212) 714-1918
E-mail: artnewyork@aol.com
http://www.offbroadwayonline.com

American Alliance for Theatre and Education (AATE)
7475 Wisconsin Avenue
Bethesda, MD 20814
Phone: (301) 951-7977
E-mail: info@aate.com
http://www.aate.com

American Association for Music Therapy (AAMT)
8455 Colesville Road
Silver Spring, MD 20910
Phone: (301) 589-3300
Fax: (301) 589-5175
E-mail: info@musictherapy.org
http://www.musictherapy.org

American Association of Community Theatre (AACT)
8402 Briar Wood Circle
Lago Vista, TX 78645
Phone: (512) 267-0711
Fax: (512) 267-0712
E-mail: info@aact.org
http://www.aact.org

American Ballet Competition (ABC)
4701 Bath Street Building 46B
Philadelphia, PA 19137
Phone: (800) 523-0961
Fax: (215) 564-4206
E-mail: randy@dancecelebration.org
http://www.dancecelebration.org

American Bandmasters Association (ABA)
c/o Dr. William J. Moody
4250 Shorebrook Drive
Columbia, SC 29206
Phone: (803) 777-2042
E-mail: wmoody@mozart.sc.edu
http://www.americanbandmasters.org

American Choral Directors Association (ACDA)
502 Southwest 38th Street
Lawton, OK 73505
Phone: (580) 355-8161
Fax: (580) 248-1465
E-mail: acda@acdaonline.org
http://www.acdaonline.org

American College Dance Festival Association (ACDFA)
1570 East Jefferson Street
Rockville, MD 20852
Phone: (301) 770-4443
Fax: (301) 468-5841
E-mail: acdfa@bellatlantic.net
http://www.acdfa.org

American Composers Alliance
73 Spring Street
New York, NY 10012
Phone: (212) 362-8900
Fax: (212) 925-6798
E-mail: info@composers.com
http://www.composers.com

American Conservatory Theatre
30 Grant Avenue
San Francisco, CA 94108
Phone: (415) 834-3200
Fax: (415) 834-3360
E-mail: sfjimmy@aol.com
http://www.act-sfbay.org

American Dance Guild (ADG)
P.O. Box 2006
Lenox Hill Station
New York, NY 10021
Phone: (212) 932-2789
E-mail: americandanceguild@hotmail.com
http://www.americandanceguild.org

American Dance Therapy Association (ADTA)
2000 Century Plaza

10632 Little Patuxent Parkway
Columbia, MD 21044
Phone: (410) 997-4040
Fax: (410) 997-4048
E-mail: info@adta.org
http://www.adta.org

**American Federation of Musicians
  (AFM)**
1501 Broadway
New York, NY 10036
Phone: (212) 869-1330
Fax: (212) 764-6134
E-mail: info@afm.org
http://www.afm.org

**American Federation of Teachers
  (AFT)**
555 New Jersey Avenue NW
Washington, DC 20001
Phone: (202) 879-4400
Fax: (202) 879-4545
E-mail: online@aft.org
http://www.aft.org

**American Federation of Television and
  Radio Artists (AFTRA)**
260 Madison Avenue
New York, NY 10016
Phone: (212) 532-0800
Fax: (212) 532-2242
E-mail: info@aftra.com
http://www.aftra.com

American Guild of Music (AGM)
P.O. Box 599
Warren, MI 48090
Phone: (248) 336-9388
E-mail: agm@americanguild.org
http://www.americanguild.org

**American Guild of Musical Artists
  (AGMA)**
1430 Broadway
New York, NY 10018
Phone: (212) 265-3687
Fax: (212) 262-9088
E-mail: agma@musicalartists.org
http://www.musicalartists.org

American Guild of Organists (AGO)
475 Riverside Drive
New York, NY 10115
Phone: (212) 870-2310
Fax: (212) 870-2163
E-mail: info@agohq.org
http://www.agohq.org

**American Guild of Variety Artists
  (AGVA)**
363 7th Avenue
New York, NY 10001
Phone: (212) 675-1003
Fax: (212) 633-0097

American Harp Society (AHS)
P.O. Box 38334
Los Angeles, CA 90038
Phone: (323) 469-3050
E-mail: kmoon@uclalumni.net
http://www.harpsociety.org

America Library Association (ALA)
50 East Huron Street
Chicago, IL 60611
Phone: (312) 944-7298
Fax: (312) 280-4380
http://www.ala.org

American Mime Theatre
61 4th Avenue
New York, NY 10003
Phone: (212) 777-1710
E-mail: mime@americanmime.org
http://www.americanmime.org

**American Musical Instrument Society
  (AMIS)**
126 Darlington Avenue
Ramsey, NJ 07446
Phone: (201) 327-8426
Fax: (608) 831-8200
E-mail: ksl@nic.com
http://www.amis.org

American Music Center (AMC)
30 West 26th Street
New York, NY 10010
Phone: (212) 366-5260
Fax: (212) 366-5265
E-mail: richard@amc.net
http://www.amc.net

American Music Conference (AMC)
5790 Armada Drive
Carlsbad, CA 92008
Phone: (760) 431-9124
Fax: (760) 438-7327
E-mail: sharonm@amc-music.org
http://www.amc-music.org

**American Music Festival Association
  (AMFA)**
P.O. Box 2987
Anaheim, CA 92814
Phone: (714) 827-4562
Fax: (562) 948-4575

American Musicological Society (AMS)
201 South 34th Street
Philadelphia, PA 19104
Phone: (888) 611-4267
Fax: (215) 573-3673
E-mail: ams@sas.upenn.edu
http://www.ams-net.org

American Place Theatre (APT)
266 West 37th Street
New York, NY 10018
Phone: (212) 594-4482
Fax: (212) 594-4208
E-mail: contact@americanplacetheatre.
  org
http://www.americanplacetheatre.org

**American Society for Jewish Music
  (ASJM)**
15 West 16th Street
New York, NY 10011
Phone: (212) 294-8328
Fax: (212) 294-6161
E-mail: asjm@cjh.org
http://www.jewishmusic-asjm.org

**American Society for Theatre Research
  (ASTR)**
1849 Cannon Drive
Columbus, OH 43210
Phone: (614) 292-7926
Fax: (614) 292-3222

**American Society of Composers and
  Publishers (ASCAP)**
1 Lincoln Plaza
New York, NY 10023
Phone: (212) 621-6000
Fax: (212) 724-9064
E-mail: info@ascap.com
http://www.ascap.com

**American Society of Journalists and
  Authors, Inc. (ASJA)**
1501 Broadway
New York, NY 10036
Phone: (212) 997-0947
Fax: (212) 768-7414
http://www. asja.org

**American Society of Music Arrangers
  and Composers (ASMAC)**
P.O. Box 17840
Encino, CA 91416
Phone: (818) 994-4661
Fax: (818) 994-6181
E-mail: properimage2000@earthlink.net
http://www.asmac.org

American Symphony Orchestra League
33 West 60th Street
New York, NY 10023
Phone: (212) 262-5161
Fax: (212) 262-5198
E-mail: league@symphony.org
http://www.symphony.org

American Theatre Arts for Youth (AFAFY)
1429 Walnut Street
Philadelphia, PA 19102
Phone: (215) 563-3501
Fax: (215) 563-1588
E-mail: atafyinfo@atafy.org
http://www.atafy.org

American Theatre Critics Association (ATCA)
c/o Theatre Service
P.O. Box 15282
Evansville, IN 47716
Phone: (812) 474-0549
Fax: (812) 476-4168
E-mail: ts@evansville.edu
http://www.americantheatrecritics.org

American Theatre Organ Society (ATOS)
P.O. Box 551081
Indianapolis, IN 46205
Phone: (317) 251-6441
Fax: (317) 251-6443
E-mail: fellenzer@atos.org
http://www.atos.org

American Viola Society (AVS)
13140 Coit Road
Dallas, TX 75240
Phone: (972) 233-9107
E-mail: info@avsnationaloffice.org
http://www.americanviolasociety.org

American Women in Radio and Television (AWRT)
8405 Greensboro Drive
McLean, VA 22102
Phone: (703) 506-3290
Fax: (703) 506-3266
E-mail: info@awrt.org
http://www.awrt.org

Art Resources in Collaboration (ARC)
123 West 18th Street
New York, NY 10011
Phone: (212) 206-6492
Fax: (212) 627-2838
http://www.eyeondance.org

Associated Actors and Artists of America (AAAA)
165 West 46th Street
New York, NY 10036
Phone: (212) 869-0358
Fax: (212) 869-1746

Association for Theatre in Higher Education (ATHE)
P.O. Box 69
Downers Grove, IL 60515
Phone: (888) 284-3737
Fax: (630) 964-1941
E-mail: info@athe.org
http://www.athe.org

Association for Women in Communications
780 Ritchie Highway
Severna Park, MD 21146
Phone: (410) 544-7442
Fax: (410) 544-4640
E-mail: pat@womcom.org
http://www.womcom.org

Association of Independent Music Publishers (AIMP)
P.O. Box 69473
Los Angeles, CA 90069
Phone: (818) 771-7301
E-mail: lainfo@aimp.org
http://www.aimp.org

Association of Theatrical Press Agents and Managers, AFL-CIO (ATPAM)
1560 Broadway
New York, NY 10036
Phone: (212) 719-3666
Fax: (212) 302-1585
E-mail: info@atpam.com
http://www.atpam.com

Audience Development Committee (AUDELCO)
876 Hillside Avenue
Rochester, NY 14618
Phone: (212) 368-6906
Fax: (212) 368-6906
http://www.harpsociety.org/resources/adap.html

Authors Guild (AG)
31 East 28th Street
New York, NY 10016
Phone: (212) 563-5904
Fax: (212) 564-5363
E-mail: staff@authorsguild.org
http://www.authorsguild.org

Ballet Theatre Foundation (BTF)
890 Broadway
New York, NY 10003
Phone: (212) 477-3030
Fax: (212) 254-5938
http://www.abt.org

Big Band Academy of America (BBAA)
1438 North Pepper Street
Burbank, CA 91505-1835
Phone: (818) 841-5447
Fax: (775) 249-5939
E-mail: mbernhar@pacbell.net

Bilingual Foundation of the Arts (BFA)
421 North Avenue
Los Angeles, CA 90031
Phone: (323) 225-4044
Fax: (323) 225-1250
E-mail: bfa99@earthlink.net
http://www.bfatheatre.org

Black Theatre Network
763 Belmont Place
Seattle, WA 98102
Phone: (352) 495-2116
Fax: (352) 495-2051
http://www.blacktheatrenetwork.org

Broadcast Music, Inc. (BMI)
320 West 57th Street
New York, NY 10019
Phone: (212) 586-2000
Fax: (212) 956-2059
E-mail: newyork@bmi.com
http://www.bmi.com

Burlesque Historical Society (BHS)
c/o Exotic World
29053 Wild Road
Helendale, CA 92342
Phone: (760) 243-5261

Caledonian Foundation (CF)
P.O. Box 4151
Sarasota, FL 34230
Phone: (800) 713-0507

Callerlab-International Association of Square Dance Callers
467 Forrest Avenue
Cocoa, FL 32922
Phone: (321) 639-0039
Fax: (321) 639-0851
E-mail: info@callerlab.org
http://www.callerlab.org

Cecchetti Council of America
23393 Meadows Avenue
Flat Rock, MI 48134

Phone: (734) 379-6710
Fax: (734) 379-3886
E-mail: info@cecchetti.org
http://www.cecchetti.org

Center for Sports and Osteopathic Medicine
317 Madison Avenue
New York, NY 10017
Phone: (212) 685-8113
Fax: (212) 697-4541
E-mail: richardbachrach@bonesdoctor.com
http://www.bonesdoctor.com

Chamber Music America (CMA)
305 7th Avenue
New York, NY 10001
Phone: (212) 242-2022
Fax: (212) 242-7955
E-mail: info@chamber-music.org
http://www.chamber-music.org

Choristers Guild (CD)
2834 West Kingsley Road
Garland, TX 75041
Phone: (972) 271-1521
Fax: (972) 840-3113
E-mail: choristers@marlcg.org
http://www.choristersguild.org

Chorus America
1156 15th Street NW
Washington, DC 20005
Phone: (202) 331-7577
Fax: (202) 331-7599
E-mail: service@chorusamerica.org
http://www.chorusamerica.org

College Music Society
312 East Pine Street
Missoula, MT 59802
Phone: (406) 721-9616
Fax: (406) 721-9419
E-mail: cms@music.org
http://www.music.org

Congress on Research in Dance (CORD)
College at Brockport
Department of Dance
350 New Campus Drive
Brockport, NY 14420
Phone: (585) 395-2590
Fax: (585) 395-5413
E-mail: qcarlson@brocksport.edu
http://cordance.org

Costume Designers Guild (CDG)
4730 Woodman Avenue
Sherman Oaks, CA 91423

Phone: (818) 905-1557
Fax: (818) 905-1560
E-mail: cdgia@earthlink.net
http://www.costumedesignersguild.com

Country Dance and Song Society of America (CDSSA)
132 Main Street
P.O. Box 338
Haydenville, MA 01039
Phone: (413) 268-7426
Fax: (413) 268-7471
E-mail: office@cdss.org
http://www.cdss.org

Country Music Association (CMA)
1 Music Circle South
Nashville, TN 37203
Phone: (615) 244-2840
Fax: (615) 726-0314
E-mail: info@cmaworld.com
http://www.cmaworld.com

Creative Music Foundation (CMF)
P.O. Box 671
Woodstock, NY 12498
Phone: (845) 679-8847
E-mail: contact@creativemusicstudio.org
http://www.creativemusicstudio.org

Dance Critics Association (DCA)
c/o Membership Services
10592 Perry Highway
Wexford, PA 15090
Phone: (412) 363-4321
Fax: (412) 363-4320
E-mail: dancecritics@hotmail.com

Dance Educators of America (DEA)
P.O. Box 607
Pelham, NY 10803
Phone: (800) 229-3868
Fax: (914) 636-5895
E-mail: DEA@DEAdance.com
http://www.deadance.com

Dance Films Association (DFA)
48 West 21st Street
New York, NY 10010
Phone: (212) 727-0764
Fax: (212) 727-0764
E-mail: dfa5@earthlink.net
http://www.dancefilmsassn.org

Dance Masters of America (DMA)
214-10 41st Avenue
P.O. Box 610533
Bayside, NY 11361
Phone: (718) 225-4013

Fax: (718) 225-4293
E-mail: dmamann@aol.com
http://www.dma-national.org

Dance Notation Bureau (DNB)
151 West 30th Street
New York, NY 10001
Phone: (212) 564-0985
Fax: (212) 216-9027
http://www.dancenotation.org

Dance Theater Workshop (DTW)
219 West 19th Street
New York, NY 10011
Phone: (212) 691-6500
Fax: (212) 633-1974
E-mail: dtw@dtw.org
http://www.dtw.org

Dance/U.S.A.
1156 15th Street NW
Washington, DC 20005
Phone: (202) 833-1717
Fax: (202) 833-2686
http://www.danceusa.org

Directors Guild of America (DGA)
7920 Sunset Boulevard
Los Angeles, CA 90046
Phone: (800) 421-4173
Fax: (310) 289-2029
http://www.dga.org

Drama Desk (DD)
244 West 54th Street, 9th Floor
New York, NY 10019
Phone: (212) 586-2600
http://www.dramadesk.com

Dramatists Guild (DG)
1501 Broadway
New York, NY 10036
Phone: (212) 398-9366
Fax: (212) 944-0420
http://www.dramatistsguild.com

Episcopal Actors' Guild of America (EAGA)
1 East 29th Street
New York, NY 10016
Phone: (212) 685-2927
Fax: (212) 685-8793
E-mail: actors_guild@msn.com
http://www.actorsguild.org

Ethnic Cultural Preservation Council (ECPC)
6500 South Pulaski Road
Chicago, IL 60629

Phone: (773) 582-5143
Fax: (773) 582-5133

The Eugene O'Neill Memorial Theater Center
305 Great Neck Road
Waterford, CT 06385
Phone: (860) 443-5378
Fax: (860) 443-9653
E-mail: info@theoneill.org
http://www.oneilltheatercenter.org

Exotic Dancers League of America (EDLA)
29053 Wild Road
Helendale, CA 92342
Phone: (760) 243-5261

Ford's Theatre Society (FTS)
511 10th Street NW
Washington, DC 20004
Phone: (202) 638-2941
Fax: (202) 347-6269
E-mail: onstage@fordstheatrse.org
http://www.fordstheatre.org

Friars Club (FC)
57 East 55th Street
New York, NY 10022
Phone: (212) 751-7272
Fax: (212) 355-0217
E-mail: webmonk@friarsclub.com
http://www.friarsclub.com

Gospel Music Association (GMA)
1205 Division Street
Nashville, TN 37203
Phone: (615) 242-0303
Fax: (615) 254-9755
E-mail: info@gospelmusic.org
http://www.gospelmusic.org

Gospel Music Workshop of America (GMWA)
3908 West Warren
Detroit, MI 48208
Phone: (313) 898-6900
Fax: (313) 898-4520
E-mail: manager@gmwa.org
http://www.gmwa.org

Graphic Artists Guild (GAG)
90 John Street
New York, NY 10038
Phone: (212) 791-3400
Fax: (212) 791-0333
http://www.gag.org

Hospital Audiences (HA)
548 Broadway
New York, NY 10012

Phone: (212) 575-7676
Fax: (212) 575-7669
E-mail: hai@hospaud.org
http://www.hospitalaudiences.org

IDEA Health and Fitness Association
6190 Cornerstone Court East
Suite 204
San Diego, CA 92121
Phone: (858) 535-8979
Fax: (858) 535-8234
E-mail: member@ideafit.com
http://www.ideafit.com

Institute of Outdoor Drama (IOD)
CB 3240, 1700 Airport Road
Chapel Hill, NC 27599
Phone: (919) 962-1328
Fax: (919) 962-4212
E-mail: outdoor@unc.edu
http://www.unc.edu/depts/outdoor

Institute of the American Musical (IAM)
121 North Detroit Street
Los Angeles, CA 90036
Phone: (323) 934-1221

The International Alliance of Theatrical Stage Employees, Moving Picture Technicians Artists, and Allied Crafts of the United States, Its Territories, and Canada (IATSE)
1430 Broadway, 20th Floor
New York, NY 10018
Phone: (212) 730-1770
http://www.iatse-intl.org

International Association of Auditorium Managers (IAAM)
635 Fritz Drive
Coppell, TX 75019
Phone: (972) 906-7441
Fax: (972) 906-7418
http://www.iaam.org

International Brotherhood of Electrical Workers (IBEW)
1125 15th Street NW
Washington, DC 20005
Phone: (202) 833-7000
Fax: (202) 467-6316
http://www.ibew.org

International Conference of Symphony and Opera Musicians (ICSOM)
4 West 31st Street
New York, NY 10001
Phone: (212) 594-1636

E-mail: rtl@icsom.org
http://www.icsom.org

International Society for Contemporary Music (ISCM)
P.O. Box 1205
New York, NY 10276
Phone: (718) 442-5225
E-mail: mcmullin@league-iscm.org
http://www.league-iscm.org

League of American Theatres and Producers (LATP)
226 West 47th Street
New York, NY 10036
Phone: (212) 764-1122
Fax: (212) 719-4389
E-mail: league@broadway.org
http://www.broadway.org

League of Historic American Theatres (LHAT)
616 Water Street
Baltimore, MD 21202
Phone: (410) 659-9533
Fax: (410) 837-9664
http://www.lhat.org

League of Resident Theatres (LORT)
1501 Broadway
New York, NY 10036
Phone: (212) 944-1501
Fax: (212) 768-0785
http://www.lort.org

Meet the Composer
75 9th Avenue
New York, NY 10011
Phone: (212) 645-6949
Fax: (212) 645-9669
http://www.meetthecomposer.org

Metropolitan Opera Association (MOA)
Lincoln Center
New York, NY 10023
Phone: (212) 362-6000
Fax: (212) 874-2659
E-mail: metinfo@visionfoundry.com
http://www.metopera.org

Metropolitan Opera Guild (MOG)
70 Lincoln Center Plaza
New York, NY 10023
Phone: (212) 769-7000
Fax: (212) 769-7007
http://www.metopera.org

Music Educators National Conference (MENC)
1806 Robert Fulton Drive

Reston, VA 20191
Phone: (703) 860-4000
Fax: (703) 860-9404
E-mail: mbrserv@menc.org
http://www.menc.org

Music Publishers Association of the
United States (MPA)
PMB 246
1562 First Avenue
New York, NY 10028
Phone: (212) 327-4044
Fax: (212) 327-4044
E-mail: mpa-admin@mpa.org
http://www.mpa.org

Music Teachers National Association
(MTNA)
441 Vine Street
Cincinnati, OH 45202
Phone: (513) 421-1420
Fax: (513) 421-2503
E-mail: mtnanet@mtna.org
http://www.mtna.org

Nashville Songwriters Association
International (NSAI)
1701 West End Avenue
Nashville, TN 37203
Phone: (800) 321-6008
Fax: (615) 256-0034
E-mail: nsai@nashvillesongwriters.com
http://www.nashvillesongwriters.com

National Academy of Popular Music
(NAPM)
330 West 58th Street
New York, NY 10019
Phone: (212) 957-9230
Fax: (212) 957-9227
E-mail: info@songwritershalloffame.org
http://www.songwritershalloffame.org

National Academy of Recording Arts
and Sciences (NARAS)
3402 Pico Boulevard
Santa Monica, CA 90405
Phone: (310) 392-3777
Fax: (310) 392-2188
E-mail: info@grammyfoundation.org
http://www.grammy.com

National Academy of Television Arts
and Sciences (NATAS)
5220 Lankershim Boulevard
North Hollywood, CA 91601
Phone: (818) 754-2810
Fax: (818) 761-2827
http://www.emmyonline.org

National Association of Broadcast
Employees and Technicians
(NABET)
501 3rd Street NW
Washington, DC 20001
Phone: (800) 882-9174
Fax: (202) 434-1426
E-mail: jclark@cwa-union.org
http://www.nabetcwa.org

National Association of Broadcasters
(NAB)
1771 N Street NW
Washington, DC 20036
Phone: (202) 429-5300
Fax: (202) 429-4199
E-mail: nab@nab.org
http://www.nab.org

National Association of Composers
USA (NACUSA)
Box 49256
Barrington Station
Los Angeles, CA 90049
Phone: (310) 838-4465
Fax: (310) 838-4465
E-mail: deonprice@aol.com
http://www.music-usa.org/nacusa

National Association of Dramatic and
Speech Arts (NADSA)
P.O. Box 561
Grambling, LA 71245
Phone: (225) 216-6803
Fax: (225) 216-6801
E-mail: info@nadsa.com
http://www.nadsa.com

National Association of Schools of
Dance (NASD)
11250 Roger Bacon Drive
Reston, VA 20190
Phone: (703) 437-0700
Fax: (703) 437-6312
E-mail: info@arts-accredit.org
http://www.arts-accredit.org

National Association of Schools of
Music (NASM)
11250 Roger Bacon Drive
Reston, VA 20190
Phone: (703) 437-0700
Fax: (703) 437-6312
E-mail: info@arts-accredit.org
http://www.arts-accredit.org

National Association of Schools of
Theatre (NAST)
11250 Roger Bacon Drive
Reston, VA 20190

Phone: (703) 437-0700
Fax: (703) 437-6312
E-mail: info@arts-accredit.org
http://www.arts-accredit.org

National Conference of Personal
Managers (NCOPM)
330 West 38th Street
New York, NY 10018
http://www.ncopm.com

National Corporate Theatre Fund
(NCTF)
1 East 53rd Street
New York, NY 10022
Phone: (212) 750-6895
Fax: (212) 750-6977
E-mail: nctfbw153@aol.com
http://www.nctf.org

National Cosmetology Association
401 North Michigan Avenue
Chicago, IL 60611
Phone: (312) 527-6757
Fax: (312) 464-6118
E-mail: nca1@sba.com
http://www.salonprofessionals.org

National Dance Association (NDA)
1900 Association Drive
Reston, VA 20191
Phone: (800) 213-7193
Fax: (703) 476-9527
E-mail: nda@aahperd.org
http://www.aahperd.org/nda

National Dance Council of America
(NDCA)
P.O. Box 22018
Provo, UT 84602
Phone: (801) 422-8124
Fax: (801) 422-0541
http://www.ndca.org

National Dance-Exercise Instructor's
Training Association (NDEITA)
5955 Golden Valley Road
Minneapolis, MN 55422
Phone: (800) 237-6242
Fax: (763) 545-2524
E-mail: ndeita@ndeita.com
http://www.ndeita.com

National Dance Institute (NDI)
594 Broadway
New York, NY 10012
Phone: (800) 875-0083
Fax: (212) 226-0761
E-mail: info@nationaldance.org
http://www.nationaldance.org

National Federation of Music Clubs (NFMC)
1336 North Delaware Street
Indianapolis, IN 46202
Phone: (317) 638-4003
Fax: (317) 638-0503
E-mail: nfmc@nfmc-music.org
http://www.nfmc-music.org

National Federation of Press Women (NFPW)
P.O. Box 5556
Arlington, VA 22205
Phone: (800) 780-2715
Fax: (703) 534-5751
E-mail: presswomen@aol.com
http://www.nfpw.org

National Movement Theatre Association (NMTA)
c/o Pontine Movement Theatre
P.O. Box 1437
Portsmouth, NH 03801
Phone: (603) 436-6660
http://www.pontine.org

National Music Publishers Association (NMPA)
475 Park Avenue South
New York, NY 10016
Phone: (646) 742-1651
Fax: (646) 742-1779
E-mail: pr@nmpa.org
http://www.nmpa.org

National Opera Association (NOA)
P.O. Box 60869
Canyon, TX 79016
Phone: (806) 651-2857
Fax: (806) 651-2958
http://www.noa.org

National Orchestral Association (NOA)
P.O. Box 7016
New York, NY 10150
http://www.nationalorchestral.org

National Performance Network (NPN)
P.O. Box 70435
New Orleans, LA 70172
Phone: (504) 595-8008
Fax: (504) 595-8006
E-mail: info@npnweb.org
http://www.npnweb.org

National Press Club (NPC)
National Press Building
529 14th Street NW
Washington, DC 20045

Phone: (202) 662-7500
Fax: (202) 662-7512
E-mail: info@npcpress.org
http://www.press.org

National Press Photographers Association (NPPA)
3200 Croasdaile Drive
Durham, NC 27705
Phone: (800) 289-6772
Fax: (919) 383-7261
E-mail: info@nppa.org
http://www.nppa.org

National Symphony Orchestra Association (NSOA)
JFK Center for the Performing Arts
2700 F Street NW
Washington, DC 20566
Phone: (800) 444-1324
Fax: (202) 416-8105
http://www.nationalsymphony.org

National Theatre Conference (NTC)
School of Theatre
University of Houston
Houston, TX 77204
Phone: (713) 743-2930
Fax: (713) 749-1420

National Theatre of the Deaf (NTD)
55 Van Dyke Avenue
Hartford, CT 06106
Phone: (800) 300-5179
Fax: (860) 550-7974
E-mail: info@ntd.org
http://ntd.org

National Theatre Workshop of the Handicapped (NTWH)
535 Greenwich Street
New York, NY 10013
Phone: (212) 206-7789
Fax: (212) 206-0200
E-mail: ntwhny@ntwh.org
http://www.ntwh.org

New Dramatists (ND)
424 West 44th Street
New York, NY 10036
Phone: (212) 757-6960
Fax: (212) 265-4738
E-mail: newdramatists@
    newdramatists.org
http://newdramatists.org

New England Theatre Conference (NETC)
Northeastern University

360 Huntington Avenue
Boston, MA 02115
Phone: (617) 424-9275
Fax: (617) 424-1057
E-mail: mail@netconline.org
http://www.netconline.org

North American Performing Arts Managers and Agents (NAPAMA)
459 Columbus Avenue
New York, NY 10024
Phone: (888) 745-8759
E-mail: info@napama.org
http://www.napama.org

Northwest Drama Conference (NDC)
Olympic College
1600 Chester Avenue
Bremerton, WA 98337
Phone: (360) 475-7315
Fax: (360) 475-7689

The O'Neill Critics Institute
c/o Dan Sullivan
The Eugene O'Neill Theater Center
305 Great Neck Road
Waterford, CT 06385
Phone: (860) 443-5378
Fax: (860) 443-9653
http://www.oneilltheatercenter.org/prog/cr
    itic/critprog.htm

The O'Neill National Theatre Institute
305 Great Neck Road
Waterford, CT 06385
Phone: (860) 443-7139
Fax: (860) 443-9653
http://nti.conncoll.edu

Opera America (OA)
1156 15th Street NW
Washington, DC 20005
Phone: (202) 293-4466
Fax: (202) 393-0735
E-mail: frontdesk@operaamerica.org
http://www.operaam.org

Organization of Professional Acting Coaches and Teachers (OPACT)
3968 Eureka Drive
Studio City, CA 91604
Phone: (323) 877-4988
Fax: (323) 877-4988

Outer Critics Circle (OCC)
101 West 57th Street
New York, NY 10019
Phone: (212) 765-8557
Fax: (212) 765-7979

Paper Bag Players (PBP)
225 West 99th Street
New York, NY 10025 USA
Phone: (212) 663-0390
E-mail: info@paperbagplayers.org
http://www.paperbagplayers.org

Playwrights Conference
534 West 42nd Street
New York, NY 10036
Phone: (212) 244-7008
Fax: (212) 967-2957

Professional Dance Teachers
    Association (PDTA)
P.O. Box 38
Waldwick, NJ 07463
Phone: (800) 462-8679
Fax: (201) 652-2599
E-mail: hoctordance@hoctordance.com
http://www.hoctordance.com

Public Relations Society of America
    (PRSA)
33 Maiden Lane
New York, NY 10038
Phone: (212) 460-1400
Fax: (212) 995-0757
http://www.prsa.org

Public Relations Student Society of
    America (PRSSA)
33 Maiden Lane
New York, NY 10038
Phone: (212) 460-1400
Fax: (212) 995-0757
http://www.prsa.org

Radio-Television News Directors
    Association & Foundation (RTNDA)
1600 K Street NW
Washington, DC 20006
Phone: (800) 80-RTNDA
Fax: (202) 223-4007
E-mail: rtnda@rtnda.org
http://www.rtnda.org

Recording Industry Association of
    America (RIAA)
1330 Connecticut Avenue NW
Washington, DC 20036
Phone: (202) 775-0101
Fax: (202) 775-7253
http://www.riaa.com

Royal Academy of Dancing
c/o Patti Ashby
1412 17th Street
Bakersfield, CA 93301

Phone: (661) 336-0160
Fax: (661) 336-0162
E-mail: info@radusa.org
http://www.radusa.org

Screen Actors Guild (SAG)
5757 Wilshire Boulevard
Los Angeles, CA 90036
Phone: (800) SAG-0767
Fax: (323) 549-6603
http://www.sag.org

Screen Extras Guild (SEG)
3253 North Knoll Drive
Los Angeles, CA 90068
Phone: (323) 851-4301

SESAC, Inc.–Nashville
55 Music Square East
Nashville, TN 37203
Phone: (615) 320-0055
Fax: (615) 329-9627
http://www.sesac.com

SESAC, Inc.–New York
152 West 57th Street
New York, NY 10019
Phone: (212) 586-3450
Fax: (212) 489-5699
http://www.sesac.com

Society of American Fight Directors
    (SAFD)
School of Theatre
6321 North Lakewood
Chicago, IL 60660
Phone: (800) 659-6579
E-mail: president@safd.org
http://www.safd.org

Society of Dance History Scholars
    (SDHS)
c/o Ginnine Cocuzza
3416 Primm Lane
Birmingham, AL 35216
Phone: (800) 748-7347
Fax: (205) 823-2760
E-mail: sdhs@eprimemanagement.net
http://www.sdhs.org

Society of Stage Directors and
    Choreographers (SSDC)
1501 Broadway
New York, NY 10036
Phone: (800) 541-5204
Fax: (212) 302-6195
E-mail: info@ssdc.org
http://www.ssdc.org

Songwriters and Lyricists Club (SLC)
P.O. Box 605
Times Plaza Station
542 Atlantic Avenue
Brooklyn, NY 11217

Songwriters Guild of America
1500 Harbor Boulevard
Weehawken, NJ 07086
Phone: (201) 867-7603
Fax: (201) 867-7535
E-mail: songwritersnj@aol.com

Special Libraries Association (SLA)
1700 18th Street NW
Washington, DC 20009
Phone: (202) 234-4700
Fax: (202) 234-2442
E-mail: sla@sla.org
http://www.sla.org

Television Audience Screen Extras
    Guild (TASEG)
Solarium Penthouse
LaFong Tower
8311 54th Avenue South
Seattle, WA 98118
Phone: (206) 725-0873

Theatre Communications Group
    (TCG)
520 Eighth Avenue
New York, NY 10018
Phone: (212) 609-5900
Fax: (212) 609-5901
E-mail: tcg@tcg.org
http://www.tcg.org

Theatre Development Fund (TDF)
1501 Broadway .
New York, NY 10036
Phone: (212) 221-0885
Fax: (212) 768-1563
E-mail: info@tdf.org
http://www.tdf.org

Theatre Guild (TG)
135 Central Park West
New York, NY 10023
Phone: (212) 873-0676
Fax: (212) 873-5972

Theatre Historical Society (THS)
York Theatre
152 North York Road
Elmhurst, IL 60126
Phone: (630) 782-1800
Fax: (630) 782-1802
E-mail: execdir@historictheatres.org
http://www.historictheatres.org

United Scenic Artists (USA)
29 West 38th Street
New York, NY 10018
Phone: (212) 581-0300
Fax: (212) 977-2011
E-mail: usa829@aol.com
http://www.usa829.org

United States Institute for Theatre
  Technology (USITT)
6443 Ridings Road
Syracuse, NY 13206
Phone: (800) 938-7488
Fax: (315) 463-6525
E-mail: info@office.usitt.org
http://www.usitt.org

United States National Institute of
  Dance (USNID)
38 South Arlington Avenue
P.O. Box 245
East Orange, NJ 07019
Phone: (973) 673-9225

University Resident Theatre
  Association (URTA)
1560 Broadway
New York, NY 10036

Phone: (212) 221-1130
Fax: (212) 869-2752
E-mail: urta@aol.com

Up With People (UWP)
1675 Broadway
Denver, CO 80202
Phone: (303) 460-7100
Fax: (303) 225-4649
E-mail: anarans@upwithpeople.org
http://www.upwithpeople.org

Women in Communications
  Foundation
355 Lexington Avenue
New York, NY 10017
Phone: (212) 297-2133
Fax: (212) 370-9047
http://www.nywici.org/foundation

World Congress of Teachers of Dancing
  (WCTD)
c/o United States National Institute of
  Dance
38 South Arlington Avenue
P.O. Box 245
East Orange, NJ 07019

Writers Guild of America East (WGA)
555 West 57th Street
New York, NY 10019
Phone: (212) 767-7800
Fax: (212) 582-1909
E-mail: info@wgaeast.org
http://www.wgaeast.org

Writers Guild of America West (WGA)
7000 West Third Street
Los Angeles, CA 90048
Phone: (800) 548-4532
Fax: (323) 782-4800
E-mail: website@wga.org
http://www.wga.org

Yiddish Theatrical Alliance (YTA)
31 East 7th Street
New York, NY 10003
Phone: (212) 674-3437

Young Concert Artists (YCA)
250 West 57th Street
New York, NY 10107
Phone: (212) 307-6655
Fax: (212) 581-8894
E-mail: yca@yca.org
http://www.yca.org

APPENDIX V
BROADWAY THEATERS

The following is a listing of Equity-affiliated Broadway theaters in New York City. They are located in Manhattan's theater district and generally specialize in lavish, commercial productions. Names, addresses, and box office phone numbers are included for each. Many theaters are represented by a common organization and share a phone number that is also used for ticket sales. When you call, simply explain what kind of information you need, and the operator will route you to the correct party. Use this list to obtain general information and to locate internships and job opportunities.

Ambassador Theatre
219 West 49th Street
New York, NY 10019
Phone: (212) 239-6200

American Airlines/Selwyn Theatre
227 West 42nd Street
New York, NY 10036
Phone: (212) 719-9393

Brooks Atkinson Theatre
256 West 47th Street
New York, NY 10036
Phone: (212) 719-4099

Ethel Barrymore Theatre
247 West 47th Street
New York, NY 10036
Phone: (212) 239-6200

Vivian Beaumont Theatre
150 West 65th Street
New York, NY 10023
Phone: (212) 787-6868

Belasco Theatre
111 West 44th Street
New York, NY 10036
Phone: (212) 239-6200

Booth Theatre
222 West 45th Street
New York, NY 10036
Phone: (212) 239-6200

Broadhurst Theatre
235 West 5th Street
New York, NY 10036
Phone: (212) 239-6200

Broadway Theatre
Broadway at 52nd Street
New York, NY 10036
Phone: (212) 239-6200

Circle in the Square
1633 Broadway
New York, NY 10019
Phone: (212) 239-6200

Cort Theatre
138 West 48th Street
New York, NY 10036
Phone: (212) 239-6200

Ford Center
213 West 42nd Street
New York, NY 10036
Phone: (212) 307-4550

Gershwin Theatre
222 West 51st Street
New York, NY 10019
Phone: (212) 586-6510

John Golden Theatre
252 West 45th Street
New York, NY 10036
Phone: (212) 239-6200

Helen Hayes Theatre
240 West 44th Street
New York, NY 10036
Phone: (212) 944-9450

Al Hirschfeld Theatre
302 West 45th Street
New York, NY 10036
Phone: (212) 239-6200

Imperial Theatre
249 West 45th Street
New York, NY 10036
Phone: (212) 239-6200

Walter Kerr Theatre
219 West 48th Street
New York, NY 10036
Phone: (212) 239-6200

Longacre Theatre
220 West 48th Street
New York, NY 10036
Phone: (212) 239-6200

Lunt-Fontanne Theatre
205 West 46th Street
New York, NY 10036
Phone: (212) 575-9200

Lyceum Theatre
149 West 45th Street
New York, NY 10036
Phone: (212) 239-6200

Majestic Theatre
247 West 44th Street
New York, NY 10036
Phone: (212) 239-6200

Marquis Theatre
1535 Broadway
New York, NY 10036
Phone: (212) 282-0100

Henry Miller
124 West 43rd Street
New York, NY 10036
Phone: (212) 239-6200

Minskoff Theatre
200 West 45th Street
New York, NY 10036
Phone: (212) 869-0550

Music Box Theatre
239 West 45th Street
New York, NY 10036
Phone: (212) 239-6200

Nederlander Theatre
208 West 41st Street
New York, NY 10036
Phone: (212) 921-8000

New Amsterdam Theatre
214 West 42nd Street
New York, NY 10036
Phone: (212) 282-2900

Eugene O'Neill Theatre
230 West 49th Street
New York, NY 10036
Phone: (212) 239-6200

Palace Theatre
1564 Broadway
New York, NY 10036
Phone: (212) 730-8200

Plymouth Theatre
236 West 45th Street
New York, NY 10036
Phone: (212) 239-6200

Richard Rodgers Theatre
228 West 46th Street
New York, NY 10036
Phone: (212) 221-1211

Royal Theatre
242 West 45th Street
New York, NY 10036
Phone: (212) 239-6200

St. James Theatre
246 West 44th Street
New York, NY 10036
Phone: (212) 239-6200

Studio 54
254 West 54th Street
New York, NY 10019
Phone: (212) 239-6200

Shubert Theatre
225 West 44th Street
New York, NY 10036
Phone: (212) 239-6200

Neil Simon Theatre
250 West 52nd Street
New York, NY 10036
Phone: (212) 757-8646

Virginia Theatre
245 West 52nd Street
New York, NY 10019
Phone: (212) 239-6200

Winter Garden
1634 Broadway
New York, NY 10019
Phone: (212) 239-6200

APPENDIX VI
OFF-BROADWAY THEATERS

The following is a listing of Off-Broadway theaters in New York City provided by Actor's Equity Association. These theaters tend to be venues for serious theater and provide an alternative to the commercial tradition of Broadway.

Names, addresses, and phone numbers are included for each. Use this list to obtain general information and to locate internship and job possibilities.

Acorn Theatre
410 West 42nd Street
New York, NY 10036
Phone: (212) 753-5959

Actor's Playhouse
100 Seventh Avenue South
New York, NY 10014
Phone: (212) 302-5200

Astor Place Theatre
434 Lafayette Street
New York, NY 10003
Phone: (212) 254-4370

Barrow Street Theatre
27 Barrow Street
New York, NY 10014
Phone: (212) 243-6565

Blue Angel Theatre
323 West 44th Street
New York, NY 10036
Phone: (212) 252-3333

Century Theatre Center
111 East 15th Street
New York, NY 10003
Phone: (212) 982-6782

Chernuchin Theatre
American Theatre of Actors
314 West 54th Street
New York, NY 10019
Phone: (212) 581-3044

Cherry Lane Theatre
38 Commerce Street
New York, NY 10014
Phone: (212) 989-2020

Culture Project
49 Bleecker Street
New York, NY 10012
Phone: (212) 253-7037

Dodger Stages
340 West 50th Street
New York, NY 10019
Phone: (646) 871-1730

Douglas Fairbanks Theatre
432 West 42nd Street
New York, NY 10036
Phone: (212) 967-7079

Daryl Roth Theatre
101 East 15th Street
New York, NY 10003
Phone: (212) 375-1110

Duffy Theatre
1553 Broadway
New York, NY 10036
Phone: (212) 445-1016

Duke Theatre on 42nd Street
229 West 42nd Street
New York, NY 10036
Phone: (646) 223-3042

45 Bleecker Street Theatre
45 Bleecker Street
New York, NY 10010
Phone: (212) 253-7017

47th Street Theatre
304 West 47th Street
New York, NY 10036
Phone: (212) 265-0794

Gramercy Theatre
127 East 23rd Street
New York, NY 10010
Phone: (212) 459-3000

John Houseman Theatre Center
450 West 42nd Street
New York, NY 10036
Phone: (212) 967-7079

Jane Street Theatre
13 Jane Street
New York, NY 10014

Joyce Theatre
175 8th Avenue
New York, NY 10011
Phone: (212) 691-9740

Little Shubert Theatre
422 West 42nd Street
New York, NY 10036
Phone: (212) 279-3559

Lucille Lortel
121 Christopher Street
New York, NY 10014
Phone: (212) 924-8689

Maverick Theater
307 West 26th Street
New York, NY 10001
Phone: (212) 967-7079

Minetta Lane
18 Minetta Lane
New York, NY 10012
Phone: (212) 420-8000

New 42nd Street Studios
229 West 42nd Street
New York, NY 10036
Phone: (212) 223-3042

New York Shakespeare Festival
425 Lafayette Street
New York, NY 10003
Phone: (212) 539-8500

Orpheum Theatre
126 Second Avenue
New York, NY 10003
Phone: (212) 477-2477

Players Theatre
115 McDougal Street
New York, NY 10012

Playhouse 91
316 East 91st Street
New York, NY 10128
Phone: (212) 831-2000

Playwrights Horizons
416 West 42nd Street
New York, NY 10036
Phone: (212) 564-1235

Promenade Theatre
2162 Broadway
New York, NY 10024
Phone: (212) 580-1313

Revelation Theatre
339 West 39th Street
New York, NY 10018
Phone: (212) 947-7000

Saint Clement's Church
423 West 46th Street
New York, NY 10036
Phone: (212) 246-7227

Second Stage Theatre
307 West 43rd Street
New York, NY 19936
Phone: (212) 787-8302

Soho Playhouse
15 Vandam Street
New York, NY 10013
Phone: (212) 691-1555

Sullivan Street Playhouse
181 Sullivan Street
New York, NY 10012
Phone: (212) 674-3838

Theatre East
211 East 60th Street
New York, NY 10022
Phone: (212) 838-9090

Theatre Four
424 West 55th Street
New York, NY 10019
Phone: (212) 757-3900

Times Square Theatre
675 8th Avenue
New York, NY 10023
Phone: (212) 206-1515

Triad Theatre
158 West 72nd Street
New York, NY 10023
Phone: (212) 787-7921

Union Square Theatre
100 East 17th Street
New York, NY 10003
Phone: (212) 505-0700

Variety Arts Theatre
110 Third Avenue
New York, NY 10003
Phone: (212) 982-5800

Village Theatre
158 Bleecker Street
New York, NY 10012

Westside Theatre
407 West 53rd Street
New York, NY 10036
Phone: (212) 315-2302

York Theatre
St. Peter's Church
53rd Street and Lexington
New York, NY 10022
Phone: (212) 935-5820

APPENDIX VII
OFF-OFF-BROADWAY THEATERS

The following is a listing of Off-Off-Broadway theaters in New York City provided by Actor's Equity Association. These theaters tend to be venues for serious theater and provide an alternative to the commercial tradition of Broadway.

Names, addresses, and phone numbers are included for each. Use this list to obtain general information and to locate internship and job possibilities.

Abingdon Theatre
212 West 38th Street
New York, NY 10018
Phone: (212) 868-2055

Access Theater Company
380 Broadway
New York, NY 10013
Phone: (212) 968-1047

All Stars Projects Arts Center
543 West 42nd Street
New York, NY 10036
Phone: (212) 941-5800

Altered Stages–29th Street Rep.
212 West 29th Street
New York, NY 10001
Phone: (212) 712-8712

American Globe Theatre
145 West 46th Street
New York, NY 10036
Phone: (212) 869-9809

American Theatre of Actors–Sargent Theatre
314 West 54th Street
New York, NY 10019
Phone: (212) 581-3044

Arclight Theatre
152 West 71st Street
New York, NY 10023
Phone: (212) 787-8716

Astoria Performing Arts Center
31-30 33rd Street
New York, NY 11106
Phone: (718) 393-7505

Atlantic Theatre 453
453 West 16th Street
New York, NY 100011
Phone: (212) 869-8530

Bank Street Theatre
155 Bank Street
New York, NY 10014
Phone: (212) 633-6533

Phil Bosakowski Theatre
(45th Street Primary Stages)
354 West 45th Street
New York, NY 10036
Phone: (212) 333-4052

Club Rare
416 West 14th Street
New York, NY 10014
Phone: (212) 675-2220

Community Services Community
207 West 133 Street
New York, NY 10030
Phone: (212) 368-9314

Connelly Theatre
220 East 4th Street
New York, NY 10009
Phone: (212) 982-3995

Creative Acting Company
122 West 28th Street
New York, NY 10001
Phone: (212) 352-2103

Creative Artist Laboratory
303 West 42nd Street, #310
New York, NY 10036
Phone: (212) 316-0400

Creative Place Theatre
750 8th Avenue
New York, NY 10036
Phone: (212) 352-2103

CSU Cultural Center
107 Suffolk Street
New York, NY 10002
Phone: (212) 260-4080

Directors Company
331 West 43rd Street
New York, NY 10036
Phone: (212) 246-5877

Emerging Artists Theatre
432 West 42nd Street
New York, NY 10036
Phone: (212) 594-1404

William Esper Studios
261 West 35th Street
New York, NY 10001
Phone: (212) 904-1350

Flea Theatre
41 White Street
New York, NY 10013
Phone: (212) 226-0051

45th Street Theatre
354 West 54th Street
New York, NY 10036
Phone: (212) 840-9705

440 Studios
440 Lafayette Street
New York, NY 10003
Phone: (212) 529-0259

14th Street YMCA
344 East 14th Street
New York, NY 10003
Phone: (212) 780-0800

Gallery Players
199 14th Street
Brooklyn, NY 11215
Phone: (718) 832-0617

Goldberg Theatre
721 Broadway
New York, NY 10003
Phone: (212) 998-1940

Greenwich Street Theatre
547 Greenwich Street
New York, NY 100013
Phone: (212) 647-7530

Greenwich Village Center
219 Sullivan Street
New York, NY 10012
Phone: (212) 354-3074

Harlem Theatre Company
473 West 150th Street
New York, NY 10031
Phone: (212) 281-0130

Harold Clurman Theatre
410 West 42nd Street
New York, NY 10036
Phone: (212) 714-2442

Henry Street Settlement
Recital Hall
466 Grand Street
New York, NY 10002
Phone: (212) 766-9205

HERE Theatre
145 6th Avenue
New York, NY 10013
Phone: (212) 647-0202

Hudson Guild Theatre
119 9th Avenue
New York, NY 10011
Phone: (212) 760-9837

Independent Theatre
52-A West 8th Street
New York, NY 10011
Phone: (212) 929-6192

Instant Theatre
122 West 26th Street
New York, NY 10001
Phone: (212) 352-2103

Irish Arts Center
553 West 51st Street
New York, NY 10019
Phone: (212) 757-3318

La MaMa Experimental Theater
74A East 4th Street
New York, NY 10003
Phone: (212) 475-7710

Lamb's Theatre
130 West 44th Street
New York, NY 10038
Phone: (212) 575-0300

Lark Studio
939 8th Avenue
New York NY 10019
Phone: (212) 246-2676

Little Theatre
5 West 64th Street
New York, NY 10023
Phone: (212) 875-4128

Frederick Loewe Theater
35 West 4th Street
New York, NY 10012
Phone: (212) 998-5131

Loewe Theatre at Hunter College
68th Street & Lexington Avenue
New York, NY 10021

Looking Glass Theatre Space
422 West 57th Street
New York, NY 10019
Phone: (212) 307-9467

Lower Tenement Museum
97 Orchard Street
New York, NY 10002
Phone: (212) 387-8302

Manhattan Theatre Source
177 MacDougal Street
New York, NY 10011
Phone: (212) 260-4698

Horace Mann Theatre
c/o Ruth Krenshka
2960 Broadway
MC 1807 Dodge Hall
New York, NY 10027
Phone: (212) 854-5343

McGinn/Cazale Theatre–Second Stage
2162 Broadway
New York, NY 10024
Phone: (212) 787-8302

Medicine Show Theatre Ensemble
549 West 52nd Street
New York, NY 10019
Phone: (212) 262-4216

Sanford Meisner Theatre
164 11th Avenue
New York, NY 10011
Phone: (212) 206-1764

Metropolitan Playhouse
220 East 4th Street
New York, NY 10009
Phone: (212) 995-8410

Muddy Cup Coffee House Theatre
388 Van Duzer Street
Staten Island, NY 10304
Phone: (718) 818-8100

National Black Theatre
2031 Fifth Avenue
New York, NY 10035
Phone: (212) 722-3800

Native Aliens Playhouse
119 West 23rd Street
New York, NY 10010
Phone: (212) 330-7043

Neighborhood Playhouse
340 East 54th Street
New York, NY 10022
Phone: (212) 888-3770

Neuwirth Theatre
5625 Arlington Avenue
Bronx, NY 10471
Phone: (718) 548-8200

New Media Repertory
512 East 89th Street
New York, NY 10021
Phone: (212) 734-5195

Ohio Theatre
66 Wooster Street
New York, NY 10012
Phone: (212) 966-4844

Ontological Hysteric Theatre
260 West Broadway
New York, NY 10013
Phone: (212) 941-8911

Pantheon Theater
303 West 42nd Street
New York, NY 10036
Phone: (212) 582-5856

Pelican Studio Theatre
750 8th Avenue
New York, NY 10036
Phone: (212) 730-2030

Producers Club–Royal Theatre
348 West 44th Street
New York, NY 10036
Phone: (212) 315-4743

Producers Club II
616 9th Avenue
New York, NY 10036
Phone: (212) 946-1242

Queens Theatre in the Park
P.O. Box 520069
Flushing, NY 11352
Phone: (718) 760-0686

Quintero Theatre–Signature Theatre Co.
630 Ninth Avenue, # 1106
New York, NY 10036
Phone: (212) 564-4959

Red Room
85 East 4th Street
New York, NY 11218
Phone: (212) 777-6088

Paul Robeson Theatre
40 Greene Avenue
Brooklyn, NY 11223
Phone: (718) 783-9794

Saint Veronica's Church
140 Christopher Street
New York, NY 10014
Phone: (212) 243-0265

Sargent Theatre
314 West 54th Street
New York, NY 10019
Phone: (212) 719-7973

78th Street Theatre Lab
236 West 78th street
New York, NY 10024
Phone: (212) 873-9050

Shelter Theatre 54
244-250 West 54th Street
New York, NY 10019
Phone: (212) 246-6555

Peter Jay Sharp Theatre @Playwrights Horizon
416 West 42nd Street
New York, NY 10036
Phone: (212) 564-1235

Sande Shurin Theatre
311 West 43rd Street
New York, NY 10036
Phone: (212) 262-6848

SITI Company Workshop
520 8th Avenue
New York, NY 10018
Phone: (212) 868-0860

SOHO REPERTORY Theatre
46 Walker Street
New York, NY 10013
Phone: (212) 941-8632

Staten Island Shakesperean Theatre
450 Brielle Avenue
Staten Island, NY 10314
Phone: (718) 605-2682

Storm Theatre
145 West 46th Street
New York, NY 10036
Phone: (212) 730-3960

Tada Theatre
15 West 28th Street
New York, NY 10001
Phone: (212) 252-1619

Teatro La Tea
107 Suffolk Street
New York, NY 10002
Phone: (212) 529-1948

Theatre @ GTT
325 West 33rd Street
New York, NY 10011
Phone: (212) 563-4437

Theatre 53-INTAR
508 West 53rd Street
New York, NY 10019
Phone: (212) 695-6134

Theatre for the New City
155 First Avenue
New York, NY 10003
Phone: (212) 254-1101

Theatre of Riverside Church
91 Claremont Avenue
New York, NY 10027
Phone: (212) 854-5343

Theatre Row-Studio
410 West 42nd Street
New York, NY 10036
Phone: (212) 71402442

Theatre Ten Ten
1010 Park Avenue
New York, NY 10028
Phone: (212) 288-3246

Theatre 3
311 West 43rd Street
New York, NY 10036
Phone: (212) 246-5877

Theatre 315
315 West 47th Street
New York, NY 10036
Phone: (212) 975-9988

Trilogy Theatre
341 West 44th Street
New York, NY 10036
Phone: (212) 489-1632

Undercroft @ Trinity Lutheran Church
31-18 37th street
Astoria, NY 11101
Phone: (718) 278-0036

Under St. Marks
94 St. Marks Place
New York, NY 10003
Phone: (212) 777-5088

Urban Stages
259 West 30th Street
New York, NY 10001
Phone: (212) 421-1380

Vital Theatre Company
432 West 42nd Street
New York, NY 10036
Phone: (212) 268-2040

Women's Interart Annex
400 West 52nd Street
New York, NY 10019
Phone: (212) 246-1050

Workshop Theatre Company
312 West 36th Street
New York, NY 10018
Phone: (212) 695-4173

WOW Café Theatre
59 East 4th Street
New York, NY 10003
Phone: (212) 777-4280

APPENDIX VIII
DINNER THEATERS

The following is a listing of dinner theaters throughout the country provided by Actor's Equity Association. Dinner theaters are restaurants in which a play is performed following a meal. Names, addresses, and phone numbers are included. Use this list to obtain general information and to locate internship and job possibilities.

CALIFORNIA

Lawrence Welk Village Theatre
8975 Lawrence Welk Drive
Escondido, CA 92026
Phone: (619) 749-3000
Fax: (619) 749-6182

COLORADO

Country Dinner Playhouse
6875 South Clinton
Englewood, CO 80110
Phone: (303) 790-9311
Fax: (303) 790-2615

FLORIDA

Alhambra Dinner Theater
12000 Beach Boulevard
Jacksonville, FL 32216
Phone: (904) 641-1212
Fax: (904) 642-3505

Golden Apple Dinner Theatre
25 North Pineapple Avenue
Sarasota, FL 33577
Phone: (941) 366-2646
Fax: (941) 354-9100

Mark Two Dinner Theatre
3376 Edgewater Drive
Orlando, FL 32804
Phone: (407) 422-3191
Fax: (407) 843-1510

The Royal Palm Dinner Theatre
303 Southeast Mizner Boulevard
Royal Palm Plaza
Boca Raton, FL 33432
Phone: (561) 392-3755
Fax: (561) 392-1443

Show Palace Dinner Theatre
16128 US Highway 19

Hudson, FL 14667
Phone: (727) 863-7949
Fax: (727) 863-2585

ILLINOIS

Drury Lane Oakbrook Theatre
100 Drury Lane
Oakbrook Terrace, IL 60181
Phone: (312) 538-3800

Drury Lane South
2500 West Drury Lane
Evergreen Park, IL 60642
Phone: (312) 799-4000

Marriott's Lincolnshire Theatre
101 Half Day Road
Lincolnshire, IL 60015
Phone: (847) 634-0204
Fax: (847) 634-7358

INDIANA

Beef 'N' Boards Dinner Theatre
9301 North Michigan
Indianapolis, IN 46268
Phone: (317) 872-9664
Fax: (317) 876-0510

MINNESOTA

Chanhassen Playhouse Dinner Theatre
501 West 78th Street
Chanhassen, MN 55317
Phone: (612) 934-1500
Fax: (612) 934-1586

Fireside Dinner Theatre
501 West 78th Street
Chanhassen, MN 55317
Phone: (612) 934-1500
Fax: (612) 934-1586

MISSOURI

The American Heartland Theatre
2450 Grand Avenue
Kansas City, MO 64108
Phone: (816) 842-9800
Fax: (816) 842-1881

The New American Theatre Company
1116 West 25th Street
Kansas City, MO 64108
Phone: (913) 649-0103
Fax: (913) 649-9743

NEW YORK

Lake George Dinner Theatre
P.O. Box 266
2110 Route 9
Lake George, NY 12845
Phone: (518) 668-2198

Westchester Broadway Theatre
1 Broadway Plaza
Elmsford, NY 10523
Phone: (914) 592-2268
Fax: (914) 592-6917

OHIO

Carousel Dinner Theatre
P.O. 7530
Akron, OH 44306
Phone: (330) 724-9855
Fax: (330) 724-2232

PENNSYLVANIA

Grand Candlelight Dinner Theatre
321 West State Street
Media, PA 19063
Phone: (610) 566-5462

APPENDIX IX
RESIDENT THEATERS

The following information, provided by Actor's Equity Association, lists Equity-affiliated resident theaters throughout the United States. These theaters operate under the LORT (League of Resident Theaters) contract. Use this listing to obtain general information and to locate internships or job possibilities.

ALABAMA

Alabama Shakespeare Festival
One Festival Drive
Montgomery, AL 36117
Phone: (334) 271-5300
Fax: (334) 271-5348
http://www.asf.net

ARIZONA

Arizona Theatre Company
P.O. Box 1631
Tucson, AZ 83702
Phone: (520) 884-8210
Fax: (520) 628-9129
http://www.aztheatreco.org

ARKANSAS

Arkansas Repertory Theatre
601 East Main Street
P.O. Box 110
Little Rock, AR 72201
Phone: (501) 378-0445
Fax: (501) 378-0012
http://www.therep.org

CALIFORNIA

American Conservatory Theatre
30 Grant Avenue
San Francisco, CA 94108
Phone: (415) 439-2429
Fax: (415) 834-3326
http://www.act-sfbay.org

Berkeley Repertory Theatre
2025 Addison Street
Berkeley, CA 94702
Phone: (510) 204-8901
Fax: (510) 841-7711
http://www.berkeleyrep.org

California Shakespeare Festival
701 Heinz Avenue
Berkeley, CA 94710
Phone: (510) 548-3422
Fax: (510) 843-9921

Center Theatre Group
601 West Temple Street
Los Angeles, CA 90012
Phone: (213) 972-7384
Fax: (213) 972-7402
http://www.taperahmanson.com

Geffen Playhouse
11693 San Vicente Boulevard, #816
Los Angeles, CA 90049
Phone: (310) 208-6500
Fax: (310) 208-0341
http://www.geffenplayhouse.com

Laguna Playhouse
P.O. Box 1747
Laguna Beach, CA 92652
Phone: (949) 497-2787
Fax: (949) 376-8185
http://www.lagunaplayhouse.com

La Jolla Playhouse
P.O. Box 12039
La Jolla, CA 92037
Phone: (858) 550-1070
Fax: (858) 550-1075
http://www.lajollaplayhouse.com

Old Globe Theatre
P.O. Box 2171
San Diego, CA 92112
Phone: (619) 231-1941
Fax: (619) 231-5879
http://www.theoldglobe.org

Pasadena Playhouse
39 South El Molino Avenue
Pasadena, CA 91101
Phone: (626) 792-8672
Fax: (626) 792-7343
http://www.pasadenaplayhouse.org

San Jose Repertory Theatre
101 Paseo de San Antonio
San Jose, CA 95113
Phone: (408) 291-2266
Fax: (408) 367-7237
http://www.sjrep.com

Shakespeare Festival/LA
1238 West First Street
Los Angeles, CA 90026
Phone: (213) 481-2273
Fax: (213) 975-0833

South Coast Repertory Theatre
Box 2197
Costa Mesa, CA 92628
Phone: (714) 708-5500
Fax: (714) 545-0391
http://www.scr.org

COLORADO

Arvada Center for the Arts
6901 Wadsworth Boulevard
Arvada, CO 8003
Phone: (720) 898-7266
Fax: (720) 898-7217

Denver Center Theatre Company
1050 13th Street
Denver, CO, 80204
Phone: (303) 893-4000
Fax: (303) 825-2117
http://www.denvercenter.org

CONNECTICUT

The Eugene O'Neil Theater Center
National Playwrights Conference
305 Great Neck Road
Waterford, CT 06385
Phone: (860) 443-5376
Fax: (860) 443-9653

Goodspeed Opera House
6 Main Street
East Haddam, CT 06423

Phone: (860) 873-8664
Fax: (860) 873-2329
http://www.goodspeed.org

Hartford Stage
50 Church Street
Hartford, CT 06103
Phone: (860) 525-5601
Fax: (860) 525-4420
http://www.hartfordstage.org

Long Wharf Theatre
222 Sargent Drive
New Haven, CT 06511
Phone: (203) 787-4284
Fax: (203) 776-2287
http://www.longwharf.org

Yale Repertory Theatre
1120 Chapel Street
P.O. Box 1257
New Haven, CT 06505
Phone: (203) 432-1234
Fax: (203) 432-8332
http://www.yale.edu/yalerep

DELAWARE

Delaware Theatre Company
200 Water Street
Wilmington, DE 19801
Phone: (302) 594-1104
Fax: (302) 594-1107
http://www.delawaretheatre.org

DISTRICT OF COLUMBIA

Arena Stage
Sixth and Main Avenue SW
Washington, DC 20024
Phone: (202) 554-9066
Fax: (202) 488-4056
http://www.arenastage.org

Ford's Theatre
511 10th Street NW
Washington, DC 20004
Phone: (202) 638-2941
http://www.fordstheatre.org

Shakespeare Theatre
516 8th Street SE
Washington, DC 20003
Phone: (202) 547-3230
Fax: (202) 547-0226
http://www.shakespearedc.org

FLORIDA

Asolo Theatre Company
5555 North Tamiami Trail

Sarasota, FL 34243
Phone: (941) 351-9010
Fax: (941) 351-5796
http://www.asolo.org

Coconut Grove Playhouse
3500 Main Highway
Miami, FL 33133
Phone: (305) 442-2662
Fax: (305) 444-6437
http://www.cgplayhouse.com

Florida Stage
Plaza del Mar
262 South Ocean Boulevard
Manalapan, FL 33462
Phone: (561) 585-3404
Fax: (561) 588-4708
http://www.floridastage.org

Maltz Jupiter Theatre
1001 East Indiantown Road
Jupiter, FL 33477
Phone: (561) 743-2666
Fax: (561) 743-0107
http://www.jupitertheatre.org

Riverside Theatre
3250 Riverside Park Drive
Vero Beach, FL 3293
Phone: (772) 231-5860
Fax: (772) 234-5298

GEORGIA

Alliance Theatre Company
1280 Peachtree Street NE
Atlanta, GA 30309
Phone: (404) 733-4650
Fax: (404) 733-4625
http://www.alliancetheatre.org

Georgia Shakespeare Festival
4484 Peachtree Road NE
Atlanta, GA 30319
Phone: (404) 504-3400
Fax: (404) 504-3414
http://www.gashakespeare.org

ILLINOIS

Court Theatre
5535 South Ellis Avenue
Chicago, IL 60637
Phone: (773) 702-7005
Fax: (773) 34-1897
http://www.courttheatre.org

Goodman Theatre Company
170 North Dearborn Street
Chicago, IL 60601

Phone: (312) 443-3811
Fax: (312) 443-3821
http://www.goodman-theatre.org

Northlight Theatre
9501 Skokie Boulevard
Skokie, IL 60077
Phone: (847) 679-9501
http://www.northlight.org

North Shore Center for the Performing Arts
9501 North Skokie Boulevard
Skokie, IL 60076
Phone: (847) 679-9501
Fax: (847) 679-1879

INDIANA

Indiana Repertory Theatre
140 West Washington Street
Indianapolis, IN 46204
Phone: (317) 635-5277
Fax: (317) 236-0767
http://www.indianarep.com

KENTUCKY

Actors Theatre of Louisville
316 West Main Street
Louisville, KY 40202
Phone: (502) 584-1265
Fax: (502) 561-3300
http://www.actorstheatre.org

MAINE

Portland Stage Company
P.O. Box 1458
Portland, ME 04104
Phone: (207) 774-1043
Fax: (207) 774-0576
http://www.portlandstage.com

MARYLAND

Center Stage
700 North Calvert Street
Baltimore, MD 21202
Phone: (410) 986-4000
Fax: (410) 539-3912
http://www.centerstage.org

MASSACHUSETTS

American Repertory Theatre
64 Brattle Street
Cambridge, MA 02138
Phone: (617) 495-2668
Fax: (617) 495-1775
http://www.amrep.org

Berkshire Theatre Festival
P.O. Box 797
Stockbridge, MA 01262
Phone: (413) 298-5536
Fax: (413) 298-3368
http://www.berkshiretheatre.org

Huntington Theatre Company
264 Huntington Avenue
Boston, MA 02115
Phone: (617) 266-7900
Fax: (617) 353-8300
http://www.huntingtontheatre.org

Merrimack Repertory Theatre
50 East Merrimack Street
Lowell, MA 01852
Phone: (978) 654-7750
Fax: (978) 654-7575
http://www.merrimackrep.org

MICHIGAN

Meadow Brook Theatre Ensemble
Oakland University
207 Wilson Hall
Rochester, MI 48309
Phone: (248) 370-3310
Fax: (248) 370-3108

MINNESOTA

Guthrie Theater
725 Vineland Place
Minneapolis, MN 55403
Phone: (612) 347-1100
Fax: (612) 347-1188
http://www.guthrietheater.org

MISSOURI

Kansas City Repertory Theatre
4949 Cherry Street
Kansas City, MO 64110
Phone: (816) 235-2727
Fax: (816) 235-5357
http://www.kcrep.org

The Repertory Theatre of St. Louis
P.O. Box 191730
130 Edgar Road
St. Louis, MO 63119
Phone: (314) 968-7340
Fax: (314) 968-9638
http://www.repstl.org

NEW JERSEY

George Street Playhouse
9 Livingston Avenue
New Brunswick, NJ 08901
Phone: (732) 846-2895
Fax: (732) 247-9151
http://www.georgestplayhouse.org

McCarter Theatre
91 University Place
Princeton, NJ 08540
Phone: (609) 258-6500
Fax: (609) 497-0369
http://www.mccarter.org

Shakespeare Theatre of New Jersey
36 Madison Avenue
Madison, NJ 07940
Phone: (973) 408-3278
Fax: (973) 408-3361

NEW MEXICO

Santa Fe Stages
105 East Marcy Street
Santa Fe, NM 87501
Phone: (505) 982-6680
Fax: (505) 982-6682

NEW YORK

Bay Street Theatre
P.O. Box 810
Sag Harbor, NY 11963
Phone: (631) 725-0818
Fax: (631) 725-0906

Capital Repertory Company
111 North Pearl Street
Albany, NY 12207
Phone: (518) 462-4531
Fax: (518) 465-0213
http://www.capitalrep.org

Geva Theatre Center
75 Woodbury Boulevard
Rochester, NY 14607
Phone: (585) 232-1366
Fax: (585) 232-4031
http://www.gevatheatre.org

Lincoln Center Theater
150 West 65th Street
New York, NY 10023
Phone: (212) 362-7600
Fax: (212) 873-0761
http://www.lct.org

Manhattan Theatre Club
311 West 43rd Street
New York, NY 10036
Phone: (212) 399-3000
Fax: (212) 399-4329
http://www.mtc-nyc.org

National Actors Theatre
Pace University
1 Pace Plaza
New York, NY 10038
Phone: (212) 748-3490
Fax: (212) 748-3510

New York Shakespeare Festival
Joseph Papp Public Theatre
425 Lafayette Street
New York, NY 10003
Phone: (212) 539-8500
Fax: (212) 539-8705

Pearl Theatre Company, Inc.
80 Saint Mark's Place
New York, NY 10003
Phone: (212) 505-3401
Fax: (212) 505-3404

Roundabout Theatre Company
231 West 39th Street
New York, NY 10018
Phone: (212) 719-9393
Fax: (212) 869-8817
http://www.roundabouttheatre.org

SITI Company
520 Eighth Avenue
New York, NY 10018
Phone: (212) 868-0860
Fax: (212) 868-0837

Studio Arena Theatre
710 Main Street
Buffalo, NY 14202
Phone: (716) 856-8025
Fax: (716) 856-3415
http://www.studioarena.org

Syracuse Stage
820 East Genesee Street
Syracuse, NY 13210
Phone: (315) 443-4008
Fax: (315) 443-9846
http://www.syracusestage.org

Theatre for a New Audience
154 Christopher Street
New York, NY 10014
Phone: (212) 229-2819
Fax: (212) 229-2911
http://www.tfana.org

NORTH CAROLINA

Charlotte Repertory Theatre
622 East 28th Street
Charlotte, NC 28205
Phone: (704) 333-8587
Fax: (704) 333-0224

North Carolina Shakespeare Festival
1014 Mill Avenue
High Point, NC 07260
Phone: (336) 841-2273
Fax: (336) 841-8627

PlayMakers Repertory Company
CB# 3235
Center for Dramatic Art
UNC Campus
Chapel Hill, NC 27599
Phone: (919) 962-1122
Fax: (919) 962-4069
http://www.playmakersrep.org

OHIO

Cincinnati Playhouse in the Park
P.O. Box 6537
Cincinnati, OH 45206
Phone: (513) 345-2242
Fax: (513) 345-2254
http://www.cincyplay.com

Cleveland Play House
8500 Euclid Avenue
Cleveland, OH 44106
Phone: (216) 795-7010
Fax: (216) 795-7005
http://www.clevelandplayhouse.com

Great Lakes Theatre Festival
1501 Euclid Avenue
Cleveland, OH 44115
Phone: (216) 241-5490
Fax: (216) 241-6315
http://www.greatlakestheater.org

OREGON

Oregon Shakespeare Festival
P.O. Box 158
Ashland, OR 97530
Phone: (541) 482-2111
Fax: (541) 482-0466

Portland Center Stage
1111 Southwest Broadway
Portland, OR 97205
Phone: (503) 248-6309
Fax: (503) 796-6509
http://www.pcs.org

PENNSYLVANIA

Arden Theatre Company
40 North 2nd Street
Philadelphia, PA 19106
Phone: (215) 922-8900

Fax: (215) 922-7011
http://www.ardentheatre.org

City Theatre Company
1300 Bingham Street
Pittsburgh, PA 15203
Phone: (412) 431-4400
Fax: (412) 431-5535
http://www.citytheatrecompany.org

The People's Light and Theatre Company
39 Conestoga Road
Malvern, PA 19355
Phone: (610) 647-1900
Fax: (610) 640-521
http://www.peopleslight.org

Philadelphia Theatre Company
230 South 15th Street
Philadelphia, PA 19102
Phone: (215) 985-1400
Fax: (215) 985-5800
http://www.phillytheatreco.com

Pittsburgh Public Theater
621 Penn Avenue
Pittsburgh, PA 15222
Phone: (412) 316-8200
Fax: (412) 316-8216
http://www.ppt.org

Prince Music Theater
100 South Broad Street
Philadelphia, PA 19110
Phone: (215) 972-1000
Fax: (215) 972-1020
http://www.princemusictheater.org

Walnut Street Theatre
825 Walnut Street
Philadelphia, PA 19107
Phone: (215) 574-3550
Fax: (215) 574-3598

Wilma Theater
265 South Broad Street
Philadelphia, PA 19107
Phone: (215) 893-9456
Fax: (215) 893-0895
http://www.wilmatheater.org

RHODE ISLAND

Trinity Repertory Company
201 Washington Street
Providence, RI 02903
Phone: (401) 351-4242
Fax: (401) 751-5577
http://www.trinityrep.com

TENNESSEE

Clarence Brown Theatre
206 McClung Tower
Knoxville, TN 37996
Phone: (865) 974-3447
Fax: (865) 974-4867
http://www.clarencebrowntheatre.com

TEXAS

Alley Theatre
615 Texas Avenue
Houston, TX 77002
Phone: (713) 228-9341
http://www.alleytheatre.org

Dallas Theater Center
3636 Turtle Creek Boulevard
Dallas, TX 75219
Phone: (214) 526-8210
Fax: (214) 521-7666
http://www.dallastheatercenter.org

UTAH

Pioneer Theatre Company
Univeristy of Utah
300 South 1400 East
Salt Lake City, UT 84112
Phone: (801) 581-6227
Fax: (801) 581-5472

Utah Shakespearean Festival
351 West Center Street
Cedar City, UT 84720
Phone: (435) 586-7880
Fax: (435) 865-8003

VERMONT

Weston Playhouse
703 Main Street
Weston, VT 05161
Phone: (802) 824-8167
Fax: (802) 824-5099

VIRGINIA

Barter Theatre
Box 867
Abingdon, VA 24212
Phone: (276) 628-2281
Fax: (276) 619-3335
http://www.bartertheatre.com

Virginia Stage
P.O. Box 3770
Norfolk, VA 23514
Phone: (757) 627-6988

Fax: (757) 628-5958
http://www.vastage.com

WASHINGTON

A Contemporary Theatre (ACT)
700 Union Street
Seattle, WA 98101
Phone: (206) 292-7660
Fax: (206) 292-7670
http://www.acttheatre.org

Intiman Theatre
201 Mercer Street
Seattle, WA 98109
Phone: (206) 269-1901
Fax: (206) 269-1928
http://www.intiman.org

Seattle Repertory
155 Mercer Street
P.O. Box 900923
Seattle, WA 98109
Phone: (206) 443-2210

Fax: (206) 443-2379
http://www.seattlerep.org

WISCONSIN

Milwaukee Repertory Theatre
108 East Wells Street
Milwaukee, WI 53202
Phone: (414) 224-1761
Fax: (414) 224-8987
http://www.milwaukeerep.com

APPENDIX X
STOCK THEATERS

The following information, provided by Actor's Equity Association, lists selected Equity-affiliated stock theaters throughout the country. Contact information is included for each, as is the distinction between resident and nonresident theaters. (Resident theaters hire actors for the season; nonresident, for the performance.) Use this listing to obtain general information and to locate internships and job possibilities.

CALIFORNIA

California Musical Theatre (Resident Musical)
Wells Farco Pavilion–Music Circus
1419 H Street
Sacramento, CA 95814
Phone: (916) 557-1999
http://www.californiamusicaltheatre.com
Office:
1510 J Street
Sacramento, CA 95814
Phone: (916) 446-5880
Fax: (916) 446-1370

La Marinda Theatre (Nonresident Dramatic Stock)
14900 La Mirada Boulevard
La Mirada, CA 90638
Phone: (714) 994-6318
http://www.mccoyrigby.com
Office:
McCoy Rigby Entertainment
110 East Wilshire Avenue
Fullerton, CA 92832
Phone: (714) 525-8388
Fax: (714) 525-1352

CONNECTICUT

Westport Country Playhouse (Nonresident Dramatic Stock)
P.O. Box 629
Westport, CT 006881
Phone: (203) 227-5137
Fax: (203) 221-7482
http://www.westportplayhouse.org

GEORGIA

Theatre of the Stars (Musical Stock and Unit Attractions)
Fabulous Fox Theatre
660 Peachtree Street
Atlanta, GA 30355

Phone: (404) 252-8690
http://www.theatreofthestars.com
Office:
P.O. Box 11749
Atlanta, GA 30355
Phone: (404) 252-8960
Fax: (404) 252-1460

MAINE

Ogunquit Playhouse (Nonresident Dramatic Stock)
P.O. Box 2092
Ogunquit, ME 03907
Phone: (207) 646-2402
Fax: (207) 646-4732
http://www.ogunquitplayhouse.org
Office:
c/o Southcoast Rep
125 Bow Street
Portsmouth, NH 03801

Maine State Music Theatre (Resident)
22 Elm Street
Brunswick, ME 04011
Phone: (207) 725-1199
Fax: (207) 725-1199
http://www.msmt.org

MARYLAND

Olney Theatre (Nonresident Dramatic Stock)
2001 Olney-Sandy Lane Springs Road
Olney, MD 20832
Phone: (301) 924-4485
Fax: (301) 924-2654
http://www.olneytheatre.org

MASSACHUSETTS

Cape Playhouse (Nonresident Dramatic Stock)
P.O. Box 2001

Dennis, MA 03638
Phone: (508) 385-3838
Fax: (508) 385-8162
http://www.capeplayhouse.com

North Shore Music Theatre (Nonresident Dramatic Stock)
62 Dunham Road
Beverly, MA 01915
Phone: (978) 232-7241
Fax: (978) 921-7874
http://www.nsmt.org

Williamstown Theatre Festival (Resident)
1000 Main Street
Williamstown, MA 01267
Phone: (413) 697-3377
http://www.wtfestival.org
Office:
P.O. Box 517
Williamstown, MA 01267
Phone: (413) 458-3200
Fax: (413) 458-3147

Nikos Stage (Resident)
P.O. Box 517
Williamstown, MA 01267
Phone: (413) 458-3200
Fax: (413) 458-3147

MICHIGAN

Barn Theatre (Resident-Independent)
11351 West M-96
Augusta, MI 49012
Phone: (269) 731-4121
Fax: (269) 731-2306
http://www.barntheatre.com

MINNESOTA

Old Log Theater (Resident-Independent)
5185 Meadville Street

Greenwood, MN 55331
Phone: (952) 474-5951
http://www.oldlog.com
Office:
P.O. Box 250
Excelsior, MN 55331
Phone: (952) 474-5951
Fax: (952) 474-1290

MISSOURI

Kansas City Starlight Theatre (Musical Stock and Unit Attractions)
600 Starlight Road
Kansas City, MO 64132
Phone: (816) 363-7827
http://www.kcstarlight.com
Office:
Starlight Theatre Association of Kansas City
6601 Swope Parkway
Kansas City, MO 64132
Phone: (816) 363-7827
Fax: (816) 444-2117

The MUNY at Forest Park (Musical Stock and Unit Attractions)
St. Louis, MO 63112
Phone: (314) 361-1900
http://www.muny.com
Office:
Municipal Theatre Association
Forest Park
St. Louis, MO 63112
Phone: (314) 361-1900
Fax: (314) 361-0090

NEW HAMPSHIRE

The Barnstormers (Resident)
Box 434
Tamworth, NH 03886
Phone: (603) 323-8661
Fax: (603) 323-3351
http://www.barnstormerstheatre.com

Peterborough Players (Resident)
P.O. Box 118
55 Hadley Road
Peterborough, NH 03458
Phone: (603) 924-9344
Fax: (603) 924-5359
http://www.peterboroughplayers.org

NEW JERSEY

Paper Mills Playhouse (Nonresident Dramatic Stock)
Brookside Drive

Milburn, NJ 07041
Phone: (973) 379-3636
Fax: (973) 376-0825

NORTH CAROLINA

Flat Rock Playhouse (Resident)
2661 Greenville Highway
P.O. Box 310
Flat Rock, NC 28731
Phone: (828) 693-0403
Fax: (828) 693-6795
http://www.flatrockplayhouse.org

OHIO

Blue Jacket (Outdoor Dramatic Stock)
First Frontier Theatre
Casar's Ford Park
520 South Stringtown Road
Xenia, OH 45385
http://www.bluejacketdrama.com
Office:
First Frontier, Inc.
P.O. Box C
50 South Detroit Street
Xenia, OH 45385
Phone: (937) 376-4358
Fax: (937) 376-5364

Tecumseh (Outdoor Dramatic Stock)
Sugar Loaf Mountain Amphitheatre
5968 Marietta Road
Chillicothe, OH 45601
http://www.tecumsehdrama.com
Office:
The Scioto Society, Inc.
216 Freshour
P.O. Box 73
Chillicothe, OH 45601
Phone: (740) 775-4100
Fax: (740) 775-4349

PENNSYLVANIA

Allenberry Playhouse (Resident-Independent)
P.O. Box 7
Boiling Springs, PA 17007
Phone: (717) 258-3211
Fax: (717) 960-5280
http://www.allenberry.com

Mountain Playhouse (Resident)
7690 Somerset Pike
Jennerstown, PA 15547
Phone: (814) 629-9201
Fax: (814) 629-6221
http://www.mountainplayhouse.com

Office Address
P.O. Box 205
Jennerstown, PA 15547

Pittsburgh Civic Light Opera (Resident Musical)
Benedum Center
719 Liberty Avenue
Pittsburgh, PA 15222
Phone: (412) 281-3973
Fax: (412) 281-5339
http://www.pittsburghclo.org

Totem Pole Playhouse (Resident)
95555 Golf Course Road
Caldonia State Park
Fayetteville, PA 17222
Phone: (717) 352-2162
Fax: (717) 352-8870
Office Address
10290 Golf Course Road
P.O. Box 603
Fayetteville, PA 17222
http://www.totempoleplayhouse.com

TEXAS

Bass Performance Hall (Nonresident Dramatic Stock)
525 Commerce Street
Fort Worth, TX 76102
Phone: (817) 212-4280
http://www.casamanana.org

Casa Mañana Theatre (Nonresident Dramatic Stock)
3201 West Lancaster
Fort Worth, TX 76107
Phone: (817) 332-2272
http://www.casamanana.org
Office:
300 West 3rd Street
Fort Worth, TX 76107
Phone: (817) 332-2272
Fax: (817) 332-5711

Dallas Summer Musicals (Musical Stock and Unit Attractions)
Music Hall at Fair Park
900 First Avenue
Dallas, TX 75210
Phone: (214) 691-7200
http://www.dallassummermusicals.org
Office:
P.O. Box 710336
Dallas, TX 75371
Phone: (214) 421-5678
Fax: (214) 428-4526

VERMONT

St. Michael's Playhouse (Resident)
St. Michael's College
Colchester, VT 05439
Phone: (802) 654-2617
Fax: (802) 654-2685

http://www.academics.smcvt.edu/
    playhouse

WISCONSIN

Peninsula Theatre (Resident)
West 4351 Peninsula Players Road

Fish Creek, WI 54212
Phone: (773) 777-2904
Fax: (773) 427-8012
http://www.peninsulaplayers.com

APPENDIX XI
U.S. ORCHESTRAS

The following is a listing provided by the American Symphony Orchestra League (ASOL) of selected orchestras of various sizes located throughout the United States. Names, addresses, phone numbers, and Web sites have been included when available. Use this listing to obtain general information, locate internships, and inquire about auditions and job possibilities. To find orchestras not included in this listing, visit the ASOL Web site at http://www.symphony.org.

ALABAMA

Alabama Symphony Orchestra
3621 6th Avenue South
Birmingham, AL 35222
Phone: (205) 251-6929
http://www.alabamasymphony.org

Huntsville Symphony Orchestra
P.O. Box 2400
Huntsville, AL 35804
Phone: (256) 539-4818
http://www.hso.org

Mobile Symphony
257 Dauphin Street
Mobile, AL 36652
Phone: (251) 432-7080
http://www.mobilesymphony.org

Tri-State Community Orchestra
909 South Saint Andrew's Street
Dothan, AL 36301
Phone: (334) 792-7197
http://www.seartsalliance.org

Tuscaloosa Symphony Orchestra
P.O. Box 20001
Tuscaloosa, AL 35402
Phone: (205) 752-5515
http://www.tsoonline.org

ALASKA

Anchorage Symphony Orchestra
400 D Street, #230
Anchorage, AK 99501
Phone: (907) 274-8668
http://www.anchoragesymphony.org

Fairbanks Symphony
P.O. Box 82104
Fairbanks, AK 99708
Phone: (907) 474-5733
http://www.fairbankssymphony.org

Juneau Symphony
P.O. Box 21236
Juneau, AK 99802
Phone: (907) 586-4676
http://www.juneausymphony.org

ARIZONA

Flagstaff Symphony Orchestra
113 East Aspen Avenue
Suite A
Flagstaff, AZ 86001
Phone: (928) 774-5107
http://www.flagstaffsymphony.org

Mesa Symphony Orchestra
P.O. Box 1308
Mesa, AZ 85211
Phone: (480) 827-2143
http://www.mesasymphony.org

The Phoenix Symphony
455 North 3rd Street
Suite 390
Phoenix, AZ 85004
Phone: (602) 495-1117
http://www.phoenixsymphony.org

Sierra Vista Symphony Orchestra
P.O. Box 895
Sierra Vista, AZ 85636
Phone: (520) 515-5408
http://www.svsymphony.org

**Southern Arizona Symphony
  Orchestra**
P.O. Box 43131
Tucson, AZ 85733
Phone: (520) 323-7166
http://www.sasomusic.org

Symphony of the West Valley
10451 Palmeris Drive
Suite 210
Sun City, AZ 95373

Phone: (623) 972-4484
http://www.westvalleysymphony.org

Tucson Symphony Orchestra
2175 North Sixth Avenue
Tucson, AZ 85705
Phone: (520) 792-9155
http://www.tucsonsymphony.org

ARKANSAS

Arkansas Symphony Orchestra
P.O. Box 7328
Little Rock, AR 72217
Phone: (501) 666-1761
http://www.arkansassymphony.org

Fort Smith Symphony
P.O. Box 3151
Fort Smith, AR 72913
Phone: (479) 452-7575
http://www.fortsmithsymphony.org

Hot Springs Music Festival
634 Prospect Avenue
Hot Springs, AR 71901
Phone: (501) 623-4763
http://www.hotmusic.org

North Arkansas Symphony Orchestra
P.O. Box 1243
Fayetteville, AR 72702
http://www.nasymphony.org

Pine Bluff Symphony Orchestra
P.O. Box 1594
Pine Bluff, AR 71613
Phone: (870) 536-7666

South Arkansas Symphony
315 East Oak Street
Suite 206
El Dorado, AR 71730
Phone: (870) 862-0521
http://www.southarkansassymphony.com

CALIFORNIA

Asia America Symphony
608 Silver Spur Road
Rolling Hills Estates, CA 90274
Phone: (310) 377-8977

Bakersfield Symphony Orchestra
1328 34th Street
Bakersfield, CA 93301
Phone: (661) 323-7928
http://www.bakersfieldsymphony.org

Berkeley Symphony Orchestra
1942 University Avenue
Suite 207
Berkeley, CA 94704
Phone: (510) 841-2800
http://www.berkeleysymphony.org

Cabrillo Music Festival
104 Walnut Avenue
Suite 206
Santa Cruz, CA 95060
http://www.cabrillomusic.org

Chamber Orchestra of the South Bay
P.O. Box 2095
Palos Verdes, CA 90274
Phone: (310) 373-3151
http://www.palosverdes.com/
    chamberorchestra

Claremont Symphony Orchestra
P.O. Box 698
Claremont, CA 91711
Phone: (909) 593-5620
http://www.claremontso.org

Fremont Symphony Orchestra
P.O. Box 104
Fremont, CA 94537
http://www.fremontsymphony.org

Hewlett-Packard Symphony Orchestra
436 River Rock Court
San Jose, CA 95136
http://www.yefchak.com/hpsymphony

Imperial Valley Symphony
P.O. Box 713
El Centro, CA 92244-0713
http://faculty.imperial.cc.ca.us/users/
    music/IVSCurrent.htm

La Jolla Symphony and Chorus
9500 Gilman Drive
UCSD BOX 0361
La Jolla, CA 92093

Phone: (858) 534-4637
http://www.lajollasymphony.com

Livermore-Amador Symphony
P.O. Box 1049
Livermore, CA 94551
Phone: (925) 447-3672
http://www.livamsymph.org

Long Beach Symphony Orchestra
110 West Ocean Boulevard
Suite 22
Long Beach, CA 90802
Phone: (562) 491-3599
http://www.lbso.org

Los Angeles Chamber Orchestra
707 Wilshire Boulevard
Suite 1850
Los Angeles, CA 90017
Phone: (213) 622-7001
http://www.laco.org

Los Angeles Philharmonic
151 South Grand Avenue
Los Angeles, CA 90012
Phone: (213) 972-7300
http://www.laphil.com

Mission Chamber Orchestra
P.O. Box 32872
San Jose, CA 95152
http://www.missionchamber.org

Modesto Symphony Orchestra
911 Thirteenth Street
Modesto, CA 95354
Phone: (209) 523-4156
http://www.modestosymphony.org

Monterey Symphony
P.O. Box 3965
Carmel, CA 93921
Phone: (831) 624-8511
http://www.montereysymphony.org

Music in the Mountains
530 Searls Avenue
Suite A
Nevada City, CA 95959
Phone: (530) 265-6173
http://www.musicinthemountains.org

Napa Valley Symphony
860 Kaiser Road
Suite E
Napa, CA 94558
Phone: (707) 226-6872
http://www.napavalleysymphony.org

New West Symphony Orchestra
2100 East Thousand Oaks Boulevard
Suite D
Thousand Oaks, CA 91362
Phone: (805) 497-5800
http://www.newwestsymphony.org

North State Symphony
California State University
400 West First Street
Chico, CA 95929
Phone: (209) 523-4156
http://www.modestosymphony.org

Nova Vista Symphony
P.O. Box 60312
Sunnyvale, CA 94088-0312
Phone: (408) 530-0700
http://www.novavista.org

Oakland East Bay Symphony
400 29th Street
Suite 501
Oakland, CA 94609
Phone: (510) 444-0801
http://www.oebs.org

Orange County's Pacific Symphony
3631 S Harbor Blvd
Suite 100
Santa Ana, CA 92704
Phone: (714) 755-5788
http://www.pacificsymphony.org

Palisades Symphony Orchestra
1081 Palisair Place
Pacific Palisades, CA 90272
Phone: (714) 755-5788
http://www.pacificsymphony.org

The Pasadena Pops Orchestra
87 North Raymond Avenue
Suite 500
Pasadena, CA 91103
Phone: (626) 792-7677
http://www.pasadenapops.com

The Pasadena Symphony
2500 East Colorado Blvd
Suite 260
Pasadena, CA 91107
Phone: (626) 793-7172
http://www.pasadenasymphony.org

Peninsula Pops Orchestra
3790 El Camino Real Estate
Suite 341
Palo Alto, CA 94306
Phone: (650) 856-8432
http://www.peninsulapops.org

Redwood Symphony
1031 16th Avenue
Redwood City, CA 94063
http://www.redwoodsymphony.org

Sacramento Chamber Orchestra
P.O. Box 214193
Sacramento, CA 95821
http://www.sacchamberorch.org

Sacramento Philharmonic Orchestra
3400 Third Avenue
P.O. Box 5236
Sacramento, CA 95817
Phone: (916) 732-9045
http://www.sacramentophilharmonic.org

San Bernadino Symphony
1811 North D Street
San Bernardino, CA 92405
Phone: (909) 381-5388
http://www.sanbernardinosymphony.org

San Diego Symphony
1245 Seventh Avenue
San Diego, CA 92101
http://www.sandiegosymphony.com

San Fernando Valley Symphony
20210 Haynes Street
Winnetka, CA 91306
http://www.sfvsymphony.com

San Francisco Chamber Orchestra
P.O. Box 591566
San Francisco, CA 94159
Phone: (415) 248-1640
http://www.sfchamberorchestra.org

San Francisco Sinfonietta
830 York Street
San Francisco, CA 94110
http://www.sfsinfonietta.org

San Francisco Symphony
201 Van Ness Avenue
Davies Symphony Hall
San Francisco, CA 94102
http://www.sfsymphony.org

San Jose Chamber Orchestra
1034 Bennett Way
San Jose, CA 95125
Phone: (408) 293-6060
http://www.missionchamber.org

San Luis Obispo Symphony
P.O. Box 658
San Luis Obispo, CA 93406

Phone: (805) 543-3533
http://www.slosymphony.com

Santa Barbara Symphony Orchestra
1900 State Street
Suite G
Santa Barbara, CA 93101
Phone: (805) 898-9626
http://www.thesymphony.org

Santa Rosa Symphony
50 Santa Rosa Avenue
Suite 410
Santa Rosa, CA 95404
Phone: (707) 546-8742
http://www.santarosasymphony.com

Shasta Symphony Orchestra
P.O. Box 496006
Redding, CA 96049

South Coast Symphony
13642 Winthrope Street
Santa Ana, CA 92705
Phone: (714) 731-8079
http://www.southcoastsymphony.org

Stockton Symphony
46 West Fremont Street
Stockton, CA 95202
Phone: (209) 951-0196
http://www.stocktonsymphony.org

Symphony Silicon Valley
P.O. Box 790
San Jose, CA 95106
Phone: (408) 286-2600
http://www.symphonysiliconvalley.org

Tennessee Valley Orchestra
611 Springfield Way
Mill Valley, CA 94941
http://www.tennesseevalleyorchestra.org

Ventura Music Festival
89 South California Street
Ventura, CA 93001
Phone: (805) 648-3146
http://www.vcmfa.org

West Coast Symphony
1812 La Coronilla Drive
Santa Barbara, CA 93109
Phone: (805) 962-6609
http://www.westcoastsymphony.com

The Women's Philharmonic
44 Page Street
Suite 604D
San Francisco, CA 94102

Phone: (707) 824-0228
http://www.womensphil.org

COLORADO

Arapahoe Philharmonic
2100 West Littleton Boulevard
Suite 250
Littleton, CO 80120
Phone: (303) 781-1892
http://www.arapahoe-phil.org

Aspen Music Festival and School
2 Music School Road
Aspen, CO 81611
Phone: (970) 925-3254
http://www.aspenmusicfestival.com

Boulder Philharmonic Orchestra
2995 Wilderness Place
Suite 100
Boulder, CO 80301
Phone: (303) 449-1343
http://www.peakarts.org

Colorado Music Festival
900 Baseline Road, Cottage 100
Boulder, CO 80302
Phone: (303) 449-1397
http://www.coloradomusicfest.org

Colorado Springs Philharmonic
P.O. Box 60730
Colorado Springs, CO 80960
Phone: (719) 226-9130
http://www.csphilharmonic.org

Colorado Symphony Orchestra
Denver Place, North Tower
999 18th Street
Suite 2055
Denver, CO 80202
Phone: (303) 292-5566
http://www.coloradosymphony.org

Fort Collins Symphony Orchestra
P.O. Box 1963
Fort Collins, CO 80522
Phone: (970) 482-4823
http://www.fcsymphony.org

Grand Junction Symphony Orchestra
Box 3039
Grand Junction, CO 81502
Phone: (970) 243-787
http://www.gjsymphony.org

Greeley Philharmonic Orchestra
P.O. Box 1535
Greeley, CO 80632

Jefferson Symphony Orchestra
1801 Jackson Street
Golden, CO 80401
Phone: (303) 278-4237
http://www.jeffersonsymphony.org

Longmont Symphony Orchestra
P.O. Box 74
Longmont, CO 80502
http://longmontsymphony.org

National Repertory Orchestra
P.O. Box 6336
Breckenridge, CO 80424
Phone: (970) 453-5825
http://www.nromusic.com

Pueblo Symphony Association
301 North Main
Suite 106
Pueblo, CO 81003
http://www.pueblosymphony.org

San Juan Symphony
P.O. Box 1073
Durango, CO 81302
http://www.sanjuansymphony.com

Symphony in the Valley
P.O. Box 1831
Glenwood Springs, CO 81602
Phone: (970) 920-4314

CONNECTICUT

American Classical Orchestra
284 Davis Road
Fairfield, CT 06825
Phone: (203) 396-0199
http://www.amerclassorch.org

Danbury Symphony
256 Main Street
Danbury, CT 06810
Phone: (203) 748-1716
http://www.danbury.org

Eastern CT Symphony Orchestra, Inc.
289 State Street
New London, CT 06320
Phone: (860) 443-2876
http://www.ectsymphony.org

Greater Bridgeport Symphony Orchestra
446 University Avenue
Bridgeport, CT 06604
http://www.bridgeportsymphony.org

Greenwich Symphony Orchestra
P.O. Box 35
Greenwich, CT 06836
Phone: (203) 859-2664
http://www.greenwichsym.org

Hartford Symphony Orchestra
228 Farmington Avenue
Hartford, CT 06105
Phone: (860) 246-8742
http://www.hartfordsymphony.org

New Haven Symphony Orchestra
70 Audubon Street
New Haven, CT 06510
Phone: (203) 865-0831
http://www.newhavensymphony.org

Norwalk Symphony Orchestra
1 Park Street
Norwalk, CT 06851
Phone: (203) 847-8844
http://www.norwalksymphony.org

Ridgefield Symphony Orchestra
P.O. Box 289
90 East Ridge
Suite C
Ridgefield, CT 06877
Phone: (203) 438-3889
http://www.ridgefieldsymphony.org

Stamford Symphony Orchestra
263 Tresser Boulevard
1 Stamford Plaza
Stamford, CT 06901
Phone: (203) 325-1407
http://www.stamfordsymphony.org

Waterbury Symphony Orchestra
P.O. Box 1762
Waterbury, CT 06721
Phone: (203) 697-2261
http://www.wallingfordsymphony.org

West Hartford Symphony Orchestra
P.O. Box 370036
West Hartford, CT 06137
Phone: (203) 574-4283
http://www.waterburysymphony.org

DELAWARE

Delaware Symphony Orchestra
P.O. Box 1870
Wilmington, DE 19899
Phone: (302) 656-7442
http://www.desymphony.org

DISTRICT OF COLUMBIA

National Symphony Orchestra
John F. Kennedy Center for the
    Performing Arts
Washington, DC 20566
Phone: (202) 416-8000
http://www.kennedy-center.org

U.S. Congressional Philharmonic Orchestra
c/o FAA-Operational Evolution
490 L'Enfant Plaza SW
Washington, DC 20024

FLORIDA

Alhambra Orchestra
7007 Loch Isle Drive South
Miami Lakes, FL 33014
Phone: (305) 668-9260
http://www.alhambramusic.org

Atlantic Classical Orchestra
1766 Northeast Jensen Beach Boulevard
Jensen Beach, FL 34957
Phone: (772) 234-1304

Big Bend Community Orchestra
1345 Thomasville Road
Tallahassee, FL 32303
http://www.bbco.org

Brevard Symphony Orchestra
P.O. Box 361965
Melbourne, FL 32936
Phone: (321) 242-2024
http://www.brevardsymphony.com

Central Florida Symphony Orchestra
416 Southeast Fort King Street
Ocala, FL 34471
Phone: (352) 351-1606
http://www.cfsymphony.com

Charlotte Symphony Orchestra
P.O. Box 495831
Port Charlotte, FL 33949
Phone: (941) 625-5996
http://www.charlottesymphony.com

Flagler Symphonic Society
P.O. Box 350033
Palm Coast, FL 32135
Phone: (386) 447-8911
http://www.flaglersymphonicsociety.org

Florida Orchestra
101 South Hoover Boulevard
Suite 100
Tampa, FL 33609

Florida West Coast Symphony Orchestra
709 North Tamiami Trail
Sarasota, FL 34236
Phone: (941) 953-4252
http://www.fwcs.org

Imperial Symphony Orchestra
P.O. Box 2623
Lakeland, FL 33806
Phone: (863) 688-3743
http://www.imperialsymphony.org

Jacksonville Symphony Orchestra
300 West Water Street
Suite 200
Jacksonville, FL 32202
Phone: (904) 354-5479
http://www.jaxsymphony.org

Key West Symphony Orchestra
P.O. Box 774
Key West, FL 33041

The Naples Philharmonic
5833 Pelican Bay Boulevard
Naples, FL 34108
Phone: (239) 597-1900
http://thephil.org

New World Symphony
541 Lincoln Road, 4th Floor
Miami Beach, FL 33139

Orlando Philharmonic Orchestra
812 East Rollins Street
Orlando, FL 32803
Phone: (407) 896-6700
http://www.orlandophil.org

Pensacola Symphony Orchestra
P.O. Box 1752
Pensacola, FL 32591
Phone: (850) 435-2533
http://www.pensacolasymphony.com

Philharmonic Orchestra of NW Florida
P.O. Box 25
Fort Walton Beach, FL 32549

Southwest Florida Symphony
4560 Via. Royale
Suite 2
Fort Myers, FL 33919
http://www.swflso.org

Symphony of the Americas
199 North Ocean Boulevard
Suite 200
Pompano Beach, FL 33062
Phone: (954) 545-0088

Tallahassee Symphony Orchestra
1345 Thomasville Road
Tallahassee, FL 32303
http://www.tsolive.org

Venice Symphony
P.O. Box 1561
Venice, FL 34284
Phone: (941) 488-1010
http://www.thevenicesymphony.org

GEORGIA

Albany Symphony Orchestra
P.O. Box 70065
Albany, GA 31708
Phone: (229) 430-6799
http://www.albanysymphony.org

Atlanta Symphony Orchestra
1293 Peachtree Street NE
Suite 300
Atlanta, GA 30309
Phone: (404) 733-4900
http://www.atlantasymphony.org

Augusta Symphony Orchestra
P.O. Box 579
Augusta, GA 30903
Phone: (706) 826-4705
http://www.augustasymphony.org

Cobb Symphony Orchestra
P.O. Box 680993
Marietta, GA 30068
Phone: (770) 426-1509
http://www.cobbsymphony.com

Columbus Symphony Orchestra
P.O. Box 1499
Columbus, GA 31902
http://www.csoga.org

DeKalb Symphony Orchestra
P.O. Box 1313
Tucker, GA 30085
Phone: (404) 299-4341
http://www.dekalbsymphony.com

Gwinnett Philharmonic Association, Inc.
P.O. Box 920159
Norcross, GA 30010
Phone: (770) 418-1115
http://www.gwinnettphilharmonic.org

La Grange Symphony Orchestra
P.O. Box 2321
La Grange, GA 30241
Phone: (706) 882-0662

HAWAII

Honolulu Symphony Orchestra
650 Iwilei Road
Suite 202
Honolulu, HI 96817
Phone: (808) 524-0815
http://www.honolulusymphony.com

IDAHO

Boise Philharmonic Association, Inc.
516 South Ninth Street
Boise, ID 83702
http://www.boisephilharmonic.org

Idaho Falls Symphony
450 A Street
Suite A
Idaho Falls, ID 83402
Phone: (208)529-1080
http://www.srv.net/~ifsymph

Idaho State Civic Symphony
P.O. Box 8099
Pocatello, ID 83209
Phone: (208) 234-1587
http://www.thesymphony.us

Magic Philharmonic Orchestra
P.O. Box 939
Burley, ID 83318
Phone: (208) 678-0404

Magic Valley Symphony Orchestra
P.O. Box 1805
Twin Falls, ID 83303
Phone: (208) 733-2291

Meridian Symphony Orchestra
P.O. Box 1016
Meridian, ID 83680
Phone: (208) 939-9371
http://www.meridiansymphony.org

ILLINOIS

Champaign-Urbana Symphony Orchestra
701 Devonshire Drive
Champaign, IL 61820
http://www.cusymphony.org

Chicago Chamber Orchestra
332 South Michigan Avenue

Suite 1143
Chicago, IL 60604
Phone: (312) 922-5570
http://www.chicagochamberorchestra.org

Chicagoland Pops Orchestra
Rosemont Theater
5400 North River Road
Rosemont, IL 60018
Phone: (847) 825-7677
http://www.chicagolandpops.com

Chicago Sinfonietta
70 East Lake Street
Suite 226
Chicago, IL 60601
Phone: (312) 236-3681
http://chicagosinfonietta.org

Chicago Symphony Orchestra
220 South Michigan Avenue
Chicago, IL 60604
Phone: (312) 294-3333
http://www.cso.org

Civic Orchestra of Chicago
220 South Michigan Avenue
Chicago, IL 60604
Phone:(312) 294-3333
http://www.cso.org

Danville Symphony Orchestra
2917 North Vermillion Street
Danville, IL 61832
http://www.danvillesymphonyorchestra.org

Elgin Symphony Orchestra
20 DuPage Court
Elgin, IL 60120
Phone: (847) 888-4000
http://www.elginsymphony.org

Elmhurst Symphony Orchestra
P.O. Box 345
Elmhurst, IL 60126
Phone: (630) 941-0202
http://www.elmhurstsymphony.org

**Evanston Symphony Orchestra
Association**
P.O. Box 778
Evanston, IL 60204
Phone: (847) 864-8804
http://www.evanstonsymphony.org

Grant Park Orchestra and Chorus
205 East Randolph Street
Chicago, IL 60601
Phone: (312) 742-7638
http://www.grantparkmusicfestival.com

Illinois Philharmonic Orchestra
377 Artists Walk
Park Forest, IL 60466
Phone: (708) 481-7774
http://www.ipomusic.org

Illinois Symphony Orchestra
P.O. Box 5191
524 1/2 East Capital Avenue
Springfield, IL 62705
http://www.ilsymphony.org

Illinois Valley Symphony Orchestra
9 Oakdale Court
Spring Valley, IL 61362
http://www.ivso.org

Millikin-Decatur Symphony
1184 West Main Street
Millikin University
Decatur, IL 62522

Music of the Baroque
111 North Wabash Avenue
Suite 810
Chicago, IL 60602
Phone: (312) 551-1414
http://www.baroque.org

New Philharmonic
425 Fawell Boulevard
Glen Ellyn, IL 60137
http://www.cod.edu/ArtsCntr/new_phil.htm

Northbrook Symphony Orchestra
899 Skokie Boulevard
Suite LL 12
Northbrook, IL 60062
Phone: (847) 272-0755
http://www.northbrooksymphony.org

Northwest Symphony Orchestra
1100 West Northwest Highway
Suite 205
Mount Prospect, IL 60056
Phone: (847) 965-7271
http://www.northwestsymphony.org

Peoria Symphony Orchestra
Foster Arts Center
203 Harrison Street
Peoria, IL 61602
Phone: (309) 637-2787
http://www.peoriasymphony.org

Quincy Symphony Orchestra
428 Maine Street
Suite 270
Quincy, IL 62301

Phone: (217) 222-2856
http://users.adams.net/~qsoa

Rockford Symphony Orchestra
711 North Main Street
Riverfront Museum Park
Rockford, IL 61103
Phone: (815) 965-0049
http://www.rockfordsymphony.com

Symphonic Pops Orchestra of Chicago
1765 George Court
Glenview, IL 60025
Phone: (847) 729-1893

Waukegan Symphony Orchestra
39 Jack Benny Drive
Waukegan, IL 60087
http://www.wheaton.edu/Conservatory/
ensembles/symphony

West Suburban Symphony Society
P.O. Box 565
Hinsdale, IL 60522
Phone: (630) 887-SING
http://www.westsubsymphony.org

**Wheaton Symphony Orchestra and
Chorus**
344 Spring Avenue
Glen Ellyn, IL 60137-4826
http://www.wheaton.edu/Conservatory/
ensembles/symphony

INDIANA

Anderson Symphony Orchestra
1124 Meridian Plaza Suite C
P.O. Box 741
Anderson, IN 46015
Phone: (765) 644-2111
http://www.andersonsymphony.org

Bloomington Pops Orchestra
P.O. Box 7611
Bloomington, IN 47407
Phone: (812) 336-8747
http://www.bloomingtonpops.org

Carmel Symphony Orchestra
P.O. Box 761
Carmel, IN 46082
Phone: (317) 844-9717
http://www.carmelsymphony.org

Columbus Indiana Philharmonic
315 Franklin
Columbus, IN 47201
http://www.thecip.org

Evansville Philharmonic Orchestra
530 Main Street
P.O. Box 84
Evansville, IN 47701
Phone: (812) 425-5050
http://www.evansvillephilharmonic.org

Fort Wayne Philharmonic Orchestra
2340 Fairfield Avenue
Fort Wayne, IN 46807
Phone: (260) 744-1700
http://www.fortwaynephilharmonic.com

Grace Community Orchestra
200 Seminary Drive
Winona Lake, IN 46590
Phone: (574) 372-5100
http://www.gcorchestra.org

Indianapolis Symphony Orchestra
32 East Washington Street
Suite 600
Indianapolis, IN 46204
Phone: (317) 262-5224
http://www.indianapolissymphony.org

Lafayette Symphony Orchestra
P.O. Box 52
Lafayette, IN 47902
Phone: (765) 742-6463
http://lso.nlci.com

LaPorte County Symphony Orchestra
P.O. Box 563
LaPorte, IN 46350
Phone: (219) 325-0666
http://www.lcso.net

Manchester Symphony Orchestra
P.O. Box 113
Manchester, IN 46962
Phone: (260) 982-5331

Marion Philharmonic Orchestra
P.O. Box 272
Marion, IN 46952
Phone: (765) 662-0012
http://www.marionphil.com

Muncie Symphony Orchestra
c/o Ball State University
2000 University Avenue
Muncie, IN 47306
Phone: (765) 285-5531
http://www.munciesymphony.org

New World Youth Orchestras, Inc.
Northwest Indiana Symphony Orchestra
1040 Ridge Road

Munster, IN 46321
Phone: (317) 229-2365
http://nwyso.org

Richmond Symphony Orchestra
P.O. Box 982
380 Hub Etchison Parkway
Richmond, IN 47375
Phone: (765) 966-5181
http://www.richmondsymphony.org

South Bend Symphony Orchestra
120 West LaSalle Avenue
Suite 404
South Bend, IN 46601
Phone: (574) 232-6343
http://www.southbendsymphony.com

Terre Haute Symphony Orchestra
25 North Sixth Street
Terre Haute, IN 47807
Phone: (812) 242-8476
http://www.thso.org

IOWA

Cedar Rapids Symphony Orchestra
119 3rd Avenue SE
Cedar Rapids, IA 52401
Phone: (319) 366-8203
http://www.crsymphony.org

Central Iowa Symphony
P.O. Box C
Ames, IA 50014
http://www.cisymphony.org

Clinton Symphony Orchestra
P.O. Box 116
Clinton, IA 52733
http://www.clintonsymphony.org

Des Moines Community Orchestra
P.O. Box 1796
Des Moines, IA 50301
Phone: (515) 964-4562
http://www.desmoinescommunityorchestra.
org

Des Moines Symphony
221 Walnut Street
Des Moines, IA 50309
Phone: (515) 280-4000
http://www.dmsymphony.org

Dubuque Symphony Orchestra
1633 Main Street
P.O. Box 881
Dubuque, IA 52004

Phone: (563) 557-1677
http://www.dubuquesymphony.org

Muscatine Symphony Orchestra
P.O. Box 573
Muscatine, IA 52761
Phone: (563) 263-8895
http://www.muscatinesymphony.org

Northwest Iowa Symphony Orchestra
498 Fourth Avenue NE
Sioux Center, IA 51250
Phone: (712) 722-6230
http://www.siouxcitysymphony.org

Ottumwa Symphony Orchestra
P.O. Box 173
Ottumwa, IA 52501
Phone: (641) 684-7628

Quad City Symphony Orchestra
327 Brady Street
Davenport, IA 52801
Phone: (563) 322-0931
http://www.qcsymphony.com

**Sioux City Symphony Orchestra
Association**
P.O. Box 754
Sioux City, IA 51102
Phone: (712) 277-2111
http://www.siouxcitysymphony.org

Southeast Iowa Symphony Orchestra
Iowa Wesleyan College
601 North Main Street
Mount Pleasant, IA 52641
http://www.geocities.com/seiso.geo/seiso4.
html

Wartburg Community Symphony
Box 3
Waverly, IA 50677
Phone: (800) 772-2085
http://www.wartburg.edu/music/symphony.
html

Waterloo-Cedar Falls Symphony
Gallagher-Bluedorn PAC
Cedar Falls, IA 50614
Phone: (319) 273-3373
http://www.wcfsymphony.org

KANSAS

Kansas City Civic Orchestra
P.O. Box 224
Shawnee Mission, KS 66201
http://www.kccivic.org

Lawrence Chamber Orchestra
940 New Hampshire Street
Lawrence, KS 66044

**Newton Mid-Kansas Symphony
    Orchestra**
P.O. Box 245
Newton, KS 67117
Phone: (316) 283-0814

Salina Symphony
P.O. Box 792
Salina, KS 67402
Phone: (785) 823-8309
http://www.salinasymphony.org

Topeka Symphony Orchestra
P.O. Box 2206
Topeka, KS 66601-2206
http://www.topekasymphony.org

Wichita Symphony Orchestra
Century II Concert Hall
225 West Douglas
Suite 207
Wichita, KS 67202
Phone: (316) 267-5259
http://www.wso.org

KENTUCKY

Bowling Green Chamber Orchestra
1046 Elm Street
P.O. Box 1408
Bowling Green, KY 42102
Phone: (270) 846-BGCO
http://www.bgchamberorchestra.org

**Bowling Green Western Symphony
    Orchestra**
500 East Main Street
Bowling Green, KY 42101
Phone: (270) 745-7681

Lexington Philharmonic Orchestra
ArtsPlace
161 North Mill Street
Lexington, KY 40507
Phone: (859) 233-4226
http://www.lexphil.org

The Louisville Orchestra
300 West Main Street
Suite 100
Louisville, KY 40202-2930
Phone: (502) 587-8681
http://www.louisvilleorchestra.org

The Owensboro Symphony
122 East 18th Street
Owensboro, KY 42303

Phone: (270) 684-0661
http://www.owensborosymphony.org

Paducah Symphony Orchestra
P.O. Box 1763
Paducah, KY 42002
Phone: (270) 444-0065
http://www.paducahsymphony.com

LOUISIANA

Acadiana Symphony Orchestra
P.O. Box 53632
412 Travis Street
Lafayette, LA 70505
http://www.acadianasymphony.org

Baton Rouge Symphony
161 Third Street
Baton Rouge, LA 70801
Phone: (225) 383-0500
http://www.brso.org

Louisiana Philharmonic Orchestra
225 Baronne Street
Suite 910
New Orleans, LA 70112
Phone: (504) 523-6530
http://www.lpomusic.com

Monroe Symphony Orchestra
P.O. Box 4353
Monroe, LA 71211
http://www.bayou.com/symphony

Rapides Symphony Orchestra
1101 4th Street
Suite 201
Alexandria, LA 71301-8534
Phone: (318) 442-9709

Shreveport Symphony Orchestra
P.O. Box 205
Shreveport, LA 71162-0205
Phone: (318) 222-7496
http://www.shreveportsymphony.com

MAINE

Bangor Symphony Orchestra
51A Main Street
Bangor, ME 04401
Phone: (207) 942-5555
http://www.bangorsymphony.com

Midcoast Symphony Orchestra
P.O. Box 86
Brunswick, ME 04011
Phone: (207) 371-2028
http://www.midcoastsymphony.org

Portland Symphony Orchestra
477 Congress Street
P.O. Box 3573
Portland, ME 04104
Phone: (207) 773-6128
http://www.portlandsymphony.com

MARYLAND

Annapolis Symphony Orchestra
801 Chase Street
Suite 204
Annapolis, MD 21401
Phone: (410) 269-1132
http://www.annapolissymphony.org

Baltimore Chamber Orchestra
5807 Harford Road
Baltimore, MD 21214
Phone: (410) 426-0157
http://www.baltchamberorch.org

Baltimore Symphony Orchestra
1212 Cathedral Street
Baltimore, MD 21201
Phone: (410) 783-8000
http://www.baltimoresymphony.org

The Columbia Orchestra
P.O. Box 2323
Columbia, MD 21045-1323
Phone: (410) 465-8777
http://www.columbiaorchestra.org

**Jewish Community Center Symphony
    Orchestra**
6125 Montrose Road
Rockville, MD 20852
Phone: (301) 881-0100
http://www.jccso.org

Maryland Symphony Orchestra
13 South Potomac Street
Hagerstown, MD 21740
Phone: (301) 797-4000
http://www.marylandsymphony.org

Mid-Atlantic Symphony Orchestra
P.O. Box 3687
Ocean City, MD 21843
http://www.midatlanticsymphony.org

National Philharmonic
401 Fleet Street
Suite 101
Rockville, MD 20850
Phone: (301) 493-9283
http://www.nationalphilharmonic.org

Prince George's Philharmonic
Orchestra
P.O. Box 1111
Riverdale, MD 20738
http://pgphilharmonic.org

Susquehanna Symphony Orchestra
P.O. Box 485
Forest Hill, MD 21050
Phone: (410) 838-6465
http://www.ssorchestra.org

Washington Pro Musica
607 McNeill Road
Silver Spring, MD 20910
Phone: (202) 722-4881

MASSACHUSETTS

Boston Classical Orchestra
P.O. Box 152
Newton, MA 02468
Phone: (617) 423-3883
http://www.bostonclassicalorchestra.org

Boston Landmarks Orchestra
168 Brattle Street
Cambridge, MA 02138
Phone: (617) 520-2200
http://www.landmarksorchestra.org

Boston Modern Orchestra Project
9 Birch Street
Roslindale, MA 02131
Phone: (617) 363-0396
http://www.bmop.org

Boston Philharmonic Orchestra
295 Huntington Avenue
Suite 210
Boston, MA 02115
Phone: (617) 236-0999
http://www.bostonphil.org

Boston Symphony Orchestra
301 Massachusetts Avenue
Symphony Hall
Boston, MA 02115
http://www.bso.org

Brockton Symphony Orchestra
P.O. Box 143
Brockton, MA 02303-0143
Phone: (508) 588-3841
http://www.brocktonsymphony.org

Cape Ann Symphony Orchestra
P.O. Box 1343
Gloucester, MA 01931
http://www.capeannsymphony.org

Cape Symphony Orchestra, Inc.
712A Main Street
Fiddlers Green
Yarmouth Port, MA 02675
Phone: (508) 362-1111
http://www.capesymphony.org

Longwood Symphony Orchestra
P.O. Box 886
Brookline, MA 02446
Phone: (508) 877-3928
http://www.longwoodsymphony.org

Melrose Symphony Orchestra
P.O. Box 715
Melrose, MA 02176-3714
http://www.melrosesymphony.org

New Bedford Symphony Orchestra
488 Pleasant Street
P.O. Box 2053
New Bedford, MA 02741-2053
Phone: (508) 999-6276
http://www.nbsymphony.org

New England Philharmonic
1906 Massachusetts Avenue
Cambridge, MA 02140
Phone: (617) 868-1222
http://www.nephilharmonic.org

New England String Ensemble
P.O. Box 2012
599 North Avenue
Suite 8
Wakefield, MA 01880
Phone: (781) 224-1117
http://www.newenglandstringensemble.org

New Philharmonia
Orchestra/Massachusetts
P.O. Box 610384
Newton Highlands, MA 02461
Phone: (617) 527-9717
http://www.newphil.org

Newton Symphony Orchestra
230 Central Street
Newton, MA 02466
Phone: (617) 965-2555
http://www.newtonsymphony.org

The Orchestra of Indian Hill
36 King Street
P.O. Box 1484
Littleton, MA 01460
Phone: (978) 486-9524
http://www.indianhillmusic.org

Pioneer Valley Symphony
91 Main Street

Greenfield, MA 01301
Phone: (413) 773-3664
http://www.pvso.org

Plymouth Philharmonic Orchestra
16 Court Street
Plymouth, MA 02360
Phone: (508) 746-8008
http://www.plymouthphilharmonic.com

Pro Arte Chamber Orchestra of Boston
99 Bishop Allen Drive
Cambridge, MA 02139
Phone: (617) 661-7067
http://www.proarte.org

Quincy Symphony Orchestra
P.O. Box 2
Wollaston, MA 02170
Phone: (217) 222-2856
http://www.adams.net/~qsoa

Springfield Symphony Orchestra
75 Market Place
Springfield, MA 01103
Phone: (413) 733-2291
http://www.springfieldsymphony.org

Symphony by the Sea
Box 1425
Marblehead, MA 01945
Phone: (978) 745-4955
http://www.symphonybythesea.org

Symphony Pro Musica
P.O. Box 332
Hudson, MA 01749
http://symphonypromusica.org

Waltham Philharmonic Orchestra
P.O. Box 1188
Waltham, MA 02454-1188
http://www.wphil.org

MICHIGAN

Adrian Symphony Orchestra
110 South Madison
Adrian, MI 49221
Phone: (517) 264-3121
http://www.aso.org

Ann Arbor Symphony Orchestra
527 East Liberty
Suite 208B
Ann Arbor, MI 48104
Phone: (734) 994-4801
http://www.a2so.com

Battle Creek Symphony Orchestra
P.O. Box 1613

Battle Creek, MI 49016
Phone: (269) 963-1911
http://www.musiccenterscmi.com/
  symphony/symphonyconcerts.htm

Cadillac Symphony Orchestra
P.O. Box 435
Cadillac, MI 49601
Phone: (231) 775-8870

Dearborn Symphony Orchestra
P.O. Box 2063
Dearborn, MI 48123
Phone: (313) 565-2424
http://www.dearbornsymphony.org

Detroit Symphony Orchestra
3711 Woodward
Detroit, MI 48201
http://www.detroitsymphony.com

Flint Institute of Music
1025 East Kearsley Street
Flint, MI 48503
http://www.thefim.com

Grand Rapids Symphony
300 Ottawa NW
Suite 100
Grand Rapids, MI 49503
Phone: (616) 454-9451
http://www.grsymphony.org

Greater Lansing Symphony Orchestra
230 North Washington Square
Suite 100
Lansing, MI 48933
http://www.lansingsymphony.org

Holland Symphony Orchestra
150 East 8th Street
Holland, MI 49423
Phone: (616) 494-0256
http://www.hollandsymphony.org

Kalamazoo Symphony Orchestra
359 South Kalamazoo Mall
Suite 100
Kalamazoo, MI 49007
http://www.kalamazoosymphony.com

Midland Symphony Orchestra
1801 West Saint Andrews Drive
Midland Center for the Arts
Midland, MI 48640
http://www.mcfta.org/symphony_orchestra

Plymouth Symphony Society
P.O. Box 6379
Plymouth, MI 48170

Phone: (734) 451-2112
http://www.plymouthsymphony.org

Saginaw Bay Symphony Orchestra
P.O. Box 415
310 North Johnson
Suite 216
Saginaw, MI 48606
Phone: (989) 755-6471
http://www.saginawbayorchestra.com

Traverse Symphony Orchestra
121 East Front Street
Suite 301
Traverse City, MI 49684
http://www.tso-online.org

Warren Symphony Orchestra
4504 East Nine Mile Road
Warren, MI 48091
Phone: (586) 754-2950
http://www.warrensymphony.org

West Shore Symphony Orchestra
425 West Western Avenue
Suite 409
Muskegon, MI 49440
Phone: (231) 726-3231
http://www.wsso.org

Ypsilanti Symphony Orchestra
P.O. Box 970942
Ypsilanti, MI 48197
Phone: (734) 480-4579

MINNESOTA

Allegro Orchestral Association
P.O. Box 189
Wayzata, MN 55391

Austin Symphony Orchestra
604 13th Avenue SW
Austin, MN 55912
Phone: (507) 433-5647

Bloomington Symphony Orchestra
1800 West Old Shakopee Road
Bloomington, MN 55431
Phone: (952) 563-8573
http://www.bloomingtonsymphony.org

Civic Orchestra of Minneapolis
P.O. Box 50604
Minneapolis, MN 55405
Phone: (612) 332-4842
http://www.civicorchestrampls.org

Duluth Superior Symphony Orchestra
506 West Michigan Street

Duluth, MN 55802
Phone: (218) 733-7575
http://www.dsso.com

Lake Superior Chamber Orchestra
P.O. Box 434
Duluth, MN 55801
http://www.lakesuperiorchamberorchestra.
  org

Mankato Symphony Orchestra
P.O. Box 645
Mankato, MN 56002
Phone: (507) 625-8880
http://www.symphony.mankato.com

Metropolitan Symphony Orchestra
P.O. Box 581213
Minneapolis, MN 55458
Phone: (651) 645-4283
http://www.msoa.net

Minnesota Orchestra
1111 Nicollet Mall
Minneapolis, MN 55403
Phone: (612) 371-5600
http://www.minnesotaorchestra.org

Minnesota Philharmonic Orchestra
P.O. Box 6116
Minneapolis, MN 55406
Phone: (612) 656-5676
http://www.mnphil.org

St. Cloud Symphony Orchestra
P.O. Box 234
Saint Cloud, MN 56302
Phone: (320) 257-3114
http://www.stcloudsymphony.com

The Saint Paul Chamber Orchestra
408 Saint Peter Street
The Hamm Building
Saint Paul, MN 55102
Phone: (651) 292-3248
http://www.thespco.org

MISSISSIPPI

Gulf Coast Symphony
P.O. Box 542
Biloxi, MS 39533
Phone: (228) 435-9800
http://www.gulfcoastsymphony.net

Meridian Symphony Orchestra
P.O. Box 2171
Meridian, MS 39302
Phone: (601) 693-2787
http://www.meridianms.org

Mississippi Symphony Orchestra
P.O. Box 2052
Jackson, MS 39225
Phone: (601) 960-1565
http://www.msorchestra.com

Tupelo Symphony Orchestra
P.O. Box 474
Tupelo, MS 38802
Phone: (662) 842-8433
http://www.tupelosymphony.com

MISSOURI

Gateway Festival Orchestra
722 Elkington Lane
St. Louis, MO 63132
Phone: (314) 569-0371

Independence Symphony Orchestra
P.O. Box 2193
Independence, MO 64055
http://www.indepsymphony.org

Kansas City Symphony
1020 Central
Suite 300
Kansas City, MO 64105
Phone: (816) 471-1100
http://www.kcsymphony.org

Lee's Summit Symphony Orchestra
206 Southeast Ridgeview Drive
P.O. Box 352
Lee's Summit, MO 64063
http://www.lssymphony.org

Liberty Symphony Orchestra
P.O. Box 30
Liberty, MO 64069
Phone: (816) 781-7700

Northland Symphony Orchestra
P.O. Box 12255
Kansas City, MO 64152
Phone: (816) 759-1260
www.northlandsymphony.com

Ozark Festival Orchestra
P.O. Box 778
Monett, MO 65708
Phone: (417) 235-3135

Philharmonia of Greater Kansas City
P.O. Box 14448
Kansas City, MO 64152
http://www.kcphilharmonia.org

Saint Louis Philharmonic Orchestra
P.O. Box 220437

Saint Louis, MO 63122
Phone: (314) 421-3600
http://www.stlphilharmonic.org

Saint Louis Symphony Orchestra
718 North Grand Boulevard
Powell Symphony Hall
Saint Louis, MO 63103
Phone: (314) 533-2500
http://www.slso.org

Sedalia Symphony Orchestra Society
1711 West 10th Street
P.O. Box 1833
Sedalia, MO 65302
Phone: (660) 827-6091

Springfield Symphony Orchestra
1536 East Division
Springfield, MO 65803
Phone: (417) 864-6683
http://www.springfieldmosymphony.org

MONTANA

Billings Symphony Orchestra
201 North Broadway
Suite 350
Billings, MT 59101
Phone: (406) 252-3610
http://www.billingssymphony.org

Bozeman Symphony
P.O. Box 1174
Bozeman, MT 59771
Phone: (406) 585-9774
http://symphony.gomontana.com

Butte Symphony
P.O. Box 725
Butte, MT 59703-0725
Phone: (406) 723-5590
http://www.buttesymphony.us

Glacier Symphony and Chorale
c/o Myra Appel, CPA
P.O. Box 4223
Whitefish, MT 59937
http://www.glaciersymphonychorale.org

Great Falls Symphony
P.O. Box 1078
Great Falls, MT 59403
Phone: (406) 453-4102
http://www.gfsymphony.org

Helena Symphony Society
P.O. Box 1073
Helena, MT 59624

Phone: (406) 442-1860
http://www.helenasymphony.org

Missoula Symphony Orchestra
P.O. Box 8301
225 West Front Street
Missoula, MT 59807
http://www.missoulasymphony.org

NEBRASKA

Lincoln Symphony Orchestra
233 South 13th Street
Suite B102
Lincoln, NE 68508
Phone: (402) 476-2211
http://www.lincolnsymphony.com

Omaha Municipal Orchestra
209 South 19th Street
Suite 477
Omaha, NE 68102
Phone: (402) 330-4442

Omaha Symphony
1605 Howard Street
Omaha, NE 68102-2705
Phone: (402) 342-3836
http://www.omahasymphony.org

NEVADA

Carson City Symphony
P.O. Box 2001
Carson City, NV 89702
http://members.aol.com/ccsymphony

Foundation Orchestra Assocation
P.O. Box 3279
Reno, NV 89505
Phone: (775) 348-1818
http://www.foundationorchestra.org

The Las Vegas Philharmonic
3271 South Highland Drive, #702
Las Vegas, NV 89109
Phone: (702) 258-5438
http://www.lasvegasphilharmonic.com

Reno Chamber Orchestra
P.O. Box 547
Reno, NV 89504
Phone: (775) 348-9413
http://www.renochamberorchestra.org

Reno Philharmonic Orchestra
925 Riverside Drive
Suite 3
Reno, NV 89503

Phone: (775) 323-6393
http://www.renophilharmonic.com

Reno Pops Orchestra
P.O. Box 20952
Reno, NV 89515-0952
Phone: (775) 345-0567

NEW HAMPSHIRE

Lakes Region Symphony Orchestra
P.O. Box 721
Meredith, NH 03253
Phone: (603) 279-3324
http://www.lrso.org

New Hampshire Philharmonic Orchestra
83 Hanover Street, 4th Floor
Manchester, NH 03101
Phone: (603) 647-6476
http://www.nhphilharmonic.org

New Hampshire Symphony Orchestra
1087 Elm Street
Suite 306
Manchester, NH 03101
Phone: (603) 669-3559
http://www.nhso.org

NEW JERSEY

Bay-Atlantic Symphony
59 East Commerce Street
Bridgeton, NJ 08302
Phone: (856) 451-1169
http://www.bayatlanticsymphony.org

Bergen Philharmonic Orchestra
P.O. Box 174
Teaneck, NJ 07666
Phone: (201) 837-1980
http://www.bpo.ar88.net

Colonial Symphony
246 B Madisonville Road
Basking Ridge, NJ 07920
http://www.colonialsymphony.org

Garden State Philharmonic
150 Brick Boulevard
Brick, NJ 08723
Phone: (732) 451-0064
http://www.gardenstatephilharmonic.com

The Haddonfield Symphony
41 South Haddon Avenue
Suite 7
Haddonfield, NJ 08033

Phone: (856) 429-1880
http://www.haddonfield-symphony.org

High Mountain Symphony at William Paterson University
300 Pompton Road
Hunziker Hall 104
Wayne, NJ 07470
http://ww2.wpunj.edu/culture/index_culture.html

Jubilate Deo Chorale & Orchestra
631 Market Street
Camden, NJ 08102
Phone: (856) 583-6156
http://www.jdco.org

Monmouth Symphony Orchestra
P.O. Box 1302
Wall, NJ 07719
Phone: (732) 842-9000
http://www.monsym.org

New Jersey Symphony Orchestra
2 Central Avenue
Newark, NJ 07102
Phone: (973) 624-3713
http://www.njsymphony.org

New Sussex Symphony
P.O. Box 859
Newton, NJ 07860
Phone: (973) 579-6465

Ocean City Pops Orchestra
c/o City of Ocean City
901 Asbury Avenue
Ocean City, NJ 08226
Phone: (609) 525-9291
http://www.oceancitypops.org

Philharmonic of Southern New Jersey
P.O. Box 1750
Cherry Hill, NJ 08034
Phone: (856) 779-2600
http://www.psnj.org/concerts.html

Philharmonic Orchestra of New Jersey
50 Mount Bethel Road
P.O. Box 4064
Warren, NJ 07059
Phone: (908) 226-7300
http://www.ponj.org

Plainfield Symphony Orchestra
P.O. Box 5093
Plainfield, NJ 07061
http://www.plainfieldsymphony.org

Princeton Symphony Orchestra
P.O. Box 250
Princeton, NJ 08542
Phone: (609) 497-0020
http://www.princetonsymphony.org

Ridgewood Symphony Orchestra
P.O. Box 176
Ridgewood, NJ 07451
http://www.ridgewoodsymphony.org

NEW MEXICO

Las Cruces Symphony at NMSU
P.O. Box 1622
Las Cruces, NM 88004
http://www.lascrucessymphony.com

New Mexico Symphony Orchestra
P.O. Box 30208
Albuquerque, NM 87190
Phone: (505) 881-9590
http://www.nmso.org

Roswell Symphony Orchestra
Executive West Office Plaza
1717 West Second Street
Roswell, NM 88201-2027
Phone: (505) 623-5882
http://www.roswellsymphony.org

Santa Fe Community Orchestra
551 West Cordova
Santa Fe, NM 87505
Phone: (505) 466-4879
http://www.sfco.org

Southwest Symphony Orchestra
P.O. Box 101
Hobbs, NM 88241
Phone: (505) 738-1041

NEW YORK

Albany Symphony Orchestra
19 Clinton Avenue
Albany, NY 12207
Phone: (518) 465-4755
http://www.albanysymphony.com

American Composers Orchestra
240 West 35th Street
Suite 405
New York, NY 10001
http://www.americancomposers.org

American Symphony Orchestra
333 West 39th Street
Suite 1101
New York, NY 10018

Phone: (212) 868-9276
http://www.americansymphony.org

Amherst Symphony Orchestra
P.O. Box 1083
Williamsville, NY 14231
http://www.amherst.ny.us/News/symphony.
asp

Astoria Symphony
25-90 35th Street
Suite 6J
Astoria, NY 11103
Phone: (718) 204-9034
http://www.astoriamusic.org

Binghamton Philharmonic
31 Front Street
Binghamton, NY 13905
Phone: (607) 722-6717
http://www.binghamtonphilharmonic.org

Bronx Arts Ensemble Orchestra
100 Van Cortlandt Park–Golf House
Bronx, NY 10471
Phone: (718) 601-7399
http://www.bronxartsensemble.org

Brooklyn Philharmonic Orchestra
138A Court Street
Brooklyn, NY 11201
Phone: (718) 488-5700
http://www.brooklynphilharmonic.org

Brooklyn Symphony Orchestra
P.O. Box 20334
Brooklyn, NY 11201
http://www.brooklynsymphonyorchestra.
org

Buffalo Philharmonic Orchestra
499 Franklin Street
Buffalo, NY 14202
Phone: (716) 885-0331
http://www.bpo.org

Catskill Symphony Orchestra
P.O. Box 14
Oneonta, NY 13820
Phone: (607) 436-2670
http://www.catskillsymphony.org

Chappaqua Orchestra
P.O. Box 461
Chappaqua, NY 10514
Phone: (914) 921-4642
http://www.chappaquaorchestra.org

Empire State Pops Orchestra
130 Garth Road

Suite 123
Scarsdale, NY 10583
Phone: (914) 723-2694

Forest Hills Symphony Orchestra
The Queens Festival Orchestra
   Association
2502 Navy Place
Bellmore, NY 11710
Phone: (516) 785-2532

Genesee Symphony
P.O. Box 391
Batavia, NY 14021
http://www.geneseesymphony.com

Glens Falls Symphony Orchestra
P.O. Box 2036
Glens Falls, NY 12801
Phone: (518) 793-1348
http://www.glensfallssymphony.org

Greenwich Village Orchestra
P.O. Box 910
New York, NY 10113
Phone: (212) 932-0372
http://www.gvo.org

Lake Placid Sinfonietta
Box 1303
Lake Placid, NY 12946
Phone: (518) 523-2051
http://web.northnet.org/
   lakeplacidsinfonietta

Long Island Philharmonic
One Huntington Quadrangle
Suite 2C21
Melville, NY 11747
Phone: (631) 293-2222.
http://www.liphilharmonic.com

Music Company Orchestra
P.O. Box 132
Saratoga Springs, NY 12866
http://www.geocities.com/mcomusic

The New York Philharmonic
10 Lincoln Center Plaza
Avery Fisher Hall
New York, NY 10023-6973
http://www.newyorkphilharmonic.org

New York Pops, Inc.
881 Seventh Avenue
Suite 903
New York, NY 10019
Phone: (212) 765-7677
http://www.newyorkpops.org

New York Repertory Orchestra
949 West End Avenue
Suite 4D
New York, NY 10025
http://www.nyro.org

New York Scandia Symphony
P.O. Box 583
New York, NY 10150
Phone: (212) 927-1596

Orchard Park Symphony
P.O. Box 332
Orchard Park, NY 14127
Phone: (716) 559-4000

Orchestra of St. Luke's
330 West 42nd Street, 9th Floor
New York, NY 10036
Phone: (212) 594-6100
http://www.oslmusic.org

**Orchestra of the Southern Finger
   Lakes**
P.O. Box 15
Corning, NY 14830
Phone: (607) 936-2873
http://www.osfl.org

Orpheus Chamber Orchestra
490 Riverside Drive, 11th Floor
New York, NY 10027
http://www.orpheusnyc.org

The Park Avenue Chamber Symphony
605 Park Avenue
New York, NY 10021
Phone: (212) 570-1200
http://www.chambersymphony.com

Richmond County Orchestra
300 Howard Avenue
Flynn Hall #105A
Staten Island, NY 10301
Phone: (718) 390-4306
http://www.richmondcountyorchestra.8k.
   com

Rochester Philharmonic Orchestra
108 East Avenue
Rochester, NY 14604
http://www.rpo.org

Sound Symphony
20 Nevinwood Place
Huntington Station, NY 11746
Phone: (631) 549.3881
http://www.soundsymphony.org

Staten Island Symphony Orchestra
1 Campus Road
Staten Island, NY 10301
Phone: (718) 390-3426
http://www.sisymphony.org

Syracuse Symphony Orchestra
411 Montgomery Street
Suite 40
Syracuse, NY 13202
Phone: (315) 424-8222
http://www.syracusesymphony.org

Utica Symphony Orchestra
505 Henry Street
Utica, NY 13502
Phone: (315) 732-5146

Westchester Philharmonic
123 Main Street
Suite 702
White Plains, NY 10601
Phone: (914) 682-3707
http://www.westchesterphil.org

Woodstock Chamber Orchestra
P.O. Box 711
Woodstock, NY 12498
Phone: (845) 246-6195

NORTH CAROLINA

Asheville Symphony Orchestra
P.O. Box 2852
Asheville, NC 28802
http://www.ashevillesymphony.org

Charlotte Civic Orchestra
P.O. Box 11334
Charlotte, NC 28220
Phone: (704) 344-0098
http://www.charlottecivicorchestra.org

Charlotte Symphony
201 South College Street
Suite 110
Charlotte, NC 28244
Phone: (704) 972-2003
http://www.charlottesymphony.org

Fayetteville Symphony Orchestra
P.O. Box 53234
Fayetteville, NC 28305
http://www.fayettevillesymphony.org

Hendersonville Symphony Orchestra
P.O. Box 1811
Hendersonville, NC 28793
Phone: (828) 679-5884
http://www.hendersonvillesymphony.org

North Carolina Symphony
2 East South Street
Raleigh, NC 27601
Phone: (919) 733-2750
http://www.ncsymphony.org

Raleigh Civic Symphony & Chamber
NCSU Music Department
P.O. Box 7311
Raleigh, NC 27695
http://www.ncsu.edu

Salisbury Symphony Orchestra
P.O. Box 4264
Salisbury, NC 28145
Phone: (704) 637-4314
http://www.salisburysymphony.org

Western Piedmont Symphony
243 Third Avenue NE
Suite 1-N
Hickory, NC 28601
Phone: (828) 324-8603
http://www.wpsymphony.org

Wilmington Symphony Orchestra
4608 Cedar Avenue
Building 2, Suite 105
Wilmington, NC 28403
Phone: (910) 791-9262
http://www.wilmingtonsymphony.org

Winston-Salem Symphony
680 West Fourth Street
Suite 101
Winston-Salem, NC 27101
Phone: (336) 725-1035
http://www.wssymphony.org

NORTH DAKOTA

Bismarck-Mandan Symphony Orchestra
215 North 6th
Bismarck, ND 58501
Phone: (701) 258-8345
http://www.bismarckmandansymphony.org

Fargo-Moorhead Symphony Orchestra
P.O. Box 1753
Fargo, ND 58107-1753

Greater Grand Forks Symphony
P.O. Box 7084
Grand Forks, ND 58202
Phone: (218) 233-8397
http://www.fmsymphony.org

OHIO

Akron Symphony Orchestra
17 North Broadway Street
Akron, OH 44308
http://www.akronsymphony.org

Ashland Symphony Orchestra
P.O. Box 13
Ashland, OH 44805
Phone: (419) 289-5115

Canton Symphony Orchestra
1001 Market Avenue North
Canton, OH 44702-1024
Phone: (330) 452-3434
http://www.cantonsymphony.org

Cincinnati Chamber Orchestra
1406 Elm Street
Cincinnati, OH 45210
Phone: (513) 723-1182
http://www.cincychamberorch.com

Cincinnati Symphony Orchestra
1241 Elm Street
Music Hall
Cincinnati, OH 45202
Phone: (513) 621-1919
http://www.cincinnatisymphony.org

Cleveland Chamber Symphony
Cleveland State University
2121 Euclid Avenue
Cleveland, OH 44115
http://www.clevelandchambersymphony.
org

The Cleveland Orchestra
Severance Hall
11001 Euclid Avenue
Cleveland, OH 44106
Phone: (216) 231-7300
http://www.clevelandorchestra.com

The Cleveland Pops Orchestra
2400 Mercantile Road
Beachwood, OH 44122
Phone: (216) 765-7677
http://www.clevelandpops.com

The Columbus Symphony Orchestra
55 East State Street
Columbus, OH 43215
Phone: (614) 228-8600
http://www.columbussymphony.com

Columbus Women's Orchestra
P.O. Box 14722
Columbus, OH 43214

Phone: (614) 470-0098
http://www.vanderbilt.edu/~bingham/
    CWO.html

Dayton Philharmonic Orchestra
Performance Place
109 North Main Street
Suite 200
Dayton, OH 45402
http://www.daytonphilharmonic.com

Hamilton-Fairfield Symphony
23 South Front Street
Hamilton, OH 45011
Phone: (513) 895-5151
http://www.hfso.org

**Land of Legend Philharmonic
    Orchestra**
208 Beechwood Drive
Granville, OH 43023
Phone: (740) 587-7704

The Lima Symphony Orchestra
133 North Elizabeth
Metro Center Building, First Floor
Lima, OH 45801
Phone: (419) 422-5701
http://www.limasymphony.com

Mansfield Symphony Orchestra
Renaissance Performing Arts Association,
    Inc
P.O. Box 789
Mansfield, OH 44901
Phone: (419) 522-2726
http://www.rparts.org

Ohio Valley Symphony
P.O. Box 424
Gallipolis, OH 45631
http://www.jscs.org

ProMusica Chamber Orchestra
243 North Fifth Street
Suite 202
Columbus, OH 43215
Phone: (614) 464-0066
http://www.promusicacolumbus.org

Red {an orchestra}
28815 Aurora Road
Cleveland, OH 44139
Phone: (440) 519-1733
http://www.redanorchestra.org

**Southeastern Ohio Symphony
    Orchestra**
P.O. Box 42

New Concord, OH 43762
http://fates.cns.muskingum.edu/~seoso/

Springfield Symphony Orchestra
300 South Fountain Avenue
P.O. Box 1374
Springfield, OH 45501
Phone: (937) 325-8100
http://www.springfieldsym.org

Stow Chamber Orchestra
3134 Peterboro Drive
Stow, OH 44224
Phone: (330) 678-0029
http://www.stowchamberorchestra.org

The Toledo Symphony
1838 Park Wood Avenue
Suite 310
Toledo, OH 43624
Phone: (419) 246-8000
http://www.toledosymphony.com

Tuscarawas Philharmonic
P.O. Box 406
New Philadelphia, OH 44663
http://www.tuscarawasphilharmonic.org

Westerville Symphony
P.O. Box 478
Westerville, OH 43086
Phone: (614) 890-5523
http://www.westervillesymphony.org

Youngstown Symphony Orchestra
260 Federal Plaza West
Youngstown, OH 44503
Phone: (330) 744-4269
http://www.youngstownsymphony.com

OKLAHOMA

Bartlesville Symphony Orchestra
P.O. Box 263
Bartlesville, OK 74005
Phone: (918) 336-7717
http://www.bartlesvillesymphony.org

Enid Symphony Orchestra
300 West Cherokee
Suite 100
Enid, OK 73701
Phone: (508) 237-9646

Lawton Philharmonic Orchestra
P.O. Box 1473
Lawton, OK 73502
http://www.lawtonphil.org

Oklahoma City Philharmonic
428 West California Avenue
Suite 210
Oklahoma City, OK 73102
Phone: (405) 232-7575
http://www.okcphilharmonic.org

OREGON

Britt Festival Orchestra
216 West Main Street
P.O. Box 1124
Medford, OR 97501
Phone: (541) 779-0847
http://www.brittfest.org

Eugene Symphony Orchestra
115 West 8th
Suite 115
Eugene, OR 97401
Phone: (541) 687-9487
http://www.eugenesymphony.org

**Mid-Columbia Sinfonietta Chamber
    Orchestra**
5590 Trout Creek Road
Parkdale, OR 97041
http://w3.gorge.net/mdstg/CGOA.htm

Mt. Hood Pops Orchestra
P.O. Box 1641
Gresham, OR 97030
Phone: (503) 669-1937

Oregon East Symphony
424 South Main
Pendleton, OR 97801
Phone: (541) 276-0320

Oregon Symphony
921 Southwest Washington Street
Suite 200
Portland, OR 97205
Phone: (503) 228-4294
http://www.orsymphony.org

Rogue Valley Symphony
1250 Siskiyou Boulevard
SOU Music Hall
Ashland, OR 97520
Phone: (541) 552-6398
http://www.rvsymphony.org

Sunriver Music Festival
P.O. Box 4308
Sunriver, OR 97707
Phone: (541) 593-1084
http://www.sunrivermusic.org

PENNSYLVANIA

Allentown Symphony Orchestra
23 North Sixth Street
Allentown, PA 18101
http://www.allentownsymphony.org

Altoona Symphony Orchestra
P.O. Box 483
1331 12th Avenue
Altoona, PA 16603
Phone: (814) 943-2500
http://www.altoonasymphony.org

Central Pennsylvania Symphony
P.O. Box 55
Hummelstown, PA 17036
http://www.centralpasymphony.org

**The Chamber Orchestra of
Philadelphia**
1520 Locust Street
Suite 500
Philadelphia, PA 19102
Phone: (215) 545-5451
http://www.chamberorchestra.org

**Delaware Valley Philharmonic
Orchestra**
409 Hood Boulevard
Fairless Hills, PA 19030
http://www.dvpo.org

Erie Philharmonic Orchestra
1006 State Street
Erie, PA 16501
Phone: (814) 455-1375
http://www.eriephil.org

Hanover Symphony Orchestra
1150 Carlisle Street
PMB 151
Hanover, PA 17331
Phone: (717) 633-6720

Harrisburg Symphony Association
800 Corporate Circle
Suite 101
Harrisburg, PA 17110
Phone: (717) 545-5527
http://www.harrisburgsymphony.org

Hershey Symphony Orchestra
P.O. Box 93
Hershey, PA 17033
Phone: (717) 533-8449
http://www.hersheysymphony.org

Johnstown Symphony Orchestra
227 Franklin Street

Suite 302
Johnstown, PA 15901
Phone: (814) 535-6738
http://www.johnstownsymphony.org

Kennett Symphony/Chester County
P.O. Box 72
Kennett Square, PA 19348
Phone: (610) 444-6363
http://www.symphony.kennett.net

Lancaster Symphony Orchestra
P.O. Box 1281
Lancaster, PA 17608-1281
Phone: (717) 291-6440
http://www.lancastersymphony.org

Lehigh Valley Chamber Orchestra
961 Marcon Boulevard
Suite 112
Allentown, PA 18109
Phone: (610) 266-8555
http://www.lvco.org

McKeesport Symphony Orchestra
P.O. Box 354
McKeesport, PA 15134
Phone: (412) 664-2854
http://www.mckeesportsymphony.org

Nittany Valley Symphony
P.O. Box 1375
444 East College Avenue
State College, PA 16804
Phone: (814) 231-8224
http://www.nvs.org

**Northeastern Pennsylvania
Philharmonic**
957 Broadcast Center
Avoca, PA 18641
http://www.nepaphil.org

North Penn Symphony Orchestra
P.O. Box 694
Lansdale, PA 19446
Phone: (215) 368-9800
http://www.northpennsymphony.org

Peter Nero and the Philly Pops
252 South 16th Street
Philadelphia, PA 19102
Phone: (215) 546-6400
http://www.phillypops.com

The Philadelphia Orchestra
260 South Broad Street, 16th Floor
Philadelphia, PA 19102

Phone: (215) 893-1900
http://www.philorch.org

Pittsburgh Symphony Orchestra
600 Penn Avenue
Heinz Hall
Pittsburgh, PA 15222
Phone: (412) 392-4900
http://www.pittsburghsymphony.org

Pottstown Symphony Orchestra
P.O. Box 675
Pottstown, PA 19464
Phone: (610) 326-8742
http://www.pottstownsymphony.org

Reading Symphony Orchestra
147 North Fifth Street
Reading, PA 19601
Phone: (610) 373-7557
http://www.readingsymphony.org

Schuylkill Symphony Orchestra
P.O. Box 1310
Pottsville, PA 17901
Phone: (570) 628-2632
http://www.schuylkillsymphony.com

Warminster Symphony Orchestra
P.O. Box 117
Warminster, PA 18974
http://www.warmsymphony.org

Warren Civic Orchestra
c/o Victoria Hanson
418 Water Street
Warren, PA 16365
Phone: (814) 726-6307

Washington Symphony Orchestra
64 South Main Street
Box 306
Washington, PA 15301
Phone: (724) 263-6752
http://www.washsym.org

Westmoreland Symphony Orchestra
105 North Pennsylvania Avenue
Greensburg, PA 15601
Phone: (724) 837-1850
http://www.westmorelandsymphony.org

West Shore Symphony Orchestra
P.O. Box 125
Mechanicsburg, PA 17055
Phone: (231) 726-3231
http://www.wsso.org

Williamsport Symphony Orchestra
360 Market Street

Williamsport, PA 17701
Phone: (570) 322-0227
http://www.williamsportsymphony.com

York Symphony Orchestra
10 North Beaver Street
York, PA 17401
http://www.yorksymphony.org

RHODE ISLAND

Rhode Island Philharmonic
222 Richmond Street
Suite 112
Providence, RI 02903
Phone: (401) 831-3123
http://www.ri-philharmonic.org

SOUTH CAROLINA

Florence Symphony Orchestra
  Association
P.O. Box 3211
Florence, SC 29502
http://www.florencesymphony.com

The Greater Spartanburg
  Philharmonic
P.O. Box 1274
385 South Spring Street
Spartanburg, SC 29306
Phone: (864) 948-9020
http://www.sparklenet.com/
    musicfoundation

Greenville Symphony Orchestra
200 South Main Street
Greenville, SC 29601
Phone: (864) 232-0344
http://www.greenvillesymphony.org

Hilton Head Orchestra
P.O. Drawer 5757
Hilton Head Island, SC 29938
Phone: (843) 842-2055
http://www.hhorchestra.org

Long Bay Symphony Orchestra
1551 21st Avenue North
Myrtle Beach, SC 29577
Phone: (843) 448-8379
http://www.longbaysymphony.com

South Carolina Philharmonic
1237 Gadsden Street
Suite 102
Columbia, SC 29201
Phone: (803) 771-7937
http://www.scphilharmonic.com

SOUTH DAKOTA

Black Hills Symphony Orchestra
P.O. Box 2246
Rapid City, SD 57709-2246
Phone: (605) 348-4676
http://www.bhsymphony.org

South Dakota Symphony
300 North Dakota Avenue
Suite 116
Sioux Falls, SD 57104
Phone: (605) 335-7933
http://www.sdsymphony.org

TENNESSEE

Bryan Symphony Orchestra
P.O. Box 185
Cookeville, TN 38503
http://www.bryansymphony.org

Chattanooga Symphony & Opera
  Association
630 Chestnut Street
Chattanooga, TN 37402
Phone: (423) 267-8583
http://www.chattanoogasymphony.org

Germantown Symphony Orchestra
P.O. Box 38038
Germantown, TN 38183
http://www.germantownsymphony.org

Iris Chamber Orchestra
Germantown Performing Arts Center
1801 Exeter Road
Germantown, TN 38138
Phone: (901) 757-7256
http://gpacweb.com/iris

Jackson Symphony Orchestra
P.O. Box 3429
Jackson, TN 38303
Phone: (731) 427-6440
http://www.jso.tn.org

Johnson City Symphony
P.O. Box 533
3201 Bristol Highway
Johnson City, TN 37601
http://www.jcsymphony.com

Knoxville Symphony Orchestra
P.O. Box 360
Knoxville, TN 37901-0360
Phone: (865) 523-1178
http://www.knoxvillesymphony.com

Memphis Symphony Orchestra
3100 Walnut Grove Road
Suite 501
Memphis, TN 38111
Phone: (901) 324-3627
http://www.memphissymphony.org

Nashville Chamber Orchestra
2002 Blair Boulevard
Nashville, TN 37212
Phone: (615) 783-1200
http://www.nco.org

The Nashville Symphony
2000 Glen Echo Road
Suite 204
Nashville, TN 37215
http://www.nashvillesymphony.org

Sewanee Summer Music Festival
735 University Avenue
Sewanee, TN 37383
Phone: (931) 598-1225
http://sewaneetoday.sewanee.edu/ssmf

Symphony of the Mountains
1200 East Center Street
Kingsport Renaissance Center
Kingsport, TN 37660
Phone: (423) 392-8423
http://www.symphonyofthemountains.org

Tennessee Philharmonic Symphony
  Orchestra
P.O. Box 36
Murfreesboro, TN 37133
Phone: (615) 898-1862
http://www.tnphilharmonic.com

TEXAS

Abilene Philharmonic
402 Cypress
Suite 130
Abilene, TX 79601
Phone: (325) 677-6710
http://www.abilene.com/philharmonic

Amarillo Symphony
P.O. Box 2586
Amarillo, TX 79105
Phone: (806) 376-8782
http://www.amarillosymphony.org

Austin Symphony Orchestra
1101 Red River
Austin, TX 78701
Phone: (512) 476-6064
http://www.austinsymphony.org

Baytown Symphony Orchestra
P.O. Box 818
511 South Whiting Street
Baytown, TX 77522-2217
Phone: (281) 425-6350

Big Spring Symphony Orchestra &
**   Chorus**
P.O. Box 682
808 Scurry Street
Big Spring, TX 79721
Phone: (423) 264-7223
http://www.bigspringsymphony.com

Brazosport Symphony Orchestra
400 College Drive
Center for the Arts & Sciences
Clute, TX 77531
Phone: (979) 265-7661
http://bcfas.org/symphony

Brazos Valley Symphony Orchestra
P.O. Box 3524
Bryan, TX 77805
Phone: (979) 779-6100
http://www.bvso.org

Conroe Symphony Orchestra
304 North Main
Conroe, TX 77301
http://www.conroesymphony.org

Corpus Christi Symphony Orchestra
P.O. Box 495
Corpus Christi, TX 78403
http://www.ccsymphony.org

Dallas Symphony Orchestra
2301 Flora Street
Schlegel Administrative Suites
Dallas, TX 75201
Phone: (214) 692-0203
http://www.dallassymphony.com

East Texas Symphony Orchestra
P.O. Box 6323
Tyler, TX 75711
Phone: (903) 526-3876
http://www.etso.org

El Paso Symphony Orchestra
P.O. Box 180
El Paso, TX 79942
http://www.epso.org

Fort Worth Symphony Orchestra
Maddox-Muse Administrative Building
330 East Fourth Street
Suite 200
Fort Worth, TX 76102

Phone: (817) 665-6500
http://www.fwsymphony.org

Houston Symphony
615 Louisiana Street
Houston, TX 77002
Phone: (713) 224-4240
http://www.houstonsymphony.org

Irving Symphony Orchestra
225 East John Carpenter Freeway
Suite 120
Irving, TX 75062
Phone: (972) 831-8818
http://www.irvingsymphony.com

Las Colinas Symphony Orchestra
1300 Walnut Hill
Suite #106
Phone: (972) 580-1566
Irving, TX 75038-3032
http://www.lascolinassymphony.org

Lubbock Symphony Orchestra
1313 Broadway
Suite 2
Lubbock, TX 79401
Phone: (806) 762-1688
http://www.lubbocksymphony.org

Midland-Odessa Symphony/Chorale
3100 LaForce Boulevard
Midland, TX 79711
Phone: (432) 563-0921
http://www.mosc.org

Mid-Texas Symphony Orchestra
Texas Lutheran University
Box 3216
Seguin, TX 78155
Phone: (830) 372-8089
http://www.mtsymphony.org

Orchestra X, Inc.
1302 Waught Drive, #132
Houston, TX 77019-4946
Phone: (713) 225-6729

Plainview Symphony Orchestra
P.O. Box 1857
Plainview, TX 79072
Phone: (806) 291-1063

Plano Symphony Orchestra
2701-C West 15th Street
Suite 187
Plano, TX 75075
http://www.planosymphony.org

Richardson Symphony Orchestra
800 East Campbell Road
Suite 122
Richardson, TX 75081
http://www.richardsonsymphony.org

San Angelo Symphony Orchestra
P.O. Box 5922
San Angelo, TX 76902
http://www.sanangelosymphony.org

San Antonio Symphony
230 East Houston
San Antonio, TX 78205
Phone: (325) 658-5877
http://www.sasymphony.org

The Symphony of Southeast Texas
4345 Phelan Boulevard
Suite 105
Beaumont, TX 77707
Phone: (409) 892-2257
http://www.sost.org

Temple Symphony Orchestra
P.O. Box 4241
Temple, TX 76503
http://www.templesymphony.org

Valley Symphony Orchestra
P.O. Box 2832
Mcallen, TX 78502
Phone: (956) 393-2293
http://www.valleyorchestra.org

Victoria Symphony Orchestra
2112 North Navarro
Victoria, TX 77901
Phone: (361) 576-4500
http://www.victoriasymphony.com

Waco Symphony Orchestra
P.O. Box 1201
Waco, TX 76703
Phone: (254) 754-0851
http://www.wacosymphony.com

Wichita Falls Symphony Orchestra
1300 Lamar
Wichita Falls, TX 76301
Phone: (940) 723-6202
http://wfso.org

UTAH

Murray Symphony Orchestra
6285 South 725 East
Murray, UT 84107
http://www.geocities.com/
    murraysymphony

The Orchestra of Southern Utah
P.O. Box 312
Cedar City, UT 84721
Phone: (435) 867-8501
http://www.orchestraofsouthernutah.org

Utah Symphony & Opera
123 West South Temple
Maurice Abravanel Hall
Salt Lake City, UT 84101
Phone: (801) 533-5626
http://www.utahsymphony.org

VERMONT

Vermont Symphony Orchestra
2 Church Street
Suite 19
Burlington, VT 05401
Phone: (802) 864-5741
http://www.vso.org

VIRGINIA

Alexandria Symphony Orchestra
2121 Eisenhower Avenue
Suite 608
Alexandria, VA 22314
Phone: (703) 548-0885
http://www.alexsym.org

Arlington Symphony
4238 Wilson Boulevard, #3064
Arlington, VA 22203-1823
Phone: (703) 528-1817
http://www.arlingtonsymphony.org

Eclipse Chamber Orchestra
6017 Jewell Court
Alexandria, VA 22312-3030
http://www.eclipseco.com

Fairfax Symphony Orchestra
1505 Farm Credit Drive
Suite 100
McLean, VA 22102
Phone: (703) 893-8646
http://www.mclean-orchestra.org

Loudoun Symphony
P.O. Box 4478
Leesburg, VA 20177
Phone: (703) 771-8287
http://www.loudounsymphony.org

Lynchburg Symphony Orchestra
621 Court Street
Lynchburg, VA 24504
Phone: (434) 845-6604
http://www.lynchburgsymphony.com

McLean Orchestra
P.O. Box 760
McLean, VA 22101
Phone: (703) 893-8646
http://www.mclean-orchestra.org

McLean Symphony
PMB 172
1350 Beverly Road
Suite 115
McLean, VA 22101
http://www.mclean-symphony.org

Old Bridge Chamber Orchestra
9331 Main Sail Drive
Burke, VA 22015
Phone: (703) 794-9530
http://www.obco.org

Piedmont Regional Orchestra
P.O. Box 509
Warrenton, VA 20188
Phone: (540) 270-3168
http://www.prorchestra.org

Prince William Symphony Orchestra
4320 Ridgewood Center Drive
Woodbridge, VA 22192
Phone: (703) 580-8562
http://www.pwso.org

Richmond Philharmonic, Inc.
8100 Three Chopt Road
Suite 238
Richmond, VA 23229
Phone: (804) 673-7400
http://www.richmondphilharmonic.org

Richmond Symphony
300 West Franklin Street
Suite 103E
Richmond, VA 23220
Phone: (804) 788-4717
http://www.richmondsymphony.com

Roanoke Symphony Orchestra
541 Luck Avenue
Suite 200
Roanoke, VA 24016
Phone: (540) 343-6221
http://www.rso.com

Virginia Beach Symphony Orchestra
P.O. Box 2544
Virginia Beach, VA 23450
Phone: (757) 671-8611
http://www.vbso.org

Virginia Symphony
861 Glenrock Road

Suite 200
Norfolk, VA 23502
Phone: (757) 892-6366
http://www.virginiasymphony.org

Williamsburg Symphonia
P.O. Box 400
Williamsburg, VA 23185
http://www.williamsburgsymphonia.org

York River Symphony Orchestra
P.O. Box 1044
Yorktown, VA 23692
http://www.yrso.org

WASHINGTON

Bellevue Philharmonic
P.O. Box 1582
Bellevue, WA 98009
Phone: (425) 455-4171
http://www.bellevuephil.org

Bremerton Symphony Orchestra
532 5th Street #16
P.O. Box 996
Bremerton, WA 98337
Phone: (360) 373-1722
http://www.bremertonsymphony.org

Everett Symphony Orchestra
1507 Wall Street
Everett, WA 98201
Phone: (425) 257-8382
http://www.everettsymphony.org

Northwest Symphony Orchestra
P.O. Box 16231
Seattle, WA 98126
http://www.northwestsymphonyorchestra.
   org

Olympia Symphony Orchestra
3400 Capitol Boulevard South
Suite #203
Olympia, WA 98501
Phone: (360) 753-0074
http://www.olympiasymphony.com

Port Angeles Symphony Orchestra
P.O. Box 2148
Port Angeles, WA 98382
Phone: (360) 457-5579
http://www.olypen.com/pasymphony

Rainier Symphony
P.O. Box 58182
Seattle, WA 98138
http://www.rainiersymphony.org

Seattle Philharmonic Orchestra
P.O. Box 177
Seattle, WA 98111
Phone: (206) 528-6878
http://www.seattlephil.com

Seattle Symphony
200 University Street
P.O. Box 21906
Seattle, WA 98111
Phone: (206) 215-4700
http://www.seattlesymphony.org

Skagit Symphony
P.O. Box 1302
Mount Vernon, WA 98273
Phone: (360) 848-9336
http://www.skagitsymphony.com

Spokane Symphony Orchestra
818 West Riverside
Suite 100
Spokane, WA 99201
Phone: (509) 326-3136
http://www.spokanesymphony.org

Vancouver Symphony Orchestra
P.O. Box 525
Vancouver, WA 98666-0525
Phone: (360) 735-7278
http://www.vancouversymphony.org

Walla Walla Symphony
P.O. Box 92
Walla Walla, WA 99362
Phone: (509) 529-8020
http://www.wwsymphony.com

Whatcom Symphony Orchestra
P.O. Box 28895
Bellingham, WA 98228
Phone: (360) 756-6752
http://www.whatcomsymphony.com

Yakima Symphony Orchestra
32 North 3rd Street, #333
Yakima, WA 98901
Phone: (509) 248-1414
http://symphony.artsyakima.org

WEST VIRGINIA

Huntington Symphony Orchestra
P.O. Box 2434
Huntington, WV 25725
Phone: (304) 525-0670
http://www.huntingtonsymphony.org

West Virginia Symphony Orchestra
P.O. Box 2292
Charleston, WV 25328
Phone: (304) 561-3552
http://www.wvsymphony.org

Wheeling Symphony
1025 Main Street
Suite 811
Wheeling, WV 26003
Phone: (304) 232-6191
http://www.wheelingsymphony.com

WISCONSIN

Beloit Janesville Symphony Orchestra
P.O. Box 185
Beloit, WI 53512-0185
Phone: (608) 363-2554
http://www.beloit.edu/~bjso/inside/
    performance.htm

**Central Wisconsin Symphony
    Orchestra**
P.O. Box 65
933A Main Street
Stevens Point, WI 54481
Phone: (715) 345-CWSO
http://www.cwso.org

Chippewa Valley Symphony
316 Eau Claire Street
Eau Claire, WI 54701
Phone: (715) 832-6366
http://www.cvsymphony.org

Fox Valley Symphony
111 West College Avenue
Suite 550
Appleton, WI 54911
Phone: (920) 968-0300
http://www.foxvalleysymphony.com

Green Bay Symphony Orchestra
P.O. Box 222
Green Bay, WI 54305
Phone: (920) 435-3465
http://www.greenbaysymphony.com

La Crosse Symphony Orchestra
3217 Commerce Street
La Crosse, WI 54603
Phone: (608) 783-2121
http://www.lacrossesymphony.org

Madison Symphony Orchestra
6314 Odana Road

Madison, WI 53719
http://www.madisonsymphony.org

Milwaukee Symphony Orchestra
700 North Water Street
Suite 700
Milwaukee, WI 53202-4278
Phone: (414) 291-6010
http://www.milwaukeesymphony.org

Oshkosh Symphony Orchestra
P.O. Box 522
Oshkosh, WI 54902
Phone: (920) 233-7510
http://www.folklib.net/wi/oso

Racine Symphony Orchestra
P.O. Box 1874
Racine, WI 53401
Phone: (262) 636 9285
http://www.racinesymphony.org

Sheboygan Symphony Orchestra
921 North 8th Street
Suite 208
Sheboygan, WI 53081
Phone: (920) 452-1985
http://www.sheboygansymphony.org

Waukesha Symphony Orchestra
P.O. Box 531
217 Wisconsin Avenue
Waukesha, WI 53187
Phone: (262) 547-1858
http://www.waukeshasymphony.org

Wisconsin Chamber Orchestra
22 North Carroll Street
Suite 104
Madison, WI 53703
Phone: (608) 257-0638
http://www.wcoconcerts.org

WYOMING

Cheyenne Symphony Orchestra
P.O. Box 851
Cheyenne, WY 82003
Phone: (307) 778-8561
http://www.cheyennesymphony.org

Wyoming Symphony Orchestra
111 West Second Street
Suite 103
Casper, WY 82601
Phone: (307) 266-1478
http://www.wyomingsymphony.com

APPENDIX XII
CANADIAN ORCHESTRAS

The following is a selected listing of Canadian orchestras provided by the American Symphony Orchestra League. Names, addresses, phone numbers, and Web sites have been included when available. Use this listing to obtain general information, locate internships, and inquire about auditions and job possibilities. Orchestras are listed alphabetically by province. To find more Canadian orchestras, visit the American Symphony Orchestra League website at http://www.symphony.org.

ALBERTA

Calgary Philharmonic Orchestra
205 8th Avenue SE
Calgary, AB T2G OK9
Phone: (403) 571-0270
http://www.cpo-live.com

ONTARIO

National Arts Centre Orchestra
53 Elgin Street
P.O. Box 1534 Station B
Ottawa, ON K1P 5W1
http://www.nac-cna.ca

Royal Conservatory Orchestra
90 Croatia Street
Toronto, ON M6H 1K9
Phone: (416) 408-2824
http://www.rcmusic.ca

Symphony Hamilton
Box 89007
991 King Street West
Hamilton, ON L8S 4R5
Phone: (905) 526-6690
http://www.symphonyhamilton.ca

Toronto Symphony Orchestra
212 King Street West
Suite 550
Toronto, ON M5H 1K5
Phone: (416) 593-7769
http://www.tso.ca

Windsor Symphony Orchestra
487 Ouellette Avenue
Windsor, ON N9A 4J2
Phone: (519) 973-1238
Fax: (519) 973-0764
http://www.windsorsymphony.com

QUEBEC

Orchestre Symphonique de Montreal
260 Boulevard de Maisonneuve Ouest
Montreal, QC H2X 1Y9
Phone: (514) 842-9951
http://www.osm.ca

APPENDIX XIII
BALLET COMPANIES

The following is a listing of selected ballet companies throughout the United States. Names, addresses, phone numbers, e-mail addresses, and Web sites are included (when available) for each. Use this listing to obtain general information, locate internships, and inquire about auditions and job possibilities.

ALABAMA

Alabama Ballet
2726 1st Avenue South
Birmingham, AL 35233
Phone: (205) 322-4300
http://www.alabamaballet.org

Alabama Dance Theater
P.O. Box 11327
Montgomery, AL 36111
Phone: (334) 241-2590
Fax: (334) 241-2504
http://www.alabamadancetheatre.com

Mobile Ballet
Mobile Ballet, Inc.
4351 Downtowner Loop North
Mobile, AL 36609
Phone: (251) 342-2241
http://www.mobileballet.org

Montgomery Ballet Performing Company
3009 East Shirley Lane
Montgomery, AL 36117
Phone: (334) 409-0522

ALASKA

Alaska Dance Theatre
2602 Gambell Street
Anchorage, AL 99503
Phone: (907) 277-9591
Fax: (907) 274-3078
http://www.alaskadancetheatre.com

ARIZONA

Ballet Arizona
3645 East Indian School Road
Phoenix, AZ 85018
Phone: (602) 381-0184
http://www.balletaz.org

Yuma Ballet Theatre
P.O. Box 1275
Yuma, AZ 85366
Phone: (928) 341-1925
Fax: (928) 783-0538
http://www.yumaballet.org

ARKANSAS

Ballet Arkansas
7509 Cantrell Road
Little Rock, AR 72207
Phone: (501) 664-9509
http://www.balletarkansas.org

Western Arkansas Ballet
1310 North 32 Street
P.O. Box 10071
Fort Smith, AR 72917
Phone: (479) 785-0152
http://www.waballet.org

CALIFORNIA

Ballet Pacifica
1824 Kaiser Avenue
Irvine, CA 92614
Phone: (949) 851-9930
Fax: (949) 851-9974
http://www.balletpacifica.org

Ballet Theatre San Juan
40 North First Street
San Jose, CA 95113
Phone: (408) 288-2820
Fax: (408) 933-9570
http://www.balletsanjose.org

Berkeley Ballet Theater
2640 College Avenue
Berkeley, CA 94704
Phone: (510) 843-4687
Fax: (510) 843-2606
http://www.berkelyballet.com

Berkeley City Ballet
1800 Dwight Way
Berkeley, CA 94703
Phone: (510) 841-8913
Fax: (510) 841-0546
http://www.berkeleycityballet.org

California Ballet Company
4819 Ronson Court
San Diego, CA 92111
Phone: (858) 560-5676
http://www.californiaballet.org

California Riverside Ballet
3840 Lemon Street
Riverside, CA 92501
Phone: (951) 787-7850
http://www.crballet.org

Fresno Ballet
1401 North Wishon Avenue
Fresno, CA 93728
Phone: (559) 23-DANCE
http://www.fresnoballet.org

Lines Contemporary Ballet
26 7th Street
San Francisco, CA 94103
Phone: (415) 863-1248
http://www.linesballet.org

Los Angeles Chamber Ballet
Santa Monica, CA 90401
Phone: (310) 453-4952

Mendocino Ballet
205 South State Street
Ukiah, CA 95482
Phone: (707) 463-2290
http://www.mendocinoballet.org

Oakland Ballet
130 Linden Street
Oakland, CA 94607
Phone: (510) 452-9288
http://www.oaklandballet.org

Pasadena Dance Theatre
1985 East Locust Street
Pasadena, CA 91107
Phone: (626) 683-3459
http://www.pasadenadance.org

Sacramento Ballet
1631 K Street
Sacramento, CA 95814
Phone: (916) 552-5800
Fax: (916) 552-5815
http://www.sacballet.org

San Francisco Ballet
455 Franklin Street
San Francisco, CA 94102
Phone: (415) 861-5600
http://www.sfballet.org

San Jose Ballet Silicon Valley
40 North First Street
San Jose, CA 95113
Phone: (408) 288-2820
http://www.balletsanjose.org

San Jose/Cleveland Ballet Council
40 North First Street
San Jose, CA 95113
Phone: (408) 288-2830
Fax: (408) 993-9570
http://www.geocities.com/~sjcb_council

Santa Clara Ballet Company
3123 Millar Avenue
Santa Clara, CA 95051
Phone: (408) 247-9178
http://www.geocities.com/Vienna/Strasse/
7530/SCBallet.html

Santa Cruz Ballet Theatre
2800 South Rodeo Gulch Road
Soquel, CA 95073
Phone: (831) 477-1606
http://www.santacruzballettheatre.org

State Street Ballet
322 State Street
Santa Barbara, CA 93101
Phone: (805) 965-6066
Fax: (805) 965-3590
E-mail: ssbdance@aol.com
http://www.statestreetballet.com

COLORADO

Aspen Santa Fe Ballet
0245 Sage Way
Aspen, CO 81611
Phone: (970) 925-7175
Fax: (970) 925-1127
http://www.aspensantafeballet.com

Colorado Ballet
1278 Lincoln Street
Denver, CO 80203
Phone: (303) 837-8888

Fax: (303) 861-7174
http://www.coloradoballet.org

Colorado Dance Alliance
P.O. Box 1717
Eastlake, CO 80614
Phone: (303) 331-2457
http://www.codance.org

Colorado Dance Theatre
813 8th Street
Greeley, CO 80631
Phone: (970) 356-7104
http://www.fortnet.org/CDT

CONNECTICUT

Connecticut Ballet
20 Acosta Street
Stamford, CT 06902
Phone: (203) 964-1211
Fax: (203) 961-1928
http://www.hartnet.org/artsinct/MT_CT_
Ballet.html

DELAWARE

Mid-Atlantic Ballet
108A East Main Street
P.O. Box 161
Newark, DE 19715
Phone: (302) 266-6362
http://www.midatlanticballet.org

DISTRICT OF COLUMBIA

Capitol Ballet Company
1200 Delafield Place NW
Washington, DC 20011
Phone: (202) 882-4039

Washington Ballet
3515 Wisconsin Avenue NW
Washington, DC 20016
Phone: (202) 362-3606
Fax: (202) 362-1311
E-mail: wballet@washingtonballet.org
http://www.washingtonballet.org

FLORIDA

Ballet Florida
500 Fern Street
West Palm Beach, FL 33401
Phone: (561) 659-1212
Fax: (561) 659-2222
http://www.balletflorida.com

Ballet Northwest Florida
310 Perry Avenue

Fort Walton Beach, FL 32547
Phone: (850) 478-4749

Ballet Spectacular
59 Northwest 25th Avenue
Miami, FL 33125
Phone: (305) 642-8000

Bay Ballet Theatre
401 East Jackson Street
Tampa, FL 33602
Phone: (813) 222-8850

Florida Ballet of Jacksonville
123 East Forsyth Street
Jacksonville, FL 32202
Phone: (904) 353-7518

Fort Lauderdale Ballet Classique
508 Northeast 43rd Street
Fort Lauderdale, FL 33334
Phone: (954) 537-4195
http://www.fortlauderdaleballet.com

Miami City Ballet
Ophelia & Juan Js Roca Center
2200 Liberty Avenue
Miami Beach, FL 33139
Phone: (305) 929-7000
http://www.miamicityballet.org

Northwest Florida Ballet
28 Palafox Place
Pensacola, FL 32502
Phone: (850) 478-4749

Sarasota Ballet of Florida
5555 North Tamiami Trail
Sarasota, FL 34243
Phone:(941) 359-0099
http://www.sarasotaballet.org

Tallahassee Ballet
P.O. Box 772
Tallahassee, FL 32302
Phone: (850) 222-1287
Fax: (850) 224-7681
E-mail: office@tallaballet.com
http://www.tallaballet.com

GEORGIA

Atlanta Ballet
1400 West Peachtree Street NW
Atlanta, GA 30309
Phone: (404) 873-5811
http://atlantaballet.com

Augusta Ballet Company
P.O. Box 3828

Augusta, GA 30914
Phone: (706) 261-0555
Fax: (706) 261-0551
http://www.augustaballet.org

Festival Ballet Company
416 Eagles Landing Parkway
Stockbridge, GA 30281
Phone: (770) 507-2775
Fax: (770) 507-9182
http://www.festivalballetatlanta.com

Georgia Ballet
1255 Field Parkway
Marietta, GA 30066
Phone: (770) 528-0881
Fax: (770) 528-0891
http://www.georgiaballet.org

HAWAII

Hawaii State Ballet
1418 Kapiolani Boulevard
Honolulu, HI 96814
Phone: (808) 947-2755
http://www.hawaiistateballet.com

IDAHO

Ballet Idaho
501 South 8th Street
Boise, ID 83702
Phone: (208) 343-0556
Fax: (208) 424-3129
E-mail: info@balletidaho.org
http://www.balletidaho.org

ILLINOIS

Ballet Chicago
218 South Wabash Avenue
Chicago, IL 60604
Phone: (312) 251-8838
E-mail: info@balletchicago.org
http://www.balletchicago.org

Ballet Entre Nous
1237 Ridgewood Drive
Highland Park, IL 60035
Phone: (847) 432-1510
http://www.balletentrenous.org

Joffrey Ballet of Chicago
70 East Lake Street
Chicago, IL 60601
Phone: (312) 739-0120
Fax: (312) 739-0119
http://www.joffrey.com

Peoria Ballet Company
8800 North Industrial Road
Peoria, IL 61615
Phone: (309) 690-7990
Fax: (309) 690-7991
E-mail: info@peoriaballet.com
http://www.peoriaballet.com

USA Ballet
1615 East Empire
Bloomington, IL 61701
Phone: (309) 665-0300
Fax: (309) 665-0021
E-mail: info@usaballet.org
http://www.usaballet.org

INDIANA

Anderson Young Ballet Theatre
29 East Dillon Street
Anderson, IN 46016
Phone: (765) 643-2184

Ballet Internationale
502 North Capitol Avenue
Indianapolis, IN 46204
Phone: (317) 637-8979
Fax: (317) 637-1637

Butler Ballet
Jordan College of Fine Arts
4600 Sunset Avenue
Indianapolis, IN 46208
Phone: (800) 368-6852
http://www.butler.edu/dance

Evansville Dance Theatre
333 Plaza East Boulevard
Evansville, IN 47715
Phone: (812) 473-8937
Fax: (812) 473-0392
http://www.edtdance.org

Fort Wayne Ballet, Inc.
437 East Berry Street
Fort Wayne, IN 46802
Phone: (260) 424-6574
Fax: (260) 424-2789
E-mail: info@fwdc.org
http://www.fwdc.org

IOWA

Gateway Contemporary Ballet
223 5th Avenue South
Clinton, IA 52732
Phone: (563) 242-1002
http://www.gatewayballet.org

KANSAS

Metropolitan Ballet of Wichita
939 South Glendale Street
Wichita, KS 67218
Phone: (316) 687-5880

KENTUCKY

Lexington Ballet
161 North Mill Street
Lexington, KY 40507
Phone: (859) 233-3925
http://www.lexingtonballet.org

The Louisville Ballet
315 East Main Street
Louisville, KY 40202
Phone: (502) 583-2623

LOUISIANA

Baton Rouge Ballet Theatre
P.O. Box 82288
Baton Rouge, LA 70884
Phone: (225)766-8379
http://www.brballet.org

Shreveport Metropolitan Ballet
520 Olive Street
Shreveport, LA 71104
Phone: (318) 459-1457
http://www.shreveportmetropolitanballet.
    org

MARYLAND

Ballet Theatre of Annapolis
Metropolitan Ballet Theatre, Inc.
10076 Darnestown Road
Rockville, MD 20850
Phone: (301) 762-1757
E-mail: contact@
    metropolitanballettheatre
http://www.metropolitanballettheatre.com

MASSACHUSETTS

The Amherst Ballet Theatre Company
29 Strong Street
Amherst, MA 01002
Phone: (413) 549-1555
http://www.amherstballet.org

Boston Ballet
19 Clarendon Street
Boston, MA 02116
Phone: (617) 695-6954
http://www.bostonballet.org

Boston Chamber Ballet
Newton Center, MA 02459
Phone: (617) 244-0441

MICHIGAN

Ann Arbor Civic Ballet
525 East Liberty Street
Ann Arbor, MI 48104
Phone: (734) 668-8066

Grand Rapids Civic Ballet Company
341 Ellsworth Avenue SW
Grand Rapids, MI 49503
Phone: (616) 454-4771

Kalamazoo Ballet Company
431 East South Street
Kalamazoo, MI 49007
Phone: (269) 343-3027
Fax: (269) 342-8788
http://www.kalamazoomi.com/ballet.htm

Rose Marie Floyd Contemporary Civic Ballet
939 North Main Street
Royal Oak, MI 48067
Phone: (248) 546-7484
http://www.rosemariefloyd.com/civic_ballet_company.html

MINNESOTA

Minnesota Ballet
301 West First Street
Suite 800
Duluth, MN 55802
Phone: (218) 529-3742
Fax: (218) 529-3744
http://www.minnesotaballet.org

MISSISSIPPI

Ballet Mississippi
201 East Pascagoula Street
Jackson, MS 39201
Phone: (601) 960-1560
http://www.balletmississippi.com

MISSOURI

Alexandra Ballet Company
68E Four Seasons Center
Chesterfield, MO 63017
Phone: (314) 469-6222
E-mail: alexandra@alexandraballet.com
http://www.alexandraballet.com

Kansas City Ballet
1601 Broadway
Kansas City, MO 64108
Phone: (816) 931-2232
Fax: (816) 931-1172
http://www.kcballet.org

St. Louis Ballet
218 THF Boulevard
Chesterfield, MO 63005
Phone: (636) 537.1950
Fax: (636) 537.2578
E-mail: info@stlouisballet.org
http://www.stlouisballet.org

NEBRASKA

Lincoln Midwest Ballet Company
P.O. Box 30126
Lincoln, NE 68503
Phone: (401) 441-0739

Omaha Theater Company Ballet
2001 Franam Street
Omaha, NE 68102
Phone: (401) 345-2503

NEVADA

Nevada Ballet
1651 Inner Circle
Las Vegas, NV 89134
Phone: (702) 243-2623
Fax: (702) 804-0365
http://www.nevadaballet.com

Nevada Festival Ballet
1790 West Fourth Street
Reno, Nevada 89503
Phone: (775) 785-7915
http://www.aci.net/nfb

NEW HAMPSHIRE

Ballet New England
135 Daniel Street
Portsmouth, NH 03801
Phone: (603) 430-9309
http://www.balletnewengland.org

NEW JERSEY

American Repertory Ballet Company
80 Albany Street
New Brunswick, NJ 08901
Phone: (732) 249-1254
Fax: (732) 249-8475
http://www.arballet.org

Atlantic Contemporary Ballet Theatre
713 West Moss Hill Road
Egg Harbor, NJ 08215
Phone: (609) 748-6625
Fax: (609) 748-1068
http://www.acbt.org

Irine Fokine Ballet Company
33 Chestnut Street
Ridgewood, NJ 07450
Phone: (201) 652-9653
Fax: (201) 652-9286
http://www.fokineballet.com

New Jersey Ballet
15 Microlab Road
Livingston, NJ 07039
Phone: (973) 597-9600
Fax: (973) 597-9442
E-mail: njballet@aol.com
http://www.njballet.org

NEW MEXICO

Aspen Santa Fe Ballet
550-B Saint Michael's Drive
Phone: (505) 983-5591
Fax: (505) 992-1027
http://aspensantafeballet.com

Ballet Theatre International
40 Paige
Los Alamos, NM 87544
Phone: (505) 672-9808
Fax: (505) 672-9035

NEW YORK

American Ballet Theatre
890 Ballet Broadway
New York, NY 10003
Phone: (212) 477-3030
Fax: (212) 254-5938
http://www.abt.org

Ballet Manhattan
61 West 62 Street, 17M
New York, NY 10023
Phone: (212) 586-2699

Ballet Tech
890 Broadway
New York, NY 10003
Phone: (212) 777-7710
Fax: (212) 353-0936
E-mail: info@ballettech.org
http://www.ballettech.org

Brooklyn Ballet
145 Hicks Street
Brooklyn, NY
Phone: (718) 246-0146
E-mail: brooklynballet@earthlink.net

Dance Theatre of Harlem
466 West 152 Street
New York, NY 10031
Phone: (212) 690-2800
Fax: (212) 690-8736
http://www.dancetheatreofharlem.org

Dance Theatre of Long Island
105 Sheldon Road
Ithaca, NY 14850
E-mail: lbrantley@clarityconnect.com

Ithaca Ballet
105 Sheldon Road
Ithaca, NY 14850
Phone: (607) 257-6066
E-mail: lbrantley@clarityconnect.com

Mid Hudson Ballet Company
4 Old Route 9
Fishkill, NY 12524
Phone: (845) 897-2667
Fax: (845) 897-7052
http://www.estelleandalfonso.com

New Amsterdam Ballet
290 Riverside Drive
New York, NY 10025
Phone: (212) 678-0320

New York City Ballet
New York State Theater
20 Lincoln, NY 10023
Phone: (212) 870-5656
Fax: (212) 870-7791
http://www.nycballet.com

NORTH CAROLINA

Charlotte City Ballet
P.O. Box 472082
Charlotte, NC 28247
Phone: (704) 708-4474
Fax: (704) 845-1180

Greensboro Ballet
200 North Davie Street
Greensboro, NC 27401
Phone: (336) 333-7480
Fax: (336) 333-7482
http://www.greensboroballet.com

North Carolina Dance Theatre
800 North College Street
Charlotte, NC 28206
Phone: (704) 372-0101
Fax: (704) 372-0260
http://www.ncdance.org

Raleigh Dance Theatre
P.O. Box 33691
Raleigh, NC 27636
Phone: (919) 834-1058
Fax: (919) 829-1493
E-mail: raleighdance@worldnet.att.net

OHIO

Ashland Regional Ballet
130 East Main Street
Ashland, OH 44805
Phone: (419) 289-3581
Fax: (419) 281-7579
E-mail: opus@ashlandregionalballet.org
http://www.ashlandregionalballet.org

Canton Ballet Company
Cultural Center for the Arts
1001 Market Avenue North
Canton, OH 44709
Phone: (330) 455-7220
Fax: (330) 455-6977
E-mail: cantonballet@cantonballet.com
http://www.cantonballet.com

Cincinnati Ballet
1555 Central Parkway
Cincinnati, OH 45214
Phone: (513) 621-5219
Fax: (513) 621-4844
E-mail: cballet@cincinnatiballet.com
http://www.cincinnatiballet.com

Dayton Ballet
140 North Main Street
Dayton, OH 45402
Phone: (937) 449-5060
Fax: (937) 461-8353
E-mail: info@daytonballet.org
http://www.daytonballet.org

Ohio Ballet
354 East Market Street
Akron, OH 44325
Phone: (330) 972-7900
Fax: (330) 972-7902
http://www.ohioballet.org

Toledo Ballet
5001 Monroe Street
Toledo, OH 43623
Phone: (419) 471.0049

Fax: (419) 471-9005
E-mail: nburgoine@toledoballet.net
http://www.toledoballet.net

OKLAHOMA

Ballet Oklahoma
7421 North Classen Boulevard
Oklahoma City, OK 73116
Phone: (405) 843-9898
Fax: (405) 843-9894

Tulsa Ballet Theatre
4512 South Peoria
Tulsa, OK 74105
Phone: (918) 749-6030
Fax: (918) 749-0532
E-mail: admin@tulsaballet.org
http://www.tulsaballet.org

Western Oklahoma Ballet Theatre
P.O. Box 1593
Clinton, OK 73601
Phone: (580) 323-7400

OREGON

Eugene Ballet Theatre
P.O. Box 11200
Eugene, OR 97440
Phone: (541) 485-3992
Fax: (541) 687-5745
E-mail: eballet@eugeneballet.org
http://www.eugeneballet.org

Medford Civic Ballet
9 Hawthorne Street
Medford, OR 97504
Phone: (541) 772-1362
E-mail: dancemcs@aol.com

Metro Dancers
9933 Southeast Pine Street
Portland, OR 97216
Phone: (503) 408-0604
Fax: (503) 408-0495
E-mail: info@pdmextroarts.org
http://www.pdmextroarts.org

PENNSYLVANIA

Allegheny Ballet Company
P.O. Box 369
Altoona, PA 16603
Phone: (841) 943-6081
Fax: (841) 944-7713

Ballet Guild of Lehigh Valley
556 Main Street
Bethlehem, PA 18018

Phone: (610) 865-0353
Fax: (610) 865-2698
http://www.bglv.org

Berks Ballet
1701 Fairview Street
Reading, PA 19606
Phone: (610) 373-1245
Fax: (610) 373-7757
E-mail: berksballet@fast.net

Central Pennsylvania Youth Ballet
5 North Orange Street
P.O. Box 1773
Carlisle, PA 17013
Phone: (717) 245-1190
Fax: (717) 245-1189
E-mail: info@cpyb.org
http://www.cpyb.org

Cumberland Dance Company
18 South Enola Drive
Enola, PA 17025
Phone: (717) 732-2172
E-mail: cumberlanddance@panoline.com
http://www.cumberlanddance.org

Gainesville Ballet
P.O. Box 907115
Gainesville, PA 30503
Phone: (770) 534-6282
Fax: (770) 532-4241

Lake Erie Ballet
701 Holland Street
Erie, PA 16501
Phone: (814) 864-1580
E-mail: info@lakeerieballet.com
http://www.lakeerieballet.com

Pennsylvania Ballet
1101 South Broad Street
Philadelphia, PA 19147
Phone: (215) 551-7000
Fax: (215) 551-7224
http://www.paballet.org

Philadelphia Dance Conservatory
6918 Bustleton Avenue
Philadelphia, PA 19149
Phone: (215) 708-1194
Fax: (215) 357-0406

Pittsburgh Ballet Theatre
2900 Liberty Avenue
Pittsburgh, PA 15201
Phone: (412) 281-0360
Fax: (412) 281-9901
http://www.pbt.org

RHODE ISLAND

Festival Ballet Providence
825 Hope Street
Providence, RI 02906
Phone: (401) 353-1129
Fax: (401) 353-8853
E-mail: info@festivalballet.com
http://www.festivalballet.com

State Ballet of Rhode Island
52 Sherman Avenue
Lincoln, RI 02865
Phone: (401) 334-2560
Fax: (401) 334-0412
http://www.stateballet.com

SOUTH CAROLINA

Charleston Ballet Theatre
477 Kings Street
Charleston, SC 29403
Phone: (843) 723-7334
Fax: (843) 723-9099
E-mail: cbtbahr@aol.com
http://www.charlestonballet.org

Columbia City Ballet
P.O. Box 11898
Columbia, SC 29211
Phone: (803) 799-7605
Fax: (803) 799-7928
E-mail: ccballet@bellsouth.net
http://www.columbiacityballet.com

Greenville Ballet
P.O. Box 8702
Greenville, SC 29607
Phone: (864) 235-6456
Fax: (864) 235-6440
http://www.greenvilleballet.org

Robert Ivey Ballet
1910 Savannah Highway
Charleston, SC 29407
Phone: (843) 556-1343
Fax: (843) 573-0960
E-mail: ribart@mindspring.com

South Carolina Ballet
P.O. Box 8702
Greenville, SC 29607
Phone: (864) 235-6456
Fax: (864) 235-6440

TENNESSEE

Appalachian Ballet Company
215 West Broadway

Maryville, TN 37801
Phone: (865) 982-8463
Fax: (865) 982-8463

Ballet Memphis
7950 Trinity Road
Memphis, TN 38018
Phone: (901) 737-7322
Fax: (901) 737-7037
http://www.balletmemphis.org

Ballet Tennessee
John A. Patten Arts Center
3202 Kelly's Ferry Road
Chattanooga, TN 37419
Phone: (423) 821-2055
Fax: (423) 821-2156
E-mail: ballettenn@aol.com
http://www.ballettennessee.org

Nashville Ballet
3630 Redmon Street
Nashville, TN 37209
Phone: (615) 297-2966
Fax: (615) 297-9972
http://www.nashvilleballet.org

TEXAS

Abilene Ballet Theatre
1265 North Second
Abilene, TX 79601
Phone: (915) 675-0303

Allegro Ballet of Houston
1570 South Dairy Ashford
Houston, TX 77077
Phone: (281) 496-4670
E-mail: glendabrown@allegroballet.com
http://www.allegroballet.com

Ballet Arlington
1303 West Abram
Arlington, TX 76013
Phone: (817) 465-4644
E-mail: press@balletarlington.org
http://www.balletarlington.org

Corpus Christi Ballet
1621 North Mesquite
Corpus Christi, TX 78401
Phone: (361) 882-4588
Fax: (361) 881-9291
E-mail: ccballet@aol.com

Dallas Metropolitan Ballet
6815 Hillcrest
Dallas, TX 75205
Phone: (214) 361-0278

Fax: (509) 692-2678
http://www.dallasmetroballet.com

Fort Worth Dallas Ballet
6845 Green Oaks Road
Fort Worth, TX 76116
Phone: (817) 763-0207
Fax: (817) 763-0624
http://www.fwdballet.org

Houston Ballet
1921 West Bell
Houston, TX 77019
Phone: (713) 523-6300
Fax: (713) 523-4038
E-mail: info@houstonballet.org
http://www.houstonballet.org

Houston Dance Theatre
15775 Bammel Village Drive
Houston, TX 77014
Phone: (281) 444-9698
Fax: (281) 444-8317
E-mail: director@balletonline.com
http:// www.balletonline.com

Lone Star Ballet
1000 S. Polk Street
Amarillo, TX 79101
Phone: (806) 372-2463
Fax: (806) 372-3131
E-mail: lonestarballet@arn.net
http://www.lonestarballet.org

San Antonio Metropolitan Ballet
2800 Northeast Loop 410
San Antonio, TX 78218
Phone: (210) 656-1334
Fax: (210) 656-1256

Wichita Falls Ballet Theatre
1717 Grant Street
Wichita Falls, TX 76309
Phone: (940) 322-5538
Fax: (940) 322-5538

UTAH

Utah Ballet Company
University of Utah Department of Ballet
330 South 1500 East
Salt Lake City, UT 84112
Phone: (801) 581-8231
Fax: (801) 581-5442
E-mail: info@ballet.utah.edu
http://www.ballet.utah.edu

Utah Regional Ballet
P.O. Box 321

American Fork, UT 84003
Phone: (801) 756-7581
Fax: (801) 756-6545

VIRGINIA

Bristol Ballet Company
628 Cumberland Street
Bristol, VA 24201
Phone: (540) 699-6051
Fax: (540) 699-9330

Center for Ballet Arts
11215 H Lee Highway
Fairfax, VA 22030
http://www.centerforballetarts.com

Chamber Ballet
P.O. Box 1568
Williamsburg, VA 23187
Phone: (757) 229-1717
Fax: (757) 229-7997

Concert Ballet of Virginia
P.O. Box 25502
Richmond, VA 23260

Reston Conservatory Ballet
2254 L Hunters Woods Plaza Road
Reston, VA 20191
Phone: (703) 715-8366
Fax: (703) 715-8302
http://www.conservatoryballet.com

Richmond Ballet
407 East Canal Street
Richmond, VA 23219
Phone: (804) 344-0906
Fax: (804) 344-0901
E-mail: einfo@richmondballet.com
http://www.richmondballet.com

Southwest Virginia Ballet
305 East Calhoun Street
Salem, VA 24153
Phone: (540) 387-3978

Virginia Ballet Theatre
134 West Olney Road
Norfolk, VA 23510
Phone: (757) 622-4822
http://www.chm.net/ballet

WASHINGTON

Dance Theatre Northwest
2811 Bridgeport Way West
University Place
Tacoma, WA 98466

Mid-Columbia Regional Ballet
P.O. Box 326
Richland, WA 99352
Phone: (509) 946-5417
Fax: (509) 946-5417
E-mail: mcb@tricityarts.org
http://www.tricityarts.org/mcrb.html

Pacific Northwest Ballet
301 Mercer Street
Seattle, WA 98109
Phone: (206) 441-9411
Fax: (206) 441-2440
http://www.pnb.org

Peninsula Dance Theatre
515 Chester Avenue
Bremerton, WA 98377
Phone: (360) 377-6214

WEST VIRGINIA

Charleston Ballet
822 Virginia Street East
Charleston, WV 25301
Phone: (304) 342-6541
Fax: (304) 345-1134
E-mail: chballet@newwave.net
http://www.thecharlestonballet.com

Mid-Ohio Valley Ballet
1311 Ann Street
P.O. Box 4204
Parkersburg, WV 26104
Phone: (304) 422-5538
Fax: (304) 422-6730

WISCONSIN

Madison Ballet
2822 Index Road
Madison, WI 53713
Phone: (608) 278-7990
Fax: (608) 278-7992
E-mail: madisonballet@prodigy.net
http://www.madisonballet.org

Milwaukee Ballet
504 West National Avenue
Milwaukee, WI 53204
Phone: (414) 643-7677
Fax: (414) 649-4066
http://www.milwaukeeballet.org

APPENDIX XIV
U.S. OPERA COMPANIES

The following listing of opera companies throughout the United States was provided by Opera America. Names, addresses, phone numbers, and Web sites are included (when available) for each. Use this listing to obtain general information, locate internships, and inquire about auditions and job possibilities. Companies are listed alphabetically by state.

ALABAMA

Opera Birmingham
Birmingham Music Cooperative
1807 Third Avenue North
Birmingham, AL 35203
Phone: (205) 322-6737
http://www.operabirmingham.org

Mobile Opera
257 Dauphin Street
Mobile, AL 36602
Phone: (251) 432-6772
http://www.mobileopera.org

ALASKA

Anchorage Opera
1507 Spar Avenue
Anchorage AK 99501
Phone: (907) 279-2557
http://www.anchorageopera.org

ARIZONA

Arizona Opera Company
4600 North 12th Street
Phoenix, AZ 85014
Phone: (602) 266-7464
http://www.azopera.com

ARKANSAS

Wildwood Park for the Performing Arts
20919 Denny Road
Little Rock, AR 72223
Phone: (501) 821-7275
http://www.wildwoodpark.org

CALIFORNIA

Jarvis Conservatory
1711 Main Street
Napa, CA 94559
Phone: (707) 255-5445
http://www.jarvisconservatory.com

Long Beach Opera
100 West Broadway
Suite 110
Long Beach, CA 90802
Phone: (562) 439-2580
http://www.longbeachopera.org

Los Angeles Opera
135 North Grand Avenue
Los Angeles, CA 90012
Phone: (213) 972-7219
http://www.losangelesopera.com

Lyric Company of San Diego
610 A Street
Suite #101
San Diego, CA 92101
Phone: (619) 231-5714
http://www.lyricoperasandiego.com

Opera Pacific
600 West Warner Avenue
Santa Ana, CA 92707
Phone: (714) 546-6000
http://www.operapacific.org

Musical Traditions
Paul Dresher Ensemble
333 Valencia Street
San Francisco, CA 94103
Phone: (415) 558-9540
http://www.dresherensemble.org

Opera Pacific
600 West Warner Avenue
Santa Ana, CA 92707
Phone: (714) 546-6000
http://www.operapacific.org

Pacific Repertory Opera
P.O. Box 14760
San Luis Obispo, CA 93406
Phone: (805) 541-5369
http://www.kcbx.net/~pro

Sacramento Opera
P.O. Box 161027
Sacramento, CA 95816
Phone: (916) 737-1000
http://www.sacopera.org

San Diego Opera
18th Floor, Civic Center Plaza
San Diego, CA 92101
Phone: (619) 232-7636
http://www.sdopera.com

San Francisco Opera
301 Van Ness Avenue
San Francisco, CA 94102
Phone: (415) 861-4008
http://www.sfopera.com

Townsend Opera Players
P.O. Box 4519
Modesto, CA 95352
Phone: (209) 523-6426
http://www.townsendoperaplayers.com

COLORADO

Central City Opera House Association
400 South Colorado Boulevard
Suite 530
Denver, CO 80246
Phone: (303) 292-6700
http://www2.centralcityopera.org

Opera Colorado
695 South Colorado Boulevard
Denver, CO 80246
Phone: (303) 778-1500
http://www.operacolorado.org

CONNECTICUT

Connecticut Grand Opera
307 Atlantic Street
Stamford, CT 06901
Phone: (203) 327-2867
http://www.ctgrandopera.org

Connecticut Opera Association
226 Farmington Avenue
Hartford, CT 06105
Phone: (860) 527-713
http://www.connecticutopera.org

DELAWARE

Opera Delaware
P.O. Box 432
Wilmington, DE 19899
Phone: (302) 658-8063
http://www.operade.org

DISTRICT OF COLUMBIA

Washington National Opera
2600 Virginia Avenue NW
Washington, DC 20037
Phone: (202) 295-2420
http://www.dc-opera.org

FLORIDA

Florida Grand Opera
Arturo di Filippi Educational Center
1200 Coral Way
Miami, FL 33145
Phone: (305) 854-1643
http://www.fgo.org

Gold Coast Opera
3501 Southwest Davie Road
Fort Lauderdale, FL 33314
Phone: (954) 201-6578
http://www.goldcoastopera.org

Orlando Opera
1111 North Orange Avenue
Orlando, FL 32804
Phone: (407) 426-1717
http://www.orlandoopera.org

Palm Beach Opera
415 South Olive Avenue
West Palm Beach, FL 33401
Phone: (561) 833-7888
http://www.pbopera.org

Pensacola Opera
P.O. Box 1790
Pensacola, FL 32591
Phone: (850) 433-6737
http://www.pensacolaopera.com

Sarasota Opera
61 North Pineapple Avenue
Sarasota, FL 34236
Phone: (941) 366-8450
http://www.sarasotaopera.org

GEORGIA

Augusta Opera Company
P.O Box 240
Augusta, GA 30903
Phone: (404) 826-4710
http://www.augustaopera.com

Atlanta Opera Center
728 West Peachtree Street NW
Atlanta, GA 30308
Phone: (404) 881-8801
http://www.atlantaopera.org

HAWAII

Hawaii Opera Theatre
987 Waimanu Street
Honolulu, HI 96814
Phone: (808) 596-7372
http://www.hawaiiopera.org

IDAHO

Opera Idaho
501 South 8th Street
Boise, ID 83702
Phone: (208) 345-3531
http://www.operaidaho.org

ILLINOISS

Chicago Opera Theater
70 East Lake Street
Chicago, IL 60601
Phone: (312) 704-8420
http://www.chicagooperatheater.org

Lyric Opera of Chicago
20 North Wacker Drive
Chicago, IL 60606
Phone: (312) 332-2244
http://www.lyricopera.com

INDIANA

Indianapolis Opera
250 East 38th Street
Indianapolis, IN 46205
Phone: (317) 283-3531
http://www.indyopera.org

IOWA

Des Moines Metro Opera, Inc.
106 West Boston Avenue
Indianola, IA 50125
Phone: (515) 961-6221
http://www.dmmo.org

KENTUCKY

Kentucky Opera
101 South Eighth Street
Louisville, KY 40202
Phone: (502) 584-4500
http://www.kyopera.org

LOUISIANA

New Orleans Opera
305 Baronne Street
New Orleans, LA 70112
Phone: (504) 524-1018
http://www.neworleansopera.org

Shreveport Opera
212 Texas Street
Suite 101
Shreveport, LA 71101
Phone: (318) 227-9503
http://www.shreveopera.org

MAINE

Portland Opera Repertory Theatre
P.O. Box 7733
Portland, ME 04112
Phone: (207) 879-7678
http://www.portopera.org

MARYLAND

Baltimore Opera Company
Lyric Opera House
110 West Mount Royal Avenue
Suite 306
Baltimore, MD 21201
Phone: (410) 625-1600
http://www.baltimoreopera.com

MASSACHUSETTS

Berkshire Opera Company
297 North Street
Pittsfield, MA 01201
Phone: (413) 442-9955
http://www.berkshireopera.org

Boston Lyric Opera
45 Franklin Street
Boston, MA 02110
Phone: (617) 542-4912
http://www.blo.org

Opera Boston
25 Kingston Street
Boston, MA 02111
Phone: (617) 451-3388
http://www.operaboston.org

MICHIGAN

Michigan Opera Theatre
Detroit Opera House
1526 Broadway
Detroit, MI 48226
Phone: (313) 961-2500
http://www.motopera.org

Pine Mountain Music Festival
P.O. Box 406
Hancock, MI 49930
Phone: (906) 482-1542
http://www.pmmf.org

MINNESOTA

Minnesota Opera Company
620 North First Street
Minneapolis, MN 55401
Phone: (612) 333-2700
http://www.mnopera.org

Nautilus Music-Theater
308 Prince Street
St. Paul, MN 55101
Phone: (651) 298-9913

MISSISSIPPI

Mississippi Opera
Mississippi Arts Center
P.O. Box 1551
Jackson, MS 39215
Phone: (601) 960-1526
http://www.msopera.org

MISSOURI

Lyric Opera of Kansas City
1029 Central
Avenue of the Arts
Kansas City, MO 64105
Phone: (816) 471-7344
http://www.kc-opera.org

Opera Theater of Saint Louis
539 Garden Avenue
Saint Louis, MO 63119
Phone: (314) 961-0171
http://www.opera-stl.org

Springfield Regional Opera
400 South Street
Springfield, MO 65806
Phone: (417) 863-1960
http://www.sropera.com

NEBRASKA

Opera Omaha
1625 Farnam Street
Omaha, NE 68102
Phone: (402) 346-7372

NEVADA

Nevada Opera
P.O. Box 3256
Reno, NV 89505
Phone: (775) 786-4046
http://www.nevadaopera.com

NEW JERSEY

Boheme Opera
P.O. Box 4157
Trenton, New Jersey 08610
Phone: (609) 581-9551
http://www.bohemeopera.com

NEW HAMPSHIRE

Opera North
20 West Park Street
Lebanon, NH 03766
Phone: (603) 448-4141
http://www.operanorth.org

NEW MEXICO

Opera Southwest
P.O. Box 27671
Albuquerque, NM 87125
Phone: (505) 243-0591
http://www.operasouthwest.org

Santa Fe Opera
P.O. Box 2408
Santa Fe, NM 87504
Phone: (505) 986-5955
http://www.santafeopera.org

NEW YORK

America Opera Projects
South Oxford Space
138 South Oxford Street
Brooklyn, NY 11217
Phone: (718) 398-4024
http://www.operaprojects.org

Center for Contemporary Opera
P.O. Box 258
New York, NY 10044
Phone: (212) 758-2757
http://www.conopera.org

Chautauqua Opera NYC (September-May)
P.O. Box 20425
Greeley Square Station
New York, NY 10001
Phone: (212) 779-3177
http://opera.ciweb.org

Chautauqua Opera (June-August)
P.O. Box Q
Chautauqua, NY 14722
Phone: (716) 357-6286
http://opera.ciweb.org/contact.html

Encompass New Opera Theatre
138 South Oxford Street
Brooklyn, NY 11217
Phone: (718) 398-4675
http://www.encompassopera.org

Glimmerglass Opera
Lake Road
Cooperstown, NY 13326
Phone: (607) 547-2255
http://www.glimmerglass.org

Lake George Opera Company
480 Broadway
Saratoga Springs, NY 12866
Phone: (518) 584-6018
http://www.lakegeorgeopera.org

Metropolitan Opera
Lincoln Center
New York, NY 10023
Phone: (212) 799-3100
http://www.metoperafamily.org

Music Theatre Group
30 West 26th Street
Suite 1001
New York, NY 10010
Phone: (212) 366-5260
http://www.musictheatregroup.org

New York City Opera
New York State Theater at Lincoln Center
New York, NY 10023
Phone: (212) 870-5597
http://www.nycopera.com

Opera Rochester
875 East Main Street
Rochester, NY 14605-2747
Phone: (585) 546-3080
http://www.operarochester.org

Syracuse Opera
P.O. Box 1223
Syracuse, NY 13201
Phone: (315) 475-5915
http://www.syracuseopera.com

Tri-Cities Opera
315 Clinton Street
Binghamton, NY 13905
Phone: (607) 729-3444
http://www.tricitiesopera.com

Vineyard Theatre
108 East 15th Street
New York City, NY 10003
Phone: (212) 353-3366
http://www.vineyardtheatre.org

NORTH CAROLINA

Asheville Lyric Opera
2 South Pack Square
Asheville, NC 28801
Phone: (828) 236-0670
http://www.ashevillelyric.org

Greensboro Opera Company
P.O. Box 29031
Greensboro, NC 27429
Phone: (336) 273-9472
http://www.greensboroopera.org

Opera Carolina
345 North College Street
Charlotte, NC 28202
Phone: (704) 332-7177
http://www.operacarolina.org

Piedmont Opera Theatre
900 West First Street
Winston-Salem, NC 27101
Phone: (336) 725-7101
http://www.piedmontopera.org

NORTH DAKOTA

Fargo-Moorhead Opera
Black Building
114 Broadway
Fargo, ND 58102
Phone: (701) 239-4558
http://www.fmopera.org

OHIO

Cincinnati Opera
Music Hall
1243 Elm Street
Cincinnati, OH 45202
Phone: (513) 241-2742
http://www.cincinnatiopera.org

Cleveland Opera
1422 Euclid Avenue
Suite 1052
Cleveland, OH 44115
Phone: (216) 575-0903
http://www.clevelandopera.org

Dayton Opera
138 North Main Street
Dayton, OH 45402
Phone: (937) 228-7591
http://www.daytonopera.org

Lyric Opera Cleveland
P.O. Box 93046
Cleveland, Ohio 44101
Phone: (216) 685-5976
http://www.lyricoperacleveland.org

Opera Columbus
Opera Columbus Center
177 East Naghten Street
Columbus, OH 43215
Phone: (614) 461-8101
http://www.operacolumbus.org

SORG Opera
The Commercial Building
65 South Main Street
Middletown, OH 45044
Phone: (513) 425-0180
http://www.sorgopera.org

Toledo Opera
425 Jefferson Avenue
Suite 415
Toledo, OH 43604
Phone: (419) 255-7464
http://www.toledoopera.org

OKLAHOMA

Tulsa Opera
1610 South Boulder
Tulsa, OK 74119
Phone: (918) 582-4035
http://www.tulsaopera.com

OREGON

Eugene Opera
P.O. Box 11200
Eugene, OR 97440
Phone: (541) 485-3985
http://www.eugeneopera.com

Portland Opera
211 Southeast Caruthers Street
Portland, OR 97214
Phone: (503) 241-1407
http://www.portlandopera.org

Seattle Opera
P.O. Box 9248
Seattle, WA 98109
Phone: (206) 389-7600
http://www.seattleopera.org

PENNSYLVANIA

Opera Company of Philadelphia
1420 Locust Street
Philadelphia, PA 19102
Phone: (215) 893-3600
http://www.operaphilly.com

Opera Theater of Pittsburgh
P.O. Box 110108
Pittsburgh, PA 15232
Phone: (412) 624-3500
http://www.operatheaterpittsburgh.org

Pittsburgh Opera Office
801 Penn Avenue
Pittsburgh, PA 15222
Phone: (412) 281-0912
http://www.pittsburghopera.org

TENNESSEE

Chattanooga Symphony & Opera
630 Chestnut Street
Chattanooga, TN 37402
Phone: (423)-267-8583
http://www.chattanoogasymphony.org

Knoxville Opera
P.O. Box 16
Knoxville, TN 37901
Phone: (865) 524-0795
http://www.knoxvilleopera.com

Nashville Opera Association
Nashville Opera Association
3628 Trousdale Drive
Nashville, TN 37204
Phone: (615) 832-5242
http://www.nashvilleopera.org

Opera Memphis
Clark Opera Memphis Center
6745 Wolf River Parkway
Memphis, TN 38120
Phone: (901) 257-3100
http://www.operamemphis.org

TEXAS

Amarillo Opera
P.O. Box 447
Amarillo, TX 79178

Phone: (806) 372-7464
http://www.amarilloopera.org

Austin Lyric Opera Box Office
901 Barton Springs Road
Austin, TX 78704
Phone: (512) 472-5992
http://www.austinlyricopera.org

Dallas Opera
8350 North Central Expressway
Dallas, TX 75206
Phone: (214) 443-1043
http://www.dallasopera.org

El Paso Opera
1035 Belvidere Street
El Paso, TX 79912
Phone: (915) 581-5534
http://www.epopera.org

Fort Worth Opera Association
3505 West Lancaster Avenue
Fort Worth, TX 76102
Phone: (817) 731-0833
http://www.fwopera.org

Houston Grand Opera
510 Preston Street
Houston, TX 77002
Phone: (713) 546-0200
http://www.houstongrandopera.org

Lyric Opera of San Antonio
1344 South Flores
San Antonio, TX 78205
Phone: (210) 225-5972
http://www.lyricoperasa.com/opera

Lyric Opera of Waco
760 Austin Avenue
Waco, Texas 76710

Phone: (254) 756-7372
http://www.lyricoperaofwaco.org

Opera in the Heights
P.O. Box 7887
Houston, TX 77270
Phone: (713) 861-5303
http://www.operaintheheights.org

UTAH

Utah Festival Opera Company
59 South 100 West
Logan, UT 84321
Phone: (435) 750-0300
http://www.ufoc.org

Utah Symphony Opera
Abravanel Hall
123 West South Temple
Salt Lake City, UT 84101
Phone: (801) 533-5626
http://www.utahsymphonyopera.org

VIRGINIA

Ash Lawn Opera Festival
2000 Holiday Drive
Charlottesville, VA 22901
Phone: (434) 293-4500
http://www.ashlawnopera.org

Opera Roanoke
Jefferson Center
541 Luck Avenue
Roanoke, VA 24016
Phone: (540) 982-2742
http://www.operaroanoke.org

Virginia Opera
P.O. Box 2580
Norfolk, VA 23501
Phone: (757) 627-9545
http://www.vaopera.org

WASHINGTON

Spokane Opera
P.O. Box 8558
Spokane, WA 99203-0558
Phone: (509) 533-1150
http://www.spokaneopera.com

Tacoma Opera
917 Pacific Avenue
Tacoma, WA 98402
Phone: (253) 627-7789
http://www.tacomaopera.com

WEST VIRGINIA

West Virginia Symphony Orchestra
P.O. Box 2292
Charleston, WV 25328
Phone: (304) 561-3552
http://www.wvsymphony.org

WISCONSIN

Florentine Opera Company
700 North Water Street
Suite 950
Milwaukee, WI 53202
Phone: (414) 291-5700
http://www.florentineopera.org

Madison Opera
333 Glenway Street
Madison, WI 53705
Phone: (608) 238-8085
http://www.madisonopera.org

Skylight Opera
158 North Broadway
Milwaukee, WI 53202
Phone: (414) 291-7811
http://www.skylightopera.com

APPENDIX XV
CANADIAN OPERA COMPANIES

The following is a listing of selected opera companies in Canada provided by Opera America, the premier organization for the opera community. Names, addresses, phone numbers, and Web sites are included when available. Use this listing to obtain general information, located internships, and inquire about auditions and job possibilities. Companies are listed alphabetically by province.

ALBERTA

Banff Centre for the Arts
107 Tunnel Mountain Drive
Box 1020
Banff, AB T1L 1H5
Phone: (403) 762-6100
http://www.banffcentre.ca

Calgary Opera
#601, 237-8 Avenue SE
Calgary, AB T2G 5C3
Phone: (403) 262-7286
http://www.calgaryopera.com

Edmonton Opera
Winspear Centre
9720-102 Avenue
Edmonton, AB T5J 4B2
Phone: (780) 424-4040
http://www.edmontonopera.com

BRITISH COLUMBIA

Modern Baroque Opera Company
1895 Venables Street
Vancouver, BC V5L 2H6
Phone: (604) 216-1114
http://www.modernbaroque.com

Pacific Opera Victoria
1815 Blanshard Street
Victoria, BC V8T 5A4
Phone: (250) 382-1641
http://www.pov.bc.ca

Vancouver New Music
837 Davie Street
Vancouver, BC V6Z 1B7
Phone: (604) 633-0861
http://www.newmusic.org

Vancouver Opera
835 Cambie Street
Vancouver, BC V6B 2P4
Phone: (604) 682-2871
http://www.vanopera.bc.ca

MANITOBA

Manitoba Opera
380 Graham Avenue
Winnipeg, MB R3C 4K2
Phone: (204) 942-7479
http://www.manitobaopera.mb.ca

ONTARIO

Autumn Leaf Performance
P.O. Box 1231 Station F
Toronto, ON M4Y 2V8
Phone: (416) 831-9675
http://www.autumnleaf.com

Canadian Opera
227 Front Street East
Toronto, ON M5A 1E8
Phone: (416) 363-6671
http://www.coc.ca

Opera Atelier
St. Lawrence Hall
157 King Street East, 4th Floor
Toronto, ON M5C 1G9
Phone: (416) 703-3767
http://www.operaatelier.com

Opera Lyra Ottowa
2 Daly Avenue
Ottawa, ON K1N 6E2
Phone: (613) 233-9200
http://www.operalyra.ca

Opera Hamilton
105 Main Street East
Hamilton, ON L8N 1G6
Phone: (905) 527-7627
http://www.operaontario.com

Opera Kitchener-Waterloo
101 Frederick Street
Kitchener, ON N2H 6R2
Phone: (519) 578-5573
http://www.operaontario.com

Royal Opera Canada
Toronto Centre for the Arts
5040 Yonge Street
Toronto ON M2N 6R8
Phone: (416) 322-0456
http://www.royaloperacanada.com

Royal Opera Canada
Living Arts Center
4141 Living Arts Drive
Mississauga, ON L5B 4B8
Phone: (416) 322-0456
http://www.royaloperacanada.com

Queen of Puddings Music Theatre
55 Mill Street
Case Goods Building
Toronto, ON M5A 3C4
Phone: (416) 203-4149
http://www.queenofpuddingsmusictheatre.com

Soundstreams Canada
219 Dufferin Street
Toronto, ON M6K 1Y9
Phone: (416) 504-1282
http://www.soundstreams.ca

Tapestry New Opera Works
55 Mill Street
The Cannery
Toronto, ON M5A 3C4
Phone: (416) 537-6066
http://www.tapestrynewopera.com

QUEBEC

Chants Libres
1908 Rue Panet

Bureau 303
Montreal, QC H2L 3A2
Phone: (514) 841-2642
http://www.chantslibres.org

Compagnie Musicale La Nef
1899 Avenue Desjardins, Bureau 203
Montreal, QC H1V 2G8

Phone: (514) 523-3095
http://www.la-nef.com

L'Opéra de Montréal
260 Boulevard de Maisonneuve Ouest
Montreal, QC H2X 1Y9
Phone: (514) 985-2222
http://www.operademontreal.com

Opéra de Québec
1220, Avenue Taché
Québec, QC G1R 3B4
Phone: (418) 529-4142
http://www.operadequebec.qc.ca

APPENDIX XVI
ARTS COUNCILS AND AGENCIES

The following is a list of federal, regional, and state arts councils and agencies. Names, addresses, phone and fax numbers, and Web sites (when available) are included for each. Use this list to obtain general industry information, find out about state and federal programs, and locate internships, fellowships, and grants.

FEDERAL

Americans for the Arts
1000 Vermont Avenue NW
Washington, DC 20005
Phone: (202) 371-2830
Fax: (202) 371 0424
http://ww3.artsusa.org

New York Office
One East 53rd Street
New York, NY 10022
Phone: (212) 223-2787
Fax: (212) 980-4857
http://ww3.artsusa.org

National Assembly of State Arts Agencies
1029 Vermont Avenue NW
Washington, DC 20005
Phone: (202) 347-6352
Fax: (202) 737-0526
E-mail: nasaa@nasaa-arts.org
http://www.nasaa-arts.org

National Endowment for the Arts
1100 Pennsyvlania Avenue NW
Washington, DC 20506
Phone: (202) 682-5400
http://www.arts.gov

REGIONAL

Arts Midwest (IL, IN, IA, MI, MN, ND, OH, SD, WI)
2908 Hennepin Avenue
Minneapolis, MN 55408
Phone: (612) 341-0755
Fax: (613) 341-0902
http://www.artsmidwest.org

Consortium for Pacific Arts & Cultures (AS, CM, GU)
735 Bishop Street
Honolulu, HI 96813
Phone: (808) 946-7381
Fax: (808) 955-2722

District of Columbia (DC) Commission on the Arts and Humanities
410 Eighth Street NW
Washington, DC 20004
Phone: (202) 724-5613
Fax: (202) 727-4135
http://dcarts.dc.gov

Mid-America Arts Alliance (AR, KS, MO, NE, OK, TX)
2018 Baltimore
Kansas City, MO 64105
Phone: (816) 421-1388
Fax: (816) 421-3918
http://www.maaa.org

Mid Atlantic Arts Foundation (DE, DC, MD, NJ, NY, PA, VI, VA, WV)
201 North Charles Street
Suite 401
Baltimore, MD 21201
Phone: (410) 539-6656
Fax: (410) 837-5517
http://www.midatlanticarts.org

New England Foundation for the Arts (CT, ME, MA, NH, RI, VT)
145 Tremont Street
Boston, MA 02111
Phone: (617) 951-0010
Fax: (617) 951-0016
http://www.nefa.org

Southern Arts Federation (AL, FL, GA, KY, LA, MS, NC, SC, TN)
1800 Peachtree Street NW
Suite 808
Atlanta, GA 30309
Phone: (404) 874-7244
Fax: (404) 873-2148
http://www.southarts.org

Western States Arts Federation (AK, AZ, CA, CO, HI, ID, MT, NM, NV, OR, UT, WA, WY)
1743 Wazee Street
Denver, CO 80202
Phone: (303) 629-1166
Fax: (303) 629-9717
http://www.westaf.org

STATE

Alabama State Council on the Arts
201 Monroe Street
Montgomery, AL 36130
Phone: (334) 242-4076
Fax: (334) 240-3269
http://www.arts.state.al.us

Alaska State Council on the Arts
411 West 4th Avenue
Suite 1E
Anchorage, AK 99501
Phone: (907) 269-6610
Fax: (907) 269-6601
http://www.eed.state.ak.us/aksca

Arkansas Arts Council
1500 Tower Building
323 Center Street
Little Rock, AR 72201
Phone: (501) 324-9766
Fax: (501) 324-9207
http://www.arkansasarts.com

Arizona Commission on the Arts
417 West Roosevelt Street
Phoenix, AZ 85003
Phone: (602) 255-5882
Fax: (602) 256-0282
http://www.arizonaarts.org

California Arts Council
1300 I Street
Suite 930
Sacramento, CA 95814
Phone: (916) 322-6555
Fax: (916) 322-6575
http://www.cac.ca.gov

Colorado Council on the Arts
1380 Lawrence Street
Suite 1200

Denver, CO 80204
Phone: (303) 866-2723
Fax: (303) 866-4266
http://www.coloarts.state.co.us

Arts Division Connecticut Commission on Culture and Tourism
One Financial Plaza
755 Main Street
Hartford, CT 06103
Phone: (860) 256-2800
Fax: (860) 256-2811
http://www.cultureandtourism.org/arts

Delaware Division of the Arts
Carvel State Office Building
820 North French Street
Wilmington, DE 19801
Phone: (302) 577-8278
Fax: (302) 577-6561
http://www.artsdel.org

Florida Division of Cultural Affairs
Department of State, The Capitol
1001 DeSoto Park Drive
Tallahassee, FL 32301
Phone: (850) 245-6470
Fax: (850) 245-6492
http://www.florida-arts.org

Georgia Council for the Arts
260 14th Street NW
Atlanta, GA 30318
Phone: (404) 685-2787
Fax: (404) 685-2788
http://www.web-dept.com/gca

Hawaii State Foundation on Culture and the Arts
250 South Hotel Street
Honolulu, HI 96813
Phone: (808) 586-0300
Fax: (808) 586-0308
http://www.state.hi.us/sfca

Idaho Commission on the Arts
2410 North Old Penitentiary Road
P.O. Box 83720
Boise, ID 83720-0008
Phone: (208) 334-2119
Fax: (208) 334-2488
http://www.arts.idaho.gov

Illinois Arts Council
100 West Randolph Street
Suite 10-500
Chicago, IL 60601
Phone: (312) 814-6750
Fax: (312) 814-1471
http://www.state.il.us/agency/iac

Indiana Arts Commission
150 West Market Street
Suite 618
Indianapolis, IN 46204
Phone: (317) 232-1268
Fax: (317) 232-5595
http://www.in.gov/arts

Iowa Arts Council
Capitol Complex
600 East Locust
Des Moines, IA 50319
Phone: (515) 281-4451
Fax: (515) 242-6498
http://www.iowaartscouncil.org

Kansas Arts Commission
Jayhawk Tower
700 Southwest Jackson
Suite 1004
Topeka, KS 66603
Phone: (785) 296-3335
Fax: (785) 296-4989
http://arts.state.ks.us

Kentucky Arts Council
Old Capitol Annex
300 West Broadway
Frankfort, KY 40601
Phone: (502) 564-3757
http://www.kyarts.org

Louisiana Division of the Arts
P.O. Box 44247
Baton Rouge, LA 70804
Phone: (225) 342-8180
Fax: (225) 342-8173
http://www.crt.state.la.us/arts

Maine Arts Commission
193 State Street
Augusta, ME 04333
Phone: (207) 287-2724
Fax: (207) 287-2725
http://www.mainearts.com

Maryland State Arts Council
175 West Ostend Street
Suite E
Baltimore, MD 21230
Phone: (410) 767-6555
Fax: (410) 333-1062
http://www.msac.org

Massachusetts Cultural Council
10 Saint James Avenue
Boston, MA 02116
Phone: (617) 727-3668
Fax: (617) 727-0044
http://www.massculturalcouncil.org

Michigan Council for Arts and Cultural Affairs
702 West Kalamazoo
P.O. Box 30705
Lansing, MI 48909
Phone: (517) 241-4011
Fax: (517) 241-3979
http://www.michigan.gov/hal/0,1607,
7-160-17445_19272—-,00.html

Minnesota State Arts Board
Park Square Court
400 Sibley Street
St. Paul, MN 55101
Phone: (651) 215-1600
Fax: (651) 215-1602
http://www.arts.state.mn.us

Missouri Arts Council
111 North 7th Street
St. Louis, MO 63101
Phone: (314) 340-6845
Fax: (314) 340-7215
http://www.missouriartscouncil.org

Mississippi Arts Commission
239 North Lamar Street
Suite 207
Jackson, MS 39201
Phone: (601) 359-6030
Fax: (601) 359-6008
http://www.arts.state.ms.us

Montana Arts Council
City County Building
316 North Park Avenue
P.O. Box 202201
Helena, MT 59620
Phone: (406) 444-6430
Fax: (406) 444-6548
http://www.art.state.mt.us

Nebraska Arts Council
Joslyn Carriage House
3838 Davenport Street
Omaha, NE 68131
Phone: (402) 595-2122
Fax: (402) 595-2334
http://www.nebraskaartscouncil.org

Nevada Arts Council
716 North Carson Street
Carson City, NV 89701
Phone: (775) 687-6680
Fax: (775) 687-6688
http://dmla.clan.lib.nv.us/docs/arts

New Hampshire State Council on the Arts
$2\frac{1}{2}$ Beacon Street

Concord, NH 03301
Phone: (603) 271-2789
Fax: (603) 271-3584
http://www.state.nh.us/nharts

New Jersey State Council on the Arts
225 West State Street
P.O. Box 306
Trenton, NJ 08625
Phone: (609) 292-6130
Fax: (609) 989-1440
http://www.njartscouncil.org

New Mexico Arts
228 East Palace Avenue
Santa Fe, NM 87501
Phone: (505) 827-6490
Fax: (505) 827-6043
http://www.nmarts.org

New York State Council on the Arts
175 Varick Street
New York, NY 10014
Phone: (212) 627-4455
Fax: (212) 620-5911
http://www.nysca.org

North Carolina Arts Council
Department of Cultural Resources
Jenkins House
221 East Lane Street
Raleigh, NC 27699
Phone: (919) 733-2821
Fax: (919) 733-4834
http://www.ncarts.org

North Dakota Council on the Arts
1600 East Century Avenue
Bismarck, ND 58503
Phone: (701) 328-7590
Fax: (701) 328-7595
http://www.state.nd.us/arts

Ohio Arts Council
727 East Main Street
Columbus, OH 43205
Phone: (614) 466-2613
Fax: (614) 466-4494
http://www.oac.state.oh.us

Oklahoma Arts Council
Jim Thorpe Building
P.O. Box 52001-2001
Oklahoma City, OK 73152
Phone: (405) 521-2931

Fax: (405) 521-6418
http://www.oklaosf.state.ok.us/~arts

Oregon Arts Commission
775 Summer Street NE
Suite 200
Salem, OR 97301
Phone: (503) 986-0082
Fax: (503) 986-0260
http://www.oregonartscommission.org/
    main.php

Pennsylvania Council on the Arts
216 Finance Building
Harrisburg, PA 17120
Phone: (717) 787-6883
Fax: (717) 783-2538
http://www.pacouncilonthearts.org

Rhode Island State Council on the Arts
One Capitol Hill
Providence, RI 02908
Phone: (401) 222-3880
Fax: (401) 222-3018
http://www.arts.ri.gov

South Carolina Arts Commission
1800 Gervais Street
Columbia, SC 29201
Phone: (803) 734-8696
Fax: (803) 734-8526
http://www.state.sc.us/arts

South Dakota Arts Council
Office of the Arts
800 Governors Drive
Pierre, SD 57501
Phone: (605) 773-3131
Fax: (605) 773-6962
http://www.artscouncil.sd.gov

Tennessee Arts Commission
Citizens Plaza
401 Charlotte Avenue
Nashville, TN 37243
Phone: (615) 741-1701
Fax: (615) 741-8559
http://www.arts.state.tn.us

Texas Commission on the Arts
P.O. Box 13406
Capitol Station
Austin, TX 78711
Phone: (512) 463-5535

Fax: (512) 475-2699
http://www.arts.state.tx.us

Utah Arts Council
617 East South Temple Street
Salt Lake City, UT 84102
Phone: (801) 236-7555
Fax: (801) 236-7556
http://arts.utah.gov

Vermont Arts Council
136 State Street
Drawer 33
Montpelier, VT 05633
Phone: (802) 828-3291
Fax: (802) 828-3363
http://www.vermontartscouncil.org

Virginia Commission for the Arts
223 Governor Street
Richmond, VA 23219
Phone: (804) 225-3132
Fax: (804) 225-4327
http://www.arts.virginia.gov

Washington State Arts Commission
711 Capital Way Street
P.O. Box 42675
Olympia, WA 98504
Phone: (360) 753-3860
Fax: (360) 586-5351
http://www.arts.wa.gov

West Virginia Commission on the Arts
1900 Kanawha Boulevard East
Charleston, WV 25305
Phone: (304) 558-0240
Fax: (304) 558-2779
http://www.wvculture.org/arts/artsindex.
    aspx

Wisconsin Arts Board
101 East Wilson Street
Madison, WI 53702
Phone: (608) 266-0190
Fax: (608) 267-0380
http://www.arts.state.wi.us/static

Wyoming Arts Council
2320 Capitol Avenue
Cheyenne, WY 82002
Phone: (307) 777-7742
Fax: (307) 777-5499
http://wyoarts.state.wy.us

GLOSSARY

The following is a list of abbreviations, acronyms, and industry jargon that will prove helpful to individuals interested in theater and the performing arts. Entries are listed alphabetically.

AAAA Associated Actors and Artists of America
AAMT American Association for Music Therapy
AATE American Alliance for Theatre and Education
ACA American Composers Alliance
ACDA American Choral Directors Association
ACDFA American College Dance Festival Association
ACF American Choral Foundation
ACFA Associated Councils for the Arts
ACM Academy of Country Music
ACSTA American Center for Stanislavski Theatre Art
ACTF American Conservatory Theatre Foundation
ADF American Dance Festival
ADG American Dance Guild
ADTA American Dance Therapy Association
ADTR Academy of Dance Therapists Registered
advance A prepayment of monies against future royalties or fees
AE Account Executive
AEA Actors' Equity Association
affiliate A broadcast station that belongs to a network; for example, WABC in New York and KABC in Los Angeles are both affiliates of the ABC network
AFM American Federation of Musicians
AFT American Federation of Teachers
AFTRA American Federation of Television and Radio Artists
agent The person who represents actors and actresses to help them obtain jobs
AGMA American Guild of Musical Artists
AGO American Guild of Organists
AGVA American Guild of Variety Artists
AIOF American Israel Opera Foundation
AMA American Marketing Association
AMC American Music Center
AMC American Music Conference
AMFA American Music Festival Association
AMIS American Musical Instrument Society
AMS American Musicological Society
AMSA American Music Scholarship Association
angel A person who gives money or backs a theatrical production
ANTA American National Theatre and Academy
APT American Place Theatre
apprentice A person just beginning to learn a skill

arbitron ratings A television and radio rating service that indicates what percentage of people are viewing or listening to a particular show or station. Commercial rates are often based on these ratings
ARC Art Resources in Collaboration
arrangement The adaptation of a song for a performance or a recording
A.R.T./NY Alliance of Resident Theatres/New York
AS Actors Studio
ASA Acoustical Society of America
ASCAP American Society of Composers and Publishers
ASJA American Society of Journalists and Authors, Inc.
ASMA American Society of Music Arrangers
ASOL American Symphony Orchestra League
assignment The transfer of rights from a songwriter to publisher
ASTR American Society for Theatre Research
ATAFY American Theatre Arts for Youth
ATAS Academy of Television Arts and Sciences
ATCA American Theatre Critics Association
ATHE Association for Theatre in Higher Education
ATOS American Theatre Organ Society
ATPAM Association of Theatrical Press Agents and Managers, AFL-CIO
AUDELCO Audience Development Committee
AVS American Viola Society
AWRT American Women in Radio and Television
AWTF American Writers Theatre Foundation
b & w glossy Used by publicists, press agents, and public relations people when putting together press kits. It is an 8×10 glossy photograph of their client that can be used for reproduction purposes in newspapers or magazines
BBAA Big Band Academy of America
BFA Bilingual Foundation of the Arts
bio A biography of a client put together by press agents, publicists, or public relations people
biling The position, size, and/or order of an actress's or actor's name on a marquee, in advertisements, and in programs
blocking The onstage movements suggested by the director for actors or actresses in a theatrical production
BMI Broadcast Music, Inc.
book A collection of samples done by someone in either the art or writing field to show prospective employers an applicant's potential. Also known as a portfolio
booking agent Business representative responsible for seeking and securing venues for performers and entertainers
BTF Ballet Theatre Foundation

CA:APVE   Chorus America: Association of Professional Vocal Ensembles

CAG   Catholic Actors Guild of America

CAG   Concert Artists Guild

camera-ready   The condition of everything in an ad being ready for a printer to produce a print of the advertising. Nothing has to be retouched

campaign   A series of advertisements used to promote and advertise a product or group of products

cast   The list of characters in a theatrical, film, or television production

casting   Choosing and hiring the actors and actresses to star in a theatrical production, television show or movie

catalog   The collection of songs to which a music publisher owns the rights

CCA   Cecchetti Council of America

CDSSA   Country Dance and Song Society of America

CESA   Cultural Exchange Society of America

CG   Choreographers Guild

charts   Lists of current hits, found in the trade magazines

circulation   The number of copies of a newspaper or magazine that are distributed

CMA   Chamber Music America

CMA   Country Music Association

CMS   College Music Society

CNDW   Coalition for National Dance Week

commission   A percentage of artist's fee paid to agents and managers for representing the artist's interests

contractor   The person who hires session musicians for a recording session

copyright   A legal protection granted to an author or composer for the exclusive rights to his or her work

costumes   Clothing and accessories worn by actors and actresses to help them look the part that they are playing

copywriter   The person who develops the words used in advertisements, brochures, marketing, and promotional pieces

CORD   Congress on Research in Dance

CORST   Council of Resident Summer Theatres

COS   Central Opera Service

CPM   Conference of Personal Managers

CSA   Casting Society of America

CT   Choreographers Theatre

CT   Composers Theatre

cue   A signal for an actor, actress, or production person to take a specific action or an instruction given by a stage manager or director

curtain line   The line on the stage where the curtain for each act falls

DCA   Dance Critics Association

DD   Drama Desk

DEA   Dance Educators of America

demo   Demonstration tape, CD, or videotape used for selling a tune, act, group, or the like

DFA   Dance Films Association

DG   Dramatists Guild

DGA   Directors Guild of America

DMF   Dance Magazine Foundation

DNB   Dance Notation Bureau

doubling   An actor or actress taking more than one part in a play

dressing the house   A method of selling tickets in a box office that makes a theater look fuller than it really is

dress rehearsal   The rehearsal in a theatrical production in which everything, including costumes, makeup, lighting, sound, and special effects, is tried out just as if the play was actually going on in front of an audience

DT   The Drama Tree

DTW   Dance Theater Workshop

EAGA   Episcopal Actor's Guild of America

ECPC   Ethnic Cultural Preservation Council

EDLA   Exotic Dancers League of America

EOMTC   Eugene O'Neill Memorial Theater Center

Equity   Actors' Equity Association

FC   Friars Club

FCC   Federal Communications Commission

FED   Foundation for Ethnic Dance

FFD   Fund for Dance

FTS   Ford's Theatre Society

FX   Effects

GAG   Graphic Artists Guild

gig   A job for musicians

GMA   Gospel Music Association

GMWA   Gospel Music Workshop of America

HAI   Hospital Audiences

HAU   Hebrew Actors Union

HCC   Hollywood Comedy Club

house curtain   The curtain that opens and closes and separates an audience from the stage

hype   Extensive publicity used to promote people, products, or events. Hype is not always true

IAAM   International Association of Auditorium Managers

IAM   Institute of the American Musical

IASTA   Institute for Advanced Studies in the Theatre Arts

IASTE   International Alliance of Theatrical Stage Employees and Moving Picture Machine Operators of the U.S. and Canada

IAU   Italian Actors Union

IBEW   International Brotherhood of Electrical Workers

ICSOM   International Conference of Symphony and Opera Musicians

IDEA   International Dance-Exercise Association

IOD   Institute of Outdoor Drama

IPRA   International Public Relations Association

ITI/US   International Theatre Institute of the United States

ITS   Italian Thespian Society

jingle   The music in a commercial advertisement

KCA   Kentucky Callers Association

LAPT   League of American Theatres and Producers

LHAT   League of Historic American Theatres

librettist   A person who writes librettos

libretto   The book in an opera

LIMS   Laban/Bartenieff Institute of Movement Studies

literary agent   The person who tries to sell a playwright's work

LOBTP   League of Off Broadway Theatres and Producers

local   The local affiliation in a particular geographic area of a national or international union

LOPTTP   League of Professional Theatre Training Programs

LORT   League of Resident Theaters

LOS   Little Orchestra Society

LSF   Lloyd Shaw Foundation

lyrics   The words of a song

matinee   An afternoon performance of a theatrical production

MENC   Music Educators National Conference

MOA   Metropolitan Opera Association

MOG   Metropolitan Opera Guild

MTC   Meet the Composer

MTNA   Music Teachers National Association

NAB   National Association of Broadcasters

NABET   National Association of Broadcast Employees and Technicians

NADSA   National Association of Dramatic and Speech Arts

NAPM   National Academy of Popular Music

NARAS   National Academy of Recording Arts and Sciences

NAS   National Academy of Songwriters

NASD   National Association of Schools of Dance

NASM   National Association of Schools of Music

NAST   National Association of Schools of Theatre

NATAS   National Academy of Television Arts and Sciences

NCHC   National Clogging and Hoedown Council

NCTF   National Corporate Theatre Fund

ND   New Dramatists

NDA   National Dance Association

NDCA   National Dance Council of America

NDEITA   National Dance-Exercise Instructor's Training Association

NDI   National Dance Institute

NEA   Nashville Entertainment Association

Nielsen ratings   A television rating service

NETC   New England Theatre Conference

network   A group of television or radio stations affiliated and interconnected for simultaneous broadcast of the same programming

NFMC   National Federation of Music Clubs

NFPW   National Federation of Press Women

NMPA   National Music Publishers Association

NOA   National Opera Association

NOA   National Orchestral Association

nonresident theater   Theater for which actors are hired on a per-performance basis

not-for-profit theaters and companies   Theaters, orchestras, and ballet and opera companies that are set up to provide a community service and do not make a profit for any one person or company. These organizations are usually sustained by donations, grants, and other fundraising efforts

notices   Reviews for a production

NPC   National Playwrights Conference

NPC   National Press Club

NPN   National Performance Network

NPPA   National Press Photographers Association

NSAI   Nashville Songwriters Association, International

NSDC   National Square Dance Convention

NSOA   National Symphony Orchestra Association

NTC   National Theatre Conference

NTD   National Theatre of the Deaf

NTWH   National Theatre Workshop of the Handicapped

NWDC   Northwest Drama Conference

NYDCC   New York Drama Critics Circle

OA   Opera America

OCC   Outer Critics Circle

OPACT   Organization of Professional Acting Coaches and Teachers

opening night   The night a performance formally opens to the public

option   An agreement between a producer and a playwright that gives the producer the exclusive right to produce the play within a certain amount of time

PBP   Paper Bag Players

PD   Public Domain or Program Director

PDTA   Professional Dance Teachers Association

PFA   Pianists Foundation of America

PG   Producers Group

pit   The area in front of the stage where the orchestra sits

playwright   The person who writes the script for a play

portfolio   A collection of sample pieces done by someone in the creative field (either a writer or artist) that is put together into a book so that prospective employers can get an idea of their potential

PR   Public Relations

press kit   A promotional kit containing publicity, photographs, and other materials used by publicists, press agents, and public relations people to help publicize a client

preview   A performance of a production that is given before the actual opening of a show

promo   Promotion

PRSA   Public Relations Society of America

public domain   Songs or other works that have no copyright or whose copyright has expired

PRSSA   Public Relations Student Society of America

RAD   Royal Academy of Dancing, United States Branch

resident theater   Seasonal theater for which a group of actors is hired to perform during the entire season and is assigned set roles

RIAA   Recording Industry Association of America

royalties   Monies paid periodically for the sales of records, sheet music, and other copyrighted material

royalty statement   An itemized accounting of earnings for songwriters or recording artists

RTNDA   Radio Television News Directors Association

SAFD   Society of American Fight Directors

SAG   Screen Actors Guild

SCA   Screen Composers of America

scale   The minimum wages that can be paid to a union member

script   A theatrical production's story written in a special way so that the character's names are either next to or above their lines. It may also include stage directions

SDG   Sacred Dance Guild

SDHS   Society of Dance History Scholars

SEG   Screen Extras Guild

SLC   Songwriters and Lyricists Club

SSDC   Society of Stage Directors and Choreographers

stage presence   The way an actor or actress stands and moves while on stage

standby or stand-in   An actor or actress who must be available to go on for a scheduled actor or actress in a production. They must usually call in at a specified amount of time before curtain time to see if they are needed for that night's performance

STC   Southwestern Theatre Conference

STT   Save the Theatres

TA   Theatre Authority

TAMT   The American Mime Theatre

TCEO   Theatre Committee for Eugene O'Neill

TCG   Theatre Communications Group

TDF   Theatre Development Fund

TE   Theatre in Education

TG   Theatre Guild

THS   Theatre Historical Society

TJMS   Traditional Japanese Music Society of the City University of New York

Tony Awards   Annual awards given to those in the theater for excellence in various categories

tour   A series of concerts, usually in different geographical locations

trades   Newspapers and magazines that are geared to a specific industry—in this case, the theater and performing arts

understudy   An actor or actress who substitutes for another actor or actress when he or she is not able to act in a performance

union card   A card that is used to identify members of specific unions

URTA   University Resident Theatre Association

USA   United Scenic Artists

USABDA   United States Amateur Ballroom Dancers Association

USDA   United Square Dancers of America

USITT   United States Institute for Theatre Technology

UWP   Up With People

venue   A hall, auditorium, theater, arena, or club where theatrical productions or concerts are presented

WGA   Writers Guild of America

WIC   Women in Communications, Inc.

YCA   Young Concerts Artists

YTA   Yiddish Theatrical Alliance

BIBLIOGRAPHY

A. BOOKS

There are thousands of books written on all aspects of theater and the performing arts. The books listed below are separated into general categories, with the subject matter of many overlapping into other categories.

These books can be found in bookstores or libraries. If your local library does not have the books you want, you might ask your librarian to order them for you through the interlibrary loan system.

This list is meant as a beginning. For other books that might interest you, look in the performing arts section of bookstores and libraries. You can also check *Books in Print* (found in the reference section of libraries) for other books on the subject.

ACTING AND DIRECTING

Barton, Robert. *Acting: Onstage and Off.* Belmont, Calif.: Wadsworth Publishing, 2005.

Blumenfield, Robert. *Accents: A Manuel for Acting.* Milwaukee: Amadeus Press, 2004.

Caldarone, Marina. *Actions: The Actor's Thesaurus.* New York: Theatre Communications Group, 2004.

Chubbuck, Ivana. *The Power of the Actor.* East Rutherford, N.J.: Penguin Group, 2005.

Cohen, Robert. *Acting Professionally: Raw Facts about Careers in Acting.* Burr Ridge, Ill.: McGraw-Hill Higher Education, 2003.

Elgin, Kathy. *Theatre and Entertainment: Shakespeare's World.* Minneapolis: Compass Point, 2004.

Greene, Alexis. *Le Lortel: The Queen of Off Broadway.* Milwaukee: Amadeus Press, 2004.

Gussow, Mel. *Micahel Gambon: A Life in Acting.* New York: Applause Theatre Book Publishers, 2005.

Hester, John. *Stage Acting Techniques: A Practical Guide.* Alameda, Calif.: Crowood Press, Limited, 2004.

Jazwinski, Peter. *Act Now!: A Step-by-Step Guide to Becoming a Working Actor.* New York: Crown Publishing Group, 2003.

Jones, Robert Edmond. *The Dramatic Imagination: Reflections and Speculations of the Arts of the Theatre.* New York: Routledge, 2004.

Kanner, Ellie. *How Not to Audition: Avoiding the Common Mistakes Most Actors Make.* Hollywood, Calif.: Lone Eagle Publishing, 2003.

Kellow, Brian. *The Bennetts: An Acting Family.* Lexington: University Press of Kentucky, 2004.

Kohlhaas, Karen. *The Monologue Audition: A Practical Guide for Actors.* Milwaukee: Amadeus Press, 2004.

Levy, Gavin. *112 Acting Games: A Comprehensive Workbook of Theatre Games for Developing Acting Skills.* Colorado Springs, Colo.: Meriwether Publishing, 2005.

Martinez, Tony. *An Agent Tells All: An Uncensored Look at the Business of Acting.* Beverly Hills, Calif.: Hit Team Publishing, 2005.

McDonnell, Kathleen. *Putting on a Show: Theater for Young People.* Toronto: Second Story Press, 2005.

Moss, Larry. *The Intent to Live: Achieving Your True Potential as an Actor.* Westminster, Wd.: Bantam Books, 2004.

Salt, Chrys. *Make Acting Work.* London: Methuen Publishing Limited, 2004.

Schulman, Michael. *Play the Scene: The Ultimate Collection of Contemporary and Classic Scenes and Monologues.* New York: St. Martin's Press, 2005.

Simon, Ali. *Masking Unmasked: Four Approaches to Basic Acting.* New York: Palgrave Macmillan, 2004.

Thomsom, Peter. *On Actors and Acting.* Exeter, U.K.: University of Exeter Press, 2003.

Watson-Guptill Publications Staff. *Living on Stage.* New York: Watson-Guptill Publications, Inc., 2004.

Wienir, David. *Making It on Broadway: Actors' Tales of Climbing to the Top.* New York: Allworth Press, 2004.

Wroe, Craig. *An Actor Prepares . . . to Live in New York City: How to Live Like a Star Before You Become One.* Pompton Plains, N.J.: Amadeus Press, 2004.

BALLET

Cooper, Bill. *The Royal Ballet: In House.* New York: Theatre Communications Group, 2004.

Gottlieb, Robert. *George Balanchine: The Ballet Maker.* New York: Harper Trade, 2004.

Teachout, Terry. *All in the Dances: A Brief Life of George Balanchine.* San Diego, Calif.: Harcourt Trade Publishers, 2004.

DANCE

Cruz, Barbara, C. *Alvin Ailey: Celebrating African-American Culture in Dance.* Berkeley Heights, N.J.: Enslow Publishers, 2004.

Garafola, Lynn. *Legacies of Twentieth-Century Dance.* Middletown, Conn.: Wesleyan University Press, 2005.

DIRECTING

Baldwin, Chris. *Stage Directing: A Practical Guide.* Marlborough, U.K.: Crowood Press, 2003.

Braun, Kazimierz. *Theatre Directing—Art, Ethics, Creativity.* Lewiston, N.Y.: Edwin Mellen Press, 2000.

Frerer, Lloyd Anton. *Directing for the Stage.* Burr Ridge, Ill.: McGraw-Hill Higher Education, 2003.

Hodge, Francis. *Play Directing: Analysis, Communication, and Style.* Boston: Allyn & Bacon, Inc., 2004.

Reich, Russell. *Notes on Directing.* New York: RCR Creative Press, 2003.

CLASSICAL MUSICIANS AND ORCHESTRAS

Drew, Lucas. *Everything You Always Wanted to Know about the Symphony Orchestra.* Boca Raton, Fla.: Edwin F. Kalmus & Company, Inc., 1992.

Getzinger, Donna, and Feldsenfeld, Daniel. *Johannes Brahms and the Twilight of Romanticism.* Greensboro, N.C.: Morgan Reynolds Incorporated, 2004.

Hirzy, Ellen C. *Working with the Music Director: A Handbook for Board Members, Executive Directors, and Music Directors.* New York: American Symphony Orchestra League, 1999.

Morrison, Richard. *Orchestra: The LSO: A Century of Triumphs and Turbulence.* New York: Faber & Faber 2004.

Todd, R. Larry *Mendelssohn: A Life in Music.* New York: Oxford University Press, 2005.

Whiting, Jim. *The Life and Times of George Frederic Handel.* Hockessin, Del.: Mitchell Lane Publishers, 2003.

———. *The Life and Times of Igor Stravinsky.* Hockessin, Del.: Mitchell Lane Publishers, 2004.

Zannos, Susan. *The Life and Times of Ludwing Van Beethoven.* Hockessin Del.: Mitchell Lane Publishers, 2003.

COMEDY

Benjava, Gustav. *The Divine Comedian.* Philadelphia: Xlibris Corporation, 2004.

Hentzell, Tim. *So, You're A Comedian, Tell Me a Joke.* Morrisville, N.C.: *Lulu.com:* 2004.

Makinson, Robert. *How to Be a Comedian Handbook.* Brooklyn, N.Y.: R. B. Makinson, 2002.

Murray, Ken. *Life on a Pogo Stick: Autobiography of a Comedian.* Temecula, Calif.: Textbook Publishers, 2003.

Vance, Jeffrey. *Harold Lloyd: Master Comedian.* New York: Harry N. Abrams, 2002.

White, Karyn Ruth. *Your Seventh Sense: How to Think Like a Comedian.* Denver: LifeStar, 2004.

ENTERTAINMENT LAW

Butler, Joy R. *The Musician's Guide through the Legal Jungle: Answers to Frequently Asked Questions about Music Law.* Arlington, Va.: Sashay Communications, 2002.

Isaacs, Sidney C. *The Law Relating to Theatres, Music-Halls and Other Public Entertainments and to the Performers Therein, Including the Law of Musical and Dramatic Copyright, No. 1.* Holmes Beach, Fla.: Gaunt, Inc., 1999.

Parker, Nigel. *Music Business: A Professional Guide to Infrastructure, Practice and Law of the Industry.* Poole, U.K.: Palladian Law Publishing, Ltd., 2004.

Platinum Millennium Publishing Staff. *101 Music Business Contracts – Updated Edition – Preprinted Binder/CD-ROM Set: Containing over 100 Contracts and Agreements for Recording Artist, Musicians, Record Companies, Managers, Songwriters, Labels, Producers, Indies and Any and All Others in the Music Industry: Entertainment Law at Its Best!:* Waterbury, Conn.: Platinum Millennium, 2002.

Settle, Alfred Towers, and Frank H. Baber. *The Law of Public Entertainments: Theaters, Music and Dancing, Stage Plays, Cinematographs, Copyright, Sunday Performances, Children, Theatrical Cases, and Specimen Contracts.* Buffalo, N.Y.: William S. Hein & Company, 2003.

Soocher, Stan. *They Fought the Law: Rock Music Goes to Court.* New York: Music Sales Corporation, 2004.

MUSIC AND THEATER CRITICISM

Billington, Michael. *One Night Stands: A Critic's View of Modern British Theatre.* New York: Theatre Communications Group, 2002.

Hornby, Richard. *Mad about Theatre.* New York: Applause Theatre Book Publishers, 2000.

Wingell, Richard. *Writing about Music.* East Rutherford, N.J.: Prentice Hall, 2001.

MUSIC BUSINESS

Brabec, Jeffrey. *Music, Money, and Success: The Insider's Guide to Making Money in the Music Industry.* New York: Music Sales Corporation, 2004.

Colley, Craig W. *You Can Make Money in Music: Everything a Musician Needs to Know to Become Steadily Employed as a Live Performer.* Milwaukee: Hal Corporation, 1991.

Curran, Mark. *Getting Gigs!: The Musician's and Singer's Survival Guide to Booking Better Paying Jobs with or without an Agent.* Simi Valley, Calif.: New Media Digital, Inc., 2004.

Field, Shelly. *Career Opportunities in the Music Industry.* New York: Facts On File, 2004.

Frascogna, Xavier M. *This Business of Artist Management.* New York: Watson-Guptill Publications, 2004.

Grant, A. *Music Business: It's All about the Music, Right?* Lincoln, Neb.: iUniverse, Inc., 2005.

Harris, Kevin. *Inside Music 2005: The Insider's Guide to the Industry.* London: Ebury Press, 2004.

Kusek, David. *The Future of Music.* Boston: Berklee Press Publications, 2005.

Moore, Steve. *The Truth about the Music Business: A Grassroots Business and Legal Guide.* Boston: Course Technology, Inc., 2005.

Platinum Millennium. *How to Make A Fortune in the Music Industry by Doing It Yourself: Your Personal Step-by-Step Guide to Having a Successful Career in the Music Business. A-K-A How to Sell Music, Book Shows and Get Noticed!* Waterbury, Conn.: Platinum Millennium, 2005.

———. *The Music Business: How YOU Can Make $500,000 or More a Year in the Music Industry by Doing It Yourself!* Bridgeport, Conn.: Platinum Millennium, 2005.

Rudsenske, Scott J. *Music Business Made Simple: A Guide to Becoming a Recording Artist.* New York: Music Sales Corporation, 2004.

Wilson, Lee. *Making It in the Music Business: The Business and Legal Guide for Songwriters and Performers.* New York: Allworth Press, 2004.

MUSIC PUBLISHING

Beall, Eric. *Making Music Make Money: An Insider's Guide to Becoming Your Own Music Publisher.* Boston: Berklee Press Publications, 2003.

Howard, George. *Music Publishing 101.* Milwaukee: Hal Leonard Corporation, 2004.

Kashif, ed. *Kashif's Music Publishing Source Guide.* Venice, Calif.: Brooklyn Boy Books, 1998.

Sellars, Paul. *Publishing Music Online.* New York: Music Sales Corporation, 2004.

Smith, Regina. *Music Publishing 101: Crash Course.* Miami: No Walls Production & Publishing, 2001.

Whitsett, Tim. *Music Publishing: The Real Road to Music Business Success.* Vallejo, Calif.: artistpro.com, 2001.

MUSIC THERAPY

Crowe, Barbara J. *Music and Soulmaking: Toward a New Theory of Music Therapy.* Lanham, Md.: Scarecrow Press, 2004.

Glassman, Lorna R. *Here Comes the Music Lady.* Bloomington, Ind.: AuthorHouse, 2004.

Michel, Donald E., and Joseph Pinson. *Music Therapy in Principle and Practice.* Springfield, Ill.: Charles C. Thomas Publisher, 2005.

Robbins, Clive. *Journey into Creative Music Therapy.* Saint Louis, Mo.: MMB Music, Inc., 2005.

Smeijsters, Henk. *Sounding the Self: Analogy in Improvisational Music Therapy.* Gilsum, N.H.: Barcelona Publishers, 2005.

OPERA

Bradley, Ian. *Oh Joy! Oh Rapture.* New York: Oxford University Press, 2005.

Douglas, Nigel. *The Joy of Opera.* London: Andre Deutsch, 2005.

Kopp, Richard. *Notes on This Evening's Opera.* Bloomington, Ind.: AuthorHouse, 2005.

Kramer, Lawrence. *Opera and Modern Culture: Wagner and Strauss.* Berkeley: University of California Press, 2004.

Russell, P. Craig. *The P. Craig Russell Library of Opera Adaptations. Vol. 3.* New York: N B M Publishing Company, 2004.

Ottenberg, Eve. *The Widow's Opera.* Bloomington, Ind.: AuthorHouse, 2005.

PLAYWRIGHTING

Cassady, Marsh. *Playwriting Step by Step.* San Jose, Calif.: Resource Publications, Incorporated, 2003.

Catron, Louis E. *The Elements of Playwriting.* Prospect Heights, Ill.: Waveland Press, 2001.

Dromgoole, Dominic. *The Full Room: An A-Z of Contemporary Playwriting.* London: Methuen Publishing Limited, 2004.

Greig, Noel. *Playwriting: A Practical Guide.* New York: Routledge, 2005.

Hatcher, Jeffrey. *The Art and Craft of Playwriting.* Cincinnati: F & W Publications, 2000.

Macgowan, Kenneth. *A Primer of Playwriting.* Temecula, Calif.: Textbook Publishers, 2003.

Shamas, Laura A. *Playwriting for Theater, Film and Television.* Cincinnati: F & W Publications, 2003.

PUBLICITY, PUBLIC RELATIONS, AND PROMOTION

Alterman, Glenn. *Promoting Your Acting Career: A Step-by-Step Guide to Opening the Right Doors.* New York: Allworth Press, 2004.

Austin, Pam, and Bob Austin. *Getting Free Publicity: The Secrets of Successful Press Relations.* Oxford, U.K.: How To Books, 2005.

Baker, Bob. *Guerrilla Music Marketing Handbook: 201 Self-Promotion Ideas for Songwriters, Musicians & Bands.* Colorado Springs, Col.: Spotlight Publishing, 2001.

Britt, Shawnassey Howell. *The Independent Record Label's Plain and Simple Guide to Music Promotion.* Jackson, Miss.: One Horse Publishing, 2004.

Fletcher, Tana, and Julia Rockler. *Getting Publicity.* Bellingham, Wash.: Self-Counsel Press, Inc., 2004.

Hamilton, Joni. *The Beginner's Guide to Publicity.* Wheaton, Ill.: Synoia Digital Press, 2005.

Kalmar, Veronika. *Label Launch: A Guide to Independent Record Recording, Promotion, and Distribution.* New York: St. Martin's Press, 2002.

Kolb, Bonita. *Marketing for Cultural Organisations: New Strategies for Attracting Audiences to Classical Music,*

Dance, Museums, Theatre and Opera. Boston: International Thomson Business Press, 2004.

Lathrop, Ted. *This Business of Music Marketing and Promotion. Revised and Updated Edition.* New York: Billboard Books, 2003.

McArthur, Nancy. *How to Do Theatre Publicity.* Berea, Ohio: Good Ideas Company, 1978.

Reilly, Andrew. *An Actor's Business: How to Market Yourself as an Actor No Matter Where You Live.* Boulder, Col.: Sentient Publications, 2004.

Sinnett, Clair. *Actors Working: The Actor's Guide to Marketing Success.* El Segundo, Calif.: Actors Working Books, 2004.

Summers, Jodi. *Making and Marketing Music.* New York: Allworth Press, 2004.

SONGWRITING

Blume, Jason. *6 Steps to Songwriting Success: The Comprehensive Guide to Writing and Marketing Hit Songs.* New York: Watson-Guptill Books, 2004.

Byers, Dave. *Songwriting Fundamentals: Discover the Joy of Songwriting.* Gaithersburg, Md.: Singature Imprint, 2004.

DeMain, Bill. *In Their Own Words: Songwriters Talk about the Creative Process.* Westport, Conn.: Greenwood Press, 2004.

Dion, Frank. *Fingers Bleed: Learn How to Write a Song in about 15 Minutes and Increase Your Chances of Becoming a Rock-n-roll Superstar.* North Charleston, S.C.: BookSurge, 2004.

Dominic, Serene. *Burt Bacharach: Song by Song.* New York: Music Sales Corporation, 2004.

Hirschhorn, Joel. *Complete Idiot's Guide to Songwriting 2.* East Rutherford, N.J.: Penguin, 2004.

Hooper, Caroline. *Learn Songwriting.* Tulsa, Okla.: EDC Publishing, 2004.

Pincus, Lee. *The Songwriter's Success Manual.* Mattituck, N.Y.: Amereon, 2004.

Rooksby, Rikky. *Melody: How to Write Great Tunes.* San Francisco: Backbeat Books, 2004.

STAGECRAFT

Civardi, Giovani. *Drawing Scenery: Landscapes, Seascapes and Buildings.* Tunbridge Wells, U.K.: Search Press, Limited, 2004.

Crabtree, Susan. *Scenic Art for the Theatre: History, Tools, and Techniques.* San Diego: Elsevier Science & Technology Books, 2004.

Essig, Linda. *Lighting and the Design Idea.* Belmont, Calif.: Wadsworth Publishing, 2004.

Gillette, J. Michael. *Theatrical Design and Production: An Introduction to Scene Design and Construction, Lighting, Sound, Costume, and Makeup.* New York: McGraw-Hill, 2004.

Gustafson, David Eldon. *Position: Anchoring Yourself and Mastering Stagecraft.* Upland, Calif.: InfoDynamics Publication, 2003.

Kramer, Wayne. *The Mind's Eye: Theatre and Media Design from the Inside Out.* Portsmouth, N.H.: Heinemann, 2004

MacCoy, Peter. *Essentials of Stage Management.* New York: Routledge, 2004.

McDonagh, Joe. *Opening Night.* Studio City Calif.: Players Press, Inc., 2003.

Orton, Keith. *Model Making for the Stage: A Practical Guide.* Marlborough, U.K.: Crowood Press, Limited, 2005.

Pallin, Gail. *Stage Management: The Essential Handbook.* New York: Theatre Communications Group, Inc., 2004.

Richmond, Susan. *Further Steps in Stagecraft.* Studio City, Calif.: Players Press, Inc., 2003.

Sofer, Andrew. *The Stage Life of Props.* Ann Arbor.: University of Michigan Press, 2003.

Swift, Charles I. *Introduction to Stage Lighting: The Fundamentals of Theatre Lighting Design.* Colorado Springs Colo.: Meriwether Publishing, 2004.

White, Christine A. *Computer Visualization for the Theatre: 3D Modeling for Designers.* San Diego: Elsevier Science & Technology Books, 2003.

Wilson, Andy. *Making Stage Props: A Practical Guide.* Marlborough, U.K.: Crowood Press, Limited, 2003.

THEATRICAL MAKEUP

Hawker, Yvonne. *Make-up Designory's Beauty Make-up.* Burbank, Calif.: Make-up Designory, 2004.

Vinther, Janus. *Special Effects Make-Up.* New York: Routledge, 2003.

B. PERIODICALS

Magazines, newspapers, membership bulletins, and newsletters are an essential tool for keeping yourself informed and current on topics related to your field of interest. They are also an important source of information about job opportunities.

Use this list as a starting point. It is by no means a complete listing. Check your local library and newspaper/magazine store for other periodicals of interest.

CHAMBER MUSIC

Chamber Music Magazine
Chamber Music America
305 Seventh Avenue, 5th Floor
New York, NY 10001
Phone: (212) 242-2022
E-mail: info@chamber-music.org
http://www.chamber-music.org

CIRCUS AND MAGIC

Magic: The Magazine for Magicians
Stagewrite Publishing Incorporated
6220 Stevenson Way
Las Vegas, NV 89120
Phone: (702) 789-0099
Fax: (702) 798-0220
E-mail: publisher@magicmagazine.com
http://www.magicmagazine.com

CRITICS, REVIEWS, AND NEWS

Entertainment Weekly
Time & Life Building
Rockefeller Center
New York, NY 10020
Phone: (212) 522-1212
Fax: (212) 467-1396
http://www.ew.com

Rolling Stone
Wenner Media Incorporated
1290 Avenue of the Americas
New York, NY 10104
Phone: (212)484-1616
Fax: (212) 767-8209
http://www.rollingstone.com

Victory Review
P.O. Box 2254
Tacoma, WA 98401
Phone: (253) 428-0832
Fax: (253) 660-3263
E-mail: victory@nwlink.com
http://www.victorymusic.org

DANCE AND CHOREOGRAPHY

Attitude: The Dancers' Magazine
1040 Park Place
Brooklyn, NY 11213
E-mail: dancegiantsteps@hotmail.com
Phone: (718) 773-3046
http://www.geocities.com/danceattitude

Ballet Review
37 West 12th Street
New York, NY 10011
Phone: (212) 924-5183
http://www.ballet-dance.com
http://www.balletreview.com

Dance Chronicle
270 Madison Avenue
New York, NY 10016
Phone: (212) 696-9000
http://www.dekker.com

Dance Magazine
333 7th Avenue
New York, NY 10001
Phone: (212) 979-4803
http://www.dancemagazine.com

DANCE THERAPY

American Journal of Dance Therapy
American Dance Therapy Association
2000 Century Plaza
10632 Little Patuxent Parkway
Columbia, MD 21044
Phone: (410) 997-4040
Fax: (410) 997-4048
E-mail: info@adta.org
http://www.adta.org

HALLS, ARENAS, CLUBS, AND OTHER VENUES

Amusement Business
P.O. Box 24970
Nashville, TN 37202
Phone: (615) 321-4250
Fax: (615) 327-1574
http://www.amusementbusiness.com

Facility Magazine
4425 West Airport Freeway
Irving, TX 75062
Phone: (972) 255-8020
Fax: (972) 255-9582

MUSICIANS

The American Organist Magazine
American Guild of Organists
475 Riverside Drive
New York, NY 10115
Phone: (800) AGO-5115

Guitar Player
460 Park Avenue South
New York, NY 10016
Phone: (212) 378-0400
Fax: (212) 378-2149
http://www.guitarplayer.com

Guitar World
1115 Broadway
New York, NY 10010
Phone: (212) 807-7100
http://www.guitarworld.com

Harp Magazine
8737 Colesville Road
Silver Springs, MD 20910
Phone: (301) 588-4114
Fax: (301) 588-5531
http://www.harpmagazine.com

Hit Parader
210 Route 4
Paramus, NJ 07652
Phone: (973) 843-4004
http://www.hitparader.com

Independent Musician Magazine
1067 Market Street
San Francisco, CA 94103
Phone: (415) 503-0340
http://www.immagazine.com

International Musician
American Federation of Musicians
1501 Broadway
New York, NY 10036
Phone: (212) 869-1330
http://www.afm.org

JazzTimes
8737 Colesville Road
Silver Spring, MD 20910
Phone: (301) 588-4114
Fax: (301) 588-2009
http://www.jazztimes.com

Keyboard Magazine
2800 Campus Drive
San Mateo, CA 94403
Phone: (650) 513-4300
Fax: (650) 513-4642
http://www.keyboardonline.com

Music Trades
P.O. Box 432
Englewood, NJ 07631
Phone: (201) 871-1965
http://www.musictrades.com

OPERA

Opera Journal
National Opera Association
P.O. Box 60869
Canyon, TX 79016
Phone: (806) 651-2857
Fax: (806) 651-2958
http://www.noa.org

Opera News
Metropolitan Opera Guild
70 Lincoln Center Plaza
New York, NY 10023
Phone: (212) 769-7080
http://www.operanews.com

ORCHESTRAS

Symphony
American Symphony Orchestra League
33 West 60th Street, 5th Floor
New York, NY 10023
Phone: (212) 262-5161
Fax: (212) 262-5198
http://www.symphony.org

PERFORMING ARTS— GENERAL

Arts Management
Radius Group, Inc.
110 Riverside Drive
New York, NY 10024
Phone: (212) 579-2039
Fax: (212) 579-2049
http://www.artsmanagementnews.com

BCA News
Business Committee for the Arts, Inc.
29-27 Queens Plaza North
Long Island City, NY 11101
Phone: (718) 482-9901
Fax: (718) 482-9911
E-mail: info@bcainc.org
http://www.bcainc.org

IEG Sponsorship Report
IEG, Inc.
640 North LaSalle
Chicago, IL 60610
Phone: (312) 944-1727
Fax: (312) 944-1897
E-mail: ieg@sponsorship.com

Journal of Arts Management Law and Society
Heldref Publications
1319 18th Street NW
Washington, DC 20036
Phone: (202) 296-6267
Fax: (202) 296-5149
E-mail: tch@heldref.org
http://www.heldref.org/jamls.php

Performing Arts Magazine
Performing Arts Network
10350 Santa Monica Boulevard
Los Angeles, CA 90025
Phone: (310) 551-1115

Fax: (310) 551-2079
E-mail: info@performingartsmagazine.
    com
http://www.performingartsmagazine.com

Performing Arts Journal
MIT Press
P.O. Box 260
Village Station
New York, NY 10014
Phone: (212) 243-3885
E-mail: journals-info@mit.edu
http://mitpress.mit.edu/PAJ

PUBLIC RELATIONS, PUBLICITY, AND GENERAL PROMOTION

Contacts: The Media Pipeline for PR People
Mercomm, Inc.
550 Executive Boulevard
Ossining, NY 10562
Phone: (914) 923-9400
Fax: (914) 923-9484

Public Relations Journal
PRSA
33 Maiden Lane
New York, NY 10038
Phone: (212) 460-1400
Fax: (212) 995-0757
http://www.prsa.org

TALENT AND WRITING

Acoustic Guitar Magazine
220 West End Avenue
San Rafael, CA 94901
Phone: (415) 485-6946
Fax: (415) 485-0831
http://www.acousticguitar.com

American Songwriters Magazine
50 Music Square West
Nashville, TN 37203
Phone: (615) 321-6096
Fax: (615) 321-6097
http://www.americansongwriter.com

ASCAP in Action
American Society of Composers and
    Publishers (ASCAP)
1 Lincoln Plaza
New York, NY 10023
Phone: (212) 621-6000
http://www.ascap.com

BMI: The Many Worlds of Music
Broadcast Music Inc. (BMI)

320 West 57th Street
New York, NY 10019
Phone: (212) 586-2000
http://www.bmi.com

Downbeat Magazine
102 North Haven Road
Elmhurst, IL 60126
Phone: (800) 535-7496
http://www.downbeat.com

Songwriter's Market
Writer's Digest Books
4700 East Galbraith Road
Cincinnati, OH 45236
Phone: (513) 531-2690
E-mail: songmarket@fwpubs.com

TEACHING

American Music Teacher
441 Vine Street
Cincinnati, OH 45202
Phone: (513) 421-1420
Fax: (513) 421-2503
E-mail: mtnanet@mtna.org

Music Educators Journal
MENC: The National Association for
    Music Education
1806 Robert Fulton Drive
Reston, VA 20191
Phone: (703) 860-4000
E-mail: mbrserv@menc.org
http://www.menc.org

Teaching Music
MENC: The National Association for
    Music Education
1806 Robert Fulton Drive
Reston, VA 20191 USA
Phone: (703) 860-4000
E-mail: mbrserv@menc.org

THEATER

American Alliance for Theater & Education Newsletter
Theatre Department
Arizona State University
P.O. Box 872002
Tempe, AZ 85287
Phone: (480) 965-6064
Fax: (480) 965-5351
E-mail: aate.info@asu.edu
http://www.aate.com

American Drama
American Drama Institute
University of Cincinnati

Cincinnati, OH 45221
Phone: (513) 556-3914
Fax: (513) 556-5960
E-mail: american.drama@uc.edu

American Theater
Theatre Communications Group
520 Eighth Avenue
New York, NY 10018
Phone: (212) 609-5900
Fax: (212) 609-5901
E-mail: tcg@tcg.org , orders@tcg.org
http://www.tcg.org

Curtain Up (**webzine**)
http://www.curtainup.com

The Drama Review
The MIT Press
5 Cambridge Center
Cambridge, MA 02142
Phone: (800) 405-1619
Fax: (617) 258-6779
E-mail: journals-info@mit.edu
http://mitpress.mit.edu

Dramatics **Magazine**
Educational Theatre Association
2343 Auburn Avenue
Cincinnati, OH 45219
Phone: (513) 421-3900
Fax: (513) 421-7077
E-mail: pubs@edta.org

Dramatics Magazine
International Thespian Society
2343 Auburn Avenue
Cincinnati, OH 45219
Phone: (513) 429-3900
Fax: (513) 421-7077
E-mail: pubs@edta.org

Dramatists Guild Quarterly
Dramatists Guild Resource Directory
The Dramatists Guild of America, Inc.
1501 Broadway
New York, NY 10036
Phone: (212) 398-9366
Fax: (212) 944-0420

Dramatists Sourcebook
Theatre Communications Group
520 Eighth Avenue
New York, NY 10018
Phone: (212) 609-5900
Fax: (212) 609-5901
E-mail: tcg@tcg.org
http://www.tcg.org

Eugene O'Neill Review
Suffolk University
Department of English
Boston, MA 02114
Phone: (617) 573-8272
Fax: (617) 624-0157
E-mail: istrange@acad.suffolk.edu

Institute of Outdoor Drama Newsletter
CB 3240
1700 Airport Road
Chapel Hill, NC 27599
Phone: (919) 962-1328
Fax: (919) 962-4212
E-mail: outdoor@unc.edu
http://www.unc.edu/depts/outdoor

Preview Theater Magazine
Hogan Communications
150 East Olive Avenue
Burbank, CA 91502
Phone: (818) 848-4876
Fax: (818) 848-4995

Stage Directions
Lifestyle Ventures L.L.C.
250 West 57th Street
New York, NY 10107
Phone: (212) 265-8890
Fax: (212) 265-8908
E-mail: stagedir@aol.com
http://www.stage-directions.com

Stages
Curtains Inc.
301 West 45th Street
New York, NY 10036
Phone: (212) 245-9186

Theatrical Index
888 8th Avenue
New York, NY 10019
Phone: (212) 586-6343

THEATER-PRODUCTION

Entertainment Design
Primedia Business
249 West 17th Street
New York, NY 10011
Phone: (212) 462-3300
Fax: (212) 367-8345
http://www.etecnyc.net

Lighting Dimensions Magazine
Primedia Business
32 West 18th Street
New York, NY 10011
Phone: (212) 229-2084

Fax: (212) 229-2084
http://www.lightingdimensions.com

Make-Up Artist Magazine
4018 Northeast 112th Avenue
Vancouver, WA 98682
Phone: (360) 882-3488
Fax: (360) 885-1836
http://www.makeupmag.com

Stage Directions
Lifestyle Ventures L.L.C.
250 West 57th Street
New York, NY 10107
Phone: (212) 265-8890
Fax: (212) 265-8908
E-mail: stagedir@aol.com
http://www.stage-directions.com

Stages
Curtains Inc.
301 West 45th Street
New York, NY 10036
Phone: (212) 245-9186

Theatre Crafts International
Amusement Business
P.O. Box 24970
Nashville, TN 37202
Phone: (615) 321-4250
Fax: (615) 327-1574
http://www.amusementbusiness.com

Theatre Design and Technology
U.S. Institute for Theatre Technology
3001 Springcrest Drive
Louisville, KY 40241
Phone: (502) 426-1211
Fax: (502) 423-7467
E-mail: info@office.usitt.org
http://www.usitt.org

TOURING

Pollstar Directories
4697 West Jacquelyn Avenue
Fresno, CA 93722
Phone: (559) 271-7900
Fax: (559) 271-7979
E-mail: info@pollstar.com
http://www.pollstar.com

TRADES

Backstage
VNU Business Media USA
770 Broadway
New York, NY 10003
Phone: (646) 654-5000

Back Stage West
VNU Business Media USA
770 Broadway

New York, NY 10003
Phone: (646) 654-5000

Billboard
770 Broadway
New York, NY 10003
Phone: (646) 654-4400
Fax: (646) 654-4681
http://www.billboard.com

Daily Variety
Reed Business Information

249 West 17th Street
New York, NY 10011
Phone: (212) 337-6900
Fax: (212) 337-6977

The Hollywood Reporter
5055 Wilshire Boulevard
Los Angeles, CA 90036
Phone: (323) 525-2000
Fax: (323) 525-2377
http://www.hollywoodreporter.com

SHOW BUSINESS NEWS

Variety
Reed Business Information
5700 Wilshire Boulevard
Los Angeles, CA 90036
Phone: (323) 857-6600
Fax: (323) 965-2475

INDEX

ABOUT THE AUTHOR

Shelly Field is a nationally recognized motivational speaker, career expert, stress management specialist, personal career and life coach, and author of more than 25 bestselling books in the business and career fields.

Her books help people find careers in a wide variety of areas including the hospitality, music, sports, and communications industries; casinos and casino hotels; advertising and public relations; theater, the performing arts, and entertainment; animal rights; health care; writing; and art. She is a frequent guest on local, regional, and national radio, cable, and television talk, information, and news shows and has also given numerous print interviews and personal appearances.

Field is a featured speaker at conferences, conventions, expos, corporate functions, spousal programs, employee training and development sessions, career fairs, casinos, and events nationwide. A former comedienne, she adds a humorous spin whether speaking on empowerment; motivation; stress management; staying positive; careers; attracting, retaining, and motivating employees; or customer service. Her presentations, "STRESS BUSTERS: Beating the Stress in Your Work and Your Life" and "The De-stress Express," are popular around the country.

A career consultant to businesses, educational institutions, employment agencies, women's groups, and individuals, Field is sought out by executives, celebrities, and sports figures for personal life and career coaching and stress management.

In her role as a corporate consultant to businesses throughout the country, she provides assistance with human resources issues such as attracting, retaining, and motivating employees, customer service training, and stress management in the workplace.

President and CEO of the The Shelly Field Organization, a public relations, marketing, and management firm that handles national clients, she has represented celebrities in the sports, music, and entertainment industries as well as authors, businesses, and corporations.

For media inquiries, information about personal appearances, seminars, or workshops, please contact The Shelly Field Organization at P.O. Box 711, Monticello, NY 12701 or visit http://www.shellyfield.com.